C1252

BEDFORD OB

(and other post-war K/M/O passenger-carrying vehicles)

PUBLISHED BY

THE PSV CIRCLE

APRIL 2013

C1252/2

FOREWORD

This publication lists all known information about Bedford OB chassis, along with other passenger-carrying vehicles based on chassis from Bedford's post-war K/M/O range of goods models, regardless of whether they had been so bodied from new, or subsequently rebuilt for passenger use.

This publication is dedicated to David Gray, 1933 – 2013, former long-serving Honorary Publications Editor of the PSV Circle, who died just as the the draft was being prepared for print. His contribution, as with so many Circle publications, has been considerable and in this case took the form of the data extracted both from Vauxhall and Duple official records. Thanks are also offered to Maurice Bateman, John Bennett, Derek Bradfield, David Corke, Richard Evans, Mike Eyre, Mike Fenton, Richard Gadsby, Roger Grimley, Tony Holdsworth, Derek Jones, Alan Lambert, Ron Maybray, Alan Mills, Chris Taylor, Peter Tulloch, Fred Ward and Roger Warwick who have assisted throughout the Bedford project; among others consulted were Phil Baldwin, Darryl Bellamy, Colin Bull, John Carman, Andrew Higgs, Murray Jessop, Ian Manning, Sean Millar and the late Geoff Bruce. Our thanks to the Association for the Research and Study of the History of Transportation in Greece must also be placed on record. In addition to the Vauxhall and Duple records, we have consulted other body builders' and motor tax records and we extend our thanks to the many people who have collected this information over a period of many years. The publication has been coordinated and compiled by Colin Martin.

The main section of this publication is presented in eight columns as follows:-
1. Vehicle chassis number
2. An * if a specific note relates to this vehicle or a # if a general note applies
3. Original vehicle registration mark (may have subsequently been re-registered)
4. Body manufacturer
5. Body number or use if not a PSV body
6. Seating capacity
7. Date the vehicle was new – where known, this is the date of first licensing or entry into service.
8. First operator / county code / fleet number (if used)

Photographs have been taken or supplied by JH Aston, John Clarke collection, Alan Cross, John Gillham, Donald Hudson, RF Mack, Roy Marshall, Colin Martin, Geoffrey Morant courtesy Richard Morant, Phil Moth, New Zealand Motor Bodies courtesy Snow Cumming collection, Norris-Cull collection, The Omnibus Society, JF Parke, David Richardson, Mr Konstantinos Rellos family collection courtesy Rodolivos Publications, Brian Schieb, John Shearman collection, DHD Spray, Bruce Tilley and Peter Tulloch collection.

Contents:
Foreword	Page	2
Introduction	"	3
Bedford OB (pre-war)	"	10
Bedford OB (post-war)	"	11
Self-Build OBs	"	223
Bedford OL	"	224
Bedford ML	"	239
Bedford K and JCV	"	242
Beadle Chassisless Vehicles	"	245
Registration and chassis number cross reference	"	247
Historical County codes	"	274
Overseas & other codes used in this publication	"	275

Note:

This is one of a wide range of publications produced by the PSV Circle primarily as a service to its members. The information contained herein includes information provided from numerous reliable sources. Considerable time and effort is taken to ensure that the content of this publication is as complete and accurate as possible, but no responsibility can be accepted for any errors or omissions. However, please tell us if you discover any!

Any general comments, updates or corrections to this publication may be sent to the Publications Manager, PSV Circle, Unit GK, Leroy House, 436 Essex Road, London N1 3QP or via email to publications.manager@psv-circle.org.uk. Details of how to join the PSV Circle and a list of all our current publications can be obtained from the PSV Circle website – www.psv-circle.org.uk.

ISBN: 978-1-908953-12-4

Published by the PSV Circle.
© The PSV Circle March 2013

C1252/3

INTRODUCTION

Vauxhall Motors was formed in 1907 as a re-naming of Vauxhall Ironworks which had diversified into motor car production in the early years of the 20th century. The Ironworks Company had taken its name from the area of London in which it had been based, but car production had necessitated new premises and the move to Luton in Bedfordshire had been completed two years before the 1907 re-naming.

Half a century earlier than many other British motor manufacturers found themselves in foreign ownership, Vauxhall Motors was purchased by the burgeoning US-based General Motors (GM) company in 1925.

Two years earlier GM had established an assembly facility for Chevrolet commercials in Hendon, North West London. Vauxhall car production continued at Luton, that plant producing no commercials at that time. That was to change in 1929 when Chevrolet production moved to Luton; GM's best selling UK commercial chassis at that time was the 6-cylinder 30cwt LQ. Although essentially a goods model, the LQ was also a popular choice for bus and coach operators requiring a chassis suitable for 14-seat coachwork.

By 1930 marketing material was making references to Bedford Chevrolet models. Those who have researched the company's history in detail have found no documented evidence as to why the name Bedford was adopted; it can only be assumed that it was derived from the county in which Luton was situated. The name clearly found favour in the GM camp as in 1931 a new range of commercials was introduced using simply the Bedford name.

The development of the Bedford range during the 1930s is documented in companion publication C1250; C1251 continued the story through the wartime years, with particular emphasis on the OWB model. This publication continues the record of Bedford production into the early 1950s, with its main focus on Bedford's well-known OB chassis.

Bedford had introduced the K, M and O range of models in the summer of 1939, offering commercial chassis with payloads ranging from 30cwt to 5ton; these were essentially goods models, although the 4 and 5 ton O series had a variant intended specifically for passenger-carrying applications, the OB. Production of all these models ceased abruptly after just a few months when, as with all major UK manufacturing facilities, the resources of the Luton plant were committed to the war effort.

The K/M/O range was to re-appear in October 1945, with the OB alone going on to reach a production total of more than 12,500 chassis over the following five years. Chassis numbers for the range, with all models intermingled, had begun at 1001 in 1939 and reached 10856 when production was suspended. Chassis number 10857 was used for the prototype OWB in 1942 (see C1251), and the range recommenced from chassis 11001 late in 1945. The K/M/O range continued in production until February 1953, with chassis numbers then having passed 260000. The OB however ceased production rather earlier, in November 1950, its demise being attributable to the introduction of Bedford's S range of commercials, and in particular the SB which offered a seating capacity of 33 as opposed to 29 for standard OB-based coaches.

In order that this volume may present a full record of the production of the OB model, details of the small number of pre-war vehicles (already listed in publication C1250) are repeated and updated herein. Also included are all post-war K/M/O goods chassis known to have carried passenger bodies, either from new or as a result of subsequent modification.

Further volumes are planned to continue the record of Bedford bus and coach production.

The Bedford OB in more detail

The OB chassis was constructed to allow UK bodies of some 24ft 4ins in length, and with a width of 7ft 6ins, the maximum then legally permitted. (Bodies for vehicles delivered to Guernsey were restricted to a width of 7ft, while dimensions of some export vehicles were rather greater than UK regulations permitted). The wheelbase was 14ft 6ins. As with all members of the K/M/O range, the standard power unit for the OB was Bedford's highly successful 3519cc 27.34hp ("28hp") 6-cylinder engine, originally introduced in 1938 for the re-vamped W-series model range. An improved version of the power unit, known as the Extra Duty engine, appeared in 1950, producing 84 bhp, rather than the 74 bhp of the original version. A few vehicles were fitted from new with Perkins P6 29.4hp oil engines, and rather more were converted later in their lives; unfortunately our records of the vehicles so equipped are incomplete, but those that are known are indicated in specific Notes.

As explained in C1251, under the Ministry of War Transport regime, Bedford had been chosen as the supplier of single-deck buses to essential users, with delivery commencing in 1942. The OWB, the basis of these 32-seat utility vehicles, was mechanically identical to the OB, but OW chassis were numbered in a separate series to those of their peace-time equivalents. 3389 OWB chassis are believed to have been built.

One feature which set both the OB and OWB apart from the corresponding goods models was the mounting of the engine at a slight angle to the main chassis frames; this was to facilitate the propeller shaft and the differential being offset to the nearside, thus permitting the central passenger gangway to be set lower in the bodywork, effectively giving greater headroom. The lower floor level and longer wheelbase of the OB (compared to the OL) led to a number of OB chassis finding use as prison vans, horse-boxes, pantechnicons and mobile libraries.

Distinguishing OWBs from OBs is not always easy, and while the body style is generally the key feature, this too has its pitfalls; Duple for example produced some of their final batch of OWB bodies to a "relaxed Utility" pattern, and continued to produce bodies of the same style for a batch of early post-war OBs. Conversely Mulliner and SMT both continued to produce Utility style bodies on OB chassis for some customers; those by Mulliner, primarily for Government Departments and export orders, were still being built in 1948.

As detailed in C1251 many OWBs and Bedford wartime goods chassis were rebuilt in the early post-war years and fitted with coach bodies. Once rebuilt these vehicles were virtually indistinguishable from OBs. It is also very difficult to distinguish an OL fitted with passenger bodywork from an OB; this is almost certainly why it has been recorded elsewhere that 375 Perkins-engined OBs were supplied to Argentina in 1950; as these are not recorded in Vauxhall's OB records, it is likely that they were OLs. The guide on page 100 of C1251 may assist in such identification.

At the time when an extract from Vauxhall's official records was made on behalf of the PSV Circle, the OB was almost at the end of its construction period and chassis numbers had reached 147488. A few OBs were built in the following weeks for overseas customers and the highest chassis number confirmed for an OB is 154721.

As mentioned in C1251, a feature of the chassis designation and/or numbering system which cannot as yet be explained is the addition of a code (either 57 or 58) as a suffix to the model (eg OB/57) or as a prefix to the chassis number (eg 58/12345). Similar codings apply to other Bedford models. OWBs are also sometimes quoted with 57 or 58 codings. These codes are not commonly seen and are not used in this publication.

Production Statistics

Vauxhall's own records (which for convenience will subsequently be referred to as 'Bedford records') indicate that 12,693 post-war OB chassis were produced; they were therefore leaving the Luton production line at an average rate of over 50 per week throughout the main 5 year production run. Of this total some 5,500 chassis were exported. Of the UK vehicles, approximately 6,275 were bodied for passenger use (including around 425 for the Armed Forces and Government Departments), while some 450 received goods bodywork.

In this publication coverage of the UK PSV deliveries is particularly comprehensive, less so for the other categories, with more than half of the overseas vehicles recorded only by chassis number and destination.

With so many vehicles supplied to the UK market, almost every community had at least one OB in its midst. In the late 1940s, car ownership remained at a low level and the population was generally dependent upon public transport for travel to work, for shopping, or for social purposes; most therefore had direct contact with their local OB(s). This has resulted in the vehicle being recognised as having iconic status, and has in turn led to more than 150 vehicles being preserved, many still in operational condition, and with a handful returned to full PSV status, even though it is 62 years since the newest of them left the factory.

The cost of a new chassis in 1945 was around £400 and complete with 29-seat coach body the total was around £1,325. Today, fully restored vehicles can change hands for 40 times that sum.

Bodies for UK vehicles

The mention of an OB will for many immediately trigger an image of a Duple Vista coach body. This is not surprising as Duple supplied more than 4,200 coach bodies for OB chassis. While most were Vistas, materials shortages late in 1948 led to the temporary substitution of the Mark V Service Coach body, omitting the sliding "sunshine" roof of the Vista and the side moulding flares which helped to characterise the former. Duple also produced some 340 bus bodies for OBs supplied to the UK market, along with a similar number of bus bodies to overseas customers.

More details of Duple bodies on OB chassis can be found on pages 6 to 8.

Approximate totals from other leading coachbuilders were as follows:

Mulliner	1240
SMT	290
Plaxton	210
Thurgood	95
Pearson	90
Beadle	75

(The Mulliner and SMT totals will be rather higher tham the figures shown above as between them these two builders almost certainly built a further 200 bodies on OB chassis for the Royal Air Force, Royal Navy and other Government customers. Those from Mulliner were to the Utility design while SMT moved to a "relaxed utility" style; Mulliner also probably produced rather more bodies for overseas customers than have been recorded.)

No fewer than 65 other coachbuilders supplied new bodies for UK OB chassis. Some of these also closely resembled the Vista; as Duple was working to full capacity, it appears to have raised no objections to such unauthorised cloning. Mis-identification has unsurprisingly occurred in a number of cases and Duple records have proved invaluable in compiling this listing. The standard OB coach seated 29; 27 seats was also a popular option, primarily for those coaches to be used on touring work, while the small number of fully-fronted coach bodies could generally accommodate 30.

The sudden cessation of OWB production and the reversion to OB chassis late in 1945 resulted in body-builders having not completed their Ministry of War Transport contractual obligations. Duple bodies 41481 – 41549 to the "relaxed Utility" design, were therefore completed for civilian customers on OB chassis, while SMT and Mulliner continued to fulfil their war-time orders on OB chassis for the Service Departments, possibly as many as 200 in the case of SMT.

Exports

All UK manufacturers were under great pressure to export as many of their products as possible in the early post war years. Bedford was certainly successful in so doing, with some 5,500 OB chassis going to overseas customers, spread over 5 continents. In many cases it was only the chassis which were exported although Duple and Mulliner attracted significant export orders, and BOAC deployed Churchill-bodied coaches at some overseas locations (including some built to a width of 8ft). Duple's export bodies ranged from Vista coaches to a variety of bus bodies, including the metal-framed Almet model; this was available in ckd form and could seat up to 38 passengers with an option of two doors. (A few Almet bodies found their way to UK customers.)

Some of the main export markets, and approximate quantities supplied, were as follows:

Australia	1400
Belgium	120
Ceylon	100
Denmark	180
Egypt	170
Finland	120
India	575
Ireland	80
Malaya	180
New Zealand	210

Although no details are known, it is recorded that one OB chassis operating in Karachi received an open-top double-deck body.

(Note: Bedford records generally show only the destination port for exported vehicles, and we have used that information in these listings where no fuller customer details are known; it should be noted that the port does not necessarily indicate that the vehicle was supplied to a customer in that vicinity, and indeed, in some cases the vehicle eventually entered service with an operator in an adjoining country.)

Forward control conversions

Around 120 new OB chassis are known to have been converted to forward control to facilitate the fitting of full-front bodies for UK customers: Plaxton was the primary coachbuilder for such conversions. While some 50 OBs are specifically recorded as forward control service buses in Australia and New Zealand, the number of such conversions in those countries is thought to have been significantly higher. Known vehicles may be identified in the main listing by the F prefix to the seating code. Vehicles known to have been converted to forward control later in their lives are identified in specific notes.

Self-build OBs

There are six recorded instances of operators or agents, possibly frustrated by the waiting times for new OB chassis, having built their own chassis to OB specifications and seemingly using standard new Bedford components. These are included in this volume.

Bedford-Beadles

In addition to building 75 bodies for conventional OB chassis, JC Beadle of Dartford introduced a range of lightweight chassisless vehicles, starting with 4 prototypes in 1946. These fully-fronted, forward- control buses variously used running units of Bedford, Commer, Dennis, Leyland and Morris manufacture. As the running units for the Bedford vehicles were from the K/M/O range, the 54 vehicles using such units are also documented in this volume. It must however be stressed that the vehicles themselves were NOT of Bedford manufacture.

Specific Notes on the accompanying listings

Some of the bodies built by Mulliner have styles which look rather bus-like, although fitted out as coaches. Understandably a few have previously been recorded as DP—F; all were actually intended for coach use and the C—F designation is used for all such vehicles.

Where what is believed to be an incorrect chassis number has previously been published or is taken from a formal record, it is included in the main listing with a cross-reference to what is believed to be the correct version. The version shown in the extract from Bedford records is always taken to be correct.

Around 100 vehicles are shown in various notes as being recorded with chassis numbers which cannot be traced in Bedford records. The official records were colour-coded to distinguish OBs from OLs and other models in the range and took the form of a card index. It is possible that some codings were incorrect, or that cards had been temporarily removed from the file when the extract was made. The fact that a number is untraced does not necessarily mean that it is incorrect.

Bedford chassis were produced in numerical sequence. The approximate date of manufacture may therefore be inferred from those numbers. (This is certainly NOT the case with Duple body numbers.) In many cases, particularly of overseas vehicles, dates new (ie to service) are not known and may have routinely been up to a year after the chassis left Luton, due to shipping delays and in some cases having bodies built in the destination country. Even within the UK, despite the appetite for new coaches, some smaller body-builders also took many months to complete orders.

Before "permanent" registration numbers were introduced in New Zealand in 1965, registrations changed approximately every five years. Registrations quoted for New Zealand vehicles are the earliest known (with later numbers, where known, covered by notes). In some cases these may not have been the vehicle's original registration.

As recorded in C1251, the inclusion of 32 seats in bus bodies on OB chassis was a dispensation agreed when the utility body design was approved in 1942. Normal Construction and Use rules would have permitted only 30 seats. Some OBs were still being supplied to UK civilian users with 32-seats as late as 1947, but withdrawal of the dispensation resulted in all such vehicles being down-seated to 30 (and often 28) when they were subsequently offered for their annual Certificate of Fitness examinations. Such individual down-seatings are not recorded in this publication. (It is actually likely that rather more of the 1945/46 OBs with bus bodies were new as 32-seaters than are shown herein.)

Duple bodies on the Bedford OB.

Although the lists which follow identify some 70 coachbuilders supplying passenger bodies for Bedford OB chassis for the UK market, as explained in C1250 Duple bodywork has almost always been synonymous with Bedford chassis and the post-war Bedford OB was no exception. As Duple bodied more than 4,500 OBs for UK customers, about 68% of the OB chassis supplied with passenger bodies, a brief guide to the Hendon manufacturer's offerings may be helpful.

Service Buses

The first 69 post-war OB chassis bodied by Duple had in fact been ordered as Bedford OWBs with Utility bodywork. This was part of the final Ministry of War Transport order on Duple for single-deck vehicles – see C1251 for more details. During construction of the final batch of OWBs, Duple began to replace the Utility body with what was unofficially known as the "relaxed utility" body, taking advantage of improved supply of materials as the war drew to a close. While the final batch of OWBs was a mixed bunch in terms of body styling, all 69 of the OBs built to complete this order (body numbers 41481 to 41549) had the relaxed style of utility bodywork.

The Duple Mark II

The relaxed utility body became known as the Mk II (implying that the Utility was regarded as the Mk I). The Mark II nominally had 32 seats in pairs all facing forwards with the emergency door at the centre rear of the body and a sliding passenger door at the front. The waistrail was straight and the front and rear domes were panel beaten in a well proportioned shape, the front dome featuring a large single destination screen. The bodywork was timber framed and panelled in aluminium, with five half-drop windows for ventilation. The seating was constructed of steel tubular framing with leather covered cushions. By 1947 Duple had built some 250 MK II bodies, but was overwhelmed with orders for its Vista coach. Early in that year, Mulliner took over production of buses to the Mk II design; these continued to be built at their Birmingham site until the end of OB production. These Mulliner-built bodies were referred to in Bedford advertisements as the Mk III. (Mulliner built these alongside bodies to the original Utility design, some still with slatted wooden seats, which continued to find favour with Governmental and overseas customers, although a few continued to find their way to UK civilian customers.)

The Duple Mk IV

The "Universal type Mark IV, 30 passenger service bus".... "for home and export" was introduced in 1948. It had a straight waistrail and deeper windows fitted with sliding ventilators. The emergency door was placed behind the driver, allowing five seats across the rear of the bodywork. Single inward facing seats were provided over the rear wheel arches. At least some Mk IVs had metal-framed bodies.

The Duple Almet

The Almet was an all metal body as the names suggests, designed for service overseas where timber framed bodies were unsuitable. It was supplied ckd for local assembly; the whole body was in six main sections. Some 20 of these bodies were supplied to UK Government customers, some later passing to PSV operators. For overseas customers the three basic variants were front entrance, front and rear entrance and front entrance with rear emergency door. The body was suitable for left hand or right hand drive chassis and a variety of seating arrangements were offered with up to 38 seats! The seats had tubular metal frames with cushions in "double tropically treated brown hide", although metal slatted seats were available.

Other Export Models

Duple was of course willing to construct non-standard models; among these were batches for operators in East Africa where the bodies, resembling the Mk II design for the forward end, were divided into two compartments, each with its own door; upholstered seats graced the front compartment while those at the rear were of the slatted timber design.

The Duple Vista

While the name Vista can be traced back to 1936 as an offering on Bedford WTB chassis, a new design of the same name was introduced for the short-lived pre-war OB. In January 1946 "Bus and Coach" magazine carried an advertisement for the Bedford-Duple "Vista" Luxury Coach. The first examples entered service in March 1946. A 26 seat model (usually actually 27) was offered at £1,265 and the 29 seater at £1,275. Both were offered painted in two colours. The Vista was subject to regular modifications throughout its production up to 1952.The earliest Vista coach bodies had a passenger door which slid inside the bodywork when opened; the emergency door was directly opposite, behind the driver and hinged outwards. The waistrail was curved and the window pillars

sloped back slightly giving the characteristic Duple shape. The bodywork was timber framed and panelled in aluminium, with seven full-drop windows for ventilation. In addition the centre section of the roof slid open. The seating was constructed of steel tubular framing with moquette covered cushions. The early bodies had destination glasses of the pre-war shape and this feature was continued in the SMT built coach bodies which were to Duple design.

The most obvious change to the coach body was the fitting of the passenger door to slide on the outside of the bodywork (from mid-1946, after only 46 to the original design had been constructed), but there were minor improvements to the fittings and trim in most years. A better standard of seating, with a full headrest was soon available and later optional features such as glazed roof quarter panels were offered. For 1949 the rear end was re-designed, with framing introduced below the boot doors which had hitherto extended to the bottom of the vehicle.

Once again, pressures on Duple production capacity resulted in an agreement for another coachbuilder to assist in meeting orders. In this case SMT was allowed to build coach bodies to the Vista design for supply to customers in Scotland and those northerly parts of England within its normal sphere of supply and support. This agreement led to the building of a further 218 Vista style bodies between mid-1947 and mid-1948.

(SMT built a further 45 bodies to the Vista design for rebodying OWB chassis – see Circle publications B1701 (part 2) and C1251 for details; these 260 bodies added further to the dominance of the Vista design.)

The Duple Mk V Service Coach

In late 1948 the Mark V service coach was offered in response to a Government directive regarding luxury features, and the need to conserve materials; this was the Vista without the distinctive side trim and some hitherto standard features, including the sliding roof panels. The Mk V remained in production for only four months, Vista production resuming in March 1949.

(A small number of Vista bodies produced between 1947 and 1950 were of a simplified form resembling the Mk V; these were seemingly built to customers' own requirements and were in effect customized Vistas.)

The Duple Sportsman

Although it did not enter production, Duple produced just one vehicle, using the Sportsman name, to a very different design for the shorter Bedford OL chassis. This vehicle most unusually had external timber framing. Vehicles subsequently produced on OL chassis for David MacBrayne had coachwork to a similar profile, but with conventional body construction.

(Photos courtesy of Allan Condie, Tim Machin, Omnibus Society Collection (John Clarke), Peter Tulloch Collection)

BIBLIOGRAPHY

The Bedford OB and OWB by John Woodhams, published by DPR Marketing and Sales in 1986

Bedford Volume 1 (Bedford and British Chevrolet 1923 – 1950) by Stuart Broach and Alan Townsin, published by Venture Publications in 1995

Bedford Buses of the 1930s and 1940s by Alan Earnshaw, published by Trans-Pennine Publishing in 2000

Bedford Buses and Coaches since 1931, published by Vauxhall Motors Ltd in 1979

PSV Circle Publication B1701 Scottish Bodybuilders and Minibus Converters, published in two parts in 2008, giving full details of all SMT bodies

C1252/10

PRE-WAR OB

This listing of pre-war Bedford OBs appeared in C1250. It is repeated here for the convenience of readers in order that all OBs may appear in a single volume.

39/OB/1* DBM 59   Duple   3713/2 C26F   -/39   Vauxhall (test vehicle)

3996	?	Duple	5929/2	C29F	-/39	Supplied to Yeates (dealer), Loughborough
5422	DOD 550	Duple	7384/2	C26F	7/40	Southern National, Exeter (DN) 501
5490	CBL 502	Thurgood	737	C26F	11/39	Herring Bros, Wokingham (BE)
5530	BDT 659	Duple	6861/2	C26F	4/40	A Sykes, Camblesforth (WR)
5543	SS 5610	Duple	6865/2	C29F	1/41	Stark's Bus Service, Dunbar (EL) B5
5560	EAO 177	Thurgood	739	B26F	11/39	B Mandale, Greystoke (CU)
5826	DS 2275	Duple	6866/2	C29F	-/39	W Ramsay jnr, Peebles (PB)
5844	FYY 830	Duple	6701/2	C26F	3/40	Keith & Boyle (London) Ltd {Orange Luxury Coaches}, London SE11 (LN) Thalia
5899	SO 6882	Duple	6864/2	C29F	-/39	J Dean Jnr, Findhorn (MR)
6047	SS 5568	Duple	6888/2	C26F	7/40	Stark's Bus Service, Dunbar (EL) B4
6059	* DOD 533	Duple	7364/2	C26F	1/40	Western National, Exeter (DN) 435
6083	* DOD 547	Duple	7379/2	C26F	9/40	Southern National, Exeter (DN) 498
6112	BVG 190	Watson		C26F	11/40	J Phillips & Son, Rhostyllen (DH)
6189	* DOD 545	Duple	7382/2	C26F	9/40	Southern National, Exeter (DN) 496
6220	DOD 546	Duple	7378/2	C26F	9/40	Southern National, Exeter (DN) 497
6402	DOD 543	Duple	7377/2	C26F	9/40	Southern National, Exeter (DN) 494
6430	CBU 418	?		C30-	7/40	Oldham Corporation Education Dept (XLA)
6595	DOD 544	Duple	7381/2	C26F	9/40	Southern National, Exeter (DN) 495
6607	FYY 832	Duple	8387/2	C26F	3/40	Keith & Boyle (London) Ltd {Orange Luxury Coaches}, London SE11 (LN) Athenia
6708	DOD 549	Duple	7383/2	C26F	7/40	Southern National, Exeter (DN) 500
6727	* FYF 798	Stening		B24-	-/39	London County Council (XLN) 339
6998	DOD 530	Duple	7367/2	C26F	2/40	Western National, Exeter (DN) 432
7100	DOD 532	Duple	7366/2	C26F	2/40	Western National, Exeter (DN) 434
7122	DOD 548	Duple	7380/2	C26F	7/40	Southern National, Exeter (DN) 499
7224	* DOD 531	Duple	7365/2	C26F	2/40	Western National, Exeter (DN) 433
7464	?	Thurgood	743	(van)	10/39	Allen & Hanbury Ltd, Ware (XHT)
8918	DOD 552	Duple	7386/2	C26F	7/40	Southern National, Exeter (DN) 503
8951	* DOD 534	Duple	7368/2	C26F	2/40	Western National, Exeter (DN) 436
9011	DOD 551	Duple	7385/2	C26F	7/40	Southern National, Exeter (DN) 502
9022	DOD 553	Duple	7387/2	C26F	7/40	Southern National, Exeter (DN) 504
9038	FYY 833	Duple	8389/2	C26F	3/40	Keith & Boyle (London) Ltd {Orange Luxury Coaches}, London SE11 (LN) Claudia II
9056	DOD 537	Duple	7371/2	C26F	3/40	Western National, Exeter (DN) 439
9074	DOD 535	Duple	7369/2	C26F	3/40	Western National, Exeter (DN) 437
9077	FYY 831	Duple	8386/2	C26F	3/40	Keith & Boyle (London) Ltd {Orange Luxury Coaches}, London SE11 (LN) Astoria
9083	DOD 536	Duple	7370/2	C26F	3/40	Western National, Exeter (DN) 438
?	HI 4180	-		B26F	-/40	R Campion {Princess Bus Service}, Clonmel (EI)

Notes:

39/OB/1 (DBM 59)   passed to GW & A Nesbit {Nesbit Bros}, Somerby (LE) 9/52
6059   (DOD 533)   exported to Cyprus and re-registered TV 430 1/56
6083   (DOD 547)   exported to Cyprus and re-registered TX 301 4/56
6189   (DOD 545)   rebuilt as forward control to FC28F configuration 6/54
6727   (FYF 798)   based at Joyce Green Hospital, Dartford
7224   (DOD 531)   exported to Cyprus and re-registered TV 819 -/56
8951   (DOD 534)   exported to Cyprus and re-registered TV 413 1/56

C1252/11

POST-WAR OB

11003					Exported to Ceylon
11004					Exported to New Zealand
11005					Exported to Ceylon
11006					Exported to New Zealand
11007					Exported to Ceylon
11008	* P.351	Auckland TB	FB33F	5/47	Auckland Transport Board (O-NZ) 316
11009	* 2900	Tonna	B31F	4/47	Route Bus Service (Fortunato Micallef), Rabat (O-M)
11010 - 11013					Exported to Ceylon
11014					Exported to New Zealand
11015	* P.962	Transport BS	B35F	-/46	Transport BS Ltd, Auckland (O-NZ) 21
11016	* P1.133	Pomeroy	B33F	-/47	Buses Ltd, Hamilton (O-NZ) 46
11017, 11018					Exported to Ceylon
11019	BJT 171	Duple	41493 B28F	11/45	RW Toop, WJ Ironside & PW Davis {Bere Regis & District}, Dorchester (DT)
11020	FTG 392	Duple	41497 B29F	11/45	R Thomas {East Glam Motors}, Nelson (GG)
11021	* FTG 400	Duple	41498 B29F	7/46	FR Williams {Victoria Motorways}, Treorchy (GG)
11022					Exported to Ceylon
11023	BJT 170	Duple	41491 B28F	11/45	RW Toop, WJ Ironside & PW Davis {Bere Regis & District}, Dorchester (DT)
11024	BUD 279	Duple	41488 B32F	4/46	House Bros (Watlington) Ltd (OX)
11025	HKX 377	Duple	41483 B32F	10/45	Pilot Coaches (High Wycombe) Ltd (BK)
11026					Exported to Melbourne (O-AUS)
11027	* EBM 615	Duple	41990 B32F	-/45	Vauxhall (experimental vehicle)
11028	JM 5699	Duple	41484 B30F	-/45	S Mitchell & Son, Kendal (WT)
11029	CUX 527	Duple	41482 B32F	11/45	WA Thomas {Plowden Valley Motor Services}, Bishop's Castle (SH)
11030	GYB 993	Duple	41485 B32F	1/46	H Gratton, Burnham-on-Sea (SO) B4
11031	CUX 528	Duple	41481 B29F	11/45	RB & R Charles (Charles Bros) {Charles Motor Services}, Cleobury Mortimer (SH)
11032	GYB 640	Duple	41487 B32F	5/46	C Sandford, Langport (SO)
11033	DCJ 474	Duple	41486 B32F	10/45	PHE Tummey {Llangrove Coach Services}, Llangrove (HR)
11034	EWX 274	Duple	41496 B32F	12/45	G Pyne {White Coach Tours}, Starbeck (WR)
11035	BJT 168	Duple	41489 B28F	11/45	RW Toop, WJ Ironside & PW Davis {Bere Regis & District}, Dorchester (DT)
11036	FTG 99	Duple	41501 B32F	12/45	Steven Probert (Aberdare) Ltd (GG)
11037	* V1.632	?	?	-/--	Howie Motors, Ohura (O-NZ)
11038					Exported to New Zealand
11039	CUX 591	Duple	41492 B28F	12/45	AE Freeman, Munslow (SH)
11040					Exported to New Zealand
11041	BJT 169	Duple	41490 B28F	11/45	RW Toop, WJ Ironside & PW Davis {Bere Regis & District}, Dorchester (DT)
11042	?	SMT	B32F	c12/45	Air Ministry (Royal Air Force) (GOV)
11043	EWX 273	Duple	41494 B32F	12/45	G Pyne {White Coach Tours}, Starbeck (WR)
11044					Exported to New Zealand
11045	* RAF 208529	SMT	B32F	c12/45	Air Ministry (Royal Air Force) (GOV)
11046	* RAF 119773	SMT	B32F	c12/45	Air Ministry (Royal Air Force) (GOV)
11047	* RAF 119779	SMT	B32F	c12/45	Air Ministry (Royal Air Force) (GOV)
11048	* RAF 119780	SMT	B32F	c12/45	Air Ministry (Royal Air Force) (GOV)
11049	* RAF 120733	SMT	B32F	c12/45	Air Ministry (Royal Air Force) (GOV)
11050	?	SMT	B32F	c12/45	Air Ministry (Royal Air Force) (GOV)
11051	7243	G Zammit	B32F	8/46	Unscheduled Bus Service (O-M)
11052, 11053					Exported to New Zealand
11054	* P.350	Magee	FB33F	-/46	Auckland Transport Board (O-NZ) 315
11055					Exported to New Zealand
11056					Exported to Ceylon
11057					Exported to New Zealand
11058	* ?	Eaddy & Taylor	C23F	-/47	Gibson's Motors, New Plymouth (O-NZ)
11059	7242	Sultana	B31F	3/47	Unscheduled Bus Service (O-M)
11060	?	?	B--F	-/--	Madge Motors Ltd, Palmerston North (O-NZ)
11061	HKK 593	Duple	41505 B32F	12/45	CJ Newman & Son, Hythe (KT)
11062	FTG 393	Duple	41500 B32F	2/46	DH Selby & E Jones, Port Talbot (GG)

11063	EOT 404	Duple	41518	B32F	12/45	Odiham Motor Services Ltd (HA)
11064	KEV 836	Duple	41508	B32F	11/45	CJW Sage, Great Bromley (EX)
11065	?	?	?	?	-/--	Asiatic Petrol Co, unknown overseas location
11066	?	Duple	41887	B32F	-/--	Asiatic Petrol Co, Borneo
11067	* ?	Duple	41883	B32F	-/45	Asiatic Petrol Co, Rotterdam (O-NL)
11068	* ?	SMT		B32F	c12/45	Air Ministry (Royal Air Force) (GOV)
11069	* ?	SMT		B32F	-/45	Air Ministry (Royal Air Force) (GOV)
11070	* RAF 208539	SMT		B32F	c12/45	Air Ministry (Royal Air Force) (GOV)
11071	* RAF 208536	SMT		B32F	c12/45	Air Ministry (Royal Air Force) (GOV)
11072	* RAF 208543	SMT		B32F	c12/45	Air Ministry (Royal Air Force) (GOV)
11073	* RAF 119776	SMT		B32F	c12/45	Air Ministry (Royal Air Force) (GOV)
11074	* RAF 208541	SMT		B32F	c12/45	Air Ministry (Royal Air Force) (GOV)
11075	* RAF 208544	SMT		B32F	c12/45	Air Ministry (Royal Air Force) (GOV)
11076	?	Duple	41888	B32F	-/--	Asiatic Petrol Co, Borneo
11077	?	Duple	41885	B32F	-/--	Asiatic Petrol Co, unknown overseas location
11078	?	Duple	41884	B32F	-/--	Asiatic Petrol Co, Rotterdam (O-NL)
11079	?	Duple	41886	B32F	-/--	Asiatic Petrol Co, Curacao (O-YV)
11080	EWX 943	Duple	41512	B30F	1/46	Clifford Lunn, Rothwell (WR)
11081	BVL 338	Duple	41510	B32F	11/45	W Hutson, North Hykeham (LI)
11082	CPM 450	Duple	41495	B30F	11/45	AH & JH Sargent {East Grinstead Motor Coaches}, East Grinstead (ES) 05
11083	EU 7942	Duple	41517	B32F	10/45	Ford & Reames, Brynmawr (BC)
11084						Exported to New Zealand
11085						Exported to Malta
11086						Exported to New Zealand
11087						Exported to Ceylon
11088, 11089						Exported to Malta
11090						Exported to New Zealand
11091	* 634	Mallia		B30C	8/47	Unscheduled Bus Service (O-M)
11092	CBX 810	Duple	41499	B29F	11/45	J & T Thomas {Thomas Bros}, Llangadog (CR)
11093	* ?	Duple	41882	B28F	-/--	Nyasaland Transport Co Ltd, Blantyre (O-EAN)
11094	JJO 656	Duple	41503	B32F	12/45	GR Freeman, Faringdon (BE)
11095	LRE 642	Duple	41519	B32F	12/45	Greatrex Motor Coaches Ltd, Stafford (ST) 28 Chaffinch
11096	* CNV 668	Duple	41535	B32F	4/46	Rushden Motors Ltd (NO)
11097	CRX 546	Duple	41504	B26F	1/46	Thames Valley, Reading (BE) 437
11098	ATL 885	Duple	41507	B32F	12/45	C Gresswell, Billingborough (KN)
11099	DAY 499	Duple	41537	B30F	12/45	R, SL & AH Wheildon (R Wheildon & Sons), Castle Donington (LE) 3
11100	3241	Mallia		B30F	5/47	Route Bus Service (O-M)
11101	3065	Mallia		B30F	3/48	Route Bus Service, Gozo (O-M)
11102	1421	Bonavia		B31F	2/47	Route Bus Service (O-M)
11103	* P.352	Auckland TB		FB33F	-/47	Auckland Transport Board (O-NZ) 317
11104	FTG 353	Duple	41502	B32F	12/45	J Jenkins, Skewen (GG)
11105	CFW 829	Duple	41525	B32F	1/46	RW Appleby, Conisholme (LI)
11106	DDL 874	Duple	41506	B32F	1/46	Mrs M Groves (W Groves & Sons), East Cowes (IW)
11107	LRE 641	Duple	41513	B32F	12/45	Greatrex Motor Coaches Ltd, Stafford (ST) 27 Bullfinch
11108	?	SMT		B32F	c12/45	Air Ministry (Royal Air Force) (GOV)
11109	* RAF 208545	SMT		B32F	c12/45	Air Ministry (Royal Air Force) (GOV)
11110	* RAF 208542	SMT		B32F	c12/45	Air Ministry (Royal Air Force) (GOV)
11111	* s.306	NZMB		B24F	10/46	New Zealand Railways Road Services (O-NZ) 1448
11112, 11113						Exported to Ceylon
11114	P.353	Auckland TB		FB33F	-/48	Auckland Transport Board (O-NZ) 318
11115						Exported to Ceylon
11160		see 111666				
11654 - 11656						Exported to Ceylon
11657	CPY 821	Duple	41521	B32F	12/45	Saltburn Motor Services Ltd, Saltburn (NR) 3
11658	CPY 822	Duple	41514	B32F	12/45	Saltburn Motor Services Ltd, Saltburn (NR) 4
11659	FRM 88	Duple	41516	B32F	12/45	E Thomas, Dearham (CU)
11660	BJT 217	Duple	41509	B32F	12/45	CA Adams (Adams Bros) {Victory Tours}, Sixpenny Handley (DT)
11661	EUY 356	Duple	41515	B30F	12/45	GE Rouse, Blockley (GL)
11712	LRE 640	Duple	41511	B32F	12/45	Greatrex Motor Coaches Ltd, Stafford (ST) 26 Goldfinch
11713	DMR 835	Duple	41910	B32F	1/46	Norton's Motors (Malmesbury) Ltd (WI)

C1252/13

11714	GRO 205	Duple	41527	B32F	1/46	London, Midland & Scottish Railway Co {LMS}, Watford (XHT)
11715, 11716						Exported to Ceylon
11717	s.771	NZMB		B24F	10/46	New Zealand Railways Road Services (O-NZ) 1447
11718						Exported to Ceylon
11719 - 11722						Exported to New Zealand
11723	GRO 206	Duple	41528	B32F	1/46	London, Midland & Scottish Railway Co {LMS}, Watford (XHT)
11724	* ?	Magee		B32-	-/49	Edgar Jim, Waipawa (O-NZ)
11725	* p.339	Auckland TB		FB33F	-/47	Auckland Transport Board (O-NZ) 304
11726						Exported to New Zealand
11727	* RAF 209744	?		B32F	c12/45	Air Ministry (Royal Air Force) (GOV)
11728	* RAF 209732	Mulliner		B32F	c12/45	Air Ministry (Royal Air Force) (GOV)
11729	* RAF 209733	?		B32F	c12/45	Air Ministry (Royal Air Force) (GOV)
11730	* RAF 209731	Mulliner		B32F	c12/45	Air Ministry (Royal Air Force) (GOV)
11731	EUE 421	Duple	42125	C29F	3/46	T Payne, Bedworth (WK)
12001	CUX 589	Duple	41524	B32F	12/45	J Jervis, Wellington (SH)
12002	DYS 933	Duple	41526	B20FM	1/46	SCWS Ltd {The Skye Transport Co}, Portree (IV)
12003	ENX 893	Duple	41534	B32F	1/46	Wainfleet Motor Services Ltd, Nuneaton (WK)
12004	CFW 833	Duple	41531	B32F	1/46	E & F Adams {E Adams & Son}, Saltfleet (LI)
12005	CRX 547	Duple	41523	B26F	1/46	Thames Valley, Reading (BE) 438
12006	CDT 759	Duple	41532	B32F	1/46	ER Dodd {Selwyn Motors}, Belton (KN)
12007	FUP 521	Duple	41522	B32F	3/46	Shaw Bros {Bonnie Heather}, Byers Green (DM)
12008	?	?		B--F	-/--	Air Ministry (Royal Air Force) (GOV)
12009	* RAF 209734	?		B32F	-/--	Air Ministry (Royal Air Force) (GOV)
12010	?	?		B--F	-/--	Air Ministry (Royal Air Force) (GOV)
12011	?	Duple	41725	B--F	-/--	Original operator unknown (O-CL)
12012						Exported to New Zealand
12013	?	Duple	41731	B--F	-/--	Original operator unknown (O-CL)
12014						Exported to Ceylon
12015						Exported to New Zealand
12016	p.617	North Shore		B33F	-/47	North Shore Transport Co Ltd, Takapuna (O-NZ) 17
12017	* CE 7021	?		?	8/46	Panadura Motor Transit, Panadura (O-CL)
12018						Exported to New Zealand
12019	FDD 863	Duple	41901	B32F	1/46	AH, V & Mrs E Fluck {Fluck & Sons}, Notgrove (GL)
12020	VV 9042	Duple	41533	B32F	12/45	RG & T Wesley, Stoke Goldington (BK)
12021	CJY 317	Duple	41536	B32F	12/45	Millbrook Steamboat & Trading Co Ltd (CO)
12022	AGS 215	Duple	41539	B32F	11/45	A & C McLennan, Spittalfield (PH) 19
12023	JVT 330	Duple	41530	B32F	12/45	AJ, WH & LW Jeffreys {W Jeffreys & Sons}, Goldenhill (ST)
12024	CUX 592	Duple	41529	B31F	12/45	H Carter {Reliance}, Ironbridge (SH)
12025	JS 6924	Duple	41538	B32F	1/46	P MacAulay, Carloway, Lewis (RY)
12026	FFD 480	Duple	42122	C29F	3/46	J Green, Brierley Hill (ST)
12028	* ?	Benton		B33F	-/47	Northern Motor Bus Co, Whangarei (O-NZ) 12
12031	?	Duple	41726	B--F	-/--	Original operator unknown (O-CL)
12033	?	Duple	41729	B--F	-/--	Original operator unknown (O-CL)
12035	* ?	Auckland TB		FB33F	-/48	Auckland Transport Board (O-NZ) 335
12038	* s.307	NZMB		B24F	10/46	New Zealand Railways Road Services (O-NZ) 1449
12040	?	Duple	41728	B--F	-/--	Exported to unknown overseas location
12041	s.903	NZMB		B24F	5/47	New Zealand Railways Road Services (O-NZ) 1459
12044	?	Duple	41727	B--F	-/--	Original operator unknown (O-CL)
12047	* RAF 209737	?		B32F	-/--	Air Ministry (Royal Air Force) (GOV)
12049	* (RAF 208548 ?)	?		B32F	-/--	Air Ministry (Royal Air Force) (GOV)
12052	* RAF 209741	?		B32F	-/--	Air Ministry (Royal Air Force) (GOV)
12054	GBP 628	Duple	41520	B32F	12/45	Hare & Sons (Arundel) Ltd (WS)
12057	FUP 567	Duple	41542	B32F	1/46	J Iveson & Son, Esh (DM)
12059	* 1292	Guernsey Motors		B32F	3/46	Guernsey Motors (CI) 2
12061	BNL 673	Duple	41543	B32F	12/45	Bedlington & District Luxury Coaches Ltd, Ashington (ND)
12064	HKX 651	Duple	41902	B32F	1/46	AG Varney, Buckingham (BK)
12066	LRE 794	Duple	41545	B32F	12/45	H Nickolls, Milford (ST) 3
12068	FTG 446	Duple	41909	B32F	3/46	EP John {Kenfig Motors}, Kenfig Hill (GG)
12071	EDK 965	Duple	42114	C27F	4/46	WE Taylor, Castleton (LA)
12072		see 12702				

C1252/14

12073	P.369	Auckland TB		FB33F	12/48	Auckland Transport Board (O-NZ) 34
12074	P.354	Auckland TB		FB33F	-/48	Auckland Transport Board (O-NZ) 19
12076	* P.576	Suburban		B33F	9/47	Suburban Buses Ltd, Te Papapa (O-NZ) 35
12078	?	NZMB		B24F	4/47	New Zealand Railways Road Services (O-NZ) 1455
12079		see 12709				
12080	?	Duple	41730	B--F	-/--	Original operator unknown (O-CL)
12081	* P.575	Suburban		B33F	9/47	Suburban Buses Ltd, Te Papapa (O-NZ) 34
12083	?	NZMB		B24F	10/46	New Zealand Railways Road Services (O-NZ) 1445
12085						Exported to Ceylon
12092	* P.126	Eaddy & Taylor		B33F	4/47	Howick Bus Co Ltd, Auckland (O-NZ) 4
12095						Exported to Ceylon
12097	s1.116	NZMB		B24F	4/47	New Zealand Railways Road Services (O-NZ) 1458
12099	?	NZMB		B24F	4/47	New Zealand Railways Road Services (O-NZ) 1457
12702	* ?	NZMB		B24F	-/47	New Zealand Railways Road Services (O-NZ) 1456
12704						Exported to Ceylon
12706						Exported to unknown location via Crown Agents
12709	* v1.828	Suburban		B33F	9/47	Suburban Buses Ltd, Te Papapa (O-NZ) 33
12710	ASD 961	Duple	42106	C29F	4/46	D Blane {Blane's Motor Coach Services}, Kilmarnock (AR)
12712	EU 7948	Duple	41547	B32F	11/45	WC Fouracre {Embassy Motors}, Brynmawr (BC)
12714	* FT 5651	Duple	42100	C29F	3/46	TH Taylor {Taylor Bros}, North Shields (ND)
12715	EWY 35	Duple	41546	B32F	1/46	J Cowgill & Sons, Lothersdale (WR)
12717	CUX 614	Duple	41540	B28F	1/46	JW, WHF & GW Lloyd, Oswestry (SH) 11
12718	BNL 642	Duple	42107	C29F	3/46	W Smith {Safeway Coaches}, Bedlington Station (ND)
12720	GV 9865	Duple	42102	C29F	3/46	M & H Murfet, Barrow (CM)
12722	* CE 5575	Duple	41735	B--F	3/46	Original operator unknown (O-CL)
12723	EWY 61	Duple	41541	B32F	12/45	F & A Wigmore {Excelsior}, Dinnington (WR)
12725						Exported to Ceylon
12727	?	Duple	41732	B--F	-/--	Original operator unknown (O-CL)
12728, 12730, 12731, 12733						Exported to Ceylon
12735	?	Duple	41737	B--F	-/--	Original operator unknown (O-CL)
12736	?	Mulliner		B--F	-/--	Air Ministry (Royal Air Force) (GOV)
12738	?	Mulliner		B--F	-/--	Air Ministry (Royal Air Force) (GOV)
12740	* RAF 208547	SMT		B32F	c1/46	Air Ministry (Royal Air Force) (GOV)
12742	* (RAF 208548 ?)	SMT		B32F	c1/46	Air Ministry (Royal Air Force) (GOV)
12743	* RAF 209739	Mulliner		B32F	-/46	Air Ministry (Royal Air Force) (GOV)
12744	* RAF 208549	SMT		B32F	c1/46	Air Ministry (Royal Air Force) (GOV)
12745	* RAF 208552	?		B32F	-/--	Air Ministry (Royal Air Force) (GOV)
12746	?	Mulliner		B--F	-/--	Air Ministry (Royal Air Force) (GOV)
12748	* RAF 208551	?		B32F	-/--	Air Ministry (Royal Air Force) (GOV)
12749	* RAF 208550	SMT		B32F	c1/46	Air Ministry (Royal Air Force) (GOV)
12751	?	Mulliner		B--F	-/--	Air Ministry (Royal Air Force) (GOV)
12753	* CE 7292	?		-33-	9/46	Original operator unknown (O-CL)
12754	HKK 709	Duple	42101	C27F	4/46	Pilcher's Coaches Ltd, Chatham (KT)
12756	GTB 539	Duple	42105	C27F	4/46	KS Harvey {Pilot}, Maghull (LA)
12758	HLX 832	Duple	42117	C27F	4/46	Keith & Boyle (London) Ltd {Orange Luxury Coaches}, London EC2 (LN) Clara
12759	GRR 19	Duple	41908	B32F	2/46	Major's Coaches Ltd {Red Bus Service}, Worksop (NG)
12761	?	Duple	41736	B--F	-/--	Original operator unknown (O-CL)
12762	?	Duple	41739	B--F	-/--	Original operator unknown (O-CL)
12764						Exported to Ceylon
12765		see 12766				
12766	* ?	Duple	41734	B--F	-/--	Original operator unknown (O-CL)
12767	EUY 592	Duple	41904	B32F	1/46	Mrs ME Ward {Ward's Super de Luxe}, Sidemoor (WO)
12769	JV 9032	Duple	42119	C29F	5/46	FA & WR Stark (FA Stark and Sons), Tetney (LI)
12771	NS 1953	Duple	41549	B32F	12/45	D O'Brien, Bettyhill (SU)
12772	HLX 831	Duple	42116	C27F	4/46	Keith & Boyle (London) Ltd {Orange Luxury Coaches}, London EC2 (LN) Alma
12774						Exported to Ceylon
12775	?	Duple	41733	B--F	-/--	Original operator unknown (O-CL)
12777						Exported to Ceylon
12779						Exported to unknown location via Crown Agents
12780	DAY 752	Duple	42108	C29F	3/46	Mrs KA Smeeton, Great Bowden (LE)
12782	HWE 475	Plaxton	?	FC30F	4/46	Law Bros Ltd, Sheffield (WR)

12784	* DCA 574	Duple	41905	B32F	4/46	HP Phillips, Glyn Ceiriog (DH)
12785	LMG 988	Duple	42103	C29F	3/46	H Burch, Harrow Weald (MX)
12787						Exported to Ceylon
12788	?	Duple	41748	B32F	-/46	Anglo Iranian Oil Co, Abadan (O-IR)
12790	?	Duple	41738	B--F	-/--	Original operator unknown (O-CL)
12792						Exported to unknown location via Crown Agents
12793	FUP 993	Duple	42170	C29F	6/46	FC Head, Coxhoe (DM)
12795	KPD 329	Duple	42112	C27F	4/46	HR Richmond {Epsom Coaches}, Epsom (SR)
12797	FUP 522	Duple	42121	C29F	6/46	Shaw Bros {Bonnie Heather}, Byers Green (DM)
12798	GJH 766	Duple	42110	C29F	3/46	F Heaton {Rush Green Coaches}, Langley (HT)
12800						Exported to Ceylon
13015		see 11009				
13402						Exported to Ceylon
13404						Exported to unknown location via Crown Agents
13405	?	Duple	41747	B32F	-/46	Anglo Iranian Oil Co, Abadan (O-IR)
13406	* RAF 208553	?		B32F	-/--	Air Ministry (Royal Air Force) (GOV)
13407	* RAF 208554	?		B32F	-/--	Air Ministry (Royal Air Force) (GOV)
13408	?	Mulliner		B--F	-/--	Air Ministry (Royal Air Force) (GOV)
13410	?	Mulliner		B--F	-/--	Air Ministry (Royal Air Force) (GOV)
13411	JRA 580	Duple	42104	C27F	4/46	WE Pashley, Bradwell (DE)
13413	CUX 760	Duple	42109	C29F	3/46	A Price {Excelsior}, Wrockwardine Wood (SH)
13415	DJF 671	Duple	42113	C29F	1/46	Mrs GH Clayton (Clayton Bros) {The Royal Blue}, Leicester (LE)
13416	CDT 772	Duple	41903	B30F	1/46	A Hopley & F Richardson {Majestic}, Thorne (WR)
13418, 13419, 13421						Exported to Ceylon
13422	?	Duple	41746	B32F	-/46	Anglo Iranian Oil Co, Abadan (O-IR)
13423	FDD 832	Duple	41548	B32F	1/46	EC Young {Cotswold Coaches}, Stow-on-the-Wold (GL)
13425	JE 7906	Duple	41935	B32F	2/46	JW Brown {Marquis Service}, Guyhirn (CM)
13427	SS 6192	Duple	42120	C29F	5/46	J Ewart, Haddington (EL)
13428	DBE 346	Duple	42111	C29F	4/46	G Lewis {Daisy Bus Service}, Broughton (LI)
13430, 13431						Exported to unknown location via Crown Agents
13433						Exported to Ceylon
13434	?	Duple	41750	B32F	-/46	Anglo Iranian Oil Co, Abadan (O-IR)
13435	GRR 436	Duple	41911	B32F	2/46	LW Evans, East Kirkby (NG) 2
13437	GJH 2	Duple	41907	B32F	2/46	EG Hewitt {Premier Coaches}, Watford (HT)
13439	FUP 499	Duple	41906	B32F	1/46	H Frazer Ltd {Dale Coaches}, Swalwell (DM)
13440	FNG 931	Duple	41923	B30F	2/46	WT Jarvis, Swaffham (NK)
13442, 13443						Exported to Ceylon
13445						Exported to unknown location via Crown Agents
13446	?	Duple	41752	B32F	-/46	Anglo Iranian Oil Co, Abadan (O-IR)
13448	* RAF 208559	SMT		B32F	c1/46	Air Ministry (Royal Air Force) (GOV)
13449	?	Mulliner		B--F	-/--	Air Ministry (Royal Air Force) (GOV)
13451	?	Mulliner		B--F	-/--	Air Ministry (Royal Air Force) (GOV)
13452	* RAF 208556	SMT		B32F	c1/46	Air Ministry (Royal Air Force) (GOV)
13454, 13455						Exported to unknown location via Crown Agents
13457						Exported to Ceylon
13458	?	Duple	41759	B32F	-/46	Anglo Iranian Oil Co, Abadan (O-IR)
13459	* RAF 208564	SMT		B32F	c1/46	Air Ministry (Royal Air Force) (GOV)
13461	?	Mulliner		B--F	-/--	Air Ministry (Royal Air Force) (GOV)
13463	* RAF 208557	SMT		B32F	c1/46	Air Ministry (Royal Air Force) (GOV)
13464	* RAF 208555	SMT		B32F	c1/46	Air Ministry (Royal Air Force) (GOV)
13466						Exported to Ceylon
13467, 13469						Exported to unknown location via Crown Agents
13470	?	Duple	41756	B32F	-/46	Anglo Iranian Oil Co, Abadan (O-IR)
13471	* RAF 208566	?		B32F	-/--	Air Ministry (Royal Air Force) (GOV)
13472	* RAF 208558	SMT		B32F	c1/46	Air Ministry (Royal Air Force) (GOV)
13473	?	Mulliner		B--F	-/--	Air Ministry (Royal Air Force) (GOV)
13475	* (RAF 208565 ?)	SMT		B32F	c1/46	Air Ministry (Royal Air Force) (GOV)
13476	HLX 839	Duple	42132	C27F	5/46	Keith & Boyle (London) Ltd {Orange Luxury Coaches}, London EC2 (LN) Myra
13478	KHK 178	Duple	41912	B32F	1/46	CR Pyman, Stambourne (EX)
13480	* LMY 893	Duple	42124	C29F	4/46	WD Hall Ltd, London SW19 (LN)
13481	* HLX 833	Duple	42118	C27F	4/46	Keith & Boyle (London) Ltd {Orange Luxury Coaches}, London EC2 (LN) Diana

13483, 13484, 13486   Exported to unknown location via Crown Agents
13487   ?   Duple   41755   B32F   -/46 Anglo Iranian Oil Co, Abadan (O-IR)
13488   DDL 924   Duple   41917   B32F   2/46 MJ Wavell {Enterprise Bus Service}, Newport (IW)
13490   * DDL 928   Duple   42162   C29F   3/46 Fountain Garage Ltd, Cowes (IW)
13492   HKX 654   Duple   41544   B32F   1/46 JRG Dell {Rover Bus Service}, Lye Green (BK) 5
13493   XG 8276   Duple   42123   C29F   4/46 Lambert & Co, Middlesbrough (NR)
13495, 13496   Exported to unknown location via Crown Agents
13498   * CE 7885   ?   ?   10/46 Original operator unknown (O-CL)
13499   ?   Duple   41749   B32F   -/46 Anglo Iranian Oil Co, Abadan (O-IR)
13500   * RAF 95848   Mulliner   B32F   -/-- Air Ministry (Royal Air Force) (GOV)
13715   * ?   ?   B--F   -/-- Unknown Government Department (GOV)
14121   * ?   ?   B--F   -/-- Unknown Government Department (GOV)
14202   ?   Mulliner   B--F   -/-- Air Ministry (Royal Air Force) (GOV)
14204   * RAF 95849   Mulliner   B32F   -/-- Air Ministry (Royal Air Force) (GOV)
14205   ?   Mulliner   B--F   -/-- Air Ministry (Royal Air Force) (GOV)
14207   ?   Mulliner   B--F   -/-- Air Ministry (Royal Air Force) (GOV)
14208   * RAF 95850   Mulliner   B32F   -/-- Air Ministry (Royal Air Force) (GOV)
14210   * RAF 208561 SMT   B32F   c1/46 Air Ministry (Royal Air Force) (GOV)
14211   ?   Duple   41757   B32F   -/46 Anglo Iranian Oil Co, Abadan (O-IR)
14212   ?   Mulliner   B--F   -/-- Air Ministry (Royal Air Force) (GOV)
14214   ?   Mulliner   B--F   -/-- Air Ministry (Royal Air Force) (GOV)
14216   * RAF 208560 SMT   B32F   c1/46 Air Ministry (Royal Air Force) (GOV)
14217   * RAF 208563 SMT   B32F   c1/46 Air Ministry (Royal Air Force) (GOV)
14219   * RAF 95851   Mulliner   B32F   -/-- Air Ministry (Royal Air Force) (GOV)
14220   * RAF 208562 SMT   B32F   c1/46 Air Ministry (Royal Air Force) (GOV)
14222   Exported to unknown location via Crown Agents
14223   ?   Duple   41754   B32F   -/46 Anglo Iranian Oil Co, Abadan (O-IR)
14224, 14226, 14228, 14229   Exported to unknown location via Crown Agents
14231, 14232, 14234   Exported to Ceylon
14235   ?   Duple   41758   B32F   -/46 Anglo Iranian Oil Co, Abadan (O-IR)
14236   Exported to unknown location via Crown Agents
14237, 14238, 14240, 14241   Exported to Ceylon
14243, 14245, 14246, 14248   Exported to unknown location via Crown Agents
14249   Exported to Ceylon
14250   Exported to unknown location via Crown Agents
14251   #?   Mulliner   41805   B32F   -/46 Anglo Iranian Oil Co, Abadan (O-IR)
14252 - 15254   Exported to unknown location via Crown Agents
14255   Exported to Ceylon
14256 - 14258   Exported to unknown location via Crown Agents
14259   ?   Duple   41760   B32F   -/46 Anglo Iranian Oil Co, Abadan (O-IR)
14260, 14262, 14264, 14265   Exported to unknown location via Crown Agents
14267, 14268   Exported to Ceylon
14270   Exported to unknown location via Crown Agents
14271   ?   Duple   41751   B32F   -/46 Anglo Iranian Oil Co, Abadan (O-IR)
14272, 14274, 14276, 14277, 14279, 14280, 14282   Exported to unknown location via Crown Agents
14283   ?   Duple   41761   B32F   -/46 Anglo Iranian Oil Co, Abadan (O-IR)
14284   Exported to Ceylon
14286   * ?   ?   -30-   -/-- Original operator unknown (O-CL)
14288, 14289   Exported to unknown location via Crown Agents
14291   Exported to Ceylon
14292, 14294   Exported to unknown location via Crown Agents
14295   ?   Duple   41762   B32F   -/46 Anglo Iranian Oil Co, Abadan (O-IR)
14296   HLX 836   Duple   42130   C27F   4/46 Keith & Boyle (London) Ltd {Orange Luxury Coaches},
                                                          London EC2 (LN) Matilda
14297   HLX 834   Duple   42128   C27F   4/46 Keith & Boyle (London) Ltd {Orange Luxury Coaches},
                                                          London EC2 (LN) Eva
14298   HLX 840   Duple   42131   C27F   5/46 Keith & Boyle (London) Ltd {Orange Luxury Coaches},
                                                          London EC2 (LN) Miranda
14300   HLX 835   Duple   42129   C27F   4/46 Keith & Boyle (London) Ltd {Orange Luxury Coaches},
                                                          London EC2 (LN) Laura
15001   BJT 471   Duple   42177   C29F   5/46 SC Sheasby {South Dorset Coaches}, Corfe Castle
                                                          (DT)
15003   HLX 838   Duple   42127   C27F   4/46 Keith & Boyle (London) Ltd {Orange Luxury Coaches},
                                                          London EC2 (LN) Gloria

C1252/17

15005	HLY 557	Duple	42134	C27F	5/46 Keith & Boyle (London) Ltd {Orange Luxury Coaches}, London EC2 (LN) Sara
15007					Exported to unknown location via Crown Agents
15008					Exported to Ceylon
15010					Exported to unknown location via Crown Agents
15011	?	Duple	41753	B32F	-/46 Anglo Iranian Oil Co, Abadan (O-IR)
15012					Exported to unknown location via Crown Agents
15014	GL 8583	Duple	42137	C29F	4/46 CJ & IH Fale, Combe Down (SO)
15015					Exported to unknown location via Crown Agents
15017	?	?	(shop ?)		-/-- Navy, Army & Air Force Institutes (NAAFI) (XLN)
15018, 15019, 15021, 15022, 15024					Exported to unknown location via Crown Agents
15025	?	Duple	41763	B32F	-/46 Anglo Iranian Oil Co, Abadan (O-IR)
15026, 15028					Exported to unknown location via Crown Agents
15030					Exported to Ceylon
15031					Exported to unknown location via Crown Agents
15032					Exported to Ireland
15034					Exported to unknown location via Crown Agents
15035	ID 3507	?		B26F	-/46 J McGirr {McGirr Bus Service], Arvagh (EI)
15037					Exported to unknown location via Crown Agents
15038	#?	Mulliner	41813	B32F	-/46 Anglo Iranian Oil Co, Abadan (O-IR)
15039	BJT 894	Duple	42169	C29F	5/46 RW Toop, WJ Ironside & PW Davis {Bere Regis & District}, Dorchester (DT)
15041	FUP 615	Duple	41925	B32F	1/46 Dixon Bros {The Witbank}, Lanchester (DM) 11
15043	J 11590	Duple	42115	C29F	3/46 RH Barney & AA Allo {Pioneer Coaches}, St Helier, Jersey (CI) 4
15044	HGP 514	Duple	41914	B16F	1/46 Adelphi Players, London NW8 (XLN)
15045	HHN 10	Duple	41924	B32F	2/46 Favourite Direct Services Ltd, Bishop Auckland (DM) 4
15047	BJT 892	Duple	42161	C29F	5/46 RW Toop, WJ Ironside & PW Davis {Bere Regis & District}, Dorchester (DT)
15048	HKM 15	Duple	41920	B28F	1/46 CD Smith & Sons, Brenzett (KT)
15050	HLX 837	Duple	42126	C27F	4/46 Keith & Boyle (London) Ltd {Orange Luxury Coaches}, London EC2 (LN) Dora
15051	?	Duple	41764	B32F	-/46 Anglo Iranian Oil Co, Abadan (O-IR)
15052	HLY 556	Duple	42133	C27F	5/46 Keith & Boyle (London) Ltd {Orange Luxury Coaches}, London EC2 (LN) Olga
15054	* CRX 857	Duple	42136	C29F	3/46 W & G Chandler, Wantage (BE)
15056	GPT 17	?		B32F	1/46 F Lockey & Son, St Helens Auckland (DM)
15057	* J 11593	Duple	42171	C29F	4/46 RH Barney & AA Allo {Pioneer Coaches}, St Helier, Jersey (CI)
15058	* FT 5681	Duple	42236	C29F	6/46 TH Taylor {Taylor Bros}, North Shields (ND)
15060	HKL 61	Duple	41913	B32F	1/46 HE Thomsett, Deal (KT)
15061	* FT 5666	Duple	42179	C29F	4/46 G Chapman {Priory Motor Coach Co}, North Shields (ND) 36
15063	JDH 518	Duple	41922	B32F	1/46 Pearson's Motorways Ltd, Walsall (ST)
15064	#?	Mulliner	41789	B32F	-/46 Anglo Iranian Oil Co, Abadan (O-IR)
15065	#?	Duple	41839	B28D	-/46 Uganda Transport Co Ltd, Kampala (O-EAU)
15066	#A 4826	Duple	41836	B32F	9/46 Kenya Bus Services (Mombasa) Ltd (O-EAK) 20
15067	#A 4827	Duple	41837	B32F	9/46 Kenya Bus Services (Mombasa) Ltd (O-EAK) 21
15068	#?	Duple	41845	B28D	-/46 Uganda Transport Co Ltd, Kampala (O-EAU)
15069					Exported to Melbourne (O-AUS)
15070	* A 4828	Duple	41838	B32F	9/46 Kenya Bus Services (Mombasa) Ltd (O-EAK) 22
15072	DDL 929	Duple	42165	C29F	3/46 Fountain Garage Ltd, Cowes (IW)
15074	* CRX 858	Duple	42135	C29F	3/46 W & G Chandler, Wantage (BE)
15075	* CSA 234	Duple	41915	B32F	1/46 J Thomson Ross, Huntly (AD)
15076	BNL 929	Duple	42166	C29F	3/46 R Tait, Kirkwhelpington (ND)
15078	BJT 890	Duple	42139	C29F	4/46 RW Toop, WJ Ironside & PW Davis {Bere Regis & District}, Dorchester (DT)
15079	FUP 954	Duple	42222	C29F	5/46 H Frazer Ltd {Dale Coaches}, Swalwell (DM)
15081	EF 7578	Duple	41953	B32F	3/46 Richardson Bros, West Hartlepool (DM)
15082	?	Duple	41766	B32F	-/46 Anglo Iranian Oil Co, Abadan (O-IR)
15083	BJT 472	Duple	42176	C29F	5/46 SC Sheasby {South Dorset Coaches}, Corfe Castle (DT)
15085	* GEL 502	Duple	42220	C29F	5/46 Shamrock & Rambler Motor Coaches Ltd, Bournemouth (HA)

C1252/18

15087	* GEL 500	Duple	42213 C29F	5/46	Shamrock & Rambler Motor Coaches Ltd, Bournemouth (HA)
15088	PS 1407	Duple	42186 C29F	4/46	W Thomson, Sandwich (SD)
15089	EJ 7671	Duple	42239 C29F	6/46	E & J Lloyd-Jones {Lloyd-Jones Bros}, Pontrhydygroes (CG)
15091	HUC 194	Duple	42174 C27F	5/46	GJ Miller {GJ Miller & Son}, Cirencester (GL)
15092	BNL 930	Duple	42167 C29F	3/46	R Tait, Kirkwhelpington (ND)
15094	FPW 26	Duple	42180 C29F	5/46	JC Brown {Norfolk Coachways}, Attleborough (NK)
15095	?	Duple	41774 B32F	-/46	Anglo Iranian Oil Co, Abadan (O-IR)
15096	BJT 470	Duple	42175 C29F	5/46	W Dean & Sons {Swanage Coaches}, Chickrell (DT)
15098	BJT 891	Duple	42160 C29F	5/46	RW Toop, WJ Ironside & PW Davis {Bere Regis & District}, Dorchester (DT)
15100	HAF 798	Duple	41927 B32F	3/46	TW Mundy (TW Mundy & Son) {Silver Queen}, Camborne (CO)
15430	* P.766	Transport BS	B35F	-/46	Transport BS Ltd, Auckland (O-NZ) 30
15901	ACF 54	Duple	42163 C29F	5/46	HC Chambers & Son Ltd {Chambers & Sons}, Bures (WF)
15902	CVN 208	Duple	42172 C29F	4/46	TA Howard, Whitby (NR)
15904	GHN 942	Duple	41919 B32F	1/46	Summerson Bros {The Eden}, West Auckland (DM)
15905	CSA 472	Duple	42164 C29F	5/46	JAS McIntyre, Bucksburn (AD)
15907	BST 173	Duple	41930 B20F(M?)	3/46	Ardgour & Acharacle Motor Services Ltd, Fort William (IV)
15908	?	Duple	41778 B32F	-/46	Anglo Iranian Oil Co, Abadan (O-IR)
15909	BJT 893	Duple	42168 C29F	5/46	RW Toop, WJ Ironside & PW Davis {Bere Regis & District}, Dorchester (DT)
15911	GV 9759	Duple	41926 B32F	2/46	L Keeble, Bildeston (WF)
15913	EOT 784	Duple	42178 C29F	4/46	Odiham Motor Services Ltd (HA)
15914	EP 8950	Duple	41918 B32F	2/46	HM Bunford, Trefeglwys (MO)
15915	FTG 536	Duple	41929 B32F	3/46	DT & R Davies {Cream Line Services}, Tonmawr (GG)
15917	* CUJ 38	Duple	41999 B32F	3/46	Salopia Saloon Coaches Ltd, Whitchurch (SH) 42
15918	BJT 889	Duple	42138 C29F	3/46	RW Toop, WJ Ironside & PW Davis {Bere Regis & District}, Dorchester (DT)
15920	JRA 476	Duple	41938 B32F	2/46	N Frost {Felix Bus Service}, Stanley (DE)
15921	#?	Mulliner	41783 B32F	-/46	Anglo Iranian Oil Co, Abadan (O-IR)
15922	HAF 797	Duple	41916 B32F	6/46	WF Berriman {Berriman' Motor Service}, Troon (CO)
15924	GHN 938	Duple	41928 B32F	2/46	JW Robinson, Low Etherley (DM)
15959	* KPD 956	Duple	42173 C29F	6/46	Ripley Motor Works Ltd, Ripley (SR)
15960	CJY 533	Duple	42198 C29F	5/46	Plymouth Co-operative Society (DN) 503
15961	?	?	B--F	-/--	Air Ministry (Royal Air Force) (GOV)
15963	* RAF 208642	SMT	B32F	c2/46	Air Ministry (Royal Air Force) (GOV)
15964	?	?	B--F	-/--	Air Ministry (Royal Air Force) (GOV)
15966	* RAF 209765	?	B32F	-/--	Air Ministry (Royal Air Force) (GOV)
15967	?	Duple	41765 B32F	-/46	Anglo Iranian Oil Co, Abadan (O-IR)
15968	* RAF 209766	Mulliner	B32F	-/--	Air Ministry (Royal Air Force) (GOV)
15970	* RAF 209779	Mulliner	B32F	-/--	Air Ministry (Royal Air Force) (GOV)
15972	* RAF 208595	SMT	B32F	c2/46	Air Ministry (Royal Air Force) (GOV)
15973	* RAF 209768	Mulliner	B32F	-/--	Air Ministry (Royal Air Force) (GOV)
15974	* RAF 208567	?	B32F	-/--	Air Ministry (Royal Air Force) (GOV)
15976	* RAF 209776	?	B32F	-/--	Air Ministry (Royal Air Force) (GOV)
15977	* RAF 208634	SMT	B32F	-/--	Air Ministry (Royal Air Force) (GOV)
15979	* RAF 209770	?	B32F	-/--	Air Ministry (Royal Air Force) (GOV)
15980	?	Duple	41769 B32F	-/46	Anglo Iranian Oil Co, Abadan (O-IR)
15981	?	Mulliner	B--F	-/--	Air Ministry (Royal Air Force) (GOV)
15982	* RAF 208568	?	B32F	-/--	Air Ministry (Royal Air Force) (GOV)
15983	* RAF 208578	?	B32F	-/--	Air Ministry (Royal Air Force) (GOV)
15984	* RAF 209767	Mulliner	B32F	-/--	Air Ministry (Royal Air Force) (GOV)
15985	* RAF 209773	Mulliner	B32F	-/--	Air Ministry (Royal Air Force) (GOV)
15986	* RAF 208569	?	B32F	-/--	Air Ministry (Royal Air Force) (GOV)
15988	* RAF 209772	Mulliner	B33F	-/46	Air Ministry (Royal Air Force) (GOV)
15990	* RAF 209777	Mulliner	B32F	-/--	Air Ministry (Royal Air Force) (GOV)
15991	* RAF 209763	Mulliner	B32F	-/46	Air Ministry (Royal Air Force) (GOV)
15992	* RAF 208629	?	B32F	-/--	Air Ministry (Royal Air Force) (GOV)
15994	* RAF 209769	Mulliner	B32F	-/--	Air Ministry (Royal Air Force) (GOV)
15995	* RAF 208575	?	B32F	-/--	Air Ministry (Royal Air Force) (GOV)

15997	* RAF 208570	?		B32F	-/--	Air Ministry (Royal Air Force) (GOV)
15998	?	Duple	41768	B32F	-/46	Anglo Iranian Oil Co, Abadan (O-IR)
15999	* RAF 208571	?		B32F	-/--	Air Ministry (Royal Air Force) (GOV)
16601	* RAF 208572	Mulliner		B32F	-/46	Air Ministry (Royal Air Force) (GOV)
16603	* RAF 209761	?		B32F	-/--	Air Ministry (Royal Air Force) (GOV)
16604	* RAF 208581	?		B32F	-/--	Air Ministry (Royal Air Force) (GOV)
16605	* RAF 209778	Mulliner		B32F	-/--	Air Ministry (Royal Air Force) (GOV)
16607	* RAF 209775	Mulliner		B32F	-/46	Air Ministry (Royal Air Force) (GOV)
16608	* RAF 209790	Mulliner		B32F	-/46	Air Ministry (Royal Air Force) (GOV)
16610	* RAF 208579	?		B32F	-/--	Air Ministry (Royal Air Force) (GOV)
16611	?	Duple	41767	B32F	-/46	Anglo Iranian Oil Co, Abadan (O-IR)
16612	* RAF 208621	?		B32F	-/--	Air Ministry (Royal Air Force) (GOV)
16614	* RAF 208596	SMT		B32F	c3/46	Air Ministry (Royal Air Force) (GOV)
16616	* RAF 209795	?		B32F	-/--	Air Ministry (Royal Air Force) (GOV)
16617	* RAF 209782	?		B32F	-/--	Air Ministry (Royal Air Force) (GOV)
16618	* RAF 208597	SMT		B32F	c3/46	Air Ministry (Royal Air Force) (GOV)
16620	* RAF 208639	SMT		B32F	c3/46	Air Ministry (Royal Air Force) (GOV)
16621	* RAF 209784	?		B--F	-/--	Air Ministry (Royal Air Force) (GOV)
16623	* RAF 208618	?		B32F	-/--	Air Ministry (Royal Air Force) (GOV)
16624	?	Duple	41771	B32F	-/46	Anglo Iranian Oil Co, Abadan (O-IR)
16625	* RAF 208643	SMT		B32F	c3/46	Air Ministry (Royal Air Force) (GOV)
16627	* RAF 208580	?		B32F	-/--	Air Ministry (Royal Air Force) (GOV)
16629	* RAF 208635	?		B32F	-/--	Air Ministry (Royal Air Force) (GOV)
16630	* RAF 208622	?		B32F	-/--	Air Ministry (Royal Air Force) (GOV)
16631	* ?	?		B--F	-/--	Air Ministry (Royal Air Force) (GOV)
16633	* RAF 208608	SMT		B32F	c3/46	Air Ministry (Royal Air Force) (GOV)
16634	* RAF 208607	SMT		B32F	c3/46	Air Ministry (Royal Air Force) (GOV)
16636	* RAF 208612	?		B32F	-/--	Air Ministry (Royal Air Force) (GOV)
16637	#?	Mulliner	41802	B32F	-/46	Anglo Iranian Oil Co, Abadan (O-IR)
16638	* RAF 208632	?		B32F	-/--	Air Ministry (Royal Air Force) (GOV)
16639	* RAF 208592	SMT		B32F	-/46	Air Ministry (Royal Air Force) (GOV)
16640	?	?		B--F	-/--	Air Ministry (Royal Air Force) (GOV)
16641	* RAF 208900	?		B32F	-/--	Air Ministry (Royal Air Force) (GOV)
16642	* RAF 209792	?		B32F	-/--	Air Ministry (Royal Air Force) (GOV)
16643	* RAF 208609	SMT		B32F	c3/46	Air Ministry (Royal Air Force) (GOV)
16644	* RAF 208633	?		B32F	-/--	Air Ministry (Royal Air Force) (GOV)
16645	* RAF 208604	SMT		B32F	c3/46	Air Ministry (Royal Air Force) (GOV)
16646	?	Duple	41770	B32F	-/46	Anglo Iranian Oil Co, Abadan (O-IR)
16647	* RAF 208577	?		B32F	-/--	Air Ministry (Royal Air Force) (GOV)
16648	* RAF 208605	SMT		B32F	c3/46	Air Ministry (Royal Air Force) (GOV)
16649	* RAF 208576	?		B32F	-/--	Air Ministry (Royal Air Force) (GOV)
16650	* RAF 208574	?		B32F	-/--	Air Ministry (Royal Air Force) (GOV)
16651	* RAF 208610	SMT		B32F	c3/46	Air Ministry (Royal Air Force) (GOV)
16652	* RAF 208602	SMT		B32F	c3/46	Air Ministry (Royal Air Force) (GOV)
16653	?	?		B--F	-/--	Air Ministry (Royal Air Force) (GOV)
16654	#?	Mulliner	41819	B32F	-/46	Anglo Iranian Oil Co, Abadan (O-IR)
16655	* (RAF 208582 ?)	SMT		B32F	c3/46	Air Ministry (Royal Air Force) (GOV)
16656	* RAF 208603	SMT		B32F	c3/46	Air Ministry (Royal Air Force) (GOV)
16657	* RAF 208583	SMT		B32F	c3/46	Air Ministry (Royal Air Force) (GOV)
16658	* RAF 208584	SMT		B32F	c3/46	Air Ministry (Royal Air Force) (GOV)
16659	* RAF 208606	SMT		B32F	c3/46	Air Ministry (Royal Air Force) (GOV)
16660	* RAF 208591	SMT		B32F	c3/46	Air Ministry (Royal Air Force) (GOV)
16661	* RAF 208611	SMT		B32F	c3/46	Air Ministry (Royal Air Force) (GOV)
16662	#?	Mulliner	41803	B32F	-/46	Anglo Iranian Oil Co, Abadan (O-IR)
16663	* RAF 208640	SMT		B32F	c3/46	Air Ministry (Royal Air Force) (GOV)
16664	* RAF 208636	?		B32F	-/--	Air Ministry (Royal Air Force) (GOV)
16665	* RAF 208599	SMT		B32F	c3/46	Air Ministry (Royal Air Force) (GOV)
16666	* RAF 208638	SMT		B32F	c3/46	Air Ministry (Royal Air Force) (GOV)
16667	* RAF 208585	SMT		B32F	c3/46	Air Ministry (Royal Air Force) (GOV)
16668	* RAF 209771	Mulliner		B32F	-/--	Air Ministry (Royal Air Force) (GOV)
16669	* RAF 209774	Mulliner		B32F	-/--	Air Ministry (Royal Air Force) (GOV)
16670	#?	Mulliner	41800	B32F	-/46	Anglo Iranian Oil Co, Abadan (O-IR)
16671	* RAF 208600	SMT		B32F	c3/46	Air Ministry (Royal Air Force) (GOV)
16672	* RAF 208587	SMT		B32F	c3/46	Air Ministry (Royal Air Force) (GOV)

16673	* RAF 208586	?		B32F	-/--	Air Ministry (Royal Air Force) (GOV)
16674	* RAF 208588	SMT		B32F	c3/46	Air Ministry (Royal Air Force) (GOV)
16675	* RAF 208613	?		B32F	-/--	Air Ministry (Royal Air Force) (GOV)
16676	* RAF 209780	?		B32F	-/--	Air Ministry (Royal Air Force) (GOV)
16677	* RAF 208589	SMT		B32F	c3/46	Air Ministry (Royal Air Force) (GOV)
16678	?	Duple	41772	B32F	-/46	Anglo Iranian Oil Co, Abadan (O-IR)
16679	* RAF 208590	SMT		B32F	c3/46	Air Ministry (Royal Air Force) (GOV)
16680	* RAF 208593	SMT		B32F	c3/46	Air Ministry (Royal Air Force) (GOV)
16681	* RAF 209781	?		B32F	-/--	Air Ministry (Royal Air Force) (GOV)
16682	* RAF 208594	SMT		B32F	c3/46	Air Ministry (Royal Air Force) (GOV)
16683	* RAF 209785	?		B32F	-/--	Air Ministry (Royal Air Force) (GOV)
16684	* (RAF 208601	?)SMT		B32F	c3/46	Air Ministry (Royal Air Force) (GOV)
16685	* RAF 209783	?		B32F	-/--	Air Ministry (Royal Air Force) (GOV)
16686	?	Duple	41776	B32F	-/46	Anglo Iranian Oil Co, Abadan (O-IR)
16687	?	Duple	41931	B32F	-/--	Navy, Army & Air Force Institutes (NAAFI) (XLN)
16688	?	Duple	41932	B32F	-/--	Navy, Army & Air Force Institutes (NAAFI) (XLN)
16689	* 5190800	Duple	41933	B32F	-/--	Navy, Army & Air Force Institutes (NAAFI) (XLN)
16690	#?	Duple	41843	B28D	-/46	Uganda Transport Co Ltd, Kampala (O-EAU)
16691	#?	Duple	41842	B28D	-/46	Uganda Transport Co Ltd, Kampala (O-EAU)
16692	#?	Duple	41840	B28D	-/46	Uganda Transport Co Ltd, Kampala (O-EAU)
16693	?	Duple	41773	B32F	-/46	Anglo Iranian Oil Co, Abadan (O-IR)
16694	#?	Duple	41841	B28D	-/46	Uganda Transport Co Ltd, Kampala (O-EAU)
16695	IH 5806	O'Doherty		B20F	1/47	Londonderry & Lough Swilly (LY) 26
16696	WI 2117	(Kenneally ?)		B30R	-/46	W Kenneally {Kenneally Bus Service}, Johnstown (EI)
16697	?	Duple	41934	B32F	-/--	Navy, Army & Air Force Institutes (NAAFI) (XLN)
16698	IH 5807	O'Doherty		B20F	1/47	Londonderry & Lough Swilly (LY) 27
16699	IH 5808	O'Doherty		B20F	-/47	Londonderry & Lough Swilly (LY) 28
16700						Exported to Port Elizabeth (O-ZA)
17201	#?	Mulliner	41780	B32F	-/46	Anglo Iranian Oil Co, Abadan (O-IR)
17202	JC 7732	Duple	41981	B32F	5/46	Mrs M Ellis, Llanllechid (CN)
17203	DJU 210	Duple	42185	C29F	5/46	Machin's Garage Ltd, Ashby-de-la-Zouch (LE)
17204	JS 6963	Duple	41942	B32F	-/46	DW MacDonald, Garrabost, Lewis (RY)
17205	BTY 187	Duple	42197	C29F	6/46	J Dickinson, Gunnarton (ND)
17206	* CJY 538	Duple	42215	C29F	6/46	Plymouth Co-operative Society (DN) 508
17207	CDP 236	Duple	41987	B32F	5/46	Reading Corporation (BE) 18
17208	CVN 71	Duple	41951	B32F	3/46	JJ Longstaff, Mirfield (WR)
17209	#?	Mulliner	41781	B32F	-/46	Anglo Iranian Oil Co, Abadan (O-IR)
17210	CDP 232	Duple	41983	B32F	5/46	Reading Corporation (BE) 13
17211	CJY 534	Duple	42199	C29F	5/46	Plymouth Co-operative Society (DN) 504
17212	GTB 564	Duple	42182	C29F	5/46	JH Battersby & Son Ltd {Blue Belle Coaches}, Morecambe (LA)
17213	ADO 270	Duple	41939	B32F	2/46	F Rose, Holbeach Drove (LI)
17214	#CVN 153	Plaxton	?	FC29F	12/46	Hardwick's Services Ltd, Snainton (NR)
17215	J 11592	Duple	42184	C29F	4/46	RH Barney & AA Allo {Pioneer Coaches}, St Helier, Jersey (CI)
17216	DCA 643	Duple	41943	B32F	3/46	RN & A Jones {Bryn Melyn Motor Service}, Llangollen (DH)
17217	#?	Mulliner	41786	B32F	-/46	Anglo Iranian Oil Co, Abadan (O-IR)
17218	BCT 54	Duple	41937	B32F	2/46	WJ Simmons {Reliance Coaches}, Great Gonerby (KN) 21
17219	* GEL 503	Duple	42219	C27F	5/46	Shamrock & Rambler Motor Coaches Ltd, Bournemouth (HA)
17220	FP 4207	Duple	42183	C29F	9/46	Mrs AM Glenn {Central Coaches}, Uppingham (RD) 4
17221	FPW 92	Duple	41940	B32F	2/46	WT Jarvis, Swaffham (NK)
17222	BCT 55	Duple	41936	B32F	2/46	WJ Simmons {Reliance Coaches}, Great Gonerby (KN) 22
17223	* GEL 509	Duple	42229	C27F	5/46	Shamrock & Rambler Motor Coaches Ltd, Bournemouth (HA)
17224	CJY 532	Duple	42196	C29F	5/46	Plymouth Co-operative Society (DN) 502
17225	?	Duple	41775	B32F	-/46	Anglo Iranian Oil Co, Abadan (O-IR)
17226						Exported to Port Elizabeth (O-ZA)
17227 - 17231						Exported to Malaya
17232						Exported to Port Elizabeth (O-ZA)
17233	#?	Mulliner	41790	B32F	-/46	Anglo Iranian Oil Co, Abadan (O-IR)

17234, 17235						Exported to Malaya
17236						Exported to Port Elizabeth (O-ZA)
17237 - 17240						Exported to Malaya
17241	?	Duple	41777	B32F	-/46	Anglo Iranian Oil Co, Abadan (O-IR)
17242	DCJ 776	Duple	42193	C29F	5/46	Miss I Baynham, Ross-on-Wye (HR)
17243	DCJ 777	Duple	42194	C29F	5/46	Miss I Baynham, Ross-on-Wye (HR)
17244	EUE 798	Duple	42189	C29F	5/46	J Lloyd & Son Ltd, Nuneaton (WK)
17245	BVG 722	Duple	42192	C27F	12/46	HA & Mrs ME Roberts {Red Car Service}, Norwich (NK)
17246	CJY 531	Duple	42191	C29F	5/46	Plymouth Co-operative Society (DN) 501
17247	* GYC 892	Duple	42187	C29F	5/46	JA Wintle {Wintle & Murray}, Bower Hinton (SO)
17248	JC 7734	Duple	41979	B32F	5/46	CJ Roberts {Purple Motors}, Bethesda (CN)
17249	#?	Mulliner	41779	B32F	-/46	Anglo Iranian Oil Co, Abadan (O-IR)
17250 - 17254						Exported to Malaya
17255	CVA 242	Duple	42190	C29F	5/46	McAteer & Son, Broomhouse (LK)
17256	HLY 564	Duple	42188	C27F	5/46	Shamrock & Rambler Motor Coaches Ltd, Bournemouth (HA)
17257	#?	Mulliner	41782	B32F	-/46	Anglo Iranian Oil Co, Abadan (O-IR)
17258	1833	Strachan		B32F	6/46	Guernsey Motors (CI) 7
17259	* GEL 507	Duple	42223	C27F	5/46	Shamrock & Rambler Motor Coaches Ltd, Bournemouth (HA)
17260	FBJ 870	Duple	41941	B32F	3/46	B Beeston & Sons Ltd, East Bergholt (EK)
17261	KPC 658	Duple	41949	B32F	2/46	Safeguard Coaches Ltd, Guildford (SR)
17262	FPW 27	Duple	42195	C27F	6/46	Culling & Son (Norwich) Ltd {Claxton & District}, Claxton (NK)
17263	* CJY 535	Duple	42210	C29F	5/46	Plymouth Co-operative Society (DN) 505
17264	* GEL 510	Duple	42232	C27F	5/46	Shamrock & Rambler Motor Coaches Ltd, Bournemouth (HA)
17265	#?	Mulliner	41784	B32F	-/46	Anglo Iranian Oil Co, Abadan (O-IR)
17266	DCA 644	Duple	41944	B32F	3/46	RN & A Jones {Bryn Melyn Motor Service}, Llangollen (DH)
17267	EUY 994	Duple	41969	B32F	3/46	AE Collins {Favourite}, Lye (WO)
17268	CJY 536	Duple	42211	C29F	5/46	Plymouth Co-operative Society (DN) 506
17269	HKN 750	Duple	42235	C29F	7/46	PWJ Jessop, Frinstead (KT)
17270	EF 7577	Duple	41952	B32F	3/46	Richardson Bros, West Hartlepool (DM)
17271	CPN 183	Duple	41991	B30F	6/46	D Bowles, Albourne Green (ES)
17272	* GEL 504	Duple	42218	C27F	5/46	Shamrock & Rambler Motor Coaches Ltd, Bournemouth (HA)
17273	#?	Mulliner	41788	B32F	-/46	Anglo Iranian Oil Co, Abadan (O-IR)
17274	BS 2268	Duple	42224	C27F	6/46	JG Nicolson, Kirkwall (OK)
17275	* GEL 508	Duple	42231	C27F	5/46	Shamrock & Rambler Motor Coaches Ltd, Bournemouth (HA)
17276	* FUP 669	Duple	42225	C29F	6/46	Anderson Bros {Blue Belle}, Evenwood (DM)
17277	CJY 537	Duple	42212	C29F	5/46	Plymouth Co-operative Society (DN) 507
17278	* GEL 501	Duple	42216	C27F	5/46	Shamrock & Rambler Motor Coaches Ltd, Bournemouth (HA)
17279	FUP 817	Duple	41960	B32F	3/46	Bond Bros {Imperial Motor Services}, Willington (DM)
17280	* JTT 719	Duple	41974	B32F	5/46	CB Foxworthy {Dart Bus Service}, Stoke Gabriel (DN)
17281	#?	Mulliner	41785	B32F	-/46	Anglo Iranian Oil Co, Abadan (O-IR)
17282	EF 7580	Duple	41955	B32F	3/46	Richardson Bros, West Hartlepool (DM)
17283	GYC 330	Duple	41948	B32F	3/46	HR, J & Miss V Gunn {Safeway Services}, South Petherton (SO)
17284	* FUP 723	Duple	42214	C29F	3/46	Braithwaite Tours Ltd, Stockton-on-Tees (DM)
17285	CDP 231	Duple	41982	B32F	4/46	Reading Corporation (BE) 12
17286	KTW 91	Duple	42228	C29F	6/46	L Hall & Sons, Maldon (EX)
17287	FT 5679	Duple	42221	C29F	6/46	G Chapman {Priory Motor Coach Co}, North Shields (ND) 37
17288	* GEL 505	Duple	42217	C27F	5/46	Shamrock & Rambler Motor Coaches Ltd, Bournemouth (HA)
17289	#?	Mulliner	41795	B32F	-/46	Anglo Iranian Oil Co, Abadan (O-IR)
17290	FVF 4	Duple	42230	C29F	6/46	WJ Rasberry {Gayton & District Bus Service}, Grimston (NK)
17291	JC 7729	Duple	41975	B32F	7/46	JW Hughes {Deiniolen Motors}, Deiniolen (CN)
17292	JE 7984	Duple	41962	B32F	6/46	T Canham & Sons (Services) Ltd, Whittlesey (CM)
17293	DWV 82	Duple	42227	C29F	6/46	E Drew, Highworth (WI)

C1252/22

17294	FT 5680	Duple	42233	C29F	6/46 G Chapman {Priory Motor Coach Co}, North Shields (ND) 38
17295	* GEL 506	Duple	42226	C27F	5/46 Shamrock & Rambler Motor Coaches Ltd, Bournemouth (HA)
17296	EF 7579	Duple	41954	B32F	3/46 Richardson Bros, West Hartlepool (DM)
17297	?	Duple	41879	B32F	-/46 Gibraltar Motor Hire Services (O-GBZ)
17298	RAF 208627	?		B32F	-/-- Air Ministry (Royal Air Force) (GOV)
17299	RAF 208614	SMT		B32F	c5/46 Air Ministry (Royal Air Force) (GOV)
17300	RAF 208615	SMT		B32F	c5/46 Air Ministry (Royal Air Force) (GOV)
18701	* RAF 209793	?		B32F	-/-- Air Ministry (Royal Air Force) (GOV)
18702	* RAF 208616	SMT		B32F	-/-- Air Ministry (Royal Air Force) (GOV)
18703	* RAF 209786	?		B32F	-/-- Air Ministry (Royal Air Force) (GOV)
18704	* RAF 208617	SMT		B32F	c5/46 Air Ministry (Royal Air Force) (GOV)
18705	#?	Mulliner	41787	B32F	-/46 Anglo Iranian Oil Co, Abadan (O-IR)
18706	* RAF 209794	?		B32F	-/-- Air Ministry (Royal Air Force) (GOV)
18707	JE 7925	Duple	41945	B32F	3/46 CJ Smith {Bluebell}, March (CM)
18708	SJ 1042	Duple	41946	B32F	3/46 F Kerr Newton {Newton's Motors}, Brodick, Arran (BU)
18709	CVN 564	Duple	42234	C29F	6/46 Saltburn Motor Services Ltd, Saltburn (NR) 6
18710	GV 9861	Duple	41947	B32F	3/46 GF Burgoin (Haverhill) Ltd {Grey Pullman Coaches} (WF)
18711	* JRA 737	Plaxton	?	FC30F	3/46 HD Andrew {Anchor Coaches}, Tideswell (DE)
18712	* DVJ 22	Duple	41965	B30F	5/46 S Smith {Smith's Motors}, Bitterley (SH)
18713	#?	Mulliner	41806	B32F	-/46 Anglo Iranian Oil Co, Abadan (O-IR)
18714	* ?	?		B--F	-/46 Admiralty (Royal Navy) (GOV)
18715	* RAF 208631	?		B32F	-/-- Air Ministry (Royal Air Force) (GOV)
18716	* RAF 208624	?		B32F	-/-- Air Ministry (Royal Air Force) (GOV)
18717	* RAF 209797	?		B32F	-/-- Air Ministry (Royal Air Force) (GOV)
18718	* RAF 209787	?		B32F	-/-- Air Ministry (Royal Air Force) (GOV)
18719	* RAF 209788	?		B32F	-/-- Air Ministry (Royal Air Force) (GOV)
18720	* RAF 209789	Mulliner		B32F	-/46 Air Ministry (Royal Air Force) (GOV)
18721	#?	Mulliner	41801	B32F	-/46 Anglo Iranian Oil Co, Abadan (O-IR)
18722	* RAF 209791	?		B32F	-/-- Air Ministry (Royal Air Force) (GOV)
18723	* ?	?		B32F	-/-- Air Ministry (Royal Air Force) (GOV)
18724	* RAF 208625	?		B32F	-/-- Air Ministry (Royal Air Force) (GOV)
18725	* ?	?		B--F	-/-- Air Ministry (Royal Air Force) (GOV)
18726	* RAF 208619	?		B32F	-/-- Air Ministry (Royal Air Force) (GOV)
18727	* RAF 209798	?		B32F	-/-- Air Ministry (Royal Air Force) (GOV)
18728	* RAF 208620	?		B32F	-/-- Air Ministry (Royal Air Force) (GOV)
18729	?	Duple	41880	B32F	-/46 Gibraltar Motor Hire Services (O-GBZ)
18730	* RAF 208623	?		B32F	-/-- Air Ministry (Royal Air Force) (GOV)
18731	* RAF 208626	?		B32F	-/-- Air Ministry (Royal Air Force) (GOV)
18732	RAF 208630	?		B32F	-/-- Air Ministry (Royal Air Force) (GOV)
18733	* RAF 209799	?		B32F	-/46 Air Ministry (Royal Air Force) (GOV)
18734	* RAF 209804	?		B32F	-/-- Air Ministry (Royal Air Force) (GOV)
18735	* RAF 208641	SMT		B32F	c5/46 Air Ministry (Royal Air Force) (GOV)
18736	* RAF 209796	?		B32F	-/-- Air Ministry (Royal Air Force) (GOV)
18737	?	Duple	41881	B32F	-/46 Gibraltar Motor Hire Services (O-GBZ)
18738	* RAF 208628	?		B32F	-/-- Air Ministry (Royal Air Force) (GOV)
18739	MME 738	Duple	42240	C27F	6/46 E Evans {Evan Evan Tours}, London WC1 (LN)
18740	CUX 995	Duple	41980	B28F	5/46 GA Darrall {Supreme}, Dawley (SH)
18741	DDM 262	Duple	41998	B32F	6/46 WG Richardson & Sons, Buckley (FT)
18742	DBE 95	Duple	41970	B32F	5/46 F Hunt, Alford (LI)
18743	JV 9375	Duple	41968	B32F	6/46 HH Milton, Waddingham (LI)
18744	CDP 233	Duple	41984	B32F	5/46 Reading Corporation (BE) 15
18745	#?	Mulliner	41791	B32F	-/46 Anglo Iranian Oil Co, Abadan (O-IR)
18746	HB 6144	Duple	41972	B30F	6/46 Morlais Services Ltd, Merthyr Tydfil (GG) 40
18747	GPT 199	Duple	41959	B32F	6/46 Bond Bros {Imperial Motor Services}, Willington (DM)
18748	HB 6145	Duple	41973	B30F	6/46 Morlais Services Ltd, Merthyr Tydfil (GG) 41
18749	LMY 760	Duple	42243	C29F	7/46 Fallowfield & Britten Ltd, London E8 (LN)
18750	HB 6146	Duple	41963	B30F	6/46 Morlais Services Ltd, Merthyr Tydfil (GG) 42
18751	GYD 39	Duple	41967	B32F	5/46 FE Partridge, Winsham (SO)
18752	HCV 212	Duple	41964	B30F	4/46 WA Tremain, Zelah (CO)
18753	#?	Mulliner	41794	B32F	-/46 Anglo Iranian Oil Co, Abadan (O-IR)

18754	BNL 894	Duple	41966	B32F	3/46	JH Batty & Sons {Wansbeck Motor Services}, Ashington (ND) 5
18755	CUX 804	Duple	41961	B30F	3/46	RW Carpenter {Valley Motor Services}, Bishop's Castle (SH)
18756	KPE 959	Duple	41997	B30F	6/46	L Rhees {Tillingbourne Valley Coaches}, Chilworth (SR)
18757	FTG 628	Duple	41957	B32F	5/46	Thomas & James Ltd, Port Talbot (GG)
18758	GDE 687	Duple	41977	B32F	6/46	DJ Morrison Ltd, Tenby (PE) 22
18759	SB 6704	Duple	42277	C27F	7/46	Dunoon Motor Services Ltd, Dunoon (AL)
18760	GV 9970	Thurgood	126	B30F	11/46	HS Theobald & Son, Long Melford (WF)
18761	#?	Mulliner	41792	B32F	-/46	Anglo Iranian Oil Co, Abadan (O-IR)
18762	* RAF 208637	?		B32F	-/--	Air Ministry (Royal Air Force) (GOV)
18763	IP 4862	Ryan		B26F	-/47	L Bowers {Suir Valley Service}, Fiddown (EI)
18764	#?	Mulliner	41793	B32F	-/46	Anglo Iranian Oil Co, Abadan (O-IR)
18765						Exported to Ireland
18766	FTG 629	Duple	41956	B32F	6/46	J & EH Jones (D Jones & Son) {Pantdu Garage}, Pantdu (GG)
18767	FTG 630	Duple	41958	B32F	6/46	J & EH Jones (D Jones & Son) {Pantdu Garage}, Pantdu (GG)
18768	#?	Mulliner	41797	B32F	-/46	Anglo Iranian Oil Co, Abadan (O-IR)
18769						Exported to Ireland
18770	#?	Duple	41849	B28D	-/46	Uganda Transport Co Ltd, Kampala (O-EAU)
18771	#?	Mulliner	41798	B32F	-/46	Anglo Iranian Oil Co, Abadan (O-IR)
18772	HB 6147	Duple	41971	B30F	6/46	Morlais Services Ltd, Merthyr Tydfil (GG) 43
18773	KPE 455	Duple	41950	B28F	2/46	Safeguard Coaches Ltd, Guildford (SR)
18774	LMY 770	Duple	42247	C29F	7/46	Fallowfield & Britten Ltd, London E8 (LN)
18775	#?	Duple	41846	B28D	-/46	Uganda Transport Co Ltd, Kampala (O-EAU)
18776	#?	Mulliner	41804	B32F	-/46	Anglo Iranian Oil Co, Abadan (O-IR)
18777	#?	Duple	41847	B28D	-/46	Uganda Transport Co Ltd, Kampala (O-EAU)
18778	#?	Mulliner	41796	B32F	-/46	Anglo Iranian Oil Co, Abadan (O-IR)
18779	#?	Duple	41844	B28D	-/46	Uganda Transport Co Ltd, Kampala (O-EAU)
18780	CTH 200	Duple	41976	B32F	6/46	D Jones & Sons {Dan Jones}, Carmarthen (CR) 1
18781	BTY 202	Duple	41993	B32F	1/46	WF Wilkinson {Swift Motor Service}, Ashington (ND)
18782	#?	Mulliner	41799	B32F	-/46	Anglo Iranian Oil Co, Abadan (O-IR)
18783	#?	Duple	41848	B28D	-/46	Uganda Transport Co Ltd, Kampala (O-EAU)
18784	?	?		(shop ?)	-/--	Navy, Army & Air Force Institutes (NAAFI) (XLN)
18785	#?	Mulliner	41807	B32F	-/46	Anglo Iranian Oil Co, Abadan (O-IR)
18786	* 5190808	?		(shop ?)	-/--	Navy, Army & Air Force Institutes (NAAFI) (XLN)
18787	CDY 294	Duple	41989	B32F	6/46	John Dengate & Sons Ltd, Beckley (ES) 16
18788	HWE 562	Plaxton	?	FC30F	4/46	Law Bros Ltd, Sheffield (WR)
18789	#?	Mulliner	41812	B32F	-/46	Anglo Iranian Oil Co, Abadan (O-IR)
18790	?	?		(shop ?)	-/--	Navy, Army & Air Force Institutes (NAAFI) (XLN)
18791	* 6062632	?		(shop ?)	-/--	Navy, Army & Air Force Institutes (NAAFI) (XLN)
18792	BTY 203	Duple	41994	B30F	6/46	WF Wilkinson {Swift Motor Service}, Ashington (ND)
18793						Exported to Port Elizabeth (O-ZA)
18794	#?	Mulliner	41808	B32F	-/46	Anglo Iranian Oil Co, Abadan (O-IR)
18795	DBE 653	Duple	41992	B32F	6/46	C Barker {Grayscroft Coaches}, Mablethorpe (LI)
18796						Exported to Port Elizabeth (O-ZA)
18797						Exported to Ireland
18798						Exported to Port Elizabeth (O-ZA)
18799	#?	Mulliner	41809	B32F	-/46	Anglo Iranian Oil Co, Abadan (O-IR)
18800	#?	Mulliner	41810	B32F	-/46	Anglo Iranian Oil Co, Abadan (O-IR)
19801	SB 6705	Duple	42276	C27F	7/46	Dunoon Motor Services Ltd, Dunoon (AL)
19802	CDP 234	Duple	41985	B32F	5/46	Reading Corporation (BE) 16
19803	#?	Mulliner	41817	B32F	-/46	Anglo Iranian Oil Co, Abadan (O-IR)
19804, 19805						Exported to Port Elizabeth (O-ZA)
19806	#?	Mulliner	41815	B32F	-/46	Anglo Iranian Oil Co, Abadan (O-IR)
19807						Exported to Port Elizabeth (O-ZA)
19808	CDP 235	Duple	41986	B32F	5/46	Reading Corporation (BE) 17
19809	* CUJ 30	Duple	42242	B30F	6/46	RG, FJ, DA & K Cooper {G Cooper & Sons}, Oakengates (SH)
19810	#?	Mulliner	41814	B32F	-/46	Anglo Iranian Oil Co, Abadan (O-IR)
19811						Exported to Demerara (O-BRG)
19812	?	Mulliner		B--F	-/--	Admiralty (Royal Navy) (GOV)
19813	#?	Mulliner	41811	B32F	-/46	Anglo Iranian Oil Co, Abadan (O-IR)

19814	?	Mulliner		B--F	-/--	Admiralty (Royal Navy) (GOV)
19815	HHA 433	Duple	42244	C29F	5/46	Gliderways Coaches Ltd, Smethwick (ST)
19816	DCO 99	Duple	42258	C29F	5/46	Heybrook Bay Motor Services Ltd, Down Thomas (DN)
19817	#?	Mulliner	41816	B32F	-/46	Anglo Iranian Oil Co, Abadan (O-IR)
19818	?	Mulliner		B--F	-/--	Admiralty (Royal Navy) (GOV)
19819	?	Mulliner		B--F	-/--	Admiralty (Royal Navy) (GOV)
19820	#?	Mulliner	41818	B32F	-/46	Anglo Iranian Oil Co, Abadan (O-IR)
19821	?	Mulliner		B--F	-/--	Admiralty (Royal Navy) (GOV)
19822	?	Mulliner		B--F	-/--	Admiralty (Royal Navy) (GOV)
19823	?	Mulliner		B--F	-/--	Admiralty (Royal Navy) (GOV)
19824	#?	Mulliner		B32F	-/46	Anglo Iranian Oil Co, Abadan (O-IR)
19825	* 812 RN	Mulliner		B28F	-/46	Admiralty (Royal Navy) (GOV)
19826	* RAF 209802	Mulliner		B32F	-/--	Air Ministry (Royal Air Force) (GOV)
19827	* ?	Mulliner		B--F	-/--	Admiralty (Royal Navy) (GOV)
19828	?	Duple	41878	B32F	-/46	Iraq Petroleum Co, Haifa (O-IL)
19829	?	Mulliner		B--F	-/--	Admiralty (Royal Navy) (GOV)
19830	?	Mulliner		B--F	-/--	Admiralty (Royal Navy) (GOV)
19831	?	Duple	41877	B32F	-/46	Iraq Petroleum Co, Haifa (O-IL)
19832	* 698 RN	Mulliner		B32F	-/46	Admiralty (Royal Navy) (GOV)
19833	?	Mulliner		B--F	-/--	Admiralty (Royal Navy) (GOV)
19834	?	Duple	41876	B32F	-/46	Iraq Petroleum Co, Haifa (O-IL)
19835	?	Mulliner		B--F	-/--	Admiralty (Royal Navy) (GOV)
19836	?	Mulliner		B--F	-/--	Admiralty (Royal Navy) (GOV)
19837	?	Mulliner		B--F	-/--	Admiralty (Royal Navy) (GOV)
19838	?	Duple	41875	B32F	-/46	Iraq Petroleum Co, Haifa (O-IL)
19839	?	Mulliner		B--F	-/--	Admiralty (Royal Navy) (GOV)
19840	?	Mulliner		B--F	-/--	Admiralty (Royal Navy) (GOV)
19841	LA-11-85	?		C24D	7/46	Companhia Hoteleira de Monte Estoril (O-P)
19842	?	Mulliner		B--F	-/--	Admiralty (Royal Navy) (GOV)
19843	?	Mulliner		B--F	-/--	Admiralty (Royal Navy) (GOV)
19844	* RAF 209803	Mulliner		B32F	-/--	Air Ministry (Royal Air Force) (GOV)
19845	BL-11-83	?		DP28D	5/46	João Ferreira das Neves, Guimarães (O-P) 10
19846	?	Mulliner		B--F	-/--	Admiralty (Royal Navy) (GOV)
19847	* ?	Mulliner		B--F	-/--	Admiralty (Royal Navy) (GOV)
19848	HH-11-88	Pereira & Fausto Crespo		B29D	5/46	Empresa de Viação e Comércio de Alenquer (O-P) 14
19849	?	Mulliner		B--F	-/--	Admiralty (Royal Navy) (GOV)
20801	* 718 RN	Mulliner		B32F	-/46	Admiralty (Royal Navy) (GOV)
20802	* DC-11-81	?		B30D	5/46	Auto Viação Feirense, Lourosa (O-P) 7
20803	* RAF 209801	Mulliner		B32F	-/--	Air Ministry (Royal Air Force) (GOV)
20804	?	Mulliner		B--F	-/--	Admiralty (Royal Navy) (GOV)
20805						Exported to Lima (O-PE)
20806	?	Mulliner		B--F	-/--	Admiralty (Royal Navy) (GOV)
20807	* 744 RN	Mulliner		B32F	-/--	Admiralty (Royal Navy) (GOV)
20808	?	Mulliner		B32F	-/--	Admiralty (Royal Navy) (GOV)
20809						Exported to Lima (O-PE)
20810	?	Mulliner		B--F	-/--	Admiralty (Royal Navy) (GOV)
20811	* ?	Mulliner		B32F	-/--	Admiralty (Royal Navy) (GOV)
20812						Exported to Copenhagen (O-DK)
20813	?	Mulliner		B--F	-/--	Admiralty (Royal Navy) (GOV)
20814	* ?	Mulliner		B--F	-/46	Admiralty (Royal Navy) (GOV)
20815	?	Mulliner		B--F	-/--	Admiralty (Royal Navy) (GOV)
20816						Exported to Santiago (O-RCH)
20817	?	Mulliner		B--F	-/--	Admiralty (Royal Navy) (GOV)
20818	?	Mulliner		B--F	-/--	Admiralty (Royal Navy) (GOV)
20819						Exported to Santiago (O-RCH)
20820	#?	Duple	41850	B28D	-/46	Uganda Transport Co Ltd, Kampala (O-EAU)
20821	* CUJ 29	Duple	42241	B30F	6/46	RG, FJ, DA & K Cooper {G Cooper & Sons}, Oakengates (SH)
20822	BNL 674	Duple	42270	C29F	6/46	Bedlington & District Luxury Coaches Ltd, Ashington (ND)
20823						Exported to Montevideo (O-ROU)
20824	LMY 681	Duple	42245	C29F	5/46	Essex County Coaches Ltd, London E15 (LN)
20825	FUP 794	Duple	42250	C29F	3/46	A Gillingham {Diamond Bus Services}, Lanchester (DM)

C1252/25

20826					Exported to Montevideo (O-ROU)
20827	FTX 237	Duple	42001	B32F	6/47 LG Potter, Skewen (GG)
20828	CRV 436	Duple	42280	C29F	7/46 CW Hutfield, Gosport (HA)
20829	BUD 522	Duple	42257	C29F	8/46 OA Slatter, Long Hanborough (OX) 20
20830	GV 9866	Duple	42251	C29F	7/46 EF Long, Glemsford (WF)
20831	DJ 9464	Duple	42269	C29F	7/46 G Murray {Jubilee Coaches}, St Helens (LA)
20832	EBC 221	Duple	42340	C29F	8/46 CLW Harris {Majestic}, Leicester (LE)
20833	BNL 675	Duple	42273	C29F	7/46 Bedlington & District Luxury Coaches Ltd, Ashington (ND)
20834	GYD 353	Duple	42267	C29F	6/46 H Gratton, Burnham-on-Sea (SO) B5
20835	BJT 901	Duple	42246	C29F	6/46 HG Barlow & GE Phillips {Barlow, Phillips & Co}, Yeovil (SO)
20836	MHX 450	Duple	42268	C29F	7/46 Fallowfield & Britten Ltd, London E8 (LN)
20837	BJT 902	Duple	42261	C29F	6/46 HG Barlow & GE Phillips {Barlow, Phillips & Co}, Yeovil (SO)
20838	CTH 201	Duple	41978	B32F	6/46 D Jones & Sons {Dan Jones}, Carmarthen (CR) 2
20839	HHA 431	Duple	42278	C29F	4/46 Gliderways Coaches Ltd, Smethwick (ST)
20840	FDG 107	Duple	42260	C29F	7/46 CAJ Scarrott {Luxury Coaches}, Stow-on-the-Wold (GL)
21301	FDG 108	Duple	42266	C29F	7/46 CAJ Scarrott {Luxury Coaches}, Stow-on-the-Wold (GL)
21302	KTW 212	Duple	42253	C29F	6/46 RW Hooks & Co {Harwich & District}, Great Oakley (EX)
21303	JHU 830	Duple	42255	C27F	6/46 TJ King {Monarch Coaches}, Bristol (GL)
21304	DBE 773	Duple	42264	C29F	6/46 JE Vessey, Hibaldstow (LI)
21305	* HHA 434	Duple	42283	C29F	4/46 Gliderways Coaches Ltd, Smethwick (ST)
21306	CUJ 46	Duple	42254	C29F	6/46 TH & T Hyde {T Hyde & Son}, Welsh Frankton (SH)
21307	HHA 435	Duple	42285	C29F	7/46 Gliderways Coaches Ltd, Smethwick (ST)
21308	LMY 725	Duple	42287	C29F	6/46 RG Flexman {Flexman's Coaches}, Southall (MX)
21309	CPM 963	Duple	42291	C29F	6/46 AH & JH Sargent {East Grinstead Motor Coaches}, East Grinstead (ES) 06
21310	LMY 682	Duple	42259	C29F	5/46 Essex County Coaches Ltd, London E15 (LN)
21311	FUP 795	Duple	42006	B32F	7/46 J Iveson & Son, Esh (DM)
21325 – 21336		#			Exported to Melbourne (O-AUS)
21409	LMY 254	Duple	42249	C29F	7/46 Garner's Coaches Ltd, London W5 (LN)
21420	MME 174	Duple	42248	C29F	6/46 AC Susans {Fountain Luxury Coaches}, Twickenham (MX)
21468	* GMN 699	Duple	42292	C29F	6/46 WJ Purvis {Marguerite Rose}, Douglas (IM)
21484	GV 9928	Duple	42256	C29F	7/46 NS Rule, Boxford (WF)
21493	HRL 25	Duple	42000	B32F	6/46 WA Hawkey & Sons Ltd, Wadebridge (CO)
21505	* GYD 80	Duple	42252	C29F	3/46 Quantock Hauliers Ltd, Watchet (SO)
21516	BCT 188	Duple	42275	C29F	6/46 J Hodson, Navenby (LI)
21528	GNK 593	Thurgood	133	C29F	7/46 CW Sworder, Walkern (HT)
21539	JRA 710	Plaxton	?	FC30F	6/46 HD Andrew {Anchor Coaches}, Tideswell (DE)
21551	FDG 343	Duple	42308	C29F	7/46 TEA Bowles {Bowles Coaches}, Ford (GL)
21567	* GTC 651	Duple	42262	C29F	6/46 EN Hadwin, Ulverston (LA)
21576	GYD 354	Duple	42265	C29F	6/46 H Gratton, Burnham-on-Sea (SO) B6
21588	* JDH 858	Duple	42271	C29F	6/46 Mrs FG Mason, Darlaston (ST)
21599	FUO 92	Duple	42274	C29F	6/46 J, EM & AB Geddes {Burton Cars}, Brixham (DN)
21611	DJU 532	Duple	42263	C29F	6/46 OC Bishop, Coalville (LE)
21622	LRF 714	Duple	42294	C29F	7/46 Greatrex Motor Coaches Ltd, Stafford (ST) 29
21634	BNL 676	Duple	42281	C29F	6/46 Bedlington & District Luxury Coaches Ltd, Ashington (ND)
21650	HHA 432	Duple	42282	C29F	4/46 Gliderways Coaches Ltd, Smethwick (ST)
21658	?	Mulliner		B--F	-/-- Admiralty (Royal Navy) (GOV)
21670	HHA 436	Duple	42288	C29F	7/46 Gliderways Coaches Ltd, Smethwick (ST)
21681					Exported to British Guiana
21693	FVF 160	Duple	42272	C29F	12/46 G Hubbard {Burnham Coaches}, Burnham Market (NK)
21704	?	Mulliner		B--F	-/-- Admiralty (Royal Navy) (GOV)
21716	BJT 943	Duple	42279	C29F	6/46 CA Adams (Adams Bros) {Victory Tours}, Sixpenny Handley (DT)
21731	H-4510	?		B21-	-/46 Simon Ødegården, Ødegårdens Verk (O-N)
21741	?	Mulliner		B--F	-/-- Admiralty (Royal Navy) (GOV)
21752	HRL 75	Duple	42284	C29F	7/46 WJ Crowle, Crackington Haven (CO)
21770 - 21781					Exported to Melbourne (O-AUS)
21824					Exported to British Guiana

21836	FO 4654	Duple	42304	C29F	7/46	TA Owen, Knighton (RR)
21847	?	Mulliner		B--F	-/--	Admiralty (Royal Navy) (GOV)
21859	KTW 846	Duple	42290	C27F	7/46	Mrs LA Bennett {Went's Coaches}, Boxted (EX)
21874						Exported to Lisbon (O-P)
21884	?	Mulliner		B--F	-/--	Admiralty (Royal Navy) (GOV)
21896	GOH 80	Duple	42286	C29F	7/46	H Brown, Birmingham (WK)
21907						Exported to Malaya
21919	EBM 760	Duple	41995	B32F	6/46	FM Bailey, Turvey (BD)
21929	?	Mulliner		B--F	-/--	Admiralty (Royal Navy) (GOV)
21941	GOE 257	Duple	42297	C29F	6/46	Eatonways Ltd, Birmingham (WK)
21957						Exported to Lisbon (O-P)
21967	?	Mulliner		B--F	-/--	Admiralty (Royal Navy) (GOV)
21978	GYD 502	Duple	42289	C29F	7/46	Binding & Payne Ltd {Dorothy's Coaches}, Clevedon (SO)
21989						Exported to Malaya
22001	GOE 259	Duple	42300	C29F	6/46	Eatonways Ltd, Birmingham (WK)
22012	?	Mulliner		B--F	-/--	Admiralty (Royal Navy) (GOV)
22024	FWR 199	Duple	42293	C29F	7/46	JC Turner, Todmorden (WR)
22039						Exported to Lisbon (O-P)
22049 *	?	Mulliner		B--F	-/--	Admiralty (Royal Navy) (GOV)
22061	FWR 300	Duple	42299	C29F	7/46	MA Hargreaves (Morley) Ltd (WR) 14
22072						Exported to Malaya
22083	HRL 178	Duple	42301	C29F	8/46	Willis (Central Garage) Ltd, Bodmin (CO)
22094	?	Mulliner		B--F	-/--	Admiralty (Royal Navy) (GOV)
22167	BRS 603	Duple	42295	C29F	6/46	WN Stott {Caledonian Tours}, Aberdeen (AD)
22182						Exported to Lisbon (O-P)
22192	?	Mulliner		B--F	-/--	Admiralty (Royal Navy) (GOV)
22204	FUO 264	Duple	42296	C29F	7/46	Way & Son, Crediton (DN)
22216						Exported to Malaya
22228	1864	Strachan		B32F	7/46	Guernsey Motors (CI) 8
22239	?	Mulliner		B--F	-/--	Admiralty (Royal Navy) (GOV)
22251	GOE 258	Duple	42298	C29F	6/46	Eatonways Ltd, Birmingham (WK)
22266						Exported to Lima (O-PE)
22276	?	Mulliner		B--F	-/--	Admiralty (Royal Navy) (GOV)
22287	FT 5794	Duple	42305	C29F	7/46	TH Taylor {Taylor Bros}, North Shields (ND)
22299						Exported to Malaya
22311	YJ 8446	Plaxton	?	FC30F	6/46	R Dickson jnr, Dundee (AS) 8
22323	?	Mulliner		B--F	-/--	Admiralty (Royal Navy) (GOV)
22334 *	EOU 856	Duple	42310	C29F	7/46	AE Butler {Sunshine Coaches}, Bagshot (SR)
22349						Exported to Lima (O-PE)
22360	DET 51	Duple	42303	C29F	7/46	C Riley, Rotherham (WR)
22371	GPT 154	Duple	42306	C29F	7/46	JH Dowson {Safety Coach Service}, Frosterley (DM)
22384						Exported to Malaya
22396	CPM 895	Duple	42307	C29F	6/46	PG Warren, Ticehurst (ES)
22407 *	FUO 534	Duple	42316	C29F	8/46	WJ Redwood, Hemyock (DN)
22418	YJ 8447	Plaxton	?	FC30F	7/46	R Dickson jnr, Dundee (AS) 9
22433						Exported to Santiago (O-RCH)
22443	?	Mulliner		B--F	-/--	Admiralty (Royal Navy) (GOV)
22455	?	Mulliner		B--F	-/--	Admiralty (Royal Navy) (GOV)
22467						Exported to Port Elizabeth (O-ZA)
22479	?	Mulliner		B--F	-/--	Admiralty (Royal Navy) (GOV)
22490	?	Mulliner		B--F	-/--	Admiralty (Royal Navy) (GOV)
22501	?	Mulliner		B--F	-/--	Admiralty (Royal Navy) (GOV)
22516	T-3916	?		B29-	12/46	Eira Auto, Nesset (O-N)
22526	?	Mulliner		B--F	-/--	Admiralty (Royal Navy) (GOV)
22539						Exported to Port Elizabeth (O-ZA)
22553, 22562						Exported to Malaya
22571						Exported to Lagos (O-WAN)
22584	YJ 8524	Thurgood	150	C29F	7/46	Beat & Ferrier, Dundee (AS)
22637 - 22648						Exported to Bombay (O-IND)
22733	K-7162	?		B29-	12/46	Lyngdal Bilselskap, Lydngal (O-N)
22747, 22760, 22774						Exported to Lagos (O-WAN)
22783	EWD 229	Duple	42309	C29F	7/46	JC Arnold, Twogates (WK)
22792	JHA 264	Burlingham	?	C29F	10/46	JE Morris {Bearwood Coaches}, Bearwood (ST)

22804	* HWJ 180	Willmott		C26F	5/46	E Jeffcock, Sheffield (WR)
22821	V-3883	?		B29-	11/46	Original operator unknown (O-N)
22835, 22848, 22861						Exported to Rangoon (O-BUR)
22870	YJ 8332	Plaxton	?	FC30F	6/46	R Dickson jnr, Dundee (AS) 6
22879	GNK 274	Duple	42313	C27F	7/46	Crain's Garage Ltd, St Albans (HT)
22892	* EU 8097	Duple	42312	C29F	6/46	WC Fouracre {Embassy Motors}, Brynmawr (BC)
22909						Exported to Santiago (O-RCH)
22923, 22935						Exported to Rangoon (O-BUR)
22949						Exported to Demerara (O-BRG)
22958	#?	Duple	41854	B28D	-/46	Uganda Transport Co Ltd, Kampala (O-EAU)
22967						Exported to Uganda
22980	#?	Duple	41852	B28D	-/46	Uganda Transport Co Ltd, Kampala (O-EAU)
22997	#?	Mulliner		B32F	-/46	Anglo Iranian Oil Co, Abadan (O-IR)
23011	#?	Duple	41851	B28D	-/46	Uganda Transport Co Ltd, Kampala (O-EAU)
23024	#?	Duple	41853	B28D	-/46	Uganda Transport Co Ltd, Kampala (O-EAU)
23037	JRB 953	Duple	42327	C29F	7/46	E, E & H Webster {E Webster & Sons}, Hognaston (DE)
23046	* HUU 430	Duple	42314	C27F	8/46	George Ewer & Co Ltd {Grey Green}, London N16 (LN)
23055	FT 5795	Duple	42311	C29F	7/46	TH Taylor {Taylor Bros}, North Shields (ND)
23068	HPP 774	Thurgood	152	C29F	7/46	Pilot Coaches (High Wycombe) Ltd (BK)
23085	#?	Mulliner		B32F	-/46	Anglo Iranian Oil Co, Abadan (O-IR)
23099	?	?	?		-/--	Challis, London SW19 (GLN)
23112	EDL 140	Duple	42322	C29F	6/46	West Wight Motor Bus Co Ltd, Totland Bay (IW)
23196	EDL 141	Duple	42323	C29F	6/46	West Wight Motor Bus Co Ltd, Totland Bay (IW)
23206	* KFC 820	(Duple ?)		C29F	5/46	PC Skinner {Percival's Coaches}, Oxford (OX) 17
23215	HUU 427	Duple	42317	C27F	8/46	George Ewer & Co Ltd {Grey Green}, London N16 (LN)
23228	* DDT 244	Duple	42318	C29F	7/46	GH Ennifer Ltd {Blue Ensign}, Doncaster (WR)
23245	#?	Mulliner		B32F	-/46	Anglo Iranian Oil Co, Abadan (O-IR)
23259	KBB 767	Plaxton	?	FC30F	7/46	G Galley (Galley's Motors), Newcastle (ND)
23272	JDH 917	Duple	42339	C29F	7/46	Dawson's Motorways Ltd, Walsall (ST)
23285	HPP 773	Thurgood	151	C29F	7/46	Pilot Coaches (High Wycombe) Ltd (BK)
23294	HUU 431	Duple	42348	C27F	6/46	George Ewer & Co Ltd {Grey Green}, London N16 (LN)
23303	JUM 717	Plaxton	?	FC30F	6/46	JA Hudson Ltd, Leeds (WR)
23316	* KBB 766	Plaxton	(16 ?)	FC30F	7/46	G Galley (Galley's Motors), Newcastle (ND)
23333	#?	Mulliner		B32F	-/46	Anglo Iranian Oil Co, Abadan (O-IR)
23347	JDH 813	Duple	42338	C29F	6/46	Dawson's Motorways Ltd, Walsall (ST)
23359	BTY 348	Duple	42319	C29F	7/46	C Moffit, Acomb (ND) 21
23373	FDG 128	Duple	42320	C29F	7/46	FJR Harvey {Harvey's Coaches}, Chedworth (GL)
23382	* 1560	Mulliner		B32F	5/46	Sarre Transport Ltd, St Peter Port, Guernsey (CI) 5
23391	GPT 208	Duple	42321	C29F	8/46	Scurr's Motor Services Ltd, Stillington (DM)
23404	CUJ 619	Duple	42346	C29F	7/46	DJ Hampson {Hampson's Luxury Coaches}, Oswestry (SH)
23421	#?	Mulliner		B32F	-/46	Anglo Iranian Oil Co, Abadan (O-IR)
23435						Exported to Rangoon (O-BUR)
23446, 23459						Exported to Port Elizabeth (O-ZA)
23464	#?	Mulliner		B32F	-/46	Anglo Iranian Oil Co, Abadan (O-IR)
23475	MME 742	Duple	42324	C29F	8/46	LC Davis & Sons Ltd, London SW16 (LN)
23489	* CVH 239	Duple	42325	C29F	6/46	Hanson's Buses Ltd, Huddersfield (WR) 211
23496	BPR 402	Duple	42336	C29F	8/46	RW Toop, WJ Ironside & PW Davis {Bere Regis & District}, Dorchester (DT)
23504	CVH 240	Duple	42326	C29F	6/46	Hanson's Buses Ltd, Huddersfield (WR) 212
23643, 23654						Exported to Port Elizabeth (O-ZA)
23658	BPR 403	Duple	42337	C29F	8/46	RW Toop, WJ Ironside & PW Davis {Bere Regis & District}, Dorchester (DT)
23673	#?	Mulliner		B32F	-/46	Anglo Iranian Oil Co, Abadan (O-IR)
23684	* BTY 380	Plaxton	149	C30F	7/46	W Smith {Safeway Coaches}, Bedlington Station (ND)
23697	BPR 400	Duple	42332	C29F	8/46	RW Toop, WJ Ironside & PW Davis {Bere Regis & District}, Dorchester (DT)
23704	BPR 401	Duple	42333	C29F	8/46	RW Toop, WJ Ironside & PW Davis {Bere Regis & District}, Dorchester (DT)
23712	FTX 453	Duple	42328	C29F	8/46	Humphreys Garages (Pontypridd) Ltd (GG)
23731	#?	Mulliner		B32F	-/46	Anglo Iranian Oil Co, Abadan (O-IR)
23743, 23755						Exported to Port Elizabeth (O-ZA)
23761	#?	Mulliner		B32F	-/46	Anglo Iranian Oil Co, Abadan (O-IR)
23772	#?	Mulliner		B32F	-/46	Anglo Iranian Oil Co, Abadan (O-IR)

23785	EDL 256	Duple	42335	C29F	8/46	WC & RP Shotter (GA Shotter & Son), Brighstone (IW)
23792	BPR 398	Duple	42330	C29F	8/46	RW Toop, WJ Ironside & PW Davis {Bere Regis & District}, Dorchester (DT)
23800	?	Mulliner		B--F	-/--	Admiralty (Royal Navy) (GOV)
23819	#?	Mulliner		B32F	-/46	Anglo Iranian Oil Co, Abadan (O-IR)
23830						Exported to Port Elizabeth (O-ZA)
23843						Exported to Uganda
23848	#?	Mulliner		B32F	-/46	Anglo Iranian Oil Co, Abadan (O-IR)
23860	HI-12-00	F B Russo		B27D	8/46	Manuel Martins e Sebastião Martins, Évora (O-P) 36
23873	BPR 399	Duple	42331	C29F	8/46	RW Toop, WJ Ironside & PW Davis {Bere Regis & District}, Dorchester (DT)
23880	EDL 257	Duple	42334	C29F	8/46	WC & RP Shotter (GA Shotter & Son), Brighstone (IW)
23888	* ?	Mulliner		B--F	-/--	Admiralty (Royal Navy) (GOV)
23907						Exported to Lisbon (O-P)
23918, 23930						Exported to Uganda
23937	* II-12-01	?		B29D	1/47	José Rodrigues Novo, Águeda (O-P) 7
23947						Exported to Lisbon (O-P)
23960	1558	Mulliner		B32F	5/46	Sarre Transport Ltd, St Peter Port, Guernsey (CI) 1
23966	LMY 449	Duple	42343	C29F	6/46	Essex County Coaches Ltd, London E15 (LN)
23974	?	Mulliner		B--F	-/--	Admiralty (Royal Navy) (GOV)
23992	HE-11-99	?		B26D	8/46	Auto Viação de Souto, Souto (O-P) 3
24018 - 24029						Exported to Stockholm (O-S)
24111, 24123						Exported to Uganda
24129	FE-12-03	F B Russo		B27D	8/46	Manuel Martins e Sebastião Martins, Évora (O-P) 35
24139						Exported to Lima (O-PE)
24154	DWV 260	Duple	42342	C29F	8/46	G Keen {Enterprise}, Heddington (WI)
24161	* EYG 100	Duple	42341	C29F	8/46	WR & P Bingley, Kinsley (WR)
24185	?	Mulliner		B--F	-/--	Admiralty (Royal Navy) (GOV)
24191						Exported to Lima (O-PE)
24202, 24215						Exported to Uganda
24221, 24232						Exported to Lima (O-PE)
24245	FT 5784	Plaxton	8	FC30F	7/46	TH Taylor {Taylor Bros}, North Shields (ND)
24252	HUU 432	Duple	42352	C27F	8/46	George Ewer & Co Ltd {Grey Green}, London N16 (LN)
24260	?	Mulliner		B--F	-/--	Admiralty (Royal Navy) (GOV)
24279						Exported to Santiago (O-RCH)
24290, 24303						Exported to Uganda
24309, 24320						Exported to Santiago (O-RCH)
24333	BTY 63	Duple	42349	C29F	3/46	C Moffit, Acomb (ND) 19
24340	1557	Mulliner		B32F	5/46	Sarre Transport Ltd, St Peter Port, Guernsey (CI) 2
24346	?	Mulliner		B--F	-/--	Admiralty (Royal Navy) (GOV)
24367						Exported to Santiago (O-RCH)
24378, 24391						Exported to Ireland
24397, 24408						Exported to Iraq
24422	* JS 7166	Mitchell (Stornoway)		B28F	10/46	J Mitchell {Mitchell's Transport Parcel Service}, Stornoway (RY)
24428	* JS 7297	Mitchell (Stornoway)		B28F	6/47	J Mitchell {Mitchell's Transport Parcel Service}, Stornoway (RY)
24436	* ?	Mulliner		B--F	-/--	Admiralty (Royal Navy) (GOV)
24455	#?	Mulliner		B32F	-/46	Anglo Iranian Oil Co, Abadan (O-IR)
24466, 24479						Exported to Ireland
24485	#?	Mulliner		B32F	-/46	Anglo Iranian Oil Co, Abadan (O-IR)
24497	#?	Mulliner		B32F	-/46	Anglo Iranian Oil Co, Abadan (O-IR)
24510	HUU 426	Duple	42347	C27F	8/46	George Ewer & Co Ltd {Grey Green}, London N16 (LN)
24517	BRS 638	Duple	42345	C29F	6/46	DW Stott {Daisy Tours}, Aberdeen (AD)
24525	?	Mulliner		B--F	-/--	Admiralty (Royal Navy) (GOV)
24540						Exported to Santiago (O-RCH)
24554, 24567						Exported to Rangoon (O-BUR)
24573	H-7232	Funnemark		B---	11/46	Isnius Aspheim, Vestre Melum (O-N)
24583						Exported to Santiago (O-RCH)
24596	DSR 500	Duple	43028	C29F	8/46	A Melville, Kirriemuir (AS)
24604	BJN 475	Duple	42390	C29F	8/46	Westcliff Belle Ltd, Southend-on-Sea (EX)
24612	DJU 831	Duple	42350	C29F	8/46	CLW Harris {Majestic}, Leicester (LE)
24631						Exported to Santiago (O-RCH)
24642, 24655						Exported to Rangoon (O-BUR)

C1252/29

24671						Exported to Santiago (O-RCH)
24684	MME 743	Duple	42351	C29F	8/46	LC Davis & Sons Ltd, London SW16 (LN)
24691	JUM 543	Duple	42356	C29F	8/46	TS Heaps & Sons, Leeds (WR)
24699	FT 5785	Plaxton	9	FC30F	8/46	TH Taylor {Taylor Bros}, North Shields (ND)
24761 - 24772						Exported to Melbourne (O-AUS)
24789	?	Strachan	?		-/--	Original operator unknown (O-B)
24803						Exported to Santiago (O-RCH)
24814, 24827						Exported to Rangoon (O-BUR)
24833, 24844						Exported to Santiago (O-RCH)
24857	LMY 450	Duple	42344	C29F	6/46	Essex County Coaches Ltd, London E15 (LN)
24864	BAG 574	Duple	42372	C29F	8/46	D Blane {Blane's Motor Coach Services}, Kilmarnock (AR)
24872	GL 9200	(Heaver ?)		C26F	11/46	LH Prescott {City Coaches}, Bath (SO)
24890						Exported to Lisbon (O-P)
24902, 24915						Exported to Malaya
24921, 24932						Exported to Lima (O-PE)
24945	GOM 412	Burlingham	?	B26F	3/47	Sugden's Garage Ltd, Birmingham (WK)
24952	JTT 965	Duple	42360	C29F	6/46	AE Townsend {Townsend's Tours}, Torquay (DN)
24959	HUU 428	Duple	42353	C27F	8/46	George Ewer & Co Ltd {Grey Green}, London N16 (LN)
24979, 24990						Exported to Lima (O-PE)
25003						Exported to Malaya
25009						Exported to Lisbon (O-P)
25020						Exported to Santiago (O-RCH)
25033	JTT 964	Duple	42359	C29F	6/46	AE Townsend {Townsend's Tours}, Torquay (DN)
25040	AMS 944	Duple	42375	C27F	8/46	W Alexander, Falkirk (SN) W192
25048	EF 7666	Duple	42369	C29F	8/46	Bee-Line Roadways (Teeside) Ltd, West Hartlepool (DM)
25067						Exported to Lima (O-PE)
25078	HUU 429	Duple	42355	C27F	8/46	George Ewer & Co Ltd {Grey Green}, London N16 (LN)
25091	MME 744	Duple	42361	C29F	8/46	LC Davis & Sons Ltd, London SW16 (LN)
25097, 25108						Exported to Lisbon (O-P)
25121	EF 7664	Duple	42367	C29F	8/46	Bee-Line Roadways (Teeside) Ltd, West Hartlepool (DM)
25128	BTY 64	Duple	42374	C29F	3/46	C Moffit, Acomb (ND) 20
25136	MME 745	Duple	42362	C29F	8/46	LC Davis & Sons Ltd, London SW16 (LN)
25155	* ?	Mulliner		B--F	-/--	Admiralty (Royal Navy) (GOV)
25166	EF 7665	Duple	42368	C29F	8/46	Bee-Line Roadways (Teeside) Ltd, West Hartlepool (DM)
25179	GPT 206	Duple	42363	C29F	8/46	Scurr's Motor Services Ltd, Stillington (DM)
25185	* 818 RN	Mulliner		B28F	-/46	Admiralty (Royal Navy) (GOV)
25196	* 813 RN	Mulliner		B28F	-/46	Admiralty (Royal Navy) (GOV)
25245	NS 1984	Duple	42378	C27F	9/46	Sutherland Transport & Trading Co Ltd, Lairg (SU)
25252	GPT 207	Duple	42364	C29F	8/46	Scurr's Motor Services Ltd, Stillington (DM)
25260	?	Mulliner		B--F	-/--	Admiralty (Royal Navy) (GOV)
25279	?	Mulliner		B--F	-/--	Admiralty (Royal Navy) (GOV)
25290	CUJ 655	Duple	42381	C29F	8/46	JT, FW & GE Whittle {JT Whittle & Sons}, Highley (SH)
25303	* CUJ 656	Duple	42384	C29F	8/46	JT, FW & GE Whittle {JT Whittle & Sons}, Highley (SH)
25309	?	Mulliner		B--F	-/--	Admiralty (Royal Navy) (GOV)
25320	?	Mulliner		B--F	-/--	Admiralty (Royal Navy) (GOV)
25333	* FAB 202	Duple	42377	C27F	8/46	AE Collins {Favourite}, Lye (WO)
25340	ACF 181	Thurgood	169	C29F	8/46	WT Norfolk, Nayland (WF)
25348	?	Mulliner		B--F	-/--	Admiralty (Royal Navy) (GOV)
25367	* ?	Mulliner		B--F	-/--	Admiralty (Royal Navy) (GOV)
25373	* 751 RN	Mulliner		B28F	-/--	Admiralty (Royal Navy) (GOV)
25378	* ?	Mulliner		B--F	-/--	Admiralty (Royal Navy) (GOV)
25391	?	Mulliner		B--F	-/--	Admiralty (Royal Navy) (GOV)
25397, 25408, 25479, 25490, 25503						Exported to Ireland
25510	* LWL 252	Willmott		C26F	11/46	PC Skinner {Percival's Coaches}, Oxford (OX)
25518	DBU 78	Santus		C25F	7/46	Shearings Tours Ltd, Oldham (LA)
25549	DBU 594	Challenger		C25F	1/47	Shearings Tours Ltd, Oldham (LA)
25560	KPU 730	Mulliner		B32F	5/46	City Coach Co Ltd, Brentwood (EX) B20
25568						Exported to Ireland
25574	LMY 462	Duple	42400	C27F	8/46	Garner's Coaches Ltd, London W5 (LN)
25580	CUJ 654	Duple	42379	C29F	8/46	SC & J Vagg {Vagg's Motors}, Knockin Heath (SH)

C1252/30

25587	KPU 859	Mulliner		B32F	5/46	City Coach Co Ltd, Brentwood (EX) B21
25592	* EDL 283	Duple	42392	C29F	8/46	Mrs V Pearce {White Heather}, Ryde (IW) 4
25599	* GUO 114	Willmott		C26F	9/46	CG & L Burgoyne (Burgoyne Bros) {Grey Cars}, Sidmouth (DN)
25606	DBU 79	Challenger		C26F	9/46	Shearings Tours Ltd, Oldham (LA)
25613	XS 5822	Duple	42398	C29F	9/46	Young's Bus Service Ltd, Paisley (RW) 160
25621	HUU 433	Duple	42354	C27F	8/46	George Ewer & Co Ltd {Grey Green}, London N16 (LN)
25669	?	Mulliner		B--F	-/--	Admiralty (Royal Navy) (GOV)
25677, 25689, 25702, 25715, 25725				#		Exported to Hong Kong
25774						Exported to Malaya
25787	BTY 533	Duple	42373	C27F	8/46	WF Wilkinson {Swift Motor Service}, Ashington (ND)
25799	* EBM 606	Duple	?	B32F	6/46	Vauxhall (staff bus)
25809, 25821, 25834, 25847, 25857				#		Exported to Hong Kong
25869						Exported to Rangoon (O-BUR)
25878	KVW 60	Thurgood	166	C29F	7/46	Rose Bros {Primrose}, Chelmsford (EX) 4
25893	GUR 623	Duple	42401	C29F	8/46	TH Kirby, Bushey Heath (HT)
25905, 25917, 25930, 25943, 25953						Exported to Rangoon (O-BUR)
25966	EF 7663	SMT		B28F	5/46	Bee-Line Roadways (Teeside) Ltd, West Hartlepool (DM)
25979						Exported to Rangoon (O-BUR)
26003	* EBM 615	Duple	?	B--F	-/--	Luton Car Deliveries, Luton (XBD)
26009	U 277	?		?	-/46	Original operator unknown (O-S)
26010 - 26020						Exported to Stockholm (O-S)
26041, 26049						Exported to Rangoon (O-BUR)
26062 #						Exported to Hong Kong
26075						Exported to Malaya
26087						Exported to Rangoon (O-BUR)
26098						Exported to Malaya
26104	?	Mulliner		B--F	-/--	Admiralty (Royal Navy) (GOV)
26112	GEL 714	Harrington	?	C29F	8/46	CJ Pounds {Charlie's Cars}, Bournemouth (HA) 53
26124	HWJ 622	Duple	42389	C29F	8/46	JW Fantom, Sheffield (WR)
26158 #						Exported to Hong Kong
26169						Exported to Ireland
26178	DMO 246	Duple	44365	C29F	2/47	Windsorian Motor Coach Services Ltd, Windsor (BE) 46
26184, 26197, 26207						Exported to Ireland
26219	FAA 921	Duple	44218	C29F	8/46	A Matthews & Sons {Greyfriars Services}, Winchester (HA)
26233	DWV 776	Duple	42391	C29F	8/46	Burrett & Wells Ltd, Melksham (WI)
26245	* 855 RN	Mulliner	K2/98	B32F	-/46	Admiralty (Royal Navy) (GOV)
26279	BPR 500	Duple	42395	C29F	8/46	HS Rendell {Cosy Coaches}, Parkstone (DT)
26291	CUJ 652	Duple	42387	C29F	8/46	WH & W Lowe (JE Lowe & Sons) {Tulip Coaches}, Hadley (SH)
26304	* CUJ 657	Duple	42382	C29F	7/46	JT, FW & GE Whittle {JT Whittle & Sons}, Highley (SH)
26317	JAF 830	Strachan		C26F	4/47	Newquay Motor Co Ltd {Red & White Tours} (CO)
26327	?	Mulliner		B--F	-/--	Admiralty (Royal Navy) (GOV)
26339	?	Mulliner		B--F	-/--	Admiralty (Royal Navy) (GOV)
26352	?	Mulliner		B--F	-/--	Admiralty (Royal Navy) (GOV)
26365	?	Mulliner		B--F	-/--	Admiralty (Royal Navy) (GOV)
26388	* GUR 985	Thurgood	171	C29F	10/46	HV Richmond, Barley (HT)
26400	HWJ 621	Duple	42388	C29F	8/46	JW Fantom, Sheffield (WR)
26413	DAW 41	Duple	42380	C29F	8/46	SC & J Vagg {Vagg's Motors}, Knockin Heath (SH)
26426	GOG 877	Duple	42385	C29F	8/46	E Newton {Gaby Glide}, Birmingham (WK) 2
26436	* ?	Mulliner		B--F	-/--	Admiralty (Royal Navy) (GOV)
26449	?	Mulliner		B--F	-/--	Admiralty (Royal Navy) (GOV)
26462	?	Mulliner		B--F	-/--	Admiralty (Royal Navy) (GOV)
26474	?	Mulliner		B--F	-/--	Admiralty (Royal Navy) (GOV)
26484	* CUJ 658	Duple	42383	C29F	8/46	JT, FW & GE Whittle {JT Whittle & Sons}, Highley (SH)
26496	HAR 648	Thurgood	241	C29F	11/46	WJ Carter, Royston (HT)
26509	DET 94	Duple	42409	C29F	7/46	E Thornton & Sons {Alma Coaches}, Thurcroft (WR)
26522	EDL 284	Duple	42393	C29F	9/46	Mrs V Pearce {White Heather}, Ryde (IW) 5
26532	* 808 RN	Mulliner		B28F	-/46	Admiralty (Royal Navy) (GOV)
26545	?	Mulliner		B--F	-/--	Admiralty (Royal Navy) (GOV)
26558	?	Mulliner		B--F	-/--	Admiralty (Royal Navy) (GOV)
26570	* ?	Mulliner		B--F	-/--	Admiralty (Royal Navy) (GOV)

26597 - 26608					Exported to Melbourne (O-AUS)
26621	?	Duple	46140	C29F	-/47 British Embassy, Ankara (O-TR)
26628	GOG 878	Duple	42386	C29F	9/46 E Newton {Gaby Glide}, Birmingham (WK)
26641	* E-45613	Hainje		B30-	-/47 Schutte, Zwolle (O-N) 13
26654	* JVT 965	?		B28F	6/46 William Tatton & Co Ltd, Leek (ST)
26664					Exported to Lisbon (O-P)
26677	?	Mulliner		B--F	-/-- Admiralty (Royal Navy) (GOV)
26690	* E-45614	Hainje		B30-	-/47 Schutte, Zwolle (O-N) 14
26712					Exported to Lisbon (O-P)
26724	JP 6522	Santus		FC29F	9/47 W Liptrot (Coaches) Ltd, Bamfurlong (LA)
26736					Exported to Antwerp (O-B)
26748	KTW 855	Thurgood	167	C29F	7/46 Rose Bros {Primrose}, Chelmsford (EX) 3
26758	?	Duple	46133	B32F	-/-- Shell Petroleum Co, Bachaquera (O-YV)
26772	?	Mulliner		B--F	-/-- Admiralty (Royal Navy) (GOV)
26786	?	Duple	46132	B32F	-/-- Shell Petroleum Co, Bachaquera (O-YV)
26808	?	Duple	46130	B32F	-/-- Shell Petroleum Co, Cabimas (O-YV)
26820	* CVH 317	Roberts		C29F	5/46 Chapman's Ivy Coaches Ltd, Milnsbridge (WR)
26833	?	Duple	46131	B32F	-/-- Shell Petroleum Co, Cabimas (O-YV)
26846	KPU 871	Mulliner		B32F	5/46 City Coach Co Ltd, Brentwood (EX) B22
26856	* HD-12-07	?		DP26D	8/46 Empresa Lopes e Matos, Pontes de Monfalim (O-P) 18
26869	* 796 RN	Mulliner		B32F	-/46 Admiralty (Royal Navy) (GOV)
26882	K-1264	?		B27-	11/46 Topdalens Bilruter AS, unknown location (O-N)
26887 - 26898					Exported to Buenos Aires (O-RA)
26952	O-6015	?		B---	-/46 Original operator unknown (O-N)
26964	JK 9188	Duple	43161	C29F	6/46 Thorogood {Berkeley Coaches}, Eastbourne (ES)
26977	H-876	?		B30-	4/47 Lars Økter, Skien (O-N)
26990	DSR 391	Duple	43027	C29F	6/46 A Melville, Kirriemuir (AS)
27000	F-12454	?		?	5/47 PL Al Rutebillag, Ål (O-N)
27013	?	Mulliner		B--F	-/-- Admiralty (Royal Navy) (GOV)
27026	L-14144	?		?	2/47 Sverre Haga's Bilruter, Høyland (O-N)
27048	K-8137	?		?	2/47 Torkel Bakke og Sigurd Sigbjørnsen (Bakkeruta) (O-N)
27060	?	?		van	5/48 WT Henley's Telegraph Works Co Ltd, London EC1 (GLN)
27073	B-15531	?		?	-/46 Original operator unknown (O-N)
27086	#				Exported to Hong Kong
27096	* ?	?		?	12/46 Original operator unknown (O-N)
27157	#				Exported to Hong Kong
27170	D-3521	Mæhlum		B29-	6/47 Magne Bjerke, Åsmarka (O-N)
27182	?	Duple	46127	B32F	-/-- Shell Petroleum Co, La Concepcion (O-YV)
27192	K-1672	?		?	3/47 Original operator unknown (O-N)
27204					Exported to Port Elizabeth (O-ZA)
27217	H-409	?		?	2/47 Original operator unknown (O-N)
27229					Exported to Malaya
27240					Exported to Oslo (O-N)
27250 - 27261					Exported to Bombay (O-IND)
27325					Exported to Malaya
27338	?	Duple	46128	B32F	-/-- Shell Petroleum Co, La Concepcion (O-YV)
27350	?	Duple	46125	B32F	-/-- Shell Petroleum Co, Mene Grande (O-YV)
27360	?	Duple	46126	B32F	-/-- Shell Petroleum Co, Mene Grande (O-YV)
27372					Exported to Malaya
27385	L-11530	?		B---	2/47 Original operator unknown (O-N)
27398	?	Duple	46134	B32F	-/-- Nigerian Motor Transport Union, Lagos (O-WAN)
27408					Exported to Lisbon (O-P)
27421	?	Duple	46135	B32F	-/-- Nigerian Motor Transport Union, Lagos (O-WAN)
27434, 27446					Exported to Lisbon (O-P)
27456					Exported to Tangier (O-MA)
27468					Exported to unknown location in Near East
27481, 27503					Exported to Lisbon (O-P)
27522					Exported to Iraq
27528, 27542					Exported to Lisbon (O-P)
27552					Exported to Iraq
27564					Exported to unknown location in Near East
27577					Exported to Iraq
27590					Exported to unknown location in Near East

C1252/32

27600						Exported, possibly to Lima (O-PE)
27613						Exported to Lisbon (O-P)
27626						Exported, possibly to Lima (O-PE)
27638						Exported to Tangier (O-MA)
27648	I-5002	?	B---	3/47		Original operator unknown (O-N)
27660, 27673, 27686						Exported to unknown location in Near East
27696						Exported to Syria
27709, 27732, 27735, 27744						Exported to unknown location in Near East
27756	?	Mulliner	B--F	-/--		Admiralty (Royal Navy) (GOV)
27769, 27782, 27792						Exported to unknown location in Near East
27805						Exported to Antwerp (O-B)
27818, 27830						Exported to unknown location in Near East
27840						Exported to Tel Aviv (O-IL)
27852	BPR 501	Duple	42396	C29F	8/46	HS Rendell {Cosy Coaches}, Parkstone (DT)
27874 - 27885						Exported to Sydney (O-AUS)
27937						Exported to unknown location in Near East
27950	?	?		van	8/46	Thorpe, Beeston (GNG)
27958						Exported to unknown location in Near East
27969	KTW 236	Mulliner		B32F	6/46	City Coach Co Ltd, Brentwood (EX) B23
27978, 27990, 28000						Exported to Iraq
28012	GUR 941	Duple	42403	C29F	9/46	TH Kirby, Bushey Heath (HT)
28025						Exported to Syria
28038	* FAA 987	Duple	42397	C29F	9/46	PW Lambert {Little Wonder Coaches}, Petersfield (HA)
28048						Exported to Syria
28060	BJD 5	Duple	43207	C26F	7/46	London Co-operative Society, London E7 (LN) 663
28073, 28085, 28095						Exported to Tel Aviv (O-IL)
28108	GUR 622	Duple	42402	C29F	9/46	TH Kirby, Bushey Heath (HT)
28120						Exported to Tel Aviv (O-IL)
28134	GEL 792	Harrington	?	C29F	9/46	CJ Pounds {Charlie's Cars}, Bournemouth (HA) 54
28144						Exported to Jerusalem (O-IL)
28157	BRS 719	Duple	43005	C27F	9/46	F F & F Ltd, Aberdeen (AD)
28170						Exported to Jerusalem (O-IL)
28182						Exported to Tel Aviv (O-IL)
28192						Exported to Antwerp (O-B)
28204	FAA 238	Duple	44324	C29F	7/46	Hants & Sussex Motor Services Ltd, Emsworth (HA) 101
28217	#					Exported to Hong Kong
28226	FAA 239	Duple	43081	C29F	7/46	Liss & District Omnibus Co Ltd, Liss (HA) 102
28234	GVO 765	Duple	42029	B32F	7/46	South Notts Bus Co Ltd, Gotham (NG) 29
28242	#					Exported to Hong Kong
28250	FAA 240	Duple	44322	C29F	7/46	Sunbeam Coaches (Loxwood) Ltd (WS) 103
28258	DJB 117	Duple	43007	C27F	9/46	JC Chastell & DG Gray {The Dean Bus Service}, Cookham Dean (BE)
28269	FAA 241	Duple	44321	C29F	7/46	Liss & District Omnibus Co Ltd, Liss (HA) 104
28288	FAA 242	Duple	44323	C29F	7/46	Sunbeam Coaches (Loxwood) Ltd (WS) 105
28304	#?	RE&C		B33F	-/46	WJ Wheeler & Sons Ltd, Penrose (O-NZ)
28349	FAA 243	Duple	44325	C29F	7/46	Hants & Sussex Motor Services Ltd, Emsworth (HA) 106
28356	HAL 511	Duple	44240	C29F	10/46	JHP Morley (P Morley & Sons), Edwinstowe (NG)
28376	KTW 237	Mulliner		B32F	6/46	City Coach Co Ltd, Brentwood (EX) B24
28406	HXB 716	Duple	43010	C27F	9/46	Keith & Boyle (London) Ltd {Orange Luxury Coaches}, London EC2 (LN) Viola
28413	BRS 856	Duple	43006	C29F	9/46	JA Noble, Aberdeen (AD)
28435	BRS 718	Duple	43004	C27F	9/46	WC Ledingham, Aberdeen (AD)
28451	HXB 720	Duple	43014	C27F	9/46	Keith & Boyle (London) Ltd {Orange Luxury Coaches}, London EC2 (LN) Annette
28461	* KNW 455	Duple	42357	C29F	9/46	TS Heaps & Sons, Leeds (WR)
28468	DAJ 216	Duple	43003	C29F	6/46	JC Pickering {Saltburn Motor Services}, Saltburn (NR) 7
28482	DAW 346	Burlingham	?	DP32F	10/46	JT, FW & GE Whittle {JT Whittle & Sons}, Highley (SH)
28500	EDL 285	Duple	42394	C29F	9/46	Mrs V Pearce {White Heather}, Ryde (IW) 3
28507	* FAA 244	Duple	44326	C29F	7/46	BS Williams, Emsworth (HA) 107
28512	* FOY 321	Duple	43218	C27F	9/46	JE & HE Jewell {Jewell's Coaches}, Croydon (SR)
28529	LRF 654	Duple	43217	C29F	9/46	Black & White Tours (Bilston) Ltd (ST)
28545	* EBM 616	Mulliner		B28F	-/46	Vauxhall (experimental vehicle)

28556	FOY 323	Duple	43220	C29F	9/46	JE & HE Jewell {Jewell's Coaches}, Croydon (SR)
28563	HXB 714	Duple	43008	C27F	9/46	Keith & Boyle (London) Ltd {Orange Luxury Coaches}, London EC2 (LN) Vera
28577	FOY 322	Duple	43219	C29F	9/46	JE & HE Jewell {Jewell's Coaches}, Croydon (SR)
28595	HWJ 649	Duple	43000	C27F	9/46	JO Andrew Ltd, Sheffield (WR)
28602	HXB 711	Duple	43011	C27F	9/46	Keith & Boyle (London) Ltd {Orange Luxury Coaches}, London EC2 (LN) Sheila
28607	* DJB 279	Duple	42399	C29F	8/46	Tom Tappin Ltd {Travel Rambler}, Wallingford (BE)
28621	?	Mulliner		B30F	10/46	Cementation Co Ltd, Bentley (XWR)
28625	HWJ 650	Duple	43001	C27F	9/46	JO Andrew Ltd, Sheffield (WR)
28640	* HXB 719	Duple	43015	C27F	9/46	Keith & Boyle (London) Ltd {Orange Luxury Coaches}, London EC2 (LN) Minerva
28650	HXB 717	Duple	43016	C27F	9/46	Keith & Boyle (London) Ltd {Orange Luxury Coaches}, London EC2 (LN) Ella
28657	* HXB 724	Duple	43021	C27F	9/46	Keith & Boyle (London) Ltd {Orange Luxury Coaches}, London EC2 (LN) Olivette
28672	HXB 725	Duple	43023	C27F	9/46	Keith & Boyle (London) Ltd {Orange Luxury Coaches}, London EC2 (LN) Henriette
28689	* KPH 478	Duple	42407	C29F	9/46	Ben Stanley Ltd, Hersham (SR)
28697		see 28607				
28701	* GUR 664	Thurgood	168	C29F	8/46	BC Cannon Ltd, Puckeridge (HT)
28713	HXB 712	Duple	43009	C27F	9/46	Keith & Boyle (London) Ltd {Orange Luxury Coaches}, London EC2 (LN) Stella
28763 - 28767						Exported to Stockholm (O-S)
28768	C 323	?		?	1/47	JE Karlsson, Knaby (O-S)
28769 - 28774						Exported to Stockholm (O-S)
28797	HXB 713	Duple	43013	C27F	9/46	Keith & Boyle (London) Ltd {Orange Luxury Coaches}, London EC2 (LN) Tessa
28808	?	Mulliner		B31F	-/46	Cementation Co Ltd, Bentley (XWR)
28821	?	Mulliner		B--F	-/--	Admiralty (Royal Navy) (GOV)
28843, 28854						Exported to Antwerp (O-B)
28861						Exported to Syria
28867	EBT 172	Duple	42408	C29F	9/46	Kemp Bros {KB Coaches}, Withernsea (ER)
28879	HXB 715	Duple	43012	C27F	9/46	Keith & Boyle (London) Ltd {Orange Luxury Coaches}, London EC2 (LN) Wanda
28890	* HXB 718	Duple	43017	C27F	9/46	Keith & Boyle (London) Ltd {Orange Luxury Coaches}, London EC2 (LN) Erica
28914	?	?		?	-/--	Ministry of Supply (GOV)
28921	HXB 726	Duple	43022	C27F	9/46	Keith & Boyle (London) Ltd {Orange Luxury Coaches}, London EC2 (LN) Rosette
28928	#					Exported to Hong Kong
28940, 28951						Exported to Antwerp (O-B)
28963	?			B---	9/46	Sir Robert McAlpine & Sons Ltd (contractor), London W1
28975	FAB 463	Plaxton	194	FC30F	10/46	Mrs ME Ward {Ward's Super de Luxe}, Sidemoor (WO)
28987	HXB 723	Duple	43020	C27F	9/46	Keith & Boyle (London) Ltd {Orange Luxury Coaches}, London EC2 (LN) Lucette
28999	?	?		van	7/46	East Bros, Lochee (GAS)
29011	#?	?		?	-/--	Mulliners Ltd, Birmingham (XWK)
29059						Exported to Iraq
29128 - 29139						Exported to Melbourne (O-AUS)
29143, 29154						Exported to Antwerp (O-B)
29165	EX 5566	Plaxton	19	FC30F	12/46	WJ Haylett {Felix Coaches}, Great Yarmouth (NK) 2
29176	GUO 82	Duple	42404	C29F	9/46	Ruby Tours Ltd, Paignton (DN)
29188	DAJ 178	Duple	43037	C29F	4/47	W Bickerton, Kirkby Wiske (NR)
29200	GFD 322	Duple	43034	C29F	9/46	B Davenport {Bestway Coaches}, Netherton (WO)
29213	?	?		?	-/--	Ministry of Supply (GOV)
29224						Exported to Iraq
29236, 29247						Exported to Antwerp (O-B)
29261	GUO 83	Duple	42405	C29F	9/46	Ruby Tours Ltd, Paignton (DN)
29273	HXB 722	Duple	43018	C27F	9/46	Keith & Boyle (London) Ltd {Orange Luxury Coaches}, London EC2 (LN) Georgiette
29285	GUO 84	Duple	42406	C29F	9/46	Ruby Tours Ltd, Paignton (DN)

C1252/34

29297	HXB 721	Duple	43019	C27F	9/46	Keith & Boyle (London) Ltd {Orange Luxury Coaches}, London EC2 (LN) Fleurette
29424	#?	?		?	-/--	Mulliners Ltd, Birmingham (XWK)
29430						Exported to Antwerp (O-B)
29436	* K-17856	Roset		B33-	-/47	ZVTM, Terneuzen (O-NL) 16
29442	FRW 67	Duple	43043	C26F	7/46	AJ Elliott {Elliott Bros}, Coventry (WK)
29460	KTW 238	Mulliner		B32F	6/46	City Coach Co Ltd, Brentwood (EX) B25
29466	EX 5508	Plaxton	18	FC30F	8/46	WJ Haylett {Felix Coaches}, Great Yarmouth (NK) 1
29472	FUY 580	Whitson	?	C27F	3/47	Samuel Johnson (Supreme) Ltd, Stourbridge (WO)
29478	#?	?		?	-/--	Mulliners Ltd, Birmingham (XWK)
29484	KHU 176	Lee		C29F	5/47	G Feltham & Sons Ltd {Kingswood Queen}, Kingswood (GL)
29490	* K-17857	Roset		B33-	-/47	ZVTM, Terneuzen (O-NL) 17
29496	* K-17858	Roset		B33-	-/47	ZVTM, Terneuzen (O-NL) 18
29502	1951	Mulliner		B32F	9/46	Sarre Transport Ltd, St Peter Port, Guernsey (CI) 6
29507	JHA 136	Plaxton	95	FC30F	8/46	Gilbert & Houghton Ltd {Swallow Coaches}, Smethwick (ST)
29513	* DBU 341	Plaxton	52	FC30F	8/46	Ralph Renton Ltd, Hollinwood (LA)
29519	DFU 224	Plaxton	35	FC30F	9/46	JR Mellers, Goxhill (LI)
29525	#?	?		?	-/--	Mulliners Ltd, Birmingham (XWK)
29543	GPT 390	Plaxton	29	FC30F	9/46	C McCune, Stockton-on-Tees (DM)
29573	* K-17859	Roset		B33-	-/47	ZVTM, Terneuzen (O-NL) 19
29581						Exported to Rangoon (O-BUR)
29593	?	Mulliner		B31F	-/--	Cementation Co Ltd, Bentley (XWR)
29605	DFU 400	Duple	43038	C29F	10/46	F Troop, Barton-on-Humber (LI)
29617						Exported to Iraq
29629	* FHP 782	Plaxton	14	FC30F	9/46	R Bolton {Red Horse Coaches}, Coventry (WK)
29641	#?	?		?	-/--	Mulliners Ltd, Birmingham (XWK)
29653	* HTB 728	A Mulliner		C20F	3/47	E Mayers {Kenilworth Tours}, Litherland (LA)
29665	HWJ 484	Duple	43143	C29F	8/46	Sansam Bros (Sheffield) Ltd (WR)
29676, 29688						Exported to Rangoon (O-BUR)
29700	FAA 863	Strachan		C29F	9/46	Lovegrove & Lovegrove Ltd, Silchester (HA)
29712	GFJ 632	Duple	43125	C29F	9/46	Greenslades, Exeter (DN)
29724	?	?		van	10/46	H Joscelynes, Braintree (GEX)
29736	?	?		?	-/--	Ministry of Supply (GOV)
29748	ECR 57	Duple	43033	C29F	9/46	PFV Summerbee {Sumerbee's Motor Coaches}, Southampton (HA)
29780	GFD 323	Duple	43035	C29F	9/46	B Davenport {Bestway Coaches}, Netherton (WO)
29785						Exported to Rangoon (O-BUR)
29794	JBH 400	Thurgood	170	C29F	9/46	JRG Dell {Rover Bus Service}, Lye Green (BK) 6
29806	* BCB 785	Duple	50974	C27F	9/48	Fraser Motors (Accrington) Ltd (LA)
29818	?	?		?	-/--	OMT, unknown location, East Africa
29942	HG 8641	Plaxton	62	FC30F	10/46	D Tattersall Ltd, Padiham (LA)
29948	* HLB 149	Duple	45061	B32F	6/46	Delco-Remy-Hyatt {DRH Car Radio}, London SW1 (XLN)
29956, 29979						Exported to Rangoon (O-BUR)
30055	FAB 498	Duple	43069	C29F	10/46	AL Yarranton Snr & AL Yarranton Jnr {Eardiston Coaches}, Eardiston (WO)
30061	?	?		?	-/--	Ministry of Supply (GOV)
30067						Exported to Malta
30073	* KNW 639	Duple	42358	C29F	9/46	TS Heaps & Sons, Leeds (WR)
30079	* EBT 240	(Roe ?)	?	B32F	9/46	G Crosby {Red & White Bus}, Hunmanby (ER)
30085	* HUW 164	Duple	?	C26F	7/46	Ansell's Coaches Ltd, London SE5 (LN)
30093	EDL 375	Duple	43029	C29F	9/46	H Paul (H Paul & Son), Ryde (IW) 1
30104	KVX 739	Thurgood	176	B28F	9/46	GS Wright, Harlow (EX)
30117	EDL 376	Duple	43030	C29F	3/47	H Paul (H Paul & Son), Ryde (IW) 2
30124	GTE 289	Plaxton	143	FC30F	10/46	T Towler (Lytham) Ltd (LA)
30130	GAD 141	Duple	43041	C29F	9/46	FB & WE Pulham {Pulham & Sons}, Naunton (GL)
30136	JAF 831	Strachan		C26F	4/47	Newquay Motor Co Ltd {Red & White Tours} (CO)
30143, 30154						Exported to Rangoon (O-BUR)
30157 - 30168						Exported to Copenhagen (O-DK)
30226	3117	Mulliner		B33F	8/46	Guernsey Railways (CI) 78
30237	2103	Duple	46143	B32F	1/47	Route Bus Service (O-M)
30245	?	?		h/box	5/47	Miss RF Vinning, Greens Norton (GNO)

30253	2059	Duple	46144 B32F	1/47	Route Bus Service (N Micallef), Qormi (O-M)
30262	GMN 799	Duple	43032 C29F	7/46	Quayle's Garage Ltd {Marguerite Motors}, Douglas (IM)
30274	BBV 84	SMT	C27F	7/47	Roberts Tours (Blackburn) Ltd (LA)
30284, 30292					Exported to Malta
30294	#?	Elliot	C10-	-/--	OMT, unknown location, East Africa
30299	2374	Brincat	B31F	6/47	Route Bus Service (O-M)
30307	* DBU 386	Plaxton	53 FC30F	9/46	Ralph Renton Ltd, Hollinwood (LA)
30313	DAW 475	Duple	43052 C29F	10/46	JT, FW & GE Whittle {JT Whittle & Sons}, Highley (SH)
30325					Exported to Malta
30332	DJB 406	Duple	43502 C29F	10/46	GE Hedges {Reliance Motor Services}, Newbury (BE) 16
30340	* GMN 798	Duple	43031 C29F	7/46	Quayle's Garage Ltd {Marguerite Motors}, Douglas (IM)
30356	DCO 557	Duple	43050 C29F	10/46	Embankment Motor Co (Plymouth) Ltd (DN)
30364	?	?	?	-/--	Ministry of Supply (GOV)
30373	* KPJ 389	Duple	43039 C29F	10/46	Cooke's Coaches (Stoughton) Ltd (SR)
30379					Exported to Malta
30381	2980	Aquilina	B32F	9/48	Route Bus Service (O-M)
30382	* KTW 244	Mulliner	B32F	8/46	City Coach Co Ltd, Brentwood (EX) B31
30385	BJD 4	Duple	43206 C26F	7/46	London Co-operative Society, London E7 (LN) 662
30400	?	?	?	-/--	Ministry of Supply (GOV)
30404	?	?	van	8/47	Ipswich Co-operative Society (GSK)
30424	2441	Aquilina	B32F	7/49	Route Bus Service (F Vassallo), Rabat (O-M)
30436	11043	?	B32F	-/49	Medical and Health Department (O-M)
30485	4101	Mulliner	B32F	9/46	Sarre Transport Ltd, St Peter Port, Guernsey (CI) 3
30504	?	?	?	-/--	Ministry of Supply (GOV)
30523	JP 6878	NMU	FC30F	7/48	R Gray (Gray Bros) {Streamline Coaches}, Wigan (LA)
30541 - 30552					Exported to Sydney (O-AUS)
30553					Exported to Malta
30583	IP 5113	Ryan	B26F	-/47	Cullinane, Castlecomer (EI)
30590					Exported to Ireland
30644		see 30664			
30658	DNR 53	Duple	43044 C29F	10/46	RH Reeve, Fleckney (LE)
30664	* EGD 448	?	B28F	8/46	Original operator
30671	BJD 7	Duple	43209 C29F	7/46	London Co-operative Society, London E7 (LN) 665
30689	BJD 6	Duple	43208 C29F	7/46	London Co-operative Society, London E7 (LN) 664
30698	DBD 150	Duple	43055 C29F	10/46	York Bros (Northampton) Ltd (NO) 11
30706					Exported to Ireland
30716	JE 8712	Duple	46303 C29F	10/46	JW Brown {Marquis Service}, Guyhirn (CM)
30731	HDE 733	Mulliner	B31F	4/47	J Edwards (Edwards Bros), Crymych (PE)
30802	HXB 727	Duple	43025 C27F	9/46	Keith & Boyle (London) Ltd {Orange Luxury Coaches}, London EC2 (LN) Suzette
30816	?	?	?	-/--	Ministry of Supply (GOV)
30860	?	?	?	-/--	Ministry of Supply (GOV)
30930					Exported to Lisbon (O-P)
30932					Exported to unknown overseas location
30934					Exported to Lisbon (O-P)
30949	?	?	?	-/--	Ministry of Supply (GOV)
30956					Exported to unknown overseas location
30960	DCO 554	Duple	43047 C29F	10/46	Embankment Motor Co (Plymouth) Ltd (DN)
30962 - 30973					Exported to Melbourne (O-AUS)
30974	DJB 410	Duple	43026 C29F	9/46	WF Carter & Sons Ltd {Alpha Coaches}, Maidenhead (BE)
30983					Exported to unknown location in Near East
31000	DFU 435	Duple	43045 C27F	10/46	HA Kemp, Burgh-on-Bain (LI)
31007	DJB 379	Duple	43053 C29F	10/46	L Stevens, Charney Bassett (BE)
31013	JMA 17	Plaxton	76 FC30F	2/47	Altrincham Coachways Ltd (CH)
31020					Exported to Ireland
31026					Exported to Lisbon (O-P)
31037	FWT 646	Duple	43036 C29F	10/46	F & A Wigmore {Excelsior}, Dinnington (WR)
31049					Exported to Lisbon (O-P)
31097	HXB 728	Duple	43024 C29F	9/46	Keith & Boyle (London) Ltd {Orange Luxury Coaches}, London EC2 (LN) Yvette
31103	* KTW 243	Mulliner	B32F	8/46	City Coach Co Ltd, Brentwood (EX) B30
31109	K-18984	Roset	B33-	-/47	ZVTM, Terneuzen (O-NL) 20

C1252/36

31115						Exported to Lisbon (O-P)
31121	* KNW 902	Plaxton	162	FC30F	10/46	Wallace Arnold, Leeds (WR)
31145	* DAW 473	Duple	43059	C29F	10/46	WH & W Lowe (JE Lowe & Sons) {Tulip Coaches}, Hadley (SH)
31152, 31154						Exported to Lisbon (O-P)
31157	EDA 693	Mulliner		B30F	10/46	Worthington Motor Tours Ltd, Wolverhampton (ST)
31160	* JUO 874	Whitson	?	C26F	4/47	EG Butter {Sid Valley Coaches}, Sidmouth (DN)
31172						Exported to Iraq
31208	?	?	?		-/--	Ministry of Supply (GOV)
31248	KNU 581	Duple	43086	C27F	11/46	J Cunliffe, R Spencer & GA Gibbins {Park Hire}, Chapel-en-le-Frith (DE)
31261	DCO 556	Duple	43049	C29F	10/46	Embankment Motor Co (Plymouth) Ltd (DN)
31297	GPT 775	Duple	44383	C29F	10/46	F Lockey & Son, St Helens Auckland (DM)
31299 - 31310						Exported to Buenos Aires (O-RA)
31328	L-34207	DO&D		B30D	11/46	GVU, Utrecht (O-NL) 36
31332- 31343						Exported to Melbourne (O-AUS)
31347	?	?	?		-/--	Ministry of Supply (GOV)
31359	?	?	?		-/--	Ministry of Supply (GOV)
31374						Exported to Iraq
31380	3460	Mulliner		B32F	9/46	Sarre Transport Ltd, St Peter Port, Guernsey (CI) 4
31390	DMO 247	Duple	44364	C29F	2/47	Windsorian Motor Coach Services Ltd, Windsor (BE) 47
31396	GPT 488	Duple	43058	C29F	10/46	HJ Annforth, South Stanley (DM)
31420						Exported to Tel Aviv (O-IL)
31636	KTW 241	Mulliner		B32F	8/46	City Coach Co Ltd, Brentwood (EX) B28
31645	JWA 348	Duple	43057	C29F	10/46	EH Sims, Sheffield (WR)
31650	KTW 240	Mulliner		B32F	8/46	City Coach Co Ltd, Brentwood (EX) B27
31655	GPT 490	Duple	43063	C29F	10/46	R & J Armstrong and Mrs M Wardle {Cowling's Bus Service}, Ebchester (DM) 11
31679	* DCO 558	Duple	43051	C29F	10/46	Embankment Motor Co (Plymouth) Ltd (DN)
31689						Exported to Tel Aviv (O-IL)
31896	FWU 231	Duple	43002	C29F	10/46	W Simpson, Ripon (WR) 1
31908	3118	Mulliner		B33F	9/46	Guernsey Railways (CI) 19
32004	KPJ 390	Duple	43040	C29F	10/46	Cooke's Coaches (Stoughton) Ltd (SR) 25
32073 #						Exported to Hong Kong
32078	DCO 555	Duple	43048	C29F	10/46	Embankment Motor Co (Plymouth) Ltd (DN)
32083	DCO 553	Duple	43046	C29F	10/46	Embankment Motor Co (Plymouth) Ltd (DN)
32146	?	Duple	46136	B32F	-/46	Odulola Bros, Lagos (O-WAN)
32150	* EGD 150	(Mulliner ?)		B28F	8/46	C Fitzpatrick {Azure Blue Line}, Dunoon (AL)
32155	KTW 239	Mulliner		B32F	8/46	City Coach Co Ltd, Brentwood (EX) B26
32161	?	?	?		-/--	Ministry of Education (GOV)
32165						Exported to Antwerp (O-B)
32172	?	Duple	46137	B32F	-/46	Odulola Bros, Lagos (O-WAN)
32180						Exported to Iraq
32185	* FDV 210	Duple	44377	C29F	4/47	ST Wills, Atherington (DN)
32190	BTY 823	Duple	43060	C29F	8/46	M Charlton & Sons, Fourstones (ND) 9
32195	FTX 773	Duple	44731	C29F	10/46	WJ, BA & R Edwards, Talbot Green (GG)
32205						
32206	JE 8578	Duple	43042	C29F	10/46	T Canham & Sons (Services) Ltd, Whittlesey (CM)
32207	GPT 491	Duple	43064	C29F	10/46	R & J Armstrong and Mrs M Wardle {Cowling's Bus Service}, Ebchester (DM) 12
32213	KUA 185	Duple	43094	C29F	10/46	George Barker & Sons (Scarborough) Ltd (NR)
32273	?	?	?		8/46	Sir Robert McAlpine & Sons Ltd (contractor), London W1
32274						Exported to Rangoon (O-BUR)
32298	HHN 751	Duple	43070	C29F	10/46	Anderson Bros {Blue Belle}, Evenwood (DM)
32306 #						Exported to Hong Kong
32319 - 32322						Exported to Melbourne (O-AUS)
32323	* Q.489.923	CAC	M31.34	B35F	8/47	PJ O'Brien, Gympie, Qld (O-AUS)
32324 - 32328						Exported to Melbourne (O-AUS)
32329	* WVF.767	CAC	M31.26	B--F	7/47	Green Coach Lines, Hobart, Tas (O-AUS)
32330						Exported to Melbourne (O-AUS)
32353	HKA 648	(Pearson ?)		B32F	8/46	Sunniways Coaches (Pearsons of Liverpool) Ltd (LA)
32359	* KTW 242	Mulliner		B32F	8/46	City Coach Co Ltd, Brentwood (EX) B29
32366						Exported to Ireland

32368	* GZ-60875	Met		B29	-/46	TESO, Den Burg (O-NL) 3
32381						Exported to Ireland
32426	* J 6986	Mulliner		B32F	6/47	Jersey Motor Transport (CI) 57
32433	* DBD 151	Duple	43056	C29F	11/46	York Bros (Northampton) Ltd (NO) 12
32463, 32469						Exported to Ireland
32497	?	?		l/stock	8/46	Harvey Bros, Coningsby (GLI)
32534, 32553						Exported to Ireland
32563	SL 2970	Duple	43061	C29F	10/46	W Dawson, Sauchie (CK)
32564	JLG 991	Plaxton	75	FC30F	11/46	Altrincham Coachways Ltd (CH)
32583	GPT 718	Plaxton	175	FC30F	10/46	C McCune, Stockton-on-Tees (DM)
32598						Exported to Ireland
32620 - 32631						Exported to Melbourne (O-AUS)
32633	EDA 691	Mulliner		B32F	9/46	Worthington Motor Tours Ltd, Wolverhampton (ST)
32744, 32758						Exported to Ireland
32764	* GPT 492	Duple	43065	C29F	10/46	R & J Armstrong and Mrs M Wardle {Cowling's Bus Service}, Ebchester (DM) 14
32771	?	?		l/stock	8/46	Harvey Bros, Coningsby (GLI)
32772	GTE 551	Plaxton	114	FC30F	10/46	Rossendale Division Carriage Co, Bacup (LA)
32773						Exported to Ireland
32787, 32795						Exported to Lisbon (O-P)
32802						Exported to Georgetown (O-MAL)
32809	* DBU 688	Plaxton	246	FC30F	3/47	Gregory & Richards Ltd, Oldham (LA)
32823	#EF 7778	Duple	42371	C29F	10/46	Bee-Line Roadways (Teeside) Ltd, West Hartlepool (DM)
32836	SB 6785	Duple	43066	C29F	11/46	West Coast Motor Service Co, Campbeltown (AL)
32850						Exported to Georgetown (O-MAL)
32874	#EF 7779	Duple	43062	C29F	10/46	Bee-Line Roadways (Teeside) Ltd, West Hartlepool (DM)
32884	GPT 489	Duple	43068	C29F	10/46	J Armstrong, Thirsk (NR)
32896, 32913						Exported to Georgetown (O-MAL)
32932	BTY 626	Duple	43075	C29F	10/46	R Armstrong, Westerhope (ND) 40
32947	?	(SMT ?)	?		9/46	Dunbarton County Council (XDB)
32960	BTY 627	Duple	43076	C29F	10/46	R Armstrong, Westerhope (ND) 41
32976	EDA 694	Mulliner		B28F	10/46	Worthington Motor Tours Ltd, Wolverhampton (ST)
32996	JAF 832	Strachan		C26F	5/47	Newquay Motor Co Ltd {Red & White Tours} (CO)
33001	CRV 983	Duple	44296	C29F	10/46	FC Smith {Smith Bros}, Funtley (HA)
33016	* GUO 398	Duple	43073	C29F	10/46	SJ Wakley {Rambler Bus Services}, Axminster (DN)
33030	* JKX 555	Thurgood	244	C29F	12/46	JRG Dell {Rover Bus Service}, Lye Green (BK) 8
33038	* ?	?	?		8/46	Eastern National, Chelmsford (EX)
33073	AJL 289	Duple	43074	C29F	10/46	GAS Longland, Crowland (LI)
33079	?	?		l/stock	-/46	Harvey Bros, Coningsby (GLI)
33098	ACF 680	Thurgood	242	C29F	11/46	F Goldsmith (Sicklesmere) Ltd (WF)
33111	DAJ 846	Plaxton	197	C28F	12/46	HG Sage, Burry Port (CR)
33125	FUY 579	Whitson	?	C27F	3/47	Samuel Johnson (Supreme) Ltd, Stourbridge (WO)
33140	CFR 735	Plaxton	60	FC30F	3/47	Marshall & Son (Blackpool) Ltd (LA)
33154	?	?	?		-/--	Ministry of Supply (GOV)
33170	KVW 948	Mulliner		B32F	9/46	City Coach Co Ltd, Brentwood (EX) B32
33185	* CTH 636	Duple	44334	C29F	10/46	D Davies {Brechfa Express}, Felingwm (CR)
33206	FAC 527	Duple	43072	C29F	10/46	JC Arnold, Twogates (WK)
33224	KHU 996	Lee		C29F	6/47	G Feltham & Sons Ltd {Kingswood Queen}, Kingswood (GL)
33264	* CVH 241	Duple	42329	C29F	10/46	Hanson's Buses Ltd, Huddersfield (WR) 213
33287	?	?	?		-/--	Ministry of Supply (GOV)
33337	* BTY 656	Duple	43054	C29F	12/46	JH Batty & Sons {Wansbeck Motor Services}, Ashington (ND) 8
33365	DAW 474	Duple	43067	C29F	10/46	JT, FW & GE Whittle {JT Whittle & Sons}, Highley (SH)
33376	3458	Mulliner		B32F	9/46	Sarre Transport Ltd, St Peter Port, Guernsey (CI) 9
33380 - 33391						Exported to Bombay (O-IND)
33400	FT 5828	Plaxton	34	FC30F	2/47	TH Taylor {Taylor Bros}, North Shields (ND)
33417	FFS 247	SMT		B--F	1/47	Scottish Association of Boys Clubs, Edinburgh (XMN)
33441	#KUA 510	Duple	43508	C29F	8/46	George Barker & Sons (Scarborough) Ltd (NR)
33456	?	?	?		-/--	Ministry of Supply (GOV)
33485	* HFM 28	Beadle	C161	B28F	11/47	Crosville MS, Chester (CH) S2
33499	YJ 8939	Plaxton	206	C27F	11/46	R Dickson jnr, Dundee (AS) 7

C1252/38

33512	?	Mulliner		?	-/--	Admiralty (Royal Navy) (GOV)
33565 - 33576						Exported to Melbourne (O-AUS)
33589	KVW 949	Mulliner		B32F	9/46	City Coach Co Ltd, Brentwood (EX) B33
33603	?	?		?	-/--	Ministry of Supply (GOV)
33617	BTY 628	Duple	43077	C29F	10/46	R Armstrong, Westerhope (ND) 42
33634	* EMJ 62	Thurgood	243	C29F	11/46	GE Costin, Dunstable (BD)
33646	FT 5829	Plaxton	33	FC30F	2/47	TH Taylor {Taylor Bros}, North Shields (ND)
33659	CRG 517	SMT		C29F	5/47	James Paterson & Co (Motor Hirers) Ltd, Aberdeen (AD)
33678						Exported to Lisbon (O-P)
33692	?	?		?	-/--	Ministry of Supply (GOV)
33706	* BTY 631	Duple	43080	C29F	1/47	R Armstrong, Westerhope (ND) 45
33723	DAJ 738	Plaxton	193	C29F	1/47	Hardwick's Services Ltd, Snainton (NR)
33737	* GBJ 375	?		C25F	12/46	EJ Hayward {Safety Coaches}, Eye (EK)
33750	GTE 552	Plaxton	115	FC30F	2/47	Rossendale Division Carriage Co, Bacup (LA)
33767						Exported to unknown overseas location
33781	?	?		?	-/--	Ministry of Supply (GOV)
33795	#KUA 181	Duple	43090	C29F	10/46	George Barker & Sons (Scarborough) Ltd (NR)
33812	KVW 950	Mulliner		B32F	10/46	City Coach Co Ltd, Brentwood (EX) B34
33826	BTY 630	Duple	43079	C29F	1/47	R Armstrong, Westerhope (ND) 44
33839	KVW 951	Mulliner		B32F	9/46	City Coach Co Ltd, Brentwood (EX) B35
33856						Exported to unknown overseas location
33870	?	?		?	-/--	Ministry of Supply (GOV)
33884	#KUA 187	Duple	43096	C29F	10/46	George Barker & Sons (Scarborough) Ltd (NR)
33901	KNU 857	Duple	43085	C29F	10/46	ET White & Sons Ltd, Calver (DE)
33915	* BTY 629	Duple	43078	C29F	1/47	R Armstrong, Westerhope (ND) 43
33928	EDA 696	Mulliner		B28F	10/46	Worthington Motor Tours Ltd, Wolverhampton (ST)
33945	?	?		?	-/--	Ministry of Education (GOV)
33958						Exported to Lisbon (O-P)
33970	GOM 82	Duple	43084	C29F	10/46	H Brown, Birmingham (WK)
33990	* KUA 182	Duple	43091	C29F	10/46	George Barker & Sons (Scarborough) Ltd (NR)
34004	FT 5820	Plaxton	32	FC30F	1/47	TH Taylor {Taylor Bros}, North Shields (ND)
34017	* MML 496	Duple	43083	C27F	10/46	AR & Mrs EF Thorne {Thorne Bros}, London SW2 (LN)
34034	K-18874	Touw		B31-	-/47	Picavet, Nieuw Namen (O-NL) 4
34048	?	?		?	-/--	Ministry of Education (GOV)
34062	DAW 471	Duple	43088	C29F	11/46	RH & SJ Foxall {Robert Foxall & Sons}, Bridgnorth (SH)
34079	BJR 268	Plaxton	255	C29F	12/46	W Smith {Safeway Coaches}, Bedlington Station (ND)
34093	EBU 13	Pearson		C26F	7/47	Shearings Tours Ltd, Oldham (LA)
34106	* DTP 308	Reading	4347	C29F	7/47	The Don Motor Coach Co Ltd, Southsea (HA)
34123	L-34209	Hoogeveen		B31-	6/47	GVU, Utrecht (O-NL) 21
34137	?	?		?	-/--	Ministry of Education (GOV)
34151	KUA 183	Duple	43092	C29F	10/46	George Barker & Sons (Scarborough) Ltd (NR)
34168						Exported to Rangoon (O-BUR)
34182	EDA 695	Mulliner		B28F	11/46	Worthington Motor Tours Ltd, Wolverhampton (ST)
34195	K-18927	De Groot		B31-	3/47	AMZ-De Baar & Leendertse, Wemeldinge (O-NL) 48
34300 - 34311, 34372 - 34383						Exported to Melbourne (O-AUS)
34441	?	?		B30-	10/47	Sir Robert McAlpine & Sons Ltd (contractor), London W1
34455	KVW 952	Mulliner		B32F	10/46	City Coach Co Ltd, Brentwood (EX) B36
34469	KUA 186	Duple	43095	C29F	10/46	George Barker & Sons (Scarborough) Ltd (NR)
34479	KVW 953	Mulliner		B32F	10/46	City Coach Co Ltd, Brentwood (EX) B37
34529	KUA 184	Duple	43093	C29F	10/46	George Barker & Sons (Scarborough) Ltd (NR)
34543	GFJ 867	Duple	43087	C29F	11/46	Knight Bros, Exeter (DN)
34549	* FO 4711	Mulliner		B32F	10/46	CT Sargeant {Sargeant's Motors}, Builth Wells (RR)
34562	KUA 189	Duple	43098	C29F	10/46	George Barker & Sons (Scarborough) Ltd (NR)
34575	?	?		?	-/--	OMT, unknown location, East Africa
34602	EX 5500	Duple	43100	C29F	10/46	Reynolds Garage Ltd {Metropolitan Coaches}, Great Yarmouth (NK)
34616	KUA 188	Duple	43097	C29F	10/46	George Barker & Sons (Scarborough) Ltd (NR)
34630	EX 5201	Duple	43101	C29F	10/46	Reynolds Garage Ltd {Metropolitan Coaches}, Great Yarmouth (NK)
34636	BJR 802	ACB		C29F	4/47	EA Raisbeck & Sons, Bedlington (ND)
34649	KUA 190	Duple	43099	C29F	10/46	George Barker & Sons (Scarborough) Ltd (NR)
34662	CDB 322	Plaxton	(271 ?)	C29F	1/47	Houldsworth Motors Ltd, Bramhall (CH)

34674	?	?	?	-/--	Ministry of Supply (GOV)
34680	?	?	?	-/--	Ministry of Supply (GOV)
34686					Exported to Jerusalem (O-IL)
34692	FWU 584	Plaxton	222 FC30F	2/47	GW Castle, Holmfirth (WR) 8
34706	JHY 308	Duple	42015 B32F	10/46	Bristol Corporation Electricity Dept (XGL)
34720					Exported to Jerusalem (O-IL)
34726	CDP 768	Pearson	C26F	4/47	AE Smith {Smith's Coaches}, Reading (BE)
34733	FAC 726	Duple	43102 C29F	11/46	Priory Garage & Coaches Ltd, Leamington Spa (WK)
34740	DAW 472	Duple	43089 C29F	11/46	RH & SJ Foxall {Robert Foxall & Sons}, Bridgnorth (SH)
34753	DTP 149	Duple	43335 C29F	6/47	The Don Motor Coach Co Ltd, Southsea (HA)
34766	?	?	?	-/--	Ministry of Supply (GOV)
34775					Exported to Jerusalem (O-IL)
34781	HKD 875	Pearson	C26F	6/47	Sunniways Coaches (Pearsons of Liverpool) Ltd (LA) 5
34795	EJW 75	Mulliner	B28F	10/46	Worthington Motor Tours Ltd, Wolverhampton (ST)
34809	MMH 618	Duple	43104 C29F	3/47	L Adnams Ltd {Adnams Safety Coaches}, London SW19 (LN) 1042
34815	DAW 349	Mulliner	B32F	8/46	RG, FJ, DA & K Cooper {G Cooper & Sons}, Oakengates (SH)
34826	#HUP 158	?	van	10/47	Original operator unknown
34828	* DBU 689	Plaxton	245 FC30F	3/47	Ralph Renton Ltd, Hollinwood (LA)
34843	MMT 865	Duple	43109 C27F	-/47	Garner's Coaches Ltd, London W5 (LN)
34853	?	?	?	-/--	Ministry of Supply (GOV)
34864	#				Exported to Hong Kong
34870	* BHV 793	Duple	44361 C29F	10/46	Lacey's (East Ham) Ltd, London E6 (LN)
34884	* CFR 878	(KW ?)	C27F	3/47	Lansdowne Motors Ltd, Fleetwood (LA)
34898	2441	Mulliner	B32F	10/46	Guernsey Motors (CI) 14
34904	* FFS 855	Duple	46350 C29F	5/47	W Alexander, Falkirk (SN) W193
34917	LPC 851	Duple	43103 C29F	3/47	L Adnams Ltd {Adnams Safety Coaches}, London SW19 (LN) 1041
34930	MMH 619	Duple	43105 C29F	3/47	L Adnams Ltd {Adnams Safety Coaches}, London SW19 (LN) 1043
34943	?	?	?	-/--	Ministry of Supply (GOV)
34958	MMP 812	Duple	43146 C29F	11/46	Essex County Coaches Ltd, London E15 (LN)
34972	GPT 883	Duple	43106 C29F	10/46	JR & V Cleasby, Langley Moor (DM)
34991	HFJ 153	Duple	43126 C29F	3/47	Greenslades, Exeter (DN)
34997	FT 5892	Duple	43138 C29F	10/46	G Chapman {Priory Motor Coach Co}, North Shields (ND) 41
35029	JWA 809	Duple	43115 C29F	11/46	WH & F Crossland, Sheffield (WR)
35042	* DBK 944	White Heather	C25F	5/47	White Heather Transport Ltd, Southsea (HA) 4
35046 - 35057					Exported to Bombay (O-IND)
35115	2411	Mulliner	B32F	10/46	Guernsey Motors (CI) 12
35125					Exported to Iran
35131	KPK 951	?	B32F	10/46	Lipscombe {Dorking Coaches}, Dorking (SR)
35143	DAW 589	Mulliner	B28F	9/46	Corvedale Motor Services Ltd, Ludlow (SH) 2
35155					Exported to Jerusalem (O-IL)
35161	MMT 861	Duple	43111 C27F	10/46	Fox & Hart Ltd {Hounslow Star Coaches}, Hounslow (MX)
35168	261	Mulliner	B32F	10/46	Guernsey Motors (CI) 15
35179	MMT 866	Duple	43110 C27F	10/46	Garner's Coaches Ltd, London W5 (LN)
35192	FSC 186	SMT	C29F	5/47	M Moore, Jedburgh (RH)
35203	DAW 551	Mulliner	SP64 B29F	11/46	SC & J Vagg {Vagg's Motors}, Knockin Heath (SH)
35215					Exported to Oslo (O-N)
35223	MMT 862	Duple	43112 C27F	10/46	Fox & Hart Ltd {Hounslow Star Coaches}, Hounslow (MX)
35233	* BHV 792	Duple	44360 C29F	10/46	Lacey's (East Ham) Ltd, London E6 (LN)
35245	JM 6548	SMT	C29F	5/47	CA Smith {Silver Badge}, Bowness-on-Windermere (WT)
35257	DVJ 760	Mulliner	B32F	10/46	AW Tipping {Victory}, Lower Wyche (WO)
35267	OML 127	SMT	B28F	10/47	BEA, Ruislip (MX) 1111
35281	FT 5885	Duple	43108 C29F	2/47	G Chapman {Priory Motor Coach Co}, North Shields (ND) 40
35291	* FT 5884	Duple	43107 C29F	-/--	G Chapman {Priory Motor Coach Co}, North Shields (ND) 39
35304	Z-12271	?	B25-	5/47	David Skjelbred, Kodal (O-N)

C1252/40

35310	MMT 863	Duple	43113	C27F	10/46	Fox & Hart Ltd {Hounslow Star Coaches}, Hounslow (MX)
35324	HFJ 152	Duple	43127	C29F	3/47	Greenslades, Exeter (DN)
35338	EDL 448	Duple	43120	C29F	3/47	Moss Motor Tours (Sandown, I.W.) Ltd (IW)
35344	?	?		B30-	11/46	Sir Robert McAlpine & Sons Ltd (contractor), London W1
35357	BHV 741	Duple	43134	C29F	10/46	Grange & Sons {Broadway Coaches}, London E6 (LN)
35370	DVJ 759	Mulliner		B32F	10/46	AW Tipping {Victory}, Lower Wyche (WO)
35383	MMP 811	Duple	43144	C29F	11/46	Essex County Coaches Ltd, London E15 (LN)
35393						Exported to Iran
35399	* JKE 386	Mulliner		B32F	12/46	GR Ayers, Dover (KT)
35413	FHO 494	?		B32F	12/46	DG Grace {Graceline Coaches}, Alresford (HA)
35427	* MMT 864	Duple	43114	C29F	4/47	Fox & Hart Ltd {Hounslow Star Coaches}, Hounslow (MX)
35433	DNT 570	Plaxton	226	FC30F	3/47	Jones Coachways Ltd, Market Drayton (SH) 10
35446	EDL 446	Duple	43118	C29F	1/47	Moss Motor Tours (Sandown, I.W.) Ltd (IW)
35459	DVJ 767	Mulliner		B32F	10/46	WE Morgan {Wye Valley Motors}, Hereford (HR)
35472	JKJ 957	Mulliner		B32F	12/46	HE Thomsett, Deal (KT)
35482						Exported to Iran
35488	FT 5894	Duple	43140	C29F	10/46	G Chapman {Priory Motor Coach Co}, North Shields (ND) 43
35573 - 35584						Exported to Copenhagen (O-DK)
35681 - 35682						Exported to Melbourne (O-AUS)
35683	* ?	Syd Wood		B36F	-/50	Original operator unknown (O-AUS)
35684 - 35692						Exported to Melbourne (O-AUS)
35737		see 35757				
35753	C 200	?		?	10/48	Uppsala Läns Bussbolag, Gamla Uppsala (O-S)
35754 - 35756						Exported to Stockholm (O-S)
35757	* D 171	?		?	10/49	Näshulta Omnibus, Eskilstuna (O-S)
35758 - 35764						Exported to Stockholm (O-S)
35802	* EJW 258	Mulliner		B28F	11/46	Worthington Motor Tours Ltd, Wolverhampton (ST)
35816	HXX 633	Duple	43133	C29F	11/46	Bradshaw's Super Coaches Ltd, London SE18 (LN)
35822	EJW 257	Mulliner		B28F	11/46	Worthington Motor Tours Ltd, Wolverhampton (ST)
35823		see 35802				
35835	DAW 469	Duple	43122	C29F	11/46	RG, FJ, DA & K Cooper {G Cooper & Sons}, Oakengates (SH)
35848	HBP 852	Duple	43116	C29F	11/46	AW Buckingham {Buck's Luxury Coaches}, Worthing (WS)
35861	DAW 470	Duple	43121	C29F	11/46	RG, FJ, DA & K Cooper {G Cooper & Sons}, Oakengates (SH)
35871	?	?		lorry	-/46	R Davies Haulage Ltd, London E14 (GLN)
35882						Exported to Iran
35891	EDL 447	Duple	43119	C29F	1/47	Moss Motor Tours (Sandown, I.W.) Ltd (IW)
35905	?	?		?	9/46	J Bradshaw & Sons Ltd, Sturton-by-Stow (GLI)
35911	* FFY 628	?		C29F	8/47	Howard Coaches Ltd, Southport (LA)
35924	GFD 442	Duple	43123	C27F	11/46	Holden's Garage Ltd, Netherton (WO)
35937	CDB 323	Plaxton	270	C29F	1/47	Houldsworth Motors Ltd, Bramhall (CH)
35950	JCV 645	Strachan		C27F	5/47	LJ Ede {Roselyn Coaches}, Par (CO)
35960						Exported to Iran
35966	HXX 632	Duple	43132	C27F	11/46	Bradshaw's Super Coaches Ltd, London SE18 (LN)
35988	?	?		?	10/46	Fisher Filling Station, Birmingham (GWK)
36003	HFJ 148	Duple	43128	C29F	3/47	Greenslades, Exeter (DN)
36005	* DNT 569	Plaxton	225	C30F	3/47	RG, FJ, DA & K Cooper {G Cooper & Sons}, Oakengates (SH)
36013	DNT 571	Plaxton	227	FC30F	3/47	CH Butter, Childs Ercall (SH)
36026	HRR 192	Plaxton	249	FC30F	3/47	Mrs R Butler (Butler Bros), Kirkby-in-Ashfield (NG)
36039	EF 7955	Plaxton	250	FC30F	3/47	Longhorn & Peterson {L&P Luxury Coaches}, West Hartlepool (DM)
36049						Exported to Iran
36055	HXX 631	Duple	43131	C27F	11/46	Bradshaw's Super Coaches Ltd, London SE18 (LN)
36069	EDL 445	Duple	43117	C29F	12/46	Moss Motor Tours (Sandown, I.W.) Ltd (IW)
36083	BJR 803	ACB		C29F	4/47	EA Raisbeck & Sons, Bedlington (ND)
36089	FT 5896	Duple	43142	C29F	10/46	G Chapman {Priory Motor Coach Co}, North Shields (ND) 45

36102	#DBU 836	Plaxton	652 C29F	6/47	Gregory & Richards Ltd, Oldham (LA)
36115	?	?	van	9/46	E Ritt, London E15 (GLN)
36128	FAC 892	Duple	43124 C29F	11/46	Charles L Hull Ltd, Hockley Heath (WK)
36138					Exported to Iran
36144	CDP 769	Pearson	C29F	4/47	AE Smith {Smith's Coaches}, Reading (BE)
36155	FT 5895	Duple	43141 C29F	11/47	G Chapman {Priory Motor Coach Co}, North Shields (ND) 44
36166	FOT 432	Wadham	C27F	5/47	Creamline Motor Services (Bordon) Ltd (HA)
36178	FAB 930	Mulliner	B30F	11/46	LJ Aston, Kempsey (WO) 7
36187	HAR 557	Duple	43129 C29F	10/46	JR Street, Hertford (HT)
36203	HAR 556	Duple	43130 C29F	11/46	JR Street, Hertford (HT)
36215	* HFJ 149	Duple	43189 C29F	3/47	Greenslades, Exeter (DN)
36232	MMP 170	Duple	43135 C29F	11/46	J Hanslip {Broadway Coaches}, London N8 (LN)
36233					Exported to Lima (O-PE)
36245	GUO 778	Duple	43137 C27F	4/47	AW Burfitt & WRP Lewis {Blue Coaches}, Ilfracombe (DN)
36257	FT 5893	Duple	43139 C29F	1/47	G Chapman {Priory Motor Coach Co}, North Shields (ND) 42
36269	MMP 169	Duple	43136 C29F	11/46	J Hanslip {Broadway Coaches}, London N8 (LN)
36280	#DBU 788	Plaxton	294 C29F	4/47	Joseph Dyson Ltd {Broadway Motors}, Oldham (LA)
36293	?	?	?	-/--	OMT, unknown location, East Africa
36304	?	?	?	-/--	OMT, unknown location, East Africa
36315					Exported to Lima (O-PE)
36320	DAW 766	Mulliner	B30F	11/46	RG, FJ, DA & K Cooper {G Cooper & Sons}, Oakengates (SH)
36333	DBK 623	Duple	44295 C29F	3/47	TS Bruce {Imperial Saloon Coaches}, Portsmouth (HA)
36335	* ?	?	(C29F ?)	-/--	Original operator unknown
36345	DBD 500	Hasker	C29F	10/46	TG Dilks, Desborough (NO)
36358	GUP 364	Thurgood	246 C29F	12/46	GH, S & JB Atkinson (GH Atkinson & Sons) {General Omnibus Services}, Chester-le-Street (DM)
36369	?	?	goods	10/47	Docks Haulage Ltd, Southampton (GHA)
36382	JKK 952	Plaxton	247 FC30F	4/47	GR Ayers, Dover (KT)
36400	GUP 365	Thurgood	245 C29F	12/46	GH, S & JB Atkinson (GH Atkinson & Sons) {General Omnibus Services}, Chester-le-Street (DM)
36407					Exported to Antwerp (O-B)
36415	?	?	lorry	9/47	R Davies Haulage Ltd, London E14 (GLN)
36424	HBP 872	Duple	43148 C29F	11/46	EJ Carter {Reliance Coaches}, Plummers Plain (WS)
36435	MMP 813	Duple	43145 C29F	11/46	Essex County Coaches Ltd, London E15 (LN)
36447	FO 4712	Mulliner	B32F	10/46	CT Sargeant {Sargeant's Motors}, Builth Wells (RR)
36458	CFR 879	(KW ?)	C27F	4/47	Lansdowne Motors Ltd, Fleetwood (LA)
36471	* HMN 347	Plaxton	23 C29F	3/47	EC Hamill, Onchan (IM)
36482	DNT 59	Mulliner	B32F	12/46	SC & J Vagg {Vagg's Motors}, Knockin Heath (SH)
36494					Exported to Antwerp (O-B)
36500	EJW 259	Mulliner	B28F	1/47	Worthington Motor Tours Ltd, Wolverhampton (ST)
36585 - 36596, 36693 - 36703					Exported to Melbourne (O-AUS)
36704	sa23.704	CAC	? B33F	-/--	Original operator unknown (O-AUS)
36812	CHS 896	Mulliner	B28F	2/47	Daniel Ferguson Ltd {Victor}, Renfrew (RW) 15
36824	HYK 991	Duple	43167 C29F	3/47	Fallowfield & Britten Ltd, London E8 (LN)
36836	EJW 260	Mulliner	B28F	1/47	Worthington Motor Tours Ltd, Wolverhampton (ST)
36847	LPB 723	Duple	43152 C29F	5/47	RG Harwood, Weybridge (SR) 5
36860, 36871, 36883					Exported to Lisbon (O-P)
36893	* GTJ 947	Plaxton	200 FC30F	1/47	Mercers (Longridge) Ltd (LA)
36901	MMP 814	Duple	43147 C29F	11/46	Essex County Coaches Ltd, London E15 (LN)
36913	DVJ 859	Mulliner	B32F	10/46	IL Arnould, Fleur-de-Lys (MH)
36924	SY 8240	SMT	C29F	5/47	William Allan & Sons, Gorebridge (MN)
36936	BES 876	Cadogan	B32F	7/47	A & W McKercher {Aberfeldy Motor Coaches}, Aberfeldy (PH)
36949	#				Exported to Hong Kong
36960					Exported to Lisbon (O-P)
36972	3341	Brincat	B31F	1/49	Route Bus Service (O-M)
36978	?	?	van	10/47	CA Wells Ltd, London E2 (GLN)
36995	LPB 722	Duple	43153 C29F	5/47	RG Harwood, Weybridge (SR) 6
37002	JKE 392	Duple	44772 C29F	12/46	RF Harrington {Melody Motor Coaches}, Chatham (KT)
37015	KPK 549	Duple	43157 C29F	11/46	EJ Rapley Ltd, Dorking (SR)

C1252/42

37026	HBP 999	Duple	43155	C27F	11/46	CC Lansdell {King of the Road Coaches}, Worthing (WS)
37038	HBP 873	Duple	43156	C27F	11/46	J Mitchell, Warnham (WS)
37049	* HCD 465	Duple	43151	C29F	11/46	T Camping, Brighton (ES)
37061						Exported to Alexandria (O-ET)
37067						Exported to Malaya
37080	CFN 623	Duple	43149	C29F	11/46	GEA Fox, Ramsgate (KT)
37091	CFN 624	Duple	43150	C29F	11/46	GEA Fox, Ramsgate (KT)
37104	JKE 165	Duple	43154	C27F	11/46	W Johnson {Busy Bee}, Strood (KT)
37115	MMT 879	Duple	43163	C27F	11/46	WJ Ray {Ray Coaches}, Edgware (LN)
37126						Exported to Malaya
37138	SJ 1120	SMT		C29F	6/47	Gordon Bros {Gordon's Motors}, Lamlash (BU)
37150	* KUB 745	Plaxton	201	C29F	12/46	George Barker & Sons (Scarborough) Ltd (NR)
37155						Exported to Alexandria (O-ET)
37168	EGG 792	SMT		B28F	2/47	Northern Roadways Ltd, Glasgow (LK)
37180	GTF 644	Duple	44284	C27F	4/47	J Yates {West Coaster}, Morecambe (LA)
37193	EGG 791	SMT		B28F	2/47	Northern Roadways Ltd, Glasgow (LK)
37204	* DNT 731	Duple	41990	B32F	2/47	JT, FW & GE Whittle {JT Whittle & Sons}, Highley (SH)
37216	?	?	?		-/--	Ministry of Supply (GOV)
37227	#					Exported to Hong Kong
37239						Exported to Palestine
37245	MMP 808	Duple	43158	C29F	11/46	Oliver Taylor (Coaches) Ltd, Caterham (SR)
37258	MMT 880	Duple	43162	C27F	11/46	WJ Ray {Ray Coaches}, Edgware (LN)
37276	MMP 809	Duple	43159	C29F	11/46	Oliver Taylor (Coaches) Ltd, Caterham (SR) 16
37290	* MMP 815	Duple	43160	C29F	4/47	Valliant Direct Coaches Ltd, London W5 (LN)
37298	* RRF 799	Hughes		C29F	6/49	H Byrne (Byrne Bros) {Moorland Safety Coach}, Leek (ST)
37304	?	?	?		-/--	Ministry of Supply (GOV)
37339						Exported to Palestine
37501 - 37512						Exported to Bombay (O-IND)
37681 - 37692						Exported to Melbourne (O-AUS)
37729 - 37740						Exported to Buenos Aires (O-RA)
37816	DAW 746	Duple	43176	C29F	11/46	PM Moss, Wem (SH)
38168	GDD 200	Thurgood	247	C29F	1/47	EC Young {Cotswold Coaches}, Stow-on-the-Wold (GL)
38178	HYK 993	Duple	43169	C29F	3/47	Fallowfield & Britten Ltd, London E8 (LN)
38188	HYK 992	Duple	43168	C29F	3/47	Fallowfield & Britten Ltd, London E8 (LN)
38198	MMT 507	Duple	43165	C29F	11/46	Garner's Coaches Ltd, London W5 (LN)
38208	MMT 508	Duple	43164	C29F	11/46	Garner's Coaches Ltd, London W5 (LN)
38218	MMT 506	Duple	43166	C29F	11/46	Garner's Coaches Ltd, London W5 (LN)
38228	ACF 272	Duple	43173	C29F	11/46	GF Burgoin (Haverhill) Ltd {Grey Pullman Coaches} (WF)
38238						Exported to Tangier (O-MA)
38248	?	?	?		-/--	Ministry of Supply (GOV)
38257	GNG 61	Duple	43175	C29F	4/47	SA Abel (S & G Abel) {Abel's Coaches}, Wells-next-the Sea (NK)
38267	CVD 695	Duple	43171	C27F	4/47	J & W Wilson (Undertakers) Ltd, Hamilton (LK)
38277	EKU 726	Duple	43172	C29F	11/46	Feather Bros Ltd, Bradford (WR)
38287	SB 6826	Duple	43180	C29F	11/46	Dunoon Motor Services Ltd, Dunoon (AL)
38297	MMT 878	Duple	43181	C29F	3/47	Fallowfield & Britten Ltd, London E8 (LN)
38307	GAD 781	Duple	43174	C29F	11/46	Eric Harrison, Broadway (WO)
38317	HXX 972	Duple	43188	C29F	11/46	Rose Transport Co Ltd, London N6 (LN)
38327						Exported to Tangier (O-MA)
38337	?	?	?		-/--	Ministry of Supply (GOV)
38346	SB 6828	Duple	43179	C29F	11/46	Dunoon Motor Services Ltd, Dunoon (AL)
38356	MMP 578	Duple	43185	C29F	11/46	EA Winwood, London E10 (LN)
38366	MMP 579	Duple	43186	C29F	11/46	EA Winwood, London E10 (LN)
38376	HUO 108	Duple	43192	C29F	11/46	W Stevens & Sons {The Harrier}, Modbury (DN) 7
38386	* HFJ 150	Duple	43202	C29F	3/47	Regent Coaches (Teignmouth) Ltd (DN)
38396	EUY 855	Duple	43071	C29F	4/47	G Woodward {Mascot Coaches}, Malvern (WO)
38406	SB 6825	Duple	43178	C29F	11/46	Dunoon Motor Services Ltd, Dunoon (AL)
38416						Exported to Montevideo (O-ROU)
38426	?	?	?		-/--	Ministry of Supply (GOV)
38435	MMT 875	Duple	43182	C29F	3/47	Fallowfield & Britten Ltd, London E8 (LN)
38445	HYB 40	Duple	43194	C29F	11/46	BJ Chinn {English Rose Coaches}, Wincanton (SO)

C1252/43

38455						Exported to Montevideo (O-ROU)
38465	HUO 221	Duple	41988	B30F	11/46	St Michael's Convent, Ingsdon (XDN)
38475	SB 6827	Duple	43177	C29F	11/46	Dunoon Motor Services Ltd, Dunoon (AL)
38485	HFJ 151	Duple	43190	C29F	3/47	Regent Coaches (Teignmouth) Ltd (DN)
38495	GAD 559	Duple	44418	C29F	11/46	SK & F Silvey (Silvey's Coaches}, Epney (GL)
38516						Exported to Alexandria (O-ET)
38520	MMT 876	Duple	43183	C29F	12/46	Fallowfield & Britten Ltd, London E8 (LN)
38524	HYB 288	Duple	44359	C29F	12/46	EG Bryant, Monksilver (SO)
38531						Exported to Alexandria (O-ET)
38544	CVD 148	Duple	43170	C29F	12/46	William Stokes & Sons, Carstairs (LK)
38554	* FWW 742	Duple	44951	C29F	12/46	Walton & Helliwell Ltd, Mytholmroyd (WR)
38564	SK 3033	Duple	43639	C27F	1/47	ES Dunnet {Dunnet's Motors}, Keiss (CS)
38574	MMT 877	Duple	43184	C29F	3/47	Fallowfield & Britten Ltd, London E8 (LN)
38584	* LHK 325	Duple	43191	C29F	6/47	Ongar Motors & Transport Co Ltd, Ongar (EX)
38594						Exported to Lima (O-PE)
38604	MMP 585	Duple	43187	C29F	2/47	Universal Coaches Ltd, London N9 (LN)
38613	HB 6362	Duple	44732	C29F	4/47	DJ Davies {Wheatsheaf Motors}, Merthyr Tydfil (GG)
38623						Exported to Lima (O-PE)
38633	DAJ 590	Duple	43200	C29F	1/47	Crowe Bros, Osmotherley (NR)
38643	HUO 222	Duple	43193	C29F	12/46	CA Gayton {Gayton's Coaches}, Ashburton (DN)
38653	JAF 415	Duple	43195	C29F	12/46	Pearce's Motors Ltd, Polperro (CO)
38663	JAF 235	Duple	43196	C29F	12/46	WT Blewett {Crimson Tours}, St Ives (CO)
38673	HB 6361	Duple	44733	C29F	4/47	DJ Davies {Wheatsheaf Motors}, Merthyr Tydfil (GG)
38683						Exported to Iran
38693	JAF 236	Duple	43197	C29F	12/46	WT Blewett {Crimson Tours}, St Ives (CO)
38702	GAD 560	Duple	46398	C29F	11/46	SK & F Silvey (Silvey's Coaches}, Epney (GL)
38712						Exported to Iran
38722	HXY 214	Duple	43210	C29F	12/46	A Jones {Popular Coaches}, London E14 (LN)
38732	HXY 215	Duple	43211	C29F	12/46	A Jones {Popular Coaches}, London E14 (LN)
38742	JP 5946	Duple	44101	C29F	2/47	H Tootle, Skelmersdale (LA)
38752	* HYB 284	Duple	43198	C29F	12/46	Quantock Hauliers Ltd, Watchet (SO)
38764	HYB 285	Duple	43199	C29F	12/46	Quantock Hauliers Ltd, Watchet (SO)
38772						Exported to Tangier (O-MA)
38782	EP 9387	Duple	43204	C27F	12/46	Mid-Wales Motorways Ltd, Newtown (MO) 37
38791	KVT 119	Duple	42003	B32F	1/47	Sutton Motors (Stoke-on-Trent) Ltd, Kidsgrove (ST)
38861 - 38872, 38957 - 38968						Exported to Melbourne (O-AUS)
39089 - 39100						Exported to Bombay (O-IND)
39101						Exported to Tangier (O-MA)
39111	KVT 120	Duple	42004	B32F	1/47	Sutton Motors (Stoke-on-Trent) Ltd, Kidsgrove (ST)
39121	GON 500	Duple	43203	C27F	1/47	Sandwell Motor Co Ltd, Birmingham (WK)
39131	GKF 464	Duple	43212	C27F	12/46	M McAdam, Liverpool (LA)
39141	FNP 336	Duple	47408	B32F	1/47	Mrs ME Ward {Ward's Super de Luxe}, Sidemoor (WO)
39151	KVT 63	Duple	42002	B32F	1/47	Sutton Motors (Stoke-on-Trent) Ltd, Kidsgrove (ST)
39161						Exported to Alexandria (O-ET)
39171	EBC 883	Duple	43254	C29F	12/46	Provincial Garage (Leicester) Ltd (LE) B1
39180	FO 4777	Duple	47407	B32F	12/46	TA Owen, Knighton (RR)
39190						Exported to Alexandria (O-ET)
39200	KVT 121	Duple	42005	B32F	1/47	Sutton Motors (Stoke-on-Trent) Ltd, Kidsgrove (ST)
39210	JKJ 555	Duple	43214	C29F	1/47	Craker Southland Coaches Ltd, Bromley (KT) 8
39220	GKF 465	Duple	43213	C27F	12/46	M McAdam, Liverpool (LA)
39230	EP 9388	Duple	43205	C27F	12/46	Mid-Wales Motorways Ltd, Newtown (MO) 38
39240	* FWY 494	Duple	43215	C27F	3/47	WR & P Bingley, Kinsley (WR)
39250						Exported to Alexandria (O-ET)
39260	* FWY 495	Duple	43216	C27F	3/47	WR & P Bingley, Kinsley (WR)
39269	* HYC 60	Duple	?	B26F	3/47	Mrs P Baulch {Chard & District Motor Services}, Chard (SO)
39279						Exported to Alexandria (O-ET)
39289	FWW 743	Duple	44952	C29F	12/46	Walton & Helliwell Ltd, Mytholmroyd (WR)
39299	EJW 714	Duple	46731	C29F	3/47	Worthington Motor Tours Ltd, Wolverhampton (ST) 114
39309	GRU 158	Harrington	20	C29F	4/47	CJ Pounds {Charlie's Cars}, Bournemouth (HA) 55
39319	EJW 715	Duple	46732	C29F	3/47	Worthington Motor Tours Ltd, Wolverhampton (ST) 115
39329	GRU 159	Harrington	?	C29F	4/47	CJ Pounds {Charlie's Cars}, Bournemouth (HA) 56
39339						Exported to Antwerp (O-B)
39349	* BES 700	SMT		C29F	6/47	D McIntoch & Sons, Errol (PH)

C1252/44

39358	ECJ 65	Duple	42376	C29F	1/47 CD Bounds {Golden Wings Coaches}, Hereford (HR)
39368	P-39748	Jongerius		B33-	3/47 NAO, Roermond (O-NL) 36
39378	DNT 90	Mulliner		B28F	12/46 WR & T Hoggins (WR Hoggins & Sons) {Pilot}, Wrockwardine Wood (SH)
39388	HCD 607	Duple	44292	C29F	12/46 RG Johnston {Unique Coaches}, Brighton (ES)
39398	ECJ 116	Mulliner		B28F	12/46 BG & CJ Howse (Howse & Son), Aldsworth (GL)
39408	FO 4785	Mulliner		B32F	12/46 CT Sargeant {Sargeant's Motors}, Builth Wells (RR)
39418	GUP 30	Duple	44665	C29F	12/46 G Westwell, Felling-on-Tyne (DM) 3
39428	?	?		?	-/-- Anglo-Egyptian Oilfields, Suez (O-ET)
39438	* DAW 552	Mulliner		B29F	11/46 SC & J Vagg {Vagg's Motors}, Knockin Heath (SH)
39447	HUU 721	Duple	44378	C29F	11/46 T Tilling, London (LN) 2281
39457	?	?		?	-/-- Anglo-Egyptian Oilfields, Suez (O-ET)
39467	* HUU 722	Duple	44379	C29F	12/46 T Tilling, London (LN) 2282
39477	DNT 26	Duple	43229	C29F	12/46 JT, FW & GE Whittle {JT Whittle & Sons}, Highley (SH)
39487	EBC 909	Duple	43255	C29F	1/47 Provincial Garage (Leicester) Ltd (LE) B2
39497	* GTJ 245	Plaxton	212	C29F	1/47 W Robinson & Sons, Great Harwood (LA)
39507	DNT 49	Mulliner		B32F	11/46 RG, FJ, DA & K Cooper {G Cooper & Sons}, Oakengates (SH)
39517	?	Duple	46129	B32F	-/-- Shell Petroleum Co, Lagunillas (O-YV)
39527	DAW 922	Mulliner		B30F	11/46 RG, FJ, DA & K Cooper {G Cooper & Sons}, Oakengates (SH)
39538	* FHO 456	?		B32F	12/46 CET Gregory Ltd, Hook (HA)
39551					Exported to Santiago (O-RCH)
39564	DUT 345	Thurgood	280	C29F	2/47 W Housden, Loughborough (LE) 2
39572	GBJ 205	Duple	43465	C29F	12/46 BR Shreeve Ltd {Belle Coaches}, Lowestoft (EK)
39583	ACF 672	Thurgood	248	C29F	1/47 GF Burgoin (Haverhill) Ltd {Grey Pullman Coaches} (WF)
39596	GTJ 246	Plaxton	269	C29F	2/47 W Robinson & Sons, Great Harwood (LA)
39609	?	?		?	-/-- OMT, unknown location, East Africa
39623	AWG 991	SMT		C29F	6/47 W Alexander, Falkirk (SN) W200
39636					Exported to Alexandria (O-ET)
39649	DNT 241	Mulliner		B32F	12/46 RG, FJ, DA & K Cooper {G Cooper & Sons}, Oakengates (SH)
39657	DNT 27	Duple	43223	C29F	12/46 JP Arthur & Sons Ltd, Oswestry (SH)
39668	AWG 989	SMT		C29F	6/47 W Alexander, Falkirk (SN) W195
39681	AWG 990	SMT		C29F	6/47 W Alexander, Falkirk (SN) W196
39694	?	?		?	-/-- OMT, unknown location, East Africa
39708	* MMP 584	Duple	43821	C29F	12/46 Unique Hire Service Ltd, London E10 (LN)
39721					Exported to Santiago (O-RCH)
39734	JKM 83	?		B28F	-/47 CH & RB Barrow {Margate & District}, Margate (KT)
39742	MMT 524	Duple	44165	C29F	2/47 Venture Transport (Hendon) Ltd, London NW2 (LN)
39753	HPO 501	Duple	43604	C27F	12/46 CF Gates {Silver Queen Coaches}, Worthing (WS)
39766	* JKJ 971	?		B26F	12/46 RH Sims {Marion Coaches}, Margate (KT)
39779	?	?		?	-/-- OMT, unknown location, East Africa
39793	KHT 566	Duple	43264	C29F	4/47 CW Jordan {Maple Leaf}, Bristol (GL)
39806					Exported to Alexandria (O-ET)
39819	HYE 552	Duple	44667	C29F	5/47 Cream Coaches Ltd, London E8 (LN) 12
39827	DUT 448	Duple	43472	C29F	2/47 WG Deacon & FC Hardy {Lilac Coaches}, Barlestone (LE)
39838	CVH 988	Plaxton	281	C29F	1/47 Hanson's Buses Ltd, Huddersfield (WR) 218
39850	* FOR 732	?		B28F	3/47 WG Davies {Fleet Coaches}, Fleet (HA)
39862	?	Duple	47463	B32F	-/-- Original operator unknown (O-TT)
39876	HHN 980	Duple	43082	C29F	12/46 GE Brown & Son {GNE Motor Services}, Darlington (DM)
39889					Exported to Alexandria (O-ET)
39925 - 39936, 39985 - 39996					Exported to Melbourne (O-AUS)
40069 - 40080					Exported to Buenos Aires (O-RA)
40153 - 40164					Exported to Melbourne (O-AUS)
40202	* CVH 986	Plaxton	282	C29F	1/47 Hanson's Buses Ltd, Huddersfield (WR) 216
40212	SJ 1081	SMT		C29F	5/47 D Stewart {Stewart's Motors}, Corriecravie, Arran (BU)
40223	KRA 504	Duple	43809	C29F	12/46 HS North, Derby (DE) 36
40236	CVH 987	Plaxton	283	C29F	1/47 Hanson's Buses Ltd, Huddersfield (WR) 217
40249					Exported to Lagos (O-WAN)
40263	* EMJ 334	Duple	44382	C29F	1/47 GE Costin, Dunstable (BD)

C1252/45

40276					Exported to Alexandria (O-ET)
40289	HUO 376	Duple	43368	C29F	12/46 A Turner, Chulmleigh (DN)
40297	* HUU 723	Duple	44380	C29F	1/47 T Tilling, London (LN) 2283
40308	LPC 62	Duple	43350	C29F	2/47 HR Richmond {Epsom Coaches}, Epsom (SR)
40321	GON 800	Duple	43379	C29F	3/47 Dalton's Garage Ltd, Birmingham (WK)
40334					Exported to Lagos (O-WAN)
40349					Exported to Montevideo (O-ROU)
40361	EX 5621	Duple	43685	C29F	1/47 EA Sayers {Violet Coaches}, Great Yarmouth (NK)
40371	EDL 475	Duple	43626	C29F	1/47 Seaview Services Ltd, Seaview (IW) 9
40380	BCK 190	Duple	46589	C29F	1/47 Woodcock's British Tours Ltd, Heskin (LA)
40391	ECY 458	Duple	46491	C29F	1/47 Swan Motor Co Ltd, Swansea (GG)
40401	HXW 113	Duple	44863	C29F	2/47 Cliff's Saloon Coaches Ltd, London SE9 (LN)
40410	HPO 431	Duple	43745	C29F	12/46 FH Kilner (Transport) Ltd, Loxwood (WS) 108
40421	CRD 36	Duple	44490	C29F	1/47 AE Smith {Smith's Coaches}, Reading (BE)
40431					Exported to Tanganyika
40439					Exported to Montevideo (O-ROU)
40451	* JAU 10	Duple	43526	C29F	12/46 A Skill {Skill's Coaches}, Nottingham (NG) 3
40461	KUB 11	Duple	46536	C27F	1/47 Roy Neill Ltd, Leeds (WR)
40470	DBU 530	Duple	43838	C27F	12/46 Shearings Tours Ltd, Oldham (LA)
40481	* KVK 89	Duple	44478	C29F	1/47 E Marshall & Co Ltd {Crown Coaches}, Birtley (ND) 67
40491	* HYE 553	Duple	44668	C29F	5/47 Cream Coaches Ltd, London E8 (LN) 14
40500	* DFW 90	Duple	42067	B32F	5/47 Enterprise (Scunthorpe) Passenger Services Ltd {Enterprise} (LI) 136
40511	GNY 509	Duple	46530	C29F	3/47 AE & FR Brewer {Brewer's Motor Services}, Caerau (GG)
40521					Exported to Tanganyika
40529					Exported to Santiago (O-RCH)
40541	* BCK 189	Duple	46588	C29F	2/47 Woodcock's British Tours Ltd, Heskin (LA)
40551	FDK 570	Duple	44866	C27F	4/47 Yelloway Motor Services Ltd, Rochdale (LA)
40560	MMT 525	Duple	44381	C29F	1/47 Liss & District Omnibus Co Ltd, Liss (HA) 113
40571	DNT 28	Duple	44417	C29F	1/47 Salopia Saloon Coaches Ltd, Whitchurch (SH) 43
40581	EGG 790	Duple	42069	B32F	1/47 Northern Roadways Ltd, Glasgow (LK)
40590	OML 125	Duple	42070	B32F	10/47 BEA, Ruislip (MX) 1109
40601	* KVK 51	Duple	42065	B32F	1/47 E Marshall & Co Ltd {Crown Coaches}, Birtley (ND) 66
40611					Exported to Santiago (O-RCH)
40619					Exported to Tanganyika
40631	* MMY 847	Duple	44678	C29F	5/47 RG Flexman {Flexman's Coaches}, Southall (MX)
40641	EX 5626	Duple	44680	C29F	1/47 Norfolk Motor Services Ltd, Great Yarmouth (NK) 135
40650	ACF 669	Duple	42046	B30F	12/46 W Norfolk & Sons, Nayland (WF)
40661	DNT 147	Duple	43252	C29F	1/47 AL, GH & PJ Jones & EO Bullock (AL Jones & Co) {Victoria Coaches}, Madeley (SH) 5
40671	ECJ 144	Duple	43251	C29F	1/47 AE Bengry {Primrose Motor Services}, Leominster (HR)
40680	CBW 522	Duple	45077	B32F	1/47 HC Kemp, Woodcote (OX)
40691	HYC 918	Duple	46585	C29F	7/47 Burnell's Motors Ltd {Lorna Doone Coaches}, Weston-super-Mare (SO)
40701	?	?	?		-/-- OMT, unknown location, East Africa
40709					Exported to Tangier (O-MA)
40721	MRF 301	Duple	43237	C29F	1/47 GH Austin & Sons Ltd {Happy Days}, Stafford (ST) 54
40731	EGG 789	Duple	42068	B32F	1/47 Northern Roadways Ltd, Glasgow (LK)
40740	EBC 980	Duple	43470	C29F	1/47 WH Smith, Leicester (LE)
40755	DFW 131	Duple	42022	B32F	1/47 L Parker, Bardney (LI)
40761	CRD 37	Duple	44491	C29F	1/47 AE Smith {Smith's Coaches}, Reading (BE)
40770	* HUU 724	Duple	46537	C29F	11/47 T Tilling, London (LN) 2284
40781	* GTJ 247	Plaxton	223	C29F	3/47 W Robinson & Sons, Great Harwood (LA)
40791					Exported to Tangier (O-MA)
40799					Exported to Tanganyika
40811	* JKK 322	?	-26-		1/47 Carey Bros, New Romney (KT)
40821	3090	Mulliner		B33F	2/47 Guernsey Railways (CI) 27
40830	* 3088	Mulliner		B33F	1/47 Guernsey Railways (CI) 25
40841	OML 198	SMT		B28F	10/47 BEA, Ruislip (MX) 1112
40851	* 3087	Mulliner		B33F	1/47 Guernsey Railways (CI) 23
40860	DNT 662	Plaxton	257	FC30F	3/47 RB & R Charles (Charles Bros) {Charles Motor Services}, Cleobury Mortimer (SH)
40871	HNC 867	Duple	44063	C29F	1/47 Sykes' Motor Tours Ltd, Sale (CH)

40881, 40889						Exported to Lisbon (O-P)
40901	DNT 556	Mulliner		B28F	2/47	WT & E Keeler, Wrexham (DH)
40911						Exported to Tanganyika
40920	GNY 338	Duple	47419	B32F	1/47	GB Smith, Cymmer (GG)
40931	DAW 938	Mulliner		B32F	1/47	M Davies, Ysbyty Ifan (CN)
40941	* DNT 523	Mulliner		B28F	2/47	WT Edwards {Edwards Coaches}, Joy's Green (GL)
40950						Exported to Tangier (O-MA)
40951	FO 4842	Plaxton	258	FC30F	4/47	CT Sargeant {Sargeant's Motors}, Builth Wells (RR)
40966	GUP 195	Duple	45063	B32F	12/46	Bond Bros {Imperial Motor Services}, Willington (DM)
40971	HYB 894	Duple	43259	C29F	3/47	Binding & Payne Ltd {Dorothy's Coaches}, Clevedon (SO)
40979	DNT 146	Duple	43247	C29F	1/47	H Carter {Reliance}, Ironbridge (SH)
40991	* EJW 915	Plaxton	256	FC30F	3/47	JB Box, Lower Gornal (ST)
41001						Exported to Tangier (O-MA)
41010						Exported to unknown overseas location
41022	DNT 606	Mulliner		B32F	3/47	WR & T Hoggins (WR Hoggins & Sons) {Pilot}, Wrockwardine Wood (SH)
41031	* KMA 468	Sparshatt		C29F	3/48	Northwich Transport {Haslington Coaches}, Haslington (CH)
41040	BGS 536	McLennan		C29F	c5/48	A & C McLennan, Spittalfield (PH)
41051	?	?		caravan	1/47	CL Argent & Co, Loughton (VEX)
41061	FRK 443	Duple	43938	C29F	3/47	TJ Hutchinson {Woodside Coaches}, South Norwood, London SE25 (LN)
41070	DJB 786	Duple	43562	C29F	1/47	TH Clare {Eagle Coaches}, Faringdon (BE)
41077	* DBK 461	Duple	43334	C29F	2/47	The Don Motor Coach Co Ltd, Southsea (HA)
41081						Exported to Tanganyika
41091						Exported to Rotterdam (O-NL)
41101	MMY 668	Duple	43801	C29F	12/46	FR Harris {Harris's Coaches}, Grays (EX)
41111	* FWW 745	Duple	44948	C29F	1/47	Walton & Helliwell Ltd, Mytholmroyd (WR)
41121	* FWW 744	Duple	44953	C29F	1/47	Walton & Helliwell Ltd, Mytholmroyd (WR)
41130	MEV 321	Black & White		C28F	8/47	Davis Luxury Coaches {Black & White}, London E17 (LN) 27
41142	FVC 651	Duple	43495	C29F	1/47	A Cox & FW Sephton {Godiva Coaches}, Coventry (WK)
41152	GFJ 953	Duple	46525	C29F	1/47	PW Steer {Bow Belle}, Bow (DN)
41161	3089	Mulliner		B33F	1/47	Guernsey Railways (CI) 26
41168	HUU 725	Duple	46538	C29F	11/46	T Tilling, London (LN) 2285
41172	OML 126	Duple	42071	B32F	10/47	BEA, Ruislip (MX) 1110
41182	?	?		?	-/--	OMT, unknown location, East Africa
41190	?	Mulliner		B--F	-/47	Nyasaland Transport Co Ltd, Blantyre (O-EAN)
41285 - 41296						Exported to Bombay (O-IND)
41297 - 41308, 41357 - 41368						Exported to Melbourne (O-AUS)
41502	EX 5627	Duple	44681	C29F	3/47	Norfolk Motor Services Ltd, Great Yarmouth (NK) 136
41512	* YJ 9093	Duple	43427	C29F	3/47	Andrew W Watson & Co {Watson's Tours}, Dundee (AS)
41521	JWB 274	Duple	43995	C29F	2/47	J&J Judkins {Ladybower Coaches}, Bamford (DE)
41532	BCK 328	Duple	46723	C26F	1/47	Scout MS Ltd, Preston (LA) 31
41542	FAX 325	Duple	46735	C29F	1/47	Red & White, Chepstow (MH) 719
41551	ECJ 151	Duple	44510	C29F	1/47	Miss I Baynham, Ross-on-Wye (HR)
41558	CHS 895	Mulliner		B28F	2/47	Daniel Ferguson Ltd {Victor}, Renfrew (RW) 14
41562	* FHO 790	Duple	46419	C29F	1/47	Sunbeam Coaches (Loxwood) Ltd (WS) 117
41572	# ?	Duple	41855	B28D	-/46	Uganda Transport Co Ltd, Kampala (O-EAU)
41580						Exported to Palestine
41592	GAO 522	Duple	43426	C29F	3/47	Lake Hotel Coaches Ltd, Keswick (CU)
41602	DFW 182	Duple	42023	B32F	1/47	AE Brown, Caistor (LI) 5
41611	FFS 589	Duple	43428	C29F	3/47	Reid & Mackay, Edinburgh (MN)
41622	FWO 486	Duple	46724	C29F	1/47	El Peake, Pontnewynydd (MH)
41632	DBU 536	Duple	43839	C29F	1/47	W Johnson & Sons, Shaw (LA)
41641	* DUJ 185	Mulliner		B28F	4/47	AE Freeman, Munslow (SH)
41648	FFS 548	Duple	43422	C29F	1/47	H Moore, Jedburgh (RH)
41652	* GDD 415	Duple	43289	C29F	1/47	AW Gillett {Gillett's Coaches}, Winchcombe (GL)
41662, 41670						Exported to Palestine
41682	?	Mulliner		B--F	-/47	Nyasaland Transport Co Ltd, Blantyre (O-EAN)
41692	* K-19341	Verheul	2425	B31-	4/47	SBM, Aardenburg (O-NL) 19

C1252/47

41693		see 41692				
41701	GDD 670	Mulliner		B28F	2/47	Warner's Motors Ltd, Tewkesbury (GL)
41712	HB 6539	Green (Merthyr)		B29F	5/48	Morlais Services Ltd, Merthyr Tydfil (GG) 47
41722						Exported to Palestine
41731	JUO 691	Duple	46406	C27F	3/47	T & W Parker {Blue Coaches}, Ilfracombe (DN)
41738	FAX 324	Duple	46734	C29F	1/47	Red & White, Chepstow (MH) 718
41742	DNT 533	Mulliner		B30F	4/47	Corvedale Motor Services Ltd, Ludlow (SH) 4
41752						Exported to Antwerp (O-B)
41760	* K-19343	Verheul	2427	B31-	5/47	SBM, Aardenburg (O-NL) 21
41771	?	Mulliner		B--F	-/47	Nyasaland Transport Co Ltd, Blantyre (O-EAN)
41781	FHO 595	Duple	46705	C27F	2/47	RH Tombs & J Drake {Orchid Coaches}, Totton (HA)
41790	LNO 177	Duple	46319	C29F	2/47	Wiffen's Coaches Ltd, Finchingfield (EX)
41801	JKK 426	Duple	43899	C27F	1/47	FB Hawke, Strood (KT)
41811	* JKM 536	?		van	5/47	H Gilbert, Tunbridge Wells (KT)
41821	HYB 646	Duple	46708	C29F	1/47	AG Bowerman, Taunton (SO)
41828	DUN 903	Duple	43599	C29F	1/47	JB Pye Ltd, Rhos-on-Sea (DH)
41832	GSM 722	Mulliner		B32F	2/47	T Rae & Sons {Boreland Bus Service}, Boreland (DF)
41842						Exported to Antwerp (O-B)
41850	* K-19342	Verheul	2426	B31-	5/47	SBM, Aardenburg (O-NL) 20
41862	JC 8317	Mulliner		B28F	1/47	CJ Roberts {Purple Motors}, Bethesda (CN) 6
41872	#HNF 802	Junction		C28F	12/46	B Wolfenden, Manchester (LA)
41881	EAY 848	Abbott		C26F	7/47	L Pole & Sons Ltd, Syston (LE)
41892	?	?		van	12/46	DJ Woodgate, Birmingham (GWK)
41902	JKM 55	Thurgood	281	C29F	3/47	WE Penfold {Penfold & Brodie}, Green Street Green (KT)
41911	FOU 728	Wadham		C29F	8/47	Creamline Motor Services (Bordon) Ltd (HA)
41918	?	?		goods	11/46	Holdsworth & Hanson, Halifax (GWR)
41922	EJW 713	Duple	44514	C29F	2/47	Worthington Motor Tours Ltd, Wolverhampton (ST) 113
41932	?	Mulliner		B--F	-/--	Shell Petroleum Co, unknown overseas location
41940	?	Mulliner		B--F	-/--	Shell Petroleum Co, unknown overseas location
41952	DBD 933	Duple	43484	C29F	4/47	F Coales, Aldwincle (NO)
41962	HXX 828	Duple	46367	C29F	4/47	Cliff's Saloon Coaches Ltd, London SE9 (LN)
41971	DJ 9730	Duple	43646	C29F	3/47	G Murray {Jubilee Coaches}, St Helens (LA)
41982	GRU 63	?		C26-	3/47	Miss L Foott {Rossmore Bus Co}, Sandbanks (DT)
41992	?	Mulliner		B--F	-/--	Shell Petroleum Co, unknown overseas location
42001	GPW 48	Duple	43780	C29F	2/47	H & I Jarvis, Downham Market (NK)
42008	* FWY 311	Plaxton	600	C25F	2/47	G Pyne {White Coach Tours}, Starbeck (WR)
42012	DNT 675	Plaxton	313	FC30F	6/47	Mrs A Martlew, RW & A Ashley {Martlew & Sons}, Donnington Wood (SH)
42022	?	Mulliner		B--F	-/--	Shell Petroleum Co, unknown overseas location
42032	EG 7358	Duple	46762	C29F	1/47	E Shaw, Maxey (SP)
42044	KVK 224	Duple	46703	C29F	7/47	G Galley {Galley's Motors}, Newcastle (ND)
42056	FNP 411	Duple	43614	C29F	2/47	LJ Aston, Kempsey (WO) 8
42067	GOP 992	Duple	44977	C27F	2/47	Smith's Imperial Coaches Ltd, Birmingham (WK) 1
42077	* DAP 807	Duple	43654	C27F	2/47	LB Atkins {Beacon Motor Coach Services}, Crowborough (ES)
42089	FDK 571	Duple	44867	C27F	4/47	Yelloway Motor Services Ltd, Rochdale (LA)
42101	GDD 479	Duple	46586	C29F	1/47	FJR Harvey {Harvey's Coaches}, Chedworth (GL)
42112	GAA 940	Lee		B26F	1/48	BS Williams, Emsworth (HA) 25
42122	FNP 909	Duple	44760	C27F	3/47	Samuel Johnson (Supreme) Ltd, Stourbridge (WO)
42134	CVH 989	Plaxton	284	C29F	4/47	Hanson's Buses Ltd, Huddersfield (WR) 219
42146	HMN 152	Duple	43660	C29F	12/46	WH Shimmin & Co Ltd, Douglas (IM)
42157	MMY 696	Duple	44239	C29F	1/47	JWH, EAG & WHR Hall {Hall Bros} {Ickenham Coaches}, Hillingdon (MX)
42167	HRH 50	Duple	46763	C29F	1/47	DW Burn, H Tyler & EG Russell {Grey de Luxe}, Kingston-upon-Hull (ER)
42179	BBV 148	Duple	44575	C29F	1/47	Ribblesdale Coachways Ltd, Blackburn (LA)
42191	EHR 74	Duple	43557	C29F	1/47	PJ & D Card, Devizes (WI)
42202	JX 9550	Duple	44950	C29F	1/47	O & C Holdsworth Ltd, Halifax (WR)
42212	#?	Duple	41857	B28D	-/46	Uganda Transport Co Ltd, Kampala (O-EAU)
42224	#?	Duple	41856	B28D	-/46	Uganda Transport Co Ltd, Kampala (O-EAU)
42236	* SB 6907	Duple	43433	C29F	3/47	C Fitzpatrick {Azure Blue Line}, Dunoon (AL)
42247	DFW 207	Duple	46363	C29F	1/47	WK Harsley {Excelsior Coaches}, Scotter (LI)
42257	JP 5950	Duple	44102	C29F	1/47	Stringfellow Bros {Silver Queen}, Wigan (LA)

C1252/48

42269	* JX 9549	Duple	44949	C29F	1/47	O & C Holdsworth Ltd, Halifax (WR)
42281	* HUU 726	Duple	46539	C29F	1/47	T Tilling, London (LN) 2286
42292	DNT 674	Plaxton	310	FC30F	3/47	SC & J Vagg {Vagg's Motors}, Knockin Heath (SH)
42302						Exported to Santiago (O-RCH)
42314	DAV 614	Mulliner		B28F	1/47	JD Smith, Inverurie (AD)
42326	HYF 906	Duple	42095	B32F	2/47	Camden Coaches Ltd, Edgware (MX)
42337	DNT 672	Plaxton	311	FC30F	4/47	JW, WHF & GW Lloyd, Oswestry (SH) 15
42347	HYB 984	Duple	44687	C29F	2/47	AG Bowerman, Taunton (SO)
42359	BES 790	Cadogan		C29F	6/47	A & C McLennan, Spittalfield (PH)
42370	* ?	?		B--F	-/--	Unknown Government Department (GOV)
42371	SY 8104	Duple	43450	C29F	2/47	William Allan & Sons, Gorebridge (MN)
42382						Exported to Santiago (O-RCH)
42392	?	Mulliner		B--F	-/47	Nyasaland Transport Co Ltd, Blantyre (O-EAN)
42404	?	Mulliner		B--F	-/47	Nyasaland Transport Co Ltd, Blantyre (O-EAN)
42416	CHJ 76	Duple	43868	C29F	1/47	LA Daniel {West Leigh Motor Coaches}, Leigh-on-Sea (EX)
42427	* GMA 904	Mulliner		B28F	1/47	Altrincham Coachways Ltd (CH)
42437	AWG 999	SMT		C29F	7/47	W Alexander, Falkirk (SN) W208
42449	DDM 783	Duple	43605	C29F	1/47	Rhyl United Coachways Ltd, Rhyl (FT) 4B
42461	* BCK 329	Duple	46873	C26F	1/47	Scout MS Ltd, Preston (LA) 32
42472	MMY 680	Duple	43799	C27F	1/47	TG Green {Empress Motor Coaches}, London W6 (LN)
42490	* HND 739	Duple	44067	C29F	3/47	Martin's Coaches Ltd, Salford (LA)
42501 - 42512						Exported to Bombay (O-IND)
42549 - 42560, 42633 - 42644						Exported to Melbourne (O-AUS)
42765 - 42776						Exported to Copenhagen (O-DK)
42804	AWG 997	SMT		C29F	7/47	W Alexander, Falkirk (SN) W206
42816	DNT 673	Plaxton	312	FC30F	5/47	DJ Hampson {Hampson's Luxury Coaches}, Oswestry (SH)
42822						Exported to Alexandria (O-ET)
42827	GAO 595	Mulliner		B28F	3/47	E Hartness {Hartness Bus & Coach Service}, Penrith (CU)
42839	* FDV 383	Duple	?	C27F	4/47	T & W Parker {Blue Coaches}, Ilfracombe (DN)
42851	SY 8172	Duple	43430	C29F	2/47	W Hunter, Loanhead (MN)
42862						Exported to Alexandria (O-ET)
42872	?	Mulliner		B--F	-/47	Nyasaland Transport Co Ltd, Blantyre (O-EAN)
42884	# ?	Duple	41858	B28D	-/46	Uganda Transport Co Ltd, Kampala (O-EAU)
42896	JWE 41	Duple	43292	C27F	2/47	Hirst & Sweeting Ltd, Sheffield (WR)
42907	JCV 30	Duple	46722	C29F	4/47	WH Hawkey, Newquay (CO)
42917	* FHO 864	Duple	44686	C29F	1/47	D Jones {Doug Jones Coaches}, Winchester (HA)
42929	GAO 861	SMT		C29F	6/47	Lake Hotel Coaches Ltd, Keswick (CU)
42941	FWW 924	Duple	43514	C29F	4/47	JW Moore {Favourite}, Cawood (WR)
42952	FWO 611	Duple	46737	C29F	1/47	Red & White, Chepstow (MH) 811
42961						Exported to Iran
42971	DNT 417	Duple	45013	C29F	1/47	JT, FW & GE Whittle {JT Whittle & Sons}, Highley (SH)
42981	DPY 113	Duple	43590	C29F	2/47	AW Robinson {Ryedale Motor Services}, Pickering (NR)
42987	* HYY 900	?		C25F	4/47	British South American Airways, London SW1 (XLN)
43007	* MRF 632	Duple	46892	C29F	2/47	Wells Motor Services Ltd, Biddulph (ST) 20
43018	* JWB 892	Duple	43297	C29F	2/47	EH Sims, Sheffield (WR)
43028	FWO 612	Duple	46736	C29F	1/47	Red & White, Chepstow (MH) 812
43038						Exported to Iran
43048						Exported to Alexandria (O-ET)
43060	* DBD 907	Duple	43283	C29F	1/47	F Abbott, Great Doddington (NO)
43072	* OML 813	Duple	44005	C29F	1/47	CG Lewis {CG Lewis Safety Coaches}, London SE10 (LN)
43077		see 43007				
43087	KVT 385	?		B28F	1/47	William Tatton & Co Ltd, Leek (ST)
43097	2819	Mulliner		B32F	3/47	Sarre Transport Ltd, St Peter Port, Guernsey (CI) 11
43109	SX 5925	SMT		C29F	6/47	Browning's Luxury Coaches Ltd, Whitburn (WL) 4
43121	# SME 96	SMT		C25F	6/47	BEA, Ruislip (MX) 1107
43132						Exported to Alexandria (O-ET)
43142						Exported to Tel Aviv (O-IL)
43154	CRG 736	SMT		C29F	8/47	James Paterson & Co (Motor Hirers) Ltd, Aberdeen (AD)
43166	2818	Mulliner		B32F	3/47	Sarre Transport Ltd, St Peter Port, Guernsey (CI) 12

C1252/49

43177	LPB 4	Duple	43348	C29F	2/47	GF & BS Graves {GF Graves & Son}, Redhill (SR)
43187	* HTB 80	Duple	44858	C27F	4/47	Kia-Ora Motor Services Ltd, Morecambe (LA)
43194		see 43494				
43199	#SME 97	SMT		C25F	6/47	BEA, Ruislip (MX) 1108
43211	YJ 9291	SMT		C29F	5/47	T Cosgrove, Dundee (AS) 2
43222						Exported to unknown location in Near East
43232						Exported to Antwerp (O-B)
43244	SJ 1125	SMT		C29F	7/47	F Kerr Newton {Newton's Motors}, Brodick, Arran (BU)
43256	KVT 540	Mulliner		B30F	-/47	William Tatton & Co Ltd, Leek (ST)
43267	CRG 682	SMT		C29F	6/47	JW Duguid {Swallow Tours}, Aberdeen (AD)
43277	* HUO 688	Duple	46540	C27F	1/47	Western National, Exeter (DN) 535
43289	EJW 804	Duple	46872	C29F	3/47	Don Everall Ltd, Wolverhampton (ST)
43301	#DNT 419	Duple	41996	B32F	1/47	WR & T Hoggins (WR Hoggins & Sons) {Pilot}, Wrockwardine Wood (SH)
43312	* P-39749	Jongerius		B33-	7/47	NAO, Roermond (O-NL) 37
43322	FSP 300	SMT		C29F	7/47	R Cameron, Cowdenbeath (FE)
43334	KVK 678	Duple	46704	C29F	8/47	G Galley (Galley's Motors), Newcastle (ND)
43346	GNY 718	Duple	44356	C29F	3/47	JL Roberts, Maerdy (GG)
43357	JHN 116	Duple	46894	C29F	2/47	GE Brown & Son {GNE Motor Services}, Darlington (DM) 12
43367	2851	Mulliner		B32F	3/47	Sarre Transport Ltd, St Peter Port, Guernsey (CI) 13
43379	FSC 723	Mulliner		B28F	5/47	St Cuthbert's Co-operative Association Ltd, Edinburgh (MN) 1
43391	EMJ 999	Duple	46587	C29F	2/47	OA Bartle & Co, Potton (BD) B/47/1
43402	HNN 810	Duple	43527	C29F	2/47	JG Lewis, Cropwell Butler (NG)
43412	2877	Mulliner		B32F	4/47	Sarre Transport Ltd, St Peter Port, Guernsey (CI) 10
43426	FER 241	Duple	42016	B32F	2/47	Premier Travel Ltd, Cambridge (CM) 23
43436	HDE 657	Mulliner	T6	B28F	4/47	DH Roberts & Sons {Pioneer Motor Services}, Newport (PE)
43447	#SME 271	SMT		C25F	8/47	BEA, Ruislip (MX) 1118
43457	ECJ 282	Duple	42012	B32F	2/47	WE Morgan {Wye Valley Motors}, Hereford (HR)
43469	* HDE 542	Duple	46990	C29F	3/47	GF Rees, Neyland (PE)
43477	CCL 687	Duple	43690	C29F	3/47	RG Brown {Broadland Luxury Coaches}, Norwich (NK)
43487	GUP 978	?		goods	4/47	Durham County Constabulary (GDM)
43494	* DMO 248	Duple	44366	C29F	4/47	Windsorian Motor Coach Services Ltd, Windsor (BE) 48
43502	BCK 330	Duple	46874	C26F	2/47	Scout MS Ltd, Preston (LA) 33
43513	KHT 345	Duple	44035	C26F	4/47	AH Fielding {Empress Coaches}, Bristol (GL)
43527	* DMO 349	Duple	45078	B32F	2/47	AV Cole {Blue Bus Service}, Windsor (BE)
43536	JM 6731	SMT		C29F	7/47	T Robinson, Appleby (WT)
43550	FSF 507	SMT		C29F	6/47	St Cuthbert's Co-operative Association Ltd, Edinburgh (MN) 2
43558	NS 2050	SMT		C27F	7/47	Sutherland Transport & Trading Co Ltd, Lairg (SU)
43568	OML 825	Duple	44547	C29F	2/47	Lewis Cronshaw Ltd, London NW4 (LN)
43579	EDL 618	Duple	43633	C29F	6/47	Shotters Ltd, Brighstone (IW)
43590	* OML 915	Duple	43798	C29F	9/47	F Jacobs {Criterion Coaches}, London E12 (LN)
43613 - 43624						Exported to Melbourne (O-AUS)
43781 - 43792						Exported to Bombay (O-IND)
43906	OML 912	Duple	46528	C27F	1/47	E Evans {Evan Evan Tours}, London WC1 (LN)
43918	MNU 929	Reeve & Kenning		C29F	7/48	JT Branson, Brampton (DE)
43932	?	?		van	1/47	R Davies Haulage Ltd, London E14 (GLN)
43945	GTJ 612	Duple	44934	C29F	3/47	Broughton & Walker Ltd, Great Harwood (LA)
43955	#HNF 805	Junction		C28F	7/47	B Wolfenden, Manchester (LA)
43970	YJ 9064	Duple	46366	C29F	3/47	Andrew W Watson & Co {Watson's Tours}, Dundee (AS)
43981	JUO 324	Duple	46524	C29F	3/47	Sidmouth Motor Co & Dagworthy, Sidmouth (DN)
43993	FWX 161	Duple	46906	C29F	3/47	JB Maddison {Drake's Tours}, Scholes (WR)
44006	FWX 723	Duple	43293	C29F	3/47	JW Kitchin & Sons Ltd, Pudsey (WR)
44017	DBX 152	Duple	46216	C29F	3/47	DS & WJ Davies {Davies Bros}, Pencader (CR)
44026	BCK 331	Duple	46875	C26F	4/47	Scout MS Ltd, Preston (LA) 34
44036	JKK 668	Duple	43492	C29F	2/47	GR Ayers, Dover (KT)
44045	BTK 624	Duple	43485	C29F	3/47	FC Hoare {Bluebird Coaches}, Chickrell (DT)
44062	JM 6497	Duple	43655	C29F	2/47	E Nelson & Son, Arnside (WT)
44072	HB 6538	Green (Merthyr)		B29F	4/48	Morlais Services Ltd, Merthyr Tydfil (GG) 46
44084	--E 599	Plaxton	201	van	11/47	Bateman, Birmingham (GWK)

C1252/50

44096	* HUO 689	Duple	46541	C27F	3/47	Western National, Exeter (DN) 536
44107	* GTJ 613	Duple	44935	C29F	3/47	Broughton & Walker Ltd, Great Harwood (LA) 3
44117	DNT 420	Duple	42013	B32F	3/47	Mrs MH & CJ Elcock, Ironbridge (SH)
44129	* EBD 856	Hasker		C26F	6/48	Stockwood Motors Ltd, Corby (NO)
44141	SX 5901	Duple	43444	C27F	3/47	Browning's Luxury Coaches Ltd, Whitburn (WL) 3
44152	HMN 569	?		van	5/47	Clucas Laundry (1948) Ltd, Tromode (GIM)
44170	EHR 801	Duple	43558	C29F	3/47	CCV Crook {Blue & Ivory Coaches}, Swindon (WI)
44175	MVW 62	?		goods	12/47	Essex County Council (GEX)
44181	* EBX 77	?		C29F	5/48	TS Jenkins, Llanelly (CR)
44194	EFU 70	Plaxton	205	C29F	9/47	C, JE, T & T Hudson {Hudson's Bus Co}, Horncastle (LI)
44202	HYF 531	Duple	44816	C29F	3/47	United Service Transport Co Ltd, London SW9 (LN) 1064
44212	FWX 846	Duple	43294	C29F	3/47	JW Kitchin & Sons Ltd, Pudsey (WR)
44222	?	?		van	1/47	L Benson, Kingston-upon-Hull (GER)
44242	LPD 906	Strachan		C26F	5/47	Mears Motors Ltd, Richmond (SR)
44252	EWF 402	Plaxton	287	C29F	4/47	E Milburn {Leavening Motor Services}, Leavening (ER)
44257	?	Mulliner		B--F	-/47	Nyasaland Transport Co Ltd, Blantyre (O-EAN)
44262	BJR 450	Duple	45029	B32F	3/47	CR Robson, Smelting Syke (ND) 16
44276	DCX 256	Plaxton	285	C29F	4/47	Hanson's Buses Ltd, Huddersfield (WR) 221
44286	GOV 398	Duple	43298	C29F	2/47	JH & IV McLaughlin {Stockland Garage}, Birmingham (WK)
44297	JPP 455	Thurgood	286	C29F	3/47	Mrs HV Wall, Kingsey (BK)
44306	?	Mulliner		B--F	-/47	Nyasaland Transport Co Ltd, Blantyre (O-EAN)
44309	* OML 742	Duple	44281	C29F	2/47	CJ Greenough {Dartford Coaches}, Dartford (KT)
44347	* EBE 307	Scunthorpe Motors		C28F	5/47	G & C Johnson (Claxby) Ltd (LI)
44357	HYF 530	Duple	44815	C29F	3/47	United Service Transport Co Ltd, London SW9 (LN) 1063
44362	?	?		van	5/47	Clucas Laundry (1948) Ltd, Tromode (GIM)
44369	JWE 211	Thurgood	285	C29F	4/47	Mrs G Hibberd, Sheffield (WR)
44380	?	?		h/box	2/47	Taylor of Rottingdean Ltd (GES)
44387	DNT 422	Duple	43240	C29F	3/47	Corvedale Motor Services Ltd, Ludlow (SH) 12
44395	* HUO 690	Duple	46543	C27F	2/47	Western National, Exeter (DN) 537
44404	?	?		van	1/47	R Davies Haulage Ltd, London E14 (GLN)
44415	BCK 551	Duple	44541	C26F	3/47	Scout MS Ltd, Preston (LA) 36
44421	* HYF 378	Duple	44432	C29F	2/47	George Ewer & Co Ltd {Grey Green}, London N16 (LN)
44432						Exported to Lima (O-PE)
44438	* OML 743	Duple	43795	C29F	5/47	Universal Coaches Ltd, London N9 (LN)
44444	* OML 543	Duple	46605	C29F	4/47	FH Kilner (Transport) Ltd, Horsham (WS) 110
44450						Exported to Lima (O-PE)
44456	GOV 399	Duple	43299	C29F	2/47	JH & IV McLaughlin {Stockland Garage}, Birmingham (WK)
44466	OMP 143	Duple	47586	C25F	10/47	BEA, Ruislip (MX) 1114
44476	LBB 234	Plaxton	17	FC30F	5/47	G Galley (Galley's Motors), Newcastle (ND)
44508	?	?		van	6/47	Mitchell, Kingston-upon-Hull (GER)
44514	GDF 4	Duple	43258	C29F	3/47	A & R Crew {Majestic Coaches}, Staple Hill (GL)
44519	LPB 250	Duple	44690	C29F	3/47	ER Gudge {Comfy Coaches}, Farnham (SR)
44526	OML 665	Duple	43792	C29F	3/47	D Evans {Maroon Coaches}, London E18 (LN)
44534	DBX 677	Thomas & Thomas		B32F	6/47	DS & WJ Davies {Davies Bros}, Pencader (CR) 25
44537						Exported to Antwerp (O-B)
44540	* HYE 927	Duple	44861	C29F	5/47	V Bingley (Bingley Bros) {Sceptre Coaches}, London W6 (LN)
44551	* HUO 691	Duple	46542	C27F	2/47	Western National, Exeter (DN) 538
44561	GDG 368	Longwell Green		C27F	7/47	SG Wiltshire {Princess Mary Coaches}, Staple Hill (GL)
44583	HFJ 147	Duple	43360	C29F	3/47	Greenslades, Exeter (DN)
44586	DMO 351	Duple	43967	C29F	3/47	Tom Tappin Ltd {Travel Rambler}, Wallingford (BE)
44639	?	?		van	-/47	Lush & Cook Ltd (dyers), London E9 (GLN)
44645	* EJ 8108	Duple	47602	C29F	5/47	E & J Lloyd-Jones {Lloyd-Jones Bros}, Pontrhydygroes (CG)
44650	DNT 421	Duple	43763	C29F	3/47	E, G, FJC & W Smith {W Smith & Sons}, Donnington Wood (SH)
44656	JX 9673	Plaxton	272	C29F	4/47	O & C Holdsworth Ltd, Halifax (WR)
44663	ECJ 389	Duple	46436	C29F	4/47	WE Morgan {Wye Valley Motors}, Hereford (HR)

C1252/51

44669	LTW 251	Duple	44695	C29F	3/47	LC Hunt & West {Safeway}, London E17 (LN)
44678	BJR 679	Duple	43755	C29F	3/47	R Armstrong, Westerhope (ND) 46
44683	HNK 95	Duple	44689	C29F	2/47	Twentieth Century Travel Ltd, Borehamwood (HT)
44687	BTK 866	Duple	44259	C29F	3/47	SC Sheasby {South Dorset Coaches}, Corfe Castle (DT)
44699	* HXW 496	Duple	44666	C29F	3/47	Charing Cross Motors Ltd, London WC1 (LN)
44703	OML 312	Duple	44692	C29F	3/47	CJ Elms, Phillips & Brown {Elms Coaches}, London N17 (MX)
44710	* PRF 167	Willenhall		FC29F	7/48	Mrs FG Mason, Darlaston (ST)
44714	EDL 708	Duple	43634	C29F	5/47	Shotters Ltd, Brighstone (IW)
44720	GUP 942	SMT		C27F	4/47	W Guest {Billingham Car Co}, Billingham-on-Tees (DM)
44727	?	Mulliner		B--F	-/--	Anglo Iranian Oil Co, Abadan (O-IR)
44739	* HUO 683	Duple	46547	C27F	3/47	Southern National, Exeter (DN) 530
44749	* DBE 812	Beadle	C112	B30F	10/47	Lincolnshire RCC, Bracebridge Heath (KN) 669
44761	* HUO 693	Duple	46545	C27F	3/47	Western National, Exeter (DN) 540
44767	* P-36194	Jongerius		B33-	7/47	Jacobs, Nuth (O-NL) 12
44775	* HUO 692	Duple	46544	C27F	2/47	Western National, Exeter (DN) 539
44784	* HNE 512	?		C29F	6/47	A Mayne & Son Ltd, Manchester (LA)
44798	JKM 270	Duple	43353	C27F	3/47	LW Bowser Ltd, Sundridge (KT)
44805	HRR 422	Duple	43834	C29F	4/47	GW Wright {GW Wright & Sons}, Keyworth (NG)
44821	?	Mulliner		B--F	-/--	Anglo Iranian Oil Co, Baghdad (O-IRQ)
44827						Exported to Kingston (O-JA)
44834	SW 7187	SMT		C29F	7/47	W & A Campbell, Gatehouse of Fleet (KK)
44840	?	?		van	1/47	CA Wells Ltd, London E2 (GLN)
44845	* BBV 351	SMT		C29F	5/47	Ribblesdale Coachways Ltd, Blackburn (LA)
44857	* HUO 684	Duple	46546	C27F	3/47	Southern National, Exeter (DN) 531
44863	* FWX 696	?		C28F	5/47	FW Balme {Balme's Coaches}, Otley (WR)
44871	LPB 748	Whitson	?	C29F	5/47	Green Luxury Coaches (Walton) Ltd, Walton-on-Thames (SR)
44880	SJ 1113	Mulliner	T2	B28F	4/47	EK Ribbeck & Son, Brodick, Arran (BU)
44894	HNK 47	Duple	43574	C27F	2/47	Albanian Coaches Ltd, St Albans (HT) 1
44901 - 44912						Exported to Buenos Aires (O-RA)
44973 - 44984						Exported to Bombay (O-IND)
45093	* v1.805	NZMB		C20F	8/47	New Zealand Railways Road Services (O-NZ) 1504
45094	P.578	Suburban		B33F	-/48	Suburban Buses Ltd, Te Papapa (O-NZ) 37
45095	* P1.398	Pomeroy		B33F	-/48	Buses Ltd, Hamilton (O-NZ) 47
45096	s.92	NZMB		C20F	8/47	New Zealand Railways Road Services (O-NZ) 1503
45097	s.216	NZMB		C20F	8/47	New Zealand Railways Road Services (O-NZ) 1506
45098	* P.619	North Shore		B33F	-/47	North Shore Transport Co Ltd, Takapuna (O-NZ) 19
45099	?	NZMB		C20F	8/47	New Zealand Railways Road Services (O-NZ) 1507
45100	?	NZMB		C20F	8/47	New Zealand Railways Road Services (O-NZ) 1502
45101	s.181	NZMB		C20F	8/47	New Zealand Railways Road Services (O-NZ) 1505
45102	s.324	NZMB		C20F	8/47	New Zealand Railways Road Services (O-NZ) 1508
45103						Exported to Wellington (O-NZ)
45104	* v1.835	NZMB		C20F	9/47	New Zealand Railways Road Services (O-NZ) 1509
45177 - 45188						Exported to Copenhagen (O-DK)
45204	GNY 856	Duple	46813	C29F	3/47	DJ Thomas {Creamline}, Maesteg (GG)
45210	* H-413	?		B20FV	10/47	Original operator unknown (O-N)
45218						Exported to Malaya
45229	FOR 567	Duple	43746	C29F	2/47	Sunbeam Coaches (Loxwood) Ltd (WS) 109
45239	* DBE 808	Beadle	C108	B30F	8/47	Lincolnshire RCC, Bracebridge Heath (KN) 665
45251	FGA 566	SMT		C29F	6/47	Northern Roadways Ltd, Glasgow (LK)
45258	GPW 559	Duple	43488	C29F	7/47	MJ Eagle, Castle Acre (NK)
45266	AWG 992	SMT		C29F	6/47	W Alexander, Falkirk (SN) W201
45275	LBB 235	Plaxton	251	FC30F	5/47	G Galley (Galley's Motors), Newcastle (ND)
45289	LVW 59	Thurgood	288	C29F	4/47	FW & WE Mayhew (Mayhew Bros), Stanstead (EX)
45296	DNT 735	Mulliner	T3	B28F	3/47	Salopia Saloon Coaches Ltd, Whitchurch (SH) 44
45309						Exported to Malaya
45313	JMA 201	Duple	43597	C29F	3/47	AE Bowyer & Son Ltd, Northwich (CH)
45325	* DBE 809	Beadle	C116	B30F	3/48	Lincolnshire RCC, Bracebridge Heath (KN) 666
45335	DCX 157	Plaxton	286	C29F	4/47	Hanson's Buses Ltd, Huddersfield (WR) 222
45347						Exported to Antigua
45353	EN 8923	SMT		C29F	5/47	F Caven, Bury (LA)
45361	DNT 418	Duple	43230	C29F	3/47	JT, FW & GE Whittle {JT Whittle & Sons}, Highley (SH)

C1252/52

45372	YJ 9190	Plaxton	207	C29F	4/47	R Dickson jnr, Dundee (AS) 10
45384	#?	Duple	41860	B28D	-/46	Uganda Transport Co Ltd, Kampala (O-EAU)
45391	HTB 193	SMT		C29F	5/47	GW Haigh, Mossley (LA)
45396	DUT 149	Plaxton	288	C29F	4/47	W Parsons, Stanton-under-Bardon (LE)
45420	DMO 422	Thurgood	287	C29F	4/47	Tom Tappin Ltd {Travel Rambler}, Wallingford (BE)
45430	HMN 153	SMT		C29F	6/47	WH Shimmin & Co Ltd, Douglas (IM)
45442	AEE 158	Duple	46927	C29F	3/47	A & AE Blackbourn Ltd {Granville Tours}, Grimsby (LI) 140
45448	FER 841	Duple	46871	C29F	3/47	TJ Brown & JF Grout {Lee & District Motor Services}, Chesham (BK)
45456	* JX 9674	Plaxton	273	C29F	4/47	O & C Holdsworth Ltd, Halifax (WR)
45465	#?	?		h/box	8/47	HR Richmond {Epsom Coaches}, Epsom (GSR)
45473	H 7443	Duple	46139	C21F	7/47	OTC, Nairobi (O-EAK)
45480	* DBE 810	Beadle	C109	B30F	9/47	Lincolnshire RCC, Bracebridge Heath (KN) 667
45490	* KRB 65	Duple	46984	C29F	7/47	Midland General, Langley Mill (DE) 103
45497	#?	Duple	41863	B28D	-/46	Uganda Transport Co Ltd, Kampala (O-EAU)
45504	DBE 811	Beadle	C110	B30F	10/47	Lincolnshire RCC, Bracebridge Heath (KN) 668
45517	?	Duple	46138	C14F	-/--	OTC, Nairobi (O-EAK)
45525	?	?		showroom	8/48	Bullock, Thornhill & Sons Ltd (dyers), Macclesfield (GCH)
45537	CFV 66	SMT		C29F	6/47	S & J Wood Ltd {Seagull Coaches}, Blackpool (LA)
45541	* OML 603	Duple	43823	C29F	5/47	Essex County Coaches Ltd, London E15 (LN)
45547	NTW 911	?		C25F	9/48	Foreman, Chelmsford (XEX)
45555	?	?		h/box	9/47	T Hawkins & Sons (Epsom) Ltd (GSR)
45571	BCK 535	Duple	46876	C26F	3/47	Scout MS Ltd, Preston (LA) 35
45589	#?	Duple	41862	B28D	-/46	Uganda Transport Co Ltd, Kampala (O-EAU)
45610	* H 7442	Duple	46151	C26F	9/47	OTC, Nairobi (O-EAK)
45598	* DNT 763	Auto-Cellulose		C26F	4/47	CH Butter, Childs Ercall (SH)
45620	JPP 513	Duple	46564	C29F	3/47	F Soul (Soul Bros), Olney (BK)
45626	KUG 757	Plaxton	259	FC30F	5/47	JA Hudson Ltd, Leeds (WR)
45633	?	?		h/box	8/47	T Hawkins & Sons (Epsom) Ltd (GSR)
45638	OMP 248	Duple	47589	C25F	4/47	BEA, Ruislip (MX) 1105
45668	GPW 774	Duple	46359	C29F	4/47	JD Needs & Son {Regent Coaches}, Fakenham (NK)
45675	#?	Duple	41859	B28D	-/46	Uganda Transport Co Ltd, Kampala (O-EAU)
45691	#?	Duple	41864	B28D	-/46	Uganda Transport Co Ltd, Kampala (O-EAU)
45699	HRR 421	Duple	46993	C29F	3/47	Barton Transport, Chilwell (NG) 520
45704	ACF 72	Thurgood	289	C29F	4/47	GM & MG Challice {Challice Bros}, Newmarket (WF)
45714	HYK 192	Mulliner		T4 B32F	7/47	BOAC (LN)
45729	* (GUP 979 ?)	?		goods	4/47	Durham County Constabulary (GDM)
45742	BES 973	Cadogan		C29F	7/47	A & C McLennan, Spittalfield (PH)
45746	* BCK 647	SMT		C29F	6/47	E Barnes {Premier Motors}, Preston (LA)
45755	HYH 556	Duple	44839	C27F	3/47	Keith & Boyle (London) Ltd {Orange Luxury Coaches}, London EC2 (LN) Swift
45766	?	Mulliner		B--F	-/47	Nyasaland Transport Co Ltd, Blantyre (O-EAN)
45768	* FOR 633	Duple	46738	C29F	3/47	Venture, Basingstoke (HA) 77
45778	* FOR 634	Duple	46739	B28F	3/47	Venture, Basingstoke (HA) 78
45784	JHN 250	SMT		C29F	6/47	Percival Bros (Coaches) Ltd, Richmond (NR)
45792	HMN 253	SMT		C29F	6/47	R Scott, Douglas (IM)
45801	#?	Duple	41861	B28D	-/46	Uganda Transport Co Ltd, Kampala (O-EAU)
45815	FT 5974	Plaxton	594	FC30F	6/47	TH Taylor {Taylor Bros}, North Shields (ND)
45822	JAF 833	Strachan		C26F	5/47	Newquay Motor Co Ltd {Red & White Tours} (CO)
45826	* CBW 722	Duple	43561	C29F	4/47	JW Barnard {B & B Services}, Berkhamsted (HT)
45839	?	Mulliner		B--F	-/47	Nyasaland Transport Co Ltd, Blantyre (O-EAN)
45851	#HNF 810	Junction		C29F	2/47	B Wolfenden, Manchester (LA)
45861	DBU 887	SMT		C27F	7/47	Shearings Tours Ltd, Oldham (LA)
45873	DUT 630	Duple	43459	C29F	3/47	EA Hames, Oadby (LE)
45879	ECY 702	Duple	46741	C29F	4/47	United Welsh, Swansea (GG) 916
45887	JAF 835	Strachan		C26F	5/47	Newquay Motor Co Ltd {Red & White Tours} (CO)
45896	GRU 100	Duple	44810	C29F	7/47	Shamrock & Rambler Motor Coaches Ltd, Bournemouth (HA)
45909	GAX 9	Duple	47843	C29F	4/47	J Edwards {WJ Edwards & Son}, Tredegar (MH)
45916						Exported to Malaya
45920	* HUO 685	Duple	46548	C27F	4/47	Southern National, Exeter (DN) 532
45933						Exported to Malaya

C1252/53

45946	OMP 249	Duple	47590	C25F	4/47	BEA, Ruislip (MX) 1106
45960	?	?		van	-/--	Greenberg & Son Ltd, London W1 (GLN)
45966		see 46966				
45968	* DCX 301	Duple	46715	C29F	4/47	Hanson's Buses Ltd, Huddersfield (WR) 215
45981	?	?		h/box	10/47	T Hawkins & Sons (Epsom) Ltd (GSR)
45990	?	?		van	6/47	Hoults Ltd (removers), Newcastle-on-Tyne (GND)
45996	HYH 563	Duple	47756	C27F	3/47	St Thomas's Hospital, London SE1 (XLN)
46004	GOV 959	Duple	44978	C27F	3/47	Smith's Imperial Coaches Ltd, Birmingham (WK) 6
46011						Exported to Malaya
46015	HYH 557	Duple	44855	C27F	3/47	Keith & Boyle (London) Ltd {Orange Luxury Coaches}, London EC2 (LN) Swallow
46029	OMP 141	Duple	47587	C25F	6/48	BEA, Ruislip (MX) 1113
46039						Exported to Malaya
46063	OMP 142	Duple	47588	C25F	6/48	BEA, Ruislip (MX) 1115
46069	* GMJ 499	Thurgood	517	C29F	4/49	Nibloe Bros {N & S}, Kibworth (LE)
46077	HMN 634	Pearson		C26F	6/47	GC Gale {Gale's Western Motors}, Peel (IM)
46089	?	?		van	5/47	J Harrop Ltd, Manchester (GLA)
46100	?	?		van	2/47	Hoults Ltd (removers), Newcastle-on-Tyne (GND)
46107						Exported to Malaya
46111	* EDL 840	?		C25F	7/47	Mrs M Groves (W Groves & Sons), East Cowes (IW)
46124	* FBC 933	Churchill		C29F	8/48	E Wright, Southend (EX)
46136						Exported to Malaya
46146	* ERY 721	Duple	5989/2	C30F	3/47	Mrs GH Clayton (Clayton Bros} {The Royal Blue}, Leicester (LE)
46158	HTB 247	Duple	44944	C29F	3/47	W Robinson & Sons, Great Harwood (LA)
46164	HTB 248	Duple	44945	C29F	3/47	W Robinson & Sons, Great Harwood (LA)
46172	FCR 985	Sparshatt		C27F	c5/48	PFV Summerbee {Sumerbee's Motor Coaches}, Southampton (HA)
46181	* FBC 931	Churchill		C29F	8/48	G & K Barnes Ltd {Dauntsey Vale Coaches}, Dauntsey (WI)
46195						Exported to Malaya
46202	?	?		van	1/48	Bestway Carriers, Norton-on-Tees (GDM)
46206	GWT 533	?		h/box	1/47	A Massarella & Sons Ltd, Doncaster (GWR)
46219	?	?		van	5/47	WR Hodson, Salford (GLA)
46231						Exported to Malaya
46241	GTG 322	Thurgood	334	C29F	5/47	DJ Thomas {Creamline}, Maesteg (GG)
46253	?	?		van	9/47	T Wicks & Son, Wells (GSO)
46259	?	?		van	5/47	Bristol Haulage Co Ltd (GGL)
46267	?	?		van	5/47	J Harrop Ltd, Manchester (GLA)
46276	?	?		lorry	3/47	T Tennett & Sons, Warrington (GLA)
46290	?	?		van	2/47	Express Removals Ltd, Salford (GLA)
46297						Exported to Lagos (O-WAN)
46301	HUF 635	Whitson	?	C27F	9/47	HK Hart {Alpha Coaches}, Brighton (ES)
46314	?	?		van	7/47	W Mitchell, Kingston-upon-Hull (GER)
46326						Exported to Lagos (O-WAN)
46336	* BCK 982	SMT		C29F	7/47	Scout MS Ltd, Preston (LA)
46348	HMN 277	SMT		C29F	6/47	JW Kneen {Cornflower Motors}, Douglas (IM)
46363	* DBU 936	Plaxton	651	C29F	5/47	Joseph Dyson Ltd {Broadway Motors}, Oldham (LA)
46369	* HRT 298	Belle		C29F	6/48	BR Shreeve Ltd {Belle Coaches}, Lowestoft (EK)
46375	* 158	Duple	?	B32F	10/47	Route Bus Service (O-M)
46461 - 46472, 46581 - 46592, 46677 - 46688						Exported to Bombay (O-IND)
46706	?	?		van	2/47	R Melling, Manchester (GLA)
46709	* DBU 870	Plaxton	341	FC30F	4/47	Ralph Renton Ltd, Hollinwood (LA)
46713	* GRU 110	Duple	43943	C29F	4/47	TE Pocknell {Valerie Coaches}, Bournemouth (HA)
46724						Exported to Ireland
46727	HTB 739	Plaxton	274	C29F	5/47	Broughton & Walker Ltd, Great Harwood (LA)
46731	JCV 629	Thurgood	326	C29F	5/47	Mrs E Lidgey {Fal Service}, Tregony (CO)
46759	?	?		van	8/47	T Carey, Scunthorpe (GLI)
46764	EP 9548	Mulliner	T8	B30F	4/47	Mid-Wales Motorways Ltd, Newtown (MO)
46766	ERY 576	Duple	43333	C29F	4/47	J Peet {Tudor Coaches}, Leicester (LE)
46771	NRE 234	Duple	47765	C29F	4/47	Greatrex Motor Coaches Ltd, Stafford (ST) 32 Redshank
46779	* AHL 970	SMT		C29F	7/47	Cooper Bros (Wakefield) Ltd, Wakefield (WR)
46786						Exported to Ireland

C1252/54

46790	?	?		l/stock	7/47	Harvey Bros, Coningsby (GLI)
46801	HYC 769	Duple	47791	C29F	4/47	RJ Doble & EW Shire, Trull (SO)
46821	FDV 233	Duple	46233	C29F	4/47	J Hoare & Sons {The Ivy}, Ivybridge (DN)
46826						Exported to Malaya
46832	KHT 346	Duple	43455	C29F	3/47	Mrs A Ball (H Ball) {Eagle Coaches}, Bristol (GL)
46838	DKG 12	Duple	46814	C29F	4/47	EC Paramore {Reliance Saloon Car Service}, Cardiff (GG)
46849	HYL 143	Mulliner	T9	B32F	4/47	BOAC (LN)
46854	OMP 250	Duple	47591	C25F	6/48	BEA, Ruislip (MX) 1116
46867	JCV 525	Duple	47735	C29F	4/47	WH Hawkey, Newquay (CO)
46874						Exported to Malaya
46878	HYE 297	Duple	44462	C29F	6/47	Bradshaw's Super Coaches Ltd, London SE18 (LN)
46889	* HMN 439	Duple	44703	C29F	4/47	JA & LQ Kneen {A & L Kneen}, Douglas (IM)
46900	?	Mulliner		B--F	-/47	Nyasaland Transport Co Ltd, Blantyre (O-EAN)
46910	LVW 258	Duple	47600	C29F	4/47	Wiffen's Coaches Ltd, Finchingfield (EX)
46931	KVT 628	Duple	47736	C29F	3/47	Mrs A Lymer {Victoria Tours}, Tean (ST)
46938	?	?		l/stock	10/47	T Calvert, Stokesley (GNR)
46941	EDL 761	Duple	43637	C29F	5/47	FW Read {Read's Tours}, Ryde (IW)
46948	EMR 107	Duple	43383	C29F	4/47	J Mapson & Sons, Swindon (WI)
46955	FDV 591	Duple	47790	C29F	5/47	J Parsons & Sons, Holsworthy (DN)
46962						Exported to Malaya
46966	* KRB 66	Duple	46985	C29F	7/47	Midland General, Langley Mill (DE) 105
46977	DFW 765	Duple	47839	C29F	5/47	M Williams {Trent Motors}, Scunthorpe (LI)
46988	BST 854	Mulliner	T7	B28F	5/47	D MacLean & P MacDonald, Ardvasar (IV)
46993						Exported to Malaya
46998	JAF 834	Strachan		C26F	1/48	Newquay Motor Co Ltd {Red & White Tours} (CO)
47008	HOB 251	Duple	43380	C29F	4/47	Dalton's Garage Ltd, Birmingham (WK)
47014	FOT 214	Duple	46795	C29F	5/47	R Chisnell & Sons Ltd {King Alfred Motor Services}, Winchester (HA)
47022	GPW 568	Duple	44305	C29F	5/47	Culling & Son (Norwich) Ltd {Claxton & District}, Claxton (NK)
47031	GFD 859	Duple	46581	C29F	4/47	NC Kendrick, Dudley (WO)
47042	* HFD 609	Willenhall		C29F	1/48	NC Kendrick, Dudley (WO)
47045	HRO 281	Thurgood	290	C29F	4/47	R Hunt, Hertingfordbury (HT)
47048	HRO 1	Thurgood	328	C29F	4/47	SG Sams {SG Sams & Sons}, Hoddesdon (HT)
47054	JKM 282	Duple	43773	C29F	3/47	LR Hampshire {Eythorne & District}, Eythorne (KT)
47058	?	Mulliner		B--F	-/47	Nyasaland Transport Co Ltd, Blantyre (O-EAN)
47064	BFK 857	?		van	6/47	E Batty Ltd, Worcester (GWO)
47067	HYF 971	Duple	46787	C25F	4/47	British South American Airways, London SW1 (XLN)
47088	DDR 744	Duple	43998	C29F	8/47	Plymouth Co-operative Society (DN) 509
47092	LPC 939	Duple	43347	C29F	4/47	Ben Stanley Ltd, Hersham (SR)
47099	* JP 6376	Plaxton	584	C29F	6/47	Frostways Ltd, Kingston-upon-Hull (ER)
47102	?	?		van	8/47	Shrewsbury Transport Co Ltd (GSH)
47107	SW 7172	Mulliner	T5	B28F	3/47	W Kirkpatrick, Castle Douglas (KK)
47112	#DNT 879	Duple	43318	C29F	3/47	WR & T Hoggins (WR Hoggins & Sons) {Pilot}, Wrockwardine Wood (SH)
47116	FOR 817	Duple	46776	C29F	3/47	FH Kilner (Transport) Ltd, Loxwood (WS) 111
47122	?	Mulliner		B--F	-/47	Nyasaland Transport Co Ltd, Blantyre (O-EAN)
47126	?	Mulliner		B--F	-/47	Nyasaland Transport Co Ltd, Blantyre (O-EAN)
47133	LTW 461	Duple	46508	C29F	4/47	Leighton Coach Co Ltd, Ilford (EX)
47137	DHS 86	SMT		C29F	8/47	Daniel Ferguson Ltd {Victor}, Renfrew (RW) 18
47141	FDV 8	Duple	46954	C29F	4/47	RC & AC Hopkins {Blue Moorland Coaches}, Dawlish (DN)
47147	DNT 880	Duple	43228	C29F	4/47	A & R Parish {Parish's Motor Service}, Morda (SH)
47153	LTW 552	Duple	44750	C29F	4/47	GL Sutton {Sutton's Coaches}, Clacton (EX)
47160	?	Mulliner		B--F	-/47	Nyasaland Transport Co Ltd, Blantyre (O-EAN)
47163	LPC 938	Duple	43351	C29F	4/47	HR Richmond {Epsom Coaches}, Epsom (SR)
47172	* JTB 207	Santus		FC30F	1/48	J Monks & Sons, Leigh (LA)
47176	* NRF 268	Duple	3798/2	C25F	6/47	GH Austin & Sons Ltd {Happy Days}, Stafford (ST) 69
47182	SME 9	Whitson	?	C29F	2/47	Wright Bros (London) Ltd, London W7 (LN)
47187	JP 6242	Plaxton	254	FC30F	6/47	R Gray (Gray Bros) {Streamline Coaches}, Wigan (LA)
47193						Exported to Mombasa (O-EAK)
47200	* ECA 166	Duple	43601	C29F	4/47	Hancocks (Old Colwyn) Ltd {Royal Blue} (DH)
47206	DMO 249	Duple	44367	C29F	4/47	Windsorian Motor Coach Services Ltd, Windsor (BE) 49

47212	HYK 910	Duple	44333	C29F	4/47 George Ewer & Co Ltd {Grey Green}, London N16 (LN)
47219					Exported to Mombasa (O-EAK)
47224	ECY 703	Duple	46740	C29F	3/47 United Welsh, Swansea (GG) 917
47231	BFK 574	Duple	43615	C27F	5/47 H Burnham {Grey Coaches}, Worcester (WO)
47236	GRU 101	Duple	44811	C27F	7/47 Shamrock & Rambler Motor Coaches Ltd, Bournemouth (HA)
47241	?	?		van	7/47 Adams Dairies Ltd, Leek (GST)
47252	* PRE 759	?		C26F	7/48 AT Hardwick {Glider Coaches}, Bilston (ST)
47259	OMT 31	Duple	46388	C29F	4/47 AC Susans {Fountain Luxury Coaches}, Twickenham (MX)
47265	* FBM 339	Duple	43575	C29F	3/47 WA Tasker, Bandley (BD)
47271	FVB 383	Duple	44162	C27F	5/47 AW Bennett {Shirley Coach Services}, Croydon (SR)
47278	GDF 73	Duple	46688	C29F	5/47 ED, GE & Mrs ME Harrison {Broadway Coaches}, Broadway (WO)
47283	NRE 74	Duple	46276	C29F	4/47 B & W Hickson {Hickson Bros}, Tamworth (ST)
47290	HYK 836	Duple	44028	C29F	3/47 Camden Coaches Ltd, Edgware (MX)
47295	* DBE 815	Beadle	C114	B30F	11/47 Lincolnshire RCC, Bracebridge Heath (KN) 672
47300	* FA 8543	Duple	44317	C29F	5/47 GW Wellings, Burton-on-Trent (ST)
47305					Exported to Mombasa (O-EAK)
47311	KHT 717	Duple	43265	C29F	4/47 CW Jordan {Maple Leaf}, Bristol (GL)
47317	DCX 628	Plaxton	279	C29F	7/47 Hanson's Buses Ltd, Huddersfield (WR) 233
47322	GTG 74	Duple	46495	C29F	3/47 HG Hooper, Crynant (GG)
47330	?	?		van	6/47 Earnshaw Bros & Booth {Nu-Lyne Furniture}, Burnley (GLA)
47335	HYF 532	Duple	44822	C29F	4/47 United Service Transport Co Ltd, London SW9 (LN) 1065
47340	GDF 222	Duple	44696	C29F	4/47 CAJ Scarrott {Luxury Coaches}, Stow-on-the-Wold (GL)
47350	DBE 814	Beadle	C111	B30F	10/47 Lincolnshire RCC, Bracebridge Heath (KN) 671
47362	* ?	?		?	3/47 Smith, London N1 (LN)
47377	LVW 152	Thurgood	329	C29F	4/47 ECW Halls, Hatfield Heath (EX)
47384	?	?		van	8/47 Horwood, Aylesbury (GBK)
47393	?	?		van	7/47 Wolberg, London N1 (GLN)
47403, 47413					Exported to Malaya
47418	* SME 8	Whitson	?	C29F	5/47 Ardley Bros Ltd, London N17 (LN)
47424	?	?		van	9/47 Dunbar Transport, Chatham (GKT)
47430	?	?		van	9/47 W Sharples & Sons Ltd (removers), Lancaster (GLA)
47440	?	?		lorry	9/47 FG Alexander, London N21 (GLN)
47449	GRU 102	Duple	44840	C27F	7/47 Shamrock & Rambler Motor Coaches Ltd, Bournemouth (HA)
47459					Exported to Malaya
47468	HFM 29	Beadle	C163	B28F	11/47 Crosville MS, Chester (CH) S3
47475	LPF 249	Whitson	?	C29F	6/47 Green Luxury Coaches (Walton) Ltd, Walton-on-Thames (SR)
47484	* HNE 960	?		-27-	9/47 Sharp's Motor Services (Manchester) Ltd (LA)
47494	* DCX 627	Plaxton	650	C29F	7/47 Hanson's Buses Ltd, Huddersfield (WR) 234
47645 - 47656					Exported to Melbourne (O-AUS)
47765		see 47265			
47777 - 47788					Exported to Buenos Aires (O-RA)
47804	?	?		van	10/47 G Barnes & Son, Lincoln (GLI)
47814	* HYP 722	Duple	44112	C29F	2/48 Birch Bros Ltd, London NW5 (LN) K22
47820	?	?		l/stock	3/48 AS Burchett, Lewes (GSR)
47830					Exported to Malaya
47839	?	Mulliner		B--F	-/47 Nyasaland Transport Co Ltd, Blantyre (O-EAN)
47849	ERY 636	Duple	43473	C29F	4/47 JH Hill, Leicester (LE)
47858	?	?		van	9/48 JJ Allen Ltd (department store), Bournemouth (GHA)
47864	* DBE 817	Beadle	C117	B30F	5/48 Lincolnshire RCC, Bracebridge Heath (KN) 674
47874	* HFM 30	Beadle	C162	B28F	11/47 Crosville MS, Chester (CH) S4
47884	FOR 741	Duple	43469	C27F	3/47 A Millson, Upper Chute (HA)
47894	OMT 961	Duple	43920	C29F	5/47 Valliant Direct Coaches Ltd, London W5 (LN)
47904	HYL 144	Mulliner	T10	B32F	4/47 BOAC (LN)
47910	?	Mulliner		B--F	-/47 Nyasaland Transport Co Ltd, Blantyre (O-EAN)
47920					Exported to Lagos (O-WAN)
47930	LBB 236	Plaxton	252	FC30F	6/47 G Galley (Galley's Motors), Newcastle (ND)
47940	KBH 47	Duple	47799	C29F	4/47 JRG Dell {Rover Bus Service}, Lye Green (BK) 9

47950	BCK 552	Duple	46877	C26F	5/47	Scout MS Ltd, Preston (LA) 37
47957	?	Dews Garages		van	12/47	J Hoyle & Son, Halifax (GWR)
47967						Exported to Lagos (O-WAN)
47977	DCX 626	Plaxton	278	C29F	7/47	Hanson's Buses Ltd, Huddersfield (WR) 223
47988	GDF 748	Thurgood	332	C29F	5/47	FB & WE Pulham {Pulham & Sons}, Naunton (GL)
47998	FOT 256	Duple	44519	C29F	5/47	Sunbeam Coaches (Loxwood) Ltd (WS) 118
48005	* FDV 548	SMT	46956	C27F	4/47	CW Good {The Doves Motor Tours}, Beer (DN)
48015	?	Mulliner		B--F	-/--	Anglo Iranian Oil Co, Abadan (O-IR)
48025	?	?		van	4/48	Kirkhams Ltd, Preston (GLA)
48035	* HTD 492	Plaxton	266	C30F	6/47	Sharp's Motor Services (Manchester) Ltd (LA)
48045	GTG 438	Duple	46815	C29F	5/47	AE & FR Brewer {Brewer's Motor Services}, Caerau (GG)
48052	?	Mulliner		B--F	-/--	Anglo Iranian Oil Co, Abadan (O-IR)
48083	FFG 741	Mulliner	T16	B28F	5/47	Meldrum & Dawson, Dunfermline (FE)
48089	HYL 787	Mulliner	T23	B32F	6/47	BOAC (LN)
48098	GTG 155	Duple	46922	C29F	5/47	DT & R Davies {Cream Line Services}, Tonmawr (GG)
48106	OMT 820	Duple	47875	C29F	5/47	H Burch, Harrow Weald (MX)
48116	FOT 237	Duple	46606	C29F	4/47	BS Williams, Emsworth (HA) 122
48124	JK 9589	Duple	43653	C29F	5/47	RL & PJ Jackson {Palmerston Coaches}, Eastbourne (ES) 8
48133	?	?		goods	3/47	London Carriers, Waddon (GSR)
48140	* ?	?		(goods ?)	3/47	Britten, London E2 (GLN)
48151	?	Mulliner		B--F	-/--	Anglo Iranian Oil Co, Baghdad (O-IRQ)
48159	* DPY 708	Plaxton	296	C29F	5/47	Hardwick's Services Ltd, Snainton (NR)
48165	DUJ 197	Mulliner	T17	B32F	5/47	J Guy, Ketley Bank (SH)
48171	FOT 285	Duple	46607	C29F	5/47	Sunbeam Coaches (Loxwood) Ltd (WS) 116
48177						Exported to Ireland
48186	HUP 245	Plaxton	293	C29F	9/47	TW Stephenson {Stephenson Bros}, High Etherley (DM)
48195	?	?		van	-/-	Wright, Liverpool (GLA)
48203	AGV 194	Duple	43618	C29F	4/47	GF Burgoin (Haverhill) Ltd {Grey Pullman Coaches} (WF)
48218	BJR 825	Mulliner	T11	B28F	4/47	T Ord & Son, Alnwick (ND)
48236	?	?		van	3/48	Vickers Transport Ltd, London E9 (GLN)
48246	FKV 475	Duple	43494	C27F	4/47	H & H Motorways Ltd {Bunty}, Coventry (WK) 75
48254	?	?		van	3/48	GW Berry & Sons Ltd, London N19 (GLN)
48271	HAD 314	Plaxton	655	C30F	10/47	Almondsbury Engineers Ltd {Streamways} (GL)
48278	?	?		l/stock	11/47	J Wilson, Barnard Castle (GDM)
48286	?	?		l/stock	11/47	RE Swales, Stockton-on-Tees (GNR)
48295	HRO 150	Thurgood	330	C29F	5/47	Dye & Sons, Hertford (HT)
48301	CDB 717	Plaxton	260	C29F	5/47	Dewhurst Bros (Macclesfield) Ltd (CH)
48302	DDM 981	Thurgood	327	C29F	5/47	Rhyl United Coachways Ltd, Rhyl (FT) 5B
48315	EUK 533	Mulliner	T14	C29F	5/47	Worthington Motor Tours Ltd, Wolverhampton (ST)
48324	HYC 840	Mulliner	T12	B32F	4/47	Binding & Payne Ltd {Dorothy's Coaches}, Clevedon (SO)
48331	* ACP 562	Plaxton	275	C25F	12/47	O & C Holdsworth Ltd, Halifax (WR)
48337	KDH 801	Plaxton	289	C29F	10/47	JN & FN Boult {John Boult & Sons}, Walsall (ST) 31
48343	JC 8464	Thurgood	333	C29F	5/47	Penmaenmawr Motor Co Ltd (CN)
48351	?	?		van	3/48	London County Council (GLN)
48360	?	?		van	11/47	C Raunsley Ltd, Bradford (GWR)
48368	SMF 960	Pearson		C26F	9/47	Valliant Direct Coaches Ltd, London W5 (LN)
48377	?	?		van	5/48	W Robinson, Bridlington (GER)
48392	* HTC 600	Duple	46391	C29F	5/47	Rossendale Division Carriage Co, Bacup (LA)
48401	FDV 628	Duple	46410	C29F	5/47	Woolacombe & Mortehoe Motor Co Ltd, Woolacombe (DN)
48408	?	?		van	4/47	Earnshaw Bros & Booth {Nu-Lyne Furniture}, Burnley (GLA)
48416	HYH 570	Duple	44856	C27F	5/47	Keith & Boyle (London) Ltd {Orange Luxury Coaches}, London EC2 (LN) Siskin
48423	* EDL 638	Duple	46532	C29F	6/47	Southern Vectis, Newport (IW) 209
48433	?	?		van	10/47	McCormack, Lancaster (GLA)
48441	HYE 200	Duple	46370	C29F	6/47	Bradshaw's Super Coaches Ltd, London SE18 (LN)
48450	GVF 534	Plaxton	262	FC30F	5/47	WA Dalliston, Wells-next-the-Sea (NK)
48458	?	?		van	10/47	T Nicholson & Son, London EC2 (GLN)

C1252/57

48467	HVM 393	NMU	C25F	4/47	Sharp's Motor Services (Manchester) Ltd (LA)
48483	* ?	?	(goods ?)	3/47	City Coach Co Ltd, Brentwood (GEX)
48493	?	?	van	6/48	WJ Edwards, Luton (GBD)
48501	* EFU 375	Scunthorpe Motors	C28F	10/47	TA Everett, Atterby (LI)
48507		see 48501			
48510	KDH 802	Plaxton 290	C29F	10/47	JN & FN Boult {John Boult & Sons}, Walsall (ST) 32
48517	EF 7992	Duple 44632	C29F	4/47	Bee-Line Roadways (Teeside) Ltd, West Hartlepool (DM)
48528	?	?	van	3/48	Bool Bros Ltd, Liverpool (GLA)
48551	FDK 572	Duple 44868	C27F	4/47	Yelloway Motor Services Ltd, Rochdale (LA)
48560	HMN 658	Pearson	C26F	6/47	Crennell's Garage Ltd, Ramsey (IM)
48566					Exported to Ireland
48572	?	?	van	5/48	WS Sutton Ltd, Warrington (GLA)
48578	FOR 907	?	C29F	2/48	EH Morton {Brown Bus Service}, Lymington (HA)
48588	?	Mulliner	B--F	-/--	Anglo Iranian Oil Co, Abadan (O-IR)
48673	* v1.840	NZMB	C20F	9/47	New Zealand Railways Road Services (O-NZ) 1510
48674	s.221	NZMB	C20F	1/48	New Zealand Railways Road Services (O-NZ) 1519
48675	* s.805	NZMB	C20F	9/47	New Zealand Railways Road Services (O-NZ) 1511
48676	?	NZMB	B25F	7/48	New Zealand Railways Road Services (O-NZ) 1606
48677	?	NZMB	C20F	2/48	New Zealand Railways Road Services (O-NZ) 1520
48678	* GVT 19358	NZMB	C20F	1/48	New Zealand Railways Road Services (O-NZ) 1518
48679	* GVT 18036	NZMB	C20F	12/47	New Zealand Railways Road Services (O-NZ) 1517
48680	s.220	NZMB	C20F	12/47	New Zealand Railways Road Services (O-NZ) 1515
48681	?	NZMB	C20F	12/47	New Zealand Railways Road Services (O-NZ) 1516
48682	?	NZMB	C20F	12/47	New Zealand Railways Road Services (O-NZ) 1513
48683	?	NZMB	C20F	9/47	New Zealand Railways Road Services (O-NZ) 1512
48684	* s.322	NZMB	C20F	12/47	New Zealand Railways Road Services (O-NZ) 1514
48793 - 48804					Exported to Bombay (O-IND)
48877 - 48878					Exported to Copenhagen (O-DK)
48879	?	Ørum-Pedersen	B---	10/47	Ingv. Bak, Sundby Mors (O-DK)
48880 - 48882					Exported to Copenhagen (O-DK)
48883	J 1126	Rønne	B--C	3/48	DBJ (Bornholm Railways), Rønne (O-DK) 13
48884 - 48886					Exported to Copenhagen (O-DK)
48887	JA 8029	Ørum-Pedersen	C29C	-/48	Tejn Turistfart, Tejn (O-DK)
48888					Exported to Copenhagen (O-DK)
48904	BDO 89	Mulliner T15	B32F	4/47	JW, JT & WE Camplin {Holme Delight Bus Service}, Donington (LI)
48907	KBH 384	Thurgood 331	C29F	5/47	Pilot Coaches (High Wycombe) Ltd (BK)
48912	HYK 235	Duple 44817	C27F	5/47	United Service Transport Co Ltd, London SW9 (LN) 1066
48923	HRH 834	Duple 43330	C29F	4/47	JB & JW McMaster {JB McMaster & Sons}, Kingston-upon-Hull (ER)
48932	?	?	van	3/48	W Richardson, Stretford (GLA)
48940	DUJ 251	Duple 46438	C29F	4/47	RW Carpenter {Valley Motor Services}, Bishop's Castle (SH)
48948	* HUO 694	Duple 46549	C27F	4/47	Western National, Exeter (DN) 541
48957	?	Mulliner	B--F	-/47	Nyasaland Transport Co Ltd, Blantyre (O-EAN)
48973	* ?	?	van	10/47	AJ Cattle, London N19 (GLN)
48982					Exported to Antwerp (O-B)
48992	* NRF 301	Duple 3686/2	C26F	6/47	GH Austin & Sons Ltd {Happy Days}, Stafford (ST) 29
49001	* JWJ 16	Plaxton 263	FC30F	5/47	Law Bros Ltd, Sheffield (WR)
49008	?	?	h/box	9/47	J Ormston Longmead, Hutton Magna (GNR)
49021	HRR 553	Duple 46994	C29F	5/47	Barton Transport, Chilwell (NG) 521
49029	?	?	van	3/48	W Caudle & Co Ltd (upholsterers), Sheffield (GWR)
49039	?	Mulliner	B--F	-/47	Nyasaland Transport Co Ltd, Blantyre (O-EAN)
49048	* OMT 968	Duple 43914	C29F	5/47	Valliant Direct Coaches Ltd, London W5 (LN)
49057	* LVW 650	Duple 44699	C29F	4/47	H Sharpe, Grays (EX)
49073	EN 8955	Duple 43284	C29F	4/47	Auty's Tours Ltd, Bury (LA)
49082	P-39841	Jongerius	B33-	8/47	Autobedrijf De Valk (Fl. Habets), Valkenburg (O-NL) 52
49090	?	?	van	1/48	WG Gill, Spennymoor (GDM)
49099	FUY 950	Duple 47574	C29F	5/47	A Janes {Bert Janes}, Stourbridge (WO)
49107	DUJ 252	Duple 43764	C29F	5/47	RG, FJ, DA & K Cooper {G Cooper & Sons}, Oakengates (SH)

C1252/58

49118	HPT 47	Mulliner	T13	B32F	5/47	F Wilson, Hunwick (DM)
49126	?	Mulliner		B--F	-/47	Nyasaland Transport Co Ltd, Blantyre (O-EAN)
49135	?	?		van	6/48	G Fuller & Sons, London SE17 (GLN)
49143	DUJ 216	Duple	46437	C29F	5/47	Salopia Saloon Coaches Ltd, Whitchurch (SH) 47
49152	?	?		van	7/48	FG Alexander, London N21 (GLN)
49168	?	?		van	7/48	FG Alexander, London N21 (GLN)
49178						Exported to Santiago (O-RCH)
49186	FOT 19	Duple	43747	C29F	4/47	FH Kilner (Transport) Ltd, Horsham (WS) 114
49195	EDM 327	Pearson		C26F	10/47	W Bellis & Son, Buckley (FT)
49202	FBT 200	Wilson & Stockall		library	8/48	East Riding County Council (GER)
49213	HUP 842	Robson		C29F	3/48	SG & R Cheesey {Serene Coaches}, Brandon Colliery (DM)
49221	JYB 925	(Harrington ?)	?	C28F	1/48	DW & RC Gough {Mountaineer Coaches}, Cheddar (SO)
49230	?	?		caravan	3/48	T Whitelegg, Exeter (VDN)
49238	JMB 717	Pearson		C26F	7/47	FH Yates, Runcorn (CH)
49247	JM 6677	Plaxton	653	C29F	6/47	E Nelson & Son, Arnside (WT)
49263	CCL 888	Duple	44707	C27F	5/47	HA & Mrs ME Roberts {Red Car Service}, Norwich (NK)
49273						Exported to Santiago (O-RCH)
49281	HUR 106	Thurgood	342	C29F	7/47	CW Sworder, Walkern (HT)
49296	?	?		van	9/48	JJ Allen Ltd (department store), Plymouth (GDN)
49301	EP 9588	Duple	46439	C27F	5/47	Mid-Wales Motorways Ltd, Newtown (MO) 36
49307	?	?		van	-/--	Original operator unknown
49316	?	?		van	-/--	Original operator unknown
49325	* NRE 614	Duple	43591	C29F	5/47	Greatrex Motor Coaches Ltd, Stafford (ST) 33 Redstart
49333	?	?		van	-/--	Original operator unknown
49342	?	?		h/box	-/--	Original operator unknown
49358	ERY 722	Duple	43957	C29F	5/47	JA Swinfield {Sedate Coaches}, Leicester (LE) 3
49361		see 40361				
49368	* HFM 31	Beadle	C165	B28F	11/47	Crosville MS, Chester (CH) S5
49376	* HUO 668	Beadle	C118	B30F	10/47	Southern National, Exeter (DN) 515
49385	JCV 606	Mulliner	T18	B28F	-/47	JT Berryman, Leedstown (CO)
49392	?	?		van	-/--	Original operator unknown
49403	DRJ 92	Trans-United		C27F	3/49	JW Fieldsend Ltd, Salford (LA)
49419	HUO 669	Beadle	C119	B30F	10/47	Southern National, Exeter (DN) 516
49427	CCK 486	Duple	51313	C27F	8/48	Scout MS Ltd, Preston (LA)
49436	FOT 20	Duple	46420	C29F	4/47	FH Kilner (Transport) Ltd, Horsham (WS) 112
49476	HUO 695	Duple	46550	C27F	4/47	Western National, Exeter (DN) 542
49483	CRD 649	Duple	44492	C29F	5/47	AE Smith {Smith's Coaches}, Reading (BE)
49489	EDL 637	Duple	46531	C29F	6/47	Southern Vectis, Newport (IW) 208
49495	#JTE 323	Junction		C29F	7/48	B Wolfenden, Manchester (LA)
49503	HFM 32	Beadle	C164	B28F	11/47	Crosville MS, Chester (CH) S6
49508	?	?		van	-/--	Original operator unknown
49513	HUO 696	Duple	46551	C27F	4/47	Western National, Exeter (DN) 543
49521	EDL 639	Duple	46533	C29F	6/47	Southern Vectis, Newport (IW) 210
49530	* LBB 165	Mulliner	T22	B32F	4/47	Bedlington & District Luxury Coaches Ltd, Ashington (ND)
49536	* DBE 813	Beadle	C113	B30F	10/47	Lincolnshire RCC, Bracebridge Heath (KN) 670
49547	OMT 969	Duple	43915	C29F	5/47	Valliant Direct Coaches Ltd, London W5 (LN)
49557	CTY 605	ACB		C27F	6/48	EA Raisbeck & Sons, Bedlington (ND)
49565	KBH 173	Duple	44874	C29F	4/47	FH Crook {Sands Bus Co}, Booker (BK)
49570	* EMW 145	Lee		DP28F	7/47	Skylark Motor Services Ltd, Salisbury (WI) 6
49575	?	?		van	-/--	Original operator unknown
49582	?	?		van	-/--	Original operator unknown
49593	LPE 442	Mulliner	T27	B--F	4/47	ER Lipscomb (Holman & Son) {Dorking Coaches}, Dorking (SR)
49601	FUY 707	Duple	46917	C29F	5/47	AL Yarranton Snr & AL Yarranton Jnr {Eardiston Coaches}, Eardiston (WO)
49610	* MRA 315	SMT		C27F	7/48	GW Bull, Tideswell (DE)
49618	* FE-13-183	Auto Viação de Souto		B29D	7/47	Auto Viação de Souto, Souto (O-P) 4
49630	KHU 28	Duple	43266	C29F	4/47	CW Jordan {Maple Leaf}, Bristol (GL)
49643	HYL 789	Mulliner	T25	B32F	5/47	BOAC (LN)

49653	* KUM 173	Mulliner	T20	C28F	6/47	Enterprise (Scunthorpe) Passenger Services Ltd {Enterprise} (LI) 73
49665	GR 9196	Pearson		C26F	7/47	WH Jolly, South Hylton (DM)
49670	SJ 1119	Mulliner	T21	B28F	4/47	Gordon Bros {Gordon's Motors}, Lamlash (BU)
49677	EWN 5	Mulliner	T19	B28F	5/47	R Parkhouse & Sons, Penclawdd (GG)
49688	FUE 992	Duple	43290	C26F	4/47	AT & AE Hastilow {Tudor Rose}, Sutton Coldfield (WK)
49696	HRO 260	Duple	44710	C29F	5/47	CH Knight {Bream}, Hemel Hempstead (HT)
49705	HYL 788	Mulliner	T24	B32F	5/47	BOAC (LN)
49713	* AL-13-34	?		DP29D	7/47	Viúva Carneiro, Mêda (O-P) 6
49722	?	?		lorry	-/--	Original operator unknown
49738	* (HVU 674 ?)	?		C26F	8/47	Altrincham Coachways Ltd (CH)
49748	* JTC 395	?		lorry	3/48	Original operator unknown
49756	?	?		van	-/--	Original operator unknown
49765	ECA 231	Mulliner	T26	B32F	6/47	F Crawford, Pentre Broughton (DH)
49772	* JCV 612	Duple	44711	C29F	5/47	Pearce's Motors Ltd, Polperro (CO)
49783	ECJ 845	Duple	46440	C29F	5/47	WE Morgan {Wye Valley Motors}, Hereford (HR)
49791	* JP 6243	Plaxton	270	FC30F	6/47	R Gray (Gray Bros) {Streamline Coaches}, Wigan (LA)
49800	DFW 993	Duple	46295	C27F	5/47	T Topliss, North Kelsey (LI)
49808						Exported to Tel Aviv (O-IL)
49817	* DUJ 253	Duple	43231	C29F	5/47	JT, FW & GE Whittle {JT Whittle & Sons}, Highley (SH)
49833	LBB 237	Plaxton	253	FC30F	6/47	G Galley (Galley's Motors), Newcastle (ND)
49843	EAY 50	Duple	43474	C29F	5/47	J Randall, Asfordby (LE)
49851	SMF 604	Pearson		C26F	11/47	Valliant Direct Coaches Ltd, London W5 (LN)
49860	KUG 666	SMT		C29F	7/47	JB Midgely & Son Ltd, Leeds (WR)
49867	CFV 208	SMT		C29F	7/47	S & J Wood Ltd {Seagull Coaches}, Blackpool (LA)
49878	DUJ 254	Duple	43248	C29F	5/47	RB & R Charles (Charles Bros) {Charles Motor Services}, Cleobury Mortimer (SH)
49886	BRN 62	SMT		C29F	7/47	Scout MS Ltd, Preston (LA)
49895	CFV 237	SMT		C29F	7/47	J Abbott & Sons (Blackpool) Ltd (LA)
49903						Exported to Palestine
49912	LPD 847	Duple	43642	C29F	5/47	C Barber & Sons Ltd, Mitcham (SR) 6
49925	* OMT 537	Duple	43824	C29F	5/47	Essex County Coaches Ltd, London E15 (LN)
49930	CHJ 415	Duple	46232	C29F	5/47	R Wright {Blue & Cream Luxury Coaches}, Southend-on-Sea (EX)
49939	?	Mulliner	T29	?	5/47	Eagle Star Insurance Co, London (XLN)
49950	HKF 93	SMT		C29F	8/47	RM Walker {Margaret Sun Saloons}, Liverpool (LA)
49958	DUJ 97	Mulliner	T30	B32F	5/47	GA Darrall {Supreme}, Dawley (SH)
49967	* FOT 352	Duple	47625	C29F	5/47	Liss & District Omnibus Co Ltd, Liss (HA) 119
49976						Exported to Montevideo (O-ROU)
49986	?	?		van	-/--	Original operator unknown
49995	* LPU 624	Duple	46553	C29F	5/48	Eastern National, Chelmsford (EX) 3934
50004	HRO 679	Duple	47915	C29F	5/47	HW Hart {Hillside Coaches}, Markyate (HT) 10
50014	LPE 123	Duple	46526	C28F	5/47	GF & BS Graves {GF Graves & Son}, Redhill (SR)
50020	* JWJ 399	Plaxton	264	FC30F	6/47	Law Bros Ltd, Sheffield (WR)
50025	ACN 288	SMT		C29F	7/47	J Thirlwell & Sons {Greybird}, Gateshead (DM) 1
50034	CRD 591	Mulliner	T34	B32F	6/47	Reading Corporation (BE) 68
50043	* LPU 623	Duple	46552	C29F	5/48	Eastern National, Chelmsford (EX) 3933
50053	AHF 81	Duple	43235	C29F	8/47	CH Dorning {Wallasey Motorways}, Wallasey (CH)
50062	?	?		van	-/--	Original operator unknown
50071						Exported to Montevideo (O-ROU)
50081	FYG 4	Plaxton	292	C29F	5/47	A & JR Davison Ltd, Brighouse (WR) 8
50090	OMT 544	Duple	43916	C25F	5/47	Valliant Direct Coaches Ltd, London W5 (LN)
50099	* HMN 835	Pearson		C26F	8/47	JR McKibbin, Onchan (IM)
50109	EMR 601	Mulliner	T28	B28F	6/47	The Old Firm, Wroughton (WI)
50120	JMB 461	Plaxton	261	FC30F	7/47	R Bullock & Co (Transport) Ltd, Cheadle (CH)
50123		see 90495				
50129	?	?		van	-/--	Original operator unknown
50138	EX 5777	Duple	46930	C29F	5/47	James Calver Ltd {Seagull Coaches}, Great Yarmouth (NK)
50148	?	Mulliner	T31	?	6/47	Kent County Council (XKT)
50157	ERY 861	Duple	43471	C29F	5/47	AE Hercock, Leicester (LE)
50166						Exported to Ireland
50176	KDH 803	Plaxton	291	C29F	10/47	JN & FN Boult {John Boult & Sons}, Walsall (ST) 33
50185	?	Mulliner	T32	?	5/47	AA Stuart & Sons (Contractor), Carmyle

C1252/60

50192	EDL 808	Duple	43631	C29F	5/47	B Groves, Cowes (IW)
50204	HYL 797	Mulliner	T35	B32F	5/47	BOAC (LN)
50215	OMT 149	Duple	44715	C29F	5/47	Webber {Empire's Best}, London N22 (LN) 17
50224	P-39842	Jongerius		B33-	11/47	Autobedrijf De Valk (Fl. Habets), Valkenburg (O-NL) 53
50233	HMN 468	Duple	43661	C29F	4/47	WC Shimmin {Silver Star}, Douglas (IM) 2
50243	HOB 941	Duple	46285	C29F	5/47	Burley's Garage Ltd, Birmingham (WK)
50252	?	SMT		l/stock	2/48	JC Laycock, unknown location (GWT)
50261	* GAO 465	Duple	47705	C29F	7/47	Cumberland MS, Whitehaven (CU) 248
50271						Exported to Ireland
50280	* SMT 100	Mulliner	T48	B31F	6/47	Middlesex County Council (XMX)
50289	AHE 957	Duple	43515	C29F	6/47	W & A Cawthorne {W & A Cawthorne & Son}, Barugh (WR)
50299	* BCK 895	Duple	43270	C29F	6/47	E Barnes {Premier Motors}, Preston (LA)
50409 - 50420						Exported to Sydney (O-AUS)
50490		see 50499				
50493	* P.626	North Shore		B33F	5/48	North Shore Transport Co Ltd, Takapuna (O-NZ) 26
50494						Exported to Wellington (O-NZ)
50495	* P.577	Suburban		B33F	4/48	Suburban Buses Ltd, Te Papapa (O-NZ) 36
50496						Exported to Wellington (O-NZ)
50497	* ?	?		?	-/--	Original operator unknown (O-NZ)
50498						Exported to Wellington (O-NZ)
50499	* P.181	Auckland Bus Co		B33F	5/48	Auckland Bus Co Ltd (O-NZ) 29
50500	* P.373	Auckland TB		FB33F	6/49	Auckland Transport Board (O-NZ) 38
50501	P2.500	H & H		B29F	-/49	H & H Travel Lines Ltd, Invercargill (O-NZ) 20
50502	* P.366	Auckland TB		FB33F	11/48	Auckland Transport Board (O-NZ) 31
50503	P.337	Auckland TB		FB33F	11/48	Auckland Transport Board (O-NZ) 2
50504	* ?	?		?	-/--	AV Smith, Clevedon (O-NZ)
50557		see 45729				
50610	EWF 631	Duple	46775	C29F	6/47	H Hodgson, Duggleby (ER)
50619	* P-36198	Jongerius		B33-	-/46	Nelissen, Koningsbosch (O-NL) 4
50629	DUJ 296	Mulliner	T40	B30F	5/47	RG, FJ, DA & K Cooper {G Cooper & Sons}, Oakengates (SH)
50637	HTC 863	Plaxton	267	FC30F	7/47	T Towler (Lytham) Ltd (LA)
50646	RC 9963	Duple	47741	C29F	5/47	W Boyden, Castle Donington (LE)
50655	JC 8451	Duple	43343	C29F	5/47	MO Jones {Tryfan Ranger}, Llanwnda (CN)
50665	?	?		h/box	-/--	Original operator unknown
50674						Exported to Antigua
50683	FYG 74	Duple	43845	C27F	6/47	Ripponden & District Motors Ltd (WR) 14
50693	KHU 129	Duple	44233	C29F	5/47	Morning Star Motor Services Ltd, Bristol (GL)
50704	BJR 956	SMT		C29F	8/47	Robson & Atkinson, Stocksfield-on-Tyne (ND)
50713	* P-39843	Jongerius		B33-	11/47	Autobedrijf De Valk (Fl. Habets), Valkenburg (O-NL) 54
50722	?	?		van	-/--	Original operator unknown
50732	CDB 680	Duple	43846	C29F	6/47	EC Morley & W Pickford {Great Moor Coaches}, Stockport (CH)
50741	EM 4077	Pearson		C26F	9/47	T Lawrenson Ltd, Bootle (LA)
50750	* AFB 266	Strachan		C27F	9/47	H Little, Winsley (WI)
50760	* HYP 723	Duple	44113	C29F	2/48	Birch Bros Ltd, London NW5 (LN) K23
50768	?	Mulliner		B--F	-/--	Nyasaland Transport Co Ltd, Blantyre (O-EAN)
50775	HPT 190	Duple	44312	C29F	6/47	J&T Hunter (Washington) Ltd, Washington (DM)
50788	KKX 28	Longwell Green		C27F	7/47	Jeffways Coaches & Station Taxis Ltd, High Wycombe (BK)
50799	CCK 487	Duple	51314	C27F	8/48	Scout MS Ltd, Preston (LA)
50808						Exported to Antwerp (O-B)
50817	* JWJ 531	Duple	47680	C27F	7/47	Sheffield United Tours (WR) 153
50827	CNL 151	Duple	44187	C27F	6/47	J Walker, Wooler (ND)
50836	DUJ 436	Mulliner	T52	B29F	5/47	Corvedale Motor Services Ltd, Ludlow (SH) 6
50845	EDL 809	Duple	43987	C29F	5/47	C & W Coombes {Coombes Bros}, Shanklin (IW)
50855	HYE 554	Duple	44669	C29F	5/47	Cream Coaches Ltd, London E8 (LN) 8
50864	?	Mulliner		B--F	-/--	Nyasaland Transport Co Ltd, Blantyre (O-EAN)
50873	LEH 132	Mulliner	T56	B29F	5/47	C, WH & AR Poole {Poole Bros}, Alsagers Bank (ST) 2
50883	JAT 11	SMT		C29F	9/47	DW Burn, H Tyler & EG Russell {Grey de Luxe}, Kingston-upon-Hull (ER)
50894	HTB 410	Duple	44940	C29F	5/47	W Robinson & Sons, Great Harwood (LA)
50903	BCK 800	Duple	47976	C29F	5/47	Scout MS Ltd, Preston (LA) 39

C1252/61

50912	BCK 894	Duple	43278 C29F	6/47	E Barnes {Premier Motors}, Preston (LA)
50922	HYL 799	Mulliner	T37 B32F	5/47	BOAC (LN)
50931	BCK 799	Duple	47975 C29F	5/47	Scout MS Ltd, Preston (LA) 38
50940	HYD 134	Duple	43467 C29F	6/47	RE Wake {Wake's Services}, Sparkford (SO)
50950	* OMT 552	Duple	43828 C29F	5/47	Essex County Coaches Ltd, London E15 (LN)
50957	* HFM 33	Beadle	C167 B28F	11/47	Crosville MS, Chester (CH) S7
50968	?	?	van	7/48	JH Lunn, Edinburgh (GMN)
50978	LNW 825	Plaxton	202 C29F	12/47	Kelsall Coaches Ltd {Saffman & Beasley}, Leeds (WR)
50989	?	SMT	van	-/--	Original operator unknown
50998					Exported to Antwerp (O-B)
51001	* HMN 511	Duple	43663 C29F	6/47	Crennell's Garage Ltd, Ramsey (IM)
51008	?	?	?	-/--	OMT, Nairobi (O-EAK)
51017	CFV 128	Duple	46880 C29F	6/47	S & J Wood Ltd {Seagull Coaches}, Blackpool (LA)
51026	FFH 8	Duple	47905 C29F	5/47	HT Letheren & Son, Lydney (GL)
51036	?	?	l/stock	-/--	Original operator unknown
51045	HUO 697	Duple	47672 C27F	5/47	Western National, Exeter (DN) 544
51054	EBE 435	Plaxton	268 FC30F	6/47	RW Appleby, Conisholme (LI)
51064	BJD 815	Duple	44721 C29F	5/47	WB Clark & TV Edwarthy (Clark & Son) {Clark's Red Coaches}, London E7 (LN)
51075	EUK 534	Mulliner	T33 C29F	6/47	Worthington Motor Tours Ltd, Wolverhampton (ST)
51083	GCG 334	Lee	B26F	1/48	BS Williams, Emsworth (HA) 26
51093	HYL 800	Mulliner	T38 B32F	5/47	BOAC (LN)
51107					Exported to Malaya
51117	?	?	van	-/--	Original operator unknown
51126	JTC 12	KW	C27F	2/48	WH Robinson, Dalton-in-Furness (LA) 4
51135	ANH 252	Mulliner	T42 B28F	5/47	Mrs J Morris, Steeple Claydon (BK)
51143		see 46181			
51147	ECJ 777	Duple	46441 C29F	5/47	JH, HJ & GH Yeomans {Yeomans Motors}, Canon Pyon (HR) 60
51154	JCV 917	Duple	46234 C29F	5/47	MTD Weston, East Looe (CO)
51163	HTC 577	Duple	47990 C29F	6/47	W Robinson & Sons, Great Harwood (LA)
51174	CRD 678	Duple	44493 C29F	5/47	AE Smith {Smith's Coaches}, Reading (BE)
51185	EUK 535	Mulliner	T44 C29F	7/47	Worthington Motor Tours Ltd, Wolverhampton (ST)
51196	* P-36202	Jongerius	B33-	-/47	Ploemen-Schols, Meerssen (O-NL) 4
51198		see 51196			
51203					Exported to Malaya
51213	HYL 798	Mulliner	T36 B32F	5/47	BOAC (LN)
51222	BJR 643	Duple	43622 C29F	5/47	CR Robson, Smelting Syke (ND) 18
51231	* DBE 816	Beadle	C115 B30F	11/47	Lincolnshire RCC, Bracebridge Heath (KN) 673
51241	EAY 605	Thurgood	340 C30F	7/47	AW & JW Farrow (AW Farrow & Son), Melton Mowbray (LE)
51253	CDB 799	Duple	46401 C29F	6/47	W Kirkpatrick {Pride of the Road}, Marple (CH)
51257	LPU 625	Duple	46554 C29F	5/48	Eastern National, Chelmsford (EX) 3935
51269	DBU 888	Duple	43841 C27F	6/47	Shearings Tours Ltd, Oldham (LA)
51280	DUJ 483	Duple	46443 C29F	5/47	WH & W Lowe (JE Lowe & Sons) {Tulip Coaches}, Hadley (SH)
51295					Exported to Lisbon (O-P)
51305	* BDO 338	Duple	44226 C29F	5/47	JR Flatt & Sons Ltd, Long Sutton (LI)
51312	?	?	?	-/--	OTC, Nairobi (O-EAK)
51321	LVW 952	Duple	47571 C29F	5/47	RW Hooks & Co (Harwich & District), Great Oakley (EX)
51331	* KUM 172	Duple	47969 C29F	6/47	Wallace Arnold, Leeds (WR)
51340					Exported to Lisbon (O-P)
51349	OMT 834	Duple	46841 C29F	5/47	Northern Roadways Ltd, Glasgow (LK)
51359	* HYK 236	Duple	44818 C27F	5/47	United Service Transport Co Ltd, London SW9 (LN) 1067
51370	OMT 551	Duple	43917 C29F	5/47	Valliant Direct Coaches Ltd, London W5 (LN)
51379	ECJ 897	Duple	46442 C29F	5/47	PHE Tummey {Llangrove Coach Services}, Llangrove (HR)
51388	GVP 875	Duple	43300 C29F	8/47	Burley's Garage Ltd, Birmingham (WK)
51398	EN 8956	Duple	43285 C29F	5/47	Auty's Tours Ltd, Bury (LA)
51407	HYH 912	Duple	44870 C27F	5/47	WF Butler {Sydenham Coaches}, London SE26 (LN)
51415					Exported to Antigua
51424	* DRX 296	Mulliner	T43 B28F	5/47	Frowen & Hill Ltd {Borough Bus Service}, Windsor (BE)

C1252/62

51433						Exported to Santiago (O-RCH)
51442	HTB 411	Duple	44941	C29F	5/47	W Robinson & Sons, Great Harwood (LA)
51452	HYM 685	Duple	44562	C29F	6/47	Fallowfield & Britten Ltd, London E8 (LN)
51461	HTC 578	Duple	47991	C29F	6/47	W Robinson & Sons, Great Harwood (LA)
51470	SK 3073	Mulliner	T39	B30F	5/47	DB Morrison, Castletown (CS)
51479 *	EX 5760	Duple	43686	C29F	5/47	CG Yaxley, Great Yarmouth (NK)
51489	?	SMT		van	-/--	Original operator unknown
51497	FFS 901	Duple	47960	C29F	6/47	W Alexander, Falkirk (SN) W194
51506	?	?		?	-/--	OMT, unknown location, East Africa
51516	HRR 973	Duple	44391	C29F	5/47	FL Lees {Lees Motorways}, Worksop (NG) B47
51525						Exported to Santiago (O-RCH)
51534	HRR 995	Duple	46995	C29F	7/47	Barton Transport, Chilwell (NG) 522
51544	EDL 640	Duple	47830	C29F	6/47	Southern Vectis, Newport (IW) 211
51555	EU 8535	Duple	46816	C29F	6/47	WC Fouracre {Embassy Motors}, Brynmawr (BC)
51564	HPT 191	Duple	47985	C27F	5/47	Mayfair Luxury Coaches Ltd, Gateshead (DM)
51573	HVM 103	SMT		C29F	7/47	AF Wetnall, Manchester (LA)
51583	DBU 902	Duple	43844	C29F	6/47	G Barlow & Sons Ltd, Oldham (LA)
51592	DBX 579	Duple	43584	C27F	6/47	JD Evans & CA Jones {Gwalia Bus Service}, Llanybyther (CR)
51601	?	?		?	-/--	OMT, unknown location, East Africa
51611	DBU 889	Duple	43842	C27F	6/47	Shearings Tours Ltd, Oldham (LA)
51620						Exported to Lisbon (O-P)
51628 *	CDB 896	Plaxton	269	FC30F	7/47	Dewhurst Bros (Macclesfield) Ltd (CH)
51638	EMR 335	Longwell Green		C28F	7/47	G Hillman {Typhoon Coaches}, Westbury (WI)
51649	GDV 133	Duple	43509	C29F	5/47	Waverley Motor Coach Tours Ltd, Paignton (DN)
51658	?	?		van	-/--	Original operator unknown
51668	FYG 148	Duple	47968	C29F	5/47	JJ Longstaff, Mirfield (WR)
51678	?	?		l/stock	-/--	Original operator unknown
51687	KHU 470	Duple	44234	C29F	5/47	Morning Star Motor Services Ltd, Bristol (GL)
51696						Exported to Lisbon (O-P)
51709	DVN 715	Plaxton	271	C26F	9/47	R Turner, Grangetown (NR)
51720						Exported to Tel Aviv (O-IL)
51727	BES 789	Duple	48069	C29F	6/47	A & C McLennan, Spittalfield (PH)
51734	LVW 953	Mulliner	T47	B29F	5/47	RW Hooks & Co {Harwich & District}, Great Oakley (EX)
51757	LPU 627	Duple	47669	C29F	6/47	Eastern National, Chelmsford (EX) 3937
51768	JAF 836	Strachan		C26F	2/48	Newquay Motor Co Ltd {Red & White Tours} (CO)
51775	HMN 426	Duple	43662	C29F	4/47	JA Moore {Moore's Motors}, Port Erin (IM)
51784	JAT 12	Duple	43577	C27F	6/47	Endsleigh College, Kingston-upon-Hull (XER)
51790	HRO 821	Mulliner	T49	B26F	6/47	Picton & Gibbs {Vanguard Coaches}, Watford (HT)
51800	JWE 876	Duple	43996	C29F	6/47	J Green, Sheffield (WR)
51809	?	Churchill		-30-	6/47	BOAC, unknown overseas location
51818	CRD 592	Mulliner	T46	B32F	8/47	Reading Corporation (BE) 69
51828	HVM 97	Duple	44075	C29F	6/47	Claribel Motors (Ardwick) Ltd, Manchester (LA)
51839	JHN 624	Duple	46884	C29F	6/47	F Wilson, Hunwick (DM)
51848	?	Churchill		?	6/47	BOAC, unknown overseas location
51857	MEV 332	Thurgood	341	C29F	6/47	E Benjamin & E Brandon {Our Bus Service}, Grays (EX) 20
51867	DCX 424	Duple	43617	C29F	6/47	Central Garage Co (Marsden) Ltd, Uppermill (WR)
51876	EMW 59	Thurgood	339	C29F	6/47	AW Giles {Giles Transport Co}, Cricklade (WI)
51885	JX 9967	Duple	46340	C29F	6/47	Brearley's Tours Ltd, Halifax (WR)
51895	HFM 34	Beadle	C166	B28F	11/47	Crosville MS, Chester (CH) S8
51904	?	Churchill		?	6/47	BOAC, unknown overseas location
51913	MNU 931	Reeve & Kenning		C29F	7/48	CT Truman, Clowne (DE)
51923 *	FBC 930	Churchill		C29F	6/48	RS Barnes, Calne (WI)
51934	CBN 748	Duple	47965	C27F	6/47	Fairclough Bros Ltd, Horwich (LA)
51943	?	Churchill		?	6/47	BOAC, unknown overseas location
51952 *	EDL 850	Mulliner	T45	B28F	5/47	Seaview Services Ltd, Seaview (IW) 3
51956						Exported to Tel Aviv (O-IL)
51963	BBV 514	Duple	44576	C29F	6/47	J Benson (Motors) Ltd {Eagle Coaches}, Oswaldtwistle (LA)
51972 *	HRT 299	Churchill		C29F	7/48	Classic Coaches (Lowestoft) Ltd (EK)
51986 *	BBV 483	Duple	43221	C29F	6/47	Whitehurst Tours Ltd, Accrington (LA)

51991	KKX 40	Thurgood	343	C29F	7/47	TJ Brown & JF Grout {Lee & District Motor Services}, Chesham (BK)
52000	?	Churchill	?		6/48	BOAC, unknown overseas location
52009	?	?		lorry	-/--	Original operator unknown
52019	EWF 644	Duple	43904	C27F	7/47	JT Bailey {Bailey's Bus Service}, Fangfoss (ER)
52031	EED 618	Duple	47966	C29F	6/47	G Naylor & Sons {Naylor's Motor Services}, Stockton Heath (CH)
52040	BCS 981	Mulliner	T51	B28F	6/47	W Stewart {A1 Service}, Ardrossan (AR)
52049	* FCY 390	Jeffreys		C28F by	11/48	Priory Motors {Woolnough}, Swinton (LA)
52059	?	?		van	-/--	Original operator unknown
52068	GDF 789	Mulliner	T54	B28F	5/47	ACJ Perrett {Perrett's Coaches}, Shipton Oliffe (GL)
52077	?	?		van	-/--	Original operator unknown
52087	HNF 68	NMU		C29F	1/48	Sharp's Motor Services (Manchester) Ltd (LA)
52096	?	?		l/stock	-/--	Original operator unknown
52125 - 52136						Exported to Buenos Aires (O-RA)
52269 - 52280						Exported to Bombay (O-IND)
52377 - 52388						Exported to Melbourne (O-AUS)
52405	DVN 37	Duple	46322	C29F	6/47	TE Jackson, Thornton-le-Dale (NR)
52415	?	?		van	-/--	Original operator unknown
52426	* JAH 171	(Longford ?)		C29F	5/47	W Tresize {Black Cat Coach & Taxi Co}, North Walsham (NK)
52435	GVF 487	Mulliner	T53	B29F	6/47	HJ Pye {Pye's Garage}, Blakeney (NK)
52444	?	SMT		van	-/--	Original operator unknown
52454	CDY 737	Mulliner	T50	B32F	7/47	Hastings County Borough Education Dept (XES)
52463	HG 9240	Mulliner	T55	B32F	6/47	Burnley, Colne & Nelson JTC (LA) 4
52472	FBT 402	Hedon		C29F	8/47	RA Johnson {Hedon Motor Coaches}, Hedon (ER)
52482	HPT 356	Mulliner	T57	B30F	6/47	Trimdon Motor Services Ltd, Trimdon Grange (DM) 10
52491	HYR 330	Pearson		C26F	10/47	Fallowfield & Britten Ltd, London E8 (LN)
52500	GAA 872	Wadham		C29F	12/47	Creamline Motor Services (Bordon) Ltd (HA)
52510	FFS 902	Duple	47961	C29F	5/47	W Alexander, Falkirk (SN) W197
52521	?	?		l/stock	-/--	Original operator unknown
52530	?	?		van	-/--	Original operator unknown
52539	* JTB 771	NMU		C29F	7/48	AE Hargreaves {Irene}, Bolton (LA)
52549	* OMT 553	Duple	43825	C29F	6/47	Essex County Coaches Ltd, London E15 (LN)
52558	KAF 992	Strachan		C27F	5/47	LJ Ede {Roselyn Coaches}, Par (CO)
52567	EDT 208	SMT		C29F	8/47	EA Hart {Beehive Services}, Adwick-le-Street (WR)
52577	FFS 903	Duple	47962	C29F	6/47	W Alexander, Falkirk (SN) W198
52586	FFS 904	Duple	47963	C29F	6/47	W Alexander, Falkirk (SN) W199
52595	JHN 626	Duple	46886	C29F	6/47	Summerson Bros {The Eden}, West Auckland (DM)
52605	?	?		van	-/--	Original operator unknown
52616	* GAO 466	Duple	47706	C29F	7/47	Cumberland MS, Whitehaven (CU) 249
52625	HPT 381	Mulliner	T60	B32F	6/47	Bond Bros {Imperial Motor Services}, Willington (DM)
52634						Exported to Port Elizabeth (O-ZA)
52644	GRT 221	Mulliner	T58	B32F	6/47	B Beeston & Sons Ltd, East Bergholt (EK)
52653	FDK 682	Duple	47964	C29F	6/47	WE Taylor, Castleton (LA)
52662	BJR 947	Duple	44467	C29F	6/47	WM Appleby & JD Jordan {A & J Coaches}, Bedlington (ND)
52672	CFR 977	Duple	43274	C29F	6/47	J Abbott & Sons (Blackpool) Ltd (LA)
52681						Exported to Port Elizabeth (O-ZA)
52690	JHN 625	Duple	46885	C29F	6/47	Gardiner Bros, Spennymoor (DM)
52700	?	?		van	-/--	Original operator unknown
52711	HTC 661	Duple	43493	C29F	6/47	Dean & Pounder Ltd, Morecambe (LA)
52720	* GTX 3	Mulliner	T59	B32F	7/47	Thomas Bros, Port Talbot (GG)
52729						Exported to Santiago (O-RCH)
52739	JTU 457	Pearson		C26F	9/47	FH Yates, Runcorn (CH)
52748	HTD 658	SMT		C29F	6/47	W Hesford, Leigh (LA)
52757	HVM 98	Duple	44077	C29F	7/47	GW Cartledge {Supreme Red Coaches}, Rhyl (FT)
52767	* CFV 847	Trans-United		C29F	7/48	Enterprise Motors (Blackpool) Ltd (LA)
52776						Exported to Santiago (O-RCH)
52785	KUM 82	Duple	43510	C29F	6/47	Waverley Motor Coach Tours Ltd, Paignton (DN)
52795	FYG 809	Duple	48022	C29F	7/47	W Simpson, Ripon (WR) 3
52806	BBV 520	Duple	44577	C29F	6/47	Ribblesdale Coachways Ltd, Blackburn (LA)
52815	HVM 99	Duple	44069	C29F	6/47	John Boyd Motors Ltd, Manchester (LA)
52824	WI 2317	Kenneally		B30R	-/47	W Kenneally {Kenneally Bus Service}, Johnstown (EI)

C1252/64

52834	* HUO 698	Duple	47673	C27F	6/47	Western National, Exeter (DN) 545
52846	* JKO 674	Duple	44664	C29F	6/47	HF Gilbert {Medway Belle}, Strood (KT)
52852	CFV 167	Duple	46882	C27F	6/47	Batty-Holt Touring Service Ltd, Blackpool (LA)
52861						Exported to Ireland
52869	CFV 194	Duple	46881	C29F	7/47	WC Standerwick, Blackpool (LA)
52878	CFV 995	KW		C27F	3/48	Lansdowne Motors Ltd, Fleetwood (LA)
52887	DBU 890	Duple	43843	C27F	6/47	Shearings Tours Ltd, Oldham (LA)
52897	GRU 103	Duple	44841	C27F	7/47	Shamrock & Rambler Motor Coaches Ltd, Bournemouth (HA)
52906	EJF 39	Duple	44175	C29F	7/47	WH Smith, Leicester (LE)
52914	?	?		van	1/48	BOAC (LN)
52924	FWW 596	Duple	46808	C26F	6/47	West Yorkshire RCC, Harrogate (WR) 646
52933	LPU 626	Duple	46555	C29F	6/47	Eastern National, Chelmsford (EX) 3936
52941	HGK 446	Mulliner	T61	B32F	7/47	British Broadcasting Corporation {BBC}, London SW4 (XLN) B446
52950	OMT 462	Duple	43826	C29F	6/47	Essex County Coaches Ltd, London E15 (LN)
52958	?	?		?	1/48	BOAC (LN)
52976	AWG 993	SMT		C29F	7/47	W Alexander, Falkirk (SN) W202
52981	BJR 946	Duple	44481	C29F	6/47	GP Cooper {Cooper Bros}, Annitsford (ND)
52987	AWG 996	SMT		C29F	8/47	W Alexander, Falkirk (SN) W205
52994	AWG 994	SMT		C29F	7/47	W Alexander, Falkirk (SN) W203
53121 - 52132						Exported to Copenhagen (O-DK)
53303						Exported to Malaya
53313	CNL 252	SMT		C29F	8/47	Bedlington & District Luxury Coaches Ltd, Ashington (ND)
53322	AWG 995	SMT		C29F	8/47	W Alexander, Falkirk (SN) W204
53328	?	?		lorry	-/--	Original operator unknown
53340	JTB 770	NMU		C29F	3/48	Mills & Seddon, Farnworth (LA)
53347						Exported to Malaya
53356	JRL 265	Duple	47863	C29F	7/47	RC Williams {Godolphin Motors}, Godolphin (CO)
53365	HVO 387	Duple	46996	C29F	6/47	Barton Transport, Chilwell (NG) 523
53375	HYE 555	Duple	44670	C29F	7/47	Cream Coaches Ltd, London E8 (LN) 9
53385	HYN 480	Duple	44563	C29F	6/47	Fallowfield & Britten Ltd, London E8 (LN)
53401	GAX 189	Duple	46742	C29F	6/47	Ralph's Garages Ltd, Abertillery (MH) 89
53406						Exported to Basra (O-IRQ)
53411	MFC 340	Duple	43956	C29F	6/47	PC Skinner {Percival's Coaches}, Oxford (OX) (19?)
53419	* HDV 754	Tiverton		C26F	3/48	E Clatworthy {Supreme}, Tiverton (DN)
53428	* KRB 67	Duple	46986	C29F	7/47	Midland General, Langley Mill (DE) 114
53436						Exported to Basra (O-IRQ)
53445	DVN 24	Duple	44717	C29F	6/47	Saltburn Motor Services Ltd, Saltburn (NR) 8
53454	* HYN 420	Duple	44463	C29F	6/47	Bradshaw's Super Coaches Ltd, London SE18 (LN)
53464	HYN 479	Duple	44564	C29F	6/47	Fallowfield & Britten Ltd, London E8 (LN)
53474						Exported to Malaya
53483	HRO 998	Duple	43282	C29F	7/47	BC Cannon Ltd, Puckeridge (HT)
53491	JP 6523	SMT		C29F	9/47	W Liptrot (Coaches) Ltd, Bamfurlong (LA)
53500	HTC 690	Duple	48000	C29F	6/47	Kia-Ora Motor Services Ltd, Morecambe (LA)
53508	KUM 83	Duple	43511	C29F	6/47	Wallace Arnold, Leeds (WR)
53517	HKF 544	Duple	47967	C29F	6/47	CH Williams, Birkenhead (CH)
53525						Exported to Malaya
53534	* CFV 846	NMU		C29F	3/48	Enterprise Motors (Blackpool) Ltd (LA)
53544	* JYA 8	Mulliner	T41	B32F	7/47	JA Wintle {Wintle & Murray}, Bower Hinton (SO)
53554	#LNW 31	SMT		C29F	8/47	Kelsall Coaches Ltd {Saffman & Beasley}, Leeds (WR)
53563	?	?		van	-/--	Original operator unknown
53570	?	Churchill		?	6/47	BOAC, unknown overseas location
53580	GVF 900	Duple	43548	C29F	6/47	F, PW & CE Thompson {Eniway Coaches}, Dereham (NK)
53589	GDG 58	Mulliner	T62	B32F	7/47	Mrs K Riddiford, Thornbury (GL)
53597	EU 8541	Duple	46743	C29F	5/47	Griffin Motor Co Ltd, Brynmawr (BC) 106
54101 - 54112						Exported to Bombay (O-IND)
54382	JKO 590	Duple	44663	C29F	7/47	TC Cox {Streamline Coaches}, Maidstone (KT)
54391	EMR 870	Duple	43336	C29F	6/47	AEJ, HG & RH Scull {AE Scull & Sons}, Westbury (WI)
54401	HYO 97	Duple	47583	C29F	6/47	AE Pritchard (J Pritchard), London E14 (LN)
54410	BSD 139	SMT		C29F	9/47	CB Law, Prestwick (AR)
54420	EVJ 74	Duple	46444	C29F	6/47	Miss I Baynham, Ross-on-Wye (HR)

54429	HYO 197	Duple	47592	C27F	7/47	Frames Tours Ltd, London WC1 (LN) 71
54439	GDV 584	Duple	43371	C26F	6/47	Court Garages (Torquay) Ltd (DN)
54448	MEV 408	Thurgood	362	C29F	7/47	FH & DJ Rose (Rose Bros) {Primrose}, Chelmsford (EX) 8
54457	* LDH 45	Duple	47631	C29F	6/47	W Hayes jnr, Walsall (ST) 5
54467	DNV 810	Duple	46565	C29F	6/47	KW Services Ltd, Daventry (NO) B4
54477	DUJ 684	Mulliner	T63	B32F	6/47	JT, FW & GE Whittle {JT Whittle & Sons}, Highley (SH)
54486	FWP 656	Mulliner	T66	B32F	7/47	GC Slater, Malvern (WO)
54496	CFE 957	Duple	46489	C27F	7/47	L Parker, Bardney (LI)
54505	HPT 74	Mulliner	T65	B32F	7/47	Dixon Bros {The Witbank}, Lanchester (DM) 3
54515	BGS 69	SMT		C25F	8/47	Loch Katrine Steamboat Co Ltd, Callander (PH)
54524	BDO 540	Duple	47918	C29F	7/47	WG Turner {Silver Dawn}, Crowland (LI)
54534	* HTD 190	Duple	44859	C29F	7/47	Kia-Ora Motor Services Ltd, Morecambe (LA)
54543	FSP 181	Mulliner	T64	B28F	7/47	J Robertson & Son, Cardenden (FE)
54552	BRN 61	Duple	46878	C29F	7/47	Scout MS Ltd, Preston (LA)
54567	GWR 28	Duple	44942	C29F	7/47	Walton & Helliwell Ltd, Mytholmroyd (WR)
54571	BDO 574	Duple	47578	C29F	8/47	HR Cropley {Safety Coaches}, Fosdyke (LI)
54576	EMW 96	Duple	43560	C29F	7/47	L Sheppard, Broadtown (WI)
54581		see 54851				
54585	HVO 596	Duple	46997	C29F	7/47	Barton Transport, Chilwell (NG) 524
54595						Exported to Ireland
54602	BDO 539	Duple	43295	C26F	7/47	HJ Nightingale {Reliance Coaches}, Spalding (LI)
54608	DBX 862	Mulliner	T68	B30F	7/47	HE Clarke (Clarke Bros) {Capel Evan Express}, Capel Evan (CR)
54612	HMN 217	Duple	43664	C29F	1/47	Collister's Garage Ltd, Douglas (IM)
54625	GAX 531	Duple	48106	C29F	7/47	EJ Parfitt {Parfitt's Motor Services}, Rhymney Bridge (MH)
54632	SS 6556	SMT		C29F	9/47	TW Wiles, Port Seton (EL)
54640	HVO 594	Duple	43833	C29F	7/47	GW Wright {GW Wright & Sons}, Keyworth (NG)
54649	* P-35308	Jongerius		B33-	-/47	Seegers, Maastricht (O-NL) 11
54661	* LJO 756	Duple	46745	C29F	7/47	South Midland, Oxford (OX) 43
54671	GTX 263	Duple	46818	C29F	8/47	C Lewis & J Jacob, Maesteg (GG)
54680	NRF 409	Duple	43592	C29F	8/47	Greatrex Motor Coaches Ltd, Stafford (ST) 35 Dipper
54690						Exported to Ireland
54697	CNL 312	Duple	43756	C29F	7/47	R Armstrong, Westerhope (ND) 47
54703	HYD 848	Duple	43309	C29F	7/47	JH Fursland & Co Ltd {Pride of Bridgwater}, Bridgwater (SO)
54707	DUJ 933	Duple	46445	C29F	7/47	SC & J Vagg {Vagg's Motors}, Knockin Heath (SH)
54716	DJY 6	Duple	43999	C29F	7/47	Plymouth Co-operative Society (DN) 510
54727	* GWR 46	Duple	44943	C29F	7/47	Walton & Helliwell Ltd, Mytholmroyd (WR)
54735	CFX 728	Duple	46349	C29F	7/47	AH Condon {Minuet Coaches}, Hamworthy (DT)
54744	* P-36203	Jongerius		B33-	-/47	Mevis, Nuth (O-NL) 9
54756	JKT 210	Thurgood	363	C29F	7/47	WE Penfold {Penfold & Brodie}, Green Street Green (KT)
54766	FWP 769	Duple	47573	C29F	7/47	CW Shuker {Lady Edith}, Halesowen (WO)
54775	JKO 754	Duple	43774	C29F	6/47	LR Hampshire {Eythorne & District}, Eythorne (KT)
54785	HYO 690	Duple	44434	C29F	7/47	George Ewer & Co Ltd {Grey Green}, London N16 (LN)
54792						Exported to Ireland
54798	DRX 723	Duple	43501	C29F	7/47	WE Kent, Baughurst (HA)
54802	DTP 212	Mulliner	T70	B32F	7/47	J Dyer {Yellow Bus Service}, Gosport (HA)
54811	SL 3073	SMT		C29F	8/47	W Dawson, Sauchie (CK)
54822	* KRB 68	Duple	46987	C29F	7/47	Midland General, Langley Mill (DE) 134
54830	EBU 24	Duple	48128	C29F	7/47	Shearings Tours Ltd, Oldham (LA)
54839	GRU 104	Duple	44842	C27F	7/47	Shamrock & Rambler Motor Coaches Ltd, Bournemouth (HA)
54851	* P-39844	Jongerius		B33-	12/47	Autobedrijf De Valk (Fl. Habets), Valkenburg (O-NL) 55
54861	FWO 613	Duple	46744	C29F	7/47	Red & White, Chepstow (MH) 813
54870	OMT 463	Duple	43827	C29F	7/47	Essex County Coaches Ltd, London E15 (LN)
54880						Exported to Ireland
54887	HYO 981	Duple	44464	C29F	8/47	Bradshaw's Super Coaches Ltd, London SE18 (LN)
54893	DUX 337	Mulliner	T91	B32F	8/47	Jones Coachways Ltd, Market Drayton (SH) 15
54897	SME 652	Duple	43921	C29F	7/47	Valliant Direct Coaches Ltd, London W5 (LN)
54906	HYK 237	Duple	44823	C27F	7/47	United Service Transport Co Ltd, London SW9 (LN) 1068

54917	BMS 93	SMT		C29F	9/47	W Alexander, Falkirk (SN) W209
54925	AWG 998	SMT		C29F	8/47	W Alexander, Falkirk (SN) W207
54934	* D-16286	Smit Appingedam	B30-		-/47	DABO, Meppel (O-NL) 2
54946	BMS 94	SMT		C29F	9/47	W Alexander, Falkirk (SN) W210
54956	* HMN 600	Duple	43665	C29F	6/47	WJ Purvis {Marguerite Rose}, Douglas (IM)
54965	* KKX 99	Thurgood	365	C29F	7/47	CJ Arnold {Glen Coaches}, Ibstone (BK)
54978	* ?	Duple	46152	C14F	-/47	OTC, Nairobi (O-EAK)
54982	NRF 175	Duple	43238	C29F	6/47	GH Austin & Sons Ltd {Happy Days}, Stafford (ST) 39
54988	HOF 757	Duple	43464	C29F	7/47	Smith's Imperial Coaches Ltd, Birmingham (WK)
54992	HMN 994	Pearson		C26F	9/47	FH Magee (Lily of the Valley), Douglas (IM)
55021 - 55024						Exported to Copenhagen (O-DK)
55025	JA 8024	Ørum-Pedersen		C25C	8/48	Tejn Turistfart, Tejn (O-DK) 64
55026 - 55032						Exported to Copenhagen (O-DK)
55153 - 55164						Exported to Sydney (O-AUS)
55201	EF 8093	Duple	44633	C29F	7/47	Bee-Line Roadways (Teeside) Ltd, West Hartlepool (DM)
55212	HYO 263	Mulliner	T73	B32F	7/47	BOAC (LN)
55220	DTP 218	Duple	47883	C29F	7/47	White Heather Transport Ltd, Southsea (HA)
55229	CRD 593	Mulliner	T72	B30F	9/47	Reading Corporation (BE) 70
55241	* E-37754	Smit Appingedam	B29-		6/47	NWH, Zwartsluis (O-NL) 71
55251	BMS 96	SMT		C29F	9/47	W Alexander, Falkirk (SN) W212
55260	HYO 496	Duple	44435	C29F	7/47	George Ewer & Co Ltd {Grey Green}, London N16 (LN)
55270	?	?	?		-/--	OMT, unknown location, East Africa
55277	HYO 495	Duple	44565	C29F	7/47	Fallowfield & Britten Ltd, London E8 (LN)
55283	HYM 648	Duple	48144	C29F	7/47	RJ Elliott, CF Savage & L King {Sidcup Coaches}, Sidcup (KT)
55287	CCT 596	Duple	43456	C29F	7/47	AL Moore, Sleaford (LI) 8
55293	HYH 919	Duple	44851	C27F	7/47	Keith & Boyle (London) Ltd {Orange Luxury Coaches}, London EC2 (LN) Snipe
55306	* GHP 581	Duple	43564	C29F	6/47	H & H Motorways Ltd {Bunty}, Coventry (WK)
55315	BMS 95	SMT		C29F	9/47	W Alexander, Falkirk (SN) W211
55324	* E-37756	Smit Appingedam	B29-		1/48	NWH, Zwartsluis (O-NL) 72
55341	GTX 69	Thurgood	364	C29F	7/47	Mrs AM Maisey, Church Village (GG)
55349	EDL 918	Duple	43586	C29F	7/47	West Wight Motor Bus Co Ltd, Totland Bay (IW)
55357	* ?	Smit Appingedam	B30-		9/47	DABO, Meppel (O-NL) 1
55365	* LPG 191	Duple	46314	C29F	7/47	SL Hayter {Yellow Bus Service}, Stoughton (SR)
55373	* EX 5818	Duple	44682	C29F	7/47	Norfolk Motor Services Ltd, Great Yarmouth (NK) 141
55381	* JWJ 532	Duple	47681	C27F	8/47	Sheffield United Tours (WR) 154
55389	EDL 956	Duple	43630	C29F	8/47	Fountain Garage Ltd, Cowes (IW)
55397	GTX 154	Duple	46819	C29F	8/47	FD Jones {Jones Bros}, Aberaman (GG)
55405	?	Duple	46153	C14F	-/--	OTC, Nairobi (O-EAK)
55413	HDV 415	Whitson	5794	C27F	8/47	Miller & Son (Exmouth) Ltd (DN)
55421	* FWM 33	KW		C27F	2/48	Howard Coaches Ltd, Southport (LA)
55428	HYO 264	Mulliner	T75	B32F	7/47	BOAC (LN)
55443	* ?	Smit Appingedam	B29-		-/47	DABO, Meppel (O-NL) 3
55451	* KUM 998	Plaxton	203	C30F	9/47	Kelsall Coaches Ltd {Saffman & Beasley}, Leeds (WR)
55461	EKW 874	Duple	43305	C29F	7/47	Feather Bros Ltd, Bradford (WR)
55467	* HVO 691	Duple	43301	C29F	7/47	G Gittins, Mansfield Woodhouse (NG)
55473	GRT 434	Duple	43682	C29F	7/47	RO Simonds, Botesdale (EK)
55480	FDK 573	Duple	44869	C27F	7/47	Yelloway Motor Services Ltd, Rochdale (LA)
55486	HYO 265	Mulliner	T74	B32F	7/47	BOAC (LN)
55491	HYN 688	Duple	44864	C29F	8/47	Cliff's Saloon Coaches Ltd, London SE9 (LN)
55494	?	?	?		-/--	OMT, Uganda (O-EAU)
55501	HYN 461	Duple	43912	C29F	7/47	WD Hall Ltd, London SW19 (LN)
55508	JFJ 179	Tiverton		C29F	5/48	Greenslades, Exeter (DN)
55524	KHW 121	Duple	44808	C27F	7/47	JG Vincent {Severn Valley Motors}, Bristol (GL)
55531	* SME 617	Duple	46842	C29F	7/47	Northern Roadways Ltd, Glasgow (LK)
55536	DEA 230	Duple	47774	C27F	8/47	Hills Tours Ltd, West Bromwich (ST) 11
55541	GRT 457	Duple	43466	C29F	7/47	BR Shreeve Ltd {Belle Coaches}, Lowestoft (EK)
55546	* HYO 706	Duple	44700	C29F	7/47	TG Green {Empress Motor Coaches}, London E2 (LN) 1
55552	HYP 775	Duple	46600	C29F	7/47	RB Shugg {Grove Coaches}, London SW2 (LN)
55559	SME 280	Duple	44679	C29F	7/47	RG Flexman {Flexman's Coaches}, Southall (MX)
55565	HFJ 507	Duple	43361	C29F	5/47	Greenslades, Exeter (DN)

C1252/67

55572						Exported to Malaya
55579	DUJ 934	Duple	46446	C29F	9/47	W, WE & JR Fisher, Bronington (FT)
55586	HX-2428	Van Peet		B29-	1/48	TP-RopdeL, Kinderdijk (O-NL) 21
55591	FDL 69	Pearson		C26F	5/48	Shotters Ltd, Brighstone (IW)
55597	EUK 540	Mulliner	T76	C29F	7/47	Worthington Motor Tours Ltd, Wolverhampton (ST)
55604	* HNY 566	Jeffreys		B32F	2/48	Afan Transport Co Ltd, Port Talbot (GG)
55611	HYD 963	Duple	43354	C29F	8/47	BJ Chinn {English Rose Coaches}, Wincanton (SO)
55618	* DUX 74	Duple	43716	C29F	7/47	FH Davies {Victory}, St Georges (SH)
55623	FDA 122	Duple	47868	C27F	2/47	L Barnett {Pathfinder}, Coseley (ST)
55631	* GDG 467	Duple	48196	C29F	8/47	A Bayliss, Dymock (GL)
55638	EEW 974	Duple	46304	C29F	7/47	SV Robinson, Kimbolton (HN)
55644						Exported to Malaya
55651	* BBV 809	SMT		C29F	9/47	J Wearden & Sons Ltd, Blackburn (LA)
55658	DUJ 931	Duple	43232	C29F	7/47	JT, FW & GE Whittle {JT Whittle & Sons}, Highley (SH)
55665	* HTE 624	SMT		C29F	10/47	Cross Street Motors (Lancaster) Ltd {Vista Coaches}, Morecambe (LA)
55675						Exported to Biel (O-CH)
55688	JKO 758	Mulliner	T71	B30F	7/47	EJ Banks, Sturry (KT)
55695						Exported to Biel (O-CH)
55699	CST 42	Mulliner	T67	B32F	8/47	J McCormack, Kingussie (IV)
55703	HUF 454	Duple	43768	C29F	7/47	T Camping, Brighton (ES)
55709	MVW 515	Duple	48212	C29F	1/48	Ashdown's Luxury Coaches Ltd, Danbury (EX) 36
55713	FDA 256	Mulliner	T77	C29F	9/47	Worthington Motor Tours Ltd, Wolverhampton (ST)
55717	FWP 847	Duple	46992	C29F	7/47	S Wright, Kidderminster (WO)
55723	* EMW 788	Lee		B31F	10/47	Skylark Motor Services Ltd, Salisbury (WI)
55728	GDV 940	Duple	46235	C26F	7/47	H & A Sleep, Bere Alston (DN)
55732	FT 6102	SMT		C29F	11/47	G Chapman {Priory Motor Coach Co}, North Shields (ND) 46
55737		see 55739				
55739	* MHK 525	Mulliner	T78	B28F	8/47	Shell Refining & Marketing Co, Shell Haven (XEX)
55747						Exported to Kenya
55752	GDV 923	Duple	46404	C29F	7/47	PA Norman {Kingston Coach Tours}, Combe Martin (DN)
55758	FDA 258	Mulliner	T84	C29F	9/47	Worthington Motor Tours Ltd, Wolverhampton (ST)
55765	MFC 951	Duple	43563	C29F	7/47	H Crapper & Son Ltd, Oxford (OX) 33
55771						Exported to Santiago (O-RCH)
55779	JHN 744	SMT		C29F	9/47	Favourite Direct Services Ltd, Bishop Auckland (DM) 6
55786	HUR 755	Duple	43490	C29F	8/47	AE Moule {Blue Cream Coaches}, Ashwell (HT)
55792	FOT 215	Duple	46796	C29F	7/47	R Chisnell & Sons Ltd {King Alfred Motor Services}, Winchester (HA)
55799	EDL 942	Duple	44030	C29F	7/47	SH, AC, PH & AR Randall (H Randall & Sons), Bonchurch (IW)
55805	HYP 720	Duple	44110	C29F	8/47	Birch Bros Ltd, London NW5 (LN) K20
55814	LPG 154	Duple	43345	C29F	7/47	Whiteley Homes Trust, Whiteley Village (XSR)
55819	JTU 13	Pearson		C26F	1/48	AE Bowyer & Son Ltd, Northwich (CH)
55826						Exported to Kenya
55832	HYO 985	Duple	46371	C29F	7/47	Bradshaw's Super Coaches Ltd, London SE18 (LN)
55838	JHN 902	SMT		C29F	9/47	Percival Bros (Coaches) Ltd, Richmond (NR)
55845	ECA 621	Duple	43600	C29F	8/47	JB Pye Ltd, Rhos-on-Sea (DH)
55853						Exported to Santiago (O-RCH)
55858	GBY 85	Duple	44523	C29F	7/47	John Bennett (Croydon) Ltd (SR) 1
55865	* HVU 243	SMT		C29F	9/47	AB McMurray {Carsville Private Coaches}, Manchester (LA)
55871	HXJ 103	SMT		C29F	9/47	C Holt, Manchester (LA)
55877	HTD 200	Duple	44860	C29F	7/47	Kia-Ora Motor Services Ltd, Morecambe (LA)
55883	EBU 106	SMT		C29F	7/47	Holt's Transport (Royton) Ltd (LA)
55894	* FFS 856	SMT		C29F	10/47	SMT (MN) C156
55900	HFJ 575	Duple	46935	C29F	8/47	J Potter & Sons {Tor Bus Service}, Haytor (DN)
55907						Exported to Malaya
55912	?	Mulliner	T81	?	8/47	Eagle Star Insurance Co, London (XLN)
55917	GTX 194	Duple	46817	C29F	7/47	CR Dobson, Ystrad Mynach (GG)
55924	HAH 171	Duple	43688	C29F	7/47	JC Brown {Norfolk Coachways}, Attleborough (NK)
55930	?	?		?	-/--	Anglo-Egyptian Oilfields, Suez (O-ET)
55937	DRP 100	Duple	46568	C29F	7/47	York Bros (Northampton) Ltd (NO) 13

55944	GAX 587	Duple	43910	C29F	7/47	C Collier {Collier's Garage}, Abertillery (MH)
55950	DBX 850	Duple	47919	C29F	7/47	TS Jenkins, Llanelly (CR)
55956	?	Mulliner	T79	B--F	7/47	London, Midland & Scottish Railway Co {LMS}, Watford (XHT)
55964	JKO 789	Duple	46576	C27F	7/47	Pilcher's Coaches Ltd, Chatham (KT)
55976	DTP 416	Duple	47802	C29F	7/47	Southsea Royal Blue Parlour Coaches Ltd (HA) 120
55982	DTP 417	Duple	46421	C29F	7/47	Southsea Royal Blue Parlour Coaches Ltd (HA) 123
55990						Exported to Malaya
55995	* LPG 109	Duple	44691	C29F	8/47	ER Gudge {Comfy Coaches}, Farnham (SR)
56001	GDG 392	Duple	47840	C29F	8/47	LM Norton {Norton Motor Services}, Lechlade (GL)
56008	JYA 109	Duple	44279	C27F	8/47	AE Harse {Westward Ho Coaches}, Weston-super-Mare (SO)
56015	?	?		?	-/--	Anglo-Egyptian Oilfields, Suez (O-ET)
56022	CRD 594	Mulliner	T82	B30F	11/47	Reading Corporation (BE) 71
56029	GRT 516	Duple	44290	C29F	8/47	VT & J Faiers {Clarke's Service}, Felixstowe (EK)
56035	JPT 529	Robson		C29F	7/48	JS Mowbray {Diamond Bus Service}, South Moor (DM)
56041	EDT 409	Mulliner	T80	B32F	8/47	R Store {Reliance}, Stainforth (WR)
56046	SMF 407	Pearson		C26F	3/48	Valliant Direct Coaches Ltd, London W5 (LN)
56054	EMW 141	Duple	43554	C29F	8/47	CH Thomas, Calne (WI)
56060	SMF 957	Duple	43918	C25F	8/47	Valliant Direct Coaches Ltd, London W5 (LN)
56067	?	Mulliner		B---	-/--	NV de Bataafsche Petroleum Mij, Pladjoe (O-RI)
56072	JKR 163	Duple	44724	C29F	8/47	H Dineley {Rapid Rover Garages & Coaches}, Margate (KT)
56078	EUK 892	Mulliner	T83	C29F	8/47	Worthington Motor Tours Ltd, Wolverhampton (ST)
56086	?	Mulliner		B---	-/--	NV de Bataafsche Petroleum Mij, Pladjoe (O-RI)
56091	NRF 552	Duple	47575	C29F	8/47	HL, DJ, E, PG & R Stanton {Stanton Bros} {Fountain Coaches}, Tipton (ST)
56099	AEE 578	Duple	46928	C29F	8/47	A & AE Blackbourn Ltd {Granville Tours}, Grimsby (LI) 143
56110	SMF 961	Duple	43911	C29F	8/47	Modern Super Coaches Ltd, London N9 (LN)
56120	HYO 271	Mulliner	T87	B32F	8/47	BOAC (LN)
56135	JRL 513	Duple	47788	C29F	8/47	HLA & MB Truscott {Truscott Bros}, Ruan High Lanes (CO)
56141	JKR 36	Duple	43588	C29F	8/47	Ashline Ltd {Ashline Coaches}, Tonbridge (KT)
56145	EBE 788	Duple	44096	C29F	8/47	F Hunt, Alford (LI)
56149	HYP 891	Duple	48157	C29F	8/47	PJ Elliott {Sidcup Coaches}, Sidcup (KT)
56154	* FOU 936	Duple	46608	C29F	8/47	Hants & Sussex Motor Services Ltd, Emsworth (HA) 121
56160	FOU 375	Duple	43725	C29F	8/47	O Porter, Dummer (HA)
56167						Exported to Takoradi (O-WAC)
56173	* GOV 580	Duple	44590	C29F	8/47	Burley's Garage Ltd, Birmingham (WK)
56177	* GZ-25926	Jongerius		B31-	-/47	Oorbeek, Edam (O-NL) 13
56183	* FWO 614	Duple	46746	C29F	8/47	Red & White, Chepstow (MH) 814
56194	HGK 447	Mulliner	T85	B32F	-/47	British Broadcasting Corporation {BBC}, London SW4 (XLN) B447
56200	AHF 82	Duple	46447	C29F	8/47	Mather's Motors Ltd, Wallasey (CH)
56261 - 56272						Exported to Bombay (O-IND)
56393 - 56404						Exported to Copenhagen (O-DK)
56489 - 56500						Exported to Melbourne (O-AUS)
56511	EWN 368	Duple	46805	C29F	8/47	D Tulk {John Tulk & Son}, Brynhyfryd (GG)
56529	* HYP 209	Duple	44819	C27F	9/47	United Service Transport Co Ltd, London SW9 (LN) 1069
56533	HYP 560	Duple	44438	C29F	8/47	George Ewer & Co Ltd {Grey Green}, London N16 (LN)
56538	* K-19152	Verheul	2499	B31-	2/48	AMZ-De Muynck, Borssele (O-NL) 39
56542	HYO 272	Mulliner	T86	B32F	8/47	BOAC (LN)
56546	HYP 559	Duple	44566	C29F	8/47	Fallowfield & Britten Ltd, London E8 (LN)
56553						Exported to Takoradi (O-WAC)
56559	SME 624	Duple	44006	C17F	8/47	CG Lewis {CG Lewis Safety Coaches}, London SE10 (LN)
56563	HEL 160	Duple	44843	C27F	9/47	Shamrock & Rambler Motor Coaches Ltd, Bournemouth (HA)
56570	CRD 842	Duple	44494	C29F	5/47	AE Smith {Smith's Coaches}, Reading (BE)
56577	EUK 893	Duple	46733	C29F	8/47	Worthington Motor Tours Ltd, Wolverhampton (ST) 116
56583	?	?		van	12/47	Fishpool, Waltham Cross (GHT)

C1252/69

56590	DUJ 935	Duple	43765	C29F	8/47 RG, FJ, DA & K Cooper {G Cooper & Sons}, Oakengates (SH)
56597	* ?	Hoekstra		B33-	-/47 Bax, Groenlo (O-NL) 2
56605	* JWJ 533	Duple	47682	C27F	8/47 Sheffield United Tours (WR) 155
56612	BDO 644	Duple	48253	C29F	8/47 RL Cropley {Blue Glider Bus Service}, Sutterton (LI)
56619	* CFV 415	SMT		C29F	10/47 Whiteside Ltd, Blackpool (LA)
56624	DNV 983	Duple	43481	C29F	8/47 GT Owen & Sons Ltd, Upper Boddington (NO)
56629	JNA 4	Pearson		C26F	10/47 Sykes' Motor Tours Ltd, Sale (CH)
56636	BRN 361	SMT		C29F	5/48 Scout MS Ltd, Preston (LA)
56642	NRF 410	Duple	48213	C29F	8/47 Greatrex Motor Coaches Ltd, Stafford (ST) 36 Snipe
56649	HTF 74	SMT		C29F	10/47 Tower Motors Ltd, Morecambe (LA)
56659	GWR 365	SMT		C29F	10/47 G Pyne {White Coach Tours}, Starbeck (WR)
56663					Exported to Rotterdam (O-NL)
56672	FF 6737	Duple	48204	C29F	8/47 DE Davies Ltd {Welshways Tour}, Barmouth (ME)
56678	* GDG 700	Duple	44697	C29F	8/47 Mrs K Riddiford, Thornbury (GL)
56685	* HMN 601	SMT		C29F	6/47 Mrs E Clague (A & E Clague) {Esplanade de Luxe Coaches}, Douglas (IM) 1
56692	FOU 483	Duple	48211	C29F	8/47 C Bailey {Bailey's Ringwood Coaches}, Ringwood (HA)
56703	HYP 210	Duple	44820	C27F	9/47 United Service Transport Co Ltd, London SW9 (LN) 1070
56709	* L-34219	Domburg	135	B27D	2/49 GVU, Utrecht (O-NL) 2
56716	JTU 42	Duple	44662	C29F	8/47 J & H Coppenhall Ltd, Sandbach (CH)
56722	HAH 338	Duple	43683	C29F	9/47 EE Smith & Sons Ltd, Attleborough (NK)
56729	JKR 636	Duple	46918	C29F	9/47 Mrs S Solomon {Blue Rambler Coaches}, Cliftonville (KT)
56735	?	?		van	-/-- ART Ltd, location unknown
56741	DPM 371	Duple	47874	C29F	8/47 H Gilbert, Crowborough (ES)
56749	HDV 320	Duple	46237	C29F	11/47 JH Clark {Tally Ho! Coaches}, East Allington (DN)
56760	#LNW 827	ACB		C26F	12/47 Kelsall Coaches Ltd {Saffman & Beasley}, Leeds (WR)
56769	GHP 937	Duple	46351	C29F	7/47 Wainfleet Motor Services Ltd, Nuneaton (WK)
56777	EWN 18	Duple	46747	C29F	8/47 United Welsh, Swansea (GG) 918
56783	CVG 219	Duple	44708	C27F	12/48 HA & Mrs ME Roberts {Red Car Service}, Norwich (NK)
56789	LPH 403	Duple	46315	C29F	7/47 SL Hayter {Yellow Bus Service}, Stoughton (SR)
56796	MNO 290	Duple	44395	C29F	8/47 L Hall & Sons, Maldon (EX)
56802	* D-16933	Smit Appingedam		B29-	-/47 DABO, Meppel (O-NL) 5
56810	?	Mulliner	T88	?	-/-- BOAC, unknown overseas location
56814	HYO 988	Duple	46368	C29F	8/47 Bradshaw's Super Coaches Ltd, London SE18 (LN)
56818	CUD 365	Duple	44484	C29F	7/47 H Shurey, Nettlebed (OX)
56826	* BRN 190	Duple	48142	C29F	8/47 W Wrigley, Droylesden (LA)
56830	DRP 101	Duple	46569	C29F	8/47 York Bros (Northampton) Ltd (NO) 14
56837	JWJ 534	Duple	47683	C27F	8/47 Sheffield United Tours (WR) 156
56844	CNL 417	Duple	43757	C29F	8/47 R Armstrong, Westerhope (ND) 48
56849	BBV 896	SMT		C29F	10/47 W Barnes Ltd, Rishton (LA)
56854	GCE 69	Duple	48160	C29F	9/47 AE, WI & PL Harris {Progressive}, Cambridge (CM)
56860	* DTP 948	Reading	?	C27F	12/47 PW Lambert {Little Wonder Coaches}, Petersfield (HA)
56866	JDE 6	Duple	47959	C29F	9/47 DH Roberts & Sons {Pioneer Motor Services}, Newport (PE)
56870					Exported to Port Elizabeth (O-ZA)
56873	?	Churchill		?	7/47 BOAC, unknown overseas location
56881	* SMF 632	Duple	44555	C29F	7/47 AR & Mrs EF Thorne {Thorne Bros}, London SW2 (LN)
56888	?	Churchill		-30-	3/48 BOAC, unknown overseas location
56895	HDV 496	Duple	43366	C29F	8/47 RW Cure {Sunbeam Motor Tours}, Torquay (DN)
56902	KHW 501	Duple	44034	C27F	8/47 TJ King {Monarch Coaches}, Bristol (GL)
56909	DET 779	SMT		C29F	10/47 E Roe, Wickersley (WR)
56916	EX 5870	Duple	44683	C29F	8/47 Norfolk Motor Services Ltd, Great Yarmouth (NK) 146
56924					Exported to Antwerp (O-B)
56931	DRP 289	Duple	43303	C29F	8/47 ART Head {Reliance Coaches}, Lutton (NO)
56938	HYN 700	Duple	44862	C29F	9/47 V Bingley {Bingley Bros} {Sceptre Coaches}, London W6 (LN)
56944	JAR 111	Thurgood	400	C29F	8/47 Dye & Sons, Hertford (HT)
56951					Exported to Port Elizabeth (O-ZA)
56955	DUX 355	Duple	46449	C29F	8/47 AT Brown, Trench (SH)
56962	SMF 8	Duple	44195	C27F	9/47 Ardley Bros Ltd, London N17 (LN) 2
56969	HOH 922	Duple	43382	C29F	8/47 Sandwell Motor Co Ltd, Birmingham (WK)

C1252/70

56976	HYN 699	Duple	44192	C29F	9/47	AP Downs, Worcester Park (SR)
56983	JP 6500	SMT		C29F	10/47	Stringfellow Bros {Silver Queen}, Wigan (LA)
56990	EVJ 439	Duple	46453	C29F	8/47	WE Morgan {Wye Valley Motors}, Hereford (HR)
56996	HDV 416	Duple	46402	C27F	8/47	Waldron Bros {Heather Coaches}, Ilfracombe (DN)
57004	* E-37757	Smit Appingedam		B29-	-/47	NWH, Zwartsluis (O-NL) 73
57011	ECO 746	Mashford		C29F	6/48	Millbrook Steamboat & Trading Co Ltd (CO)
57018	EDL 641	Duple	47831	C29F	5/48	Southern Vectis, Newport (IW) 212
57024	EDL 973	Duple	43901	C29F	9/47	Fountain Garage Ltd, Cowes (IW)
57031	* JTU 888	Pearson		C26F	10/47	Watson's (Winsford) Motor Services Ltd (CH)
57036	JAL 123	Duple	48270	C29F	8/47	R Wain, Mansfield (NG)
57043	HDV 75	Duple	46936	C27F	7/47	Mrs WA Hart, Budleigh Salterton (DN)
57050	FEW 55	Duple	46897	C29F	9/47	H Lee {Whippet Coaches}, Hilton (HN)
57057						Exported to Freetown (O-WAL)
57064	GTX 551	Duple	48278	C29F	9/47	T Phillips, Seven Sisters (GG)
57071	JYA 630	Duple	48214	C29F	8/47	AA Woodbury, Wellington (SO)
57078	GAB 2	Duple	47723	C29F	8/47	WC Greenhill, Kidderminster (WO)
57086	EAY 881	Duple	43304	C29F	8/47	HJ & AJ Barkus (Barkus & Son), Woodhouse Eaves (LE)
57093	GTX 274	Duple	46820	C29F	9/47	RF & DT Burrows, Ogmore Vale (GG)
57100	* ?	Smit Appingedam		B29-	-/47	DABO, Meppel (O-NL) 4
57106	EVJ 441	Duple	43317	C29F	9/47	AE Bengry {Primrose Motor Services}, Leominster (HR)
57113	EFU 571	Plaxton	206	C29F	12/47	C, JE, T & T Hudson {Hudson's Bus Co}, Horncastle (LI)
57117	* SMF 410	Pearson		FC26F	3/48	Valliant Direct Coaches Ltd, London W5 (LN)
57124	GDG 877	Thurgood	397	C29F	10/47	ACJ Perrett {Perrett's Coaches}, Shipton Oliffe (GL)
57131	* P-41539	Den Oudsten	1671	B33-	5/48	Meussen, Maastricht (O-NL) 16
57138	JRL 635	Duple	47787	C29F	9/47	RA Richards {Truronian}, Truro (CO)
57145	HTE 528	Duple	48909	C29F	9/47	J Davies, Leigh (LA)
57152						Exported to Freetown (O-WAL)
57159	EDL 642	Duple	47832	C29F	6/48	Southern Vectis, Newport (IW) 213
57167	GAB 168	Plaxton	319	FC30F	9/47	Mrs ME Ward {Ward's Super de Luxe}, Sidemoor (WO)
57174	OMT 150	Duple	44716	C29F	8/47	Webber {Empire's Best}, London N22 (LN) 18
57181	?	Mulliner	T89	?	-/--	BOAC, unknown overseas location
57187	HUR 664	Duple	48250	C29F	9/47	EG Hewitt {Premier Coaches}, Watford (HT)
57194	GAB 167	Plaxton	323	FC30F	9/47	Mrs ME Ward {Ward's Super de Luxe}, Sidemoor (WO)
57199	CTY 146	Plaxton	600	FC30F	12/47	Bedlington & District Luxury Coaches Ltd, Ashington (ND)
57205	HYP 681	Mulliner	T90	B32F	8/47	British South American Airways, London SW1 (XLN)
57212	EMW 490	Duple	43556	C29F	8/47	PJ & D Card, Devizes (WI)
57219	?	Duple	46154	C14F	-/--	OTC, Nairobi (O-EAK)
57226	JMN 113	Pearson		C26F	10/47	TH Kneen Junior {The Falcon}, Douglas (IM)
57233	SMF 596	Duple	43310	C29F	9/47	LC Davis & Sons Ltd, London SW16 (LN)
57240	CFX 977	Duple	44098	C29F	8/47	T Lawley & Son {Grosvenor Coaches}, Gillingham (DT)
57252	* K-20257	Verheul	2476	B31-	3/48	SBM, Aardenburg (O-NL) 26
57257	DUX 160	Mulliner	T92	B32F	7/47	Jones Coachways Ltd, Market Drayton (SH) 14
57262	JXH 720	Pearson		C26F	4/48	Fallowfield & Britten Ltd, London E8 (LN)
57268	FSG 280	Mulliner	T93	B28F	9/47	A Dunsmuir, Tranent (EL)
57275	FWW 597	Duple	46809	C26F	9/47	West Yorkshire RCC, Harrogate (WR) 647
57279	EAY 882	Duple	43308	C29F	9/47	D Jacques, Coalville (LE)
57286	AEE 760	Plaxton	687	C29F	10/47	FA & WR Stark (FA Stark and Sons), Tetney (LI)
57293	DUX 356	Duple	46450	C29F	8/47	AJ Boulton {Arthur Boulton's Bus Service}, Cardington (SH)
57300	H 8515	Duple	46155	C21F	1/48	OTC, Nairobi (O-EAK)
57307	JYA 268	Duple	43468	C29F	8/47	RE Wake {Wake's Services}, Sparkford (SO)
57314	GWT 206	Plaxton	649	C29F	9/47	AS Howick & J Hargreaves, Hebden (WR)
57321	* KRB 69	Duple	46988	C29F	7/47	Midland General, Langley Mill (DE) 141
57329	* HZ-43871	Den Oudsten	1682	B30-	5/48	JL de Jong, Rotterdam (O-NL) 4
57336	DTP 413	Duple	44293	C29F	9/47	The Don Motor Coach Co Ltd, Southsea (HA)
57343	GAA 210	Duple	46911	C29F	9/47	Lovegrove & Lovegrove Ltd, Silchester (HA)
57349	JC 8745	Thurgood	398	C29F	9/47	Penmaenmawr Motor Co Ltd (CN)
57356	* HYR 257	Duple	43900	C29F	9/47	Camden Coaches Ltd, Edgware (MX)
57360	HPT 642	Mulliner	T94	B32F	9/47	Sherburn Hill Co-operative Society (Burn Line), Sherburn (DM)

C1252/71

57367	GRM 378	Mulliner	T97	B31F	8/47	E Hartness {Hartness Bus & Coach Service}, Penrith (CU)
57374	SMF 954	Duple	43919	C29F	9/47	Valliant Direct Coaches Ltd, London W5 (LN)
57384	* K-20256	Verheul	2475	B31-	2/48	SBM, Aardenburg (O-NL) 74
57388	CUD 568	Duple	43329	C29F	9/47	AR Taylor, Bicester (OX) 8
57395	HNG 99	Duple	43576	C29F	11/47	F Randall, Wigginhall St Mary Magdalen (NK)
57402	EMW 165	Duple	48252	C27F	9/47	H Little, Winsley (WI)
57410	JC 8509	Duple	43602	C29F	9/47	J Williams & Son {Red Garage}, Portmadoc (CN)
57417	JKR 510	Duple	46332	C29F	9/47	PJ Elliott {Sidcup Coaches}, Sidcup (KT)
57424						Exported to Georgetown (O-MAL)
57430	* JAL 30	Duple	46998	C29F	9/47	Barton Transport, Chilwell (NG) 525
57437	GWT 509	Mulliner	T95	B31F	9/47	EL Thompson {Advance}, Swinefleet (WR)
57441	GDG 717	Duple	46696	C29F	9/47	FP Russell {A Russell & Son}, Wormington (GL)
57448	HYP 901	Duple	44436	C29F	9/47	George Ewer & Co Ltd {Grey Green}, London N16 (LN)
57455	HYO 990	Duple	48346	C29F	9/47	Cliff's Saloon Coaches Ltd, London SE9 (LN)
57462	ACP 729	Ireland		C29F	3/48	Den-Roy Coaches Ltd, Hebden Bridge (WR)
57469	GBY 567	Duple	44524	C29F	9/47	John Bennett (Croydon) Ltd (SR) 2
57476	* E-27960	Smit Appingedam		B29-	-/48	NWH, Zwartsluis (O-NL) 74
57485	* HYP 211	Duple	44821	C27F	9/47	United Service Transport Co Ltd, London SW9 (LN) 1071
57491	?	?		van	-/--	Original operator unknown
57498	HOH 920	Plaxton	601	FC30F	1/48	EH & PH Ludlow {Ludlow Bros}, Birmingham (WK)
57505						Exported to Georgetown (O-MAL)
57511	* GWT 716	Plaxton	686	C29F	9/47	Kirkby & Sons (Harthill) Ltd (WR)
57518	KDH 804	Plaxton	209	C29F	10/47	JN & FN Boult {John Boult & Sons}, Walsall (ST) 34
57522	CFK 274	?		van	3/48	Quality Cleaners Ltd, Worcester (GWO)
57529	HYP 847	Duple	47593	C27F	9/47	Frames Tours Ltd, London WC1 (LN) 72
57536	* LPU 628	Duple	47670	C29F	9/47	Eastern National, Chelmsford (EX) 3938
57543	DUX 473	Mulliner	T96	B29F	8/47	J Williamson {The Green Bus Service}, Shrewsbury (SH)
57550	JYA 387	Duple	43390	C29F	9/47	DJ Pratten {Waverley Coaches}, Weston-super-Mare (SO)
57557	* A-35170	Smit Appingedam		B29-	-/47	ESA, Marum (O-NL) 53
57564	FFH 293	Duple	48255	C29F	9/47	FOJ & RJ Bevan (Bevan Bros){Soudley Valley Coaches}, Soudley (GL)
57572	GWT 340	Duple	43307	C29F	9/47	W Simpson, Ripon (WR) 2
57579	MNO 901	Duple	47601	C29F	9/47	Wiffen's Coaches Ltd, Finchingfield (EX)
57586						Exported to Georgetown (O-MAL)
57594	PV 8261	Duple	43314	C29F	9/47	GS Morley, Ipswich (WF)
57599	CAN 155	Duple	44722	C29F	10/47	WB Clark & TV Edworthy (Clark & Son) {Clark's Red Coaches}, London E7 (LN)
57603	KLG 70	Pearson		C29F	11/47	G West {Reliance Motor Services}, Kelsall (CH)
57610	HVR 631	Mulliner	T98	B32F	9/47	Altrincham Coachways Ltd (CH)
57617	HTE 958	SMT		C29F	12/47	E Marsden {E Marsden & Sons Motors}, Manchester (LA)
57624	CNL 566	Duple	43623	C29F	9/47	CR Robson, Smelting Syke (ND) 19
57631	CUD 724	Plaxton	212	C26F	11/47	RS Hall, Deddington (OX)
57638						Exported to Alexandria (O-ET)
57645	JTU 170	Duple	48311	C29F	9/47	AE & RI Niddrie, Middlewich (CH)
57653						Exported to Georgetown (O-MAL)
57660	HAD 151	Duple	43719	C29F	10/47	CAJ Scarrott {Luxury Coaches}, Stow-on-the-Wold (GL)
57667	XS 6185	SMT		C29F	11/47	Young's Bus Service Ltd, Paisley (RW) 161
57673	* FFS 863	SMT		C29F	11/47	SMT (MN) C163
57680	DUX 357	Duple	46452	C29F	9/47	J & HG Phillips {J Phillips & Son}, Rhostyllen (DH)
57684	* HPT 917	Mulliner	T99	B31F	9/47	F Wilson, Hunwick (DM)
57694		see 57684				
57691	* FFS 864	SMT		C29F	11/47	SMT (MN) C164
57699	JWJ 535	Duple	47684	C27F	6/49	Sheffield United Tours (WR) 157
57741	FGD 203	SMT		C29F	10/47	Northern Roadways Ltd, Glasgow (LK)
57748	HNG 625	Plaxton	282	C29F	11/47	R & WC Doughty (R Doughty & Sons) {Ever Ready}, Kings Lynn (NK)
57755						Exported to Alexandria (O-ET)
57762	FFY 776	SMT		C27F	10/47	Southport & Birkdale Motor Carriage Co {Gore}, Southport (LA)

C1252/72

57770	#					Exported to Hong Kong
57777	* KWB 5	Plaxton	283	FC30F	11/47	W, J & R Anderson (Anderson Bros), Sheffield (WR)
57784	AGV 653	Thurgood	399	B29F	9/47	WT Norfolk, Nayland (WF)
57790	PV 8172	Plaxton	619	C29F	12/47	P & M Coaches Ltd, Ipswich (WF) 36
57797	* KWB 6	Plaxton	213	FC30F	11/47	W, J & R Anderson (Anderson Bros), Sheffield (WR)
57801	* FFS 865	SMT		C29F	11/47	SMT (MN) C165
57808	* FFS 858	SMT		C29F	10/47	SMT (MN) C158
57816	* FFS 857	SMT		C29F	10/47	SMT (MN) C157
57822	#EBU 157	SMT		C29F	3/48	Gregory & Richards Ltd, Oldham (LA)
57829	KAF 484	Plaxton	618	C29F	12/47	WA Hawkey & Sons Ltd, Wadebridge (CO)
57836	?	?		?	-/--	Wilhelm Nielsen, Tórshavn (O-FR)
57843	KDH 805	Plaxton	210	C29F	10/47	JN & FN Boult {John Boult & Sons}, Walsall (ST) 35
57851	#					Exported to Hong Kong
57858	* EFU 575	Plaxton	317	C30F	1/48	HE Sheriff & SC Hayward {Star Services}, Gainsborough (LI)
57865	HPT 504	SMT		C29F	10/47	SM Pinnington & Son, Crook (DM)
57871	HVF 160	Thurgood	453	C29F	2/48	GV Carter {BM & KT Carter}, Litcham (NK)
57878	* FFS 862	SMT		C29F	11/47	SMT (MN) C162
57882	* FFS 861	SMT		C29F	11/47	SMT (MN) C161
57889	JTB 262	Plaxton	602	FC30F	12/47	WH Cornish {Wilton Garage}, Denton (LA)
57897	* FFS 860	SMT		C29F	11/47	SMT (MN) C160
57906	SMF 380	Thurgood	402	C29F	10/47	H Holmes {Horseshoe Coaches}, London N15 (LN)
57912	KLG 529	Plaxton	265	FC30F	1/48	R Bullock & Co (Transport) Ltd, Cheadle (CH)
57918	* FFS 859	SMT		C29F	10/47	SMT (MN) C159
57924	LNW 623	SMT		C29F	11/47	Wallace Arnold, Leeds (WR)
57932	?	?		van	-/--	Hedges, Blackpool (GLA)
57939	AEB 49	Duple	43321	C29F	9/47	JR Morley & Sons Ltd, Whittlesey (CM)
57946	FDL 23	Duple	44597	C29F	9/47	H Paul (H Paul & Son), Ryde (IW) 3
57952	BRN 362	SMT		C29F	5/48	Scout MS Ltd, Preston (LA)
57959	* GWT 403	Mulliner	T101	B30F	4/47	Clifford Lunn, Rothwell (WR)
57963	HNG 626	Plaxton	616	C29F	7/48	W Carter, Marham (NK)
57970	* HYR 297	Duple	44671	C25F	9/47	Cream Coaches Ltd, London E8 (LN) 11
57978	HMN 774	SMT		C29F	7/47	GW Wharton {Highlander}, Douglas (IM)
57984	KWA 729	SMT		C29F	11/47	EH Sims, Sheffield (WR)
57991	* EU 8714	Mulliner	T100	B32F	9/47	E & TW Jones (J Jones & Sons), Ystradgynlais (BC)
58000	BCB 96	Plaxton	320	FC30F	1/48	Ribblesdale Coachways Ltd, Blackburn (LA) 20
58049 - 58060						Exported to Bombay (O-IND)
58125	EJU 136	Duple	43461	C29F	9/47	JS Astill & T Jordan {Ratby Service}, Ratby (LE)
58133	FSP 327	SMT		C29F	11/47	Meldrum & Dawson, Dunfermline (FE)
58139	* HUO 686	Duple	47674	C27F	9/47	Southern National, Exeter (DN) 533
58148						Exported to Antwerp (O-B)
58157	FWO 615	Duple	46748	C29F	9/47	Red & White, Chepstow (MH) 815
58162	JWJ 536	Duple	47685	C27F	6/49	Sheffield United Tours (WR) 158
58172	HYR 1	Duple	44194	C29F	8/47	AC Coaches Ltd, London SE15 (LN)
58177	GAC 767	Duple	43462	C29F	9/47	W Hill, Stockingford (WK)
58187	SMF 605	Duple	43922	C29F	11/47	Valliant Direct Coaches Ltd, London W5 (LN)
58217	JC 8725	Duple	46448	C29F	9/47	CJ Roberts {Purple Motors}, Bethesda (CN)
58224	DUX 584	Duple	43224	C29F	9/47	SC & J Vagg {Vagg's Motors}, Knockin Heath (SH)
58228	* HYR 298	Duple	44672	C25F	1/48	Cream Coaches Ltd, London E8 (LN) 18
58232						Exported to Antwerp (O-B)
58236	GAA 232	Duple	46527	C29F	9/47	GC, FW & GR Warren {Altonian Coaches}, Alton (HA)
58240	SMY 256	Whitson	?	C29F	3/48	Wright Bros (London) Ltd, London W7 (LN)
58247	* N-20761	Van Leersum		C32F	-/47	Autobedrijf Van Dongen, Zeeland (O-NL) 6
58252	LPH 482	Duple	43346	C29F	10/47	Walton on Thames Motor Co Ltd (SR)
58259	* HEL 412	Duple	44193	C27F	1/48	Shamrock & Rambler Motor Coaches Ltd, Bournemouth (HA)
58269	FJW 101	Mulliner	T105	C28F	1/48	Worthington Motor Tours Ltd, Wolverhampton (ST)
58274	HAH 825	Duple	43691	C27F	9/47	BG Day & Sons {Red Rover}, Aldborough (NK)
58284	EKY 703	Plaxton	318	C29F	12/47	Feather Bros Ltd, Bradford (WR)
58293	DTH 960	Duple	48335	C29F	3/48	DS & WJ Davies {Davies Bros}, Pencader (CR) 26
58304	BCB 97	Plaxton	324	FC30F	3/48	Ribblesdale Coachways Ltd, Blackburn (LA) 21
58308	SMF 655	Duple	44388	C29F	9/47	Batten's Coaches Ltd, London E6 (LN)
58317	* ?	Smit Appingedam		B29-	-/48	DABO, Meppel (O-NL) 9
58328	EFU 82	Duple	46299	C29F	10/47	JS & Mrs CE Millard {Ubique Coaches}, Brigg (LI)

C1252/73

58333	GTX 584	Duple	46821	C29F	9/47	Steven Probert (Aberdare) Ltd (GG)
58342	JMN 129	Pearson		C26F	10/47	JR Crellin {Castle Rushen Motors}, Castletown (IM)
58349	OMY 837	Pearson		C26-	11/47	Heybrook Bay Motor Services Ltd, Down Thomas (DN)
58356	KHW 869	Duple	44227	C29F	10/47	H Russett {Royal Blue}, Bristol (GL)
58366	* ?	?		B30-	-/47	K Wolf, Nijmegen (O-NL) 1
58371	SMF 654	Duple	44319	C29F	9/47	Venture Transport (Hendon) Ltd, London NW2 (LN)
58381	* ?	?		(goods ?)	8/47	Venture Transport (Hendon) Ltd, London NW2 (GLN)
58390	GWU 653	Barnaby		C27F	1/48	J & R Laycock {E Laycock & Sons}, Barnoldswick (WR) 46
58401	FDL 68	Pearson		C26F	5/48	Shotters Ltd, Brighstone (IW)
58405	JC 8845	Pearson		C26F	2/48	J Williams & Son {Red Garage}, Portmadoc (CN)
58414	CRD 595	Mulliner	T102	B30F	11/47	Reading Corporation (BE) 72
58425	* E-34070	Smit Appingedam		B29-	-/48	NWH, Zwartsluis (O-NL) 76
58430	FJW 104	Mulliner	T103	C28F	1/48	Worthington Motor Tours Ltd, Wolverhampton (ST)
58439	EJF 919	Plaxton	321	FC30F	1/48	AA Mason, Leicester (LE)
58446	CJT 185	Duple	44003	C27F	10/47	Gibbs & Hillyer, Beaminster (DT)
58453	KKK 373	Plaxton	248	FC30F	3/48	GR Ayers, Dover (KT)
58463	* M-29849	Jongerius		B31-	-/47	Van Maanen, Harderwijk (O-NL) 9
58468	EF 8223	Plaxton	322	FC30F	1/48	Longhorn & Peterson {L&P Luxury Coaches}, West Hartlepool (DM)
58478	?	?		h/box	-/--	Lord Astor, Cliveden (GBK)
58487	LRA 310	Duple	48304	C29F	10/47	E, E & H Webster {E Webster & Sons}, Hognaston (DE)
58498	HOJ 662	Duple	43381	C29F	9/47	Dalton's Garage Ltd, Birmingham (WK)
58549 - 58560						Exported to Bombay (O-IND)
58598	EM 4227	Pearson		C26F	2/48	T Lawrenson Ltd, Bootle (LA)
58607	GAB 497	Duple	43723	C29F	9/47	AW Tipping {Victory}, Lower Wyche (WO)
58618	* E-48219	Jongerius		B33-	-/47	WATO, Nijverdal (O-NL) 10
58623	FJW 102	Mulliner	T104	C28F	1/48	Worthington Motor Tours Ltd, Wolverhampton (ST)
58631	CRD 978	Duple	44495	C29F	2/48	AE Smith {Smith's Coaches}, Reading (BE)
58639	EX 5874	Duple	44684	C29F	9/47	Norfolk Motor Services Ltd, Great Yarmouth (NK) 145
58646	OMY 838	Pearson		C26F	12/47	F Wightman, Saxmundham (SK)
58660	FTM 367	Duple	47837	C29F	9/47	OA Bartle & Co, Potton (BD) B/47/2
58670	CRG 991	SMT		C29F	11/47	J Simpson jnr {Heatherbell Coach Tours}, Aberdeen (AD)
58679	LPU 629	Duple	47671	C29F	1/48	Eastern National, Chelmsford (EX) 3939
58685	* ?	De Jong Groot Ammers		B30-	-/47	Janse Groot Ammers (O-NL) 2
58691	BRN 494	SMT		C29F	5/48	Scout MS Ltd, Preston (LA)
58695	EF 8165	Duple	44634	C29F	9/47	Bee-Line Roadways (Teeside) Ltd, West Hartlepool (DM)
58704	* KRB 70	Duple	46989	C29F	7/47	Midland General, Langley Mill (DE) 148
58715	* E-33637	Smit Appingedam		C29F	-/48	NWH, Zwartsluis (O-NL) 75
58720	* FFS 868	SMT		C29F	11/47	SMT (MN) C168
58729	KHN 79	SMT		C29F	11/47	Anderson Bros {Blue Belle}, Evenwood (DM)
58736	?	?		l/stock	-/--	Original operator unknown
58743	HYP 688	Mulliner	T108	B31F	9/47	BOAC (LN)
58753	* K-19049	Verheul	2488	B31-	2/48	AMZ-De Muynck, Borssele (O-NL) 36
58758	HYP 686	Mulliner	T106	B31F	9/47	BOAC (LN)
58768	DCX 738	SMT		C29F	11/47	Hanson's Buses Ltd, Huddersfield (WR) 237
58777	* JNB 53	Pearson		C26F	12/47	Altrincham Coachways Ltd (CH)
58788	HTF 255	SMT		C29F	11/47	R Wood & Sons (Tours) Ltd, Ashton-under-Lyne (LA)
58792	HYP 687	Mulliner	T107	B31F	10/47	BOAC (LN)
58801	#HFJ 834	Duple	43362	C29F	12/47	H & EA Belcher Ltd {Empress Coaches}, Teignmouth (DN)
58812	* K-20258	Verheul	2477	B31-	3/48	SBM, Aardenburg (O-NL) 27
58817	* SB 7161	SMT		C27F	11/47	Hartley's Silver Line Motors, Dunoon (AL)
58826	* JP 6591	SMT		C29F	11/47	Gray Bros (Wigan) Ltd {Streamline Coaches}, Ince (LA)
58833	EVJ 572	Mulliner	T112	B29F	10/47	JH, HJ & GH Yeomans {Yeomans Motors}, Canon Pyon (HR) 61
58840	CCT 954	Mulliner	T111	B31F	9/47	Sharpe's Motors (Heckington) Ltd (LI)
58850	* A 32264	Smit Appingedam		B29F	-/47	ESA, Marum (O-NL) 52
58855	JMN 130	Pearson		C26F	10/47	WAL Cregeen, Port Erin (IM) 1
58865	JTU 381	SMT		C29F	8/48	F Brazendale {Pride of Sale Motor Tours}, Sale (CH)
58874	BGS 538	McLennan		C29F	6/48	A & C McLennan, Spittalfield (PH)

C1252/74

58885	?	?	van	-/--	Original operator unknown
58889	* HXJ 496	SMT	C29F	11/47	Wilmslow Motor Co Ltd (CH)
58898	GR 9616	Pearson	C29F	12/47	Taylor {Blue Arrow}, Gateshead (DM)
58909	* P-34004	Jongerius	B33-	12/46	Jansen, Maastricht (O-NL) 12
58914					Exported to Port Elizabeth (O-ZA)
58923	* KLG 391	Pearson	C26F	1/48	A Mealor, Ellesmere Port (CH)
58930	JTV 774	Duple 43573	C29F	9/47	E Horton, Retford (NG)
58937	* CWH 525	?	C29F	3/48	Holden's Carriage Co Ltd, Bolton (LA)
58947	* ?	?	?	-/48	Scheven, Emmercompascuum (O-NL)
58952	HYP 690	Mulliner T110	B31F	9/47	BOAC (LN)
58962	ZH 9892	GJ Roberts	C25F	-/--	Corais Iompair Eireann, Dublin (EI) BP1
58971	HYP 689	Mulliner T109	B31F	7/47	BOAC (LN)
58985	* EMO 6	Mulliner T268	B30F	6/48	A Moore & Sons {Imperial Bus Service}, Windsor (BE)
59085, 59086					Exported to Wellington (O-NZ)
59087	* ?	NZMB	B--F	-/46	Jamieson Motors Ltd, Stratford (O-NZ) 12
59088	* ?	?	?	-/--	Madge Motors Ltd, Palmerston North (O-NZ) 16
59089	* ?	Nuttall	B29F	-/47	Madge Motors Ltd, Palmerston North (O-NZ) 8
59090	* P.680	North Shore	B33F	6/48	Waitemata Bus & Transport Co Ltd, Auckland (O-NZ) 7
59091	* P.915	Tauranga Bus Service	B46F	-/47	Tauranga Bus Service, Tauranga (O-NZ) 5
59092					Exported to Wellington (O-NZ)
59093	* ?	NZMB	B35F	2/48	New Zealand Railways Road Services (O-NZ) 1521
59094	H7.491	?	tower	-/49	Auckland Transport Board (O-NZ) 6
59095					Exported to Wellington (O-NZ)
59096	* P.358	Auckland TB	FB33F	11/48	Auckland Transport Board (O-NZ) 23
59110					Exported to Port Elizabeth (O-ZA)
59115	BMS 293	Mulliner T113	B28F	9/47	Ardgour & Acharacle Motor Services Ltd, Fort William (IV)
59120	* D-16997	Smit Appingedam	B29-	4/48	DABO, Meppel (O-NL) 32
59127	SX 6103	SMT	C29F	3/48	Browning's Luxury Coaches Ltd, Whitburn (WL) 5
59132	NPU 437	Belle	?	7/48	Benfleet & District Motor Services Ltd, Benfleet (EX)
59139	SMF 597	Duple 44385	C29F	10/47	Lacey's (East Ham) Ltd, London E6 (LN)
59151	* ?	(Den Oudsten ?)	B33-	-/48	Ghielen, Helden-Beringe (O-NL) 36
59156	?	?	van	-/--	Original operator unknown
59164	* JMN 138	SMT	C29F	10/47	Mrs E Clague (A & E Clague) {Esplanade de Luxe Coaches}, Douglas (IM) 3
59173	?	?	van	-/--	Original operator unknown
59184					Exported to Ireland
59188	SMF 585	Duple 44197	C29F	10/47	Ardley Bros Ltd, London N17 (LN) 3
59197	* CHH 508	SMT	C25F	9/47	Blair & Palmer Ltd, Carlisle (CU)
59207	* ?	?	B29-	-/47	Takens, Rolde (O-NL) 1
59213					Exported to Ireland
59221	?	?	van	-/--	Holdsworth & Hanson, Halifax (GWR)
59229	LUA 467	SMT	C29F	11/47	Wallace Arnold, Leeds (WR)
59235	FDL 43	Duple 46215	C29F	1/48	Moss Motor Tours (Sandown, I.W.) Ltd (IW)
59246	* K-4314	De Groot	B30-	-/48	Van der Klundert, Oud Vossemeer (O-NL) 5
59254	GAB 728	Duple 47873	C27F	10/47	WH Hayes {Doreen Coaches}, Lye (WO)
59261	?	?	van	-/--	Original operator unknown
59270	?	?	van	-/--	Original operator unknown
59281	* FFS 866	SMT	C29F	11/47	SMT (MN) C166
59285					Exported to Ireland
59294	CFV 617	SMT	C29F	2/48	J Abbott & Sons (Blackpool) Ltd (LA)
59305	* D-16995	Smit Appingedam	B29-	1/48	DABO, Meppel (O-NL) 20
59310					Exported to Ireland
59319	FO 5069	Duple 43964	C29F	10/47	CT Sargeant {Sargeant's Motors}, Builth Wells (RR)
59326	* FFS 867	SMT	C29F	11/47	SMT (MN) C167
59342	?	Mulliner	B--F	-/--	Shell Petroleum Co, Curacao (O-YV)
59347	GDK 39	Pearson	C26F	1/48	L Dunkerley, Royton (LA)
59357	JC 8898	Pearson	C26F	2/48	J Williams & Son {Red Garage}, Portmadoc (CN)
59366	?	?	h/box	-/--	Original operator unknown
59372	?	?	van	-/--	Flinn & Sons Ltd (dyers), Fishergate (GWS)
59378					Exported to Ireland
59382	ACP 509	Pearson	C26F	12/47	Taylor's Coaches Ltd, Mytholmroyd (WR)
59391	LUB 564	Plaxton 709	C29F	2/48	A Watson, Leeds (WR)

C1252/75

59402	?	Mulliner	B--F	-/--	Shell Petroleum Co, Curacao (O-YV)
59407	#				Exported to Hong Kong
59416	CTY 754	ACB	C26F	5/48	J Lowther {Hollings Garage & Engineering Works}, Wallsend-on-Tyne (ND)
59423	#HDF 413	Junction	C29F	6/48	EC Young {Cotswold Coaches}, Stow-on-the-Wold (GL)
59430	FSG 815	SMT	C29F	12/47	Reid & MacKay, Edinburgh (MN)
59440	?	Mulliner	B--F	-/--	Shell Petroleum Co, Curacao (O-YV)
59445	DDP 561	?	van	-/--	Huntley & Palmer, Reading (GBE)
59455	?	SMT	van	-/--	Original operator unknown
59464	HTJ 979	Pearson	C26F	1/48	H Kirkham (F Kirkham & Son), Church (LA)
59475	#				Exported to Hong Kong
59479	EX 5900	Duple 44685	C29F	10/47	Norfolk Motor Services Ltd, Great Yarmouth (NK) 147
59488	JMN 122	Pearson	C26F	10/47	M Duggan {Duggan's Motors}, Port Erin (IM)
59499					Exported to Santiago (O-RCH)
59624					Exported to Barbados
59633	?	?	van	-/--	Original operator unknown
59640	?	?	library	-/--	Original operator unknown
59647	* KHW 987	Duple 44229	C29F	1/48	H Russett {Royal Blue}, Bristol (GL)
59657					Exported to Santiago (O-RCH)
59662	?	SMT	van	-/--	Original operator unknown
59672	SMY 257	Whitson ?	C29F	3/48	Wrights Hanwell Ltd, London W7 (LN)
59681	PRF 559	Longwell Green	C27F	10/48	Greatrex Motor Coaches Ltd, Stafford (ST) 46 Silver Plover
59692					Exported to Barbados
59696	* JNB 146	Pearson	C26F	2/48	Altrincham Coachways Ltd (CH)
59705	HLJ 600	Portsmouth Aviation	C29F	8/47	Excelsior Coaches Ltd, Bournemouth (HA)
59716					Exported to Santiago (O-RCH)
59722	* KA 4910	Duple 46163	C25F	-/48	OTC, Nairobi (O-EAK) 9
59730	?	?	van	-/--	Original operator unknown
59737	* EBL 647	?	C26-	8/47	TH Clare {Eagle Coaches), Faringdon (BE)
59744	?	SMT	van	8/47	Patterson Bros, Dalry (GAR)
59754					Exported to Santiago (O-RCH)
59759	* ?	?	?	8/47	WA Noakes Ltd {Dothwell Coaches}, Pensnett (ST)
59769	?	SMT	shop	-/--	St Cuthbert's Co-operative Association Ltd, Edinburgh (GMN)
59778	KDV 440	Thurgood 541	C29F	4/49	White & Goodman (Tavistock) Ltd (DN)
59789	?	Duple 46158	C14F	-/--	OTC, Nairobi (O-EAK)
59793	* DVH 133	Duple 6173/2	C27F	12/47	Chapman's Ivy Coaches Ltd, Milnsbridge (WR) 21
59802	JPX 15	Whitson ?	C29F	4/48	J Mitchell, Warnham (WS)
59813					Exported to Santiago (O-RCH)
59818	* ?	Duple 46156	C14F	-/48	OTC, Nairobi (O-EAK)
59827	GWY 654	Motor Distributors	C29F	5/48	RJ Armitage, Flockton (WR)
59834	HUO 670	Beadle C120	B30F	11/47	Southern National, Exeter (DN) 517
59841	* GAO 467	Duple 47707	C29F	3/48	Cumberland MS, Whitehaven (CU) 250
59851					Exported to Santiago (O-RCH)
59856	JAR 559	Thurgood 405	C29F	10/47	CW Jones {Enterprise Bus Service}, Kimpton (HT)
59866	* KUM 999	ACB	C26F	3/48	Kelsall Coaches Ltd {Saffman & Beasley}, Leeds (WR)
59875	EU 8758	Duple 46749	C29F	1/48	Griffin Motor Co Ltd, Brynmawr (BC) 116
59886	?	Duple 46157	C14F	-/--	OTC, Nairobi (O-EAK)
59890	* CRD 979	Duple 44496	C29F	2/48	AE Smith {Smith's Coaches}, Reading (BE)
59899	LRB 284	Yeates ?	C29F	1/48	ET White & Sons Ltd, Calver (DE)
59910					Exported to Helsinki (O-FIN)
59915	W 124	Duple 46312	C14F	-/--	OTC, Nairobi (O-EAK)
59924	* AEE 764	Duple 48836	C29F	10/47	C Tindall, Ashby-cum-Fenby (LI)
59931	* FBT 900	SMT	C29F	12/47	HG Anfield & Sons, Bridlington (ER)
59938	DVN 754	Duple 44004	C29F	10/47	Begg's Luxury Coaches Ltd, Thornaby-on-Tees (NR)
59948					Exported to Helsinki (O-FIN)
59953	?	?	van	-/--	Original operator unknown
59963	DPM 267	Duple 43391	C27F	10/47	Killick & Vincent, Dallington (ES)
59972	DUX 601	Duple 46451	C29F	9/47	GA Williams, Cefn Mawr (DH)
59983	* KA 4909	Duple 46161	C26F	-/48	OTC, Nairobi (O-EAK) 7
59987	JNB 600	Pearson	C26F	2/48	Jackson's Holiday Tours Ltd, Blackpool (LA)
59996	JAR 954	Thurgood 407	C29F	11/47	EG Hewitt {Premier Coaches}, Watford (HT)

C1252/76

60006						Exported to Helsinki (O-FIN)
60011	* W 125	Duple	46160	C14F	-/48	OTC, Nairobi (O-EAK) 2
60020	* CWH 640	Pearson		C26F	4/48	E Nesbit, Atherton (LA)
60027	JXE 572	Duple	44844	C27F	3/48	Keith & Boyle (London) Ltd {Orange Luxury Coaches}, London EC2 (LN) Condor
60034	* EFU 361	SMT		C29F	1/48	Enterprise (Scunthorpe) Passenger Services Ltd {Enterprise} (LI) 79
60045						Exported to Helsinki (O-FIN)
60050	JAR 426	Thurgood	404	C29F	10/47	F Heaton {Rush Green Coaches}, Langley (HT)
60060	#EBU 503	Pearson		C26F	5/48	Gregory & Richards Ltd, Oldham (LA)
60069	BRN 495	SMT		C29F	5/48	Scout MS Ltd, Preston (LA)
60080	?	Duple	46159	C14F	-/--	OTC, Nairobi (O-EAK)
60084	FDA 536	Duple	48041	C29F	10/47	Worthington Motor Tours Ltd, Wolverhampton (ST)
60093	* SMF 530	Duple	46281	C29F	10/47	BC Viney {Viney's Motor Coaches}, London N15 (LN) 10
60104						Exported to Helsinki (O-FIN)
60109						Exported to Malaya
60118	GCE 413	Thurgood	403	C29F	11/47	AE, WI & PL Harris {Progressive}, Cambridge (CM)
60125	* FWX 547	Beadle	C104	B30F	1/48	West Yorkshire RCC, Harrogate (WR) 614
60132	CAN 260	Duple	44723	C29F	9/47	WB Clark & TV Edworthy (Clark & Son) {Clark's Red Coaches}, London E7 (LN)
60142						Exported to Helsinki (O-FIN)
60147	JYB 190	Duple	48861	C29F	10/47	CG Berry, Bradford-on-Tone (SO)
60157	SX 6151	SMT		C29F	3/48	Browning's Luxury Coaches Ltd, Whitburn (WL) 6
60166	?	?		van	-/--	Original operator unknown
60177						Exported to Helsinki (O-FIN)
60181	HUO 671	Beadle	C121	B30F	11/47	Southern National, Exeter (DN) 518
60190	CWH 267	Pearson		C26F	1/48	Binns Motor Coaches Ltd, Bolton (LA)
60201 - 60212						Exported to Bombay (O-IND)
60309, 60314						Exported to Helsinki (O-FIN)
60323	JYA 880	Duple	43256	C29F	9/47	CT & LT Bond {Tor Coaches}, Street (SO)
60330	CES 163	NMU		C29F	7/48	A & W McKercher {Aberfeldy Motor Coaches}, Aberfeldy (PH)
60337	* HFM 35	Beadle	C169	B28F	11/47	Crosville MS, Chester (CH) S9
60347	* E-48059	Smit Appingedam		B29-	-/48	NWH, Zwartsluis (O-NL) 78
60352	DJY 810	Duple	46238	C27F	1/48	Salcombe Motor & Marine Engineering Co Ltd (DN)
60362	SU 4894	SMT		C29F	11/47	F & J Mitchell, Luthermuir (KE)
60371	* DHS 192	SMT		C29F	12/47	McQuatter Bros, Nitshill (RW) 3
60382	GRM 491	Duple	44728	C29F	2/48	Wright Bros Coaches Ltd, Nenthead (CU)
60386	HFM 36	Beadle	C168	B28F	11/47	Crosville MS, Chester (CH) S10
60395	* DTP 878	Duple	47881	C29F	11/47	E Byng & Sons Ltd, Southsea (HA)
60406	* M-29850	Hoogeveen		B31-	-/47	Van Maanen, Harderwijk (O-NL) 10
60415	ECA 907	Duple	43594	C29F	10/47	M Peters, Leeswood (FT)
60422						Exported to Santiago (O-RCH)
60431	HUP 283	Duple	43896	C29F	10/47	Scurr's Motor Services Ltd, Stillington (DM)
60439	EBL 349	Duple	43983	C29F	10/47	TH Clare {Eagle Coaches}, Faringdon (BE)
60447	JWJ 537	Duple	47686	C27F	6/49	Sheffield United Tours (WR) 159
60455	EJU 164	Duple	44373	C29F	1/48	Machin's Garage Ltd, Ashby-de-la-Zouch (LE)
60463	EDM 203	Duple	43611	C29F	10/47	A Owen {Allandale Coaches}, Rhyl (FT)
60471	JXH 664	Duple	44439	C29F	3/48	George Ewer & Co Ltd {Grey Green}, London N16 (LN)
60479	LRA 443	Duple	43810	C29F	10/47	HS North, Derby (DE) 37
60486						Exported to Santiago (O-RCH)
60495	* JWJ 538	Duple	47687	C27F	6/49	Sheffield United Tours (WR) 160
60500		See 50500				
60503	PV 8242	Duple	46210	C29F	11/47	HC Chambers & Son Ltd {Chambers & Sons}, Bures (WF)
60512	GAA 548	Duple	47803	C29F	10/47	FH Kilner (Transport) Ltd, Horsham (WS) 115
60519	JM 7090	SMT		C29F	3/48	CA Smith {Silver Badge}, Bowness-on-Windermere (WT)
60528	* E-48218	Jongerius		B33-	-/47	WATO, Nijverdal (O-NL) 9
60536	EBL 430	Duple	46300	C29F	10/47	GE Hedges {Reliance Motor Services}, Newbury (BE) 19
60544	GTX 911	Thurgood	408	C29F	11/47	Edwards Bros (Beddau) Ltd (GG)
60552	KKM 358	Kenex		C29F	2/48	CJ Newman & Son, Hythe (KT)

60560	* HYR 587	Duple	44824	C27F	3/48	United Service Transport Co Ltd, London SW9 (LN) 1072
60568						Exported to Malaya
60576	HYN 469	Duple	47730	C27F	10/47	Evan Evans, London WC1 (LN)
60583	ANH 698	Duple	46512	C29F	10/47	RG & T Wesley, Stoke Goldington (BK)
60592	JYA 839	Duple	44688	C29F	10/47	AG Bowerman, Taunton (SO)
60600	* D-16996	Smit Appingedam		B29-	12/47	DABO, Meppel (O-NL) 26
60717	HTJ 748	SMT		C29F	1/48	T Barrett {Barley Omnibus Co}, Barley (LA)
60724	HUP 417	SMT		C29F	1/48	Bond Bros {Imperial Motor Services}, Willington (DM)
60733						Exported to Malaya
60741	#SME 553	SMT		C25F	8/47	BEA, Ruislip (MX) 1117
60749	* TMG 94	Allweather		C29F	9/47	AC Susans {Fountain Luxury Coaches}, Twickenham (MX)
60757	DEA 410	Duple	47775	C29F	10/47	Hills Tours Ltd, West Bromwich (ST) 13
60765	HBJ 10	Duple	47931	C29F	10/47	F Reeve {Red Coaches}, Lowestoft (EK)
60773	* E-48058	Smit Appingedam		B29-	-/48	NWH, Zwartsluis (O-NL) 77
60781	HTF 586	SMT		C29F	12/47	Warburton Bros (Bury) Ltd, Tottington (LA)
60788	HDV 751	Duple	46403	C27F	10/47	CT & LM Burfitt {Grey Coaches}, Ilfracombe (DN)
60797	GCG 823	Lee		B26F	2/48	Hants & Sussex Motor Services Ltd, Emsworth (HA) 27
60805	* E-18800	Kuiphuis		B31-	-/48	ONOG, Oldenzaal (O-NL) 14
60814	?	?		van	-/--	Original operator unknown
60821	* L-34220	Domburg	136	B27D	2/49	GVU, Utrecht (O-NL) 36
60830	EDT 666	Jaques		C29F	9/47	SM Wilson & Sons Ltd, Balby (WR) 9
60838	FDA 461	Duple	48794	C29F	11/47	Don Everall Ltd, Wolverhampton (ST)
60846	?	?		van	-/--	Original operator unknown
60854	JWJ 539	Duple	47688	C27F	6/49	Sheffield United Tours (WR) 161
60862						Exported to Malaya
60870	JFJ 260	Tiverton		C29F	6/48	Greenslades, Exeter (DN)
60878	?	?		van	-/--	Original operator unknown
60885	* CFV 970	Booth		C29F	3/48	ET Butterworth Ltd {Pathfinder}, Blackpool (LA)
60894	* FBC 932	Churchill		C29F	7/48	Athelstan Coaches Ltd, Malmesbury (WI)
60902	* A-39774	Smit Appingedam		B29-	-/48	ESA, Marum (O-NL) 55
60911	HYR 774	Duple	44568	C29F	1/48	Fallowfield & Britten Ltd, London E8 (LN)
60918						Exported to Rotterdam (O-NL)
60927	DUX 586	Duple	43233	C29F	10/47	JT, FW & GE Whittle {JT Whittle & Sons}, Highley (SH)
60935	* HYR 776	Duple	44567	C29F	1/48	Fallowfield & Britten Ltd, London E8 (LN)
60943	* FWM 197	Ormac		C29F	5/48	Howard Coaches Ltd, Southport (LA)
60951	CFV 677	SMT		C29F	2/48	Whittaker Bros (Blackpool) Ltd (LA)
60959						Exported to Malaya
60967	?	?		van	-/--	Original operator unknown
60975	* EAW 112	Burlingham	?	C26F	1/48	JW, WHF & GW Lloyd, Oswestry (SH) 8
60982	EMW 939	Duple	43559	C29F	10/47	RPH Hopkins {Hopkins & Sons}, Lacock (WI)
60991	* LTN 376	Mulliner	T114	B31F	10/47	Bedlington & District Luxury Coaches Ltd, Ashington (ND)
60999	?	Mulliner		B--F	-/--	Shell Petroleum Co, Lagunillas (O-YV)
61008	CNL 832	Duple	43758	C27F	10/47	R Armstrong, Westerhope (ND) 49
61015	KKX 866	Duple	43323	C29F	10/47	JW & RFP Hayfield (Hayfield Bros), Newport Pagnell (BK)
61024	?	Mulliner		B---	-/--	NV de Bataafsche Petroleum Mij, Pladjoe (O-RI)
61032	JXE 571	Duple	44828	C27F	3/48	Keith & Boyle (London) Ltd {Orange Luxury Coaches}, London EC2 (LN) Astoria II
61040	HNY 763	?		B32F	3/48	HJ Uphill, Caerau (GG)
61048	JNN 656	Duple	49444	C29F	2/48	JR Woodhouse & TH Barton {W & B Coaches}, Sandiacre (NG)
61056						Exported to Rotterdam (O-NL)
61064	* LTN 680	SMT		C29F	1/48	E Marshall & Co Ltd {Crown Coaches}, Birtley (ND) 61
61072	EBX 666	Thomas & Thomas		C29F	7/48	D Jones {Ffoshelig Coaches}, Newchurch (CR)
61079	GUY 602	Plaxton	712	C29F	5/48	Mrs ME Ward {Ward's Super de Luxe}, Sidemoor (WO)
61087	GBT 110	Roney		B28F	6/48	JH & TW Graham (Connor & Graham), Easington (ER)
61096						Exported to Malaya
61101	*					Exported to Wellington (O-NZ)
61102 - 61106						Exported to Wellington (O-NZ)
61107	* P.367	Auckland TB		FB33F	11/48	Auckland Transport Board (O-NZ) 32
61108 - 61110						Exported to Wellington (O-NZ)

C1252/78

61111	* V2.071	Tauranga Bus Service		B33F	-/48	Tauranga Bus Service, Tauranga (O-NZ) 6
61112						Exported to Wellington (O-NZ)
61189	#W 123	Duple	?	C14F	-/47	OTC, Nairobi (O-EAK)
61231	BCB 7	Duple	44548	C29F	10/47	Lewis Cronshaw Ltd, London NW4 (LN)
61236	* K-20244	Van Oers	28	B30F	6/48	Van der Klundert, Oud Vossemeer (O-NL) 6
61241	?	?		library	-/--	Derbyshire County Council (GDE)
61249	DUX 585	Duple	46454	C29F	10/47	TG Smith {Eagle Coachways}, Trench (SH)
61257	JAL 708	Duple	43331	C29F	2/48	WE, RE and RN Brumpton {WE Brumpton & Sons}, Dunham-on-Trent (NG)
61265	* CFV 678	SMT		C29F	3/48	Whiteside Ltd, Blackpool (LA)
61273						Exported to Rotterdam (O-NL)
61281	SMF 527	Duple	43923	C29F	3/48	Valliant Direct Coaches Ltd, London W5 (LN)
61289	* PRF 84	Churchill		C29C	8/48	CA Newton (B Newton & Sons) {Mayflower}, Cradley Heath (ST)
61296	OMY 385	Duple	44676	C29F	10/47	Fox & Hart Ltd {Hounslow Star Coaches}, Hounslow (MX)
61305	GRM 604	Duple	43892	C29F	11/47	E & L Titterington, Blencow (CU)
61313						Exported to Malaya
61322	OMY 386	Duple	44675	C29F	10/47	Fox & Hart Ltd {Hounslow Star Coaches}, Hounslow (MX)
61338	* LJO 757	Duple	46751	C29F	3/48	South Midland, Oxford (OX) 44
61346	MPU 504	Duple	43491	C29F	10/47	ER, TW & AC Lodge, High Easter (EX)
61354	* EWN 19	Duple	46750	C29F	10/47	United Welsh, Swansea (GG) 919
61365	JUV 297	Duple	46369	C29F	1/48	Bradshaw's Super Coaches Ltd, London SE18 (LN)
61377	JXH 663	Duple	44440	C29F	3/48	George Ewer & Co Ltd {Grey Green}, London N16 (LN)
61385						Exported to Lagos (O-WAN)
61392	KKE 282	Duple	44624	C29F	10/47	R Ovenden {Queen Coaches}, Margate (KT)
61401	* HUO 687	Duple	47675	C27F	10/47	Southern National, Exeter (DN) 534
61409	DRP 722	Duple	46566	C29F	10/47	KW Services Ltd, Daventry (NO) B5
61418	EJU 691	Yeates	?	C29F	1/48	C & M Lester (Lester Bros), Long Whatton (LE)
61425	* A-39244	Smit Appingedam		B29-	-/48	ESA, Marum (O-NL) 56
61434	EJ 8620	Duple	48332	C29F	10/47	WE Lloyd (WE Lloyd & Son) {Glan Teify Bus Services}, Pontrhydfendigaid (CG)
61442	KKE 173	Duple	46716	C29F	11/47	FA Brooks {Brookline}, Ryarsh (KT)
61446		see 61466				
61450	* ?	?		?	9/47	WA Noakes Ltd {Dothwell Coaches}, Pensnett (ST)
61458	MPU 348	Duple	44677	C29F	10/47	Thorpe Coaches Ltd, London E17 (LN)
61466	* A-39689	Smit Appingedam		B29-	-/48	ESA, Marum (O-NL) 54
61474	* E-48060	Smit Appingedam		B29-	-/48	NWH, Zwartsluis (O-NL) 79
61475	JKR 970	Duple	47934	C29F	11/47	RH Sims {Marion Coaches}, Margate (KT)
61483	?	Mulliner		?	-/--	Original operator unknown (O-WAN)
61490	HYR 7	Duple	44203	C29F	10/47	AC Coaches Ltd, London SE15 (LN)
61499	CWH 817	NMU		C29F	7/48	Brockbank & Baxter Ltd, Bolton (LA)
61507	GCG 618	Wadham		C29F	2/48	Creamline Motor Services (Bordon) Ltd (HA)
61516	CRS 44	SMT		C29F	12/47	R Cheyne {Cheyne's Motor Service}, Aberdeen (AD)
61522	CUD 647	Duple	48094	C29F	10/47	EHA Oliver, Long Hanborough (OX)
61532						Exported to Antwerp (O-B)
61540	HAD 216	Duple	43717	C29F	10/47	MJ Cox, Ellwood (GL)
61548	JAL 592	Duple	48313	C29F	10/47	Barton Transport, Chilwell (NG) 526
61556	KKE 472	Mulliner	T115	B31F	10/47	Carey Bros, New Romney (KT)
61564						Exported to Antwerp (O-B)
61572	HUO 699	Duple	47676	C27F	10/47	Western National, Exeter (DN) 546
61580						Exported to Freetown (O-WAL)
61587	ORE 359	Mulliner	T116	B29F	9/47	W Warrington, Ilam (ST)
61596	KAF 221	Duple	48322	C29F	11/47	TW Mundy (TW Mundy & Son) {Silver Queen}, Camborne (CO)
61604	LHT 543	Strachan		C27F	6/48	AH Fielding {Empress Coaches}, Bristol (GL)
61613	EJU 694	Yeates	?	C29F	12/47	R, SL & AH Wheildon (R Wheildon & Sons), Castle Donington (LE)
61620						Exported to Freetown (O-WAL)
61629						Exported to Antwerp (O-B)
61637	GNP 76	Duple	48267	C29F	11/47	JH Jakeman {Regent Coaches}, Redditch (WO)
61645	HYN 467	Duple	46355	C29F	11/47	CW Banfield, London SE15 (LN)

61653	JUP 566	Robson		C29F	3/49	SG & R Cheesey {Serene Coaches}, Brandon Colliery (DM)
61661	*D-16998	Hainje		B29-	12/47	DABO, Meppel (O-NL) 48
61669	EUN 51	Duple	43571	C29F	6/47	Mrs E Williams {Williams & Hodson}, Marchwiel (DH)
61677	MPU 394	Duple	43802	C27F	10/47	FR Harris {Harris's Coaches}, Grays (EX)
61684	CRD 596	Mulliner	T122	B32F	12/47	Reading Corporation (BE) 73
61693	DUX 587	Duple	43241	C29F	9/47	Corvedale Motor Services Ltd, Ludlow (SH) 14
61701	HEL 161	Duple	44845	C27F	10/47	Shamrock & Rambler Motor Coaches Ltd, Bournemouth (HA)
61710	HYP 721	Duple	44111	C29F	11/47	Birch Bros Ltd, London NW5 (LN) K21
61717	JAU 808	Duple	46976	C29F	5/48	A Skill {Skill's Coaches}, Nottingham (NG) 8
61733						Exported to Antwerp (O-B)
61742	?	?		van	-/--	Original operator unknown
61750	HYU 786	Duple	44701	C29F	9/47	TG Green {Empress Motor Coaches}, London E2 (LN) 2
61764	FJW 106	Mulliner	T125	C28F	3/48	Worthington Motor Tours Ltd, Wolverhampton (ST)
61769	*E-48061	Hainje		B30-	-/48	NWH, Zwartsluis (O-NL) 80
61774						Exported to Freetown (O-WAL)
61779	*OMY 384	Duple	47859	C29F	11/47	Olsen Bros {Pickwick Coaches}, Strood (KT)
61795	*CL 9649	Mulliner	T127	?	-/--	BOAC, Ceylon
61800	JAR 905	Thurgood	427	C29F	11/47	W Hodge & Sons, Much Hadham (HT)
61925	HUP 376	Mulliner	T121	B32F	10/47	Bond Bros {Imperial Motor Services}, Willington (DM)
61932	EX 6031	Plaxton	595	FC30F	2/48	WJ Haylett {Felix Coaches}, Great Yarmouth (NK) 3
61941						Exported to Antwerp (O-B)
61949	JYB 136	Mulliner	T118	B31F	10/47	H Gratton, Burnham-on-Sea (SO)
61957	*KAF 110	Thurgood	429	C29F	12/47	Banfil & Barrington, Mawnan Smith (CO)
61965						Exported to Tanganyika
61973	LPK 54	Duple	44043	C29F	3/48	Mrs AA Charman {Felday Coaches}, Ockley (SR)
61981						Exported to Antwerp (O-B)
61989	GAA 549	Duple	46609	C29F	10/47	Liss & District Omnibus Co Ltd, Liss (HA) 130
61996	EFU 247	Duple	47565	C29F	1/48	C, JE, T & T Hudson {Hudson's Bus Co}, Horncastle (LI)
62005	OMY 556	Mulliner	T117	B31F	10/47	Middlesex County Council (XMX)
62013	*LVT 317	Yeates	?	C29F	1/48	AJ, WH & LW Jeffreys {W Jeffreys & Sons}, Goldenhill (ST)
62022	EJU 319	Duple	44374	C29F	11/47	Machin's Garage Ltd, Ashby-de-la-Zouch (LE)
62029	#KGH 638	Junction		C29-	-/48	W King & Sons Ltd {Emerald Coaches}, London N1 (LN)
62038						Exported to Antwerp (O-B)
62042	?	?		van	-/--	Original operator unknown - given only as "D.G."
62047	HAD 270	Duple	46697	C29F	10/47	AH Kearsey Ltd {Kearsey's Coaches}, Cheltenham (GL) 47
62055	*JAR 976	Thurgood	428	C29F	11/47	AJ Draper, Lemsford (HT)
62063						Exported to Bangkok (O-T)
62071						Exported to Antwerp (O-B)
62081	KHY 318	Duple	44036	C27F	10/47	AH Fielding {Empress Coaches}, Bristol (GL)
62087	*FWW 598	Duple	46810	C26F	10/47	West Yorkshire RCC, Harrogate (WR) 648
62094	DDP 117	Duple	44497	C29F	2/48	AE Smith {Smith's Coaches}, Reading (BE)
62103	HAD 267	Duple	48254	C29F	11/47	A Bayliss, Dymock (GL)
62111	JDE 226	Mulliner	T120	B31F	10/47	DC Thomas & JI Jones Ltd {Precelly Motors}, Clynderwen (PE)
62120	OMY 378	Duple	44693	C29F	10/47	CJ Elms, Phillips & Brown {Elms Coaches}, London N17 (MX)
62127						Exported to Antwerp (O-B)
62136	?	Duple	48969	B31F	-/--	Trinidad Government Railways (O-TT)
62144	*ACP 730	(Ireland ?)		C29F	3/48	EA Southwell {Park Coachways}, Halifax (WR)
62152	GTX 778	Mulliner	T119	B30F	10/47	Pugh & Stanton, Ogmore Vale (GG)
62160						Exported to Thailand
62168	HNG 407	Duple	43684	C29F	11/47	SA Abel (S & G Abel) {Abel's Coaches}, Wells-next-the Sea (NK)
62176	KAF 883	Thurgood	434	C29F	1/48	CH Kinsman, Ponsanooth (CO)
62184	*ORE 944	Yeates	?	C29F	11/47	H Nickolls, Milford (ST) 4
62197, 62224						Exported to Antwerp (O-B)
62200	KPP 190	Thurgood	430	C29F	11/47	JRG Dell {Rover Bus Service}, Lye Green (BK) 11

C1252/80

62208	GWK 76	Duple	48086	C29F	9/47	Wainfleet Motor Services Ltd, Nuneaton (WK)
62217	JXA 701	Duple	48217	C29F	11/47	Pall Mall Car Hire {Pamalhire}, London SW1 (LN)
62233	FJW 108	Mulliner	T124	C29F	3/48	Worthington Motor Tours Ltd, Wolverhampton (ST)
62241	ECA 963	Duple	46501	C29F	2/48	JB Pye Ltd, Rhos-on-Sea (DH)
62249	* GAB 754	Duple	43835	C29F	1/48	CCO Powell, Dunley (WO)
62257						Exported to Tanganyika
62265	?	?		van	-/--	Original operator unknown
62273	HAD 380	Duple	43724	C27F	12/47	FR Willetts, Pillowell (GL)
62281	EFU 772	Plaxton	325	FC30F	1/48	JR Mellers, Goxhill (LI)
62288						Exported to Antwerp (O-B)
62297	OMY 410	Duple	44198	C29F	11/47	Ardley Bros Ltd, London N17 (LN) 4
62305	GTX 439	Duple	44339	C29F	11/47	FR Williams {Victoria Motorways}, Treorchy (GG)
62314	* MTW 263	Duple	44751	C29F	2/48	GL Sutton {Sutton's Coaches}, Clacton (EX)
62321						Exported to Santiago (O-RCH)
62330	* CNL 262	Weymann	W890	B20F	9/47	AB Wilson, Horsley-on-Tyne (ND)
62338	EUN 176	Duple	43595	C29F	1/48	EG Peters, Llanarmon yn Ial (FT)
62346	GTX 208	Duple	46822	C29F	10/47	Edwards Bros (Beddau) Ltd (GG)
62355						Exported to Tanganyika
62362	JBP 856	Duple	46353	C29F	1/48	AW Buckingham {Buck's Luxury Coaches}, Worthing (WS)
62370	DMO 250	Duple	44368	C29F	11/47	Windsorian Motor Coach Services Ltd, Windsor (BE) 50
62378	#EF 8132	Duple	44635	C29F	11/47	Bee-Line Roadways (Teeside) Ltd, West Hartlepool (DM)
62387						Exported to Santiago (O-RCH)
62394	JDV 317	Duple	43657	C29F	10/47	CA Gayton {Gayton's Coaches}, Ashburton (DN)
62402	HYR 522	Mulliner	T126	B31F	11/47	BOAC (LN)
62411	MPU 61	Black & White		C29F	2/48	Black & White (Walthamstow) Ltd, London E17 (LN)
62418						Exported to Santiago (O-RCH)
62427	* HTJ 913	?		van	12/47	WG Ribchester, Heywood (LA)
62435	JXE 956	Whitson	?	C29F	-/48	Robin & Rambler Coaches Ltd, London SW11 (LN)
62443	JYB 258	Duple	44201	C29F	11/47	TE Herring {W Herring & Son}, Burnham-on-Sea (SO)
62451						Exported to Tanganyika
62459	FJW 105	Mulliner	T123	C28F	3/48	Worthington Motor Tours Ltd, Wolverhampton (ST)
62467	PRF 160	Longwell Green		C27F	10/48	Greatrex Motor Coaches Ltd, Stafford (ST) 47 Golden Plover
62474	AEB 204	Duple	44709	C29F	11/47	M Green {Green Bus Service}, Thorney (CM)
62482						Exported to Santiago (O-RCH)
62491	EWV 155	Mulliner	T128	B31F	11/47	Hull & Bartlett (Nadder Valley), Tisbury (WI)
62499	KAF 151	Duple	46507	C29F	10/47	JM & CM Prout {Prout Bros}, Port Isaac (CO)
62537 - 62548						Exported to Bombay (O-IND)
62664	SO 8176	SMT		C29F	1/48	D MacKay {MacKay's Tours}, Granton-on-Spey (MR)
62671	?	Jonckheere	5509	C27-	3/48	Cuypers, Liège (O-B)
62680	GHO 170	Lee		B26F	3/48	BS Williams, Emsworth (HA) 28
62688	JAU 804	Duple	43319	C29F	5/48	A Skill {Skill's Coaches}, Nottingham (NG) 4
62696	DUX 786	Duple	46455	C29F	10/47	Salopia Saloon Coaches Ltd, Whitchurch (SH) 50
62705						Exported to Port Elizabeth (O-ZA)
62713	?	?		meat van	-/--	Original operator unknown
62721	OMY 740	Duple	43924	C29F	11/47	Valliant Direct Coaches Ltd, London W5 (LN)
62729	HFD 541	Duple	47718	C29F	11/47	JJ Field, Dudley (WO)
62736						Exported to Antwerp (O-B)
62745	HWR 616	NMU		C29F	9/48	W Simpson, Ripon (WR) 5
62753	DVH 81	SMT		C29F	12/47	Hanson's Buses Ltd, Huddersfield (WR) 238
62762	#HTG 679	Junction		C29F	8/48	WJ, BA & R Edwards, Talbot Green (GG)
62769						Exported to Helsinki (O-FIN)
62778	#DUX 945	Duple	43506	C29F	10/48	WR & T Hoggins (WR Hoggins & Sons) {Pilot}, Wrockwardine Wood (SH)
62786	?	?		van	-/--	Original operator unknown
62794	?	?		h/box	-/--	Original operator unknown
62802	* JWJ 540	Duple	47689	C27F	6/49	Sheffield United Tours (WR) 162
62810						Exported to Port Elizabeth (O-ZA)
62818	?	?		van	-/--	Original operator unknown
62826	BCB 84	SMT		C29F	12/47	NW & F Barnes & J Garside {Mark Barnes & Sons}, Haslingden (LA)
62833						Exported to Rotterdam (O-NL)

C1252/81

62842	HNG 953	Duple	43625	C27F	11/47	RT & TH Houchen, Dersingham (NK)
62850	* GAO 468	Duple	47708	C29F	3/48	Cumberland MS, Whitehaven (CU) 251
62859	CTL 67	Duple	43775	C26F	12/47	CW Blankley {Gem Luxury Coaches}, Colsterworth (KN)
62866						Exported to Helsinki (O-FIN)
62875	* CJA 520	Plaxton	603	FC30F	1/48	Melba Motors Ltd, Reddish (CH)
62885	GTX 774	Duple	48841	C29F	11/47	OE James, Port Talbot (GG)
62891	XG 9631	SMT		C29F	1/48	FL Pickering {Royal Coaches}, Thornaby-on-Tees (NR)
62899						Exported to Rotterdam (O-NL)
62907	* CJA 521	Plaxton	604	FC30F	1/48	Melba Motors Ltd, Reddish (CH)
62915	KKX 812	Duple	44875	C29F	11/47	FH Crook {Sands Bus Co}, Booker (BK)
62923	MPU 62	Black & White		C29F	3/48	Black & White (Walthamstow) Ltd, London E17 (LN) 29
62930	* ?	Jonckheere	5790	C28-	7/49	Maison Mathias Lux Sarl, Luxembourg (O-L)
62939	HYR 523	Mulliner	T130	B31F	11/47	BOAC (LN)
62947	KKE 944	Duple	48124	C27F	11/47	WG Norris, Wouldham (KT)
62956	CWH 266	SMT		C29F	1/48	Lomax Bros (Transport) Ltd, Bolton (LA)
62963						Exported to Antwerp (O-B)
62972	HYN 468	Duple	43829	C29F	11/47	Essex County Coaches Ltd, London E15 (LN)
62980	HYR 525	Mulliner	T132	B31F	11/47	BOAC (LN)
62988	* EJU 397	Mulliner	T134	B31F	10/47	Mrs KA Smeeton, Market Harborough (LE)
62996						Exported to Mombasa (O-EAK)
63004	JYB 351	Duple	44806	C29F	11/47	G Willmott Ltd {Wells City Coaches}, Wells (SO) 6
63012	HYR 524	Mulliner	T131	B31F	11/47	BOAC (LN)
63020	* LAE 275	Strachan		C26F	3/48	AH Fielding {Empress Coaches}, Bristol (GL)
63027						Exported to Mombasa (O-EAK)
63036	LVK 181	Plaxton	954	FC30F	1/48	G Galley (Galley's Motors), Newcastle (ND)
63044	EAW 280	Plaxton	327	FC30F	1/48	DJ Hampson {Hampson's Luxury Coaches}, Oswestry (SH)
63053	HVU 879	Mulliner	T136	B31F	11/47	Altrincham Coachways Ltd (CH)
63060						Exported to Antwerp (O-B)
63069	?	?		van	-/--	Faulkner & Sons, location unknown
63077	?	?		van	-/--	Original operator unknown
63085	* TMG 169	Strachan		C29F	10/47	Wright Bros (London) Ltd, London W1 (LN)
63093						Exported to Freetown (O-WAL)
63101	* (FGD 818 ?)	Mulliner	T129	B--F	11/47	SCWS Ltd, Glasgow (LK)
63109	HLJ 800	Lee		C29F	9/48	Excelsior Coaches Ltd, Bournemouth (HA)
63117	GAA 762	Mulliner	T139	B31F	10/47	CET Gregory Ltd, Hook (HA)
63124						Exported to Freetown (O-WAL)
63133	FWO 616	Duple	46752	C29F	11/47	Red & White, Chepstow (MH) 816
63141	* ?	Mulliner	T138	?	11/47	Original operator unknown
63155	* HFJ 836	Duple	43363	C29F	12/47	Greenslades, Exeter (DN)
63168						Exported to Port Elizabeth (O-ZA)
63173	GCE 422	Mulliner	T140	B31F	1/48	Premier Travel Ltd, Cambridge (CM) 13
63178	AFB 455	Mulliner	T133	C29F	11/47	G Alford & Sons, Coleford (SO)
63188	LTN 582	Mulliner	T137	B30F	10/47	GH, S & JB Atkinson (GH Atkinson & Sons) {General Omnibus Services}, Chester-le-Street (DM) 9
63198						Exported to Antwerp (O-B)
63206	LRB 158	Duple	43328	C29F	11/47	GE Taylor {My Lady Coaches}, Crich (DE)
63214	EUN 87	Mulliner	T135	B31F	11/47	A Mates, Chirk (DH)
63222						Exported to Antwerp (O-B)
63229	CDY 946	Mulliner	T142	B31F	11/47	John Dengate & Sons Ltd, Beckley (ES) 17
63236	EP 9982	Duple	46456	C29F	3/48	Mid-Wales Motorways Ltd, Newtown (MO) 45
63246	EJF 778	Duple	48981	C29F	11/47	AE Hercock, Leicester (LE)
63254						Exported to Antwerp (O-B)
63262	HYR 526	Mulliner	T149	B--F	11/47	BOAC (LN)
63270						Exported to Port Elizabeth (O-ZA)
63274	JXC 640	Duple	48218	C29F	11/47	Pall Mall Car Hire {Pamalhire}, London SW1 (LN)
63278	EOW 870	Duple	46389	C29F	11/47	PFV Summerbee {Sumerbee's Motor Coaches}, Southampton (HA)
63282	MTW 498	Mulliner	T146	B31F	11/47	Essex County Council (Borough of Barking Education) (XEX)
63287	OMY 617	Duple	47795	C29F	11/47	H & G Beach, Staines (MX)
63296	CTL 166	Duple	47579	C29F	12/47	WH Lancaster {Lancaster Bros}, Tetford (KN)
63304						Exported to Antwerp (O-B)

C1252/82

63312	JFJ 181	Tiverton		C25F	6/48	Greenslades, Exeter (DN)
63320	FJW 109	Mulliner	T145	C28F	4/48	Worthington Motor Tours Ltd, Wolverhampton (ST)
63327						Exported to Port Elizabeth (O-ZA)
63334	DPM 945	Duple	44718	C29F	11/47	AH & JH Sargent {East Grinstead Motor Coaches}, East Grinstead (ES) 08
63344	EAJ 14	Duple	44880	C29F	11/47	Saltburn Motor Services Ltd, Saltburn (NR) 9
63352	FDL 154	Duple	43587	C29F	3/48	West Wight Motor Bus Co Ltd, Totland Bay (IW)
63360						Exported to Antwerp (O-B)
63368	EEA 400	Whitson	?	C27F	3/49	Hills Tours Ltd, West Bromwich (ST)
63376	* EFU 362	Mulliner	T151	B31F	1/48	Enterprise (Scunthorpe) Passenger Services Ltd {Enterprise} (LI) 51
63384						Exported to Port Elizabeth (O-ZA)
63393	JUO 600	Duple	47690	C29F	3/48	Devon General, Torquay (DN) TCB600
63461	P2.417	NZMB		B30F	12/48	New Zealand Railways Road Services (O-NZ) 1697
63462	P1.222	NZMB		B31F	2/49	New Zealand Railways Road Services (O-NZ) 1702
63463	* P1.221	NZMB		B31F	3/49	New Zealand Railways Road Services (O-NZ) 1701
63464	* P1.223	NZMB		B31F	3/49	New Zealand Railways Road Services (O-NZ) 1703
63465	P1.036	NZMB		B30F	3/49	New Zealand Railways Road Services (O-NZ) 1700
63466	* P1.891	NZMB		B30F	12/48	New Zealand Railways Road Services (O-NZ) 1698
63467	P.372	Auckland TB		FB33F	-/49	Auckland Transport Board (O-NZ) 37
63468	P2.484	H & H		B29F	-/--	H & H Travel Lines Ltd, Invercargill (O-NZ) 1
63469	* P.375	Auckland TB		FB33F	7/49	Auckland Transport Board (O-NZ) 40
63470 - 63472						Exported to Wellington (O-NZ)
63509						Exported to Antwerp (O-B)
63517	HYR 783	Duple	44825	C27F	3/48	HJ Phillips & Sons Ltd, London SW11 (LN) 1001
63525	KKE 478	Mulliner	T143	B31F	11/47	GR Ayers, Dover (KT)
63532	KKE 704	Duple	44264	C27F	11/47	FJ Avards & Co {Avard's Coaches}, Lamberhurst (KT)
63539	HFD 643	Mulliner	T141	B28F	1/48	NC Kendrick, Dudley (WO)
63549	HUO 700	Duple	47677	C27F	11/47	Western National, Exeter (DN) 547
63557	GCG 284	Duple	47804	C29F	1/48	Hants & Sussex Motor Services Ltd, Emsworth (HA) 124
63565						Exported to Antwerp (O-B)
63595	HYR 782	Duple	44829	C27F	3/48	HJ Phillips & Sons Ltd, London SW11 (LN) 1000
63599	DMO 251	Duple	44369	C29F	11/47	Windsorian Motor Coach Services Ltd, Windsor (BE) 51
63604						Exported to Mombasa (O-EAK)
63608	DRP 900	Duple	46570	C29F	12/47	York Bros (Northampton) Ltd (NO) 15
63613	?	Jonckheere	5583	C27-	6/48	Albert van Mullem, Roosbeek (O-B)
63617	BJL 341	Yeates		?	C29F	1/48	F Rose, Holbeach Drove (LI)
63622	#HFJ 835	Duple	43364	C29F	12/47	H & EA Belcher Ltd {Empress Coaches}, Teignmouth (DN)
63628	FJW 103	Mulliner	T144	C28F	1/48	Worthington Motor Tours Ltd, Wolverhampton (ST)
63635	?	?		l/stock	-/--	Original operator unknown
63646	GBY 800	Duple	44525	C29F	11/47	John Bennett (Croydon) Ltd (SR) 3
63654	FWO 617	Duple	46753	C29F	11/47	Red & White, Chepstow (MH) 817
63662						Exported to Antwerp (O-B)
63670	JXC 985	Mulliner	T147	B31F	10/47	London County Council (XLN) 1573
63678	EAW 225	Yeates		?	C29F	1/48	Jones Coachways Ltd, Market Drayton (SH) 17
63685						Exported to Kenya
63694	HFM 37	Beadle		C170	B28F	11/47	Crosville MS, Chester (CH) S11
63702						Exported to Antwerp (O-B)
63710	* JXA 925	Duple	48110	C29F	11/47	CG Lewis {CG Lewis Safety Coaches}, London SE10 (LN)
63718	BJL 342	Yeates		?	C29F	1/48	A & WH Rose (W Rose & Son) {Brown Linnet}, Holbeach St Johns (LI)
63725	JXB 321	Whitson		?	C29F	10/47	Robin & Rambler Coaches Ltd, London SW11 (LN)
63732	* DUH 110	Duple	46823	C29F	11/47	ER Forse, Cardiff (GG)
63742	HFM 38	Beadle		C171	B28F	11/47	Crosville MS, Chester (CH) S12
63750	FTM 994	Duple	49105	C29F	1/48	C Symes {Kempstonian Coaches}, Kempston (BD)
63758						Exported to Antwerp (O-B)
63766	JXE 573	Duple	44846	C27F	3/48	Keith & Boyle (London) Ltd {Orange Luxury Coaches}, London EC2 (LN) Falcon
63774	KMA 93	Pearson		C26F	3/48	LW & J Hollinshead {Hollinshead Garage}, Kent Green (CH)
63782	?	Mulliner		?	-/--	Original operator unknown (O-WAN)

C1252/83

63792	* SML 958	Duple	44041 C29F	1/48	HV Richmond, Barley (HT)
63800					Exported to Antwerp (O-B)
63808	CNL 973	Duple	43759 C27F	11/47	R Armstrong, Westerhope (ND) 50
63816	EWV 378	Duple	44871 C29F	11/47	C Bodman, Worton (WI)
63823	* FWW 599	Duple	46811 C26F	11/47	West Yorkshire RCC, Harrogate (WR) 649
63829	GNX 530	Duple	47629 C29F	11/47	De Luxe Buses Ltd, Mancetter (WK)
63840	* LPU 615	Beadle	C133 B30F	12/47	Eastern National, Chelmsford (EX) 3925
63848	OMY 520	Duple	44199 C29F	1/48	Ardley Bros Ltd, London N17 (LN) 5
63856					Exported to Antwerp (O-B)
63864	JXC 981	Mulliner	T148 B31F	-/47	London County Council (XLN) 1572
63872	GR 9748	Pearson	C26F	-/--	G Bridges, Sunderland (DM)
63880	* HNY 868	Jeffreys	-25-	3/48	HJ Uphill, Caerau (GG)
63889	?	Mulliner	?	-/--	Original operator unknown (O-WAN)
63897	DPM 946	Duple	44719 C29F	11/47	AH & JH Sargent {East Grinstead Motor Coaches}, East Grinstead (ES) 09
63997 - 64008					Exported to Copenhagen (O-DK)
64049	SML 469	Pearson	C26F	3/48	Valliant Direct Coaches Ltd, London W5 (LN) 77
64057	HYR 527	Mulliner	T150 B--F	11/47	BOAC (LN)
64064	?	?	van	-/--	Original operator unknown
64071					Exported to Antwerp (O-B)
64081	CJT 596	Duple	44019 C29F	11/47	AC Marvin, West Stour (DT)
64089	EVJ 923	Duple	46457 C29F	1/48	JH, HJ & GH Yeomans {Yeomans Motors}, Canon Pyon (HR) 62
64097	* G60xx	Mulliner	B--F	-/47	Gibraltar Motor Hire Services (O-GBZ)
64105	EU 8793	Duple	49046 C29F	10/47	T Rees (Rees Motors) {Reliance Motors}, Llanelly Hill (BC)
64113	EBL 42	Duple	44486 C29F	12/47	EJ Spratley {Blue Star}, Mortimer (BE)
64124	JP 6751	Pearson	C26F	2/48	F Grundy, Hindley (LA)
64133					Exported to Freetown (O-WAL)
64138	DRV 931	Reading	? C27F	7/48	PW Lambert {Little Wonder Coaches}, Petersfield (HA)
64146	AGV 957	Duple	43539 C29F	12/47	HAC Claireaux {CJ Partridge & Son}, Layham (WF)
64154	LRB 750	Barnaby	C29F	4/48	Booth & Fisher Ltd, Halfway (DE) 11
64160	JXB 322	Whitson	? C29F	10/47	Robin & Rambler Coaches Ltd, London SW11 (LN)
64168	* G60xx	Mulliner	B--F	-/47	Gibraltar Motor Hire Services (O-GBZ)
64178	LRB 751	Barnaby	C29F	3/48	Booth & Fisher Ltd, Halfway (DE) 12
64186	JDE 479	Duple	44256 C29F	12/47	WG Richards {Richards Bros}, Moylgrove (PE)
64194					Exported to Helsinki (O-FIN)
64202	?	?	van	-/--	Original operator unknown
64210	GWK 493	Duple	48054 C29F	1/48	A Cox & FW Sephton {Godiva Coaches}, Coventry (WK)
64218	JNK 143	Duple	49104 C29F	12/47	JR Street, Hertford (HT)
64227					Exported to Freetown (O-WAL)
64235	BGS 537	McLennan	C29F	c5/48	A & C McLennan, Spittalfield (PH)
64243	JC 8887	Plaxton	326 FC30F	1/48	Mrs M Ellis, Llanllechid (CN)
64251	MJO 283	Duple	44720 C29F	11/47	PC Skinner {Percival's Coaches}, Oxford (OX) 20
64258	JPO 200	Duple	44205 C29F	1/48	CF Wood & Son Ltd {Enterprise Coaches}, Steyning (WS)
64265	* HB-938	?	B28F	-/47	Original operator unknown (O-FIN)
64275	JMN 132	Pearson	C26F	10/47	JWA Wightman {Sunny Hours Motors}, Onchan (IM)
64283	EJU 786	Yeates	? C29F	1/48	LD Brown {Brown's Blue Coaches}, Markfield (LE)
64291					Exported to Helsinki (O-FIN)
64299	EFU 662	Yeates	? C29F	3/48	AE Brown, Caistor (LI)
64307	* JAH 888	East Coast Motors	C29F	9/48	East Coast Motor Co Ltd {Orange Coaches}, Cromer (NK) 8
64315	KHW 578	Duple	44235 C29F	12/47	Wessex Coaches Ltd, Bristol (GL)
64324					Exported to Freetown (O-WAL)
64332	* LVK 381	Plaxton	955 FC30F	3/48	G Galley (Galley's Motors), Newcastle (ND)
64340	?	?	h/box	-/--	Original operator unknown
64348	# EF 8254	Duple	44636 C29F	1/48	Bee-Line Roadways (Teeside) Ltd, West Hartlepool (DM)
64362	GBT 103	Hedon	C29F	6/48	RA Johnson {Hedon Motor Coaches}, Hedon (ER)
64372	AGV 967	Duple	43873 C29F	12/47	AW Towler & Sons Ltd, Brandon (WF)
64380	FWM 151	Pearson	C26F	5/48	JA Barwick {Crown Motors}, Birkdale (LA)
64388					Exported to Helsinki (O-FIN)

C1252/84

64396	FFH 399	Duple	48256	C29F	1/48	FOJ & RJ Bevan (Bevan Bros) {Soudley Valley Coaches}, Soudley (GL)
64404	JYB 856	Duple	49153	C29F	1/48	E Giles {Venture}, South Petherton (SO)
64412	LTN 942	Duple	49114	C27F	12/47	Moordale Bus Services Ltd, Newcastle (ND)
64421	* G60xx	Duple	47464	C26F	-/47	Gibraltar Motor Hire Services (O-GBZ)
64429	HSM 501	SMT		C29F	12/47	M Green {Green's Motor Hirers}, Lochmaben (DF)
64437	CUD 900	Thurgood	441	C29F	1/48	RC Surman, Chinnor (OX)
64445	DVA 987	SMT		C29F	12/47	I Hutchison {Hutchison's Coaches}, Overtown (LK)
64459	KKE 986	Duple	47937	C29F	12/47	CJ Newman & Son, Hythe (KT)
64469	LRB 191	Duple	43811	C29F	12/47	HS North, Derby (DE) 38
64477	JNN 253	Duple	43645	C29F	12/47	R Wain, Mansfield (NG)
64485						Exported to Helsinki (O-FIN)
64496	BCB 50	Duple	49070	C29F	12/47	Ribblesdale Coachways Ltd, Blackburn (LA) 22
64501	GWO 53	Duple	49132	C29F	2/48	LG & CH Stephens {Stephen's Red Bus}, Tredegar (MH)
64509	FGE 384	SMT		C29F	1/48	Northern Roadways Ltd, Glasgow (LK)
64518	KKJ 933	Thurgood	436	C29F	12/47	WJ Moody, Northfleet (KT)
64533	* G60xx	Duple	47465	C26F	-/47	Gibraltar Motor Hire Services (O-GBZ)
64538	JNK 356	Thurgood	437	C29F	12/47	WJ Carter, Royston (HT)
64542	LHY 64	Lee		C29F	3/49	G Feltham & Sons Ltd {Kingswood Queen}, Kingswood (GL)
64556	KLG 48	Duple	49127	C29F	11/47	Goddard & Buckingham Ltd, Marple (CH)
64566	EUN 88	Duple	43730	C29F	12/47	DC & AN Jones (DC Jones & Sons), Ruabon (DH)
64574	KDH 806	Plaxton	208	C29F	2/48	JN & FN Boult {John Boult & Sons}, Walsall (ST) 39
64582	OE-719	?		B30F	9/48	Piippolan Auto, Pippola (O-FIN)
64597	GR 9615	Duple	49115	C29F	12/47	SF Hunter, Great Lumley (DM)
64721	* EWN 863	Duple	48329	C29F	12/47	Mrs V Williams {Richmond}, Neath (GG)
64726	SML 696	Duple	46913	C29F	12/47	WJ Ray {Ray Coaches}, Edgware (LN)
64743	* DVN 799	Duple	43619	C29F	11/47	RB Allenby {Allenby's Coaches}, Great Ayton (NR)
64749	EJU 699	Duple	43572	C29F	12/47	G Howlett, Quorn (LE) 5
64759	* GAO 469	Duple	47709	C29F	3/48	Cumberland MS, Whitehaven (CU) 252
64767						Exported to Georgetown (O-MAL)
64773	HNY 167	Duple	46754	C29F	3/48	Reliance Motors (Barry) Ltd (GG)
64783	BRN 497	Duple	49094	C29F	5/48	Scout MS Ltd, Preston (LA)
64791	EFU 655	Mulliner	T157	B31F	1/48	Enterprise (Scunthorpe) Passenger Services Ltd {Enterprise} (LI) 82
64803	T-12300	Turun Aut K		B30F	8/48	Vesman Liikenne Oy, Turku (O-FIN)
64807	SB 7183	SMT		C27F	1/48	Air Industrial Developments Ltd {Gold Line}, Dunoon (AL)
64815	SS 6690	SMT		C29F	1/48	W Cleghorn, Haddington (EL)
64823	* HTJ 347	Duple	49072	C29F	12/47	T Barrett {Barley Omnibus Co}, Barley (LA)
64832	EBU 296	Duple	49129	C29F	1/48	G Barlow & Sons Ltd, Oldham (LA)
64840						Exported to Georgetown (O-MAL)
64851	?	?		h/box	-/--	Original operator unknown
64856	DTP 877	Mulliner	T153	B31F	12/47	O Calloway {Micheldever & Stratton Bus Service}, Micheldever (HA)
64870	FO 5127	Duple	46461	C29F	12/47	TA Owen, Knighton (RR)
64880	HNY 432	Thurgood	439	C29F	1/48	Edwards Bros (Beddau) Ltd (GG)
64888	DSA 896	SMT		C27F	12/47	James Shand & Co, Tarland (AD)
64896						Exported to Helsinki (O-FIN)
64907	FGE 836	SMT		C29F	2/48	Northern Roadways Ltd, Glasgow (LK)
64912	SML 276	Thurgood	442	C29F	1/48	Modern Super Coaches Ltd, London N9 (LN)
64920	KAF 559	Duple	48323	C29F	12/47	A & G Morse {Roseland Motors}, Veryan (CO)
64929	* MVW 68	Thurgood	440	C29F	12/47	E Benjamin & E Brandon {Our Bus Service}, Grays (EX) 21
64937	* CTL 275	Mulliner	T152	B31F	12/47	AE Olive, Billinghay (LI) 31
64945						Exported to Georgetown (O-MAL)
64953	CJA 440	Duple	49068	C29F	12/47	H Edwards, Marple (CH)
64967	GUY 122	Pearson		C26F	3/48	A Janes {Bert Janes}, Stourbridge (WO)
64976	HEL 167	Duple	44847	C27F	12/47	Shamrock & Rambler Motor Coaches Ltd, Bournemouth (HA)
64985	EAW 281	Plaxton	328	FC30F	1/48	JW, WHF & GW Lloyd, Oswestry (SH) 12
64993						Exported to Helsinki (O-FIN)
65001	HOD 441	Duple	42365	C29F	3/48	J, EM & AB Geddes {Burton Cars}, Brixham (DN)

C1252/85

65009	JS 7693	Mulliner	T156 B31F	12/47	A MacRae, North Kessock (RY)
65017	* JNA 611	Mulliner	T154 B31F	11/47	Davies, Stockport (XCH)
65026	HUF 892	Duple	43770 C29F	12/47	RG Johnston {Unique Coaches}, Brighton (ES)
65034	KPP 251	Duple	47838 C29F	1/48	JRG Dell {Rover Bus Service}, Lye Green (BK) 10
65046					Exported to Georgetown (O-MAL)
65050	SJ 1168	SMT	C29F	12/47	AC Lennox & Sons {Lennox Motor Service}, Whiting Bay, Arran (BU)
65064	HNY 168	Duple	46755 C29F	3/48	Reliance Motors (Barry) Ltd (GG)
65074	SX 6203	SMT	C29F	1/48	W Douglas & Sons, Armadale (WL)
65082	JUO 601	Duple	47691 C29F	3/48	Devon General, Torquay (DN) TCB601
65091	* RA-152	?	B26F	-/48	Original operator unknown (O-FIN)
65098	SY 8483	SMT	C29F	12/47	WD Tod, Mid Calder (MN)
65106	JXD 221	Duple	48219 C29F	12/47	Pall Mall Car Hire {Pamalhire}, London SW1 (LN)
65114	SB 7180	SMT	C29F	12/47	West Coast Motor Service Co, Campbeltown (AL)
65123					Exported to Georgetown (O-MAL)
65131	GRM 914	SMT	C29F	1/48	B Mandale, Greystoke (CU)
65141	JNC 398	Pearson	C26F	3/48	JW Fieldsend Ltd, Salford (LA)
65147	HSM 535	SMT	C29F	4/48	WJ Elliott {Blue Band Bus Service}, Lockerbie (DF)
65162	CAG 37	SMT	C29F	4/48	James Dodds & Sons, Troon (AR)
65167					Exported to Georgetown (O-MAL)
65171	HUO 672	Beadle	C122 B30F	1/48	Southern National, Exeter (DN) 519
65179	EX 6000	Duple	46931 C29F	12/47	James Calver Ltd {Seagull Coaches}, Great Yarmouth (NK)
65189					Exported to Helsinki (O-FIN)
65195	CAG 89	SMT	C29F	1/48	William Stewart & Son, Stevenston (AR)
65201	* P.374	Auckland TB	FB33F	-/49	Auckland Transport Board (O-NZ) 39
65202	* P.628	North Shore	B33F	-/48	North Shore Transport Co Ltd, Takapuna (O-NZ) 28
65203	P.627	North Shore	B33F	-/48	North Shore Transport Co Ltd, Takapuna (O-NZ) 27
65204	P.622	North Shore	B33F	-/48	North Shore Transport Co Ltd, Takapuna (O-NZ) 22
65205	P2.502	H & H	B29F	-/49	H & H Travel Lines Ltd, Invercargill (O-NZ) 22
65206	* P1.191	McCullough	B29F	-/49	Whatatutu Bus Service, Whatatutu (O-NZ)
65207					Exported to Wellington (O-NZ)
65208	* P.371	Auckland TB	FB33F	6/49	Auckland Transport Board (O-NZ) 36
65209	* ?	?	B35F	-/--	Original operator unknown (O-NZ)
65210	* P.767	Transport BS	B35F	7/48	Transport BS Ltd, Auckland (O-NZ) 14
65211	* s1.047	?	?	-/--	Johnston's Blue Motors, Auckland (O-NZ) 5
65212					Exported to (O-NZ)
65311	DTH 435	Mulliner	T158 B31F	12/47	D Jones & Sons {Dan Jones}, Carmarthen (CR) 3
65319					Exported to Thailand
65328	DDP 295	Duple	44485 C29F	2/48	AE Smith {Smith's Coaches}, Reading (BE)
65336	SMF 413	Duple	44262 C29F	12/47	JWH, EAG & WHR Hall (Hall Bros) {Ickenham Coaches}, Hillingdon (MX)
65344					Exported to Helsinki (O-FIN)
65352	HPT 505	Mulliner	T155 B31F	3/48	Langley Park Motor Co {Gypsy Queen Coaches}, Langley Park (DM)
65366	JDV 754	Duple	46411 C26F	12/47	Woolacombe & Mortehoe Motor Co Ltd, Woolacombe (DN)
65372					Exported to Thailand
65376	HOM 78	Duple	44616 C29F	12/47	A Winwood {Alwyn Coaches}, Birmingham (WK)
65384	GWX 796	Pearson	C26F	4/48	JF, F, W & AH Jowett (EJ Slater & Son), Elland (WR)
65392	* TL-802	?	B30F	-/48	Original operator unknown (O-FIN)
65400	* JP 6692	NMU	C29F	9/48	A Bretherton {Crawford Coaches}, Upholland (LA)
65408	FGE 835	SMT	C29F	2/48	Northern Roadways Ltd, Glasgow (LK)
65416					Exported to Malaya
65425	BGS 433	SMT	C29F	1/48	C Christison {Christison's Bus Service}, Blairgowrie (PH)
65433	DCX 964	Duple	49100 C29F	12/47	Chapman's Ivy Coaches Ltd, Milnsbridge (WR) 22
65441					Exported to Helsinki (O-FIN)
65449	HUP 891	Plaxton	610 FC30F	1/48	C McCune, Stockton-on-Tees (DM)
65463	HNY 221	Duple	46824 C29F	12/47	Mrs SA Bebb, Llantwit Fardre (GG)
65469					Exported to Tanganyika
65473	HUO 673	Beadle	C123 B30F	1/48	Southern National, Exeter (DN) 520
65481	HUO 674	Beadle	C124 B30F	1/48	Southern National, Exeter (DN) 521
65507					Exported to Antwerp (O-B)

C1252/86

65511	EX 6148	Plaxton	596	FC30F	6/48	WJ Haylett {Felix Coaches}, Great Yarmouth (NK) 4
65515	* HUP 737	Duple	49116	C29F	12/47	JR & V Cleasby, Langley Moor (DM)
65519						Exported to Tanganyika
65523	JP 6921	Pearson		C26F	9/48	M, O & R Hart (O Hart & Sons), Coppull (LA)
65530	HUP 574	Duple	43620	C29F	12/47	G Pennington {Cosy Coaches/Meadowfield Motor Co}, Meadowfield (DM)
65538						Exported to Antwerp (O-B)
65546	GCG 886	Wadham		C29F	3/48	Creamline Motor Services (Bordon) Ltd (HA)
65553	EAW 131	Mulliner	T159	B31F	1/48	Mrs M Ellis, Llanllechid (CN)
65560	HUP 697	Plaxton	609	FC30F	12/47	Creamline Motor Services (Bordon) Ltd (HA)
65569	EUN 612	Pearson		C26F	5/48	JB Pye Ltd, Rhos-on-Sea (DH)
65577	KKE 802	Mulliner	T161	B28F	12/47	JE Mannifield {Camden Coaches}, Sevenoaks (KT)
65585	SY 8499	SMT		C29F	1/48	W Stewart, Dalkeith (MN)
65593						Exported to Port Elizabeth (O-ZA)
65601	HYN 470	Duple	43830	C29F	12/47	Essex County Coaches Ltd, London E15 (LN)
65609	KPP 253	Mulliner	T160	B31F	12/47	FW Hewitt & K Shurrock, Brill (BK)
65617	ORF 90	Duple	43324	C29F	1/48	JB Box, Lower Gornal (ST)
65625						Exported to Antwerp (O-B)
65633	FCJ 14	Duple	43939	C29F	1/48	AE Bengry {Primrose Motor Services}, Leominster (HR)
65641	* EAW 275	Duple	43234	C29F	1/48	JT, FW & GE Whittle {JT Whittle & Sons}, Highley (SH)
65649	KWB 334	Duple	49073	C29F	1/48	ET White & Sons Ltd, Calver (DE)
65666	JVU 269	NMU		C25F	11/48	AF Holden & Co Ltd, Manchester (LA)
65674	FFY 949	Duple	49139	C27F	12/47	Enterprise Tours (Southport) Ltd (LA)
65682						Exported to Antwerp (O-B)
65690	FFY 950	Duple	49140	C27F	12/47	Enterprise Tours (Southport) Ltd (LA)
65698	#EBU 223	Pearson		C25F	2/48	H Harrison, Chadderton (LA)
65826	HYR 528	Mulliner	T163	B31F	2/48	BOAC (LN)
65834	JTB 139	SMT		C27F	3/48	Parker's Motors Ltd, Grange-over-Sands (LA)
65842	CST 343	SMT		C29F	3/48	Dean Bros, Kingussie (IV) 20
65850	ATS 186	AF Smith		C25F	5/48	Andrew W Watson & Co {Watson's Tours}, Dundee (AS)
65858						Exported to Port Elizabeth (O-ZA)
65866	#I NW 829	ACB		C29F	11/47	Kelsall Coaches Ltd {Saffman & Beasley}, Leeds (WR)
65883	GDK 288	Pearson		C26F	6/48	Howarth Bros (Royton) Ltd, Royton (LA)
65891	KMB 246	Pearson		C26F	6/48	J Lofthouse {Lofty's Coaches}, Bridge Trafford (CH)
65899						Exported to Antwerp (O-B)
65907	?	?		van	11/47	Mann, Isleworth (GMX)
65915	PRF 561	Longwell Green		C27F	10/48	Greatrex Motor Coaches Ltd, Stafford (ST) 48
65923	* EEA 500	Whitson	?	C27F	6/49	Hills Tours Ltd, West Bromwich (ST)
65931	MBB 263	Plaxton	587	FC30F	9/48	G Galley (Galley's Motors), Newcastle (ND)
65940	HYR 529	Mulliner	T162	B31F	12/47	BOAC (LN)
65950	FGE 343	SMT		C27F	2/48	Lowland Motorways Ltd, Glasgow (LK) 18
65957						Exported to Port Elizabeth (O-ZA)
65963	AKS 314	SMT		C29F	1/48	A Moore & Son, Bonchester Bridge (RH)
65978	MNU 79	Allsop		C29F	5/48	Booth & Fisher Ltd, Halfway (DE) 14
65988	* FJW 110	Mulliner	T164	C26F	3/48	Worthington Motor Tours Ltd, Wolverhampton (ST)
65998						Exported to Antwerp (O-B)
66004	* HFD 945	Willenhall		FC28F	7/48	NC Kendrick, Dudley (WO)
66012	FRY 12	Willenhall		FC29F	10/48	Mrs GH Clayton (Clayton Bros) {The Royal Blue}, Leicester (LE)
66020	* JFJ 14	Duple	43365	C29F	3/48	Greenslades, Exeter (DN)
66028	* DUH 627	Whitson	?	C29F	4/48	HH Shurnhill & PS Baston {Brownhills Garage}, Cardiff (GG)
66036	GWU 913	Duple	49069	C29F	1/48	JJ Longstaff, Mirfield (WR)
66047	DBN 51	Plaxton	711	C29F	8/48	JW Nesbit, Atherton (LA)
66056						Exported to Port Elizabeth (O-ZA)
66060	MNU 80	Allsop		C29F	5/48	Booth & Fisher Ltd, Halfway (DE) 13
66075	KAH 555	East Coast Motors		C29F	6/49	East Coast Motor Co Ltd {Orange Coaches}, Cromer (NK) 5
66082	LRB 749	Barnaby		C29F	3/48	Booth & Fisher Ltd, Halfway (DE) 10
66088	#KND 388	Junction		C29F	8/49	H Ramsden Ltd, Oldham (LA)
66095						Exported to Antwerp (O-B)
66103	CST 511	Scunthorpe Motors		B26F	4/48	Macrae & Dick Ltd, Inverness (IV)
66106	HYE 762	Whitson	?	C29F	11/47	Robin & Rambler Coaches Ltd, London SW11 (LN)

C1252/87

66113	MNU 81	Allsop		C29F	5/48 Booth & Fisher Ltd, Halfway (DE) 15
66119	ORF 833	Auto-Cellulose		C27F	3/48 JW Genner, Quarry Bank (ST)
66125	FJW 114	Duple	48042	C26F	3/48 Worthington Motor Tours Ltd, Wolverhampton (ST)
66131					Exported to Port Elizabeth (O-ZA)
66138	JXC 931	Duple	44209	C24F	1/48 United Service Transport Co Ltd, London SW9 (LN) 1073
66153	* JAF 837	Strachan		C26F	2/48 Newquay Motor Co Ltd {Red & White Tours} (CO)
66156	EWV 389	Duple	43874	C29F	11/47 J Crook & Sons, Melksham (WI)
66161	LRB 222	Duple	44315	C29F	12/47 GH Watson, Church Gresley (DE)
66168	JXH 662	Duple	44437	C29F	3/48 George Ewer & Co Ltd {Grey Green}, London N16 (LN)
66174	LPL 780	Duple	44787	C29F	12/47 A Plumridge, Lowfield Heath (WS)
66180					Exported to Antwerp (O-B)
66187	* SX 6218	SMT		C29F	3/48 Browning's Luxury Coaches Ltd, Whitburn (WL) 7
66193	BGS 480	SMT		C29F	3/48 Loch Katrine Steamboat Co Ltd, Callander (PH)
66199					Exported to Port Elizabeth (O-ZA)
66207	* GRM 910	SMT		C29F	3/48 WD Sowerby {Sowerby's Tours}, Gilsland (CU)
66214	DVH 169	Duple	49284	C29F	12/47 Hanson's Buses Ltd, Huddersfield (WR) 239
66219	* DTP 929	Duple	47884	C29F	1/48 White Heather Transport Ltd, Southsea (HA)
66224	JXD 650	Duple	44763	C29F	12/47 J, J, J Jnr & E Clarke {Clarke's Luxury Coaches}, London E16 (LN)
66230	* FWM 196	KW		C27F	5/48 Howard Coaches Ltd, Southport (LA)
66236	HB 6629	Green (Merthyr)		B29F	7/48 Morlais Services Ltd, Merthyr Tydfil (GG) 49
66243	GWU 855	Duple	49271	C29F	2/48 Mexborough & Swinton (WR) 77
66249	HTJ 278	Duple	49288	C29F	3/48 W Robinson & Sons, Great Harwood (LA)
66255					Exported to Antwerp (O-B)
66262	EAW 283	Duple	44095	C29F	12/47 RH & SJ Foxall {Robert Foxall & Sons}, Bridgnorth (SH)
66268	HTJ 841	Duple	49164	C29F	12/47 AE Wheatley, Patricroft (LA) 6
66274					Exported to Accra (O-WAC)
66281	AEE 966	Duple	46929	C29F	1/48 A & AE Blackbourn Ltd {Granville Tours}, Grimsby (LI) 150
66289	KAF 882	Duple	46241	C26F	1/48 JM & CM Prout {Prout Bros}, Port Isaac (CO)
66294	* MVW 556	Thurgood	440	C29F	12/47 E Benjamin & E Brandon {Our Bus Service}, Grays (EX) 22
66299	JXC 989	Mulliner	T166	B31F	11/47 London County Council (XLN) 1574
66305	* BCB 263	Trans-United		C27F	2/48 Whitehurst Tours Ltd, Accrington (LA)
66313	ASN 465	SMT		C29F	1/48 C Elliott, Jamestown (DB)
66325	JXC 990	Mulliner	T167	B31F	11/47 London County Council (XLN) 1575
66331	MVW 285	Duple	49295	C29F	12/47 City Coach Co Ltd, Brentwood (EX) B51
66335					Exported to Antwerp (O-B)
66340	SML 144	Mulliner	T168	B31F	12/47 Middlesex County Council (XMX)
66343	SML 700	Duple	44217	C29F	12/47 Dicks, London NW10 (LN)
66353					Exported to Accra (O-WAC)
66364	JPT 4	Yeates	?	C29F	2/48 Trimdon Motor Services Ltd, Trimdon Grange (DM) 20
66368	FJW 107	Mulliner	T165	C28F	3/48 Worthington Motor Tours Ltd, Wolverhampton (ST)
66375	EDW 541	Yeates	?	C29F	2/48 R Williams, Newport (MH)
66379	JTC 248	Trans-United		C27F	7/48 Bracewells (Colne) Ltd (LA)
66388					Exported to Accra (O-WAC)
66394					Exported to Antwerp (O-B)
66398	FGE 837	SMT		C29F	2/48 Northern Roadways Ltd, Glasgow (LK)
66402	JKB 944	Pearson		C26F	7/48 Sunniways Coaches (Pearsons of Liverpool) Ltd (LA) 7
66414	LEH 339	Duple	48033	C29F	3/48 W Stonier & Sons Ltd, Goldenhill (ST)
66422	ORF 497	Yeates	?	C29F	2/48 H Nickolls, Milford (ST) 5
66430					Exported to Antwerp (O-B)
66438	* MBB 262	Plaxton	586	FC30F	6/48 G Galley (Galley's Motors), Newcastle (ND)
66446					Exported to Antwerp (O-B)
66454					Exported to Accra (O-WAC)
66458	CNL 947	Duple	49152	C27F	1/48 WF Wilkinson {Swift Motor Service}, Ashington (ND) 8
66474	HUP 859	Thurgood	445	C29F	1/48 GH, S & JB Atkinson (GH Atkinson & Sons) {General Omnibus Services}, Chester-le-Street (DM) 12
66484	KAF 912	Duple	46919	C29F	1/48 East Cornwall Co-operative Society, Saltash (CO)
66490					Exported to Biel (O-CH)
66498	CWH 340	Pearson		C26F	2/48 Enterprise Transport Ltd, Kearsley (LA)
66513 - 66524					Exported to Bombay (O-IND)
66607	#VA-189	?		B26F	6/48 Sarpon Liikenne Oy, Seinäjoki (O-FIN)

C1252/88

66614	CTY 753	ACB		C26F	5/48	J Lowther {Hollings Garage & Engineering Works}, Wallsend-on-Tyne (ND)
66622	HG 9241	Mulliner	T171	B31F	12/47	Burnley, Colne & Nelson JTC (LA) 5
66630	* JAH 570	?		C27F	7/48	WA Dalliston, Wells-next-the-Sea (NK)
66638						Exported to Accra (O-WAC)
66646	?	Mulliner		B--F	-/--	Shell Petroleum Co, Cabimas (O-YV)
66654	* KDE 525	?		C29F	10/48	GF Rees, Neyland (PE)
66664	GR 9967	Pearson		C26F	9/48	Humphrey Bros {Progressive}, Brandon Colliery (DM)
66667	GCE 842	Thurgood	444	C29F	1/48	AE, WI & PL Harris {Progressive}, Cambridge (CM)
66679	JMN 399	Pearson		C26F	1/48	WH Shimmin & Co Ltd, Douglas (IM)
66689	MTW 868	Duple	44704	C29F	2/48	EA Winwood, London E10 (LN) 17
66695	?	Mulliner		B--F	-/--	Shell Petroleum Co, Cabimas (O-YV)
66703	HTJ 279	Duple	49289	C29F	3/48	W Robinson & Sons, Great Harwood (LA) 18
66711	#SS 7023	Junction		C29F	9/48	W Ralton, Prestonpans (EL)
66720	EBL 952	Duple	44448	C29F	12/47	Windsorian Motor Coach Services Ltd, Windsor (BE) 52
66727	DVH 183	Duple	49285	C29F	1/48	Hanson's Buses Ltd, Huddersfield (WR) 240
66735						Exported to Accra (O-WAC)
66743	?	Marshall		library	-/--	Kent County Council (GKT)
66753	ASN 502	SMT		C29F	2/48	C McAteer, Dumbarton (DB)
66759						Exported to Palestine
66764	JNN 174	Duple	48314	C29F	12/47	Barton Transport, Chilwell (NG) 527
66776	JP 6750	Duple	49101	C29F	1/48	Taylor Bros, Standish (LA)
66784	* GNP 278	Duple	47658	C29F	3/48	Samuel Johnson (Supreme) Ltd, Stourbridge (WO)
66792						Exported to Palestine
66800	MVW 387	Duple	48027	C29F	4/48	Rose Bros {Primrose}, Chelmsford (EX) 1
66809	ECO 997	Mashford		C27F	7/48	Millbrook Steamboat & Trading Co Ltd (CO)
66816	MTW 879	Duple	44752	C27F	2/48	GL Sutton {Sutton's Coaches}, Clacton (EX)
66821	#H-8177	?		B26F	-/--	Niemisen Linjat Oy, Padasjoki (O-FIN)
66824	FDT 788	Jaques		C25F	-/48	SM Wilson & Sons Ltd, Balby (WR) 10
66832						Exported to Accra (O-WAC)
66842	CTY 7	Duple	49118	C27F	1/48	JH Batty & Sons {Wansbeck Motor Services}, Ashington (ND) 6
66848	FT 6281	Duple	49117	C29F	1/48	G Chapman {Priory Motor Coach Co}, North Shields (ND) 47
66856						Exported to Helsinki (O-FIN)
66861	DRV 27	Duple	46422	C29F	1/48	Triumph Coaches Ltd, Southsea (HA) 125
66873	JMN 126	Duple	49215	C29F	10/47	RH Corkill, Onchan (IM)
66883						Exported to Accra (O-WAC)
66890						Exported to Helsinki (O-FIN)
66898	HTJ 957	Duple	49098	C29F	5/48	J Lamb, Upholland (LA)
66905	ANH 831	Mulliner	T169	B31F	1/48	EJ Robinson, Stewkley (BK)
66913	JMN 127	Duple	49216	C29F	10/47	CL Kennish {Rambler Motors}, Douglas (IM)
66921	GWW 100	Duple	49350	C29F	1/48	AE Gillard, Normanton (WR)
66929	EBU 294	Duple	49137	C29F	1/48	Harrison's Tours (Oldham) Ltd (LA)
66937	FSP 898	SMT		C29F	3/48	J Birrell, Markinch (FE)
66946	HSM 543	SMT		C29F	2/48	T Rae & Sons {Boreland Bus Service}, Boreland (DF)
66953						Exported to Helsinki (O-FIN)
66958	FGD 888	SMT		C29F	2/48	Cotter's Motor Tours Ltd, Glasgow (LK)
66968	#SMY 140	SMT		C25F	2/48	BEA, Ruislip (MX) 1119
66974						Exported to Accra (O-WAC)
66982						Exported to Helsinki (O-FIN)
66993	?	Mulliner	T175	?	11/47	BOAC, unknown overseas location
66997	?	Mulliner	T176	?	11/47	BOAC, unknown overseas location
67085 - 67096						Exported to Sydney (O-AUS)
67110	JDV 789	Mulliner	T170	B31F	12/47	Balls Ltd, Newton Abbot (DN) 3
67119	* FFS 869	SMT		C25F	2/48	SMT (MN) C169
67124	* BGS 595	SMT		C29F	2/48	Loch Katrine Steamboat Co Ltd, Callander (PH)
67132	GUE 207	Yeates	?	C29F	2/48	AT & AE Hastilow {Tudor Rose}, Sutton Coldfield (WK)
67141	* JDV 561	Duple	49342	C29F	1/48	Waverley Motor Coach Tours Ltd, Paignton (DN)
67151						Exported to Helsinki (O-FIN)
67161	* JNA 920	Duple	49291	C29F	1/48	Fred Corkhill Ltd {District Hire Service}, West Didsbury (LA)
67167	EJU 822	Mulliner	T174	B31F	1/48	AA Oliver {Luxicoaches}, Loughborough (LE)
67175						Exported to Accra (O-WAC)

C1252/89

67182	HLJ 171	Harrington	?	C29F	3/48 CJ Pounds {Charlie's Cars}, Bournemouth (HA) 58
67187					Exported to Helsinki (O-FIN)
67190	* JMN 201	Mulliner	T172	B30F	10/47 J Broadbent {Safeway}, Ramsey (IM)
67196	JFJ 178	Duple	46959	C29F	5/48 Greenslades, Exeter (DN)
67204	EWN 917	Mulliner	T173	B31F	1/48 R Parkhouse & Sons, Penclawdd (GG)
67210	EBU 709	Plaxton	615	FC30F	6/48 Ralph Renton Ltd, Hollinwood (LA)
67218	JNN 712	Yeates	?	C29F	3/48 J Thomas (J Thomas & Son) {Thomas Tours}, North Muskham (NG)
67225	EBU 449	Plaxton	638	FC30F	3/48 Ralph Renton Ltd, Hollinwood (LA)
67233					Exported to Helsinki (O-FIN)
67238	* JP 7040	Pearson		C29F	7/48 H Heaps Ltd, Charnock Richard (LA)
67249					Exported to Helsinki (O-FIN)
67260	EBL 967	Mulliner	T182	B26F	1/48 JA Perry {Crescent Coaches}, Windsor (BE)
67267	KPP 918	Thurgood	454	C29F	2/48 Pilot Coaches (High Wycombe) Ltd (BK)
67274	EFU 656	Mulliner	T178	B31F	1/48 Enterprise (Scunthorpe) Passenger Services Ltd {Enterprise} (LI) 41
67279	HTJ 316	Duple	49144	C29F	1/48 IJ Curwen & Sons Ltd, Lancaster (LA)
67284	JP 6752	Duple	49102	C29F	1/48 Beacon Coaches Ltd, Upholland (LA)
67289	FDL 239	Duple	46337	C29F	1/48 Mrs V Pearce {White Heather}, Ryde (IW) 1
67293					Exported to Helsinki (O-FIN)
67297					Exported to Lagos (O-WAN)
67302	HAD 866	Duple	46691	C29F	1/48 Warner's Motors Ltd, Tewkesbury (GL)
67312	JXC 932	Duple	44210	C24F	1/48 United Service Transport Co Ltd, London SW9 (LN) 1074
67316					Exported to Helsinki (O-FIN)
67328	FBT 967	Duple	49320	C29F	1/47 JA Holt, Newport (ER)
67330		see 67336			
67336	* TM-355	?		B27F	10/48 Halikon, Sairaala (O-FIN)
67346	GWU 633	Duple	49349	C27F	1/48 G Pyne {White Coach Tours}, Starbeck (WR)
67351	HTJ 317	Duple	49145	C27F	1/48 RH Harrison, Morecambe (LA)
67359	JNE 247	Pearson		C26F	6/48 JW Fieldsend Ltd, Salford (LA)
67365	BRN 565	Duple	49147	C29F	1/48 Whittingham Mental Hospital, Goosnargh (XLA)
67370	BRN 499	Duple	49096	C29F	2/48 Scout MS Ltd, Preston (LA)
67375	BRN 654	Duple	49141	C29F	1/48 E Barnes {Premier Motors}, Preston (LA)
67378					Exported to Helsinki (O-FIN)
67383					Exported to Malaya
67388	* CWH 370	Duple	49142	C29F	1/48 W Knowles & Sons, Bolton (LA)
67396	* JFJ 198	Heaver		C25F	6/48 Taylor's Central Garage (Exeter) Ltd (DN)
67402	TM-787	?		B29F	2/49 Ketonen Pauli Oy, Nakkila (O-FIN)
67414	JNA 932	Duple	49292	C29F	1/48 WD Hartle (WD Hartle & Son), Buxton (DE)
67422	T-12651	Autohalli		B30F	-/49 Leiniön Liikenne Oy, Turku (O-FIN)
67432	CFV 827	Duple	49143	C29F	2/48 J Abbott & Sons (Blackpool) Ltd (LA)
67437	BRN 498	Duple	49095	C29F	5/48 Scout MS Ltd, Preston (LA)
67446	* FFS 874	SMT		C25F	3/48 SMT (MN) C174
67451	* FFS 870	SMT		C25F	2/48 SMT (MN) C170
67456					Exported to Malaya
67461	GWW 532	Duple	49351	C29F	1/48 A, JW, S & AJ Camplejohn (Camplejohn Bros), Darfield (WR) 22
67468	* FFS 871	SMT		C25F	2/48 SMT (MN) C171
67475	LUB 12	Duple	49359	C29F	1/48 Roy Neill Ltd, Leeds (WR)
67482	CES 721	SCWS		B28F	1/49 AS & WT Whyte {Bankfoot Motor Co}, Bankfoot (PH)
67488	CES 447	SCWS		B28F	11/48 AS & WT Whyte {Bankfoot Motor Co}, Bankfoot (PH)
67500, 67508					Exported to Helsinki (O-FIN)
67518	GWW 292	Duple	49367	C29F	1/48 W Simpson, Ripon (WR) 4
67523	FJW 113	Mulliner	T179	C28F	4/48 Worthington Motor Tours Ltd, Wolverhampton (ST)
67532	JXD 635	Mulliner	T183	B31F	11/47 London County Council (XLN) 1576
67537	HAD 953	Mulliner	T177	B28F	3/48 BE Dallow, Tewkesbury (GL)
67542					Exported to Malaya
67547	JXD 637	Mulliner	T184	B31F	11/47 London County Council (XLN) 1577
67555	LPU 616	Beadle	C134	B30F	12/47 Eastern National, Chelmsford (EX) 3926
67560	OMT 602	Duple	44200	C29F	1/48 Ardley Bros Ltd, London N17 (LN) 6
67568	JNK 713	Thurgood	446	C29F	1/48 EG Hewitt {Premier Coaches}, Watford (HT)
67574	JYB 950	Mulliner	T181	B32F	1/48 Quantock Hauliers Ltd, Watchet (SO)
67586, 67594					Exported to Helsinki (O-FIN)

C1252/90

67724		JC 8924	Mulliner	T180	B31F	2/48	Clynnog & Trevor Motor Co Ltd, Trevor (CN)
67729	*	LPU 617	Beadle	C135	B30F	12/47	Eastern National, Chelmsford (EX) 3927
67738		JDE 487	Duple	47981	C29F	2/48	WG Richards {Richards Bros}, Moylgrove (PE)
67743		JDV 912	Whitson	?	C29F	12/47	CA Gayton {Gayton's Coaches}, Ashburton (DN)
67748							Exported to Malaya
67753		HUO 675	Beadle	C125	B30F	1/48	Southern National, Exeter (DN) 522
67761	*	FDL 535	Margham		C26F	6/48	Fountain Garage Ltd, Cowes (IW)
67773	*	CTL 460	Duple	47580	C29F	1/48	AE Olive, Billinghay (LI)
67776	*	FFS 873	SMT		C25F	3/48	SMT (MN) C173
67780	*	FFS 872	SMT		C25F	3/48	SMT (MN) C172
67792		?	?		?	-/--	Iraq Petroleum Co, Basra (O-IRQ)
67800		?	Mulliner	T187	?	12/47	BOAC, unknown overseas location
67810		EAW 285	Duple	46458	C29F	1/48	E, G, FJC & W Smith {W Smith & Sons}, Donnington Wood (SH)
67815		CFV 840	Duple	49387	C29F	3/48	Batty-Holt Touring Service Ltd, Blackpool (LA)
67824		JTB 292	Duple	49148	C29F	1/48	Atkinson & Co {Dreadnought Motors}, Morecambe (LA)
67829							Exported to Antwerp (O-B)
67834		FJW 100	Duple	48793	C29F	1/48	Harman's Motor Services Ltd, Wolverhampton (ST)
67839		EJB 460	Thurgood	451	C29F	2/48	HW Pabst {Abingdon Coaches}, Abingdon (BE)
67847		GR 9682	Duple	49119	C29F	1/48	S Featonby {Shotton Bus Co}, Shotton Colliery (DM)
67852							Exported to Port Elizabeth (O-ZA)
67861		DET 961	Duple	49360	C29F	1/48	GW Bailey {Billies Coaches}, Mexborough (WR)
67866		KLG 49	Duple	49128	C29F	12/47	Goddard & Buckingham Ltd, Marple (CH)
67878							Exported to Antwerp (O-B)
67886		MTW 819	Mulliner	T185	B28F	1/48	FC Heath {Heath's Saloon Coaches}, West Bergholt (EX)
67896		GHO 786	Lee		B26F	5/48	Hants & Sussex Motor Services Ltd, Emsworth (HA) 29
67910		FDL 240	Duple	43632	C29F	1/48	B Groves, Cowes (IW)
67915							Exported to Port Elizabeth (O-ZA)
67920		JTB 140	Duple	49365	C29F	1/48	Felsted & White Ltd, Newton-le-Willows (LA)
67925		JTB 210	Duple	44207	C27F	2/48	Kia-Ora Motor Services Ltd, Morecambe (LA)
67934		GWX 156	Plaxton	696	C29F	3/48	G Pyne {White Coach Tours}, Starbeck (WR)
67938		EUN 318	Duple	43731	C29F	1/48	DC & AN Jones (DC Jones & Sons), Ruabon (DH)
67946		MVW 155	Duple	44876	C29F	12/47	Dryer's Coaches Ltd, London E17 (LN)
67952		HUO 676	Beadle	C126	B30F	2/48	Southern National, Exeter (DN) 523
67964							Exported to Antwerp (O-B)
67972		LUB 500	Plaxton	654	FC30F	2/48	JB Midgely & Son Ltd, Leeds (WR)
67982	*	HDD 119	Duple	43784	C29F	1/48	AH, V & Mrs E Fluck {Fluck & Sons}, Notgrove (GL)
67996		HUO 677	Beadle	C127	B30F	2/48	Southern National, Exeter (DN) 524
68001							Exported to Antwerp (O-B)
68006		AJV 91	Plaxton	688	C29F	2/48	FA & WR Stark (FA Stark and Sons), Tetney (LI)
68011	*	KGH 389	?		prison	11/48	Metropolitan Police, London SW1 (GLN)
68019		FJW 111	Mulliner	T186	C26F	4/48	Worthington Motor Tours Ltd, Wolverhampton (ST)
68024		?	?		van	-/--	Original operator unknown
68033		DBD 936	Beadle	C141	B30F	1/48	United Counties, Northampton (NO) 101
68039							Exported to Port Elizabeth (O-ZA)
68050		ACH 850	Duple	49493	C29F	2/48	Derby Borough Police (XDE)
68058		GOR 824	Wadham		C29F	9/48	Creamline Motor Services (Bordon) Ltd (HA)
68069		MNU 82	Allsop		C29F	5/48	Booth & Fisher Ltd, Halfway (DE) 16
68071			see 68011				
68082							Exported to Port Elizabeth (O-ZA)
68087		GNP 704	Plaxton	940	FC30F	3/48	Mrs ME Ward {Ward's Super de Luxe}, Sidemoor (WO)
68092		JTB 639	Duple	49150	C29F	1/48	T Towler (Lytham) Ltd (LA)
68097		LUA 541	Duple	49344	C29F	1/48	JA Hudson Ltd, Leeds (WR)
68173 - 68184							Exported to Melbourne (O-AUS)
68225		CTY 168	Duple	43760	C29F	3/48	R Armstrong, Westerhope (ND) 51
68230		GWX 998	Wilks & Meade		C28F	3/48	Harry Broughton & Sons Ltd, Barnoldswick (WR)
68238		FOD 25	Whitson	5858	C29F	12/47	CA Gayton {Gayton's Coaches}, Ashburton (DN)
68245		ADJ 57	Duple	49099	C29F	1/48	James Bridge (St Helens) Ltd (LA)
68256	*	GX-3488	Den Oudsten	1771	B34-	4/50	Beemster, Averhorn (O-NL) 6
68264		BRN 500	Duple	49097	C29F	2/48	Scout MS Ltd, Preston (LA)
68274		GNP 702	Plaxton	938	FC30F	3/48	Mrs ME Ward {Ward's Super de Luxe}, Sidemoor (WO)
68288		ZH 9893	GJ Roberts		C25F	-/--	Corais Iompair Eireann, Dublin (EI) BP2
68293		FHR 876	Swindon		C27F	8/48	Private Coaches Ltd {Orange Coaches}, Swindon (WI)

C1252/91

68299		HNY 337	Duple	46825	C29F	2/48 J Evans (J Evans & Sons) {Express Motors}, Kenfig Hill (GG)
68303	*	KHY 917	Duple	43267	C29F	1/48 Wessex Coaches Ltd, Bristol (GL)
68311		BRN 710	Duple	49149	C29F	1/48 Crossley & Fishwick Ltd {Enterprise}, Preston (LA)
68325	*	EJU 936	(Duple?)		C27F	3/48 L Pole & Sons Ltd, Syston (LE)
68329		EWV 655	Duple	43555	C29F	1/48 AW Haddrell {AW Haddrell & Sons}, Calne (WI)
68336		GNP 703	Plaxton	939	FC30F	3/48 Mrs ME Ward {Ward's Super de Luxe}, Sidemoor (WO)
68342	*	HG-822	Virtanen		B26F	-/47 Original operator unknown (O-FIN)
68349		JXE 641	Duple	49413	C29F	6/48 Comben, Selsdon (SR)
68355		TMG 168	Strachan		C29F	12/47 Wright Bros (London) Ltd, London W7 (LN)
68363		ZH 9894	GJ Roberts		C25F	-/-- Corais Iompair Eireann, Dublin (EI) BP3
68371	*	JOD 354	Heaver		C29F	5/48 Teign Cars Ltd, Teignmouth (DN)
68377		?	SMT		van	-/-- Pettigrew, unknown location (G??)
68382		GWP 101	Willenhall		FC29F	6/48 W Walton {Silver King Coaches}, Stourbridge (WO)
68387		DVH 210	Duple	49286	C29F	1/48 Hanson's Buses Ltd, Huddersfield (WR) 241
68391			see 68394			
68394		SML 467	Duple	44386	C29F	1/48 Lacey's (East Ham) Ltd, London E6 (LN)
68401		JDV 562	Duple	49343	C29F	1/48 Waverley Motor Coach Tours Ltd, Paignton (DN)
68407						Exported to Helsinki (O-FIN)
68414		GCG 512	Duple	46793	C29F	2/48 HT Nobbs {Nobby Bus}, Preston Candover (HA)
68435	*	DRV 140	Duple	47882	C29F	1/48 E Byng & Sons Ltd, Southsea (HA)
68441		GWW 929	Plaxton	691	C29F	3/48 Kirkby & Sons (Harthill) Ltd (WR)
68449		CJT 864	Duple	46910	C29F	1/48 E Toomer, Manswood (DT)
68457		HPW 901	Duple	43549	C29F	1/48 F Thompson {Eniway Coaches}, Dereham (NK)
68463		HNY 328	Mulliner	T192	B31F	1/48 C Lewis & J Jacob, Maesteg (GG)
68467		JTB 286	Duple	49103	C29F	2/48 J Davies, Leigh (LA)
68472						Exported to Accra (O-WAC)
68479						Exported to Helsinki (O-FIN)
68486		MNU 83	Allsop		C29F	6/48 Booth & Fisher Ltd, Halfway (DE) 17
68492	*	DPN 936	Kenex		C27F	5/48 Ruggs Ltd {Greyline Coaches}, Lewes (ES)
68499		DCX 884	Plaxton	280	C29F	2/48 Hanson's Buses Ltd, Huddersfield (WR) 261
68569		GOY 234	Duple	44520	C29F	1/48 JE & HE Jewell {Jewell's Coaches}, Croydon (SR)
68575		ERP 45	?		library	-/-- Northamptonshire County Council (GNO)
68583		GUY 393	North Worcs Garage		van	-/-- Stringer, Stourbridge (GWO)
68592	*	GWU 856	Duple	49272	C29F	2/48 Mexborough & Swinton (WR) 78
68597						Exported to Accra (O-WAC)
68601		#LNW 830	ACB		C28F	12/47 Kelsall Coaches Ltd {Saffman & Beasley}, Leeds (WR)
68606		GWW 928	Plaxton	692	C29F	10/48 Kirkby & Sons (Harthill) Ltd (WR)
68613		FCA 139	Pearson		C26F	6/48 Hancocks (Old Colwyn) Ltd {Royal Blue} (DH)
68618		GWW 930	Plaxton	690	C29F	5/48 Kirkby & Sons (Harthill) Ltd (WR)
68626		FFS 875	SMT		C25F	3/48 SMT (MN) C175
68633, 68651						Exported to Helsinki (O-FIN)
68655		CWH 694	Pearson		C26F	6/48 Enterprise Transport Ltd, Kearsley (LA)
68663	*	GWW 407	Duple	49346	C29F	1/48 L & G Kenworthy, Hoyland Common (WR)
68669		DBD 937	Beadle	C142	B30F	2/48 United Counties, Northampton (NO) 102
68677		?	SMT		bank	6/48 Clydesdale Bank, Edinburgh (GMN)
68683	*	DBD 938	Beadle	C143	B30F	2/48 United Counties, Northampton (NO) 103
68687		JFJ 261	Tiverton		C25F	6/48 Greenslades, Exeter (DN)
68692						Exported to Accra (O-WAC)
68699		LPU 618	Beadle	C136	B30F	2/48 Eastern National, Chelmsford (EX) 3928
68725						Exported to Wellington (O-NZ)
68726	*	P.338	Auckland TB		B33F	-/49 Auckland Transport Board (O-NZ) 3
68727						Exported to Wellington (O-NZ)
68728	*	?	Buckton		B--F	-/48 Buckton, location unknown (O-NZ)
68729	*	P2.499	H & H		B29F	-/48 H & H Travel Lines Ltd, Invercargill (O-NZ) 19
68730	*	P.629	North Shore		B33F	-/48 North Shore Transport Co Ltd, Takapuna (O-NZ) 29
68731		?	NZMB		B30F	12/48 New Zealand Railways Road Services (O-NZ) 1690
68732	*	?	NZMB		B30F	-/49 Original operator unknown (O-NZ)
68733		?	NZMB		B30F	10/48 New Zealand Railways Road Services (O-NZ) 1688
68734		?	NZMB		B30F	10/48 New Zealand Railways Road Services (O-NZ) 1689
68735	*	P2.100	NZMB		B30F	11/48 New Zealand Railways Road Services (O-NZ) 1691
68736	*	P3.208	NZMB		B30F	10/48 New Zealand Railways Road Services (O-NZ) 1687
68764		MNU 686	Woodall Nicholson		DP29F	5/48 Booth & Fisher Ltd, Halfway (DE) 19

C1252/92

68772	?	SMT		van	-/--	Original operator unknown
68779	HJ-288	?		B29F	-/49	Airikkala Eino, location unknown (O-FIN)
68800	HPW 180	Mulliner	T190	B31F	1/48	TH Hawes {Creake Services}, North Creake (NK)
68807	HTJ 325	Duple	49130	C29F	2/48	EM Pickwick & Sons, Radcliffe (LA)
68815	CGS 134	NMU		C29F	1/49	A & W McKercher {Aberfeldy Motor Coaches}, Aberfeldy (PH)
68823	EAJ 679	Plaxton	698	C29F	2/48	R Howard, Whitby (NR)
68835	?	Mulliner		?	-/--	Original operator unknown (O-WAN)
68838	MNU 690	Woodall Nicholson		DP29F	9/48	Booth & Fisher Ltd, Halfway (DE) 23
68842	JMN 106	Duple	49217	C29F	10/47	EC Hamill, Onchan (IM)
68845	MRA 599	Woodall Nicholson		DP29F	10/48	Booth & Fisher Ltd, Halfway (DE) 24
68850	JXD 486	Duple	44196	C29F	2/48	V Bingley (Bingley Bros) {Sceptre Coaches}, London W6 (LN)
68858	JNB 234	Duple	49293	C29F	1/48	J Middleton & Sons {Kinder Scout/Birch Vale Hire Service}, Stockport (CH)
68865						Exported to Helsinki (O-FIN)
68887	* EFW 92	Plaxton	204	C29F	5/48	Enterprise (Scunthorpe) Passenger Services Ltd {Enterprise} (LI) 37
68894	CFV 851	Duple	49151	C27F	3/48	S & J Wood Ltd {Seagull Coaches}, Blackpool (LA)
68897	#?	Jonckheere	5736	C27-	3/49	Droeshout, Berlare (O-B)
68901	* NEV 190	Whitson	?	C29F	4/48	J Wordsworth {Dix Luxury Coaches}, Dagenham (EX)
68909	?	?		van	-/--	Original operator unknown
68910		see 68901				
68915						Exported to Malaya
68919	DVH 217	Duple	49287	C19F	3/48	Hanson's Buses Ltd, Huddersfield (WR) 242
68927	MNU 687	Woodall Nicholson		DP29F	8/48	Booth & Fisher Ltd, Halfway (DE) 20
68931	HDD 187	Mulliner	T195	B31F	1/48	CH Lansdown, Tockington (GL)
68936	SML 468	Duple	44407	C29F	6/48	Universal Coaches Ltd, London N9 (LN)
68944	LVT 485	Duple	48034	C29F	2/48	JF Findlow, Biddulph (ST)
68951	?	Mulliner		B--F	-/--	Shell Petroleum Co, Maracaibo (O-YV)
68973	KKK 342	Mulliner	T204	B31F	2/48	CJ Newman & Son, Hythe (KT)
68979	* GAO 470	Duple	47710	C29F	3/48	Cumberland MS, Whitehaven (CU) 253
68987	BCB 169	Duple	49071	C29F	3/48	Ribblesdale Coachways Ltd, Blackburn (LA) 13
68995	?	Thurgood	479	van	5/48	Peake, St Albans (GHT)
69074 - 69085						Exported to Melbourne (O-AUS)
69122	?	?		van	-/--	Original operator unknown
69127	* ECO 974	Brailey & Toms		C29F	8/48	Embankment Motor Co (Plymouth) Ltd (DN)
69134						Exported to Malaya
69142	* EWN 967	Duple	46756	C29F	2/48	United Welsh, Swansea (GG) 934
69146	SS 6785	SMT		C29F	2/48	Stark's Bus Service, Dunbar (EL) B10
69151	CUD 825	Duple	44498	C29F	1/48	AE Butler, Henley-on-Thames (OX)
69158	* HZ-55742	Met		B26-	4/50	Pasteur, Den Haag (O-NL)
69180	?	?		van	-/--	Original operator unknown
69186	MNU 84	Allsop		C29F	8/48	Booth & Fisher Ltd, Halfway (DE) 18
69194	?	?		library	-/--	Staffordshire County Council (GST)
69202	?	?		l/stock	-/--	Original operator unknown
69211						Exported to Malaya
69214	JRO 375	Thurgood	461	C29F	3/48	HW Hart {Hillside Coaches}, Markyate (HT) 8
69217	JMN 128	Duple	49218	C29F	10/47	WT Moore {Queen of the Isle}, Douglas (IM) 2
69224	?	?		van	-/--	Original operator unknown
69229	SML 699	Mulliner	T202	B31F	3/48	Vandervell Products Ltd, London W3 (XLN)
69237	JEL 32	Lee		C29F	7/50	Excelsior Coaches Ltd, Bournemouth (HA)
69244						Exported to Antwerp (O-B)
69266	* EBD 300	Duple	46571	C29F	1/48	York Bros (Northampton) Ltd (NO) 16
69272	JXE 60	Duple	48220	C24F	2/48	Pall Mall Car Hire {Pamalhire}, London SW1 (LN)
69280	?	?		van	-/--	Original operator unknown
69288	?	?		van	-/--	Original operator unknown
69294	JNK 487	Duple	49414	C29F	1/48	Albanian Coaches Ltd, St Albans (HT) 4
69298	?	Mulliner		?	-/--	Original operator unknown (O-WAN)
69299		see 69266				
69303	HUP 796	Duple	49120	C29F	2/48	Bowser's Coaches Ltd, Washington (DM)
69310	JRO 101	Thurgood	452	C29F	2/48	CW Jones {Enterprise Bus Service}, Kimpton (HT)
69316	KAF 986	Mulliner	T206	B31F	1/48	Mrs J Harry, Penryn (CO)
69323	HPW 555	Duple	43689	C29F	1/48	JC Brown {Norfolk Coachways}, Attleborough (NK)

(11098) ATL885 was a fine example of the early Mk II version of the Duple bus body on the Bedford OB chassis. It joined the Gresswell's of Billingborough fleet in Lincolnshire in December 1945, possibly having been ordered as an OWB. (Omnibus Society, John C Clarke collection)

(12002) The harbour front at Portree on the Isle of Skye is the setting for another Duple Mk II bodied OB, but this time one with a large mail compartment at the rear. DYS933 was part of the SCWS owned Skye Transport fleet. (David Richardson)

(unknown) The Kampala Town Service, part of the Uganda Transport Company, acquired a number of Duple Almet bodied Bedford OBs with dual class seating arrangement. The front portion seated 8 passengers in luxury, whilst the rear compartment seated 20 passengers on slatted wooden seats. (The Omnibus Society)

(24428) Mitchell of Stornoway purchased a number of SMT body frames and used one to complete JS7297 themselves. Heavily modified in later life with rubber mounted windows, the OB is ready to depart on one of Mitchell's many island services. (Roy Marshall)

(30299) 2374 was a Maltese Bedford OB with a traditional Brincat body assembled locally for the Route Bus Service operation and seen in the spray green livery used for this service. Notice the special side panels for the engine cover, adapted to combat the intense heat. (Mike Fenton)

(30583) Irish operators have long been keen users of small Bedfords, their size no doubt suiting the narrow roads. IP5113 was a 26 seater Ryan bodied bus, purchased by Cullinane of Castlecomer, complete with the customary roof rack. (Omnibus Society, John F Parke)

(32426) The Channel Islands also saw many Bedford OBs in the early post war years, necessary to restock the war depleted fleets after German occupation. J6986 (57) was a Mulliner bodied OB that saw service with Jersey Motor Transport for a number of years. (Geoffrey Morant, courtesy Richard Morant)

(unknown) This anonymous Australian Bedford OB carries the metropolitan registration mo4266, suggesting that it was owned by an operator in the Greater Sydney conurbation. The name of the coachbuilder has not been recorded. (Omnibus Society) (unknown) Another Irish Bedford was this 1950 GJ Roberts bodied example, IP6517, owned from new by Tommy Nolan from Callan. The bus, seen in Kilkenny, is set to return to its home town. The bus appears to have a shortened rear overhang. (RF Mack, via Roy Marshall)

(unknown) Bedford OBs and even some pre war WTBs, survived well into the 1970s in some parts of Australia. Hume Street South Bus Service operated this Grice bodied example (1016) well into the 1970s, still looking very smart despite its advancing years. (Bruce Tilley) (unknown) Yet another Irish OB is seen in the shape of HI4569, another GJ Roberts bodied bus, new to Mr Campion's Princess Bus Service from Clonmel. However, by the time of this photograph the bus was serving with a Waterford based operator and is seen on the local harbour front. (Omnibus Society - John F Parke)

(36026) Plaxton bodied a considerable number of Bedford OBs, some with conventional normal control bodywork, but some with a 30 seat full fronted body, after the chassis had been converted to forward control. Seen here is HRR192 of Mrs Butler of Kirkby-in-Ashfield. (Omnibus Society, John C Clarke collection)

(37168) Northern Roadways of Glasgow, better known for their attempts to challenge the might of the larger Scottish Transport Group on the Glasgow/Edinburgh to London express services, also operated some more mundane routes in Ayrshire for which EGG792 was purchased, complete with very utility like SMT body. It is seen here with Laughton of Deerness in Orkney. (Roy Marshall)

(43918) Bedford OBs were bodied by many smaller coachbuilders and one such was Reeve & Kenning, as seen on MNU929, new to Branson of Brampton in Derbyshire. The coach later passed to Scott of Cockfield in whose livery it is seen. (John Shearman collection)

(48675) The New Zealand Railways Road Services were over the years to become the largest operator of Bedford buses in the world. NZRRS s.805 (1511) was one of a large fleet of NZMB bodied coaches that they operated and is seen when brand new. (NZMB, courtesy Snow Cumming collection)

(51083) Basil Williams built up a number of operations in the immediate post war years, one of which was Hants & Sussex, whose GCG334 (26) is seen here. It carried a Lee bus body with a modest 26 seater capacity. (Omnibus Society, DHD Spray)

(51972) A small number of operators also bodied their own coaches, sometimes new, sometimes as replacements. HRT299 was delivered to Classic Coaches of Lowestoft with a Churchill body in 1948, but in 1957 Shreeve, who controlled Tourist Coaches, converted the chassis to forward control and fitted a new body of their own design. (Omnibus Society, Roy Marshall, Norris-Cull collection)

(52824) Looking like something out of the Ark, WI2317 carries another home-built body, this time by Kenneally of Waterford, Ireland. This strange looking bus was frequently to be found on the harbour front at Waterford, as seen in this photograph. (John Gillham)

(unknown) Equally strange in appearance, at least to British eyes, were the Fishermen's Bend forward control conversions of the Bedford OB offered by CAC on the Australian market. This example served with the Warrnambool Bus Lines fleet in Victoria, where it carried fleet number 32. (Bruce Tilley)

(55819) JTU13 was bodied by Pearson of Liverpool, who built many bodies for Bedfords, some of them on converted or rebuilt chassis, others like JTU13 on orthodox OB chassis. JTU13 started life with Bowyer of Northwich, Cheshire, but later migrated to nearby Shropshire, firstly with Hampson of Oswestry, then P Edwards also from Oswestry. (Omnibus Society, Roy Marshall, Norris-Cull collection)

(57511) Butler's of Kirkby-in-Ashfield, whose HRR192 was shown earlier, also operated an OB of conventional layout with Plaxton body, GWT716, seen here. This OB had received a Perkins diesel engine by the time of the photograph, as identified by the Company's four ring emblem on the radiator. (Omnibus Society, John C Clarke collection)

(58252) A very wet looking day and few passengers in sight as Duple Vista bodied LPH482 of the Walton-on-Thames Motor Company awaits departure time on one of the Company's local services. (Roy Marshall)

(59705) Portsmouth Aviation bodied just a single Bedford OB, HLJ600. New to Excelsior Coaches of Bournemouth, well known for their trail blazing Continental tours, it later passed to Nadder Valley Coaches for whom it was operating on a stage service to Salisbury. (John Shearman collection)

(61087) This Roney bodied Bedford OB, GBT110, looks to have an unusually narrow frontal profile. It was delivered to Connor & Graham of Easington in East Yorkshire, but passed for a short while to Richardson of Hull, with whom it is seen here. (John Shearman collection)

(64307) Heavy use of beading and an arched side profile make this East Coast Motors bodied OB very distinctive. New to East Coast Motors {Orange Coaches} as their JAH888 (8), it passed to Grey & Green Coaches of Cromer, as seen here. (Omnibus Society, Norris-Cull collection)

(64299) This interesting photograph contains three Bedford OBs with three different coachbuilders and all from the same fleet, Hunt of Alford, Lincolnshire. EFU662, the main subject of the photo carried a Yeates body, JHN744 carried an SMT body, whilst DUT149 was Plaxton bodied. (Omnibus Society, Roy Marshall, John C Clarke collection)

(64888) Another SMT bodied OB was DSA896, delivered to Shand of Tarland in Aberdeenshire in December 1947 and was still operating for them in the mid 1960s. It is seen at Aboyne railway station collecting passengers for Shand's stage service. (Roy Marshall)

(65978) MNU79 was one of a fleet of six Allsop bodied buses purchased by Booth & Fisher of Halfway, near Sheffield, and used extensively on their network of services to the local coal mines. Here it is seen on a 'Private Hire' duty on August 1st 1959. (John Cockshott)

(67488) The Bankfoot Motor Company was the fleetname for AS & WT Whyte's operation from the Perthshire village of the same name. Operating stage services and mail contracts in the area, they placed two SCWS bodied OB buses into service in November 1948 and January 1949, of which CES447 is the former. (The Omnibus Society)

(67952) The Tilling Group companies bought a number of Beadle bus bodied OBs for stage services in the more rural areas served. This delightful view shows HUO676 (523), one of Southern National's allocation, taking on a heavy load for the run to Port Isaac. (Omnibus Society, JH Aston, John Clarke collection)

(68058) New to Creamline of Bordon, GOR824 was a Wadham bodied OB, one of many Wadham bodied vehicles bought by Creamline. It passed, firstly, to Heath of West Bergholt, then to George Digby of the same village and is seen on his stage service at Colchester. (TravelLens, John Shearman collection)

(72885) Many Bedford OBs became travelling shops after their useful life as PSVs had finished. Those with the less well constructed bodies often made this transition quite early in life. DBA348 carried a Trans-United body, though it has also been claimed as a Rushworth body, and was new to Hankinson of Salford before becoming a Mobile Shop. (John Shearman collection)

C1252/93

69330						Exported to Antwerp (O-B)
69352	EAW 394	Mulliner	T205	B31F	1/48	J & HG Phillips {J Phillips & Son}, Rhostyllen (DH)
69358	MNU 689	Woodall Nicholson		DP29F	9/48	Booth & Fisher Ltd, Halfway (DE) 22
69366	JXD 750	Mulliner	T197	B28F	1/48	Lawrence Bros (Transport) Ltd, London EC1 (LN)
69374	MNU 688	Woodall Nicholson		DP29F	8/48	Booth & Fisher Ltd, Halfway (DE) 21
69377	?	Jonckheere	5557	C27-	4/48	Govaert - Miny, Oostende (O-B)
69380	GOR 136	Lee		B26F	6/48	Hants & Sussex Motor Services Ltd, Emsworth (HA) 30
69388	?	?		van	-/--	Original operator unknown
69392	?	Duple	47466	C29F	-/--	Weerakoon Bros Ltd, Colombo (O-CL)
69400	JNB 888	Duple	49294	C29F	2/48	Jackson's Holiday Tours Ltd, Blackpool (LA)
69405	EWV 967	Mulliner	T198	B31F	2/48	The Old Firm, Wroughton (WI)
69409	JRO 591	Thurgood	462	C29F	4/48	EG Hewitt {Premier Coaches}, Watford (HT)
69418						Exported to Antwerp (O-B)
69438	?	?		van	-/--	Towler, Lytham (GLA)
69444	SML 623	Duple	48939	C29F	1/48	Richardson {A & W}, Harrow (MX)
69452	?	?		van	-/--	Original operator unknown
69457	?	?		van	-/--	Original operator unknown
69463						Exported to Lima (O-PE)
69467	LAE 223	Duple	44228	C29F	3/48	H Russett {Royal Blue}, Bristol (GL)
69471	SML 622	Duple	48028	C29F	3/48	H Burch, Harrow Weald (MX)
69476	?	Mulliner		B--F	-/--	Original operator unknown (O-WAN)
69483	* JXF 327	Duple	44702	C29F	1/48	TG Green {Empress Motor Coaches}, London E2 (LN)
69488	MPA 796	Duple	44518	C29F	2/48	Oliver Taylor (Coaches) Ltd, Caterham (SR)
69496	HDD 230	Duple	47595	C29F	2/48	TW Ellis & AJ Bull {The Railway Garage Co}, Moreton-in-Marsh (GL)
69504	* ?	Den Oudsten	1777	B30-	6/49	Balemans, Breda (O-NL) 14
69509	* P.630	North Shore		B33F	-/49	North Shore Transport Co Ltd, Takapuna (O-NZ) 30
69523	HTJ 280	Duple	49290	C29F	3/48	W Robinson & Sons, Great Harwood (LA) 19
69529	EBU 301	Duple	49138	C29F	2/48	Shearings Tours Ltd, Oldham (LA)
69537	* JNB 701	Mulliner	T207	B31F	1/48	Altrincham Coachways Ltd (CH)
69545	ENR 176	Duple	43460	C29F	2/48	W Housden, Loughborough (LE) 3
69552	HDD 251	Duple	43729	C26F	2/48	TAV Scadding {White Lion Motorways}, Wotton-under-Edge (GL)
69556	?	Mulliner		B---	-/--	NV de Bataafsche Petroleum Mij, Pladjoe (O-RI)
69561	JOD 87	Duple	46957	C27F	5/48	CW Good {The Doves Motor Tours}, Beer (DN)
69568						Exported to Lima (O-PE)
69573	SMY 920	Duple	48186	C29F	2/48	AR & Mrs EF Thorne {Thorne Bros}, London SW2 (LN)
69577	GCG 749	Duple	46610	C29F	2/48	Liss & District Omnibus Co Ltd, Liss (HA) 133
69590	EF 8336	Duple	44637	C29F	2/48	Bee-Line Roadways (Teeside) Ltd, West Hartlepool (DM)
69661 - 69672						Exported to Melbourne (O-AUS)
69705	KPP 706	Duple	46513	C29F	1/48	F Soul (Soul Bros), Olney (BK)
69711	JCD 176	Duple	44208	C29F	1/48	RG Johnston {Unique Coaches}, Brighton (ES)
69719	* FDL 278	Duple	43638	C29F	3/48	FW Read {Read's Tours}, Ryde (IW)
69727	JKH 531	Duple	49319	C29F	2/48	DW Burn, H Tyler & EG Russell {Grey de Luxe}, Kingston-upon-Hull (ER)
69736	* LPU 619	Beadle	C137	B30F	3/48	Eastern National, Chelmsford (EX) 3929
69739	?	Mulliner		B---	-/--	NV de Bataafsche Petroleum Mij, Pladjoe (O-RI)
69743	FJW 115	Duple	48043	C29F	3/48	Worthington Motor Tours Ltd, Wolverhampton (ST)
69754	CFV 893	Duple	49388	C29F	3/48	Batty-Holt Touring Service Ltd, Blackpool (LA)
69759	CTY 265	Duple	43695	C29F	2/48	C Frazer & Son, West Wylam (ND)
69764	GNP 813	Duple	43378	C29F	2/48	Eric Harrison, Broadway (WO)
69774	KWB 826	Duple	49074	C29F	2/48	H Sellars, Sheffield (WR) 4
69780						Exported to Lima (O-PE)
69782		see 67982				
69787	DDN 777	Duple	43752	C29F	3/48	HC Fawcett, York (NR)
69796	SML 400	Duple	44406	C29F	3/48	T & WJ Palmer {Ferndale Coaches}, London E6 (LN)
69804	BRN 791	Duple	46879	C29F	3/48	Scout MS Ltd, Preston (LA)
69813	CFV 839	Duple	49269	C29F	3/48	T Porritt & CA, PR & GW Wolstenholme, Blackpool (LA)
69821						Exported to Lima (O-PE)
69840	FT 6282	Duple	49121	C29F	1/48	TH Taylor {Taylor Bros}, North Shields (ND)
69845	JNN 573	Duple	48315	C24F	2/48	Barton Transport, Chilwell (NG) 528
69859	JUO 602	Duple	47692	C29F	3/48	Devon General, Torquay (DN) TCB602

C1252/94

69869	JXE 574	Duple	44848	C27F	3/48	Keith & Boyle (London) Ltd {Orange Luxury Coaches}, London EC2 (LN) Gannet
69878	AEP 76	Mulliner	T214	B30F	2/48	CJ Ballard {Wilson's Coaches}, Welshpool (MO)
69885	* FMJ 544	Duple	43968	C27F	2/48	Mrs EA Jarvis, Carlton (BD)
69894	GWU 857	Duple	49273	C29F	2/48	Mexborough & Swinton (WR) 79
69902	KKN 414	Thurgood	463	C29F	4/48	WJ Moody, Northfleet (KT)
69911	CTL 490	Mulliner	T213	B31F	2/48	WJ Simmons {Reliance Coaches}, Great Gonerby (KN)
69918						Exported to Lima (O-PE)
69944	LUA 591	Duple	49345	C29F	3/48	Kelsall Coaches Ltd {Saffman & Beasley}, Leeds (WR)
69949	GWW 612	Mulliner	T212	B31F	2/48	JJ Longstaff, Mirfield (WR)
69954	JS 7766	Mulliner	T211	B29F	2/48	J Mitchell {Mitchell's Transport Parcel Service}, Stornoway (RY)
69961	GCG 873	Duple	46611	C29F	2/48	Liss & District Omnibus Co Ltd, Liss (HA) 134
69970	JFJ 180	Tiverton		C29F	6/48	Greenslades, Exeter (DN)
69977	?	Mulliner	T189	?	-/--	BOAC, unknown overseas location
69986	LPU 620	Beadle	C138	B30F	3/48	Eastern National, Chelmsford (EX) 3930
69994	CTY 303	Mulliner	T203	B31F	2/48	R Tait, Kirkwhelpington (ND)
70049 - 70060						Exported to Bombay (O-IND)
70075	HLJ 273	Harrington	?	C29F	3/48	CJ Pounds {Charlie's Cars}, Bournemouth (HA) 59
70082						Exported to Lima (O-PE)
70102	JXE 462	Mulliner	T191	B31F	1/48	London County Council (XLN) 1579
70107	* JFJ 346	Heaver		C25F	8/48	Taylor's Central Garage (Exeter) Ltd (DN)
70112						Exported to Mombasa (O-EAK)
70119	JTE 35	Withnell		C29F	6/48	J Parkinson, Adlington (LA)
70128	FJW 112	Mulliner	T194	C28F	3/48	Worthington Motor Tours Ltd, Wolverhampton (ST)
70143	HUO 678	Beadle	C128	B30F	3/48	Southern National, Exeter (DN) 525
70148	HUO 679	Beadle	C129	B30F	3/48	Southern National, Exeter (DN) 526
70152	NHK 286	Thurgood	466	C29F	4/48	FW & WE Mayhew (Mayhew Bros), Stanstead (EX)
70161	VML 2	Duple	49511	C29F	2/48	Wright Bros (London) Ltd, London W7 (LN)
70168						Exported to Alexandria (O-ET)
70189	EAW 511	Duple	43225	C29F	2/48	SC & J Vagg {Vagg's Motors}, Knockin Heath (SH)
70194	JXE 879	Duple	43693	C29F	2/48	JS Smith {Central}, Sunniside (ND)
70200						Exported to Alexandria (O-ET)
70204	FJW 196	Mulliner	T193	C28F	3/48	Worthington Motor Tours Ltd, Wolverhampton (ST)
70211	JXE 459	Mulliner	T209	B31F	1/48	London County Council (XLN) 1578
70218	* EAJ 645	Plaxton	697	C29F	2/48	Hardwick's Services Ltd, Snainton (NR)
70225	EUJ 118	Plaxton	329	FC30F	7/48	Mrs A Martlew, RW & A Ashley {Martlew & Sons}, Donnington Wood (SH)
70231	JXE 463	Mulliner	T208	B31F	1/48	London County Council (XLN) 1580
70238	JXE 464	Mulliner	T210	B31F	1/48	London County Council (XLN) 1581
70245						Exported to Mombasa (O-EAK)
70283	FWF 489	Plaxton	704	C26F	2/48	E Milburn {Leavening Motor Services}, Leavening (ER)
70288	?	Mulliner	T188	?	-/--	BOAC, unknown overseas location
70294	HDD 182	Mulliner	T225	B31F	1/48	TEA Bowles {Bowles Coaches}, Ford (GL)
70298	?	Mulliner		B--F	-/--	Shell Petroleum Co, Maracaibo (O-YV)
70305	BCF 339	Thurgood	460	C29F	4/48	HS Theobald & Son, Long Melford (WF)
70306	#GC-7376	?		B32D	2/49	Transportes Guanarteme, Las Palmas (O-IC) 2
70312	BMS 931	SMT		C29F	3/48	W Alexander, Falkirk (SN) W216
70319	HEL 775	Duple	44849	C27F	2/48	Shamrock & Rambler Motor Coaches Ltd, Bournemouth (HA)
70325	JTC 526	Duple	49901	C29F	4/48	Lansdowne Garage (Morecambe) Ltd (LA)
70332	EFU 858	Mulliner	T196	B31F	3/48	Enterprise (Scunthorpe) Passenger Services Ltd {Enterprise} (LI) 27
70339						Exported to Port Elizabeth (O-ZA)
70377	GCG 874	Duple	47626	C29F	2/48	BS Williams, Emsworth (HA) 126
70382	#LUB 251	Duple	49505	C29F	2/48	George Barker & Sons {Scarborough} Ltd (NR)
70388	DVD 166	Mulliner	T226	B31F	3/48	R Wilson, Carnwath (LK)
70392						Exported to Port Elizabeth (O-ZA)
70399	SS 6786	SMT		C29F	2/48	Stark's Bus Service, Dunbar (EL) B9
70461 - 70472						Exported to Melbourne (O-AUS)
70538	BMS 98	SMT		C25F	3/48	W Alexander, Falkirk (SN) W214
70545	BMS 97	SMT		C25F	3/48	W Alexander, Falkirk (SN) W213
70550	JS 7799	SMT		C29F	3/48	J MacKenzie, Strathpeffer (RY)
70558	BMS 932	SMT		C29F	3/48	W Alexander, Falkirk (SN) W217

70565	?	Mulliner		B--F	-/--	Shell Petroleum Co, unknown overseas location
70603	BMS 99	SMT		C25F	3/48	W Alexander, Falkirk (SN) W215
70608	?	Mulliner		B--F	-/--	Shell Petroleum Co, Maracaibo (O-YV)
70614	?	Mulliner		B--F	-/--	Shell Petroleum Co, Maracaibo (O-YV)
70618	?	?		van	-/--	Original operator unknown
70619 *	?	Jonckheere	5582	C27-	6/48	Albert van Mullem, Roosbeek (O-B)
70625	?	Mulliner		B--F	-/--	Shell Petroleum Co, Labuan (O-MAL)
70632						Exported to Penang (O-MAL)
70639	KCV 355	Mulliner	T224	B30F	4/48	FJ Skinner & Sons Ltd, Millbrook (CO)
70640	?	Mulliner		B--F	-/--	Shell Petroleum Co, Maracaibo (O-YV)
70648	?	?		(goods ?)	1/48	Cotton & Sons (egg producers), unknown location
70666						Exported to Penang (O-MAL)
70697	EFW 119	Duple	49539	C29F	2/48	M Williams {Trent Motors}, Scunthorpe (LI)
70702						Exported to Malaya
70708	?	Mulliner		B--F	-/--	Anglo-Iranian Oil Co, location unknown (O-IR)
70712						Exported to Malaya
70719	KWB 936	Duple	49543	C29F	3/48	EH Sims, Sheffield (WR)
70726						Exported to Port Swettenham (O-MAL)
70733	ENR 262	Duple	49327	C29F	3/48	AA Oliver {Luxicoaches}, Loughborough (LE)
70739						Exported to Malaya
70746	JTE 36	Withnell		C29F	7/48	J Parkinson, Adlington (LA)
70753						Exported to Malaya
70791	BCB 286	Duple	49518	C29F	2/48	Harry Duckworth (Clayton-le-Moors) Ltd, Rishton (LA)
70796						Exported to Malaya
70802						Exported to Singapore
70806						Exported to Malaya
70813	5187	Mulliner	SP211	B31F	3/48	Guernsey Railways (CI) 3
70820	MVX 376	Duple	46510	C29F	2/48	J Wordsworth {Dix Luxury Coaches}, Dagenham (EX)
70827	5181	Mulliner	SP209	B31F	3/48	Sarre Transport Ltd, St Peter Port, Guernsey (CI) 14
70833	?	Duple	47474	B31F	-/--	Trinidad Government Railways (O-TT)
70840	?	Duple	47473	B31F	-/--	Trinidad Government Railways (O-TT)
70847	KHN 335	Duple	49542	C29F	1/48	F Scott {Scott's Greys Coaches}, Darlington (DM) 61
70882						Exported to Santiago (O-RCH)
70889	FWO 618	Duple	46757	C29F	2/48	Red & White, Chepstow (MH) 818
70895						Exported to Barbados
70961 - 70972						Exported to Bombay (O-IND)
71036	FFH 551	Duple	49515	C29F	2/48	WT Edwards {Edwards Coaches}, Joy's Green (GL)
71047						Exported to Barbados
71056	EAJ 680	Duple	49321	C29F	3/48	AW Robinson {Ryedale Motor Services}, Pickering (NR)
71063	ZH 9895	GJ Roberts		C29F	-/--	Corais Iompair Eireann, Dublin (EI) BP4
71071	JXH 666	Duple	44441	C29F	3/48	George Ewer & Co Ltd {Grey Green}, London N16 (LN)
71074	JNN 960	Duple	49274	C29F	2/48	JHP Morley (P Morley & Sons), Edwinstowe (NG)
71078	JYC 339	Duple	43503	C29F	3/48	WGL Waterman {Waterman Bros}, Spaxton (SO)
71113						Exported to Santiago (O-RCH)
71117	JUO 603	Duple	47693	C29F	3/48	Devon General, Torquay (DN) TCB603
71121	ZH 9896	GJ Roberts		C25F	-/49	Corais Iompair Eireann, Dublin (EI) BP5
71130	HUP 982	Duple	43698	C29F	2/48	C & E Bus Co Ltd, Annfield Plain (DM)
71141						Exported to Port Elizabeth (O-ZA)
71150	JYC 439	Duple	48911	C29F	2/48	PJ Riggs {Vista Coaches}, Clutton (SO)
71157						Exported to Port Elizabeth (O-ZA)
71165	JXE 590	Duple	44569	C29F	3/48	Fallowfield & Britten Ltd, London E8 (LN)
71168	GNP 860	Duple	49815	C29F	2/48	Eric Harrison, Broadway (WO)
71172	JXE 649	Duple	49565	C29F	2/48	Wallis Hire Service Ltd {Dartmouth Coaches}, London SE23 (LN)
71203	?	Mulliner		B--F	-/--	Shell Petroleum Co, unknown overseas location
71209	HNY 746	Mulliner	T237	B31F	3/48	W Browning, Cefn Cribbwr (GG)
71215						Exported to Accra (O-WAC)
71224	JUO 604	Duple	47694	C29F	3/48	Devon General, Torquay (DN) TCB604
71244	GUE 353	Duple	43971	C29F	2/48	RR, AW, MR & EE Whitehall {J & F Whitehall & Sons}, Nuneaton (WK)
71251						Exported to Malaya
71259	FDL 318	Duple	43627	C29F	2/48	Seaview Services Ltd, Seaview (IW) 10
71262	GCG 981	Duple	46777	C29F	2/48	BS Williams, Emsworth (HA) 127
71266	ORF 564	Duple	48031	C29F	3/48	Wells Motor Services Ltd, Biddulph (ST) 27

71297	?	Mulliner		B--F	-/--	Anglo Iranian Oil Co, Basra (O-IRQ)
71303	EAW 653	Mulliner	T227	B31F	2/48	DJ Hampson {Hampson's Luxury Coaches}, Oswestry (SH) 15
71309						Exported to Malaya
71318	FWX 549	Beadle	C106	B30F	3/48	Keighley-West Yorkshire (WR) K616
71329	* FWX 548	Beadle	C105	B30F	1/48	West Yorkshire RCC, Harrogate (WR) 615
71338						Exported to Malaya
71345	JTC 525	Duple	49902	C29F	3/48	NA Birkett Ltd {Premier}, Morecambe (LA)
71353	JXE 575	Duple	44850	C27F	3/48	Keith & Boyle (London) Ltd {Orange Luxury Coaches}, London EC2 (LN) Goldcrest
71360	?	Mulliner	T199	-30-	2/48	BOAC, unknown overseas location
71391	?	Mulliner		B--F		Shell Petroleum Co, Maracaibo (O-YV)
71397	DTH 903	Mulliner	T230	B30F	2/48	J Evans, Pontyberem (CR)
71403						Exported to Malaya
71406	* ?	?		B--F	-/--	Blue Bus Services, Masterton (O-NZ) 17
71412	HYP 724	Duple	44114	C29F	3/48	Birch Bros Ltd, London NW5 (LN) K34
71417	JXH 163	Duple	46356	C29F	2/48	CW Banfield, London SE15 (LN)
71432	?	Mulliner		B--F	-/48	Shell Petroleum Co, Maracaibo (O-YV)
71439	EAW 637	Duple	47809	C27F	2/48	Cheshire Joint Sanatorium, Market Drayton (XSH)
71447	KCV 244	Duple	48324	C29F	3/48	GG Warren, St Ives (CO)
71452						Exported to Malaya
71454	* JUO 605	Duple	47695	C29F	3/48	Devon General, Torquay (DN) TCB605
71485	LRB 790	Duple	48023	C29F	2/48	CS & R Brooks, Castle Gresley (DE)
71491						Exported to Malaya
71497	HTG 116	Thurgood	467	C29F	4/48	Edwards Bros (Beddau) Ltd (GG)
71501 - 71512						Exported to Melbourne (O-AUS)
71578	?	Mulliner		B31F	-/48	Shell Petroleum Co, Bachaquero (O-YV)
71584	KKM 182	Duple	49042	C29F	2/48	J & J Chubb {J Chubb & Son}, Wilmington (KT)
71589						Exported to Malaya
71593	#HE-71	?		B13-	-/48	Niinivuori Aulis, unknown location (O-FIN)
71598	EJB 167	Duple	44488	C29F	3/48	Tom Tappin Ltd {Travel Rambler}, Wallingford (BE)
71608						Exported to Malaya
71613	GOY 503	Duple	44521	C29F	3/48	JE & HE Jewell {Jewell's Coaches}, Croydon (SR)
71619	KWE 293	Duple	44089	C29F	3/48	A Carr {Scholey's Coaches}, Sheffield (WR)
71651	EAW 857	Duple	46459	C29F	8/48	J Jervis, Wellington (SH)
71657						Exported to Alexandria (O-ET)
71663	GWX 927	Mulliner	T231	B31F	3/48	Kirkby & Sons (Harthill) Ltd (WR)
71672	GCG 735	Duple	46794	C29F	1/48	T & J Wood {Empress Motor Service}, Worting (HA)
71683						Exported to Malaya
71692	HOM 886	Duple	47992	C29F	2/48	L & FG Myatt {Avon Coaches}, Birmingham (WK) 14
71699	JNB 858	Duple	49755	C29F	3/48	Sykes' Motor Tours Ltd, Sale (CH)
71707	J 10278	Duple	47472	C29F	2/48	CB Griss {Scarlet Pimpernel Coaches}, St Helier, Jersey (CI)
71713	HPW 985	Duple	43687	C29F	2/48	Babbage & Sons (Cromer) Ltd {Green & Grey Coaches} (NK)
71745	MVX 508	Duple	44044	C29F	2/48	Essex County Coaches Ltd, London E15 (LN)
71751						Exported to Alexandria (O-ET)
71757	CTY 580	Duple	49814	C29F	3/48	WM Appleby & JD Jordan {A & J Coaches}, Bedlington (ND)
71766	KKM 222	Duple	44000	C29F	3/48	WE Penfold {Penfold & Brodie}, Green Street Green (KT)
71772	?	Duple	47475	B31F	-/--	Trinidad Government Railways (O-TT)
71777	AJV 190	Duple	49796	C29F	3/48	FA & WR Stark (FA Stark and Sons), Tetney (LI)
71786						Exported to Malaya
71793	BJL 705	Duple	49794	C29F	3/48	HH Milson, Coningsby (LI)
71801						Exported to Malaya
71807	JTC 293	Duple	50004	C29F	3/48	W Robinson & Sons, Great Harwood (LA)
71836	HUO 680	Beadle	C130	B30F	3/48	Southern National, Exeter (DN) 527
71842						Exported to Santiago (O-RCH)
71849	MPB 550	Duple	43253	C29F	3/48	R, RG & T Warner {T Warner & Sons}, Milford (SR)
71857	?	Mulliner		B--F	-/--	Shell Petroleum Co, unknown overseas location
71863	MVX 923	Duple	44224	C29F	3/48	GW Osborne {GW Osborne & Sons}, Tollesbury (EX)
71868	FWF 646	Duple	49825	C29F	2/48	J & J Boddy {Boddy's Motors), Bridlington (ER)
71877						Exported to Lagos (O-WAN)

C1252/97

71884	JTC 267	Duple		49837	C27F	3/48 E Mayers {Kenilworth Tours}, Litherland (LA)
71894						Exported to Mombasa (O-EAK)
71898	FCJ 780	Plaxton		707	C29F	5/48 WE Morgan {Wye Valley Motors}, Hereford (HR)
71918	FJW 199	Mulliner		T218	C26F	5/48 Worthington Motor Tours Ltd, Wolverhampton (ST)
71924						Exported to Santiago (O-RCH)
71930	KMA 98	Duple		49890	C29F	2/48 Goddard & Buckingham Ltd, Marple (CH) 4
71939						Exported to Mombasa (O-EAK)
71945	?	Mulliner		T233	?	1/48 Wardle Cotton Co, Rochdale (XLA)
71950	* FBE 131	Plaxton		629	C29F	7/48 Enterprise (Scunthorpe) Passenger Services Ltd {Enterprise} (LI) 143
71959						Exported to Ireland
71966	FWS 629	Duple		49897	C29F	3/48 St Cuthbert's Co-operative Association Ltd, Edinburgh (MN) 5
71974	ZH 9897	GJ Roberts			C25F	-/49 Corais lompair Eireann, Dublin (EI) BP6
71980	EFW 91	Mulliner		T236	B31F	3/48 Enterprise (Scunthorpe) Passenger Services Ltd {Enterprise} (LI) 63
72012	MJO 923	Mulliner		T232	B31F	3/48 PC Skinner {Percival's Coaches}, Oxford (OX) 21
72018						Exported to Port Elizabeth (O-ZA)
72024	FMJ 694	Duple		48257	C29F	3/48 FD Cox {Heathway Coaches}, Kensworth (BD)
72031						Exported to Port Elizabeth (O-ZA)
72044	?	Mulliner			B--F	-/-- Anglo Iranian Oil Co, Basra (O-IRQ)
72053	VML 574	Duple		49811	C29F	3/48 British South American Airways, London SW1 (XLN)
72060	HON 255	Duple		44979	C29F	3/48 Smith's Imperial Coaches Ltd, Birmingham (WK)
72068	?	Mulliner			?	-/-- Original operator unknown (O-WAN)
72074	MNU 512	Thurgood		468	C29F	5/48 HJ Strange, Tansley (DE)
72177	SMY 864	Duple		43913	C29F	2/48 JWH, EAG & WHR Hall (Hall Bros) {Ickenham Coaches}, Hillingdon (MX)
72183	GHO 53	Duple		47805	C29F	3/48 Triumph Coaches Ltd, Southsea (HA) 128
72189						Exported to Helsinki (O-FIN)
72196	KKL 691	Duple		43754	C29F	2/48 CJ Greenough {Dartford Coaches}, Dartford (KT)
72201						Exported to Malaya
72209	JS 7796	Mulliner		T234	B29F	3/48 J Mitchell {Mitchell's Transport Parcel Service}, Stornoway (RY)
72218						Exported to Malaya
72225	KWE 337	Duple		44090	C29F	3/48 H Jackson, Walkley (WR)
72233						Exported to Malaya
72239	KMA 371	Trans-United			C27F	4/48 AE Bowyer & Son Ltd, Northwich (CH)
72272	EJB 369	Duple		44159	C29F	3/48 W & G Chandler, Wantage (BE)
72278	JXH 361	Mulliner		T241	B31F	2/48 London County Council (XLN) 1584
72284						Exported to Malaya
72291	?	Mulliner			B--F	-/48 Shell Petroleum Co, Maracaibo (O-YV)
72295	HBJ 750	Mulliner		T238	B31F	2/48 Combs Coaches Ltd, Ixworth (EK)
72304						Exported to Malaya
72313	FOD 945	Duple		46944	C29F	3/48 Falkland Garages Ltd, Torquay (DN)
72320	FAM 210	Mulliner		T228	C29F	3/48 BP Oakey, Alvescot (OX)
72328						Exported to Malaya
72334	GHO 54	Duple		46423	C29F	3/48 Triumph Coaches Ltd, Southsea (HA) 131
72366	TMG 167	Strachan			C29F	6/48 Wrights Hanwell Ltd, London W7 (LN)
72372	JNC 388	Mulliner		T240	C29F	5/48 Brierley Bros (Transport) Ltd, Salford (LA)
72373		see 72372				
72378	?	Mulliner			B31F	-/48 Shell Petroleum Co, Bachaquero (O-YV)
72385						Exported to Malaya
72389	* KWJ 773	Plaxton		598	FC30F	8/48 Law Bros Ltd, Sheffield (WR)
72398						Exported to Malaya
72407	HB 6536	Duple		46826	C29F	4/48 Morlais Services Ltd, Merthyr Tydfil (GG) 50
72414						Exported to Malaya
72422	SMY 911	Duple		46843	C29F	3/48 Northern Roadways Ltd, Glasgow (LK)
72479	KKM 90	Duple		44725	C29F	3/48 H Dineley {Rapid Rover Garages & Coaches}, Margate (KT)
72481	FJW 198	Mulliner		T219	C29F	4/48 Worthington Motor Tours Ltd, Wolverhampton (ST)
72483	?	Mulliner			B--F	-/48 Shell Petroleum Co, Maracaibo (O-YV)
72487	FDL 354	Duple		44511	C29F	3/48 Mrs M Groves (W Groves & Sons), East Cowes (IW)
72495	GNP 871	Duple		47634	C29F	3/48 CW Shuker {Lady Edith}, Halesowen (WO)
72499						Exported to Malaya

72504	* MVW 286	Duple	49296	C29F	12/47	City Coach Co Ltd, Brentwood (EX) B52
72507						Exported to Malaya
72510	FCJ 353	Duple	43732	C29F	3/48	PHE Tummey {Llangrove Coach Services}, Llangrove (HR)
72518	HC 8218	Duple	44572	C29F	3/48	AW Barrow, Eastbourne (ES)
72519	?	Duple	47476	B31F	-/--	Trinidad Government Railways (O-TT)
72543						Exported to Santiago (O-RCH)
72546	FOD 697	Duple	46405	C29F	3/48	PA Norman {Kingston Coach Tours}, Combe Martin (DN)
72548	FCY 152	Duple	48275	C29F	3/48	LG Potter, Skewen (GG)
72553	EUN 626	Duple	46502	C29F	6/48	JB Pye Ltd, Rhos-on-Sea (DH)
72558	JPT 101	Duple	49875	C29F	3/48	Mayfair Luxury Coaches Ltd, Gateshead (DM) 4
72561	FBC 465	Duple	46208	C29F	3/48	JH Cleaver {Garden City Bus Service}, Leicester (LE)
72569	SMY 919	Duple	49442	C29F	3/48	AS Stockman {Icknield Coaches}, Tring (HT)
72573	?	Duple	47479	B31F	-/--	Trinidad Government Railways (O-TT)
72578	5182	Mulliner	SP205	B28F	4/48	Sarre Transport Ltd, St Peter Port, Guernsey (CI) 15
72585	* 5183	Mulliner	SP210	B31F	5/48	Sarre Transport Ltd, St Peter Port, Guernsey (CI) 16
72612	MVX 596	Mulliner	T243	B31F	2/48	Mrs JA Fale, Rowhedge (EX)
72614	KKM 131	Duple	47770	C29F	3/48	Mrs S Solomon {Blue Rambler Coaches}, Cliftonville (KT)
72620	J 11595	Duple	49041	C29F	4/48	RH Barney & AA Allo {Pioneer Coaches}, St Helier, Jersey (CI) 2
72624	JXC 933	Duple	44211	C24F	3/48	United Service Transport Co Ltd, London SW9 (LN) 1075
72630	ORF 840	Duple	48792	C29F	3/48	Moore's Motor Services (Wombourne) Ltd (ST)
72633	J 11594	Duple	47471	C29F	4/48	RH Barney & AA Allo {Pioneer Coaches}, St Helier, Jersey (CI) 3
72641	?	Mulliner		B31F	-/--	Shell Petroleum Co, Barranquilla (O-CO)
72645	ECO 456	Duple	46236	C29F	3/48	AW Lock, Menheniot (CO)
72649	EAW 858	Duple	46460	C29F	8/48	AT Brown, Trench (SH)
72656	?	Duple	47477	B31F	-/--	Trinidad Government Railways (O-TT)
72685	FAM 313	Duple	46476	C29F	3/48	P Chaney {Queen of the Hills}, Wanborough (WI)
72689	?	Duple	47478	B31F	-/--	Trinidad Government Railways (O-TT)
72693	VML 575	Duple	48221	C29F	5/48	Pall Mall Car Hire {Pamalhire}, London SW1 (LN)
72700	JXH 400	Duple	49819	C29F	3/48	Dryer's Coaches Ltd, London E17 (LN)
72749 - 72760						Exported to Bombay (O-IND)
72824	EBD 567	Duple	46514	C29F	3/48	LJ Adams {Buckby's Coaches}, Rothwell (NO)
72828	?	Mulliner		B31F	-/--	Shell Petroleum Co, Barranquilla (O-CO)
72832	JP 6876	Duple	49519	C29F	3/48	Sharrock Bros, Newtown (LA)
72843	* JND 999	Pearson		C26F	7/48	Jackson's Holiday Tours Ltd, Blackpool (LA)
72852	?	Duple	47480	B31F	-/--	Trinidad Government Railways (O-TT)
72877	JXD 528	Mulliner	T200	B30F	4/48	BOAC (LN)
72881	?	Duple	47481	B31F	-/--	Trinidad Government Railways (O-TT)
72885	* DBA 348	Trans-United		C27F	6/48	W Hankinson, Salford (LA)
72892	* CJA 716	Duple	49891	C29F	3/48	Melba Motors Ltd, Reddish (CH)
72896	NEV 248	Duple	43540	C29F	3/48	Hicks Bros Ltd, Braintree (EX) 87
72900	?	Mulliner		B--F	-/48	Shell Petroleum Co, Maracaibo (O-YV)
72904	?	Duple	47482	B31F	-/--	Trinidad Government Railways (O-TT)
72915	ENT 808	Pearson		C29F	8/48	JT, FW & GE Whittle {JT Whittle & Sons}, Highley (SH)
72924	?	Mulliner		B--F	-/--	Anglo Iranian Oil Co, Basra (O-IRQ)
72926	ENR 294	Duple	44362	C29F	3/48	G Rudin & Son, Ibstock (LE)
72951	JYC 612	Duple	44746	C29F	4/48	WGL Waterman {Waterman Bros}, Spaxton (SO)
72955	?	Mulliner		B--F	-/--	Anglo Iranian Oil Co, Basra (O-IRQ)
72959	?	?		van	6/48	WS Tomsitt (bed manufacturer), High Wycombe (GBK)
72966	?	Duple	47470	B36F	-/48	Elyas Transport Service, Lagos (O-WAN)
72970	HDD 691	Duple	43889	C29F	3/48	Pulham & Sons (Coaches) Ltd, Bourton-on-the-Water (GL)
72974	EAW 859	Duple	43979	C29F	3/48	RG, FJ, DA & K Cooper {G Cooper & Sons}, Oakengates (SH)
72977	J 10584	Duple	49039	C29F	4/48	H Swanson {Redline Tours}, St Helier, Jersey (CI) 8
72988						Exported to Alexandria (O-ET)
72997	EY 8600	Mulliner	T246	B31F	3/48	E Pritchard (E Pritchard & Sons), Newborough (AY)
72999	# EBU 771	Pearson		C26F	7/48	Hilditch's Tours Ltd, Oldham (LA)
73015	?	?		van	6/48	WS Tomsitt (bed manufacturer), High Wycombe (GBK)

C1252/99

73023	* 5188	Mulliner	SP212	B31F	4/48	Guernsey Railways (CI) 20
73027	EFW 414	Mulliner	T244	B31F	3/48	M Williams {Trent Motors}, Scunthorpe (LI)
73031						Exported to Alexandria (O-ET)
73038	FMJ 933	Mulliner	T242	B31F	3/48	FM Bailey, Turvey (BD)
73042	* CTL 625	Mulliner	T245	B30F	3/48	JH Gelsthorpe, Branston (KN)
73046						Exported to Malaya
73049	CWH 923	Pearson		C26F	7/48	WA Smith, Tottington (LA)
73060						Exported to Accra (O-WAC)
73069						Exported to Alexandria (O-ET)
73071	HNY 768	Thurgood	475	C29F	5/48	DJ Gray {W Gray & Sons}, Tonteg (GG)
73086	TMG 197	Allweather		C27F	2/48	Wrights Hanwell Ltd, London W7 (LN)
73094						Exported to Santiago (O-RCH)
73097	JXE 570	Duple	44204	C29F	4/48	AC Coaches Ltd, London SE15 (LN)
73098	CJN 361	Duple	48351	C29F	3/48	Westcliff Belle Ltd, Southend-on-Sea (EX)
73099						Exported to Accra (O-WAC)
73113	HVF 544	Duple	43783	C29F	8/48	H Harrod, Wormgay (NK)
73118	* JUO 606	Duple	47696	C29F	3/48	Devon General, Torquay (DN) TCB606
73121						Exported to Port Elizabeth (O-ZA)
73128	ECO 384	Duple	49500	C29F	3/48	Plymouth Co-operative Society (DN) 520
73132	JTC 451	Duple	50350	C29F	3/48	W Robinson & Sons, Great Harwood (LA) 16
73141						Exported to Port Elizabeth (O-ZA)
73144	#?		Jonckheere	5587 C27-	6/48	Segers, Boortmeerbeek (O-B)
73166						Exported to Santiago (O-RCH)
73170	JCD 370	Duple	47700	C27F	3/48	Southdown, Brighton (ES) 70
73174	* 5190	Mulliner	SP214	B31F	6/48	Guernsey Railways (CI) 29
73180	LAE 622	Duple	43268	C29F	3/48	Wessex Coaches Ltd, Bristol (GL)
73185	MPB 666	Duple	43352	C29F	3/48	HR Richmond {Epsom Coaches}, Epsom (SR)
73190	J 10585	Duple	49040	C29F	4/48	WG Walker {Premier Coaches}, Grouville, Jersey (CI)
73193	FWO 619	Duple	46758	C29F	3/48	Red & White, Chepstow (MH) 819
73200	BRN 837	Duple	49904	C29F	2/48	Woodcock's British Tours Ltd, Heskin (LA)
73225 - 73236						Exported to Melbourne (O-AUS)
73336	GER 72	Duple	48064	C29F	3/48	Percival's Motors (Cambridge) Ltd (CM)
73345	?	Mulliner		?	-/--	BOAC, unknown overseas location
73370	?	Mulliner		B--F	-/--	Shell Petroleum Co, Guanta (O-YV)
73374	?	?		caravan	-/--	J Hulme, unknown location
73378	FFS 877	SMT		C25F	3/48	SMT (MN) C177
73384	?	Duple	47483	B31F	-/--	Trinidad Government Railways (O-TT)
73389	JTC 487	Duple	49903	C29F	2/48	EN Hadwin, Ulverston (LA)
73394	FCJ 354	Duple	43726	C29F	3/48	WE Morgan {Wye Valley Motors}, Hereford (HR)
73397	JYC 990	Duple	50349	C29F	4/48	HK Haybittel {Enterprise Bus Co}, Otterhampton (SO)
73407	?	Duple	47485	B31F	-/--	Trinidad Government Railways (O-TT)
73412	FFS 878	SMT		C25F	5/48	SMT (MN) C178
73425						Exported to Santiago (O-RCH)
73442	?	Mulliner		B--F	-/48	Shell Petroleum Co, Maracaibo (O-YV)
73447	ZH 7684	Duple	47484	B27F	-/48	Guinness (brewers), Dublin (XEI)
73450	FFS 876	SMT		C25F	3/48	SMT (MN) C176
73456	LVK 593	Mulliner	T252	B31F	5/48	E Marshall & Co Ltd {Crown Coaches}, Birtley (ND) 68
73461	?	Duple	47486	B31F	-/--	Trinidad Government Railways (O-TT)
73468	LBH 57	Duple	49419	C29F	3/48	Jeffways Coaches & Station Taxis Ltd, High Wycombe (BK)
73471	GNP 996	Mulliner	T251	B31F	3/48	J Morgan {John Morgan Private Hire}, Corse Lawn (WO)
73476	DVD 536	Mulliner	T253	B30F	4/48	A Duncan & Son, Law (LK)
73480	?	Duple	47487	B31F	-/--	Trinidad Government Railways (O-TT)
73489	NEV 387	Duple	48301	C29F	4/48	Wiffen's Coaches Ltd, Finchingfield (EX)
73514	?	Mulliner		B--F	-/--	Anglo Iranian Oil Co, Ahwaz (O-IR)
73518	FDT 102	Duple	50056	C29F	3/48	Leon Motor Services Ltd, Finningley (NG) 13
73522	?	Duple	47469	B36-	-/--	Elyas Transport Service, Lagos (O-WAN)
73528	AFB 730	Duple	49996	C29F	3/48	J & G Browning, Box (WI)
73533	?	Mulliner		?	-/--	Original operator unknown (O-WAN)
73538	JCD 371	Duple	47701	C27F	3/48	Southdown, Brighton (ES) 71
73541	JFJ 15	Duple	46958	C29F	3/48	Greenslades, Exeter (DN)
73548	?	Duple	47468	B36-	-/--	Elyas Transport Service, Lagos (O-WAN)

73552	CJA 707	Duple	50300	C29F	4/48	EC Morley & W Pickford {Great Moor Coaches}, Stockport (CH)
73561	FFS 879	SMT		C25F	5/48	SMT (MN) C179
73579	EJB 503	Duple	43869	C29F	3/48	L Stevens, Charney Bassett (BE)
73586	?	Duple	47467	B36-	-/--	Elyas Transport Service, Lagos (O-WAN)
73590	SMY 152	Duple	49356	C29F	4/48	AG Varney, Buckingham (BK)
73594	JXH 363	Mulliner	T294	B31F	2/48	London County Council (XLN) 1582
73600						Exported to Alexandria (O-ET)
73605						Exported to Malaya
73610	JRO 511	Duple	46725	C27F	3/48	Brunt's Coaches Ltd, Bell Bar (HT)
73613	EJB 271	Mulliner	T250	B30F	4/48	JW & SC West (West Bros) {Bray Transport}, Bray-on-Thames (BE)
73620	JXH 545	Duple	44865	C29F	4/48	Cliff's Saloon Coaches Ltd, London SE9 (LN)
73624						Exported to Accra (O-WAC)
73633						Exported to Alexandria (O-ET)
73652	FFS 880	SMT		C25F	5/48	SMT (MN) C180
73658						Exported to Accra (O-WAC)
73662	ENT 102	Duple	46462	C29F	3/48	JT, FW & GE Whittle {JT Whittle & Sons}, Highley (SH)
73666	FAM 250	Duple	48055	C29F	3/48	WJ MacPherson, South Newton (WI)
73672						Exported to Alexandria (O-ET)
73679						Exported to Malaya
73682	SS 6817	Duple	50341	C29F	4/48	J Ewart, Haddington (EL)
73685	JXL 47	Duple	48906	C25F	3/48	E Evans {Evan Evan Tours}, London WC1 (LN)
73692						Exported to Port Elizabeth (O-ZA)
73697	KMB 956	Pearson		C26F	7/48	J & H Coppenhall Ltd, Sandbach (CH) 11
73749 - 73760						Exported to Bombay (O-IND)
73837						Exported to Alexandria (O-ET)
73858	DBD 940	Beadle	C144	B30F	3/48	United Counties, Northampton (NO) 105
73865	ACP 760	Duple	49556	C29F	4/48	James Hoyle & Son, Halifax (WR) 29
73872						Exported to Port Elizabeth (O-ZA)
73881	* FWX 550	Beadle	C107	B30F	3/48	Keighley-West Yorkshire (WR) K617
73887						Exported to Santiago (O-RCH)
73892	?	Mulliner		?	-/--	BOAC, unknown overseas location
73895	* DBD 939	Beadle	C145	B30F	4/48	United Counties, Northampton (NO) 104
73901	DTH 999	Duple	50315	C29F	4/48	D Jones {Ffoshelig Coaches}, Newchurch (CR)
73906	?	Mulliner		?	-/--	BOAC, unknown overseas location
73914	?	Mulliner		B--F	-/--	Shell Petroleum Co, Guanta (O-YV)
73920	ENR 428	Mulliner	T248	B31F	4/48	CH Allen {Allen's Motor Services}, Mountsorrel (LE) 38
73942	SMY 583	Pearson		C26F	6/48	Valliant Direct Coaches Ltd, London W5 (LN)
73954	?	Mulliner		?	-/--	BOAC, unknown overseas location
73963	?	Mulliner		B--F	-/--	Shell Petroleum Co, Guanta (O-YV)
73969	BWG 40	SMT		C25F	5/48	W Alexander, Falkirk (SN) W219
73974	?	Mulliner		?	-/--	BOAC, unknown overseas location
73977	BWG 39	SMT		C25F	5/48	W Alexander, Falkirk (SN) W218
73983	GHO 322	Duple	47885	C29F	5/48	BS Williams, Emsworth (HA) 135
73988	ENR 429	Duple	46211	C29F	4/48	F & CF Laud, Mrs WC Goodhead and Mrs EM Coates (F Laud & Co), Moira (LE)
73999	SW 7449	Duple	50339	C29F	4/48	W & A Campbell, Gatehouse of Fleet (KK)
74002	?	Duple	47489	B31F	-/--	Trinidad Government Railways (O-TT)
74021	#?	Jonckheere	5635	C27-	7/48	Albert van Mullem, Roosbeek (O-B)
74022	?	Duple	47490	B31F	-/--	Trinidad Government Railways (O-TT)
74034	JMN 133	Duple	49990	C29F	10/47	W Humphreys, Laxey (IM)
74044	?	Duple	47488	B31F	-/--	Trinidad Government Railways (O-TT)
74050	* EFW 501	Plaxton	630	C29F	5/48	Enterprise (Scunthorpe) Passenger Services Ltd {Enterprise} (LI) 40
74056	SMY 916	Duple	44007	C29F	4/48	CG Lewis {CG Lewis Safety Coaches}, London SE10 (LN)
74059	?	Mulliner		B--F	-/--	Anglo Iranian Oil Co, Abadan (O-IR)
74065	GHO 321	Duple	48197	C29F	4/48	Hants & Sussex Motor Services Ltd, Emsworth (HA) 129
74070	KMA 378	Duple	49752	C29F	4/48	EE Seville, Hollingworth (LA)
74076	CVL 789	Duple	47566	C29F	4/48	L Parker, Bardney (LI)
74084	?	Mulliner		B--F	-/48	Shell Petroleum Co, Maracaibo (O-YV)
74103	MNU 336	Duple	44892	C29F	4/48	E Carter, Hales Green (DE)

C1252/101

74114	?	Mulliner		B--F	-/-- Shell Petroleum Co, Mene Grande (O-YV)
74125	?	Duple	47491	B31F	-/-- Trinidad Government Railways (O-TT)
74131	GR 9805	Duple	49876	C27F	4/48 WH Jolly, South Hylton (DM)
74137	HAO 389	Duple	50340	C29F	4/48 SH Brownrigg, Egremont (CU)
74140	?	Duple	50721	?	-/-- Trinidad Petroleum & Development Co Ltd (O-TT)
74146	JXH 650	Duple	50348	C29F	5/48 T Tilling, London (LN) 2306
74151	JRR 114	Duple	48852	C24F	4/48 Barton Transport, Chilwell (NG) 529
74157	KCV 569	Duple	43876	C29F	12/47 CN Rickard {Penryn & Falmouth Motor Co}, Penryn (CO)
74166					Exported to Lagos (O-WAN)
74184					Exported to Malaya
74196					Exported to Alexandria (O-ET)
74327	JXH 649	Duple	50347	C29F	5/48 T Tilling, London (LN) 2305
74333					Exported to Alexandria (O-ET)
74339					Exported to Malaya
74342	* ?	?		lorry	-/-- JLC Flew {Broadclyst Garage}, Broadclyst (GDN)
74348	JTC 920	Duple	49906	C29F	5/48 T Ireland & Sons, Lancaster (LA)
74354	JWR 899	Pearson		C29F	12/49 Hayes of Horsforth Ltd (WR)
74359	CFK 363	Duple	49463	C29F	5/48 CJ Marks {Blue Bus/Pride of the Pike}, Worcester (WO) 44
74363	JXH 718	Duple	50534	C29F	5/48 George Ewer & Co Ltd {Grey Green}, London N16 (LN)
74368					Exported to Malaya
74388					Exported to Port Elizabeth (O-ZA)
74399					Exported to Alexandria (O-ET)
74410	JNC 626	Trans-United		C27F	7/48 North Manchester Motor Coaches Ltd, Moston (LA)
74416					Exported to Santiago (O-RCH)
74422	GWX 192	Duple	50057	C29F	5/47 WR & P Bingley, Kinsley (WR)
74425	JXH 719	Duple	46982	C29F	5/48 Fallowfield & Britten Ltd, London E8 (LN)
74435					Exported to Port Elizabeth (O-ZA)
74441	KKM 471	Duple	46584	C29F	7/48 WE Johnson {Busy Bee Coaches}, Strood (KT)
74445	* MPB 333	Duple	48791	C29F	4/48 WD Hall Ltd, London SW19 (LN)
74450	SMY 239	Duple	50229	C29F	4/48 Ardley Bros Ltd, London N17 (LN) 7
74482	HON 861	Duple	44288	C29F	4/48 L & FG Myatt {Avon Coaches}, Birmingham (WK) 15
74490	PRE 128	Duple	43239	C29F	5/48 GH Austin & Sons Ltd {Happy Days}, Stafford (ST) 72
74497	?	Mulliner		B--F	-/-- Anglo Iranian Oil Co, Ahwaz (O-IR)
74506	SMY 262	Duple	44655	C29F	5/48 T Gibson {Lily Coaches}, London N9 (LN)
74510	?	Mulliner		B--F	-/-- Anglo Iranian Oil Co, Abadan (O-IR)
74516	LBH 757	Thurgood	474	C29F	5/48 JRG Dell {Rover Bus Service}, Lye Green (BK) 12
74522	FJW 916	Mulliner	T239	C26F	5/48 Worthington Motor Tours Ltd, Wolverhampton (ST)
74528	FJW 915	Mulliner	T235	C26F	5/48 Worthington Motor Tours Ltd, Wolverhampton (ST)
74538	KKO 193	Duple	48125	C29F	5/48 RF Harrington {Melody Motor Coaches}, Chatham (KT)
74540	PRE 333	Duple	46312	C29F	5/48 Mrs A Lymer {Victoria Tours}, Tean (ST)
74574					Exported to Malaya
74581	JXL 478	Duple	49893	C29F	3/48 CW Banfield, London SE15 (LN)
74588	?	Mulliner		B--F	-/-- Anglo Iranian Oil Co, Abadan (O-IR)
74597	JXL 376	Duple	49022	C29F	4/48 TG Green {Empress Motor Coaches}, London E2 (LN) 6
74601	?	Mulliner		B--F	-/-- Anglo Iranian Oil Co, Abadan (O-IR)
74609					Exported to Malaya
74613	KKM 733	Duple	47792	C29F	5/48 RH Sims {Marion Coaches}, Margate (KT)
74619	* JTD 999	Yeates	?	C29F	6/48 E & T Eaves {Eavesway Tours}, Ashton-in-Makerfield (LA)
74626					Exported to Malaya
74631	LAE 845	Duple	44425	C27F	5/48 TJ King {Monarch Coaches}, Bristol (GL)
74667	JYD 426	Mulliner	T349	B31F	5/48 Hutchings & Cornelius Services Ltd {H & C}, South Petherton (SO)
74672	?	Duple	50726	B31F	-/-- Trinidad Leaseholds Ltd (O-TT)
74680	?	Mulliner		B--F	-/-- Anglo Iranian Oil Co, Abadan (O-IR)
74689	CFV 994	Duple	49905	C29F	5/48 JR Freeman {B & B Luxury Coaches}, Bispham (LA)
74692	?	Mulliner		B--F	-/-- Anglo Iranian Oil Co, Abadan (O-IR)
74701 - 74712, 74761 - 74772					Exported to Bombay (O-IND)
74830	JCD 424	Duple	43769	C29F	5/48 T Camping, Brighton (ES)
74833					Exported to Mauritius
74835	FCJ 752	Duple	50310	C29F	5/48 Miss I Baynham, Ross-on-Wye (HR)

74838	* FP 4771	Duple	47911	C29F	5/48	Mrs AM Glenn {Central Coaches}, Uppingham (RD) 5
74844	?	Mulliner		B--F	-/--	Anglo Iranian Oil Co, Abadan (O-IR)
74845	BGS 721	Duple	50344	C20F	5/48	Loch Katrine Steamboat Co Ltd, Callander (PH)
74847	EJB 628	Duple	43596	C29F	5/48	OR Tibble {Pioneer Motor Services}, St Mary Bourne (HA)
74852	?	Mulliner		B--F	-/--	Shell Petroleum Co, unknown overseas location
74854	?	?		h/box	-/--	Lord Ridley, Cramlington (GND)
74856						Exported to Port Elizabeth (O-ZA)
74858		see 77858				
74895	NNO 229	Strachan		C29F	6/48	J Wordsworth {Dix Luxury Coaches}, Dagenham (EX)
74898	KTT 254	Woodall Nicholson		B29F	3/49	J, EM & AB Geddes {Burton Cars}, Brixham (DN)
74900	JXH 366	Mulliner	T304	B23F	-/49	London County Council (XLN) 1583
74902						Exported to Port Elizabeth (O-ZA)
74905	?	Mulliner		B--F	-/--	Shell Petroleum Co, Guanta (O-YV)
74909	EBD 900	Duple	46572	C29F	5/48	York Bros (Northampton) Ltd (NO) 17
74912	KCV 688	Duple	49821	C29F	5/48	EJ Tregunna, St Austell (CO)
74915	?	Mulliner		B--F	-/--	Shell Petroleum Co, Guanta (O-YV)
74918	FJW 918	Mulliner	T223	C29F	8/48	Worthington Motor Tours Ltd, Wolverhampton (ST)
74924						Exported to Mauritius
74930	CTY 811	Duple	49877	C29F	6/48	Bedlington & District Luxury Coaches Ltd, Ashington (ND)
74936	JMN 438	Duple	49991	C29F	2/48	Crennell's Garage Ltd, Ramsey (IM)
74943	DVH 434	Duple	50407	C29F	5/48	Hanson's Buses Ltd, Huddersfield (WR) 262
74947	GYG 134	Yeates	?	C29F	7/48	JW Kitchin & Sons Ltd, Pudsey (WR)
74972	JVO 390	Yeates	?	C29F	8/48	Clark's Coaches (Epperstone) Ltd (NG)
74982						Exported to Malaya
74992	GDA 721	Mulliner	T220	C28F	3/49	Worthington Motor Tours Ltd, Wolverhampton (ST)
74994	FAY 691	Yeates	100	C29F	2/49	R, SL & AH Wheildon (R Wheildon & Sons), Castle Donington (LE)
75001	?	Mulliner		B--F	-/--	Shell Petroleum Co, unknown overseas location
75010						Exported to Malaya
75013	FDL 640	Pearson		C26F	8/48	West Wight Motor Bus Co Ltd, Totland Bay (IW)
75020	JXT 615	Woodall Nicholson		C29F	1/49	Barber {Rose}, London N7 (LN)
75030	?	Mulliner		B--F	-/--	Shell Petroleum Co, unknown overseas location
75034	CPR 693	Duple	43551	C29F	5/48	Mrs VL House {Mid-Dorset Coaches}, Hilton (DT)
75035	#?	Jonckheere	5632	C27-	7/48	Houquet, De Panne (O-B)
75061	DDN 450	Duple	49803	C29F	5/48	E Hope & Sons, Terrington (NR)
75071	HTG 171	Duple	49873	C29F	5/48	G King, Cilfynydd (GG)
75081						Exported to Malaya
75084	BWG 42	SMT		C29F	6/48	W Alexander, Falkirk (SN) W221
75091	?	Mulliner		B--F	-/--	Shell Petroleum Co, unknown overseas location
75149 - 75160						Exported to Melbourne (O-AUS)
75185	K 24.518	Sorø	64	B35F	5/49	Hvidovre Rutebiler AS, Valby (O-DK)
75186 - 75196						Exported to Copenhagen (O-DK)
75245	FHR 25	Duple	46485	C29F	5/48	WH Vaughan, Chippenham (WI)
75248						Exported to Malaya
75256	* FFS 886	SMT		C25F	7/48	SMT (MN) C186
75266						Exported to Asuncion (O-PY)
75270	JM 7327	Duple	43872	C29F	5/48	E Nelson & Son, Arnside (WT)
75286		see 75256				
75297	BCB 476	Duple	44549	C29F	5/48	Lewis Cronshaw Ltd, London NW4 (LN)
75307						Exported to Malaya
75317	BWG 41	SMT		C25F	6/48	W Alexander, Falkirk (SN) W220
75320	BWG 43	SMT		C25F	6/48	W Alexander, Falkirk (SN) W222
75327						Exported to Asuncion (O-PY)
75337	PRE 587	Duple	47635	C29F	5/48	J, SJ & FJ Green, Brierley Hill (ST)
75340						Exported to Malaya
75347	HFM 42	Beadle	C175	B28F	11/47	Crosville MS, Chester (CH) S16
75357						Exported to Alexandria (O-ET)
75361	LBH 107	Duple	50042	C29F	5/48	AH Lucas {Lucasian Coaches}, Slough (BK)
75390	BCF 411	Duple	44726	C29F	7/48	AW Towler & Sons Ltd, Brandon (WF)
75400						Exported to Alexandria (O-ET)
75410	EMO 5	Mulliner	T263	B28F	5/48	A Moore & Sons {Imperial Bus Service}, Windsor (BE)
75413, 75420						Exported to Asuncion (O-PY)

Fleet	Reg	Body	Body No	Type	Date	Operator
75425	?	Duple	50727	B31F	-/--	Trinidad Petroleum & Development Co Ltd (O-TT)
75430	* FWO 620	Duple	46759	C29F	7/48	Red & White, Chepstow (MH) 820
75437	JUO 607	Duple	47698	C29F	6/48	Devon General, Torquay (DN) TCB607
75440	HFM 43	Beadle	C176	B28F	11/47	Crosville MS, Chester (CH) S17
75450	JDE 889	Mulliner	T257	B31F	4/48	Green's Motors Ltd, Haverfordwest (PE)
75453	?	Duple	50720	C25F	-/--	British South American Airways, Kingston (O-JA)
75481	FFS 881	SMT		C25F	6/48	SMT (MN) C181
75491						Exported to Malaya
75501	FDL 432	Duple	43988	C29F	5/48	Shotters Ltd, Brighstone (IW)
75504, 75511						Exported to Alexandria (O-ET)
75516	LUB 550	Duple	50055	C29F	5/48	JB Midgely & Son Ltd, Leeds (WR)
75521						Exported to Penang (O-MAL)
75524	SMY 559	Duple	46845	C29F	6/48	Northern Roadways Ltd, Glasgow (LK)
75531	BRN 963	Duple	49907	C29F	6/48	G Clayton & N Murray (Clayton & Murray) {Majestic Motors}, Preston (LA)
75541	TMG 244	Thurgood	482	C29F	6/48	H Holmes {Horseshoe Coaches}, London N15 (LN)
75544	HFM 41	Beadle	C174	B28F	11/47	Crosville MS, Chester (CH) S15
75583						Exported to Penang (O-MAL)
75590						Exported to Alexandria (O-ET)
75600	?	Mulliner		B--F	-/--	Anglo Iranian Oil Co, Abadan (O-IR)
75603	FFS 882	SMT		C25F	6/48	SMT (MN) C182
75610	FFS 883	SMT		C25F	6/48	SMT (MN) C183
75615	JXT 614	Woodall Nicholson		C29F	10/48	Dryer's Coaches Ltd, London E17 (LN)
75620	FFS 884	SMT		C25F	6/48	SMT (MN) C184
75625	JXT 960	Woodall Nicholson		C29F	10/48	N & S Coaches Ltd, Kibworth (LE)
75630	JXU 550	Woodall Nicholson		C29F	11/48	Smith, London N1 (LN)
75640	?	Mulliner		B--F	-/--	Shell Petroleum Co, unknown overseas location
75647	#?	Jonckheere	5772	C28-	5/49	R De Sloovere, Knokke aan Zee (O-B)
75671						Exported to Penang (O-MAL)
75681, 75691						Exported to Antwerp (O-B)
75697	* DBD 941	Beadle	C146	B30F	5/48	United Counties, Northampton (NO) 106
75761 - 75772						Exported to Bombay (O-IND)
75845	JXL 166	Mulliner	T259	B31F	5/48	London County Council (XLN) 1585
75850	DDP 632	Duple	44499	C29F	5/48	AE Smith {Smith's Coaches}, Reading (BE)
75855	* GHO 942	Duple	47627	C29F	5/48	BS Williams, Emsworth (HA) 136
75860	?	Mulliner		?	-/--	BOAC, unknown overseas location
75865	GWX 66	Duple	49792	C29F	5/48	JJ Longstaff, Mirfield (WR)
75875	?	Mulliner		B--F	-/--	Shell Petroleum Co, unknown overseas location
75905						Exported to Port Elizabeth (O-ZA)
75915	?	Mulliner		B--F	-/--	Shell Petroleum Co, unknown overseas location
75925	?	Mulliner		B--F	-/--	Anglo Iranian Oil Co, Abadan (O-IR)
75928	JXH 623	Mulliner	T222	B31F	6/48	BOAC (LN)
75935	ABR 143	Pearson		C26F	9/48	S Featonby {Shotton Bus Co}, Shotton Colliery (DM)
75940	ENR 840	Duple	49328	C29F	5/48	AA Oliver {Luxicoaches}, Loughborough (LE)
75945	BWG 247	SMT		C29F	7/48	W Alexander, Falkirk (SN) W232
75948	GHO 941	Duple	48198	C29F	5/48	BS Williams, Emsworth (HA) 132
75955	JXC 934	Duple	44212	C24F	5/48	United Service Transport Co Ltd, London SW9 (LN) 1076
75965	?	Mulliner		B--F	-/--	Anglo Iranian Oil Co, Abadan (O-IR)
75989	5185	Mulliner	SP206	B31F	6/48	Sarre Transport Ltd, St Peter Port, Guernsey (CI) 18
75993	DRV 685	Duple	44294	C29F	5/48	The Don Motor Coach Co Ltd, Southsea (HA)
75999	BWG 244	SMT		C25F	7/48	W Alexander, Falkirk (SN) W229
76009	JS 7853	Mulliner	T264	B31F	5/48	Hebridean Transport Ltd, Stornoway (RY)
76013						Exported to Alexandria (O-ET)
76019	SMY 560	Duple	46844	C29F	6/48	Northern Roadways Ltd, Glasgow (LK)
76023	ENT 283	Duple	47806	C29F	5/48	RW Carpenter {Valley Motor Services}, Bishop's Castle (SH)
76031						Exported to Alexandria (O-ET)
76041	GUE 785	Duple	48056	C29F	5/48	J Lloyd & Son Ltd, Nuneaton (WK) 19
76048						Exported to Alexandria (O-ET)
76066	FJW 939	Duple	48044	C29F	6/48	Worthington Motor Tours Ltd, Wolverhampton (ST)
76070	PRE 569	Duple	51148	C29F	5/48	RHJ Salisbury (Salisbury Bros) {Blackhawk Coaches}, Darlaston (ST)
76076	5184	Mulliner	SP207	B28F	6/48	Sarre Transport Ltd, St Peter Port, Guernsey (CI) 17

76087	EDW 691	Duple	50064	C29F	5/48	TR Banwell, Newport (MH)
76091						Exported to Alexandria (O-ET)
76097	JUO 608	Duple	47697	C29F	6/48	Devon General, Torquay (DN) TCB608
76101	* HNY 941	Duple	50937	C29F	5/48	Thomas & James Ltd, Port Talbot (GG)
76110						Exported to Alexandria (O-ET)
76120	HVF 750	Duple	44375	C29F	6/48	JJ Starling & Sons, North Walsham (NK)
76127						Exported to Alexandria (O-ET)
76145	* 5189	Mulliner	SP213	B31F	6/48	Guernsey Railways (CI) 28
76149	JXH 555	Duple	50245	C29F	5/48	Carshalton & Wallington Coaches Ltd, Carshalton (SR)
76155	HFM 39	Beadle	C172	B28F	11/47	Crosville MS, Chester (CH) S13
76166	ENT 731	Yeates	?	C29F	7/48	Salopia Saloon Coaches Ltd, Whitchurch (SH) 52
76170	* P-30078	Paul & Van Weelde	B31-		6/49	NAO, Roermond (O-NL) 57
76176	HFM 40	Beadle	C173	B28F	11/47	Crosville MS, Chester (CH) S14
76180	* MPB 833	Duple	46709	C29F	5/48	White's (Camberley) Ltd, Camberley (SR) 6
76188						Exported to Asuncion (O-PY)
76199	HVF 926	Duple	46214	C26F	6/48	L Votier {Mascot Coaches}, Norwich (NK)
76206						Exported to Asuncion (O-PY)
76226	BRN 958	Duple	49911	C27F	7/48	Enterprise Tours (Southport) Ltd (LA)
76230	EDM 935	Duple	43612	C29F	7/48	A Owen {Allandale Coaches}, Rhyl (FT)
76236						Exported to Port Swettenham (O-MAL)
76250						Exported to Asuncion (O-PY)
76253	JUO 609	Duple	47699	C29F	6/48	Devon General, Torquay (DN) TCB609
76257	ENT 284	Duple	47813	C29F	6/48	Salopia Saloon Coaches Ltd, Whitchurch (SH) 54
76261						Exported to Mauritius
76269	NEV 861	Duple	46335	C29F	10/49	CF Barnes (CF Barnes & Son) {Progress Coach Services}, Clacton-on-Sea (EX)
76279						Exported to Asuncion (O-PY)
76285	BWG 248	SMT		C29F	7/48	W Alexander, Falkirk (SN) W233
76325 - 76336						Exported to Bombay (O-IND)
76363	* EA-216	?		B29F	-/--	Raision Linja Oy, Raisio (O-FIN)
76397 - 76401						Exported to Melbourne (O-AUS)
76402	* 45409	CAC	?	FB31D	-/48	Emu Buses Pty Ltd, Shenton Park, WA (O-AUS) 9
76403 - 76408						Exported to Melbourne (O-AUS)
76434	CWH 558	Duple	49804	C29F	6/48	WA Smith, Tottington (LA)
76441	BWG 245	SMT		C29F	7/48	W Alexander, Falkirk (SN) W230
76448						Exported to Mauritius
76452	CPR 425	Duple	44289	C29F	6/48	HG Barlow & GE Phillips {Barlow, Phillips & Co}, Yeovil (SO)
76459						Exported to Asuncion (O-PY)
76466	BWG 246	SMT		C29F	7/48	W Alexander, Falkirk (SN) W231
76469	GWY 207	Duple	50461	C29F	5/48	J Cowgill & Sons, Lothersdale (WR)
76476	SMY 294	Duple	43903	C29F	6/48	W Grier & J Wilkinson {Lucky Line Coaches}, Edgware (MX)
76483						Exported to Penang (O-MAL)
76488	?	Mulliner		B--F	-/--	Anglo Iranian Oil Co, Abadan (O-IR)
76494	?	Mulliner		B--F	-/--	Anglo Iranian Oil Co, Abadan (O-IR)
76513	FBC 597	Duple	46209	C29F	6/48	JH Cleaver {Garden City Bus Service}, Leicester (LE)
76520	CTY 535	Duple	49961	C29F	6/48	T Anderson, Westerhope (ND)
76527						Exported to Penang (O-MAL)
76531	FFS 887	SMT		C25F	8/48	SMT (MN) C187
76538	?	Mulliner		B--F	-/--	Shell Petroleum Co, Mene Grande (O-YV)
76548	SMY 586	Duple	47865	C29F	5/48	D Evans {Maroon Coaches}, London E18 (LN)
76552						Exported to Port Swettenham (O-MAL)
76555	FFS 885	SMT		C25F	7/48	SMT (MN) C185
76562	* SO 9300	(SMT ?)		B28F	6/50	AJ Hay, Elgin (MR)
76567	?	Mulliner		B--F	-/--	Anglo Iranian Oil Co, Abadan (O-IR)
76573	?	Mulliner		B--F	-/--	Anglo Iranian Oil Co, Abadan (O-IR)
76591	* HOD 108	Duple	50009	C27F	6/48	Southern National, Exeter (DN) 568
76596						Exported to Port Swettenham (O-MAL)
76601	FED 175	Duple	50401	C29F	6/48	F Shadwell, Warrington (CH)
76613	# JFJ 259	Duple	46960	C29F	6/48	Regent Coaches (Teignmouth) Ltd (DN)
76639	?	Mulliner		B--F	-/--	Anglo Iranian Oil Co, Abadan (O-IR)
76646	JUR 493	Thurgood	483	C29F	6/48	EG Hewitt {Premier Coaches}, Watford (HT)
76653						Exported to Port Swettenham (O-MAL)

76660	JP 7018	Duple	49520 C29F	6/48	Stringfellow Bros {Silver Queen}, Wigan (LA)
76667					Exported to Port Swettenham (O-MAL)
76674	HEL 776	Duple	44812 C27F	2/48	Shamrock & Rambler Motor Coaches Ltd, Bournemouth (HA)
76678	VML 576	Duple	48222 C27F	6/48	Pall Mall Car Hire {Pamalhire}, London SW1 (LN)
76682					Exported to Port Swettenham (O-MAL)
76687	TMG 725	Duple	44893 C29F	8/48	WE & SG Blunt {Mitcham Belle Motor Coaches}, Mitcham (SR)
76696	KTO 459	Duple	47744 C29F	6/48	A Camm {Camm's Coaches}, Nottingham (NG) 6
76713 - 76724					Exported to Melbourne (O-AUS)
76827	?	Mulliner	B--F	-/--	Anglo Iranian Oil Co, Abadan (O-IR)
76840	HOP 554	Duple	44285 C29F	5/48	Dalton's Garage Ltd, Birmingham (WK)
76847	EDM 783	Duple	51159 C29F	6/48	P & O Lloyd, Bagillt (FT)
76854	JXL 547	Duple	50251 C29F	6/48	Wren's Coaches Ltd, London NW9 (LN)
76861	DVH 531	Duple	50419 C29F	6/48	Hanson's Buses Ltd, Huddersfield (WR) 263
76865	MPH 621	Woodall Nicholson	C29F	11/48	H Eastment & Sons, Church Stretton (SH)
76874	FBC 904	Duple	44515 C29F	6/48	Provincial Garage (Leicester) Ltd (LE) B3
76883	JOD 479	Duple	48285 C29F	6/48	Way & Son, Crediton (DN)
76904					Exported to Ireland
76909					Exported to Asuncion (O-PY)
76915	EUX 26	Woodall Nicholson	C29F	11/48	FH Davies {Victory}, St Georges (SH)
76922	LHT 285	Duple	49988 C29F	6/48	G Feltham & Sons Ltd {Kingswood Queen}, Kingswood (GL)
76926	GBM 302	Duple	48811 C29F	6/48	OA Bartle & Co, Potton (BD) B/48/3
76934					Exported to Asuncion (O-PY)
76941	MPE 59	Duple	47917 C29F	6/48	AT Brady {Brown Motor Services}, Forest Green (SR)
76949					Exported to Asuncion (O-PY)
76955					Exported to Ireland
76959	JXN 558	Duple	46983 C29F	6/48	Fallowfield & Britten Ltd, London E8 (LN)
76964	KKN 752	Duple	44272 C29F	7/48	HW Eglington {Island Luxury Coaches}, Sittingbourne (KT)
76988	DHS 537	Duple	50346 C29F	6/48	Daniel Ferguson Ltd {Victor}, Renfrew (RW) 19
76993					Exported to Asuncion (O-PY)
76999	ENR 935	Duple	43750 C29F	6/48	W Housden, Loughborough (LE) 4
77006	KKM 472	Duple	51039 C27F	6/48	KL Phillips, Staplehurst (KT)
77010					Exported to Port Swettenham (O-MAL)
77021	?	Duple	50748 B31F	-/--	Shell Petroleum Co, La Concepcion (O-YV)
77025	EBU 578	Duple	49895 C29F	6/48	G Barlow & Sons Ltd, Oldham (LA)
77031	?	Duple	50750 B31F	-/--	Shell Petroleum Co, Bachaquera (O-YV)
77039					Exported to Singapore
77043	JXM 468	Duple	44045 C29F	-/48	Essex County Coaches Ltd, London E15 (LN)
77048	HWR 584	Trans-United	C27F	9/48	Wild Bros Ltd, Barnoldswick (WR)
77072	* HWT 629	Woodall Nicholson	DP32F	-/--	David Brown Tractors Ltd, Meltham (XWR) 2
77077	?	Duple	50722 C27F	-/--	Original operator unknown (O-KWT)
77083					Exported to Singapore
77090	* ECO 698	Duple	46242 C29F	6/48	Blake's Bus Services Ltd, Delabole (CO)
77094	JXN 559	Duple	51042 C29F	6/48	Garner's Coaches Ltd, London W5 (LN)
77102	?	Duple	50723 C27F	-/--	Original operator unknown (O-KWT)
77109	JTD 726	Duple	49909 C29F	6/48	J Lamb, Upholland (LA)
77114					Exported to Asuncion (O-PY)
77123	BRN 962	Duple	49908 C29F	6/48	W Wrigley, Droylesden (LA)
77127	ENT 866	Duple	47807 C29F	6/48	RH & SJ Foxall {Robert Foxall & Sons}, Bridgnorth (SH)
77132					Exported to Singapore
77170	CCK 30	Duple	51161 C29F	6/48	Scout MS Ltd, Preston (LA)
77174					Exported to Asuncion (O-PY)
77179					Exported to Singapore
77184	GWX 79	Duple	50062 C27F	7/48	Clifford Lunn, Rothwell (WR)
77187	CJD 40	Duple	49392 C29F	6/48	Lansdowne Luxury Coaches, London E11 (LN)
77194					Exported to Asuncion (O-PY)
77199	FCJ 781	Duple	50311 C29F	8/48	Yeomans Private Hire Ltd, Hereford (HR) 67
77213 - 77224					Exported to Sydney (O-AUS)
77273	* ?	NZMB	C25F	-/49	Mount Cook & Southern Lakes Tourist Co, Christchurch (O-NZ)
77274	P2.485	McWhinnie	B29F	-/51	H & H Travel Lines Ltd, Invercargill (O-NZ) 2

77275 - 77277						Exported to Wellington (O-NZ)
77278	* s.424	Stratford		C20F	-/50	Gibson's Motors, New Plymouth (O-NZ) 3
77279	* P3.588	NZMB		B30F	11/48	New Zealand Railways Road Services (O-NZ) 1694
77280	* P2.416	NZMB		B30F	12/48	New Zealand Railways Road Services (O-NZ) 1696
77281	* P2.413	NZMB		B30F	11/48	New Zealand Railways Road Services (O-NZ) 1692
77282	P2.415	NZMB		B30F	11/48	New Zealand Railways Road Services (O-NZ) 1695
77283	P1.035	NZMB		B30F	3/49	New Zealand Railways Road Services (O-NZ) 1699
77284	P2.414	NZMB		B30F	11/48	New Zealand Railways Road Services (O-NZ) 1693
77395						Exported to Asuncion (O-PY)
77400	JYD 201	Duple	51166	C29F	6/48	Hull & Bartlett (Nadder Valley), Tisbury (WI)
77405	HAO 487	Duple	44729	C29F	6/48	Wright Bros Coaches Ltd, Nenthead (CU)
77409	5186	Mulliner	SP208	B28F	6/48	Sarre Transport Ltd, St Peter Port, Guernsey (CI) 19
77447						Exported to Singapore
77451						Exported to Asuncion (O-PY)
77456	GOR 376	Duple	46612	C29F	6/48	BS Williams, Emsworth (HA) 137
77461	BCB 542	Duple	50314	C29F	6/48	FJ & A Duxbury {Alan Dene Coaches}, Blackburn (LA)
77463	FDL 455	Duple	46893	C29F	6/48	SH, AC, PH & AR Randall (H Randall & Sons), Bonchurch (IW)
77470						Exported to Asuncion (O-PY)
77475	EUT 65	Duple	43523	C29F	6/48	W Boyden, Castle Donington (LE)
77479						Exported to Asuncion (O-PY)
77483	JXN 840	Duple	49962	B27F	6/48	Metropolitan Police, London SW1 (XLN)
77488	EBU 595	Duple	49894	C29F	6/48	Shearings Tours Ltd, Oldham (LA)
77495						Exported to Singapore
77530	DBW 372	Duple	46981	C29F	6/48	OA Slatter, Long Hanborough (OX) 21
77534						Exported to Asuncion (O-PY)
77539	JUR 181	Duple	48826	C27F	7/48	J Bygrave, Rushden (HT)
77544	FT 6358	Duple	49878	C29F	6/48	G Chapman {Priory Motor Coach Co}, North Shields (ND) 50
77547	CWH 821	Duple	49910	C29F	6/48	W Knowles & Sons, Bolton (LA)
77554						Exported to Santiago (O-RCH)
77559	ECO 801	Duple	49501	C29F	6/48	Plymouth Co-operative Society (DN) 521
77563						Exported to Santiago (O-RCH)
77567	ENT 876	Duple	43242	C29F	6/48	Corvedale Motor Services Ltd, Ludlow (SH) 13
77603						Exported to Santiago (O-RCH)
77607	HDF 192	Duple	47908	C29F	6/48	Mrs K Riddiford, Thornbury (GL)
77612	* HOD 109	Duple	50010	C27F	6/48	Southern National, Exeter (DN) 569
77616						Exported to Penang (O-MAL)
77621						Exported to Santiago (O-RCH)
77625	CTL 941	Duple	50041	C29F	6/48	R Kime & JH Jackson, Folkingham (LI)
77637						Exported to Santiago (O-RCH)
77640	FBC 905	Duple	44516	C29F	6/48	Provincial Garage (Leicester) Ltd (LE) B4
77642						Exported to Penang (O-MAL)
77648	FWO 621	Duple	46760	C29F	7/48	Red & White, Chepstow (MH) 821
77654	ENT 963	Duple	47808	C29F	6/48	Mrs MH & CJ Elcock, Ironbridge (SH)
77687						Exported to Santiago (O-RCH)
77691	GER 422	Duple	49029	C29F	6/48	Premier Travel Ltd, Cambridge (CM) 38
77697	JNE 878	Trans-United		C27F	8/48	Claribel Motors (Ardwick) Ltd, Manchester (LA)
77700						Exported to Penang (O-MAL)
77706						Exported to Santiago (O-RCH)
77710	* KKO 745	Duple	47949	C29F	6/48	H, C & W Sarjeant {Sarjeant Bros}, Cheriton (KT)
77719						Exported to Santiago (O-RCH)
77721	EPY 809	Plaxton	705	C29F	7/48	Hardwick's Services Ltd, Snainton (NR)
77724						Exported to Penang (O-MAL)
77727	* HOD 110	Duple	50011	C27F	6/48	Southern National, Exeter (DN) 570
77733	JPX 500	Duple	44206	C29F	7/48	CF Wood & Son Ltd {Enterprise Coaches}, Steyning (WS)
77775						Exported to Santiago (O-RCH)
77781						Exported to Santiago (O-RCH)
77794	* FHR 502	Duple	46487	C29F	6/48	PJ & D Card, Devizes (WI)
77799						Exported to Santiago (O-RCH)
77841	?	Mulliner		B--F	-/--	Shell Petroleum Co, Lagunillas (O-YV)
77845	?	Mulliner		B--F	-/--	Shell Petroleum Co, Lagunillas (O-YV)
77858	* FJW 917	Mulliner	T271	C26F	6/48	Worthington Motor Tours Ltd, Wolverhampton (ST)

C1252/107

77863	?	Mulliner		B--F	-/--	Shell Petroleum Co, Mene Grande (O-YV)
77871	* EBU 674	Plaxton	713	C29F	4/48	Joseph Dyson Ltd {Broadway Motors}, Oldham (LA)
77877	?	Mulliner		B--F	-/--	Shell Petroleum Co, Guanta (O-YV)
77882	JPT 490	Mulliner	T255	B31F	6/48	GH, S & JB Atkinson (GH Atkinson & Sons) {General Omnibus Services}, Chester-le-Street (DM) 13
77913 - 77924						Exported to Melbourne (O-AUS)
77937 - 77946						Exported to Copenhagen (O-DK)
77947	A 17.524	Sorø		B22D	6/49	De Røde Omnibusser, Søborg (O-DK)
77948						Exported to Copenhagen (O-DK)
78021 - 78032						Exported to Melbourne (O-AUS)
78087	?	Duple	50728	B31F	-/--	Original operator unknown (O-WAC)
78093						Exported to Santiago (O-RCH)
78098	LUB 359	Duple	50060	C29F	6/48	Wallace Arnold, Leeds (WR)
78126	?	Mulliner		B--F	-/--	Shell Petroleum Co, La Concepcion (O-YV)
78130						Exported to Antwerp (O-B)
78143	HUE 163	Mulliner	T287	B31F	-/48	Warwickshire Constabulary (XWK)
78148						Exported to Antwerp (O-B)
78156	NNO 186	Mulliner	T284	B31F	5/48	Essex County Council (XEX)
78162	* ?	?		B33-	-/--	CITO Tours BV, Axel (O-NL) 20
78208, 78212						Exported to Alexandria (O-ET)
78226	HOD 930	Duple	46407	C29F	5/48	SK Hill, Stibb Cross (DN)
78232						Exported to Alexandria (O-ET)
78239	JS 7899	Mulliner	T288	B30F	4/48	J Mitchell {Mitchell's Transport Parcel Service}, Stornoway (RY)
78246, 78295						Exported to Alexandria (O-ET)
78301	?	?		van	-/--	GUS Transport, London (GLN)
78310	JAH 899	Plaxton	621	C29F	7/48	JW Bunn {W Bunn & Son}, Walsingham (NK)
78316	?	?		?	-/--	Kuwait Oil Co (O-KWT)
78322	SB 7264	Duple	50345	C29F	6/48	A Cowe {R & A Cowe}, Tobermory, Mull (AL)
78337	SMY 547	Mulliner	T286	B--F	7/48	TJ Brown & JF Grout {Lee & District Motor Services}, Chesham (BK)
78375	PRE 498	Duple	51183	C29F	5/48	Greatrex Motor Coaches Ltd, Stafford (ST) 44 Kingfisher
78381, 78390, 78394						Exported to Alexandria (O-ET)
78400	AFB 939	Mulliner	T270	C29F	5/48	DR Keates, Bradford-on-Avon (WI)
78437	* ?	Wilton		DP--F	-/--	Martin & Vernon, Wanganui (O-NZ) 7
78438, 78439						Exported to Wellington (O-NZ)
78440	H7.488	?		tower	-/50	Auckland Transport Board (O-NZ) 3
78441	* ?	?		?	-/--	Original operator unknown (O-NZ)
78442	* P2.480	Crawley Ridley		B29F	3/50	Southland News Co Ltd, Invercargill (O-NZ) 19
78443 - 78445						Exported to Wellington (O-NZ)
78446	* P.359	Auckland TB		FB33F	-/50	Auckland Transport Board (O-NZ) 24
78447, 78448						Exported to Wellington (O-NZ)
78545 - 78556						Exported to Bombay (O-IND)
78586						Exported to Alexandria (O-ET)
78595	NNO 222	Mulliner	T289	B31F	6/48	H Rippingale, Gestingthorpe (EX)
78632	?	Mulliner		B---	-/--	Kuwait Oil Co (O-KWT)
78638	* JPT 541	Duple	43947	C29F	7/48	H Frazer Ltd {Dale Coaches}, Swalwell (DM)
78644, 78659						Exported to Santiago (O-RCH)
78665	JRR 830	Duple	43486	C29F	7/48	LW Evans, East Kirkby (NG) 1
78674, 78709						Exported to Santiago (O-RCH)
78715	KTV 17	Mulliner	T285	B31F	6/48	A Skill {Skill's Coaches}, Nottingham (NG) 17
78720	?	?		?	-/--	Iraq Petroleum Co, unknown overseas location
78729	* FCJ 915	Mulliner	T269	C29F	7/48	PW Jones, Burley Gate (HR)
78736, 78741, 78750						Exported to Alexandria (O-ET)
78782	?	Mulliner		B--F	-/--	Shell Petroleum Co, unknown overseas location
78792, 78801						Exported to Alexandria (O-ET)
78812	?	Mulliner		B--F	-/--	Shell Petroleum Co, unknown overseas location
78817	EUT 145	Duple	46719	C29F	6/48	A Adams (Adams & Sons) {Blue Bird}, Market Harborough (LE)
78823	SMY 590	Duple	43800	C29F	6/48	TG Green {Empress Motor Coaches}, London W6 (LN)
78830	GKV 784	Duple	47993	C29F	5/48	H & H Motorways Ltd {Bunty}, Coventry (WK)
78859	?	Mulliner		B--F	-/--	Shell Petroleum Co, unknown overseas location
78864	?	Mulliner		B--F	-/--	Shell Petroleum Co, unknown overseas location

Chassis	Reg	Body	Body#	Type	Del	Notes
78868	ENT 964	Duple	43980	C29F	6/48	RG, FJ, DA & K Cooper {G Cooper & Sons}, Oakengates (SH)
78873	DFR 95	Duple	49912	C27F	7/48	Lansdowne Motors Ltd, Fleetwood (LA)
78879	?	Mulliner		B--F	-/--	Shell Petroleum Co, unknown overseas location
78888	?	Mulliner		B--F	-/--	Shell Petroleum Co, unknown overseas location
78897	?	Duple	50729	B31F	-/--	Original operator unknown (O-WAC)
78906	JND 404	Duple	49740	C29F	7/48	A Mayne & Son Ltd, Manchester (LA)
78932	GC-7417	AICASA		B29C	4/49	AICASA, Las Palmas (O-IC)
78942						Exported to Las Palmas (O-IC)
78951	?	Duple	50724	C27F	-/--	Original operator unknown (O-KWT)
78961	* FUS 606	SMT		C24F	8/48	Erskine Paraplegic Coach Fund, Renfrew (XRW)
78968	?	Duple	50725	C27F	-/--	Original operator unknown (O-KWT)
78978	GWP 39	Duple	47633	C29F	7/48	Blackheath & District Motor Services Ltd (WO)
79007	?	Mulliner		B--F	-/--	Anglo Iranian Oil Co, Abadan (O-IR)
79022	?	Mulliner		B--F	-/--	Anglo Iranian Oil Co, Abadan (O-IR)
79028	?	Mulliner		B--F	-/--	Anglo Iranian Oil Co, Abadan (O-IR)
79037	?	Mulliner		B---	-/--	Kuwait Oil Co (O-KWT)
79043	CFK 448	?		van	7/48	Quality Cleaners Ltd, Worcester (GWO)
79049	?	Duple	50731	B31F	-/--	Original operator unknown (O-WAC)
79055	JTD 840	Duple	50247	C29F	7/48	Kia-Ora Motor Services Ltd, Morecambe (LA)
79076	?	?		B---	-/48	Gibraltar Motor Hire Services (O-GBZ)
79086	?	Mulliner		B--F	-/--	Anglo Iranian Oil Co, Abadan (O-IR)
79149 - 79160						Exported to Melbourne (O-AUS)
79221	* MNW 300	Wilks & Meade		C--F	5/48	Wounded Warriors Welfare Committee, Leeds (XWR)
79228	?	?		B---	-/48	Gibraltar Motor Hire Services (O-GBZ)
79237						Exported to Santiago (O-RCH)
79244	* CTL 967	Duple	49795	C29F	7/48	AE Olive, Billinghay (LI)
79253	HTG 528	Duple	49874	C29F	7/48	AE & FR Brewer {Brewer's Motor Services}, Caerau (GG)
79276						Exported to Santiago (O-RCH)
79282, 79290						Exported to Port Swettenham (O-MAL)
79295						Exported to Antwerp (O-B)
79304	?	Mulliner		B--F	-/--	Anglo Iranian Oil Co, Abadan (O-IR)
79317						Exported to Port Swettenham (O-MAL)
79323	?	Mulliner		B--F	-/--	Anglo Iranian Oil Co, Abadan (O-IR)
79330						Exported to Port Swettenham (O-MAL)
79347	EUT 284	Duple	47729	C29F	7/48	J Robinson & Sons (Burbage) Ltd (LE)
79355	?	Mulliner		B--F	-/--	Shell Petroleum Co, unknown overseas location
79364	J 11888	Duple	50735	C29F	7/48	H Swanson {Redline Tours}, St Helier, Jersey (CI) 9
79374	TMG 119	Duple	49888	C27F	7/48	Transport & General Workers Union, London (XLN)
79382	5192	Mulliner	SP215	B31F	7/48	Guernsey Railways (CI) 30
79394	?	Mulliner		B--F	-/--	Shell Petroleum Co, Casigua (O-YV)
79407	CCK 31	Duple	51162	C29F	8/48	Scout MS Ltd, Preston (LA)
79423	ENV 250	Duple	46573	C29F	7/48	York Bros (Northampton) Ltd (NO) 18
79431						Exported to Asuncion (O-PY)
79440	J 1879	Duple	50734	C29F	7/48	E Routier {Majestic Coaches}, St Clement, Jersey (CI)
79450	FF 6711	Duple	48205	C29F	7/48	DE Davies Ltd {Welshways Tour}, Barmouth (ME)
79458						Exported to Singapore
79470						Exported to Asuncion (O-PY)
79483	EAP 447	Duple	46360	C29F	7/48	Brookes Coaches Ltd, Heathfield (ES)
79518						Exported to Asuncion (O-PY)
79527	* HDF 343	Duple	49889	C29F	7/48	SK & F Silvey {Silvey's Coaches}, Epney (GL)
79536						Exported to Singapore
79545	SMY 587	Duple	47796	C29F	6/48	H & G Beach, Staines (MX)
79554						Exported to Asuncion (O-PY)
79563	FI 4070	Duple	50757	B31F	-/48	M Hogan {Shamrock Bus Service}, Thurles (EI) 42
79649 - 79660						Exported to Melbourne (O-AUS)
79663						Exported to Asuncion (O-PY)
79672	FFH 781	Duple	48901	C29F	7/48	Roy Grindle & Son Ltd, Cinderford (GL)
79709 - 79720						Exported to Bombay (O-IND)
79823	LUG 14	Duple	50059	C29F	7/48	Roy Neill Ltd, Leeds (WR)
79834	* HOD 111	Duple	50012	C27F	7/48	Southern National, Exeter (DN) 571
79843						Exported to Asuncion (O-PY)

79852	JPX 523	Duple	47856	C29F	8/48	AW Buckingham {Buck's Luxury Coaches}, Worthing (WS)
79892						Exported to Asuncion (O-PY)
79901	CRS 808	Duple	50338	B30F	7/48	W Hall snr, Aberdeen (AD)
79910	?	Duple	50730	B31F	-/--	Original operator unknown (O-WAC)
79928	* H-30829	Den Oudsten	1773	B30-	5/49	EVAG, Vlaardingen (O-NL) 34
79937	* JYD 619	Duple	44727	C29F	7/48	WH Foster & Son {Avalon Coaches}, Glastonbury (SO)
79980	?	Mulliner		B--F	-/--	Shell Petroleum Co, Casigua (O-YV)
79989	?	Duple	50741	B31F	-/--	Shell Petroleum Co, La Concepcion (O-YV)
80005	BCF 573	Duple	47914	C29F	7/48	NS Rule, Boxford (WF)
80006	J 3590	Duple	50736	C29F	7/48	H Swanson {Redline Tours}, St Helier, Jersey (CI) 3
80017	CTK 178	Duple	46361	C27F	7/48	HS Rendell {Cosy Coaches}, Parkstone (DT)
80061	?	Duple	50742	B31F	-/--	Shell Petroleum Co, La Concepcion (O-YV)
80074	JXN 560	Duple	50535	C29F	7/48	George Ewer & Co Ltd {Grey Green}, London N16 (LN)
80088	?	Duple	50743	B31F	-/--	Shell Petroleum Co, La Concepcion (O-YV)
80113 - 80124						Exported to Sydney (O-AUS)
80197 - 80208						Exported to Bombay (O-IND)
80275	JXP 453	Duple	49798	C29F	7/48	Cliff's Saloon Coaches Ltd, London SE9 (LN)
80316	FWM 332	Duple	50967	C29F	7/48	Howard Coaches Ltd, Southport (LA)
80322	EBX 511	Duple	50397	C29F	8/48	TS Jenkins, Llanelly (CR)
80327, 80334, 80346, 80365, 80402						Exported to Asuncion (O-PY)
80407	JOD 640	Duple	43369	C29F	7/48	AE Townsend {Townsend's Tours}, Torquay (DN)
80416	* GRK 316	Duple	44529	C29F	7/48	Bourne & Balmer (Croydon) Ltd (SR) 50
80425						Exported to Asuncion (O-PY)
80432	VML 592	Duple	48223	C27F	7/48	Pall Mall Car Hire {Pamalhire}, London SW1 (LN)
80441	* MNU 939	Duple	49818	C29F	7/48	HS North, Derby (DE)
80489						Exported to Asuncion (O-PY)
80498	* HOD 112	Duple	50013	C27F	7/48	Southern National, Exeter (DN) 572
80501	FCY 435	Duple	48274	C29F	7/48	WL Jones, Cwmavon (GG)
80509	?	?		van	-/--	H Littlewood Ltd {Littlewood's Pools}, Liverpool (GLA)
80523	JAH 463	Duple	43692	C29F	7/48	M Miller Ltd {Pye's Garage}, Blakeney (NK)
80534	LHT 721	Duple	44230	C27F	7/48	H Russett {Royal Blue}, Bristol (GL)
80580	KRL 294	Duple	49820	C29F	7/48	WA Tremain, Zelah (CO)
80589	JRH 268	Duple	49828	C29F	7/48	JB & JW McMaster {JB McMaster & Sons}, Kingston-upon-Hull (ER)
80598	* JBJ 791	Yeates	(099 ?)	C29F	5/49	RO Simonds, Botesdale (EK)
80637						Exported to Wellington (O-NZ)
80638	?	NZMB		C16F	4/49	New Zealand Railways Road Services (O-NZ) 1706
80639	?	NZMB		C16F	4/49	New Zealand Railways Road Services (O-NZ) 1705
80640	?	NZMB		C16F	4/49	New Zealand Railways Road Services (O-NZ) 1707
80641	* v.459	Eaddy & Taylor		B36F	-/48	WT & LD Morgan, Helensville (O-NZ)
80642	* H2.404	NZMB		C16F	3/49	New Zealand Railways Road Services (O-NZ) 1704
80643, 80644						Exported to Wellington (O-NZ)
80645	* P.601	North Shore		B33F	-/49	North Shore Transport Co Ltd, Takapuna (O-NZ) 1
80646	* ?	North Shore		B33F	-/49	North Shore Transport Co Ltd, Takapuna (O-NZ) 31
80647	* P.602	North Shore		B33F	12/49	North Shore Transport Co Ltd, Takapuna (O-NZ) 2
80648						Exported to Wellington (O-NZ)
80710	?	Duple	50745	B31F	-/--	Shell Petroleum Co, La Concepcion (O-YV)
80703	JP 7017	Duple	49521	C29F	7/48	R Gray (Gray Bros) {Streamline Coaches}, Wigan (LA)
80710	?	Duple	50745	B31F	-/--	Shell Petroleum Co, La Concepcion (O-YV)
80752	?	Duple	50747	B31F	-/--	Shell Petroleum Co, La Concepcion (O-YV)
80759	AJV 454	Duple	49797	C29F	7/48	A & AE Blackbourn Ltd {Granville Tours}, Grimsby (LI) 152
80765	DBW 534	Duple	44758	C29F	7/48	House Bros (Watlington) Ltd (OX)
80777	?	Duple	50744	B31F	-/--	Shell Petroleum Co, La Concepcion (O-YV)
80784	J 5296	Duple	50737	C29F	8/48	RH Barney & AA Allo {Pioneer Coaches}, St Helier, Jersey (CI)
80793	CNL 263	Duple	49879	C29F	7/48	AB Wilson, Horsley-on-Tyne (ND) 8
80837	KKR 221	Duple	47932	C29F	7/48	RH Sims {Marion Coaches}, Margate (KT)
80846	EET 261	Duple	51034	C29F	7/48	W Smart, Greasborough (WR)
80855	TMG 998	Duple	44320	C29F	7/48	Venture Transport (Hendon) Ltd, London NW2 (LN)
80863	CPR 923	Duple	51341	C29F	7/48	Mrs AM Macklin {Antelope Tours}, Sherborne (DT)
80869, 80878, 80920						Exported to Asuncion (O-PY)
80924	DBW 576	Duple	43981	C29F	7/48	RC Surman, Chinnor (OX)

C1252/110

80929						Exported to Asuncion (O-PY)
80933	GDK 317	Duple	50259	C27F	7/48	Yelloway Motor Services Ltd, Rochdale (LA)
80937						Exported to Ireland
80946	FCA 383	Duple	47810	C29F	7/48	T Williams {T Williams & Son}, Ponciau (DH)
80952	GOR 120	Duple	46706	C29F	7/48	EH Morton {Brown Bus Service}, Lymington (HA)
80955	JXN 936	Duple	49963	B27F	7/48	Metropolitan Police, London SW1 (XLN)
80964	JPT 725	Duple	43985	C29F	7/48	PJ Coulson & Sons {ABC Motor Services}, Rushyford (DM)
80969						Exported to Asuncion (O-PY)
81025 - 81036, 81061 - 81072						Exported to Melbourne (O-AUS)
81121 - 81132						Exported to Bombay (O-IND)
81181 - 81192						Exported to Melbourne (O-AUS)
81209						Exported to Asuncion (O-PY)
81218	HYP 725	Duple	44115	C29F	7/48	Birch Bros Ltd, London NW5 (LN) K35
81226	* E-18799	Domburg	146	DP33F	5/49	ONOG, Oldenzaal (O-NL) 15
81233	FEW 800	Duple	50066	C29F	7/48	H Lee {Whippet Coaches}, Hilton (HN)
81239	* JTC 648	Duple	49896	C29F	8/48	W Hawkins {Regal Motor Service}, Werneth (LA)
81244	LKX 40	Duple	48817	C29F	7/48	Mrs HV Wall, Kingsey (BK)
81251	* FWO 622	Duple	46761	C29F	7/48	Red & White, Chepstow (MH) 822
81257	JTD 714	Duple	49913	C29F	8/48	Lancashire Constabulary, Preston (XLA)
81297	PRF 48	Duple	43593	C29F	7/48	Greatrex Motor Coaches Ltd, Stafford (ST) 45 Kittiwake
81302	JXN 937	Duple	49964	B27F	7/48	Metropolitan Police, London SW1 (XLN)
81307						Exported to Helsinki (O-FIN)
81311						Exported to Ireland
81317	TM-702	?		B29F	2/49	J & M Launokorpi, Kemio (O-FIN)
81323	DEA 940	Duple	47776	C29F	7/48	Hills Tours Ltd, West Bromwich (ST)
81334	JOD 810	Duple	49887	C29F	6/48	AW Burfitt & WRP Lewis {Blue Coaches}, Ilfracombe (DN)
81343	FBE 215	Duple	43326	C29F	8/48	JE Vessey, Hibaldstow (LI)
81375	?	Duple	50749	B31F	-/--	Shell Petroleum Co, Bachaquera (O-YV)
81384	JUR 824	Duple	43969	C29F	7/48	J Maidment Ltd, Hitchin (HT)
81393	MPF 368	Duple	44419	C29F	7/48	GF & BS Graves {GF Graves & Son}, Redhill (SR)
81398						Exported to Helsinki (O-FIN)
81402	NPU 424	Duple	47603	C29F	8/48	LC Hunt & West {Safeway}, London E17 (LN)
81411	* FDL 537	Duple	48856	C29F	7/48	Moss Motor Tours (Sandown, I.W.) Ltd (IW)
81420	EU 9170	Duple	50312	C29F	6/48	C Davies & Sons {Enterprise}, Talgarth (BC)
81468	?	Mulliner		B--F	-/--	Anglo Iranian Oil Co, Abadan (O-IR)
81472	JMN 446	Duple	49992	C29F	2/48	JS Corlett (Corlett & Ekins) {Majestic}, Douglas (IM)
81477	?	Duple	50756	B31F	-/--	Trinidad Government Railways (O-TT)
81484	EPY 860	Duple	47877	C29F	7/48	Begg's Luxury Coaches Ltd, Thornaby-on-Tees (NR)
81492	?	Mulliner		B--F	-/--	Anglo Iranian Oil Co, Abadan (O-IR)
81501	?	Mulliner		?	-/--	Ministry of Supply (GOV)
81510	?	Mulliner		?	-/--	Ministry of Supply (GOV)
81550	KGH 893	Mulliner		B28F	-/49	Ministry of Works (GOV)
81560	?	Mulliner		B--F	-/--	Anglo Iranian Oil Co, Abadan (O-IR)
81568	JTE 353	Duple	50406	C29F	12/48	W Robinson & Sons, Great Harwood (LA) 14
81589	* HOD 37	Duple	50022	C27F	8/48	Western National, Exeter (DN) 548
81598	HOD 38	Duple	50021	C27F	7/48	Western National, Exeter (DN) 549
81673	H7.492	?		tower	-/49	Auckland Transport Board (O-NZ) 7
81674	* P.632	North Shore		B33F	-/49	North Shore Transport Co Ltd, Takapuna (O-NZ) 32
81675	* V2.415	?		?	-/--	Original operator unknown (O-NZ)
81676	P.636	North Shore		B33F	-/49	North Shore Transport Co Ltd, Takapuna (O-NZ) 36
81677						Exported to Wellington (O-NZ)
81678	* ?	?		?	-/49	Original operator unknown (O-NZ)
81679	P2.474	Modern		B29F	-/50	Orr's Motors Ltd, Invercargill (O-NZ) 5
81680						Exported to Wellington (O-NZ)
81681	* ?	?		B--F	8/49	Original operator unknown (O-NZ)
81682						Exported to Wellington (O-NZ)
81683	* ?	?		DP--F	-/--	Martin & Vernon, Wanganui (O-NZ) 6
81684						Exported to Wellington (O-NZ)
81769 - 81780						Exported to Melbourne (O-AUS)
81816	JOC 550	Duple	44980	C29F	8/48	Smith's Imperial Coaches Ltd, Birmingham (WK)
81822	?	Mulliner		B--F	-/--	Anglo Iranian Oil Co, Abadan (O-IR)
81829	KRL 984	Duple	46239	C29F	7/48	NH Ashton {Ashtonville Coaches}, Halwill (DN)

81836	?	Mulliner		B--F	-/--	Anglo Iranian Oil Co, Abadan (O-IR)
81847	GOR 880	Duple	46424	C29F	7/48	FH Kilner (Transport) Ltd, Horsham (WS) 138
81855	ATS 294	Duple	50343	C29F	6/48	Dee Taxis Ltd, Aberdeen (AD)
81867	TMV 990	Duple	44046	C29F	8/48	Essex County Coaches Ltd, London E15 (LN)
81905	JFJ 386	Duple	48796	C29F	8/48	SJ Wakley {Rambler Bus Services}, Axminster (DN) 9
81911	?	Mulliner		B--F	-/--	Anglo Iranian Oil Co, Abadan (O-IR)
81918	KYA 528	Duple	44202	C29F	8/48	TE Herring {W Herring & Son}, Burnham-on-Sea (SO)
81924	* HOD 39	Duple	50024	C27F	8/48	Western National, Exeter (DN) 550
81934	?	Mulliner		B---	-/--	Kuwait Oil Co (O-KWT)
81945	DBW 612	Duple	43994	C29F	8/48	RC Surman, Chinnor (OX)
81957	* JUR 879	Duple	44039	C27F	8/48	North Star Omnibus & Coach Services Ltd, Stevenage (HT)
81994	CCK 32	Duple	51163	C29F	8/48	Scout MS Ltd, Preston (LA)
82000						Exported to Asuncion (O-PY)
82007	HOD 40	Duple	50023	C27F	8/48	Western National, Exeter (DN) 551
82014						Exported to Asuncion (O-PY)
82025	EUT 160	Duple	43950	C29F	6/48	FW Bromley, Fleckney (LE)
82033	DFR 242	Duple	49914	C29F	8/48	Whittaker Bros (Blackpool) Ltd (LA)
82045	GWX 74	Duple	50058	C29F	8/48	A McDonald, Stanley, Wakefield (WR)
82084	EUJ 279	Duple	47811	C29F	8/48	T & HR Roberts, Cefn Mawr (DH)
82090						Exported to Asuncion (O-PY)
82097	JNG 108	Duple	48778	C29F	9/48	AR Newstead, East Rudham (NK)
82105						Exported to Asuncion (O-PY)
82114	* JTE 484	Duple	49915	C29F	8/48	Cross Street Motors (Lancaster) Ltd {Vista Coaches}, Morecambe (LA)
82122	CJR 255	Duple	49880	C29F	8/48	Robson & Atkinson, Stocksfield-on-Tyne (ND) 3
82134	* KYA 64	Duple	49989	C29F	8/48	GA Wall, Mark (SO)
82174	GWP 421	Duple	47632	C29F	8/48	H & WB Jones {Jones Bros}, Upton-on-Severn (WO)
82169						Exported to Asuncion (O-PY)
82181	* KTV 396	Duple	49801	C29F	9/48	R Foster {Streamline Coaches}, Grantham (KN)
82194	DBW 613	Duple	44185	C29F	7/48	EHA Oliver, Long Hanborough (OX)
82201						Exported to Asuncion (O-PY)
82208	EUJ 441	Duple	47812	C29F	8/48	JT, FW & GE Whittle {JT Whittle & Sons}, Highley (SH)
82217	JVO 148	Duple	48853	C24F	8/48	Barton Transport, Chilwell (NG) 530
82260	K-8394	Kvinesdal		?	11/48	Johannes Reiersen {Slimestadruta}, Slimestad (O-N)
82265	JYP 490	Duple	51357	B31F	9/48	Dickinson, Apsley (XHT)
82272	KAR 67	Duple	43505	C29F	8/48	Whitehead's Garage Ltd, Letchworth (HT)
82285	* JXL 560	Duple	50353	C29F	8/48	V Bingley (Bingley Bros) {Sceptre Coaches}, London W6 (LN)
82292						Exported to Alexandria (O-ET)
82299	HCG 372	Duple	44803	C29F	6/49	Creamline Motor Services (Bordon) Ltd (HA)
82373 - 82384						Exported to Melbourne (O-AUS)
82445 - 82456						Exported to Stockholm (O-S)
82488	TMG 732	Duple	44895	C29F	8/48	BC Viney {Viney's Motor Coaches}, London N15 (LN) 12
82528						Exported to Alexandria (O-ET)
82535	JXU 561	Mulliner		?	10/48	Ministry of Works (GOV)
82543	JXU 562	Mulliner		?	11/48	Ministry of Supply (GOV)
82552	JXH 630	Mulliner	T247	B31F	7/48	BOAC (LN)
82562						Exported to Alexandria (O-ET)
82568						Exported to Helsinki (O-FIN)
82575	HDG 302	Yeates	084	C29F	9/48	Pulham & Sons (Coaches) Ltd, Bourton-on-the-Water (GL)
82619	* DFR 404	Duple	49916	C29F	9/48	Whiteside Ltd, Blackpool (LA)
82626	FHR 839	Duple	44303	C27F	8/48	E Drew, Highworth (WI)
82633						Exported to Helsinki (O-FIN)
82644	?	Mulliner		B--F	-/--	Anglo Iranian Oil Co, Abadan (O-IR)
82654	JNE 607	Duple	49678	C29F	8/48	F Brazendale {Pride of Sale Motor Tours}, Sale (CH)
82659	JUR 830	Duple	48830	C29F	7/48	HW Hart {Hillside Coaches}, Markyate (HT) 11
82669	?	Mulliner		?	-/--	Original operator unknown I6154(O-WAC)
82706	HOD 41	Duple	50025	C27F	8/48	Western National, Exeter (DN) 552
82714	JVO 329	Duple	43762	C29F	8/48	CH Wright & Sons, Newark (NG)
82725	GDA 720	Mulliner	T272	C28F	10/48	Worthington Motor Tours Ltd, Wolverhampton (ST)
82732	?	Mulliner		B--F	-/--	Anglo Iranian Oil Co, Abadan (O-IR)

82738	?	Mulliner		B--F	-/--	Anglo Iranian Oil Co, Abadan (O-IR)
82743	* MPF 643	Duple	44263	C29F	8/48	Ben Stanley Ltd, Hersham (SR)
82753	?	Mulliner		B--F	-/--	Anglo Iranian Oil Co, Abadan (O-IR)
82759						Exported to Accra (O-WAC)
82798	* JXP 557	Duple	47604	C29F	7/48	Fallowfield & Britten Ltd, London E8 (LN)
82808	?	Mulliner		B--F	-/--	Anglo Iranian Oil Co, Abadan (O-IR)
82813	JTE 396	Duple	51331	C29F	8/48	R Wood & Sons (Tours) Ltd, Ashton-under-Lyne (LA)
82825	FVJ 274	Duple	43727	C29F	9/48	WE Morgan {Wye Valley Motors}, Hereford (HR)
82833	?	Mulliner		B--F	-/--	Anglo Iranian Oil Co, Abadan (O-IR)
82840	DDP 912	Duple	44500	C29F	8/48	AE Smith {Smith's Coaches}, Reading (BE)
82848	?	Duple	52570	B30F	-/--	St Madeleine Sugar, San Fernando (O-TT)
82882	?	Mulliner		B--F	-/--	Anglo Iranian Oil Co, Abadan (O-IR)
82886	NFC 850	Duple	44040	C29F	8/48	H Crapper & Son Ltd, Oxford (OX) 34
82897	CCK 529	Duple	52026	C29F	8/48	Lansdowne Garage (Morecambe) Ltd (LA) 2
82930		see 62930				
83009 - 83020						Exported to Melbourne (O-AUS)
83084						Exported to Asuncion (O-PY)
83091	FDL 655	Duple	50037	C29F	6/49	Southern Vectis, Newport (IW) 214
83100	* KYA 142	Duple	46283	C29F	10/48	Western Engineering & Motor Services {WEMS}, Weston-super-Mare (SO)
83106						Exported to unknown overseas location
83116						Exported to Asuncion (O-PY)
83157	FWO 623	Duple	51358	C29F	8/48	Red & White, Chepstow (MH) 823
83164						Exported to Asuncion (O-PY)
83176	AEP 551	Duple	47814	C29F	8/48	Mid-Wales Motorways Ltd, Newtown (MO)
83182	FDL 577	Duple	43635	C29F	8/48	Shotters Ltd, Brighstone (IW)
83195	BCB 684	Duple	44550	C29F	7/48	Lewis Cronshaw Ltd, London NW4 (LN)
83202						Exported to Asuncion (O-PY)
83244	* LKX 291	Duple	43744	C29F	7/48	JJ Raisey, Grendon Underwood (BK) 3
83250						Exported to Alexandria (O-ET)
83257	JXP 58	Mulliner	T292	B31F	7/48	London County Council (XLN) 1589
83262	* HTG 986	Mulliner	T303	B31F	8/48	Thomas Bros, Port Talbot (GG)
83272						Exported to Alexandria (O-ET)
83280	CTK 210	Duple	46269	C29F	8/48	Swanage Coaches Ltd, Chickrell (DT)
83288						Exported to Alexandria (O-ET)
83295	MRA 610	Duple	43812	C29F	8/48	HS North, Derby (DE) 39
83334	TMV 950	Duple	48187	C29F	8/48	AR & Mrs EF Thorne {Thorne Bros}, London SW2 (LN)
83340	FDL 581	Mulliner	T266	B31F	7/48	Seaview Services Ltd, Seaview (IW)
83347						Exported to Alexandria (O-ET)
83357	CJN 299	Duple	50005	C29F	8/48	Westcliff-on-Sea MS (EX)
83367	JXP 54	Mulliner	T293	B31F	7/48	London County Council (XLN) 1588
83374						Exported to Alexandria (O-ET)
83382	VML 643	Duple	48224	C27F	8/48	Pall Mall Car Hire {Pamalhire}, London SW1 (LN)
83422	JXT 903	Mulliner	T291	B31F	9/48	London County Council (XLN) 1593
83429						Exported to Alexandria (O-ET)
83436	GOR 653	Mulliner	T267	B28F	8/48	DG Grace {Graceline Coaches}, Alresford (HA)
83440	DCT 303	Mulliner	T280	B31F	9/48	Sharpe's Motors (Heckington) Ltd (LI)
83446	LUB 360	Duple	50061	C29F	8/48	Wallace Arnold, Leeds (WR)
83456	* D-8981	Groenewold		B28-	-/48	Harmanni, Assen (O-NL) 7
83467	KTA 17	Duple	49310	C29F	8/48	Heybrook Bay Motor Services Ltd, Down Thomas (DN)
83474	* E-48221	Den Oudsten	1770	B33-	5/49	WATO, Nijverdal (O-NL) 6
83501 - 83512						Exported to Melbourne (O-AUS)
83645 - 83646						Exported to Stockholm (O-S)
83647	* D335	?		?	-/--	Nashulta Omnibus, Eskilstuna (O-S)
83648 - 83656						Exported to Stockholm (O-S)
83704	JXL 558	Duple	50249	C29F	8/48	L Manny Ltd, London SW9 (LN)
83711						Exported to Helsinki (O-FIN)
83719	* EUT 619	Duple	46604	C29F	8/48	HJ & AJ Barkus (Barkus & Son), Woodhouse Eaves (LE)
83731	ABR 6	Duple	49881	C29F	8/48	SF Hunter, Great Lumley (DM)
83738						Exported to Helsinki (O-FIN)
83746	KAR 510	Duple	44037	C29F	8/48	Brunt's Coaches Ltd, Bell Bar (HT)
83754	* EUJ 502	Duple	47815	C29F	8/48	Jones Coachways Ltd, Market Drayton (SH) 22
83790	HTG 613	Mulliner	T302	B31F	9/48	J Roberts, Caerphilly (GG)

83793	DVH 837	Duple	50420	C29F	8/48	Hanson's Buses Ltd, Huddersfield (WR) 264
83800						Exported to Helsinki (O-FIN)
83817	* FJF 833	Yeates	098	C29F	7/49	BE Quinn {Quinn's Luxury Coaches}, Erith (KT)
83826						Exported to Helsinki (O-FIN)
83837	?	?		van	-/--	D Gordon & Co Ltd (dyers), Halifax (GWR)
83845						Exported to Helsinki (O-FIN)
83881	* ?	?		van	11/48	Mendip Queen Coaches Ltd, High Littleton (GSO)
83888	?	Mulliner		B--F	-/--	Anglo Iranian Oil Co, Abadan (O-IR)
83896	JMN 936	Mulliner	T281	B31F	7/48	Isle of Man Road Services Ltd, Douglas (IM) 25
83904	?	?		van	-/--	JJ Allen Ltd (department store), Bournemouth (GHA)
83908	KWJ 634	Duple	51244	C29F	8/48	Elsworth Ltd (Elsworth Social Club), Sheffield (WR)
83918	?	Mulliner		B--F	-/--	Anglo Iranian Oil Co, Abadan (O-IR)
83925	?	?		van	-/--	H Godfrey, London N7 (GLN)
83931	TMV 8	Duple	44222	C29F	9/48	E Curtis & Hearn, London NW7 (LN)
83947		see 83647				
83965	?	?		van	10/48	JJ Allen Ltd (department store), London SW1 (GLN)
83969	DVD 401	Duple	50342	C29F	8/48	J Galloway, Harthill (LK)
83978	?	Mulliner		B--F	-/--	Anglo Iranian Oil Co, Abadan (O-IR)
83987	?	Oldland		van	-/--	Parnall (shopfitters), Bristol (GGL)
83998	CTK 524	Duple	44260	C29F	9/48	SC Sheasby {South Dorset Coaches}, Corfe Castle (DT)
84005	?	Mulliner		?	-/--	Ministry of Supply (GOV)
84012	?	Mulliner		B--F	-/--	Anglo Iranian Oil Co, Abadan (O-IR)
84021	KGT 69	Mulliner		?	2/49	Ministry of Supply (GOV)
84059	5191	Mulliner	SP216	B31F	7/48	Guernsey Railways (CI) 31
84079	?	Mulliner		B--F	-/--	Anglo Iranian Oil Co, Abadan (O-IR)
84092	?	Mulliner		B--F	-/--	Anglo Iranian Oil Co, Abadan (O-IR)
84108	?	Mulliner		B--F	-/--	Anglo Iranian Oil Co, Abadan (O-IR)
84149	J 11982	Duple	50754	C29F	9/48	E Routier {Majestic Coaches}, St Clement, Jersey (CI)
84164, 84181, 84198						Exported to Asuncion (O-PY)
84201 - 84212, 84321 - 84332						Exported to Melbourne (O-AUS)
84417	* J 4442	Duple	50755	C29F	2/48	CB Griss {Scarlet Pimpernel Coaches}, St Helier, Jersey (CI)
84431, 84442, 84461						Exported to Asuncion (O-PY)
84504	KRL 771	Mulliner	T308	B28F	9/48	Grenville Motors Ltd, Camborne (CO)
84508	* ?	?		B32-	-/49	Van Koningsbruggen, Den Helder (O-NL)
84513	?	Mulliner		B--F	-/--	Belgian Air Force, Brussels (O-B)
84523	?	?		van	-/--	Currie & Co (Newcastle) Ltd (GND)
84527	GDA 700	Duple	47821	C29F	8/48	Harman's Motor Services Ltd, Wolverhampton (ST)
84534, 84541						Exported to Helsinki (O-FIN)
84544	?	SMT		van	-/--	JH Lunn, Edinburgh (GMN)
84558	GYG 936	Duple	49892	C29F	8/48	Ripponden & District Motors Ltd (WR) 7
84554						Exported to Trinidad
84596	?	Duple	52572	B30F	-/--	St Madeleine Sugar, San Fernando (O-TT)
84601						Exported to Wellington (O-NZ)
84602	P.745	Suburban		B33F	9/49	Suburban Buses Ltd, Te Papapa (O-NZ) 12
84603	* P.125	Eaddy & Taylor		B33F	5/49	Howick Bus Co Ltd, Auckland (O-NZ) 3
84604, 84605						Exported to Wellington (O-NZ)
84606	* P.631	North Shore		B33F	-/49	North Shore Transport Co Ltd, Takapuna (O-NZ) 31
84607	* ?	NZMB		C38F	-/--	Mount Cook & Southern Lakes Tourist Co, Christchurch (O-NZ)
84608 - 84611						Exported to Wellington (O-NZ)
84612	* ?	?		?	-/--	Madge Motors Ltd, Palmerston North (O-NZ) 17
84673 - 84684						Exported to Sydney (O-AUS)
84757 - 84768						Exported to Melbourne (O-AUS)
84782						Exported to Helsinki (O-FIN)
84786	HRU 62	Duple	44813	C27F	9/48	Shamrock & Rambler Motor Coaches Ltd, Bournemouth (HA)
84790	* JKD 930	Duple	50962	C29F	9/48	RM Walker {Margaret Sun Saloons}, Liverpool (LA)
84797						Exported to Helsinki (O-FIN)
84804	JUP 104	Duple	43897	C29F	8/48	Scurr's Motor Services Ltd, Stillington (DM)
84810						Exported to Helsinki (O-FIN)
84812		see 84612				
84814	GOT 286	Duple	46425	C29F	8/48	FH Kilner (Transport) Ltd, Horsham (WS) 139

84818						Exported to Lagos (O-WAN)
84823	?	Mulliner		B--F	-/--	Anglo Iranian Oil Co, Abadan (O-IR)
84867	DHS 629	Duple	52110	C29F	9/48	Daniel Ferguson Ltd {Victor}, Renfrew (RW)
84871	EMO 524	Duple	46266	C29F	9/48	GR & GK Freeman, Faringdon (BE)
84876	?	Mulliner		B--F	-/--	Anglo Iranian Oil Co, Abadan (O-IR)
84884	?	Mulliner	T254	?	9/48	Cheshire County Council (XCH)
84888	?	Mulliner		B--F	-/--	Anglo Iranian Oil Co, Abadan (O-IR)
84895	?	Mulliner		B---	-/--	Kuwait Oil Co (O-KWT)
84898	CCK 528	Duple	52038	C29F	9/48	Woodcock's British Tours Ltd, Heskin (LA)
84907	?	Mulliner		B--F	-/--	Anglo Iranian Oil Co, Abadan (O-IR)
84911	* TMV 948	Duple	44042	C29F	9/48	HV Richmond, Barley (HT)
84917						Exported to Lagos (O-WAN)
84953	LHU 605	Duple	44805	C29F	9/48	EJ Kear {Duchess}, Bristol (GL)
84958	GDA 498	Duple	52031	C29F	9/48	L Barnett {Pathfinder}, Coseley (ST)
84962						Exported to Lagos (O-WAN)
84967	?	Mulliner		B--F	-/--	Anglo Iranian Oil Co, Abadan (O-IR)
84971	KTA 435	Duple	46409	C29F	8/48	CW & WHM Terraneau, South Molton (DN)
84978	?	Mulliner		?	-/--	Original operator unknown
84983	TMV 182	Duple	52040	C29F	7/48	BEA, Ruislip (MX) 1120
84989	?	Duple	50732	B--F	-/--	Original operator unknown (O-WAC)
84998	?	Mulliner		B--F	-/--	Anglo Iranian Oil Co, Basra (O-IRQ)
85007	?	Mulliner		B--F	-/--	Anglo Iranian Oil Co, Basra (O-IRQ)
85041	ENV 309	Duple	46520	C29F	9/48	WR Lawrence, Wappenham (NO)
85047	?	?		?	-/--	Arturo Escunder, location unknown (O-IC)
85051	EUJ 593	Duple	43226	C29F	8/48	SC & J Vagg {Vagg's Motors}, Knockin Heath (SH)
85057	* ?	?		B24-	-/49	Original operator unknown (O-GR)
85061	CJR 449	Duple	50070	C29F	9/48	GP Cooper {Cooper Bros}, Annitsford (ND)
85067	* HOD 42	Duple	50026	C27F	8/48	Western National, Exeter (DN) 553
85076	* ?	?		B24-	-/49	Original operator unknown (O-GR)
85083	HWR 181	Duple	50624	C29F	9/48	M Jackson, Knaresborough (WR)
85087	?	Duple	50733	B--F	-/--	Original operator unknown (O-WAC)
85096	* 50-855	?		B28-	-/--	Original operator unknown (O-GR)
85134						Exported to Accra (O-WAC)
85143	* 54-537	?		B24-	-/49	Original operator unknown (O-GR)
85148	FCA 506	Duple	46503	C29F	9/48	JB Pye Ltd, Rhos-on-Sea (DH)
85154	* ?	?		B24-	-/--	Original operator unknown (O-GR)
85158	FDL 627	Duple	44749	C29F	9/48	Holmes Saloon Coaches Ltd, Cowes (IW)
85165						Exported to Alexandria (O-ET)
85173	PV 8831	Duple	47913	C29F	2/49	HAC Claireaux {CJ Partridge & Son}, Layham (WF)
85179						Exported to Alexandria (O-ET)
85181	JPX 867	Duple	49445	C29F	9/48	HE Bleach, Lavant (WS)
85184						Exported to Accra (O-WAC)
85220	NTW 368	Duple	48026	C29F	9/48	L Hall & Sons, Maldon (EX)
85226	* D-6194	?		B29-	-/--	Pieters {PTH}, Hoogeveen (O-NL) 4
85230	HOD 43	Duple	50027	C27F	8/48	Western National, Exeter (DN) 554
85239	AJV 656	Duple	52067	B30F	10/48	C Tindall, Ashby-cum-Fenby (LI)
85242	?	Duple	50752	B31F	-/--	Shell Petroleum Co, Bachaquera (O-YV)
85246	TMV 941	Duple	46846	C29F	9/48	Northern Roadways Ltd, Glasgow (LK)
85251	DBW 854	Duple	43749	C29F	9/48	WH Maule, Tiddington (OX)
85257	?	Duple	50764	C24F	-/--	KLM, Karachi (O-PK) 2114
85266	?	Duple	50751	B31F	-/--	Shell Petroleum Co, Bachaquera (O-YV)
85274, 85311						Exported to Helsinki (O-FIN)
85315	HB 6648	Duple	46827	C29F	9/48	Morlais Services Ltd, Merthyr Tydfil (GG) 51
85324						Exported to Helsinki (O-FIN)
85327	TMV 989	Duple	43925	C29F	9/48	Valliant Direct Coaches Ltd, London W5 (LN) 68
85332						Exported to Helsinki (O-FIN)
85342	FDL 656	Duple	50038	C29F	6/49	Southern Vectis, Newport (IW) 215
85347	TMV 35	Duple	44694	C29F	8/48	CJ Elms, Phillips & Brown {Elms Coaches}, London N17 (MX)
85353	MPG 750	Duple	43553	C27F	9/48	Walton on Thames Motor Co Ltd (SR)
85356						Exported to Helsinki (O-FIN)
85360	?	Duple	52135	C29F	-/--	Original operator unknown (O-WAN)
85400	?	Mulliner		B--F	-/--	Anglo Iranian Oil Co, Basra (O-IRQ)
85449 - 85460, 85533 - 85544						Exported to Melbourne (O-AUS)

85572	GDA 722	Mulliner	SP277	C28F	9/48	Worthington Motor Tours Ltd, Wolverhampton (ST)
85578	?	Mulliner		B--F	-/--	Anglo Iranian Oil Co, Basra (O-IRQ)
85584	SY 8812	Duple	52039	C29F	9/48	George Montgomery & Son, Musselburgh (MN)
85589	?	Mulliner		B--F	-/--	Anglo Iranian Oil Co, Abadan (O-IR)
85598	?	Spurling		van	-/--	Maple & Co Ltd (furniture manufacturers), London NW1 (GLN) 735
85604	JXC 935	Duple	44213	C24F	9/48	United Service Transport Co Ltd, London SW9 (LN) 1077
85610	* HTX 594	Jeffreys		C26F	12/48	HJ Uphill, Caerau (GG)
85613	?	Mulliner		B--F	-/--	Anglo Iranian Oil Co, Abadan (O-IR)
85617	?	Duple	50765	C24F	-/--	KLM, Karachi (O-PK) 2115
85657	?	Mulliner		B--F	-/--	Anglo Iranian Oil Co, Abadan (O-IR)
85661	JXU 606	Mulliner		B30F	-/49	Ministry of Works (GOV)
85667	?	Mulliner		B--F	-/--	Anglo Iranian Oil Co, Abadan (O-IR)
85675	?	Mulliner		?	-/--	Ministry of Supply (GOV)
85678	?	Mulliner		B--F	-/--	Anglo Iranian Oil Co, Ahwaz (O-IR)
85687	?	Mulliner		?	-/--	Ministry of Supply (GOV)
85693	?	Mulliner		?	-/--	Ministry of Supply (GOV)
85701	#KGT 68	Mulliner		?	2/49	Ministry of Supply (GOV)
85705	?	Mulliner		B--F	-/--	Anglo Iranian Oil Co, Ahwaz (O-IR)
85709						Exported to Mauritius
85746						Exported to Piraeus (O-GR)
85750	JXU 584	Mulliner		?	12/48	Ministry of Supply (GOV)
85756	* ?	?		B25-	-/--	Original operator unknown (O-GR)
85762	KGH 906	Mulliner		B30F	-/--	Royal Ordnance Factory, Chorley (GOV)
85767	* ?	?		B28-	-/--	Original operator unknown (O-GR)
85776	JTF 414	Duple	49526	C29F	8/48	J Monks & Sons, Leigh (LA)
85782	GDA 981	Mulliner	T309	C29F	3/49	Worthington Motor Tours Ltd, Wolverhampton (ST)
85788	* HHP 178	Duple	52070	B30F	7/48	Standard Motor Co Ltd, Coventry (XWK)
85792	?	?		?	-/--	V Rios, Valencia (O-E)
85796						Exported to Mauritius
85832	PRF 655	Mulliner	T275	B31F	9/48	H & J Homer & D Jones, Quarry Bank (ST)
85838	?	Mulliner		B--F	-/--	Shell Petroleum Co, unknown overseas location
85843	JXT 901	Mulliner	T305	B23F	5/49	London County Council (XLN) 1586
85850	JCD 900	Duple	43771	C29F	9/48	RG Johnston {Unique Coaches}, Brighton (ES)
85854	DCL 151	Mulliner	T282	B31F	9/48	RG Brown {Broadland Luxury Coaches}, Norwich (NK)
85863						Exported to Alexandria (O-ET)
85867	?	Duple	50766	C24F	-/--	KLM, Karachi (O-PK) 2132
85881						Exported to Alexandria (O-ET)
85883	JXT 898	Mulliner	T295	B31F	8/48	London County Council (XLN) 1591
85887						Exported to Alexandria (O-ET)
85922	* CCK 530	Duple	52127	C29F	9/48	E Barnes {Premier Motors}, Preston (LA)
85934	JXH 634	Mulliner	SP247	B31F	12/48	BOAC (LN)
85944	JXH 635	Mulliner	T229	B31F	12/48	BOAC (LN)
85949	FWO 624	Duple	52068	C29F	9/48	Red & White, Chepstow (MH) 824
85954	?	Mulliner		B---	-/--	Iraq Petroleum Co, unknown overseas location
85967	KAR 224	Duple	48821	C29F	10/48	EG Hewitt {Premier Coaches}, Watford (HT)
85976	?	Duple	52573	B30F	-/--	Route Bus Service (O-M)
86011	ATS 408	Duple	52136	C29F	8/48	J Meffan, Kirriemuir (AS)
86023	CCK 589	Duple	52080	C29F	6/49	Scout MS Ltd, Preston (LA)
86033	JNF 767	Duple	49687	C29F	9/48	JA Charnley, Wilmslow (CH)
86038	DRD 74	Duple	44501	C29F	9/48	AE Smith {Smith's Coaches}, Reading (BE)
86043	?	Mulliner		B--F	-/--	Basra Petroleum Co (O-IRQ)
86056	EUJ 691	Duple	52056	C29F	9/48	Corvedale Motor Services Ltd, Ludlow (SH) 12
86065						Exported to Accra (O-WAC)
86100	JOE 668	Duple	44975	C29F	9/48	SW Burchell {Modern Travel}, Birmingham (WK)
86137 - 86146						Exported to Melbourne (O-AUS)
86147	sa275.306	Syd Wood		B39F	-/--	Original operator unknown (O-AUS)
86148						Exported to Melbourne (O-AUS)
86292	GDA 779	Duple	52095	C29F	10/48	Worthington Motor Tours Ltd, Wolverhampton (ST)
86302	* DHJ 22	Duple	50006	C29F	9/48	Westcliff-on-Sea MS (EX)
86307	JXT 390	Duple	52150	C29F	9/48	Dryer's Coaches Ltd, London E17 (LN)
86312	?	Mulliner		B--F	-/--	Basra Petroleum Co (O-IRQ)

86325	GOT 514	Duple	49028	C29F	9/48	Hants & Sussex Motor Services Ltd, Emsworth (HA) 140
86334	?	Mulliner		?	-/--	Original operator unknown (O-WAN)
86369	LAF 186	Duple	52104	C29F	9/48	E & T Stevens {Blue Coaches}, St Ives (CO)
86381	JNG 276	Duple	46386	C29F	9/48	Culling & Son (Norwich) Ltd {Claxton & District}, Claxton (NK)
86391	KTA 713	Duple	43658	C29F	11/48	CA Gayton {Gayton's Coaches}, Ashburton (DN)
86396	DHM 69	Duple	44399	C29F	11/48	Grange & Sons {Broadway Coaches}, London E6 (LN)
86401	?	Mulliner		B--F	-/--	Basra Petroleum Co (O-IRQ)
86414	SE 6725	Duple	52174	B30F	10/48	J Kindness {Red Motor Service}, Gardenstown (BF)
86423	?	Mulliner		B--F	-/--	Original operator unknown (O-WAC)
86459	CCK 572	Duple	52128	C29F	10/48	W Tuer {Tuer's Motors}, Morland (CU)
86470	FMR 168	Duple	52130	C29F	9/48	PJ & D Card, Devizes (WI)
86480	* KGP 290	Duple	50536	C29F	4/49	George Ewer & Co Ltd {Grey Green}, London N16 (LN)
86485	LAU 18	Duple	49799	C29F	9/48	A Skill {Skill's Coaches}, Nottingham (NG) 18
86490	?	Duple	52574	B30F	-/--	Shell Petroleum Co, Suez (O-ET)
86585 - 86596						Exported to Sydney (O-AUS)
86683	NTW 330	Duple	44705	C29F	3/48	EA Winwood ,London E10 (LN) 19
86692	?	Duple	52571	B30F	-/--	Original operator unknown (O-S)
86714	#MO.673	Ansair		FB29F	-/--	Original operator unknown (O-AUS)
86727	GEW 1	Duple	52143	C29F	10/48	SV Robinson, Kimbolton (HN)
86739	GWP 577	Duple	49920	C29F	11/48	FJ Ketley, Stourport-on-Severn (WO)
86749	* LHN 146	Duple	50700	C29F	9/48	R Handley {JC Handley & Son}, Middleham (NR)
86754	EBX 831	Duple	46593	C29F	10/48	Treharne Bros, Ponthenry (CR)
86760	?	Mulliner		B--F	-/--	Shell Petroleum Co, Barranquilla (O-CO)
86772	KGT 79	Mulliner		?	4/49	Ministry of Works (GOV)
86781						Exported to Mauritius
86816	KGH 922	Mulliner		B30F	-/49	Ministry of Works (GOV)
86828	EUJ 855	Mulliner	T311	B29F	10/48	G Edwards, Bwlchgwyn (DH)
86841	JXN 938	Duple	49965	B27F	11/48	Metropolitan Police, London SW1 (XLN)
86843	* EVN 100	Duple	49823	C29F	9/48	J Armstrong, Thirsk (NR)
86858	?	Mulliner		B--F	-/--	Shell Petroleum Co, Barranquilla (O-CO)
86861	FED 399	?		lorry	11/48	Peter Walker & Son (Warrington & Burton) Ltd (brewers), Warrington (GCH)
86870						Exported to Mauritius
86904	?	Mulliner		?	-/--	Ministry of Supply (GOV)
86917	HRM 48	Duple	52155	C29F	9/48	T Young & Sons, Keswick (CU)
86927	FMR 140	Duple	46481	C29F	9/48	CH Thomas, Calne (WI)
86932	JVO 749	Duple	48854	C24F	9/48	Barton Transport, Chilwell (NG) 531
86937	?	Duple	52575	B20F	-/--	Original operator unknown (O-IRQ)
86951	FRY 295	Duple	47912	C29F	9/48	ET Straw, Leicester (LE)
86959						Exported to Mauritius
86995	#?	Mulliner		?	-/--	Ministry of Supply (GOV)
87007	FCA 555	Duple	47816	C29F	10/48	EG Peters, Llanarmon yn lal (FT)
87017	JXP 525	Duple	44852	C27F	3/49	Keith & Boyle (London) Ltd {Orange Luxury Coaches}, London EC2 (LN) Hawk
87022	FCA 498	Duple	43498	C29F	9/48	E & C Wright {E Wright & Son}, Penycae (DH)
87026						Exported to Helsinki (O-FIN)
87039	EDR 345	Duple	49369	C29F	11/48	Heybrook Bay Motor Services Ltd, Down Thomas (DN)
87048						Exported to Accra (O-WAC)
87084, 87096						Exported to Mauritius
87101 - 87112						Exported to Melbourne (O-AUS)
87245 - 87256						Exported to Bombay (O-IND)
87286						Exported to Mauritius
87291	TMV 729	Duple	47743	C29F	10/48	V Bingley (Bingley Bros) {Sceptre Coaches}, London W6 (LN)
87295						Exported to Helsinki (O-FIN)
87309	* GOT 513	Duple	46613	C29F	9/48	Hants & Sussex Motor Services Ltd, Emsworth (HA) 141
87317	LWA 121	Duple	50383	C29F	10/48	W, E & E Warrington {Eagle Coaches}, Sheffield (WR)
87352	?	?		van	-/--	Parker Knoll Ltd (furniture manufacturers), High Wycombe (GBK)
87364	JXT 381	Duple	44531	C29F	4/49	Fallowfield & Britten Ltd, London E8 (LN)
87374	CCS 330	Duple	52163	C29F	10/48	James Dodds & Sons, Troon (AR)

87379	KKT 590	Duple	47946 C29F	10/48	PG Warren, Ticehurst (ES)
87384					Exported to Helsinki (O-FIN)
87397	EUT 880	Duple	43890 C29F	9/48	R, SL & AH Wheildon (R Wheildon & Sons), Castle Donington (LE)
87406	* FDT 718	Duple	50601 C29F	9/48	TW Holling, Askern (WR)
87438	* MPF 109	Duple	48849 C29F	9/48	WD Hall Ltd, London SW19 (LN)
87451	DEA 996	Duple	47636 C29F	10/48	Mrs LM Horton {Sunbeam Coaches}, West Bromwich (ST)
87461	VML 663	Duple	47594 C29F	10/48	Frames Tours Ltd, London WC1 (LN) 73
87466	HRU 190	Duple	44814 C27F	10/48	Shamrock & Rambler Motor Coaches Ltd, Bournemouth (HA)
87471					Exported to Helsinki (O-FIN)
87485	EJ 9403	Duple	52113 C29F	10/48	WE Lloyd (WE Lloyd & Son) {Glan Teify Bus Services}, Pontrhydfendigaid (CG)
87493	KYB 8	Duple	52203 C29F	10/48	JH Fursland & Co Ltd {Pride of Bridgwater}, Bridgwater (SO)
87529	EBU 865	Duple	51332 C29F	11/48	Holt's Transport (Royton) Ltd (LA)
87536	HG-622	?	B28-	-/--	Länsilinjat Oy, Tampere (O-FIN) 3
87544	* CCK 567	Duple	52129 C27F	4/49	Enterprise Tours (Southport) Ltd (LA)
87547	CJR 455	Duple	43624 C29F	10/48	CR Robson, Smelting Syke (ND) 20
87561	KKR 815	Mulliner	T261 B28F	9/48	AE, RW & GT Gillie {A Gillie & Sons}, Aylsham (KT)
87567	FDL 676	Duple	50039 C29F	6/49	Southern Vectis, Newport (IW) 216
87579	?	Duple	50759 B31F	-/--	Shell Petroleum Co, location unknown (O-RI)
87605	#K 24.517	Sorø	60 B35D	4/49	Hvidovre Rutebiler AS, Valby (O-DK)
87618	* LMN 1	Duple	51111 C29F	5/49	P Murray {Mona's Queen}, Douglas (IM)
87625	?	Mulliner	B--F	-/--	Anglo Iranian Oil Co, Abadan (O-IR)
87633	* BCB 857	Duple	52058 C29F	10/48	Brook Electric Motors, Huddersfield (XWR)
87636	GDA 967	Duple	52100 C18F	3/49	Worthington Motor Tours Ltd, Wolverhampton (ST)
87644	KYB 46	Duple	47728 C29F	10/48	GP Fry {JH Fry & Sons}, Stratton-on-the-Fosse (SO)
87656	TMV 999	Duple	47872 C29F	10/48	HW Winfield, Tattenham Corner (SR)
87668					Exported to Accra (O-WAC)
87707	HOD 44	Duple	50028 C27F	9/48	Western National, Exeter (DN) 555
87714	?	Mulliner	B--F	-/--	Anglo Iranian Oil Co, Abadan (O-IR)
87722	GDA 780	Duple	52096 C29F	10/48	Worthington Motor Tours Ltd, Wolverhampton (ST)
87725	JPT 957	Duple	50127 B30F	12/48	Langley Park Motor Co {Gypsy Queen Coaches}, Langley Park (DM)
87733	JXN 939	Duple	49966 B27F	11/48	Metropolitan Police, London SW1 (XLN)
87745	SB 7470	Duple	52224 C29F	10/48	West Coast Motor Service Co, Campbeltown (AL)
87757					Exported to Accra (O-WAC)
87796	JXT 902	Mulliner	T296 B31F	9/48	London County Council (XLN) 1592
87921 - 87932					Exported to Sydney (O-AUS)
88019	?	Mulliner	B---	-/--	Kuwait Oil Co (O-KWT)
88026	DDB 394	Duple	50490 C29F	10/48	A Lloyd {County Motor Services}, Stockport (CH)
88030	DBW 67	Mulliner	T260 B28F	9/48	HC Kemp, Woodcote (OX)
88038	GDA 781	Duple	52097 C29F	3/49	Worthington Motor Tours Ltd, Wolverhampton (ST)
88050	JPT 677	Duple	51359 B30F	10/48	Durham County Council (Aycliffe Hospital) (XDM)
88097					Exported to Lagos (O-WAN)
88102	SH 8394	Duple	51043 C29F	-/48	W Blackie {Blackie's Garage}, Eyemouth (BW)
88109	?	Mulliner	B--F	-/--	Shell Petroleum Co, unknown overseas location
88117	MRA 602	Duple	52216 C29F	10/48	FH Doughty, Brimington (DE)
88120	HDG 325	Mulliner	T262 B28F	11/48	AH, V & Mrs E Fluck {Fluck & Sons}, Notgrove (GL)
88128	* JTF 965	Santus	FC30F	12/48	Walls Motor Tours, Wigan (LA)
88142	GDA 892	Duple	52098 C25F	5/49	Worthington Motor Tours Ltd, Wolverhampton (ST)
88152					Exported to Accra (O-WAC)
88192	JUP 326	Duple	43621 C29F	10/48	G Pennington {Cosy Coaches/Meadowfield Motor Co}, Meadowfield (DM)
88199	?	Mulliner	B--F	-/--	Anglo Iranian Oil Co, Abadan (O-IR)
88207	?	?	van	-/--	G Barnes & Son, Lincoln (GLI)
88210	* HDG 859	Whitson	6020 C29F	1/49	ACJ Perrett {Perrett's Coaches}, Shipton Oliffe (GL)
88217	?	?	l/stock	-/--	P Jennings, Bishop Monkton (GWR)
88229	KTU 882	Mulliner	T323 B--F	1/49	Shell Petroleum Co, Stanlow (XCH)
88241					Exported to Accra (O-WAC)
88281	#?	Mulliner	?	-/--	Ministry of Supply (GOV)
88288	?	Mulliner	?	-/--	Syria Petrol Co, Tripoli (O-LAR)

C1252/118

88296	?	Mulliner	?		-/--	Ministry of Supply (GOV)
88299	?	Airwork Joinery		van	-/--	Norman Ashton Ltd, Kingston-on-Hull (GER)
88306	JXH 637	Mulliner	T265	B31F	12/48	BOAC (LN)
88317	JXR 795	Duple	44299	C29F	10/48	CB Gant {Norwood Park Coaches}, London SE27 (LN)
88330						Exported to Mombasa (O-EAK)
88371	JXN 940	Duple	49367	B27F	11/48	Metropolitan Police, London SW1 (XLN)
88381	?	Mulliner	?		-/--	Syria Petrol Co, Tripoli (O-LAR)
88384	?	?		h/box	-/--	F Latham, Chobham (GSR)
88387	CTK 548	Mulliner	T276	B31F	10/48	BF & KWC Legg (F Legg & Sons), Evershot (DT)
88395	EUT 923	Duple	49329	C29F	10/48	AA Oliver {Luxicoaches}, Loughborough (LE)
88539	?	?		h/box	-/--	T Parker & Sons, Maldern Green (GCE)
88588	?	?		van	-/--	Lawrence & Hall Ltd (removers), Harrogate (GWR)
88551						Exported to Accra (O-WAC)
88595	HOD 45	Duple	50029	C29F	5/49	Western National, Exeter (DN) 556
88607	GDA 893	Duple	52099	C25F	5/49	Worthington Motor Tours Ltd, Wolverhampton (ST)
88611	?	Mulliner	?		-/--	Syria Petrol Co, Tripoli (O-LAR)
88626	* KGH 913	Mulliner		B--F	-/--	Ministry of Works (GOV)
88631	#?	Duple	50738	B31-	-/--	Iraq Petroleum Co, location unknown (O-IR)
88640	?	Mulliner	?		-/--	Ministry of Supply (GOV)
88645						Exported to Mombasa (O-EAK)
88684	?	Duple	50771	C25F	-/--	British South American Airways, Nassau (O-BS)
88691	JNG 551	Duple	46490	C29F	11/48	RJ Cole {Sunbeam Luxury Coaches}, Hevingham (NK)
88698	* BCB 872	Duple	44551	C29F	3/49	Lewis Cronshaw Ltd, London NW4 (LN)
88711	CJR 530	Duple	43696	C29F	10/48	C Frazer & Son, West Wylam (ND)
88718	?	?		van	-/--	Flinn & Sons Ltd (dyers), Fishergate (GWS)
88725	SY 8878	Duple	52217	C29F	10/48	WD Tod, Mid Calder (MN)
88731	?	Duple	50761	B36-	-/--	Shell Petroleum Co, Port of Spain (O-TT)
88775						Exported to Helsinki (O-FIN)
88782	EUJ 832	Duple	47817	C29F	10/48	AJ Boulton {Arthur Boulton's Bus Service}, Cardington (SH)
88789	CCK 590	Duple	52131	C29F	4/49	Scout MS Ltd, Preston (LA)
88802	HAA 559	Duple	47886	C29F	3/49	Hants & Sussex Motor Services Ltd, Emsworth (HA) 142
88809	JSM 272	Duple	52235	C29F	10/48	M Green {Green's Motor Hirers}, Lochmaben (DF)
88820	LUM 614	Duple	50595	C29F	1/49	Kelsall Coaches Ltd {Saffman & Beasley}, Leeds (WR)
88824						Exported to Ireland
88866						Exported to Helsinki (O-FIN)
88873	KGK 425	Duple	44853	C29F	3/49	Keith & Boyle (London) Ltd {Orange Luxury Coaches}, London EC2 (LN) Heron
88880	SMY 602	Duple	52218	C29F	10/48	Prince of Wales Hospital, London N15 (XLN)
88893	JUP 327	Duple	50114	C29F	10/48	GH, S & JB Atkinson (GH Atkinson & Sons) {General Omnibus Services}, Chester-le-Street (DM) 14
88900	HAC 980	Duple	52069	C29F	10/48	Priory Garage & Coaches Ltd, Leamington Spa (WK)
88907	* LBH 720	Duple	52226	C29F	10/48	King Edward VII Sanatorium, Midhurst (XWS)
88912	?	Mulliner	?		-/--	Original operator unknown (EI)
88956						Exported to Helsinki (O-FIN)
88963	LHW 139	Mulliner	T274	B31F	10/48	Clifton College, Bristol (XGL)
88970	GWF 290	Duple	49322	C29F	1/49	MH, JA, L & TH Downes (MH Downes & Sons), Weaverthorpe (ER)
88983	CES 473	Duple	52227	C20F	10/48	Loch Katrine Steamboat Co Ltd, Callander (PH)
88990	JOF 332	Duple	44981	C29F	10/48	Smith's Imperial Coaches Ltd, Birmingham (WK)
88997	TMV 728	Duple	43926	C29F	4/49	Valliant Direct Coaches Ltd, London W5 (LN)
89003	?	Duple	50760	B31F	-/--	Shell Petroleum Co, Balikpapan (O-RI)
89047						Exported to Helsinki (O-FIN)
89054	JXU 602	Mulliner	?		11/48	Ministry of Supply (GOV)
89061	KGT 99	Mulliner	?		4/49	Ministry of Works (GOV)
89074	VML 664	Duple	48225	C27F	10/48	Pall Mall Car Hire {Pamalhire}, London SW1 (LN)
89081	EBU 984	Duple	51333	C29F	1/49	Shearings Tours Ltd, Oldham (LA)
89090	BCB 858	Duple	52132	C29F	10/48	J Wearden & Sons Ltd, Blackburn (LA) 6
89094						Exported to Accra (O-WAC)
89111	* ?	Jonckheere	5621	C27-	7/48	Callens, De Panne (O-B)
89149 - 89152						Exported to Melbourne (O-AUS)
89153	sa373.449	CAC	M31246	B31F	-/49	Wirth, Millicent, SA (O-AUS)
89154 - 89160						Exported to Melbourne (O-AUS)

89306					Exported to Helsinki (O-FIN)	
89313	EBK 257	Duple	52228	C29F	10/48	Mrs EB Brook {Victoria Coaches}, Southsea (HA)
89320	* JMN 902	Duple	51112	C29F	7/48	TH Kneen {Stanley Motors}, Douglas (IM)
89333	FDL 713	Duple	46800	C29F	10/48	GK Nash, Ventnor (IW)
89340	TMV 726	Duple	48920	C29F	10/48	Henry Coaches Ltd, London N15 (LN) 23
89347	EUT 851	Duple	52071	C29F	1/49	CH Allen {Allen's Motor Services}, Mountsorrel (LE) 39
89357	* TMK 28	Duple	52041	C25F	1/49	BEA, Ruislip (MX) 11..
89397					Exported to Helsinki (O-FIN)	
89404	LAF 407	Duple	43877	C29F	10/48	CN Rickard {Penryn & Falmouth Motor Co}, Penryn (CO)
89411	FMR 136	Duple	43875	C29F	3/49	J Crook & Sons, Melksham (WI)
89424	MPG 970	Duple	44517	C27F	10/48	WJ Sands & Sons, Oxted (SR)
89431	FBE 853	Duple	52240	C29F	10/48	TA Everett, Atterby (LI)
89438	FO 5416	Duple	52051	C29F	10/48	TA Owen, Knighton (RR)
89444					Exported to Ireland	
89488					Exported to Helsinki (O-FIN)	
89495	HWT 93	Duple	43953	C29F	10/48	EL Thompson {Advance}, Swinefleet (WR)
89502	* HOD 46	Duple	50030	C29F	6/49	Western National, Exeter (DN) 557
89515	AGL 449	Duple	52237	C25F	11/48	CJ & IH Fale, Combe Down (SO)
89522	KAR 550	Duple	50327	C29F	10/48	Weatherley {Ruislip Luxury Coaches}, Ruislip (MX)
89529	JS 8089	Duple	52291	B30F	10/48	J Mitchell {Mitchell's Transport Parcel Service}, Stornoway (RY)
89535	NTW 706	Duple	46511	C29F	12/48	J Wordsworth {Dix Luxury Coaches}, Dagenham (EX)
89579					Exported to Helsinki (O-FIN)	
89586	JXT 481	Duple	49968	B27F	10/48	Metropolitan Police, London SW1 (XLN)
89593	KDV 477	Duple	46950	C29F	3/49	Ruby Tours Ltd, Paignton (DN)
89606	LHU 948	Duple	44316	C29F	4/49	Wessex Coaches Ltd, Bristol (GL)
89613	EUX 7	Duple	47818	C29F	10/48	Salopia Saloon Coaches Ltd, Whitchurch (SH) 57
89620	JSM 267	Duple	52239	C29F	10/48	SBW Smail, Lochmaben (DF)
89626					Exported to Ireland	
89670					Exported to Helsinki (O-FIN)	
89677	GWP 842	Duple	49482	C29F	11/48	HJ Crowther, Wychbold (WO)
89684	TMK 31	Duple	52105	B31F	1/49	Middlesex County Council (XMX)
89697	ABR 226	Duple	50148	C29F	11/48	SM Pinnington & Son, Crook (DM)
89704	HRU 269	Duple	44830	C27F	11/48	Shamrock & Rambler Motor Coaches Ltd, Bournemouth (HA)
89711	ERX 7	Mulliner	T310	B28F	12/48	A Moore & Sons {Imperial Bus Service}, Windsor (BE)
89719					Exported to Accra (O-WAC)	
89761					Exported to Helsinki (O-FIN)	
89768	EUX 8	Duple	47819	C29F	10/48	E, G, FJC & W Smith {W Smith & Sons}, Donnington Wood (SH)
89774	EBL 954	Duple	44449	C29F	10/48	Windsorian Motor Coach Services Ltd, Windsor (BE) 54
89788	?	?		van	-/--	Newday Furnishing Stores Ltd, Levenshulme (GLA)
89795	GOW 871	Duple	52576	C29F	c5/50	General Motors Ltd, Southampton (XHA)
89885 - 89896					Exported to Sydney (O-AUS)	
89982	JUP 432	Duple	44327	C29F	11/48	R & J Armstrong and Mrs M Wardle {Cowling's Bus Service}, Ebchester (DM)
89988					Exported to Mombasa (O-EAK)	
90036					Exported to Helsinki (O-FIN)	
90039	JXU 592	Mulliner		B30F	-/--	Ministry of Supply (GOV)
90046	JXU 600	Mulliner		B--F	12/48	Ministry of Supply (GOV)
90059	JXU 601	Mulliner		B--F	-/--	Ministry of Supply (GOV)
90066	DHJ 23	Duple	50007	C29F	10/48	Westcliff-on-Sea MS (EX)
90073	DDB 501	Duple	51334	C29F	3/49	Melba Motors Ltd, Reddish (CH)
90079	* KYB 376	Duple	46284	C29F	10/48	Western Engineering & Motor Services {WEMS}, Weston-super-Mare (SO) 23
90123					Exported to Helsinki (O-FIN)	
90130	LUM 613	Duple	50540	C29F	10/48	Wallace Arnold, Leeds (WR)
90137	DVH 916	Duple	50539	C29F	11/48	Ben Smith & Co {Central Garage} Ltd, Marsden (WR)
90150	JVM 873	Duple	49682	C29F	9/48	GW Cartledge {Supreme Red Coaches}, Rhyl (FT)
90157	HAA 560	Duple	46426	C29F	3/49	Hants & Sussex Motor Services Ltd, Emsworth (HA) 143
90164	EBO 431	Duple	52241	C29F	1/49	HJ Cridland Ltd, Cardiff (GG)
90172					Exported to Mombasa (O-EAK)	

90214					Exported to Helsinki (O-FIN)
90221	HRW 186	Duple	47994	C29F	3/49 H & H Motorways Ltd {Bunty}, Coventry (WK)
90228	TMV 597	Duple	52076	C29F	10/48 Venture Transport (Hendon) Ltd, London NW2 (LN)
90241	CCS 511	Duple	52269	C29F	1/49 W Stewart, Saltcoats (AR)
90249	EMO 735	Duple	44487	C29F	11/48 J Spratley (J Spratley & Sons) {Blue Star}, Mortimer (BE)
90251	JUF 74	Duple	50226	C29F	10/48 RG Johnston {Unique Coaches}, Brighton (ES) 22
90261					Exported to Takoradi (O-WAC)
90397 - 90408					Exported to Melbourne (O-AUS)
90461					Exported to Helsinki (O-FIN)
90468	* EUT 917	Duple	44333	C29F	10/48 OC Bishop, Coalville (LE)
90475	DBN 157	Duple	49411	C29F	11/48 Brockbank & Baxter Ltd, Bolton (LA)
90488	* LHN 211	Duple	50706	C29F	11/48 Braithwaite Tours Ltd, Stockton-on-Tees (DM)
90495	* DFR 686	Duple	52133	C29F	1/49 Lansdowne Motors Ltd, Fleetwood (LA)
90502	FVJ 548	Duple	52052	C29F	12/48 Miss I Baynham, Ross-on-Wye (HR)
90508					Exported to Mombasa (O-EAK)
90552	HH-436	?		B29-	-/49 Länsilinjat Oy, Tampere (O-FIN) 4
90559	EDR 561	Duple	49502	C29F	11/48 Plymouth Co-operative Society (DN) 522
90566	FBE 924	Mulliner	T312	B31F	2/49 Enterprise (Scunthorpe) Passenger Services Ltd {Enterprise} (LI) 23
90585	?	Mulliner	T277	?	9/48 BOAC, unknown overseas location
90588	?	?		van	-/-- Jones & Davies, Rhyl (GFT)
90593	HDG 574	Duple	46692	C29F	11/48 BG & CJ Howse (Howse & Son), Aldsworth (GL)
90599					Exported to Mombasa (O-EAK)
90643					Exported to Helsinki (O-FIN)
90650	* NVW 220	Duple	43537	C29F	3/49 Ashdown's Luxury Coaches Ltd, Danbury (EX) 40
90657	HAA 562	Duple	48903	C29F	3/49 Hants & Sussex Motor Services Ltd, Emsworth (HA) 144
90670	* JXT 482	Duple	49969	B27F	10/48 Metropolitan Police, London SW1 (XLN)
90677	VML 101	Duple	52107	C29F	11/48 George Wimpey (contractor), London W6
90684	* KTU 724	Duple	52261	C29F	11/48 Roberts Coaches Ltd, Crewe (CH)
90690					Exported to Takoradi (O-WAC)
90734					Exported to Helsinki (O-FIN)
90741	KAL 255	Mulliner	T315	B31F	10/48 JG Lewis, Cropwell Butler (NG)
90748	JKF 340	?		van	-/48 Bool Bros Ltd, Liverpool (GLA)
90762	JXT 896	Mulliner	T306	B23F	5/49 London County Council (XLN) 1590
90768	DDY 383	Mulliner	T273	B32F	11/48 John Dengate & Sons Ltd, Beckley (ES) 18
90775	KYB 568	Mulliner	T279	B29F	1/49 Mrs P Baulch {Chard & District Motor Services}, Chard (SO)
90781	?	Duple	52578	B30F	-/-- Original operator unknown (O-EAK)
90828					Exported to Helsinki (O-FIN)
90832	* GVE 502	Mulliner	T329	B31F	11/48 E Towgood & Sons Ltd, Sawston (CM)
90839	* KYB 378	Mulliner	T330	B31F	11/48 Western Engineering & Motor Services {WEMS}, Weston-super-Mare (SO)
90852	?	?		l/stock	-/-- A Smith, Hatfield (GHT)
90859	JXT 886	Mulliner	T278	B31F	12/48 BOAC (LN)
90861	?	?		goods	11/48 JJ Allen Ltd (department store), London SW1 (GLN)
90872	MVW 287	Duple	49297	C29F	12/47 City Coach Co Ltd, Brentwood (EX) B53
90916					Exported to Helsinki (O-FIN)
90923	?	?		goods	-/-- Jordan & Cook, Worthing (GWS)
90930	KTT 492	Mulliner	T313	B31F	1/49 J Potter & Sons Ltd {Tor Bus Service}, Haytor (DN)
90943	?	?		goods	-/-- JJ Allen Ltd (department store), Bournemouth (GHA)
90950	?	?		van	-/-- FF (Suites) Ltd (furniture manufacturers), London N1 (GLN)
90958	BGV 155	Mulliner		B31F	11/48 WA, E & V Jolly, Norton (WF)
90963	CFK 872	?		van	1/49 Quality Cleaners Ltd, Worcester (GWO)
91115	?	?		B---	-/48 Gibraltar Motor Hire Services (O-GBZ)
91122	?	?		?	11/48 Hall, Evenwood Gate (GDM)
91129	KGH 321	Duple	46372	C29F	4/49 Bradshaw's Super Coaches Ltd, London SE18 (LN)
91142	?	?		van	-/-- Hoults Ltd (removers), Newcastle-on-Tyne (GND)
91149	?	?		?	-/-- SCWS Ltd, Glasgow (GLK)
91156	?	?		van	-/-- CJ Ashman (removers), Bristol (GGL)
91162	* GEW 58	Mulliner	T314	B31F	11/48 J Paine & Co Ltd {St Neots Hotel}, St Neots (XCM)
91202	HDG 798	Duple	43888	C29F	11/48 TEA Bowles {Bowles Coaches}, Ford (GL)

91211	?	?		B---	-/48	Gibraltar Motor Hire Services (O-GBZ)
91216	* FWO 625	Duple	48902	C29F	11/48	Red & White, Chepstow (MH) 825
91223	EVN 485	Duple	44252	C29F	11/48	HD Reedman, Thirsk (NR)
91234						Exported to Colombo (O-CL)
91238	BCB 965	Duple	50975	C29F	11/48	D Whalley, Feniscowles (LA)
91251	TMG 497	Duple	46261	C29F	11/48	RJG Rolfe, Hillingdon (MX)
91289	* LPP 53	Duple	48808	C29F	11/48	Aylesbury & District Hospital Management Committee (St John's Hospital, Stone) (XBK)
91294	?	Duple	50769	B31F	-/--	Shell Petroleum Co, Casigua (O-YV)
91300	JS 8159	Duple	52292	B30F	12/48	J Mitchell {Mitchell's Transport Parcel Service}, Stornoway (RY)
91310	GOT 784	Duple	47835	C29F	11/48	Barfoot Bros {Princess Coaches}, Southampton (HA)
91313						Exported to Colombo (O-CL)
91326	DFE 392	Duple	47564	C29F	11/48	C, JE, T & T Hudson {Hudson's Bus Co}, Horncastle (LI)
91338	JXT 483	Duple	49970	B27F	10/48	Metropolitan Police, London SW1 (XLN)
91376	JXU 473	Duple	50236	C29F	11/48	AC Coaches Ltd, London SE15 (LN)
91382	?	Duple	50768	B31F	-/--	Shell Petroleum Co, Casigua (O-YV)
91388	HAA 561	Duple	46427	C29F	3/49	Hants & Sussex Motor Services Ltd, Emsworth (HA) 145
91397	DHJ 229	Duple	48352	C29F	3/49	WS Nicholls, Southend-on-Sea (EX)
91401	* ?	?		C20F	-/49	Gibson's Motors, New Plymouth (O-NZ) 4
91402 - 91403						Exported to Wellington (O-NZ)
91404	* ?	NZMB		B31F	-/50	Edwards Motors, Auckland (O-NZ) 36
91405 - 91407						Exported to Wellington (O-NZ)
91408	* ?	NZMB		C--F	10/50	Edwards Motors, Auckland (O-NZ) 35
91409	P.356	Auckland TB		B33F	-/50	Auckland Transport Board (O-NZ) 21
91410 - 91412						Exported to Wellington (O-NZ)
91521 - 91532						Exported to Melbourne (O-AUS)
91593	FVJ 664	Duple	52053	C28F	11/48	WE Morgan {Wye Valley Motors}, Hereford (HR)
91603	EUX 149	Duple	47820	C29F	11/48	JG & TC Jones (JW Jones & Sons) {Priory Motor Services}, Oakengates (SH)
91617	VML 100	Duple	52268	C29F	11/48	John Laing (contractor), Borehamwood 333
91655	KGT 74	Mulliner		B30F	1/49	Ministry of Works (GOV)
91665	?	Mulliner		B--F	-/--	Anglo Iranian Oil Co, Abadan (O-IR)
91667	?	Mulliner		?	-/--	Ministry of Supply (GOV)
91676	* HWT 531	Duple	50463	C29F	3/49	W Simpson, Ripon (WR) 6
91680	TMV 502	Duple	46977	C29F	-/--	CW Banfield, London SE15 (LN)
91691	MRB 354	Duple	52295	C29F	11/48	JH Lamb, Biggin-by-Hartington (DE)
91704	JTF 605	Duple	52263	C29F	11/48	EH Holmes, Clifton (LA) 7
91742	?	Mulliner		?	-/--	Ministry of Supply (GOV)
91750	?	Mulliner		B--F	-/--	Anglo Iranian Oil Co, Ahwaz (O-IR)
91754	?	Mulliner		?	-/--	Ministry of Supply (GOV)
91763	CDO 851	Duple	47582	C29F	11/48	H Paling, Gosberton Risegate (LI)
91767	KGH 310	Duple	52319	C29F	-/48	Camden Coaches Ltd, Edgware (MX)
91784	HWR 225	Duple	50581	C29F	11/48	A Hymas, Burton Leonard (WR)
91790	FBE 981	Duple	43761	C29F	12/48	Mrs M Applewhite, Torksey (LI)
91827	FDL 802	Duple	50040	C29F	6/49	Southern Vectis, Newport (IW) 217
91834	?	Mulliner		B--F	-/--	Anglo Iranian Oil Co, Ahwaz (O-IR)
91841	SS 7041	Duple	44269	B30F	11/48	A Dunsmuir, Tranent (EL)
91854	* TMY 485	Duple	46847	C29F	11/48	Northern Roadways Ltd, Glasgow (LK)
91861	JXU 548	Duple	44532	C29F	4/49	Fallowfield & Britten Ltd, London E8 (LN)
91874	NWL 804	Mulliner	T324	B31F	11/48	United Oxford Hospitals (Churchill Hospital), Headington (XOX)
91878	GVB 190	Duple	44522	C29F	12/48	JE & HE Jewell {Jewell's Coaches}, Croydon (SR)
91973 - 91984						Exported to Bombay (O-IND)
92057 - 92068						Exported to Melbourne (O-AUS)
92108	JOF 693	Duple	52275	C29F	11/48	A Winwood {Alwyn Coaches}, Birmingham (WK)
92114						Exported to Alexandria (O-ET)
92125	HAX 452	Duple	52302	C29F	12/48	AGH Jordan {Jordan's Motor Services}, Blaenavon (MH)
92133	* J 12613	Duple	50777	C29F	4/48	GH Candlin {Blue Coach Tours}, St Helier, Jersey (CI) 12
92140	GFH 176	Duple	52270	C29F	11/48	FC Cottrell {Cottrell's Coaches}, Mitcheldean (GL)

92153	KGH 481	Duple	49971	B27F	11/48	Metropolitan Police, London SW1 (XLN)
92157	VML 786	Duple	48226	C27F	11/48	Pall Mall Car Hire {Pamalhire}, London SW1 (LN)
92195	* KGH 695	Duple	51230	C29F	12/48	Wallis Hire Service Ltd {Dartmouth Coaches}, London SE23 (LN)
92201						Exported to Alexandria (O-ET)
92212	SK 3384	Duple	52309	C29F	2/49	ES Dunnet {Dunnet's Motors}, Keiss (CS)
92220	J 12614	Duple	50778	C29F	11/48	GH Candlin {Blue Coach Tours}, St Helier, Jersey (CI) 14
92227	* FFU 104	Duple	52294	C29F	5/49	Enterprise (Scunthorpe) Passenger Services Ltd {Enterprise} (LI) 24
92240	FRY 481	Duple	47906	C29F	12/48	CLW Harris {Majestic}, Leicester (LE) 4
92244	* HOD 113	Duple	50014	C29F	11/48	Southern National, Exeter (DN) 573
92281	KGH 483	Duple	49973	B27F	1/49	Metropolitan Police, London SW1 (XLN)
92292	?	Mulliner		B--F	-/--	Anglo Iranian Oil Co, Ahwaz (O-IR)
92298	FDL 773	Duple	48293	C29F	11/48	H Paul (H Paul & Son), Ryde (IW) 4
92306	KGH 330	Duple	51335	C29F	11/48	CW Banfield, London SE15 (LN)
92313	TMV 503	Duple	48017	C29F	11/48	AE Pritchard (J Pritchard), London E14 (LN)
92326	JVR 497	Duple	49771	C29F	11/48	AE Wheatley, Patricroft (LA) 7
92332	HDG 816	Duple	51349	C29F	12/48	R & W Febry {Sodbury Queen}, Chipping Sodbury (GL)
92383	* ?	?		B24-	-/--	Original operator unknown (O-GR)
92387	#EUX 203	Duple	43497	C29F	11/48	WR & T Hoggins (WR Hoggins & Sons) {Pilot}, Wrockwardine Wood (SH)
92396	FCY 949	Duple	52293	C29F	2/49	B Demery, Morriston (GG)
92404	JC 9621	Duple	44774	C29F	2/49	J Williams & Son {Red Garage}, Portmadoc (CN)
92411	FAY 102	Duple	51056	C29F	11/48	OC Bishop, Coalville (LE)
92424	HDG 734	Duple	44253	C27F	12/48	GJ Miller {GJ Miller & Son}, Cirencester (GL)
92428	AVV 669	Duple	52146	C29F	1/49	Manfield & Son, Northampton (XNO)
92433	FT 6526	Duple	50131	C29F	12/48	TH Taylor {Taylor Bros}, North Shields (ND)
92439	* ?	Synergatiki		B24-	-/--	Original operator unknown (O-GR)
92476	JTJ 903	Duple	50248	C29F	10/48	Kia-Ora Motor Services Ltd, Morecambe (LA)
92482	* 54-886	?		B24-	-/--	Original operator unknown (O-GR)
92493	* KTB 127	Duple	51336	DP30F	11/48	North Western Electricity Board (XLA)
92494		see 92493				
92573 - 92575						Exported to Wellington (O-NZ)
92576	P.581	Suburban		B33F	5/50	Suburban Buses Ltd, Te Papapa (O-NZ) 40
92577	* ?	NZMB		B31F	12/49	Edwards Motors, Auckland (O-NZ)
92578 - 92580						Exported to Wellington (O-NZ)
92581	?	NZMB		?	-/50	Mason, location unknown (O-NZ)
92582 - 92584						Exported to Wellington (O-NZ)
92681	MTN 233	Duple	50104	C29F	12/48	Moordale Bus Services Ltd, Newcastle (ND) 8
92688	DBN 252	Duple	52134	C29F	12/48	Knowles & Sons (Garages) Ltd, Bolton (LA)
92701	#JFJ 867	Duple	46961	C29F	3/49	Regent Coaches (Teignmouth) Ltd (DN)
92705	GTM 272	Duple	52311	C29F	1/49	C Symes {Kempstonian Coaches}, Kempston (BD)
92743	EEA 160	Duple	47777	C29F	1/49	Hills Tours Ltd, West Bromwich (ST) 28
92749	* ?	?		B24-	-/--	Original operator unknown (O-GR)
92760	* KJH 91	Duple	52287	C29F	11/48	Rosary Priory, Busheyheath (XHT)
92768	HAA 557	Duple	47605	C29F	3/49	Hants & Sussex Motor Services Ltd, Emsworth (HA) 146
92776	JP 7299	Duple	49524	C29F	12/48	S Reeves, North Ashton (LA)
92788	KUB 477	Duple	50541	C29F	11/48	Wallace Arnold, Leeds (WR)
92792	CDO 921	Duple	52082	C29F	11/48	JR Flatt & Sons Ltd, Long Sutton (LI)
92830	GTM 128	Duple	48813	C29F	12/48	GE Costin, Dunstable (BD)
92836	?	Mulliner		B--F	-/--	Anglo Iranian Oil Co, Ahwaz (O-IR)
92847	EF 8616	Duple	50689	C29F	12/48	Richardson Bros, West Hartlepool (DM)
92855	FFU 121	Duple	43320	C29F	1/49	L Parker, Bardney (LI)
92862	EUX 320	Duple	43483	C29F	11/48	W Hart, Dawley (SH)
92875	* HOD 114	Duple	50015	C29F	11/48	Southern National, Exeter (DN) 574
92879	EVA 540	Duple	52323	C29F	12/48	I Hutchison {Hutchison's Coaches}, Overtown (LK)
92917	KAL 412	Duple	52262	C29F	12/48	GW Wright {GW Wright & Sons}, Keyworth (NG)
92923	?	Duple	50770	B31F	9/49	Shell Petroleum Co, Casigua (O-YV)
92934	* KGH 482	Duple	49972	B27F	12/48	Metropolitan Police, London SW1 (XLN)
92942	* DRJ 334	Plaxton	581	C29F	3/49	Gregory & Richards Ltd, Oldham (LA)
92949	FMR 791	Duple	46583	C29F	12/48	W & G Chandler, Wantage (BE)
92962	CJR 696	Duple	44116	C29F	11/48	R Armstrong, Westerhope (ND) 64

92967						Exported to Bangkok (O-T)
93001	KGH 911	Mulliner		B30F	1/49	Ministry of Works (GOV)
93004	?	Mulliner		B---	-/--	Iraq Petroleum Co, Basra (O-IRQ)
93015	?	Mulliner		?	-/--	Ministry of Supply (GOV)
93026	?	Mulliner		?	-/--	Ministry of Supply (GOV)
93030	SU 5267	Duple	52318	C29F	12/48	Mitchell's Garage (Stonehaven) Ltd (KE)
93043	CCK 591	Duple	52315	C29F	12/48	Scout MS Ltd, Preston (LA)
93048						Exported to Accra (O-WAC)
93093	* NVW 835	Duple	52310	C29F	3/49	Ashdown's Luxury Coaches Ltd, Danbury (EX) 41
93099	* ?	?		B24-	-/--	SPAP Railways (O-GR)
93101 - 93112						Exported to Melbourne (O-AUS)
93221						Exported to Wellington (O-NZ)
93222	P.408	Auckland TB		B33F	2/50	Auckland Transport Board (O-NZ) 124
93223	P.603	North Shore		B33F	-/50	North Shore Transport Co Ltd, Takapuna (O-NZ) 3
93224	* P.604	North Shore		B33F	-/50	North Shore Transport Co Ltd, Takapuna (O-NZ) 4
93225						Exported to Wellington (O-NZ)
93226	P.403	Auckland TB		B33F	2/51	Auckland Transport Board (O-NZ) 113
93227	* P.124	Eaddy & Taylor		B33F	8/50	Howick Bus Co Ltd, Auckland (O-NZ) 2
93228	* P1.161	Buses		B--F	-/48	Buses Ltd, Hamilton (O-NZ) 18
93229	* P1.105	RE&C		B33D	-/50	Buses Ltd, Hamilton (O-NZ) 5
93230						Exported to Wellington (O-NZ)
93231	* P.809	NZMB		B31F	-/--	Shaw's Transport Ltd, Waiuku (O-NZ) 4
93232	* P1.078	Transport BS		B33F	-/50	Transport BS Ltd, Auckland (O-NL) 8
93276						Exported to Accra (O-WAC)
93284	JXT 904	Mulliner	T297	B31F	11/48	London County Council (XLN) 1594
93291	* LUM 509	Duple	50634	C29F	12/48	JA Hudson Ltd, Leeds (WR)
93304	?	?		van	-/--	Earnshaw Bros & Booth {Nu-Lyne Furniture}, Burnley (GLA)
93309	JXT 905	Mulliner	T307	B23F	-/49	London County Council (XLN) 1587
93346	?	?		van	-/--	W Sharples & Sons Ltd (removers), Lancaster (GLA)
93352	* ?	?		B24-	-/--	Original operator unknown (O-GR)
93363	* FJU 191	Whitson	?	C29F	3/49	N & S Coaches Ltd, Kibworth (LE)
93371	ERX 284	Duple	52201	C29F	12/48	GE Hedges {Reliance Motor Services}, Newbury (BE) 23
93378	TMV 505	Duple	48779	C29F	1/49	Dryer's Coaches Ltd, London E17 (LN)
93391	?	?		van	-/--	R Pedley Ltd (furniture makers), High Wycombe (GBK)
93396	FED 422	Mulliner	T325	B31F	11/48	Winwick & Newchurch Hospital Management Committee (XCH)
93433	?	SMT		van	-/--	J Barrie, Brechin (GAS)
93439	* ?	?		B24-	-/--	SPAP Railways (O-GR)
93450	ECX 79	Plaxton	622	C29F	1/49	Hanson's Buses Ltd, Huddersfield (WR) 265
93458	?	?		van	-/--	Norwich Distributors Ltd (GNK)
93465	?	?		goods	3/49	JJ Allen Ltd (department store), London SW1 (GLN)
93478	?	?		goods	10/48	Challis, London SW19 (GLN)
93483	* ?	?		goods	1/49	Mendip Queen Coaches Ltd, High Littleton (GSO)
93515	?	?		van	-/--	Crosby Spring Interiors Ltd (furniture manufactuers), St Helens (GLA)
93526	* ?	?		B24-	-/--	Original operator unknown (O-GR)
93537	?	?		van	-/--	Wilkie & Paul Ltd (metal box manufacturers), Edinburgh (GMN)
93545	CRN 90	?		lorry	4/49	HR Vaughan & Co Ltd, Preston (GLA)
93552	?	?		van	-/--	Hoults Ltd (removers), Newcastle-on-Tyne (GND)
93565	FRY 684	Duple	49014	C29F	12/48	JH Hill, Leicester (LE)
93570	DFR 655	Duple	52322	C29F	1/49	S & J Wood Ltd {Seagull Coaches}, Blackpool (LA)
93602	ECX 80	Duple	50408	C29F	12/48	Hanson's Buses Ltd, Huddersfield (WR) 266
93613	?	?		?	-/--	Jose Felix Lloret, Valencia (O-E)
93624	VML 102	Duple	52108	C29F	12/48	George Wimpey (contractor), London W6
93634	?	?		van	-/--	SCWS, Glasgow (GLK)
93639	HAA 558	Duple	46614	C29F	3/49	Hants & Sussex Motor Services Ltd, Emsworth (HA) 147
93652	DFX 57	Duple	49060	C29F	1/49	RW Toop, WJ Ironside & PW Davis {Bere Regis & District}, Dorchester (DT)
93658	RRE 325	Duple	48847	C29F	12/48	JW Genner, Quarry Bank (ST)
93686						Exported to Colombo (O-CL)

C1252/124

93695	TMK 112	Duple	50230	C29F	1/49	Ardley Bros Coaches Ltd, London N17 (LN) 9
93821 - 93832						Exported to Melbourne (O-AUS)
93956	?	?		h/box	-/--	Ms E Williams, Kingsclere (GBE)
93963	ECX 81	Duple	50409	C29F	12/48	Hanson's Buses Ltd, Huddersfield (WR) 267
93970	DUD 127	Duple	43882	C29F	12/48	R Jarvis, Middle Barton (OX)
93974	* FBU 7	Duple	51337	C29F	1/49	G Barlow & Sons Ltd, Oldham (LA)
93983	?	Duple	50782	B31-	-/--	Iraq Petroleum Co, Basra (O-IRQ)
94012	HTX 659	Duple	52324	C29F	12/48	Mrs SA Bebb, Llantwit Fardre (GG)
94020	EUX 369	Duple	47822	C29F	2/49	JT, FW & GE Whittle {JT Whittle & Sons}, Highley (SH)
94030	TMY 218	Duple	43341	C29F	4/49	P Crouch & Son, Guildford (SR)
94042	NVX 677	Duple	43878	C29F	1/49	AC Peck {Cedric Coaches}, Wivenhoe (EX)
94055	HRM 411	Duple	52325	C29F	1/49	WR Carr {WR Carr & Son}, Silloth (CU)
94059						Exported to Colombo (O-CL)
94066	?	Mulliner		B--F	-/--	Anglo Iranian Oil Co, Ahwaz (O-IR)
94096						Exported to Ireland
94105	JXT 529	Duple	48357	C29F	12/48	Fox & Hart Ltd {Hounslow Star Coaches}, Hounslow (MX)
94116	NVX 129	Duple	44706	C29F	12/48	EA Winwood, London E10 (LN) 21
94127	XS 6564	Duple	52383	C29F	1/49	Young's Bus Service Ltd, Paisley (RW) 184
94140	LAF 978	Duple	52103	C29F	1/49	HN Trewren {Marigold Coaches}, Lanner (CO)
94144	DFX 144	Duple	46804	C29F	1/49	CA Adams (Adams Bros) {Victory Tours}, Sixpenny Handley (DT)
94151	?	Duple	50781	B31F	-/--	Shell Petroleum Co, Barranquilla (O-CO)
94181						Exported to Ireland
94190	KGH 910	Mulliner		B30F	-/--	Ministry of Works (GOV)
94201	?	Mulliner		B--F	-/--	Ministry of Supply (GOV)
94212	?	Mulliner		?	-/--	Ministry of Supply (GOV)
94225	* HOD 115	Duple	50016	C29F	12/48	Southern National, Exeter (DN) 575
94229	KTB 121	Duple	52343	C29F	3/49	Atkinson & Co {Dreadnought Motors}, Morecambe (LA)
94236	?	Duple	50780	B31F	-/--	Shell Petroleum Co, Barranquilla (O-CO)
94273	* J 12830	Duple	50779	C29F	2/49	GH Candlin {Blue Coach Tours}, St Helier, Jersey (CI) 16
94276	HWR 259	Duple	50553	C29F	1/49	G Illingworth, Crigglestone (WR)
94286	KYB 835	Duple	52102	C29F	3/49	TE Herring {W Herring & Son}, Burnham-on-Sea (SO)
94297	KBP 800	Duple	52301	B31F	1/49	West Sussex County Council Education Dept (XWS)
94310	RRE 506	Duple	52368	C29F	1/49	Greatrex Motor Coaches Ltd, Stafford (ST) 39 Sandpiper
94317	GVE 574	Duple	52152	C29F	1/49	CE Loates {Loates Bros}, Bassingbourn (CM)
94321	* ?	?		B24-	-/--	SPAP Railways (O-GR)
94351	KBP 749	Duple	46778	C29F	12/48	J Mitchell, Warnham (WS)
94360	J 12829	Duple	50776	C29F	4/49	H Swanson {Redline Tours}, St Helier, Jersey (CI) 6
94371	DHJ 24	Duple	50008	C29F	12/48	Westcliff-on-Sea MS (EX)
94382	VML 797	Duple	48227	C27F	1/49	Pall Mall Car Hire {Pamalhire}, London SW1 (LN)
94396	ETH 180	Duple	52341	C29F	1/49	LT & WH Evans (E Evans & Sons), Llangennech (CR)
94509 - 94520						Exported to Bombay (O-IND)
94593	GSC 988	Duple	52340	C29F	2/49	St Cuthbert's Co-operative Association Ltd, Edinburgh (MN) 10
94600	?	Duple	52587	B28F	-/--	Original operator unknown (O-CH)
94633	?	Duple	50762	B36F	-/--	Shell Petroleum Co, Port of Spain (O-TT)
94637	KAL 652	Duple	43332	C29F	1/49	WE, RE and RN Brumpton {WE Brumpton & Sons}, Dunham-on-Trent (NG)
94648	FVJ 704	Duple	52054	C29F	12/48	PHE Tummey {Llangrove Coach Services}, Llangrove (HR)
94659	HNX 687	Duple	43482	C29F	12/48	HR Matthews {R Matthews & Son}, Lower Brailes (WK)
94672	GOU 721	Duple	47887	B30F	1/49	FH Kilner (Transport) Ltd, Horsham (WS) 148
94676		see 94677				
94677	HDG 988	Duple	47800	C29F	1/49	A Burchill (W Burchill & Sons) {Renown Coaches}, Staple Hill (GL)
94683	* GC-15-91	?		DP29D	1/49	Joaquim P Resende, Matosinhos (O-P)
94713						Exported to Georgetown (O-MAL)
94722	EUX 474	Duple	47823	C29F	2/49	W, WE & JR Fisher, Bronington (FT)
94733	* HOD 116	Duple	50017	C29F	12/48	Southern National, Exeter (DN) 576
94744	CJR 832	Duple	44117	C29F	12/48	R Armstrong, Westerhope (ND)

94757	SJ 1243	Duple	52449	C29F	1/49	AC Lennox & Sons {Lennox Motor Service}, Whiting Bay, Arran (BU)
94761	* JOH 262	Duple	52351	C29F	12/48	Birmingham City Police Social Club (XWK)
94768	GC-15-92	?		DP29D	1/49	Joaquim da Costa Ferreira, Nogueira da Maia (O-P)
94800						Exported to Georgetown (O-MAL)
94807	HWU 170	Duple	52352	C29F	12/48	FW Balme {Balme's Coaches}, Otley (WR)
94818	GDK 564	Duple	50260	C27F	1/49	Yelloway Motor Services Ltd, Rochdale (LA)
94829	TMK 638	Duple	43311	C29F	3/49	LC Davis & Sons Ltd, London SW16 (LN)
94842	KGH 484	Duple	49974	B27F	12/48	Metropolitan Police, London SW1 (XLN)
94846	GWO 876	Duple	52344	C29F	12/48	Red & White, Chepstow (MH) 876
94884						Exported to Copenhagen (O-DK)
94888						Exported to Bangkok (O-T)
94892	* EDR 793	Duple	49370	C29F	3/49	LM & HW Pridham {Pridham Bros}, Lamerton (DN)
94908	TMK 238	Duple	52106	B31F	2/49	Middlesex County Council (XMX)
94913	KGU 670	(Vincent ?)		prison	5/49	Metropolitan Police, London SW1 (GLN)
94927	?	?		prison	-/--	Metropolitan Police, London SW1 (GLN)
94931	GTM 358	Duple	48810	C29F	5/49	A Draper {Royal Blue Motor Coaches}, Luton (BD)
94938						Exported to Alexandria (O-ET)
94968	?	?		prison	-/--	Metropolitan Police, London SW1 (GLN)
94977	FBU 27	Duple	51338	C29F	1/49	G Barlow & Sons Ltd, Oldham (LA)
94988	LKK 42	Duple	48992	C29F	1/49	H & EW Kemp, Chillendon (KT)
94999	* DFR 699	Duple	52353	C29F	5/49	WC Standerwick, Blackpool (LA) 110
95012	TMK 731	Duple	46848	C29F	12/48	Northern Roadways Ltd, Glasgow (LK)
95016	KYB 989	Duple	46354	C29F	2/49	EG Bryant, Monksilver (SO)
95023	?	Duple	52588	B30-	-/--	Shell Petroleum Co, Suez (O-ET)
95052	?	Duple	52579	B20-	-/--	Trinidad National Mining (O-TT)
95062	EDR 792	Duple	49503	C29F	4/49	Plymouth Co-operative Society (DN) 523
95073	* KTB 521	Duple	52366	C29F	4/49	Leigh Manufacturing Co, Leigh (XLA)
95084	EET 572	Duple	51035	C29F	1/49	E Thornton & Sons {Alma Coaches}, Thurcroft (WR)
95097	KGH 485	Duple	49975	B27F	12/48	Metropolitan Police, London SW1 (XLN)
95149 - 95160						Exported to Sydney (O-AUS)
95305	KTT 882	Duple	52365	C29F	1/49	EJH & AJ Lovering {Lovering Bros}, Combe Martin (DN)
95312	?	Mulliner		B--F	-/--	Shell Petroleum Co, unknown overseas location
95341						Exported to Bangkok (O-T)
95350	JUP 609	Duple	50069	C29F	1/49	W Guest {Billingham Car Co}, Billingham-on-Tees (DM)
95361	MRB 765	Duple	52084	C29F	1/49	HD Andrew {Anchor Coaches}, Tideswell (DE)
95372	GOU 361	Duple	52254	C29F	1/49	Creamline Motor Services (Bordon) Ltd (HA)
95385	CBV 67	Duple	44273	C29F	1/49	Lewis Cronshaw Ltd, London NW4 (LN)
95391	* HOD 117	Duple	50018	C29F	12/48	Southern National, Exeter (DN) 577
95396	* ?	?		B24-	-/--	SPAP Railways (O-GR)
95427						Exported to Bangkok (O-T)
95437	FAY 554	Duple	44402	C29F	1/49	D Jacques, Coalville (LE)
95448	JPW 519	Duple	44268	C29F	1/49	AG Rix {Rix Bros}, Foulsham (NK)
95459	DCT 994	Duple	44410	C29F	1/49	CW Pulfrey, Great Gonerby (LI)
95472	HWT 736	Mulliner	T321	B31-	12/48	Cementation Co Ltd, Bentley (XWR)
95476	ECX 82	Duple	50410	C29F	1/49	Hanson's Buses Ltd, Huddersfield (WR) 268
95483						Exported to Alexandria (O-ET)
95512						Exported to Bangkok (O-T)
95521	DHM 352	Mulliner	T319	B32F	1/49	East Ham County Borough Council (XLN)
95532	JUP 600	Duple	50691	C29F	1/49	Trimdon Motor Services Ltd, Trimdon Grange (DM) 52
95543	HTX 753	Duple	52334	C29F	2/49	DJ Gray {W Gray & Sons}, Tonteg (GG)
95556	GSP 249	Duple	52369	C29F	1/49	Meldrum & Dawson, Dunfermline (FE)
95560	KGK 458	Mulliner	T298	B31F	11/48	London County Council (XLN) 1596
95567						Exported to Alexandria (O-ET)
95599	?	Duple	52580	B20-	-/--	Original operator unknown (O-TT)
95613 - 95624, 95781 - 95792						Exported to Melbourne (O-AUS)
95858	EUX 557	Duple	47824	C29F	2/49	AE Parker {Parkers Motor Services}, Newcastle (SH)
95869	GWF 250	Duple	51033	C29F	1/49	HG Anfield & Sons, Bridlington (ER)
95880	BGV 261	Duple	44337	C29F	1/49	GF Burgoin (Haverhill) Ltd {Grey Pullman Coaches} (WF)
95893	* DRD 382	Duple	44502	C29F	3/49	AE Smith {Smith's Coaches}, Reading (BE)
95897	JAD 198	Duple	46218	C29F	1/49	A & R Crew {Majestic Coaches}, Staple Hill (GL)
95904						Exported to Alexandria (O-ET)
95930	?	Duple	50784	B29F	-/--	Original operator unknown (O-TT)

95937	* DFR 700	Duple	52354	C29F	5/49	WC Standerwick, Blackpool (LA) 111
95949	FO 5513	Duple	47827	C29F	1/49	TA Owen, Knighton (RR)
95963	JXU 488	Duple	50246	C29F	1/49	Carshalton & Wallington Coaches Ltd, Carshalton (SR)
95977	* JP 7335	Duple	49523	C29F	1/49	W Liptrot (Coaches) Ltd, Bamfurlong (LA)
95985	KLK 495	Duple	52377	C29F	1/49	Royal Arsenal Co-operative Society, London SE18 (LN) 76
95989	?	Mulliner		B--F	-/--	Shell Petroleum Co, unknown overseas location
96015	HAB 919	Duple	47724	C29F	2/49	JC Simmons, Rock (WO)
96027	NVX 822	Mulliner	T328	B31F	2/49	Essex County Council (XEX)
96034	?	?		van	-/--	Currie & Co (Newcastle) Ltd (GND)
96050	KAL 683	Duple	49483	C24F	1/49	Barton Transport, Chilwell (NG) 532
96062	DHM 402	Mulliner	T320	B32F	1/49	East Ham County Borough Council (XLN)
96070	?	?		van	-/--	DJ Malcolm & Son, Edgware (GMX)
96100	?	?		van	-/--	WJ Nash, London E3 (GLN)
96107	?	?		van	-/--	HF Brice, London N21 (GLN)
96119	NVX 782	Mulliner	T327	B31F	2/49	Essex County Counciln) (XEX)
96133	KGK 459	Mulliner	T299	B31F	11/48	London County Council (XLN) 1597
96147	EUX 618	Duple	47825	C29F	1/49	J & HG Phillips {J Phillips & Son}, Rhostyllen (DH)
96155	KGH 720	Duple	50537	C29F	1/49	George Ewer & Co Ltd {Grey Green}, London N16 (LN)
96185	?	?		van	4/49	Tomkins Removals Ltd, Leicester (GLE)
96192	?	?		van	-/--	E Defries, London E5 (GLN)
96204	?	?		van	-/--	Maple & Co Ltd (furniture manufacturers), London NW1 (GLN)
96218	KJJ 188	Duple	51232	C29F	9/49	Wallis Hire Service Ltd {Dartmouth Coaches}, London SE23 (LN)
96232	AVV 941	Grose		shop	4/49	Bletchley Co-operative Society (GBK)
96240	FWN 91	Duple	49423	C29F	1/49	EJ Jenkins & Sons {Streamline Coaches}, Swansea (GG)
96270	CJL 35	Duple	52381	C29F	1/49	R Cropley {Safety Coaches}, Fosdyke (LI)
96277	?	Mulliner	?		-/--	Ministry of Supply (GOV)
96289	KGT 62	Mulliner		?	2/49	Ministry of Works (GOV)
96385 - 96394						Exported to Melbourne (O-AUS)
96395	sa77.771	CAC	M33 25	B33F	-/49	Graeber, SA, Lobethal (O-AUS)
96396						Exported to Melbourne (O-AUS)
96459	KGT 70	Mulliner		B30F	2/49	Ministry of Works (GOV)
96473	HWU 593	Duple	50625	C29F	1/49	JJ Longstaff, Mirfield (WR)
96481	JC 9712	Duple	43344	C29F	6/49	OR Williams & Son {Whiteways}, Waenfawr (CN)
96511	KTB 649	Duple	52378	C29F	3/49	NA Birkett Ltd {Premier}, Morecambe (LA)
96518	TMY 173	Duple	52042	C25F	2/49	BEA, Ruislip (MX) 11..
96530	TMY 277	LCMW		B26R	4/49	Middlesex County Council (XMX)
96544	* HOD 118	Duple	50019	C29F	1/49	Southern National, Exeter (DN) 578
96558	FDL 842	Duple	46338	C29F	1/49	Mrs V Pearce {White Heather}, Ryde (IW)
96568	KGT 97	Mulliner		?	4/49	Ministry of Supply (GOV)
96608	?	Mulliner		?	-/--	Ministry of Supply (GOV)
96617	?	Mulliner		?	-/--	Ministry of Supply (GOV)
96626	FWM 917	Duple	50944	C29F	3/49	Howard Coaches Ltd, Southport (LA)
96633	?	?		van	-/--	J Stubbs, Lancaster (GLA)
96645	SY 8175	Duple	52379	C29F	1/49	W Hunter, Loanhead (MN)
96649	FMW 40	Duple	46478	C27F	1/49	C Bodman, Worton (WI)
96658						Exported to Ireland
96694	?	?		goods	-/--	FG Alexander, London N21 (GLN)
96703	KGH 486	Duple	49976	B27F	1/49	Metropolitan Police, London SW1 (XLN)
96712	* HAX 657	Duple	52382	C29F	1/49	Liberty Motors Ltd, Cardiff (GG) 7
96719	TMK 639	Duple	47866	C29F	1/49	London & Southend Associated Coaches Ltd, London E17 (LN)
96726	* KMN 324	Duple	51113	C29F	11/48	WJ & WH McMullin (WJ McMullin & Son) {The Huntsman}, Douglas (IM)
96735	HDG 973	Duple	43960	C29F	3/49	WG & RA Miles {Miles Bros}, Guiting Power (GL)
96744						Exported to Ireland
96780	KGN 204	Duple	48358	C29F	1/49	Garner's Coaches Ltd, London W5 (LN)
96789	KDE 875	Duple	49075	C29F	1/49	L Williams {Blue Glider Coaches}, St Dogmaels (PE)
96798	KBP 993	Duple	44872	C27F	1/49	CF Gates {Silver Queen Coaches}, Worthing (WS)
96805	AVV 654	Duple	46519	C29F	1/49	RG & T Wesley, Stoke Goldington (BK) 28
96812	ECX 183	Duple	50411	C29F	1/49	Hanson's Buses Ltd, Huddersfield (WR) 269

96827	* DFR 701	Duple	52355	C29F	5/49	WC Standerwick, Blackpool (LA) 112
96830	?	Duple	52590	B30F	-/--	East African Railways, Dar-es-Salaam (O-EAT)
96866	DFX 458	Duple	52380	C29F	2/49	HV Fear {Wimborne Queen}, Wimborne (DT)
96875	FFU 352	Duple	52393	C29F	2/49	Enterprise (Scunthorpe) Passenger Services Ltd {Enterprise} (LI) 25
96884	?	?		van	-/--	Platt, Manchester (GLA)
96891	TMY 26	Duple	48199	C29F	1/49	H & G Beach, Staines (MX)
96898	KGH 487	Duple	49977	B27F	1/49	Metropolitan Police, London SW1 (XLN)
96907	?	?		van	-/--	Dent, Carlisle (GCU)
96916						Exported to Mauritius
96952	* HOD 119	Duple	50020	C29F	1/49	Southern National, Exeter (DN) 579
96961	TMK 430	Duple	44047	C29F	10/48	Essex County Coaches Ltd, London E15 (LN)
96970	KUO 260	Duple	47870	C29F	1/49	PW Steer {Bow Belle}, Bow (DN)
96977	HTX 890	Duple	52335	C29F	1/49	F Manning & Sons Ltd, Aberdare (GG)
96984	CCK 927	Duple	52394	C29F	4/49	Scout MS Ltd, Preston (LA)
96993	KUM 797	Duple	50542	C29F	1/49	Wallace Arnold, Leeds (WR)
97002						Exported to Mauritius
97038	TMK 272	Duple	44372	C29F	6/49	A Butler {Dorothy Coaches}, London NW11 (LN)
97047						Exported to Colombo (O-CL)
97056	JM 8031	Duple	52395	C29F	1/49	RW Stainton & Sons, Kendal (WT)
97063	FFU 347	Duple	43327	C29F	1/49	JE Vessey, Hibaldstow (LI)
97070	FO 5506	Duple	52055	C29F	2/49	HJ Yeomans {Radnorshire Motor Services}, Knighton (RR) 14
97079	LUM 520	Duple	50640	C29F	2/49	TS Heaps & Sons, Leeds (WR)
97088						Exported to Colombo (O-CL)
97318	HOD 47	Duple	50031	C29F	6/49	Western National, Exeter (DN) 558
97325	GSF 384	Duple	52454	C29F	1/49	S MacKay, Portobello (MN)
97334	VML 804	Duple	48228	C27F	2/49	Pall Mall Car Hire {Pamalhire}, London SW1 (LN)
97341	LKK 59	Duple	43589	C29F	5/49	Ashline Ltd {Ashline Coaches}, Tonbridge (KT)
97350	LLG 806	Duple	51339	C29F	1/49	W Kirkpatrick {Pride of the Road}, Marple (CH)
97366						Exported to Mauritius
97403	BCN 170	Duple	50138	C29F	1/49	J Thirlwell & Sons {Greybird}, Gateshead (DM) 2
97410	JOK 11	Duple	44286	C29F	3/49	Dalton's Garage Ltd, Birmingham (WK)
97420	* DFR 706	Duple	52360	C29F	5/49	WC Standerwick, Blackpool (LA) 117
97427	EX 6324	Duple	52114	C29F	2/49	WJ Haylett {Felix Coaches}, Great Yarmouth (NK) 5
97436	* LTF 845	?		C29F	5/50	M Hood {Auckland Coaches}, Morecambe (LA)
97452	TMK 635	Duple	46849	C29F	1/49	Northern Roadways Ltd, Glasgow (LK)
97486	?	?		B---	-/49	Gibraltar Motor Hire Services (O-GBZ)
97489	KJH 492	Duple	50330	C27F	2/49	Albanian Coaches Ltd, St Albans (HT)
97496	KGK 457	Mulliner	T301	B31F	1/49	London County Council (XLN) 1595
97603		see 97063				
97645 - 97656						Exported to Bombay (O-IND)
97698	VML 103	Duple	52109	C29F	1/49	George Wimpey (contractor), London W6
97705	LHN 475	Duple	50704	C29F	1/49	Summerson Bros {The Eden}, West Auckland (DM)
97714	FDL 869	Duple	43902	C29F	2/49	Fountain Garage Ltd, Cowes (IW)
97730	HWR 130	Duple	50631	C29F	1/49	FW Balme {Balme's Coaches}, Otley (WR)
97761	KGT 93	Mulliner		B30F	-/--	Ministry of Works (GOV)
97765	KGT 76	Mulliner		?	4/49	Ministry of Supply (GOV)
97772	KGT 96	Mulliner		B30F	4/49	Ministry of Supply (GOV)
97781	DRD 426	Duple	44503	C29F	3/49	AE Smith {Smith's Coaches}, Reading (BE)
97788	KGK 419	Duple	50252	C29F	1/49	Wren's Coaches Ltd, London NW9 (LN)
97798	ESA 920	Duple	52417	B30F	2/49	JS Simpson {Simpson's Motor Services}, Rosehearty (AD)
97814						Exported to Mauritius
97849	SB 7611	Duple	52470	C27F	5/49	Air Industrial Developments Ltd {Gold Line}, Dunoon (AL)
97853	JVU 774	Duple	49769	C29F	2/49	Wilmslow Motor Co Ltd (CH)
97860	KYC 193	Duple	51040	C29F	2/49	HC Cole, Ubley (SO)
97869	FAY 675	Duple	52376	C29F	2/49	Windridge, Sons & Riley Ltd {Victory}, Ibstock (LE) 11
97876	MRB 934	Duple	43813	C29F	3/49	HS North, Derby (DE)
97886	KGN 431	Duple	49978	B27F	1/49	Metropolitan Police, London SW1 (XLN)
97902	?	Duple	52593	B30F	-/--	East African Railways, Dar-es-Salaam (O-EAT)
97935	HWT 738	Mulliner	T322	B31-	1/49	Cementation Co Ltd, Bentley (XWR)
97939	?	?		van	-/--	Batty's Removals Ltd, London NW4 (GLN)

97946	TMK 318	Duple	44396	C29F	1/49	RG Flexman {Flexman's Coaches}, Southall (MX)
97955	* KGW 126	Duple	51231	C29F	5/49	Wallis Hire Service Ltd {Dartmouth Coaches}, London SE23 (LN)
97962	EUX 758	Duple	47826	C29F	2/49	A & R Parish {Parish's Motor Service}, Morda (SH)
97972	KGN 432	Duple	49979	B27F	4/49	Metropolitan Police, London SW1 (XLN)
97988	KGK 466	Mulliner	T300	B31F	1/49	London County Council (XLN) 1598
98022	?	?		van	-/--	C Goodman & Sons Ltd, London SE17 (GLN)
98025	?	?		van	-/--	Pleach Products Ltd, Stockport (GCH)
98032	AVV 814	Duple	54144	C29F	4/49	Manfield & Son, Northampton (XNO)
98041	TMK 282	Duple	50282	C29F	2/49	GJ Futcher {Ace Luxury Coaches}, Surbiton (SR)
98055	DHM 657	Mulliner	T318	B16FL	3/49	East Ham County Borough Council (XLN)
98065	* HOD 48	Duple	50032	C29F	1/49	Western National, Exeter (DN) 559
98074	?	Duple	52592	B30F	-/--	East African Railways, Dar-es-Salaam (O-EAT)
98269						Exported to Melbourne (O-AUS)
98270	NL.801	CAC	?	B27F	-/--	Hawthorn Bus Service, Nunawading, Vic (O-AUS) 1
98271 - 98280						Exported to Melbourne (O-AUS)
98372	?	?		h/box	-/--	W Webb, Great Bookham (GSR)
98375	SX 6518	Duple	52501	C29F	2/49	W Douglas & Sons, Armadale (WL)
98382	TMY 941	Duple	51277	C27F	2/49	Middlesex Hospital, London W1 (XLN)
98391	FAY 599	Duple	51229	C29F	2/49	Machin's Garage Ltd, Ashby-la-Zouch (LE)
98403	?	Mulliner	T344	?	3/49	East Riding County Council Education Committee (XER)
98408	?	?		van	-/--	Ciswell Bros, Loughton (GEX)
98423	?	Duple	52594	B30F	-/--	East African Railways, Dar-es-Salaam (O-EAT)
98458	?	?		van	-/--	W Fryer & Sons Ltd, Eccles (GLA)
98461	* ?	?		van	-/--	Venture Transport (Hendon) Ltd, London NW2 (GLN)
98468	* HCG 244	?		van	5/49	GC, FW & GR Warren (Warren's Transport) (removers), Alton (GHA)
98477	?	?		van	-/--	WE Brooks, Derby (GDE)
98484	MPK 639	Duple	52475	B30F	1/49	Queen Mary's Hospital, Carshalton (XSR)
98494	?	?		van	-/--	W Leek & Sons Ltd, London EC2 (GLN)
98506	?	Duple	52591	B30F	-/--	East African Railways, Dar-es-Salaam (O-EAT)
98544	* DFR 702	Duple	52356	C29F	5/49	WC Standerwick, Blackpool (LA) 113
98547	* ?	?		van	-/--	Wright Bros, Birkenhead (GCH)
98554	?	?		tilt lorry	-/--	Smart & Brown Engineering Ltd, Spennymoor (GDM)
98563	* FKW 571	Duple	52374	B--F	2/49	Bradford Corporation Education Committee (XWR) 024
98569	* DFR 703	Duple	52357	C29F	5/49	WC Standerwick, Blackpool (LA) 114
98579	JOK 660	Mulliner	T342	C29F	2/49	Ronnie Hancox Ltd {Ronnie Hancox and his Band}, Sutton Coldfield (WK)
98591						Exported to Bangkok (O-T)
98631	TMY 938	Duple	46850	C29F	2/49	Northern Roadways Ltd, Glasgow (LK)
98634	EU 9533	Duple	54091	C29F	1/49	T Rees (Rees Motors) {Reliance Motors}, Llanelly Hill (BC)
98641	?	?		van	-/--	Brittania Wire Works, Whaley Bridge (GDE)
98650	KLB 104	?		prison	11/49	Metropolitan Police, London SW1 (GLN)
98656	?	?		prison	-/--	Metropolitan Police, London SW1 (GLN)
98666	?	?		prison	-/--	Metropolitan Police, London SW1 (GLN)
98678						Exported to Mombasa (O-EAK)
98706	HWU 479	Duple	52453	B30F	2/49	Mexborough & Swinton (WR) 81
98712	* FKW 572	Duple	52375	B--F	2/49	Bradford Corporation Education Committee (XWR) 025
98720	KYC 386	Duple	47742	C29F	4/49	DS Dallas {Stuart Coaches}, Weston-super-Mare (SO)
98760	KUO 160	Duple	44512	C29F	1/49	AJ Rowsell {Otter Coaches}, Ottery St Mary (DN)
98763	* DFR 704	Duple	52358	C29F	5/49	WC Standerwick, Blackpool (LA) 115
98770	LTO 19	Duple	48077	C29F	3/49	A Skill {Skill's Coaches}, Nottingham (NG) 19
98779	* JOK 557	Duple	44614	C29F	2/49	EH Lewis {Haydn's Coaches}, Birmingham (WK)
98785	KGN 596	Duple	44214	C24F	3/49	United Service Transport Co Ltd, London SW9 (LN) 1078
98795	KGN 971	Duple	52481	C29F	2/49	R & J Armstrong and Mrs M Wardle {Cowling's Bus Service}, Ebchester (DM)
98807						Exported to Mombasa (O-EAK)
98846	TMY 939	Duple	44008	C29F	2/49	CG Lewis {CG Lewis Safety Coaches}, London SE10 (LN)
98849	FAY 797	Duple	52072	C29F	3/49	CH Allen {Allen's Motor Services}, Mountsorrel (LE) 40
98856	KJH 731	Duple	44412	C29F	2/49	TH Kirby, Bushey Heath (HT)

C1252/129

98864	HUE 382	Duple	47630	C29F	2/49 De Luxe Buses Ltd, Mancetter (WK)
98871	HWU 480	Duple	52452	B30F	2/49 Mexborough & Swinton (WR) 82
98881	LPP 549	Duple	44411	C29F	1/49 CJ Payne (CJ Payne & Son), Buckingham (BK)
98893					Exported to Mombasa (O-EAK)
98932					Exported to Asuncion (O-PY)
98935	TMY 81	Duple	49357	C29F	3/49 Feltham Transport Ltd, Bedfont (MX)
98941	HAB 891	Duple	49927	C29F	3/49 AL Yarranton Snr & AL Yarranton Jnr {Eardiston Coaches}, Eardiston (WO)
98950	* AEP 849	Duple	43776	C29F	2/49 WT Owen & Sons, Berriew (MO)
98957	GDA 982	Duple	48045	C29F	4/49 Worthington Motor Tours Ltd, Wolverhampton (ST)
98967	TMY 55	Duple	50231	C29F	4/49 Ardley Bros Coaches Ltd, London N17 (LN)
98983					Exported to Asuncion (O-PY)
99145	#H 8516	Duple	?	C28F	1/48 OTC, Nairobi (O-EAK)
99229 - 99233					Exported to Sydney (O-AUS)
99234	Q.651	Syd Wood		B37F	-/-- Surfside Bus Service, Tweeds Head, Qld (O-AUS) 5
99235 - 99240					Exported to Sydney (O-AUS)
99282	KGT 138	Mulliner		B32F	4/49 Ministry of Works (GOV)
99290	KGT 86	Mulliner		?	-/49 Ministry of Supply (GOV)
99297	* KGT 75	Mulliner		B28F	4/49 AWRE, Aldermaston (GOV)
99303	?	?		?	-/-- Ministry of Supply (GOV)
99311	CJL 130	Duple	52480	C29F	2/49 RL Cropley {Blue Glider Bus Service}, Sutterton (LI)
99318	LCV 404	Duple	52474	C29F	4/49 Harper, Son & Kellow {Reliance Bus Service}, St Agnes (CO)
99324					Exported to Asuncion (O-PY)
99365	?	Duple	52581	B30F	-/-- Trinidad Leaseholds Ltd (O-TT)
99373	JC 9825	Duple	47828	C29F	2/49 CJ Roberts {Purple Motors}, Bethesda (CN)
99380	* HFM 44	Beadle	C177	B20F	4/49 Crosville MS, Chester (CH) S20
99386	MUA 346	Duple	50543	C29F	2/49 Wallace Arnold Tours Ltd, Leeds (WR)
99394	LKJ 966	Duple	49535	C29F	3/49 GL French {Pilgrim Coaches}, Hodsoll Street (KT)
99401	DHJ 464	Duple	48353	C29F	2/49 Westcliff Belle Ltd, Southend-on-Sea (EX)
99406	Z-1743	?		B---	4/49 Original operator unknown (O-N)
99443	?	Duple	52599	B30F	-/-- CEB, Port of Spain (O-TT)
99451	FBU 117	Duple	51340	C29F	2/49 W Hawkins {Regal Motor Service}, Werneth (LA)
99458	BCN 192	Duple	50093	C29F	2/49 Mayfair Luxury Coaches Ltd, Gateshead (DM) 6
99464	HUE 400	Duple	48057	C29F	3/49 J Lloyd & Son Ltd, Nuneaton (WK)
99472	* HOD 49	Duple	50034	C29F	2/49 Western National, Exeter (DN) 560
99479	GWF 358	Duple	49834	C29F	2/49 JH & TW Graham (Connor & Graham), Easington (ER)
99484	Z-1751	?		B---	3/49 Original operator unknown (O-N)
99528	KNK 57	Duple	48825	C29F	4/49 Smiths (Buntingford) Ltd (HT)
99536	HFM 45	Beadle	C178	B20F	4/49 Crosville MS, Chester (CH) S21
99539		see 99284			
99543	GOU 888	Duple	47628	B30F	3/49 FH Kilner (Transport) Ltd, Horsham (WS) 149
99549	DHS 933	Duple	52509	C29F	3/49 Garner's Buses (Bridge of Weir) Ltd, Bridge of Weir (RW) 7
99557	SX 6525	Duple	52502	C29F	2/49 Browning's Luxury Coaches Ltd, Whitburn (WL)
99565	JS 8232	Duple	52510	B30F	4/49 Lochs Motor Transport Ltd, Stornoway (RY)
99570	* ?	?		B28-	-/49 Original operator unknown (O-GR)
99610	KGN 207	Duple	52420	C29F	3/49 Barber {Rose}, London N7 (LN)
99618	FDL 905	Duple	43636	C29F	6/49 Shotters Ltd, Brighstone (IW)
99625	JPW 964	Duple	44371	C29F	3/49 SW Groom {Park Garage Coaches}, Thursford (NK)
99631	EUX 922	Duple	49219	B32F	2/49 JT, FW & GE Whittle {JT Whittle & Sons}, Highley (SH)
99639	GOU 791	Duple	52255	C29F	12/48 Creamline Motor Services (Bordon) Ltd (HA)
99647	KFM 437	Beadle	C150	B28F	5/49 Crosville MS, Chester (CH) S22
99652					Exported to Asuncion (O-PY)
99692	EO 8906	Duple	52503	C29F	2/49 EJ Thompson {Pearl White}, Barrow-in-Furness (LA)
99699	TMK 640	Duple	46282	C29F	3/49 Lacey's (East Ham) Ltd, London E6 (LN)
99922	UHX 285	LCMW		B26R	9/49 Middlesex County Council (XMX)
99928	BWG 983	Duple	54125	C29F	4/49 W Alexander, Falkirk (SN) W234
99936	GJW 563	Duple	52506	C29F	3/49 L Barnett {Pathfinder}, Coseley (ST)
99944	FMW 503	Duple	46477	C29F	3/49 P Chaney {Queen of the Hills}, Wanborough (WI)
99949	?	Duple	50783	C25F	-/-- British South American Airways, Buenos Aires (O-RA)
99990	?	Duple	50763	B36F	-/-- Shell Petroleum Co, Port of Spain (O-TT)
99998	KGT 426	Duple	54094	C29F	3/49 Birch Bros Ltd, London NW5 (LN) K26
100005	* DFR 705	Duple	52359	C29F	5/49 WC Standerwick, Blackpool (LA) 116

C1252/130

100011	?	Mulliner		?	-/--	Ministry of Supply (GOV)
100019	?	Mulliner		?	-/--	Ministry of Supply (GOV)
100027	?	Mulliner		?	-/--	Ministry of Supply (GOV)
100032	?	?		?	-/--	Ministry of Supply (GOV)
100071	GOU 887	Duple	46428	B30F	3/49	FH Kilner (Transport) Ltd, Horsham (WS) 150
100080	TMY 107	Duple	52467	C29F	2/49	Garner's Coaches Ltd, London W5 (LN)
100087	HOD 50	Duple	50033	C29F	6/49	Western National, Exeter (DN) 561
100093	KFM 438	Beadle	C151	B20F	5/49	Crosville MS, Chester (CH) S23
100101	KTD 179	Duple	54133	C29F	3/49	J Yates {West Coaster}, Morecambe (LA)
100109	KFM 439	Beadle	C152	B20F	5/49	Crosville MS, Chester (CH) S24
100114	T-1045	?		B24-	-/49	EP Ytrelid {Skodjeruta}, Skodje (O-N)
100154	FMW 144	Duple	43377	C29F	2/49	J Button & Son, Warminster (WI)
100162	KTC 535	Duple	54073	C29F	3/49	M Hood {Auckland Coaches}, Morecambe (LA)
100169 *	EY 9025	Duple	44258	C29F	3/49	T Jones {T Jones & Sons}, Menai Bridge (AY)
100175	JNY 83	Duple	52505	C29F	2/49	WJ, BA & R Edwards, Talbot Green (GG)
100183	FAY 980	Duple	52504	C29F	3/49	WG Deacon & FC Hardy {Lilac Coaches}, Barlestone (LE)
100191	DFR 827	Duple	54074	C29F	3/49	J Abbott & Sons (Blackpool) Ltd (LA)
100196						Exported to Copenhagen (O-DK)
100236	KGN 773	Duple	44413	C29F	2/49	AJC Giles {Viola Motor Coaches}, London SE16 (LN)
100244	GGE 530	Duple	54093	C27F	4/49	SCWS Ltd, Glasgow (LK)
100251	GDA 983	Duple	48046	C29F	4/49	Worthington Motor Tours Ltd, Wolverhampton (ST)
100257 *	ATS 689	Duple	52508	C29F	1/49	GB Fyffe, Dundee (AS)
100265	EJ 9693	Duple	46590	C29F	3/49	J Edmunds {Gwalia Motors}, Llangeitho (CG)
100273 *	FFU 594	Duple	52511	C29F	4/49	Enterprise (Scunthorpe) Passenger Services Ltd {Enterprise} (LI) 85
100278 *	?	?		B28-	-/--	Original operator unknown (O-GR)
100318	HAX 828	Duple	54085	C29F	2/49	Liberty Motors Ltd, Cardiff (GG) 8
100326	KGN 597	Duple	44215	C24F	3/49	United Service Transport Co Ltd, London SW9 (LN) 1079
100333	CCS 857	Duple	54096	C29F	3/49	CB Law, Prestwick (AR)
100338	OEV 889	Duple	52507	C29F	3/49	H Rippingale, Gestingthorpe (EX)
100347 *	DFR 707	Duple	52361	C29F	5/49	WC Standerwick, Blackpool (LA) 118
100355	LWB 647	Duple	50389	C29F	2/49	CG Littlewood, Sheffield (WR)
100360 *	46-199	?		B24-	-/--	Zissis Bluras, Thessalonika (O-GR)
100400	KNN 314	Duple	54127	C29F	4/49	South Notts Bus Co Ltd, Gotham (NG) 38
100408	KMN 530	Duple	51114	C29F	1/49	R Scott, Douglas (IM)
100415	JXJ 299	Duple	54075	C29F	3/49	WA Strowger, Manchester (LA)
100421	JFD 460	Duple	49848	C29F	3/49	NC Kendrick, Dudley (WO)
100429 *	KGT 397	Duple	54071	C29F	3/49	Duval & Son Ltd, Kingston (SR) 41
100437	EJY 146	Duple	49372	C29F	11/48	Noel Coaches Ltd, Camborne (CO)
100442						Exported to Asuncion (O-PY)
100482	FRY 932	Duple	47907	C29F	3/49	CLW Harris {Majestic}, Leicester (LE)
100490	ERX 848	Duple	54115	C29F	3/49	WE Kent, Baughurst (HA)
100497 *	TMY 940	Duple	49460	C29F	3/49	H Burch, Harrow Weald (MX)
100621 - 100629						Exported to Melbourne (O-AUS)
100630 *	A917	CAC	M31295	FB29D	-/49	Proudloves Taxi & Bus Service, Albany (O-AUS)
100631, 100632						Exported to Melbourne (O-AUS)
100707	HAA 564	Duple	47888	B30F	3/49	FH Kilner (Transport) Ltd, Horsham (WS) 151
100715	HNP 27	Duple	52512	C29F	3/49	LJ Aston, Kempsey (WO) 11
100723	OHK 668	Duple	48200	C29F	3/49	Dryer's Coaches Ltd, London E17 (LN)
100728	?	?		?	-/--	Transportes Generales Comes SA, Vigo (O-E)
100768	?	Duple	52600	B30F	-/--	CEB, Port of Spain (O-TT)
100776	HAA 563	Duple	46429	B30F	3/49	FH Kilner (Transport) Ltd, Horsham (WS) 152
100783	VML 221	Duple	54135	C29F	3/49	John Laing (contractor), Borehamwood 395
100789	?	Mulliner		?	-/--	Ministry of Supply (GOV)
100797	?	Mulliner		?	-/--	Ministry of Supply (GOV)
100806	?	Mulliner		?	-/--	Ministry of Supply (GOV)
100810	?	Mulliner		B--F	-/--	Shell Petroleum Co, unknown overseas location
100850	HWW 412	Duple	51185	C29F	3/49	MA Hargreaves (Morley) Ltd (WR) 25
100858	KGT 139	Mulliner		?	-/--	Ministry of Works (GOV)
100865	KGT 78	Mulliner		B28F	4/49	Ministry of Works (GOV)
100871	?	Mulliner		?	-/--	Ministry of Supply (GOV)
100882	KGT 155	Mulliner		?	-/--	Ministry of Works (GOV)

C1252/131

100887 *	KGT 398	Duple	54134	C29F	3/49	Duval & Son Ltd, Kingston (SR) 42
100892	?	?	?	?	-/--	Transportes Generales Comes SA, Vigo (O-E)
100937 *	TMY 716	Duple	49780	C29F	3/49	Wallis Hire Service Ltd {Dartmouth Coaches}, London SE23 (LN)
100940	GEW 300	Duple	54116	C29F	3/49	H Lee {Whippet Coaches}, Hilton (HN)
100947	EVD 51	Mulliner	T373	B28F	4/49	R Wilson, Carnwath (LK)
100953	DTL 264	Duple	48866	C29F	3/49	TA Skinner {Blue Bird Coaches}, Saltby (LE)
100968	KUO 674	Duple	54114	C29F	3/49	ST Wills, Atherington (DN)
100969 *	DFR 708	Duple	52362	C29F	5/49	WC Standerwick, Blackpool (LA) 119
100973	?	Mulliner		B--F	-/--	Anglo Iranian Oil Co, Abadan (O-IR)
101170 *	HI-744	?		B20-	-/49	Lahden Linjat, Lahti (O-FIN)
101241 *	ERX 534	Mulliner	T356	B30F	3/49	AV Cole {Blue Bus Service}, Windsor (BE)
101249	SY 9044	Duple	54110	C29F	3/49	Pentland Garage Ltd, Loanhead (MN)
101256	LHN 640	Duple	50686	C29F	3/49	Favourite Direct Services Ltd, Bishop Auckland (DM) 12A
101262	KUO 888	Duple	54109	C29F	3/49	E Saunders, Winkleigh (DN)
101270	MUA 596	Duple	50596	C29F	4/49	Kelsall Coaches Ltd {Saffman & Beasley}, Leeds (WR)
101278	CBV 274	Duple	44274	C29F	3/49	Lewis Cronshaw Ltd, London NW4 (LN)
101284	?	?	?		-/--	Transportes Generales Comes SA, Vigo (O-E)
101314		see 101414				
101321		see 101421				
101324	JP 7509	Duple	49532	C29F	3/49	J Lamb, Upholland (LA)
101327	HC 9178	Duple	48840	C29F	3/49	Thorogood {Berkeley Coaches}, Eastbourne (ES)
101332	FAW 375	Duple	47829	B30F	3/49	Jones Coachways Ltd, Market Drayton (SH) 30
101339	LKK 35	Mulliner	T359	B31F	3/49	Craker Southland Coaches Ltd, Bromley (KT) 9
101345	HOD 51	Duple	50035	C29F	6/49	Western National, Exeter (DN) 562
101353	?	?		goods	-/--	Spiers, Claverdon (GWK)
101361 *	LPU 621	Beadle	C140	B30F	6/48	Eastern National, Chelmsford (EX) 3931
101366						Exported to Alexandria (O-ET)
101406	KGN 598	Duple	44216	C24F	4/49	United Service Transport Co Ltd, London SW9 (LN) 1080
101414 *	CMS 47	Duple	54129	C29F	4/49	W Alexander, Falkirk (SN) W235
101421 *	DRG 411	Duple	54117	C29F	3/49	JA Noble, Aberdeen (AD) 15
101435	KTC 642	Duple	51341	C29F	3/49	R Wood & Sons (Tours) Ltd, Ashton-under-Lyne (LA)
101443	MVK 148	Duple	50117	C29F	3/49	G Galley (Galley's Motors), Newcastle (ND)
101448						Exported to Alexandria (O-ET)
101478	FUN 309	Duple	43942	C29F	3/49	WJ Hanmer {WJ Hanmer & Sons}, Southsea (DH)
101485	GGG 269	Duple	54248	C27F	4/49	Lowland Motorways Ltd, Glasgow (LK) 19
101487	LHY 350	Duple	47727	C29F	6/49	TJ King {Monarch Coaches}, Bristol (GL)
101496	LHY 371	Mulliner	T345	B31F	2/49	Clifton College, Bristol (XGL)
101503	HWU 623	Duple	54111	C29F	4/49	Kildare Coaches Ltd, Adwick le Street (WR)
101509	HOD 52	Duple	50036	C29F	3/49	Western National, Exeter (DN) 563
101517	?	?		van	6/49	Claude-General Neon Lights Ltd, London WC2 (GLN)
101525	?	?		van	6/49	Claude-General Neon Lights Ltd, London WC2 (GLN)
101530						Exported to Alexandria (O-ET)
101555	JEL 107	Duple	44445	C29F	-/49	Excelsior Coaches Ltd, Bournemouth (HA)
101570	DUD 385	Duple	48093	C29F	3/49	S Hicks, Chalgrove (OX)
101584	TMY 806	Duple	48201	C29F	3/49	D Evans {Maroon Coaches}, London E18 (LN)
101591	FAW 46	Mulliner	T367	DP28F	2/49	T & WR Hoggins, Wrockwardine Wood (SH)
101599	CRN 158	Duple	54140	C29F	3/49	Scout MS Ltd, Preston (LA)
101607	KYC 926	Duple	54130	C27F	3/49	J & W Hawkins (Hawkins Bros) {Scarlet Pimpernel Coaches}, Minehead (SO)
101612						Exported to Alexandria (O-ET)
101649	?	Duple	52601	B30F	-/--	CEB, Port of Spain (O-TT)
101660	FWN 280	Mulliner	T357	B31F	3/49	DT & R Davies {Cream Line Services}, Tonmawr (GG)
101668	KLB 103	?		van	11/49	Metropolitan Police, London SW1 (GLN)
101677	?	Mulliner		B--F	-/--	Anglo Iranian Oil Co, Abadan (O-IR)
101690	KGN 433	Duple	49980	B27F	5/49	Metropolitan Police, London SW1 (XLN)
101699	FAW 523	Duple	49224	B30F	4/49	Shropshire County Council (XSH)
101947	?	Duple	52602	B30F	-/--	CEB, Port of Spain (O-TT)
101953 *	LPU 622	Beadle	C139	B30F	5/48	Eastern National, Chelmsford (EX) 3932
101958	HUO 681	Beadle	C131	B30F	4/49	Southern National, Exeter (DN) 528
101966 *	JEL 276	Beadle	C147	B20F	5/49	Hants & Dorset, Bournemouth (HA) 981

101975	EL-15-31	?		B30D	3/49	Empresa de Transportes Gândra, Vale de Cambra (O-P)
101982	ETH 545	Duple	52484	C29F	4/49	D Jones & Sons {Dan Jones}, Carmarthen (CR) 10
101988	HUO 682	Beadle	C132	B30F	4/49	Southern National, Exeter (DN) 529
101997	FAW 40	Duple	43871	C29F	3/49	Ms W Bartley {JR Bartley}, Selattyn (SH)
102029						Exported to Accra (O-WAC)
102035	DTL 224	Duple	44442	C29F	4/49	J Hodson, Navenby (LI)
102040	LPP 683	Duple	52476	C29F	1/49	HG Evans {Victory Coaches}, Slough (BK)
102049	GDA 985	Mulliner	T348	C27F	5/49	Worthington Motor Tours Ltd, Wolverhampton (ST)
102058 *	EL-15-32	?		B27D	3/49	Joaquim Guedes, Castro d'Aire (O-P) 14
102064	GJW 883	Mulliner	T349	C26F	6/49	Worthington Motor Tours Ltd, Birmingham (WK)
102070	DFE 708	Duple	54118	C29F	3/49	C, JE, T & T Hudson {Hudson's Bus Co}, Horncastle (LI) 25
102079	CRN 159	Duple	54141	C29F	3/49	Scout MS Ltd, Preston (LA)
102111						Exported to Colombo (O-CL)
102117	DBN 627	Duple	54208	C29F	3/49	ET Butterworth Ltd {Pathfinder}, Blackpool (LA)
102122	GDA 986	Mulliner	T369	C29F	4/49	Worthington Motor Tours Ltd, Wolverhampton (ST)
102130	DFR 987	Duple	54142	C29F	5/49	Batty-Holt Touring Service Ltd, Blackpool (LA)
102141						Exported to Alexandria (O-ET)
102146	ONO 177	Duple	46883	C27F	3/49	Mrs LA Bennett {Went's Coaches}, Boxted (EX)
102152	EM 4507	Duple	50965	C29F	4/49	T Lawrenson Ltd, Bootle (LA)
102161	GDA 984	Mulliner	T351	C29F	4/49	Worthington Motor Tours Ltd, Wolverhampton (ST)
102193						Exported to Colombo (O-CL)
102199	GJW 884	Mulliner	T350	C26F	9/49	Worthington Motor Tours Ltd, Birmingham (WK)
102204 *	LKM 55	Duple	47950	C29F	3/49	H, C & W Sarjeant {Sarjeant Bros}, Cheriton (KT)
102212	EVA 974	Mulliner	T360	B28F	3/49	R Wilson, Carnwath (LK)
102221						Exported to Alexandria (O-ET)
102228	DVY 948	Duple	50481	C29F	3/49	J Broadbent, Stamford Bridge (ER) 16
102234	HAX 824	Duple	52513	C29F	3/49	FN Morgan {Morgan's Tours}, Govilon (MH)
102243	GWF 687	Duple	52101	C29F	3/49	AH Hardcastle, Wold Newton (ER)
102277						Exported to Takoradi (O-WAC)
102281	JS 8208	Duple	54072	B30F	5/49	Western Lewis Coaches Ltd, Stornoway (RY)
102294	MPL 640	Duple	50283	C29F	3/49	Ben Stanley Ltd, Hersham (SR)
102294	FAY 954	Mulliner	T363	B31F	3/49	W Parsons, Stanton-under-Bardon (LE)
102301 - 102312						Exported to Melbourne (O-AUS)
102507	D-5666	?		B28-	-/--	Gudbrand Bakken, location unknown (O-N)
102514	FP 4997	Mulliner	T364	B31F	3/49	AL Ward, Oakham (RD)
102520 *	JNY 200	Mulliner	T366	B31F	3/49	Afan Transport Co Ltd, Port Talbot (GG)
102529	FFU 852	Mulliner	T368	B31F	3/49	G Lewis {Daisy Bus Service}, Broughton (LI)
102561						Exported to Accra (O-WAC)
102567	FMW 730	Mulliner	T375	B--F	4/49	AH Razey {Amport & District Motor Services}, Thruxton (HA)
102572 *	ETH 888	Mulliner	T374	B31F	3/49	D Jones {Ffoshelig Coaches}, Newchurch (CR)
102580	GMJ 267	Duple	48812	C29F	5/49	OA Bartle & Co, Potton (BD) B/49/4
102589	?	Mulliner		B--F	-/--	Anglo Iranian Oil Co, Abadan (O-IR)
102596 *	CRN 91	Mulliner	T372	B31F	3/49	English Electric Co Ltd, Preston (XLA)
102602	LMA 174	Duple	54143	C29F	3/49	G West {Reliance Motor Services}, Kelsall (CH)
102611	GUK 315	Mulliner	T371	C28F	5/50	Worthington Motor Tours Ltd, Birmingham (WK)
102643	?	Duple	50786	C27F	-/49	Meralli Bus Services Ltd, Nairobi (O-EAK)
102649	DNL 272	Mulliner	T370	B31F	3/49	WM Appleby & JD Jordan {A & J Coaches}, Bedlington (ND)
102654	LKM 743	Mulliner	T388	DP28F	4/49	HE Thomsett, Deal (KT)
102657		see 102654				
102662	FFU 874	Duple	54146	C29F	3/49	JA Hankins {Reliance}, Scunthorpe (LI)
102675	?	Duple	52589	B30-	-/--	Shell Petroleum Co, Suez (O-ET)
102678	LKM 379	Mulliner	T376	B31F	3/49	EG Weeks {Valedene Coaches}, Sutton Valence (KT)
102684	HWU 800	Duple	50660	C29F	3/49	R Foster & Sons, Horbury (WR)
102693	FDL 969	Duple	44099	C29F	3/49	West Wight Motor Bus Co Ltd, Totland Bay (IW)
102725	HCG 298	Duple	48133	C29F	5/49	Liss & District Omnibus Co Ltd, Liss (HA) 153
102731	?	Duple	50785	C27F	-/49	Meralli Bus Services Ltd, Nairobi (O-EAK)
102736 *	ABR 587	Duple	50149	C27F	3/49	WH Jolly, South Hylton (DM) 5
102744	FUN 310	Mulliner	T379	B31F	3/49	T Williams {T Williams & Son}, Ponciau (DH)
102753						Exported to Alexandria (O-ET)
102760	FAW 277	Duple	49220	C29F	3/49	F Jones, Cleobury North (SH)

102766	JVF 528	Duple	47678	C29F	4/49 JR Bensley, Martham (NK)
102775 *	PV 9316	Duple	52455	B30F	2/49 Fisons Ltd, Ipswich (XWF)
102969 - 102980					Exported to Melbourne (O-AUS)
103023	?	Duple	52596	B30F	-/-- East African Railways, Dar-es-Salaam (O-EAT)
103028	LCV 810	Duple	44443	C29F	4/49 Blewett's Ltd {Crimson Tours}, Hayle (CO)
103033	FAW 620	Duple	49222	C29F	6/49 ERH & HR Evason {E Evason & Sons}, Wellington (SH)
103042	JNY 332	Duple	54077	C29F	3/49 C Lewis & J Jacob, Maesteg (GG)
103051					Exported to Alexandria (O-ET)
103058	HWW 322	Mulliner	T361	C29F	5/49 Kildare Coaches Ltd, Adwick le Street (WR)
103064	CES 926	Duple	54234	C29F	-/49 C Christison {Christison's Bus Service}, Blairgowrie (PH)
103073	HWW 642	Duple	43951	C29F	4/49 W Simpson, Ripon (WR) 7
103105	?	Duple	52595	B30F	-/-- East African Railways, Dar-es-Salaam (O-EAT)
103111	NPA 308	Duple	49308	C29F	4/49 WD Hall Ltd, London SW19 (LN)
103116	KNN 377	Duple	54149	C29F	3/49 JR Woodhouse & TH Barton {W & B Coaches}, Sandiacre (NG)
103124	KGU 584	Duple	54207	C29F	3/49 Royal Arsenal Co-operative Society, London SE18 (LN) 77
103139	GJW 882	Duple	48047	C29F	4/49 Worthington Motor Tours Ltd, Wolverhampton (ST)
103142					Exported to Alexandria (O-ET)
103146	LPP 943	Duple	45212	C29F	3/49 FH Crook {Sands Bus Co}, Booker (BK)
103155	ECX 412	Duple	50412	C29F	4/49 Hanson's Buses Ltd, Huddersfield (WR) 270
103187					Exported to Colombo (O-CL)
103193	KTC 987	Duple	54210	C29F	4/49 W Robinson & Sons, Great Harwood (LA) 20
103199	OHK 973	Duple	46509	C29F	3/49 Dagenham Coaching Service, Dagenham (EX)
103206	HVC 288	Duple	47995	C27F	4/49 H & H Motorways Ltd {Bunty}, Coventry (WK)
103217					Exported to Alexandria (O-ET)
103222	AVV 882	Duple	46518	C29F	4/49 JW & RFP Hayfield (Hayfield Bros), Newport Pagnell (BK)
103228	DBN 677	Duple	51342	C27F	5/49 Lomax Bros (Transport) Ltd, Bolton (LA)
103237	HWW 650	Duple	54126	C29F	3/49 JW Kitchin & Sons Ltd, Pudsey (WR)
103240 #	?	Duple	50739	B31-	-/-- Iraq Petroleum Co, location unknown (O-IR)
103247 *	SJ 1263	?		C29F	6/49 EK Ribbeck & Son, Brodick, Arran (BU)
103269	IN 6485	Duple	50787	C29F	-/49 Culloty's Garage, Killarney (EI)
103275	CRN 136	Duple	54249	C29F	5/49 S Morris, Kirkby Lonsdale (WT)
103280 #	MUG 873	ACB		C29F	7/49 JA Hudson Ltd, Leeds (WR)
103288	TMY 493	Duple	52088	C29F	1/49 Venture Transport (Hendon) Ltd, London NW2 (LN)
103299	?	Mulliner		B--F	-/-- Anglo Iranian Oil Co, Abadan (O-IR)
103304	JAD 770	Duple	54211	C29F	4/49 RS Marchant {Marchant's Coaches}, Cheltenham (GL)
103310	KGT 888	Duple	44836	C29F	4/49 Keith & Boyle (London) Ltd {Orange Luxury Coaches}, London EC2 (LN) Widgeon
103319	KGU 652	Duple	44533	C29F	4/49 Fallowfield & Britten Ltd, London E8 (LN)
103351 *	CN 811	?	?		6/50 Original operator unknown (O-CL)
103351					Exported to Colombo (O-CL)
103357 #	MUG 874	ACB		C29F	7/49 JA Hudson Ltd, Leeds (WR)
103362	DDB 801	Duple	50488	C29F	4/49 J Middleton & Sons {Kinder Scout/Birch Vale Hire Service}, Stockport (CH) 2
103370 *	UMP 95	Mulliner	T390	?	5/49 Garner's Coaches Ltd, London W5 (LN)
103381					Exported to Alexandria (O-ET)
103386					Exported to Colombo (O-CL)
103392	JAD 798	Duple	54090	C29F	3/49 SK & F Silvey {Silvey's Coaches}, Epney (GL)
103401 *	HBY 163	Duple	44530	C29F	4/49 Bourne & Balmer (Croydon) Ltd (SR)
103433					Exported to Colombo (O-CL)
103439	BWG 540	Duple	54224	C29F	4/49 W Alexander, Falkirk (SN) W236
103444	EJY 250	Mulliner	T387	B31F	4/49 Millbrook Steamboat & Trading Co Ltd (CO)
103452	?	Mulliner		?	-/-- Original operator unknown (O-EAK)
103461					Exported to Alexandria (O-ET)
103468		see 103469			
103469	JOL 298	Duple	46317	C29F	4/49 Mrs K Poole {Evans Coaches}, Birmingham (WK)
103474	TMY 700	Duple	44048	C29F	4/49 Essex County Coaches Ltd, London E15 (LN)
103483	NPA 73	Duple	44459	C29F	4/49 ER Gudge {Comfy Coaches}, Farnham (SR)
103515	?	Mulliner		?	-/-- Original operator unknown (O-EAK)
103521	JNY 273	Mulliner	T389	B31F	4/49 AE & FR Brewer {Brewer's Motor Services}, Caerau (GG)

103526	JOL 998	Duple	52478	C29F	4/49	Smith's Imperial Coaches Ltd, Birmingham (WK)
103534	?	Duple	52603	B30F	-/--	CEB, Port of Spain (O-TT)
103543						Exported to Alexandria (O-ET)
103550	RRF 729	Duple	43316	C29F	-/49	GH Austin & Sons Ltd {Happy Days}, Stafford (ST) 51
103556	BEE 100	Duple	54215	C29F	6/49	A & AE Blackbourn Ltd {Granville Tours}, Grimsby (LI) 153
103565	HNP 301	Mulliner	T392	B31F	3/49	CW Shuker {Lady Edith}, Halesowen (WO)
103596	?	Duple	52598	B30F	-/--	East African Railways, Dar-es-Salaam (O-EAT)
103755 *	KGT 77	Mulliner		B30F	4/49	Ministry of Supply (GOV)
103819	KPO 714	Duple	54153	C29F	4/49	SW Anstey, Haslemere (SY)
103824	HNP 114	Duple	49464	C29F	4/49	LJ Aston, Kempsey (WO) 12
103833	?	Duple	52597	B30F	-/--	East African Railways, Dar-es-Salaam (O-EAT)
103841	LB-15-86	?		DP29D	3/49	Marques, Passos de Silgueiros (O-P) 11
103848 *	EJB 234	Beadle	C153	B27F	-/49	Thames Valley, Reading (BE) 512
103854	CGS 45	Duple	54206	C29F	4/49	DC Smail {James Smail}, Blairgowrie (PH)
103861	HWU 965	Duple	50636	C29F	4/49	Clifford Lunn, Rothwell (WR)
103895						Exported to Barbados
103900	DHJ 623	Duple	54261	C29F	4/49	Westcliff-on-Sea MS (EX)
103902	KGT 406	Duple	44648	C29F	4/49	J, J, J Jnr & E Clarke {Clarke's Luxury Coaches}, London E16 (LN)
103914						Exported to Barbados
103923	LB-15-85	?		DP28D	3/49	Empresa de Transportes Courense, Paredes de Coura (O-P) 7
103930	FUN 394	Mulliner	T378	B31F	4/49	Mrs MA Evans {MA Evans & Sons}, Wrexham (DH)
103936	NPF 479	Duple	54451	C29F	3/49	JH Farmer & WW Haag {Hex Hire Services}, Surbiton (SR)
103945	GWF 741	Mulliner	T377	B28F	5/49	DW Frankish, Brandesburton (ER)
103971 *	KRR 107	Allsop		FC30F	5/49	R Wain, Mansfield (NG)
103976 *	DHS 939	Duple	54247	C29F	4/49	Daniel Ferguson Ltd {Victor}, Renfrew (RW) 30
103982	KMN 531	Duple	51115	C29F	1/49	F Gash {Empress}, Douglas (IM)
103987	OHK 976	Duple	48062	C29F	4/49	ER, TW & AC Lodge, High Easter (EX)
103995	KDV 649	Duple	46941	C29F	4/49	CA Gayton {Gayton's Coaches}, Ashburton (DN)
104004						Exported to Alexandria (O-ET)
104011 *	HAA 874	Duple	46430	C29F	4/49	Hants & Sussex Motor Services Ltd, Emsworth (HA) 154
104017	EJB 242	Beadle	C154	B27F	-/49	Thames Valley, Reading (BE) 520
104026	DRD 605	Duple	44504	C29F	6/49	AE Smith {Smith's Coaches}, Reading (BE)
104059	VML 938	Duple	49808	C25F	-/50	Frames Tours Ltd, London WC1 (LN) 76
104066	KGU 658	Duple	50538	C29F	4/49	George Ewer & Co Ltd {Grey Green}, London N16 (LN)
104071	LHN 756	Duple	50696	C29F	4/49	GE Brown & Son {GNE Motor Services}, Darlington (DM)
104078	KGT 889	Duple	44837	C29F	4/49	Keith & Boyle (London) Ltd {Orange Luxury Coaches}, London EC2 (LN) Woodlark
104092						Exported to Alexandria (O-ET)
104094	HCE 426	Duple	54242	C29F	4/49	BC Kenzie, Shepreth (CM)
104097		see 104094				
104100	ECX 413	Duple	50413	C29F	4/49	Hanson's Buses Ltd, Huddersfield (WR) 271
104109 *	JEL 578	Beadle	C157	B20F	5/49	Hants & Dorset, Bournemouth (HA) 984
104143	VML 936	Duple	49809	C27F	-/50	Frames Tours Ltd, London WC1 (LN) 74
104150	JNY 521	Duple	46492	C29F	c4/49	GB Smith, Cymmer (GG)
104159						Exported to Alexandria (O-ET)
104163	TMY 494	Duple	46851	C29F	9/49	Northern Roadways Ltd, Glasgow (LK)
104172	SL 3305	Duple	54245	C29F	3/49	W Dawson, Sauchie (CK)
104179	TMY 359	Duple	54243	C29F	4/49	Wrights Hanwell Ltd, London W7 (LN)
104184	VML 232	Duple	54246	C29F	4/49	John Laing (contractor), Borehamwood 406
104191 *	JEL 277	Beadle	C148	B20F	5/49	Hants & Dorset, Bournemouth (HA) 982
104213 - 104224						Exported to Melbourne (O-AUS)
104453 *	VML 937	Duple	49807	C29F	-/50	Frames Tours Ltd, London WC1 (LN) 75
104462	GMJ 335	Duple	48807	C29F	4/49	FD Cox {Heathway Coaches}, Kensworth (BD)
104469						Exported to Alexandria (O-ET)
104473	FAW 498	Duple	49221	C29F	4/49	SC & J Vagg {Vagg's Motors}, Knockin Heath (SH)
104482	KPT 194	Duple	50082	C29F	5/49	Shaw Bros {Bonnie Heather}, Byers Green (DM)
104489	HAA 597	Duple	44431	C29F	4/49	Odiham Motor Services Ltd (HA)
104494 *	JBJ 868	Duple	48883	C29F	4/49	Mrs M Moyse {Nightingale Coaches}, Beccles (EK)

104501 *	JEL 278	Beadle	C149	B20F	5/49	Hants & Dorset, Bournemouth (HA) 983
104535	?	Duple	52604	B30F	-/--	CEB, Port of Spain (O-TT)
104543 *	NJO 669	Duple	49997	C29F	5/49	A Hudson Ltd, Bicester (OX)
104551						Exported to Alexandria (O-ET)
104555 *	FED 767	Duple	54136	C29F	5/49	G Naylor & Sons {Naylor's Motor Services}, Stockton Heath (CH)
104564	DHJ 624	Duple	54262	C29F	-/49	Westcliff-on-Sea MS (EX)
104571	GDL 14	Duple	49016	C29F	4/49	SH, AC, PH & AR Randall (H Randall & Sons), Bonchurch (IW)
104581	HWW 703	Mulliner	T393	B28F	5/49	JB Snaith {Bronte Tours}, Haworth (WR) 11
104583	ONO 975	Mulliner	T362	B28F	5/49	RW Hooks & Co {Harwich & District), Great Oakley (EX)
104617	?	Duple	52606	B30F	-/--	East African Railways, Dar-es-Salaam (O-EAT)
104625	DUD 522	Duple	46247	C29F	4/49	AR Taylor, Bicester (OX) 3
104633						Exported to Alexandria (O-ET)
104637	JNY 634	Duple	54078	C29F	4/49	F Mitchell (Coaches) Ltd, Pontypridd (GG)
104646	GGG 143	Duple	54250	C27F	5/49	SCWS Ltd, Glasgow (LK)
104653	KGN 434	Duple	49981	B27F	6/49	Metropolitan Police, London SW1 (XLN)
104659	HAA 596	Mulliner	T395	B31F	4/49	Odiham Motor Services Ltd (HA)
104665	DNL 351	Duple	43697	C29F	4/49	C Frazer & Son, West Wylam (ND)
104699	?	Duple	52605	B30F	-/--	East African Railways, Dar-es-Salaam (O-EAT)
104707	LTO 246	Duple	47745	C29F	4/49	A Camm {Camm's Coaches}, Nottingham (NG) 9
104715	?	Mulliner		B--F	-/--	Shell Petroleum Co, Curacao (O-YV)
104719	KGU 659	Duple	52423	C29F	4/49	Dryer's Coaches Ltd, London E17 (LN)
104728	MVK 501	Mulliner	T396	B31F	3/49	Moordale Bus Services Ltd, Newcastle (ND) 9
104735	ECX 430	Duple	50359	C29F	4/49	Chapman's Ivy Coaches Ltd, Milnsbridge (WR)
104740	KTD 462	Duple	52489	C29F	5/49	R Taylor, Leigh (LA)
104747	JEL 483	Duple	44831	C29F	4/49	Shamrock & Rambler Motor Coaches Ltd, Bournemouth (HA)
104781	?	Duple	52607	B30F	-/--	East African Railways, Dar-es-Salaam (O-EAT)
104789	KNA 208	Duple	49715	C29F	4/49	WD Hartle (WD Hartle & Son), Buxton (DE)
104797						Exported to Lisbon (O-P)
105005	CMS 103	Duple	54225	C29F	5/49	W Alexander, Falkirk (SN) W237
105014	AS 1930	Duple	54204	B30F	6/49	W Shaw, Glenferness (NN)
105021	GMJ 559	Mulliner	T394	B28F	4/49	Mrs EM Richards, Kingsbridge (DN)
105026	DFV 47	Duple	54258	C29F	4/49	Lansdowne Motors Ltd, Fleetwood (LA)
105033	JEL 437	Duple	46484	C29F	4/49	Excelsior Coaches Ltd, Bournemouth (HA)
105067, 105149						Exported to Mauritius
105075 *	FFU 961	Mulliner	T403	B31F	4/49	Enterprise (Scunthorpe) Passenger Services Ltd {Enterprise} (LI) 146
105083						Exported to Alexandria (O-ET)
105087 *	CBV 353	Duple	50976	C29F	5/49	Whitehurst Tours Ltd, Accrington (LA) 7
105096	HCG 20	Duple	46615	C29F	4/49	Hants & Sussex Motor Services Ltd, Emsworth (HA) 155
105103	TMY 717	Duple	47794	C29F	4/49	Gilbert's Luxury Coaches Ltd, London EC2 (LN)
105108	JDF 398	?		van	9/49	Barnby, Bendall & Co Ltd (removers), Cheltenham (GGL)
105115	FOW 692	Duple	46707	C27F	c2/49	PFV Summerbee {Sumerbee's Motor Coaches}, Southampton (HA)
105157	GCJ 251	Duple	52514	C29F	5/49	Miss I Baynham, Ross-on-Wye (HR)
105165						Exported to Alexandria (O-ET)
105169	HAA 631	Duple	54259	C29F	c3/49	Creamline Motor Services (Bordon) Ltd (HA)
105178	KYD 575	Duple	49169	C29F	5/49	CT & JN Baker (CT Baker & Son) {Weston Greys}, Weston-super-Mare (SO)
105185	MDH 681	Duple	52486	C29F	4/49	Pearson's Motorways Ltd, Walsall (ST)
105190	DFX 932	Mulliner	T397	B28F	5/49	PC Abbott, Piddletrenthide (DT)
105197	HNP 592	Duple	49854	C29F	4/49	A Janes {Bert Janes}, Stourbridge (WO)
105230	DFE 750	Duple	54217	C29F	4/49	W Hutson, North Hykeham (LI)
105239	SH 8570	Mulliner	T391	B31F	4/49	TF Buckle & Son, Duns (BW)
105247						Exported to Alexandria (O-ET)
105251	FDM 554	Duple	43606	C29F	5/49	Rhyl United Coachways Ltd, Rhyl (FT) 6B
105260						Exported to Mombasa (O-EAK)
105267	JAO 144	Duple	44730	C29F	4/49	Wright Bros Coaches Ltd, Nenthead (CU)
105272	FUN 415	Mulliner	T400	B28F	5/49	J & HG Phillips {J Phillips & Son}, Rhostyllen (DH)

105279	JBJ 728	Mulliner	T399	B30F	4/49	CE Naylor {Halesworth Blue Bus Service}, Halesworth (EK) 10
105313						Exported to Mombasa (O-EAK)
105321	KGU 600	Duple	43880	C29F	4/49	W Grier & J Wilkinson {Lucky Line Coaches}, Edgware (MX)
105329						Exported to Montevideo (O-ROU)
105333	KFM 839	Duple	54546	C29F	11/49	Crosville MS, Chester (CH) SL39
105342	IL 4579	Duple	54205	B30F	5/49	MF Cassidy {Erne Bus}, Enniskillen (FH)
105349	NNU 461	Duple	54260	C29F	5/49	FH Doughty, Brimington (DE)
105354	FAJ 749	Mulliner	T402	B30F	5/49	Hardwick's Services Ltd, Snainton (NR)
105361	DDB 847	Mulliner	T405	B29F	6/49	AE Hackett, Hazel Grove (CH)
105394						Exported to Takoradi (O-WAC)
105413 - 105424						Exported to Sydney (O-AUS)
105618	LHY 918	Duple	44237	C29F	5/49	Wessex Coaches Ltd, Bristol (GL)
105626						Exported to Montevideo (O-ROU)
105630	LKN 546	Mulliner	T398	C28F	6/49	W Bottle {Whitstable Coaches}, Tankerton (KT)
105639	KPT 197	Mulliner	T406	B32F	5/49	GH, S & JB Atkinson (GH Atkinson & Sons) {General Omnibus Services}, Chester-le-Street (DM) 18
105646	4414	Mulliner	T383	B28F	5/49	Sarre Transport Ltd, St Peter Port, Guernsey (CI) 20
105651	KDV 991	Mulliner	T401	B31F	4/49	Devon Mental Hospital, Exeter (XDN)
105658	GUK 316	Mulliner	T381	DP26F	5/50	Worthington Motor Tours Ltd, Birmingham (WK)
105693	HI 5828	Duple	50788	B31F	-/50	R Campion {Princess Bus Service}, Clonmel (EI)
105701	KPT 96	Mulliner	T404	B31F	4/49	Moordale Bus Services Ltd, Newcastle (ND) 7
105709	?	Mulliner		B--F	-/--	Shell Petroleum Co, Cabimas (O-YV)
105713	GMJ 389	Duple	48338	C29F	5/49	G Woolston {Keysonian Coaches}, Keysoe (BD)
105722 *	JEL 579	Beadle	C158	B20F	5/49	Hants & Dorset, Bournemouth (HA) 985
105729	GCJ 298	Mulliner	T409	B31F	6/49	WE Morgan {Wye Valley Motors}, Hereford (HR)
105734	JUF 637	Duple	50227	C29F	5/49	RG Johnston {Unique Coaches}, Brighton (ES)
105741	KPT 307	Duple	43898	C29F	5/49	Scurr's Motor Services Ltd, Stillington (DM)
105775						Exported to Barbados
105783	?	?		van	-/--	Wear Shipbuilders Association, Sunderland (GDM)
105791	?	Mulliner		B--F	-/--	Anglo Iranian Oil Co, Abadan (O-IR)
105795	KFM 429	Duple	54263	C29F	5/49	Crosville MS, Chester (CH) SL30
105804	ETH 984	Mulliner	T380	B31F	5/49	WJ Davies {Davies Bros}, Pencader (CR)
105811	FT 6642	Duple	50136	C29F	5/49	G Chapman {Priory Motor Coach Co}, North Shields (ND) 48
105816	HWX 243	Mulliner	T408	B31F	8/49	JJ Longstaff, Mirfield (WR)
105823	TMY 699	Duple	48921	C29F	4/49	Henry Coaches Ltd, London N15 (LN) 23
105831						Exported to Port Elizabeth (O-ZA)
105857						Exported to Barbados
105865	DRG 529	Duple	54269	C29F	4/49	James Paterson & Co (Motor Hirers) Ltd, Aberdeen (AD)
105873						Exported to Alexandria (O-ET)
105877	ECX 484	Pearson		C28F	6/49	Bottomley's Motors (Huddersfield) Ltd (WR)
105880 *	?	?		prison	9/49	Metropolitan Police, London SW1 (GLN)
105886	KKH 127	Duple	51179	C29F	6/49	Green's Auto Services (East Yorkshire) Ltd, Kingston-upon-Hull (ER)
105893	UMP 831	Duple	50065	C29F	5/49	AR & Mrs EF Thorne {Thorne Bros}, London SW2 (LN)
105898	JFJ 939	Duple	46962	C29F	5/49	Greenslades, Exeter (DN)
105905 *	JEL 580	Beadle	C159	B20F	5/49	Hants & Dorset, Bournemouth (HA) 986
105945	?	Duple	52608	B30F	-/--	East African Railways, Dar-es-Salaam (O-EAT)
105947	KGW 419	Duple	44534	C29F	5/49	Fallowfield & Britten Ltd, London E8 (LN)
105955						Exported to Izmir (O-TR)
105959 *	LHY 919	Duple	44238	C29F	5/49	Wessex Coaches Ltd, Bristol (GL)
105968 #	LHY 920	Duple	44168	C29F	5/49	Wessex Coaches Ltd, Bristol (GL)
105974	JFD 673	Mulliner	T407	B31F	6/49	Kendrick's Luxury Tours Ltd, Dudley (WO)
105979 *	JEL 581	Beadle	C160	B20F	5/49	Hants & Dorset, Bournemouth (HA) 987
105987	LDE 400	Duple	54121	B30F	6/49	Green's Motors Ltd, Haverfordwest (PE)
106225	?	Duple	52609	B30F	-/--	East African Railways, Dar-es-Salaam (O-EAT)
106233	JVF 843	Duple	48350	C29F	-/--	EE Smith & Sons Ltd, Attleborough (NK)
106241						Exported to Alexandria (O-ET)
106245	LKN 257	Duple	47793	C29F	5/49	RH Sims {Marion Coaches}, Margate (KT)
106254	KNK 870	Duple	54237	C29F	5/49	Ronsway Coaches Ltd, Hemel Hempstead (HT)
106261	?	?		van	-/--	G Worley Ltd, High Wycombe (GBK)

Chassis	Reg	Body	Body no	Type	Date	Operator
106266 *	EJB 232	Beadle	C155	B27F	-/49	Thames Valley, Reading (BE) 510
106273	JP 7562	Duple	49949	C29F	5/49	H Heaps Ltd, Charnock Richard (LA)
106308	?	Duple	52610	B30F	-/--	East African Railways, Dar-es-Salaam (O-EAT)
106316	EKG 501	Duple	54079	C29F	5/49	ER Forse, Cardiff (GG)
106324						Exported to Alexandria (O-ET)
106328	SW 7747	Duple	54279	C29F	5/49	A & W Smith, Creetown (KK)
106336	GCJ 297	Duple	52515	C29F	6/49	WE Morgan {Wye Valley Motors}, Hereford (HR)
106343 *	EJB 233	Beadle	C156	B27F	6/49	Thames Valley, Reading (BE) 511
106348	SB 7765	Duple	54276	C29F	6/49	A & P McConnachie, Campbeltown (AL)
106355	HCG 601	Duple	46431	C29F	6/49	FH Kilner (Transport) Ltd, Horsham (WS) 156
106389	?	Duple	52611	B30F	-/--	East African Railways, Dar-es-Salaam (O-EAT)
106397	GUK 317	Mulliner	T382	DP26F	5/50	Worthington Motor Tours Ltd, Birmingham (WK)
106405						Exported to Alexandria (O-ET)
106409	?	?		van	-/--	Flinn & Sons Ltd (dyers), Fishergate (GWS)
106418	?	?		van	-/--	Flinn & Sons Ltd (dyers), Fishergate (GWS)
106420 #	?	King		B33F	-/--	Tauranga Bus Service, Tauranga (O-NZ)
106425	UMP 78	Duple	44049	C29F	5/49	Essex County Coaches Ltd, London E15 (LN)
106430	ONO 711	Duple	44753	C28F	5/49	GL Sutton {Sutton's Coaches}, Clacton (EX)
106437	LKN 948	Mulliner	T411	B31F	6/49	EJ Banks, Sturry (KT)
106471	?	Duple	52612	B30F	-/--	East African Railways, Dar-es-Salaam (O-EAT)
106477		see 106479				
106479	VML 948	Duple	49810	C27F	-/50	Frames Tours Ltd, London WC1 (LN) 77
106487						Exported to Alexandria (O-ET)
106491	UMP 79	Duple	44050	C29F	5/49	Essex County Coaches Ltd, London E15 (LN)
106500	FWN 561	Duple	49425	C29F	5/49	R Parkhouse & Sons, Penclawdd (GG)
106507 *	HOD 120	Duple	54289	C29F	5/49	Southern National, Exeter (DN) 580
106512 *	DDB 891	Duple	52490	C29F	5/49	Melba Motors Ltd, Reddish (CH)
106518		see 106512				
106519 *	KDV 675	Duple	50544	C29F	6/49	Ruby Tours Ltd, Paignton (DN)
106553	TMY 718	Duple	54244	C29F	5/49	Wrights Hanwell Ltd, London W7 (LN)
106561	CBV 509	Duple	44552	C29F	5/49	Lewis Cronshaw Ltd, London NW4 (LN)
106569						Exported to Alexandria (O-ET)
106573	SRE 12	Duple	43325	C29F	5/49	JB Box, Lower Gornal (ST)
106582	KFM 430	Duple	54264	C29F	5/49	Crosville MS, Chester (CH) SL31
106587		see 106512				
106589	JEL 718	Duple	44832	C27F	5/49	Shamrock & Rambler Motor Coaches Ltd, Bournemouth (HA)
106594	EJY 737	Mulliner	T415	B28F	6/49	Pearce's Motors Ltd, Polperro (CO)
106829	DHM 769	Duple	43986	C29F	4/49	Grange & Sons {Broadway Coaches}, London E6 (LN)
106863	LKN 550	Mulliner	T413	B28F	6/49	H Dineley {Rapid Rover Garages & Coaches}, Margate (KT)
106871	MUA 633	Duple	50641	C29F	5/49	TS Heaps & Sons, Leeds (WR)
106879	?	Mulliner		B--F	-/--	Shell Petroleum Co, Cabimas (O-YV)
106882		see 106883				
106883 *	FDM 569	Mulliner	T410	B31F	5/49	P & O Lloyd, Bagillt (FT)
106892	KFM 431	Duple	54265	C29F	5/49	Crosville MS, Chester (CH) SL32
106899 #	LHY 921	Duple	44169	C29F	5/49	Wessex Coaches Ltd, Bristol (GL)
106904	?	?		van	-/--	Greaves & Thomas Ltd (furniture manfacturers), London E5 (GLN)
106911	FAW 762	Duple	49223	C29F	5/49	JT, FW & GE Whittle {JT Whittle & Sons}, Highley (SH)
106944	?	Duple	52616	B30F	-/--	East African Railways, Dar-es-Salaam (O-EAT)
106948	NPC 416	Duple	46505	C29F	5/49	HR Richmond {Epsom Coaches}, Epsom (SR)
106953	GUK 8	Duple	54336	C29F	3/49	J Leadbetter {Pinfold De-Luxe}, Bloxwich (ST)
106961						Exported to Alexandria (O-ET)
106965 *	DFV 52	Duple	54286	C29F	5/49	G Newton (Blackpool) Ltd (LA)
106974	?	Duple	52613	B30F	-/--	East African Railways, Dar-es-Salaam (O-EAT)
106981	KTC 627	Duple	54287	C29F	5/49	JF Waterhouse, Hutton (LA)
106986	UMP 695	Duple	49338	C29F	-/--	T & W Parker {Blue Coaches}, Ilfracombe (DN)
106993	HCG 581	Mulliner	T414	B29F	c6/49	A Ford & Son, Silchester (HA)
107024						Exported to Mombasa (O-EAK)
107027	TMY 495	Duple	46852	C29F	5/49	Northern Roadways Ltd, Glasgow (LK)
107035	GDL 75	Duple	48857	C29F	5/49	Moss Motor Tours (Sandown, I.W.) Ltd (IW)
107043	IF-16-04	Martins & Caetano		B29D	5/50	União de Satão e Aguiar de Beira, Satão (O-P) 16
107047 *	HOD 121	Duple	54290	C29F	5/49	Southern National, Exeter (DN) 581

107056 *	NPC 430	Mulliner	T416	B28F	6/49	AT Brady {Brown Motor Services}, Forest Green (SR)
107063						Exported to Mombasa (O-EAK)
107068	GSG 410	Duple	54288	C29F	5/49	St Cuthbert's Co-operative Association Ltd, Edinburgh (MN) 11
107075 *	HOD 122	Duple	54291	C29F	5/49	Southern National, Exeter (DN) 582
107103						Exported to Mombasa (O-EAK)
107109	LHN 967	Duple	50715	C29F	5/49	Scurr's Motor Services Ltd, Stillington (DM)
107118	EEA 480	Duple	47778	C29F	5/49	Hills Tours Ltd, West Bromwich (ST) 17
107122						Exported to Copenhagen (O-DK)
107133	HWW 580	Duple	50632	C29F	4/49	FW Balme {Balme's Coaches}, Otley (WR)
107139	KMN 532	Duple	51116	C29F	1/49	J McMullin {Mayflower}, Douglas (IM)
107147						Exported to Izmir (O-TR)
107153	ABR 752	Mulliner	T427	B31F	5/49	Cowell Bros, Southwick (DM) 14
107181	?	Duple	52615	B30F	-/--	East African Railways, Dar-es-Salaam (O-EAT)
107187	LHN 966	Mulliner	T421	B31F	5/49	Trimdon Motor Services Ltd, Trimdon Grange (DM) 56
107196						Exported to Alexandria (O-ET)
107200	SO 8770	Duple	54293	C29F	-/49	AJ Hay, Elgin (MR)
107249 - 107260						Exported to Melbourne (O-AUS)
107451	FUN 570	Mulliner	T419	B28F	5/49	Mrs E Williams {Williams & Hodson}, Marchwiel (DH)
107458	ERP 922	Duple	44770	C29F	6/49	Royal Blue Coach & Transport Ltd, Pytchley (NO)
107463						Exported to Kingston (O-JA)
107471	LHN 965	Mulliner	T417	B31F	5/49	EG James & RW Mosley {Croft Spa Motor Services}, Croft Spa (NR)
107502	?	Duple	52614	B30F	-/--	East African Railways, Dar-es-Salaam (O-EAT)
107505	?	?		van	-/--	GJ Bentley, London E17 (GLN)
107514	?	?		lorry	-/--	Peter Walker & Son (Warrington & Burton) Ltd (brewers), Warrington (GCH)
107518						Exported to Alexandria (O-ET)
107529	DNL 601	Mulliner	T418	B30F	5/49	Bedlington & District Luxury Coaches Ltd, Ashington (ND)
107536	JNY 918	Mulliner	T422	B31F	6/49	Mrs V Williams {Richmond}, Neath (GG)
107542						Exported to Izmir (O-TR)
107549	UMP 82	Duple	44053	C29F	5/49	Essex County Coaches Ltd, London E15 (LN)
107579	?	Duple	52617	B30F	-/--	East African Railways, Dar-es-Salaam (O-EAT)
107583	?	?		van	-/--	Perry Wig, Lowestoft (GSK)
107592	KRO 511	Duple	44038	C29F	-/49	Brunt's Coaches Ltd, Bell Bar (HT)
107596						Exported to Alexandria (O-ET)
107607	?	?		van	-/--	Wright Bros, Birkenhead (GCH)
107614	FAJ 851	Duple	52153	C29F	6/49	AW Robinson {Ryedale Motor Services} , Pickering (NR)
107620						Exported to Alexandria (O-ET)
107627	KGT 898	Duple	50254	C29F	5/49	V Bingley (Bingley Bros) {Sceptre Coaches}, London W6 (LN)
107655	UMP 96	Duple	52421	C29F	-/--	Fox & Hart Ltd {Hounslow Star Coaches}, Hounslow (MX)
107661	FAW 532	Duple	49227	C29F	5/49	Salopia Saloon Coaches Ltd, Whitchurch (SH) 70
107670	UMP 832	Duple	54337	C29F	5/49	H Burch, Harrow Weald (MX)
107674						Exported to Alexandria (O-ET)
107685	?	Duple	52618	B30F	-/--	East African Railways, Dar-es-Salaam (O-EAT)
107692 *	FWV 427	Duple	46483	C29F	6/49	PJ & D Card, Devizes (WI)
107699	?	?			-/--	KLM, Amsterdam (O-NL)
107705 *	HOD 128	Duple	54292	C29F	5/49	Southern National, Exeter (DN) 583
107733	JNY 766	Duple	54080	C29F	5/49	FR Williams {Victoria Motorways}, Treorchy (GG)
107741 *	LHY 923	Duple	44171	C29F	5/49	Wessex Coaches Ltd, Bristol (GL)
107748	VML 301	Duple	54358	C29F	4/49	George Wimpey (contractor), London W6
107753	?	Duple	52630	B30F	-/--	Shell Petroleum Co, unknown overseas location
107763	DRD 820	Duple	44505	C29F	5/49	AE Smith {Smith's Coaches}, Reading (BE)
107770	FWV 424	Duple	54105	C29F	5/49	AH Razey {Amport & District Motor Services}, Thruxton (HA)
107776	?	Duple	52631	B30F	-/--	Shell Petroleum Co, unknown overseas location
107783 *	LHY 922	Duple	44170	C29F	5/49	Wessex Coaches Ltd, Bristol (GL)
107849 - 107860						Exported to Bombay (O-IND)
108003	VML 949	Duple	54359	C27F	-/--	Frames Tours Ltd, London WC1 (LN) 78
108009 *	MBH 88	Duple	?	C29F	6/49	A Hudson Ltd, Bicester (OX)

108018 *	LKO 209	Duple	49998	C29F	5/49	Sidcup Coaches & Removals Ltd, Sidcup (KT)
108022						Exported to Alexandria (O-ET)
108033	DDB 959	Duple	52491	C29F	6/49	A Lloyd {County Motor Services}, Stockport (CH)
108040	FDM 695	Mulliner	T423	B30F	6/49	W Bellis & Son, Buckley (FT)
108046						Exported to Alexandria (O-ET)
108053	UMP 80	Duple	44051	C29F	5/49	Essex County Coaches Ltd, London E15 (LN)
108080	?	?		l/stock	-/--	HG Ivory, Harpenden (GHT)
108086	LKN 941	Duple	47935	C29F	6/49	Carey Bros, New Romney (KT)
108095 *	CRN 417	Duple	54385	C29F	5/49	Scout MS Ltd, Preston (LA)
108096		see 108095				
108099	?	Mulliner		B--F	-/--	Shell Petroleum Co, La Concepcion (O-YV)
108111	LTO 715	Duple	46202	C29F	7/49	JC & TA Makemson {Makemson Bros}, Bulwell (NG)
108118	ONO 84	Duple	54306	C29F	6/49	Eastern National, Chelmsford (EX) 4063
108124						Exported to Alexandria (O-ET)
108131	DFV 175	Duple	54342	C29F	6/49	Marshall & Son (Blackpool) Ltd (LA)
108161	DJT 241	Duple	44261	C29F	6/49	SC Sheasby {South Dorset Coaches}, Corfe Castle (DT)
108165	VML 976	Duple	54360	C29F	-/--	Frames Tours Ltd, London WC1 (LN) 79
108174	JRT 41	Mulliner	T424	B28F	6/49	S & V Foreman, Orford (EK)
108178	?	Mulliner		B--F	-/--	Shell Petroleum Co, Lagunillas (O-YV)
108189	TMY 719	Duple	43927	C29F	6/49	Valliant Direct Coaches Ltd, London W5 (LN)
108196	VML 977	Duple	54361	C29F	-/--	Frames Tours Ltd, London WC1 (LN) 80
108202	?	Mulliner		B--F	-/--	Shell Petroleum Co, Casigua (O-YV)
108209 *	FAJ 872	Duple	54339	C29F	3/49	Begg's Luxury Coaches Ltd, Thornaby-on-Tees (NR)
108226	KGT 895	Duple	50237	C29F	6/49	AC Coaches Ltd, London SE15 (LN)
108235	?	Mulliner		B--F	-/--	Shell Petroleum Co, Casigua (O-YV)
108239	LKO 239	Mulliner	T425	B28F	7/49	AE, RW & GT Gillie {A Gillie & Sons}, Aylsham (KT)
108247	BGV 719	Duple	44338	C29F	6/49	GF Burgoin (Haverhill) Ltd {Grey Pullman Coaches} (WF)
108276	?	Duple	52620	B30F	-/--	East African Railways, Dar-es-Salaam (O-EAT)
108282	SB 7779	Duple	54419	C29F	6/49	West Coast Motor Service Co, Campbeltown (AL)
108291	ECX 566	Duple	54362	C29F	6/49	Hanson's Buses Ltd, Huddersfield (WR) 272
108295	?	Mulliner		B--F	-/--	Shell Petroleum Co, Casigua (O-YV)
108306	UMP 81	Duple	44052	C29F	-/49	Essex County Coaches Ltd, London E15 (LN)
108312	FSR 333	Duple	54294	C29F	5/49	J Fearn, Kirriemuir (AS)
108317						Exported to Alexandria (O-ET)
108332	NPC 214	Duple	44420	C29F	6/49	GF & BS Graves {GF Graves & Son}, Redhill (SR)
108354	?	Duple	52619	B30F	-/--	East African Railways, Dar-es-Salaam (O-EAT)
108360	DNL 580	Duple	44118	C29F	6/49	R Armstrong, Westerhope (ND) 71
108369	FAW 531	Mulliner	T428	B31F	6/49	Salopia Saloon Coaches Ltd, Whitchurch (SH) 69
108373						Exported to Alexandria (O-ET)
108384	GDL 102	Duple	52482	C29F	6/49	B Groves, Cowes (IW)
108388 *	DTL 965	Mulliner	T420	B31F	9/49	WH Patch (Cream Bus Service), Stamford (KN) 17
108397						Exported to Alexandria (O-ET)
108560	BEB 121	Duple	43322	C29F	6/49	JR Morley & Sons Ltd, Whittlesey (CM)
108588	?	Duple	52621	B30F	-/--	East African Railways, Dar-es-Salaam (O-EAT)
108594 *	4426	Mulliner	T384	B28F	7/49	Sarre Transport Ltd, St Peter Port, Guernsey (CI) 21
108603	KGN 435	Duple	49982	B27F	6/49	Metropolitan Police, London SW1 (XLN)
108607						Exported to Alexandria (O-ET)
108618	FAW 994	Duple	49226	C29F	6/49	RB & R Charles (Charles Bros) {Charles Motor Services}, Cleobury Mortimer (SH)
108625	ACC 88	Duple	49225	C29F	6/49	I Jones & TH Davies {Deiniolen Motors}, Deinolen (CN)
108631						Exported to Alexandria (O-ET)
108638	KAH 535	Duple	49886	C29F	6/49	RT & TH Houchen, Dersingham (NK)
108666						Exported to Mombasa (O-EAK)
108741	ONO 85	Duple	54307	C29F	6/49	Eastern National, Chelmsford (EX) 4064
108746	JNY 771	Mulliner	T429	B31F	6/49	AE & FR Brewer {Brewer's Motor Services}, Caerau (GG)
108753	UMP 520	Duple	48188	C29F	6/49	Batten's Coaches Ltd, London E6 (LN)
108757	SB 7709	Duple	54305	C29F	6/49	C Fitzpatrick {Azure Blue Line}, Dunoon (AL)
108764	ONO 86	Duple	54308	C29F	6/49	Eastern National, Chelmsford (EX) 4065
108769						Exported to Alexandria (O-ET)
108773	?	Mulliner		B--F	-/--	Shell Petroleum Co, Maracaibo (O-YV)
108779	HNP 736	Duple	49853	C29F	6/49	CW Shuker {Lady Edith}, Halesowen (WO)

C1252/140

108782	?	Rocklyn		T---	-/--	Rocklyn Transport, Belleplaine (O-BDS)
108784	FBL 401	Duple	44489	C29F	6/49	Tom Tappin Ltd {Travel Rambler}, Wallingford (BE)
108787 *	FFW 397	Mulliner	T426	B31F	3/50	Enterprise (Scunthorpe) Passenger Services Ltd {Enterprise} (LI) 99
108791						Exported to Alexandria (O-ET)
108819	DNL 690	Duple	51049	C29F	6/49	A Atkinson, Morebattle (RH)
108824	?	?		van	8/49	Parker Knoll Ltd (furniture), High Wycombe (GBK)
108827	?	Mulliner		B--F	-/--	Shell Petroleum Co, Maracaibo (O-YV)
108830 *	HOD 53	Duple	54309	C29F	6/49	Western National, Exeter (DN) 564
108834	ECX 599	Duple	54420	C29F	6/49	Hanson's Buses Ltd, Huddersfield (WR) 273
108839						Exported to Lagos (O-WAN)
108841	KTF 235	Duple	54511	C29F	7/49	R & E Park (Morecambe) Ltd {Rambler} (LA) 2
108848 *	KGY 200	Duple	52426	C29F	6/49	George Ewer & Co Ltd {Grey Green}, London N16 (LN)
108857						Exported to Alexandria (O-ET)
108862	JDD 612	Duple	52516	C29F	6/49	Warner's Motors Ltd, Tewkesbury (GL)
108866						Exported to Alexandria (O-ET)
108872 *	HOD 54	Duple	54310	C29F	6/49	Western National, Exeter (DN) 565
108900 *	KPT 472	Duple	54102	C29F	6/49	J Iveson & Son, Esh (DM)
108901 - 108912						Exported to Melbourne (O-AUS)
109100	OPU 853	Duple	49066	C29F	7/49	CJ Warsley {Brownie Saloon Coaches}, London E9 (LN)
109101		see 109102				
109102	TMY 720	Duple	47921	C29F	3/50	Hunt & West {Safeway}, Walthamstow, London E17 (LN)
109108						Exported to Colombo (O-CL)
109112	?	?		?	5/49	Heaton, St Helens (GLA)
109119	FNT 88	Duple	49228	C29F	7/49	TH & T Hyde {T Hyde & Son}, Welsh Frankton (SH)
109123	?	Mulliner		B--F	-/--	Shell Petroleum Co, Casigua (O-YV)
109133 *	FFW 182	Duple	54311	C29F	7/49	Lincolnshire RCC, Bracebridge Heath (KN) 728
109137	?	Mulliner		B--F	-/--	Shell Petroleum Co, Casigua (O-YV)
109170	FBL 515	Mulliner	T452	B28F	6/49	Bray Transport Ltd, Bray-on-Thames (BE)
109175	MHN 255	Mulliner	T433	B30F	-/49	Percival Bros (Coaches) Ltd, Richmond (NR)
109180	FFW 224	Duple	44788	C29F	6/49	E & F Adams {E Adams & Son}, Saltfleet (LI)
109184	CRN 440	Duple	54412	C29F	6/49	E Barnes {Premier Motors}, Preston (LA)
109190	GMJ 667	Duple	44455	C29F	6/49	A Draper {Royal Blue Motor Coaches}, Luton (BD)
109209	VML 988	Duple	48229	C29F	-/48	Pall Mall Car Hire {Pamalhire}, London SW1 (LN)
109213	?	Mulliner		B--F	-/--	Shell Petroleum Co, Casigua (O-YV)
109216 *	FAJ 874	Duple	44456	C29F	4/49	J & J Boddy (Boddy's Motors), Bridlington (ER)
109220	?	Mulliner		B--F	-/--	Shell Petroleum Co, Casigua (O-YV)
109248	JLJ 127	Duple	44833	C29F	6/49	Shamrock & Rambler Motor Coaches Ltd, Bournemouth (HA)
109253	GDK 810	Duple	51355	C29F	6/49	John Boyd Motors Ltd, Manchester (LA)
109258	MHN 81	Mulliner	T431	B31F	6/49	J Jewitt & Son, Spennymoor (DM)
109262 *	FFW 398	Mulliner	T430	B31F	8/50	Enterprise (Scunthorpe) Passenger Services Ltd {Enterprise} (LI) 101
109268	CGS 339	Mulliner	T453	B31F	7/49	Achnasheen Hotel Co Ltd, Achnasheen (RY)
109275	KGT 610	Mulliner	T283	B31F	8/49	London County Council (XLN) 1599
109279	?	Mulliner		B--F	-/--	Shell Petroleum Co, Casigua (O-YV)
109281	EF 8891	Mulliner	T432	B31F	6/49	Richardson Bros, West Hartlepool (DM)
109289	GDT 255	Duple	50555	C29F	6/49	NC & E Sykes {Atlas}, Camblesforth (WR)
109295	KYD 815	Duple	46494	C27F	6/49	Osmond's Tours & Engineering Co Ltd {Curry Queen}, Curry Rivel (SO)
109330						Exported to Colombo (O-CL)
109335	JLJ 128	Duple	44834	C29F	6/49	Shamrock & Rambler Motor Coaches Ltd, Bournemouth (HA)
109342						Exported to Alexandria (O-ET)
109347	FUN 562	Duple	54104	C29F	6/49	Hancocks (Old Colwyn) Ltd {Royal Blue} (DH)
109362 *	FFW 183	Duple	54312	C29F	7/49	Lincolnshire RCC, Bracebridge Heath (KN) 729
109368	FFW 437	Mulliner	T434	B31F	6/49	WK Harsley {Excelsior Coaches}, Scotter (LI)
109374	KGT 611	Mulliner	T333	B31F	7/49	London County Council (XLN) 1600
109380	KGT 612	Mulliner	T332	B31F	5/49	London County Council (XLN) 1601
109455						Exported to Alexandria (O-ET)
109569 - 109580						Exported to Melbourne (O-AUS)
109677	EET 951	Duple	51037	C27F	6/49	W Gordon & Sons, Rotherham (WR)

109682	FWV 429	Mulliner	T455	B30F	9/49	G Keen {Enterprise}, Heddington (WI)
109686						Exported to Kingston (O-JA)
109693	PV 9371	Duple	48307	C27F	7/49	EJ Mulley {Mulley's Motorways}, Ixworth (WF) 26
109708 *	KTE 951	Duple	54521	C29F	7/49	J Lamb, Upholland (LA)
109714	UMP 531	Duple	46853	C29F	6/49	Northern Roadways Ltd, Glasgow (LK)
109720	JM 8477	Duple	54297	C29F	6/49	S Mitchell & Son, Kendal (WT)
109726 *	KAH 949	Duple	54313	C29F	7/49	Eastern Counties, Norwich (NK) BS949
109748		see 109758				
109758 *	NBB 171	Duple	50113	C29F	5/49	R Tait, Kirkwhelpington (ND)
109764	FBU 376	Duple	49697	C29F	6/49	Joseph Dyson Ltd {Broadway Motors}, Oldham (LA)
109768	?	Mulliner	B---		-/--	Kuwait Oil Co (O-KWT)
109775	?	?		prison	-/--	Metropolitan Police, London SW1 (GLN)
109790	?	?		goods	8/50	E & A Ward, London SW16 (GLN)
109798	CBV 618	Duple	50977	C29F	6/49	J Benson (Motors) Ltd {Eagle Coaches}, Oswaldtwistle (LA)
109802	KAH 950	Duple	54314	C29F	7/49	Eastern Counties, Norwich (NK) BS950
109808	JUF 808	Duple	52477	C29F	7/49	HK Hart {Alpha Coaches}, Brighton (ES)
109846	JXW 862	Duple	52650	B30F	-/49	AERE, Harwell (GOV)
109850	?	Mulliner		B--F	-/--	Shell Petroleum Co, Maracaibo (O-YV)
109857	JXW 863	Duple	52651	B30F	-/49	Ministry of Supply (GOV)
109872	JXW 870	Duple	52652	B30F	-/49	Ministry of Supply (GOV)
109878	JXW 872	Duple	52654	B30F	-/49	Ministry of Supply (GOV)
109884	JXW 865	Duple	52653	B30F	-/49	Ministry of Supply (GOV)
109890	?	?		lorry	-/--	Malmesbury & Parsons Dairies Ltd, Bournemouth (GHA)
109928	FJF 663	Duple	48305	C29F	6/49	J Smith, Leicester (LE)
109939	KKH 293	Duple	49831	C29F	6/49	DW Burn, H Tyler & EG Russell {Grey de Luxe}, Kingston-upon-Hull (ER)
109954	?	?		van	-/--	Wright Bros, Birkenhead (GCH)
109960	DFV 242	Duple	54452	C29F	6/49	Lansdowne Motors Ltd, Fleetwood (LA)
109966	SS 7237	Duple	54296	C29F	6/49	JB Stark, Dunbar (EL)
109972	KGY 199	Duple	44535	C29F	6/49	Fallowfield & Britten Ltd, London E8 (LN)
110133 - 110144						Exported to Bombay (O-IND)
110228	?	?		l/stock	-/--	TY Wightman, Grantshouse (GBW)
110230	C-17727	Jensen		B29-	12/49	Johan Carlsen, Seterstøa st. (O-N)
110238 *	FFW 309	Duple	54512	C29F	5/50	Enterprise (Scunthorpe) Passenger Services Ltd {Enterprise} (LI) 147
110252	FBX 54	Duple	51401	C29F	6/49	TS Jenkins, Llanelly (CR)
110258	GED 256	?		lorry	1/50	Peter Walker & Son (Warrington & Burton) Ltd (brewers), Warrington (GCH)
110264	KRO 517	Duple	43489	C29F	6/49	J Maidment Ltd, Hitchin (HT)
110270	CJL 647	Duple	54100	C29F	6/49	HH Milson, Coningsby (LI)
110304	CMS 316	Duple	54226	C29F	6/49	W Alexander, Falkirk (SN) W238
110308	SJ 1082	Duple	54298	C29F	8/49	D Stewart {Stewart's Motors}, Corriecravie, Arran (BU)
110316	K-8268	Gumpen		B---	9/49	AS Kvina Bilselskap, Kvina (O-N)
110318	BEP 157	Duple	49229	C29F	6/49	CJ Ballard {Wilson's Coaches}, Welshpool (MO)
110334	UMP 522	Duple	48321	C29F	-/--	Dicks, London NW10 (LN)
110340	?			prison	-/--	Metropolitan Police, London SW1 (GLN)
110346	GUK 657	Duple	50789	C29F	7/49	Worthington Motor Tours Ltd, Birmingham (WK)
110352	JP 7941	Pearson		C28F	10/49	E & T Eaves {Eavesway Tours}, Ashton-in-Makerfield (LA)
110392	FJU 810	Duple	52349	C29F	6/49	W Housden, Loughborough (LE) 5
110396	?			prison	-/--	Metropolitan Police, London SW1 (GLN)
110401	NPE 380	Mulliner	T456	B28F	10/49	Mrs AA Charman {Felday Coaches}, Ockley (SR)
110412	?	Mulliner		B---	-/--	Kuwait Oil Co (O-KWT)
110416	KRR 297	Duple	49484	C24F	6/49	Barton Transport, Chilwell (NG) 533
110422	GDL 137	Duple	43628	C29F	6/49	Seaview Services Ltd, Seaview (IW) 11
110427	FWN 795	Mulliner	T435	B28F	8/49	M, DT & I Davies {Thomas Davies & Sons}, Glyn Neath (GG)
110434	KAH 951	Duple	54315	C29F	7/49	Eastern Counties, Norwich (NK) BS951
110468						Exported to Trinidad
110472	?	?		prison	-/--	Metropolitan Police, London SW1 (GLN)
110476	?	Mulliner		B---	-/--	Kuwait Oil Co (O-KWT)
110483	UMP 697	Duple	48263	C29F	-/--	FR Harris {Harris's Coaches}, Grays (EX)

C1252/141

110498	?	?		prison	-/--	Metropolitan Police, London SW1 (GLN)
110503	KGY 252	Mulliner	T334	B31F	8/49	London County Council (XLN) 1603
110509	LRL 660	Duple	52473	C29F	7/49	Willis (Central Garage) Ltd, Bodmin (CO)
110515	?	?		prison	3/50	Metropolitan Police, London SW1 (GLN)
110556	NPE 376	Mulliner	T454	B28F	8/49	LW Bowser Ltd, Sundridge (KT)
110560	KGY 251	Mulliner	T335	B31F	6/49	London County Council (XLN) 1602
110566	LYA 166	Duple	54139	C29F	7/49	TE Herring {W Herring & Son}, Burnham-on-Sea (SO)
110575	?	Duple	52632	B28F	-/--	Shell Petroleum Co, unknown overseas location
110580	AEJ 145	Mulliner	T437	C28F	8/49	WE Lloyd (WE Lloyd & Son) {Glan Teify Bus Services}, Pontrhydfendigaid (CG)
110586	MUG 344	Duple	50652	C29F	8/49	Kelsall Coaches Ltd {Saffman & Beasley}, Leeds (WR)
110592	LKO 520	Duple	47947	C29F	7/49	PG Warren, Ticehurst (ES)
110598	EKG 702	Duple	54081	C29F	by7/49	EC Paramore {Reliance Saloon Car Service}, Cardiff (GG)
110634						Exported to Barbados
110638	JAD 832	Mulliner	T365	B28F	3/49	HJ Flint, Nettleton (WI)
110642	?	Mulliner		B--F	-/--	Shell Petroleum Co, La Concepcion (O-YV)
110649	KFM 432	Duple	54319	C29F	6/49	Crosville MS, Chester (CH) SL33
110662	DUD 762	Duple	44905	C29F	7/49	J Tanner, Sibford Gower (OX)
110668	KGY 253	Mulliner	T336	B31F	7/49	London County Council (XLN) 1604
110674	KPT 646	Duple	44604	C29F	6/49	G Pennington {Cosy Coaches/Meadowfield Motor Co}, Meadowfield (DM)
110680	KFM 433	Duple	54320	C29F	6/49	Crosville MS, Chester (CH) SL34
110932	?	Mulliner		B--F	-/--	Shell Petroleum Co, Lagunillas (O-YV)
110936 *	KNC 297	Duple	52492	C29F	7/49	J Stubbs {Empress Coaches}, Manchester (LA)
110940 *	FBL 677	Mulliner	T458	B31F	7/49	Brookhouse-Keene {Cody Coaches}, Binfield (BE)
110947 *	BGV 782	Duple	48189	C29F	-/50	Corona Coaches Ltd, Acton (WF) 24
110960	KAH 952	Duple	54316	C29F	7/49	Eastern Counties, Norwich (NK) BS952
110966	KKC 10	Duple	50970	C29F	8/49	C James {James Motor Garage}, Liverpool (LA)
110972 *	GDL 153	Duple	54324	C29F	7/49	Southern Vectis, Newport (IW) 218
110978	NS 2283	Duple	54560	C29F	9/49	P Burr, Tongue (SU)
111015	EU 9833	Duple	54525	C29F	7/49	T Rees (Rees Motors) {Reliance Motors}, Llanelly Hill (BC)
111018						Exported to unknown overseas location
111029	VML 989	Duple	48230	C29F	-/--	Pall Mall Car Hire {Pamalhire}, London SW1 (LN)
111042	KGY 255	Mulliner	T338	B31F	6/49	London County Council (XLN) 1605
111048	LRL 941	Duple	49373	C29F	6/49	FJ Skinner & Sons Ltd, Millbrook (CO)
111054	KAH 953	Duple	54317	C29F	7/49	Eastern Counties, Norwich (NK) BS953
111060 *	GUS 494	Mulliner	T462	B31F	6/49	SCWS Ltd {Smith's Motor Service}, Barrhead (RW)
111096	?	Mulliner		B--F	-/--	Shell Petroleum Co, Lagunillas (O-YV)
111110	FO 5731	Duple	52517	C29F	8/49	CT Sargeant {Sargeant's Motors}, Builth Wells (RR)
111111	FPY 228	Duple	51176	C29F	7/49	Hardwick's Services Ltd, Snainton (NR)
111119	FBD 200	Duple	46574	C29F	6/49	York Bros (Northampton) Ltd (NO) 24
111124	GDK 852	Duple	50261	C27F	7/49	Yelloway Motor Services Ltd, Rochdale (LA)
111130	BCH 280	Duple	54092	C29F	7/49	W Boyden, Castle Donington (LE)
111136	KTJ 236	Mulliner	T459	B31F	7/49	WT Taylor {Chortex}, Horwich (XLA)
111142	JXX 466	Duple	52658	B30F	-/--	Ministry of Supply (GOV)
111176	JXX 464	Duple	52657	B30F	12/49	AWRE, Aldermaston (GOV)
111181	?	Mulliner		B--F	-/--	Shell Petroleum Co, Lagunillas (O-YV)
111187	JXX 461	Duple	52656	B30F	-/49	Ministry of Supply (GOV)
111194	?	Duple	50797	B31F	-/--	Original operator unknown (O-SUD)
111206	?	Duple	52659	B30F	-/49	Ministry of Supply (GOV)
111215	?	Duple	52635	B30F	-/49	Original operator unknown (O-ET)
111218	JXX 460	Duple	52655	B30F	11/49	AERE, Harwell (GOV)
111224	KGN 436	Duple	49983	B27F	7/49	Metropolitan Police, London SW1 (XLN)
111258	DUD 810	Duple	44759	C29F	6/49	House Bros (Watlington) Ltd (OX)
111263	DUD 755	Duple	44603	C29F	7/49	EHA Oliver, Long Hanborough (OX)
111275	HYG 23	Duple	54527	C29F	9/49	Bolton-by-Bowland Motor Services Ltd (LA)
111288	UHX 131	Duple	52043	C25F	7/49	BEA, Ruislip (MX) 11..
111293						Exported to Alexandria (O-ET)
111304	?	Mulliner	T460	?	6/49	WT Taylor {Chortex}, Horwich (XLA)
111306	SB 8023	Mulliner	T457	B31F	1/50	J & H Caskie, Bowmore, Islay (AL)
111338		see 100169				
111342	MHN 192	Duple	50694	C29F	7/49	F Lockey & Son, St Helens Auckland (DM)

C1252/143

111345	SJ 1288	Mulliner	T463	B31F	8/49	Gordon Bros {Gordon's Motors}, Lamlash (BU)
111356						Exported to Lagos (O-WAN)
111370	?	Mulliner	T467	?	7/49	Sir Robert McAlpine & Sons Ltd (contractor), London W1
111375	?	Mulliner		B---	-/--	Kuwait Oil Co (O-KWT)
111382	KFM 434	Duple	54321	C29F	7/49	Crosville MS, Chester (CH) SL35
111388 *	SS 7245	Mulliner	T461	B31F	6/49	TW Wiles, Port Seton (EL)
111401 - 111406						Exported to Melbourne (O-AUS)
111407	sa30.223	Syd Wood		B41F	-/--	Original operator unknown (O-AUS)
111408 - 111412						Exported to Melbourne (O-AUS)
111666 *	v1.599	?		C29F	-/--	Martello Motors, Morrinsville (O-NZ) 2
111679	JDD 680	Duple	54450	C29F	8/49	AW Gillett {Gillett's Coaches}, Winchcombe (GL)
111691	KAH 954	Duple	54318	C29F	7/49	Eastern Counties, Norwich (NK) BS954
117000 #	HDK 60	Trans-United		C27F	11/49	W Johnson & Sons, Shaw (LA)
111704	DCL 804	Duple	47679	C29F	8/49	RG Brown {Broadland Luxury Coaches}, Norwich (NK)
111709	?	Mulliner		B---	-/--	Kuwait Oil Co (O-KWT)
111716	FUN 661	Duple	49230	C29F	7/49	F Crawford, Pentre Broughton (DH)
111722	NPD 271	Duple	43476	C29F	7/49	Cooke's Coaches (Stoughton) Ltd (SR) 17
111754						Exported to Burutu (O-WAN)
111761	FBL 756	Duple	44602	C29F	7/49	L Stevens, Charney Bassett (BE)
111773	KMN 533	Duple	51117	C29F	1/49	Crennell's Garage Ltd, Ramsey (IM)
111779	FJU 817	Duple	46720	C29F	6/49	A Adams (Adams & Sons) {Blue Bird}, Market Harborough (LE)
111786	KFM 435	Duple	54322	C29F	7/49	Crosville MS, Chester (CH) SL36
111791	?	Mulliner		B---	-/--	Kuwait Oil Co (O-KWT)
111797	DJT 376	Duple	54270	C27F	7/49	F Budden {Blue Line}, Pamphill (DT)
111804 *	LYA 231	Duple	43260	C29F	6/49	Western Engineering & Motor Services {WEMS}, Weston-super-Mare (SO) 4
111836	?	Duple	50798	B31F	-/--	Original operator unknown (O-SUD)
111843	FNT 89	Duple	49231	C29F	7/49	WH & W Lowe (JE Lowe & Sons) {Tulip Coaches}, Hadley (SH)
111855	KFM 436	Duple	54323	C29F	7/49	Crosville MS, Chester (CH) SL37
111861	GWS 139	Duple	54299	C29F	7/49	Reid & Mackay, Edinburgh (MN)
111868	JOP 710	Duple	44619	C29F	7/49	W & WJ Meddings {Yardley Coaches}, Birmingham (WK)
111873	?	Duple	52633	B31F	-/--	Shell Petroleum Co, unknown overseas location
111879	VML 302	Duple	54565	C29F	7/49	George Wimpey (contractor), London W6
111886	DTL 772	Duple	54084	C29F	7/49	Delaine Coaches Ltd, Bourne (KN) 28
111918	DNL 676	Duple	54103	C29F	7/49	JH Batty & Sons {Wansbeck Motor Services}, Ashington (ND)
111925	FPY 296	Duple	50572	C29F	7/49	R Kennedy & W Norman {Maureen Coaches}, North Ormesby (NR)
111937	HCG 946	Duple	46616	C29F	7/49	Liss & District Omnibus Co Ltd, Liss (HA) 157
111943	KRO 689	Duple	54236	C29F	7/49	H Monk, Bishop's Stortford (HT)
111950 *	ONO 89	Duple	54530	C29F	7/49	Eastern National, Chelmsford (EX) 4068
111955	?	Mulliner		B--F	-/--	Shell Petroleum Co, Lagunillas (O-YV)
111968	KGY 266	Mulliner	T352	B31F	7/49	London County Council (XLN) 1608
112001	NPD 239	Duple	46506	C29F	7/49	HR Richmond {Epsom Coaches}, Epsom (SR)
112006	FJU 950	Duple	54563	C29F	7/49	AA Oliver {Luxicoaches}, Loughborough (LE)
112011	KGY 53	Duple	44857	C29F	7/49	Cliff's Saloon Coaches Ltd, London SE9 (LN)
112019	?	Mulliner	T468	B--F	8/49	Sir Robert McAlpine & Sons Ltd (contractor), London W1
112024	HWD 978	Duple	48058	C29F	7/49	J Lloyd & Son Ltd, Nuneaton (WK)
112032 *	ONO 88	Duple	54529	C29F	7/49	Eastern National, Chelmsford (EX) 4067
112033		see 112640				
112037	?	Mulliner		B--F	-/--	Shell Petroleum Co, La Concepcion (O-YV)
112046	?	Mulliner		B--F	-/--	Shell Petroleum Co, La Concepcion (O-YV)
112050	ONO 87	Duple	54528	C29F	7/49	Eastern National, Chelmsford (EX) 4066
112080	?	Duple	52660	B30F	-/49	Ministry of Supply (GOV)
112089	?	Duple	52661	B30F	-/49	Ministry of Supply (GOV)
112097	?	Duple	52664	B30F	-/49	Ministry of Supply (GOV)
112245 - 112256						Exported to Melbourne (O-AUS)
112295	HHO 164	Duple	54687	C29F	8/49	Hants & Sussex Motor Services Ltd, Emsworth (HA)

159

C1252/144

112305	JXX 470	Duple	52662	B30F	12/49	Ministry of Supply (GOV)
112316	?	Duple	52663	B30F	-/49	Ministry of Supply (GOV)
112324	?	Mulliner		B--F	-/--	Shell Petroleum Co, La Concepcion (O-YV)
112354	LKR 32	Duple	47999	C29F	8/49	Craker Southland Coaches Ltd, Bromley (KT) 10
112363	HCG 947	Duple	49999	C29F	7/49	Hants & Sussex Motor Services Ltd, Emsworth (HA) 158
112371	GUS 247	Duple	54564	C29F	8/49	SCWS Ltd, Glasgow (LK)
112377	JAO 380	Duple	54300	C29F	8/49	E Thomas, Dearham (CU)
112387 *	HUY 97	Duple	47637	C29F	8/49	Samuel Johnson (Supreme) Ltd, Stourbridge (WO)
112392	FJB 64	Duple	48281	C29F	8/49	TH Clare {Eagle Coaches}, Faringdon (BE)
112398	FNT 449	Duple	49233	C29F	7/49	JT, FW & GE Whittle {JT Whittle & Sons}, Highley (SH)
112436 *	KNC 385	Duple	49706	C29F	8/49	J & G Finch (Newton Heath) Ltd (LA)
112445	FFW 185	Duple	54532	C29F	7/49	Lincolnshire RCC, Bracebridge Heath (KN) 731
112453	KGY 264	Mulliner	T438	B31F	7/49	London County Council (XLN) 1606
112459	LTA 86	Duple	46946	C29F	7/49	RJC Coombe {The Devon Touring Co}, Torquay (DN)
112469	UHX 286	LCMW		B26R	2/50	Middlesex County Council (XMX)
112474	KGY 265	Mulliner	T439	B31F	7/49	London County Council (XLN) 1607
112480 *	FFW 184	Duple	54531	C29F	7/49	Lincolnshire RCC, Bracebridge Heath (KN) 730
112488	Z-12273	?		B---	12/49	David Skjelbred, Kodal (O-NL)
112518	HWY 637	Duple	46788	C29F	7/49	F & A Wigmore {Excelsior}, Dinnington (WR)
112527	CRN 501	Duple	54688	C29F	7/49	Scout MS Ltd, Preston (LA)
112535	CRN 502	Duple	54702	C29F	3/50	Scout MS Ltd, Preston (LA)
112541	KNG 83	Duple	43552	C29F	9/49	W Carter, Marham (NK)
112551	LTV 21	Duple	54082	C29F	8/49	A Skill {Skill's Coaches}, Nottingham (NG) 21
112558	BVV 239	?		van	6/50	Jeffrey Sons & Co Ltd, Northampton (GNO)
112562	JDF 306	Mulliner	T478	B28F	9/49	SK & F Silvey {Silvey's Coaches}, Epney (GL)
112567	MHT 597	Duple	44231	C27F	8/49	H Russett {Royal Blue}, Bristol (GL)
112600	JTG 129	Duple	54145	C29F	5/49	LJ Summers, Gorseinon (GG)
112609 *	KTJ 201	Duple	52493	C29F	8/49	Greenacre's Transport Ltd, Leigh (LA)
112617	JTG 280	Duple	54076	C29F	8/49	LH Starkey, Ton Pentre (GG)
112623	FBX 240	Duple	54480	C29F	8/49	Precelly Motors Ltd, Clynderwen (CR)
112633	CGS 285	Duple	54301	C29F	8/49	JAT Docherty {Midland Coaches}, Auchterarder (PH)
112638	KGY 268	Mulliner	T440	B31F	7/49	London County Council (XLN) 1610
112640 *	JXW 858	Duple	?	B30F	-/49	Ministry of Supply (GOV)
112652	D-14852	Jensen		B28-	3/50	Magnus Tomterstad, Kirkenær (O-N)
112682						Exported to Mombasa (O-EAK)
112691	KGY 267	Mulliner	T441	B31F	7/49	London County Council (XLN) 1609
112699	KRR 631	Duple	43944	C29F	6/49	R Wain, Mansfield (NG)
112837	BGV 845	Duple	54251	C29F	8/49	WT Norfolk, Nayland (WF)
112847	GDL 193	Duple	54411	C29F	8/49	C Read {Grey & Red Coaches}, Ryde (IW)
112852	UHX 102	Duple	44656	C29F	8/49	T Gibson {Lily Coaches}, London N9 (LN)
112866	CRN 504	Duple	54704	C29F	9/49	Scout MS Ltd, Preston (LA)
112896	KGY 57	Duple	50271	C29F	8/49	R, RG & T Warner {T Warner & Sons}, Milford (SR)
112905	SB 7799	Duple	54690	C27F	8/49	Air Industrial Developments Ltd {Gold Line}, Dunoon (AL)
112913						Exported to Mombasa (O-EAK)
112920 *	HOD 130	Duple	54534	C29F	8/49	Southern National, Exeter (DN) 585
112929	CRN 503	Duple	54703	C29F	10/49	Scout MS Ltd, Preston (LA)
112934						Exported to Colombo (O-CL)
112937	EF 8983	Duple	50690	C29F	8/49	Richardson Bros, West Hartlepool (DM)
112943	LTA 169	Duple	54505	C27F	8/49	AW Burfitt & WRP Lewis {Blue Coaches}, Ilfracombe (DN)
112948	?	Duple	50790	B31F	-/49	Iraq Petroleum Co, Tripoli (O-LAR)
112978 *	HOD 131	Duple	54533	C29F	8/49	Southern National, Exeter (DN) 586
112987						Exported to Colombo (O-CL)
112995	KGY 270	Mulliner	T443	B31F	8/49	London County Council (XLN) 1612
113001	DFV 456	Duple	54689	C29F	8/49	Whittaker Bros (Blackpool) Ltd (LA)
113011	HHO 346	Duple	46617	C29F	8/49	Liss & District Omnibus Co Ltd, Liss (HA) 160
113016	KGY 269	Mulliner	T442	B31F	8/49	London County Council (XLN) 1611
113025 *	KJJ 516	Duple	52427	C29F	8/49	George Ewer & Co Ltd {Grey Green}, London N16 (LN)
113060 *	KUR 510	Duple	50326	C29F	8/49	Brunt's Coaches Ltd, Bell Bar (HT)
113069	FBD 211	Duple	43976	C29F	8/49	KW Services Ltd, Daventry (NO) B7
113077	KUR 123	Duple	54338	B32F	8/49	JR Street, Hertford (HT)
113083	?	Duple	50796	B26F	-/--	Anglo Iranian Oil Co, location unknown (O-IR)

C1252/145

113093	FNT 593	Duple	49232	C29F	8/49	JW, WHF & GW Lloyd, Oswestry (SH) 7
113098 *	UMP 699	Duple	51170	C29F	-/49	Essex County Coaches Ltd, London E15 (LN)
113347	KUP 10	Duple	50067	C29F	8/49	Bowser's Coaches Ltd, Washington (DM)
113382 *	HOD 129	Duple	54535	C29F	8/49	Southern National, Exeter (DN) 584
113391	HWU 996	Duple	50605	C29F	8/49	H Murgatroyd & Son, Thruscross (WR)
113399	?	Duple	52622	B30F	-/--	East African Railways, Dar-es-Salaam (O-EAT)
113405	KAH 956	Duple	54537	C29F	8/50	Eastern Counties, Norwich (NK) BS956
113415	KJJ 314	Mulliner	T447	B31F	7/49	London County Council (XLN) 1613
113420	KJJ 317	Mulliner	T444	B31F	7/49	London County Council (XLN) 1616
113429	UMP 416	Duple	44789	C29F	-/--	EA & ER Webber (Webber Bros) {Empire's Best}, London N22 (LN) 21
113434	?	Duple	50791	B31F	-/--	Iraq Petroleum Co, Tripoli (O-LAR)
113467	KJJ 318	Mulliner	T445	B31F	7/49	London County Council (XLN) 1617
113472	KJJ 315	Mulliner	T448	B31F	8/49	London County Council (XLN) 1614
113480						Exported to Mauritius
113486	KJJ 316	Mulliner	T449	B31F	7/49	London County Council (XLN) 1615
113496	KAH 955	Duple	54536	C29F	7/49	Eastern Counties, Norwich (NK) BS955
113501	UMP 532	Duple	46854	C29F	-/49	Northern Roadways Ltd, Glasgow (LK)
113509	VML 401	Duple	48231	C29F	-/--	Pall Mall Car Hire {Pamalhire}, London SW1 (LN)
113515						Exported to Alexandria (O-ET)
113546	HUE 911	Duple	48087	C29F	9/49	Wainfleet Motor Services Ltd, Nuneaton (WK)
113555	KPX 600	Duple	54696	C29F	9/49	CF Wood & Son Ltd {Enterprise Coaches}, Steyning (WS)
113563						Exported to Mauritius
113569	BKS 97	Duple	54304	C29F	8/49	M Moore, Jedburgh (RH)
113579						Exported to Mombasa (O-EAK)
113584	KSM 142	Duple	54303	C29F	9/49	J Bell {Bell's Coaches}, Langholm (DF)
113593	KJJ 319	Mulliner	T446	B31F	7/49	London County Council (XLN) 1618
113598	?	Mulliner	T469	?	7/49	Sir Robert McAlpine & Sons Ltd (contractor), London W1
113637	CRN 505	Duple	54705	C29F	9/49	Scout MS Ltd, Preston (LA)
113645						Exported to Mombasa (O-EAK)
113651	VML 290	Mulliner	T470	?	7/49	Sir Robert McAlpine & Sons Ltd (contractor), London W1
113661	FBL 779	Duple	54335	C27F	8/49	JC Chastell & DG Gray {The Dean Bus Service}, Cookham Dean (BE)
113666	HWY 682	Duple	54365	C29F	8/49	Ripponden & District Motors Ltd (WR)
113674	DFK 148	?		van	10/49	F Winwood Ltd, Worcester (GWO)
113680	E-6400	Lillehammer		B29C	11/49	Håkon Kristiansen, Lillehammer (O-N)
113701 - 113712						Exported to Sydney (O-AUS)
113861 #	GUK 135	Mulliner	SP330	C28F	1/50	Worthington Motor Tours Ltd, Birmingham (WK)
113940	UHX 191	Duple	52422	C29F	8/49	Fox & Hart Ltd {Hounslow Star Coaches}, Hounslow (MX)
113947						Exported to Colombo (O-CL)
113955	CRN 506	Duple	54716	C29F	3/50	Scout MS Ltd, Preston (LA)
113961	UHX 833	Duple	44771	C29F	8/49	Universal Coaches Ltd, London N9 (LN)
113971	?	?		prison	-/--	Metropolitan Police, London SW1 (GLN)
113976	UHX 430	Duple	52089	C29F	-/49	Venture Transport (Hendon) Ltd, London NW2 (LN)
113984	?	?		van	-/--	FG Alexander, London N21 (GLN)
114023						Exported to Colombo (O-CL)
114028	SB 7809	Duple	54691	C27F	7/49	Air Industrial Developments Ltd {Gold Line}, Dunoon (AL)
114037	?	?		library	-/--	Nottingham City Council (GNG)
114044	?	?		van	-/--	Lush & Cook Ltd (dyers), London E9 (GLN)
114053	?	Duple	52623	B30F	-/--	East African Railways, Dar-es-Salaam (O-EAT)
114058	SY 9207	Duple	54223	C29F	9/49	Fred Allan & Son, Dalkeith (MN)
114066	KAH 957	Duple	54538	C29F	8/50	Eastern Counties, Norwich (NK) BS957
114072	R-1047	Seim		B24C	5/50	Norheimsruta, location unknown (O-N)
114104	?	?		library	-/--	Derbyshire County Council (GDE)
114111	KOD 965	Duple	54113	C27F	8/49	T & W Parker {Blue Coaches}, Ilfracombe (DN)
114122	?	Mulliner		?	-/--	Original operator unknown (O-EAK)
114125	KXW 164	?		prison	4/50	Metropolitan Police, London SW1 (GLN)
114135	HC 9888	Duple	51323	C29F	9/49	RL & PJ Jackson {Palmerston Coaches}, Eastbourne (ES) 9

C1252/146

114140	?	?	van		-/--	R Davies Haulage Ltd, London E14 (GLN)
114148	JDD 920	Duple	54715	C29F	8/49	PA Grindle {Forest Greyhound}, Cinderford (GL)
114186 *	HOD 132	Duple	54539	C29F	8/49	Southern National, Exeter (DN) 587
114193	?	Mulliner		?	-/--	Original operator unknown (O-EAK)
114198	EX 6757	Duple	44922	C29F	8/49	Reynolds Garage Ltd {Metropolitan Coaches}, Great Yarmouth (NK)
114206						Exported to Mauritius
114210 *	GDL 226	Duple	52479	B30F	8/49	MJ Wavell {Enterprise Bus Service}, Newport (IW)
114217	FCO 111	Mulliner	T412	B28F	8/49	Heybrook Bay Motor Services Ltd, Down Thomas (DN)
114222	LTA 697	Duple	47871	C29F	8/49	A Turner, Chulmleigh (DN)
114230	ETP 806	Duple	54750	C29F	9/49	The Don Motor Coach Co Ltd, Southsea (HA)
114236	?	Duple	50792	B---	-/49	Iraq Petroleum Co, Tripoli (O-LAR)
114269						Exported to Mauritius
114275	GWS 463	Duple	54731	C29F	8/49	Edinburgh Corporation (MN) X2
114283 *	FNR 237	Duple	54730	C29F	8/49	AW & JW Farrow (AW Farrow & Son), Melton Mowbray (LE)
114289	HOY 263	Mulliner	T482	B31F	-/50	Bethlehem Royal Hospital, Shirley (XSR)
114299	DJT 995	Duple	46249	C29F	10/49	RW Toop, WJ Ironside & PW Davis {Bere Regis & District}, Dorchester (DT)
114304 *	DTY 19	Mulliner	T464	B28F	9/49	T Ord & Son, Alnwick (ND)
114318	?	Duple	50795	B---	-/49	Iraq Petroleum Co, Tripoli (O-LAR)
114351	?	Mulliner		B--F	-/--	Shell Petroleum Co, unknown overseas location
114365 *	HOD 133	Duple	54540	C29F	8/49	Southern National, Exeter (DN) 588
114371	UMP 698	Duple	47986	C29F	-/49	Unique Hire Service Ltd, London E10 (LN)
114381	FNT 851	Duple	49234	C29F	9/49	D & J Gittins, Crickheath (SH)
114391	EBW 49	Duple	51398	C29F	9/49	GH Dix, Freeland (OX)
114400	?	Duple	50793	B---	-/49	Iraq Petroleum Co, Tripoli (O-LAR)
114473 - 114484						Exported to Melbourne (O-AUS)
114539	KJJ 738	Duple	44826	C27F	8/49	HJ Phillips & Sons Ltd, London SW11 (LN) 1002
114547	?	Mulliner		?	-/--	Original operator unknown (O-EAK)
114555	CRN 438	Duple	54738	C29F	8/49	W Tuer {Tuer's Motors}, Morland (CU)
114565	MKX 427	Duple	46515	C29F	9/49	CJ Payne (CJ Payne & Son), Buckingham (BK)
114573	?	Mulliner		?	-/--	Original operator unknown (O-EAK)
114582	MUG 868	Duple	50545	C29F	-/49	Wallace Arnold Tours Ltd, Leeds (WR)
114622						Exported to Mauritius
114626	CGS 423	Duple	54751	C20F	9/49	Loch Katrine Steamboat Co Ltd, Callander (PH)
114632	JXX 473	Duple	52665	B30F	-/49	Ministry of Supply (GOV)
114636	JXX 475	Duple	52667	B28F	-/49	Ministry of Supply (GOV)
114640	JXX 487	Duple	52668	B30F	1/50	Ministry of Supply (GOV)
114650	?	Duple	50794	B---	-/49	Iraq Petroleum Co, Tripoli (O-LAR)
114654						Exported to Mauritius
114657	JXX 4--	Duple	52669	B30F	-/49	Ministry of Supply (GOV)
114664	JXX 474	Duple	52666	B30F	-/49	Royal Ordnance Factory, Chorley (GOV)
114671						Exported to Alexandria (O-ET)
114678	DST 478	Mulliner	T477	B31F	12/49	J Morrison, Leverburgh, Harris (IV)
114787 *	HOD 134	Duple	54541	C29F	8/49	Southern National, Exeter (DN) 589
114793	LKP 835	Mulliner	T474	B28F	8/49	G Alderson & Son, Brasted (KT)
114797						Exported to Karachi (O-PK)
114801 #	FNT 861	Duple	49235	C29F	8/49	WR & T Hoggins (WR Hoggins & Sons) {Pilot}, Wrockwardine Wood (SH)
114809						Exported to Alexandria (O-ET)
114812	SMK 294	Mulliner	T473	B--F	9/49	Truman, Hanbury & Buxton Co Ltd (Brewers), London N1 (XLN)
114818						Exported to Karachi (O-PK)
114825	FBU 493	Duple	54366	C29F	10/49	Shearings Tours Ltd, Oldham (LA)
114832						Exported to Alexandria (O-ET)
114870	NRB 122	Duple	47927	C29F	9/49	Sharpe Brothers (Beighton) Ltd (DE)
114876	KVO 148	Duple	49485	C24F	9/49	Barton Transport, Chilwell (NG) 534
114880	KAH 958	Duple	54542	C29F	8/50	Eastern Counties, Norwich (NK) BS958
114886						Exported to Karachi (O-PK)
114890	FUN 939	Mulliner	T476	B28F	9/49	E & C Wright {E Wright & Son}, Penycae (DH)
114903	KPT 903	Mulliner	T475	B28F	c7/49	GH, S & JB Atkinson (GH Atkinson & Sons) {General Omnibus Services}, Chester-le-Street (DM) 20
114907						Exported to Karachi (O-PK)

C1252/147

114914	DTY 225	Mulliner	T472	B28F	8/49	F Wright, Rothbury (ND)
114921	K-8138	OCA		B28FV	11/49	Olav G Osen {Osenruta}, Sira (O-N)
114928	KJJ 518	Duple	44536	C27F	9/49	Fallowfield & Britten Ltd, London E8 (LN)
114965	GWS 464	Duple	54732	C29F	8/49	Edinburgh Corporation (MN) X9
114971	?	?		library	-/--	Nottingham City Council (GNG)
114975						Exported to Karachi (O-PK)
114979	MUG 869	Duple	50546	C29F	-/49	Wallace Arnold Tours Ltd, Leeds (WR)
114983	S-61	?		B19-	11/49	Original operator unknown (O-N)
115073 - 115084						Exported to Melbourne (O-AUS)
115181	LMN 261	Duple	51118	C29F	7/49	TW Bryan (E Bryan) {Tynwald Ms}, Douglas (IM) 2
115184	FPY 559	Duple	44881	C29F	-/49	Saltburn Motor Services Ltd, Saltburn (NR) 12
115187						Exported to Karachi (O-PK)
115190	O-662	Arna		B---	6/50	Drosjebilcentralen, Bergen (O-N)
115197	ACC 238	Duple	44775	C29F	9/49	J Williams & Son {Red Garage}, Portmadoc (CN) Gwydyr Castle
115234						Exported to Mombasa (O-EAK)
115240	JTG 933	Duple	54717	B30F	10/49	Mrs ES Patey, Tonyrefail (GG)
115245	EVD 683	Duple	54752	C29F	-/49	P & T Tennant, Forth (LK)
115248	DPR 477	Lee		C29F	1/50	RW Toop, WJ Ironside & PW Davis {Bere Regis & District}, Dorchester (DT)
115252	T-2519	?		B---	-/50	Eira Auto, Nesset (O-N)
115259	UHX 429	Duple	46855	C29F	-/49	Northern Roadways Ltd, Glasgow (LK)
115265						Exported to Mombasa (O-EAK)
115272	?	?		library	-/--	Derbyshire County Council (GDE)
115279	W-8302	?		B---	11/49	Original operator unknown (O-N)
115286	GUS 949	Duple	54755	C29F	9/49	SCWS Ltd, Glasgow (LK)
115323						Exported to Mombasa (O-EAK)
115329	KUP 153	Duple	50115	C29F	9/49	GH, S & JB Atkinson (GH Atkinson & Sons) {General Omnibus Services}, Chester-le-Street (DM) 21
115333						Exported to Mauritius
115337	KNG 492	Duple	44300	C29F	9/49	W Kent & Sons, Aldborough (NK)
115341						Exported to Rotterdam (O-NL)
115348 *	MHT 672	Duple	44172	C29F	8/49	Wessex Coaches Ltd, Bristol (GL)
115354	HHO 324	Duple	46563	C29F	c8/49	DG Grace {Graceline Coaches}, Alresford (HA)
115361	HTM 368	Duple	54283	C29F	1/50	Marston Valley Brick Co (XBD)
115368	?	Mulliner		B--F	-/--	Basra Petroleum Co (O-IRQ)
115375	KUP 107	Mulliner	T479	B31F	8/49	W Emmerson {OK Motor Services}, Bishop Auckland (DM)
115412						Exported to Mauritius
115418	CGS 566	Duple	54762	C29F	8/49	DC Smail {James Smail}, Blairgowrie (PH)
115422	LTV 522	Duple	48078	C29F	9/49	A Skill {Skill's Coaches}, Nottingham (NG) 22
115425	KUR 857	Thurgood	596	C29F	9/49	CW Jones {Enterprise Bus Service}, Kimpton (HT)
115432	?	Mulliner		B--F	-/--	Basra Petroleum Co (O-IRQ)
115437	EU 9895	Mulliner	T486	B30F	8/49	E & TW Jones (J Jones & Sons), Ystradgynlais (BC)
115443	KND 445	Duple	49694	C29F	9/49	F & H Dean Ltd, Newton Heath (LA)
115450	?	Mulliner		B---	-/--	Original operator unknown (O-WAN)
115457	?	Duple	52640	B30F	-/49	Kuwait Oil Co (O-KWT)
115464	PV 9636	Duple	43984	C29F	9/49	P & M Coaches Ltd, Ipswich (WF) 42
115645						Exported to Lagos (O-WAN)
115651	HWX 212	Mulliner	T481	B31-	9/49	Cementation Co Ltd, Bentley (XWR)
115655	BCP 368	Duple	51187	C29F	9/49	Bottomley's Motors (Huddersfield) Ltd (WR)
115663	?	Duple	52641	B30F	-/49	Kuwait Oil Co (O-KWT)
115670	EDP 95	Duple	44506	C29F	9/49	AE Smith {Smith's Coaches}, Reading (BE)
115676	KFM 840	Duple	54547	C29F	11/49	Crosville MS, Chester (CH) SL40
115683	KFM 838	Duple	54545	C29F	11/49	Crosville MS, Chester (CH) SL38
115690	V-2158	?		B---	12/49	Original operator unknown (O-N)
115697	KUR 238	Duple	50277	C29F	9/49	EG Hewitt {Premier Coaches}, Watford (HT)
115734	?	Mulliner		?	-/--	Original operator unknown (O-WAN)
115740	LYB 121	Mulliner	T483	B31F	9/49	Quantock Hauliers Ltd, Watchet (SO)
115744	?	?		h/box	-/--	E Sunley & Son Ltd, London W1 (GLN)
115748 *	OPA 112	King & Taylor		C29F	3/50	Hutchinson {Woodside Coaches}, London SE25 (LN)
115752	S-1986	?		B---	6/50	L/L Nordfjord og Sunnmøre Billag (O-N)
115759	OPA 113	King & Taylor		C29F	3/50	Hutchinson {Woodside Coaches}, London SE25 (LN)
115765	KLB 491	Duple	54826	C27F	9/49	WF Butler {Sydenham Coaches}, London SE26 (LN)

115772	UMY 853	Duple	52086	C29F	-/--	D Evans {Maroon Coaches}, London E18 (LN)
115779	T-1031	Ødegård		B26C	5/50	Stranda og Sykkylven Billag, Stransa (O-N)
115786	PEV 885	Duple	46244	C29F	3/50	J Jarvis {Rayleigh Grey}, Rayleigh (EX)
115823						Exported to Karachi (O-PK)
115829 *	FFW 186	Duple	54548	C29F	9/49	Lincolnshire RCC, Bracebridge Heath (KN) 732
115833	GYS 708	Duple	52230	C27F	9/49	Lowland Motorways Ltd, Glasgow (LK) 8
115837 *	KND 569	Mulliner	T511	C28F	3/50	Brierley Bros (Transport) Ltd, Salford (LA)
115841	T-1040	Ødegård		B27C	2/49	Knut Græsdal, Skodje (O-N)
115848 *	FFW 187	Duple	54549	C29F	9/49	Lincolnshire RCC, Bracebridge Heath (KN) 733
115854 *	JOP 626	Duple	47771	C29F	9/49	Eatonways Ltd, Birmingham (WK)
115870	LTT 44	Mulliner	T485	B28F	9/49	Balls Ltd, Newton Abbot (DN) 5
115872	T-5927	?		B20FV	2/50	Surnadal Billag NS, Surnadal (O-N) 27
115875	MHN 442	Duple	54727	C29F	9/49	H Featherstone {Prospect Services}, Bishop Auckland (DM)
115948						Exported to Karachi (O-PK)
115954	SRF 234	Duple	52347	C29F	9/49	Mrs A Lymer {Victoria Tours}, Tean (ST)
115958	GCJ 969	Duple	54482	C29F	8/49	WE Morgan {Wye Valley Motors}, Hereford (HR)
115962	GAM 477	Duple	44291	C29F	9/49	AW Haddrell {AW Haddrell & Sons}, Calne (WI)
115966	?	Duple	52642	B30F	-/49	Kuwait Oil Co (O-KWT)
115973	DHV 216	Duple	44886	C29F	9/49	JW Armstrong & C Downey {Silvertown Coaches}, London E16 (LN)
115979	MKX 322	Duple	54742	C29F	9/49	Mrs HV Wall, Kingsey (BK)
115986	UHX 269	Duple	50000	C29F	7/49	H & G Beach, Staines (MX)
115993						Exported to Alexandria (O-ET)
116000	JHP 193	Duple	54896	C29F	4/49	H & H Motorways Ltd {Bunty}, Coventry (WK)
116032	HHO 698	Duple	46432	C29F	9/49	FH Kilner (Transport) Ltd, Horsham (WS) 161
116045	GWS 465	Duple	54733	C29F	9/49	Edinburgh Corporation (MN) X18
116053	KGU 666	Duple	49984	B27F	12/49	Metropolitan Police, London SW1 (XLN)
116065	CBV 857	Duple	50978	C29F	10/49	W Barnes Ltd, Rishton (LA)
116075	NPG 948	Duple	50284	C29F	10/49	Ben Stanley Ltd, Hersham (SR)
116085	?	?		I/stock	-/--	Marsh & Baxter Ltd (wholesale meat suppliers), Brierly Hill (GST)
116089						Exported to Alexandria (O-ET)
116261						Exported to Karachi (O-PK)
116271	NRB 262	Duple	54875	C29F	10/49	GH Watson, Church Gresley (DE)
116278	CGS 572	Duple	54894	C20F	9/49	Loch Katrine Steamboat Co Ltd, Callander (PH)
116291	FBD 788	Mulliner	T488	B28F	9/49	WR Lawrence, Wappenham (NO)
116295	FBX 535	Mulliner	T501	B30F	10/49	DS Davies {Red & Green}, New Inn (CR)
116301 *	HUY 655	Duple	49921	C29F	9/49	FJ Ketley, Stourport-on-Severn (WO)
116311 *	LWJ 679	Duple	54700	C29F	9/49	Law Bros Ltd, Sheffield (WR)
116315						Exported to Alexandria (O-ET)
116357	GVJ 41	Mulliner	T487	B28F	9/49	EJ Parfitt {Parfitt's Motor Services}, Rhymney Bridge (MH)
116367	SW 7944	Mulliner	T490	B28F	9/49	J Davidson, Auchencairn (KK)
116375	JTG 622	Mulliner	T494	B31F	9/49	AE & FR Brewer {Brewer's Motor Services}, Caerau (GG)
116386	ECX 983	Duple	50414	C29F	9/49	Hanson's Buses Ltd, Huddersfield (WR) 274
116397	MHU 193	Mulliner	T492	B31F	9/49	Clifton College, Bristol (XGL) 6
116407	HYG 911	Mulliner	T496	C29F	9/49	John Smith (Brewers), Tadcaster (XWR) 10
116411						Exported to Alexandria (O-ET)
116446	GAM 338	Duple	54876	C27F	10/49	AH Daniels, Winsley (WI)
116456	MAF 446	Duple	54462	C29F	10/49	GG Warren, St Ives (CO)
116464 *	AGR 174	Mulliner	T497	B28F	9/49	G Bridges, Sunderland (DM)
116475	MHN 509	Mulliner	T498	B28F	9/49	Summerson Bros {The Eden}, West Auckland (DM)
116486 *	HUY 856	Duple	47638	C29F	9/49	Samuel Johnson (Supreme) Ltd, Stourbridge (WO)
116496	HOD 55	Duple	54551	C29F	9/49	Western National, Exeter (DN) 566
116500	?	Duple	52643	B30F	-/--	Kuwait Oil Co (O-KWT)
116535						Exported to Karachi (O-PK)
116541	UHX 306	Strachan		C29F	-/--	FG Wilder {Golden Miller Coaches}, Feltham (MX)
116545	HOD 56	Duple	54552	C29F	9/49	Western National, Exeter (DN) 567
116553	LKT 824	Duple	44621	C27F	9/49	GR Ayers, Dover (KT)
116564	EN 9871	Duple	54904	C29F	10/49	Auty's Tours Ltd, Bury (LA)
116575	HOD 135	Duple	54550	C29F	9/49	Southern National, Exeter (DN) 590
116588						Exported to Izmir (O-TR)

C1252/149

116590	KTJ 720	Duple	54883	C29F	10/49	WA Smith, Tottington (LA)
116624						Exported to Mombasa (O-EAK)
116630	UMY 193	Strachan		C29F	11/49	Margo's (Bexleyheath) Ltd (LN)
116634	GCY 153	Duple	48272	C29F	10/49	DH Selby & E Jones, Port Talbot (GG)
116642	BEE 551	Duple	44988	C29F	2/50	A & AE Blackbourn Ltd {Granville Tours}, Grimsby (LI) 154
116653	HBT 584	Duple	49838	C29F	9/49	H, N & A Giles, RA Falkingham and F Danby {Giles Bros}, Withernsea (ER)
116664	UHX 712	Duple	46390	C29F	-/50	TG Green {Empress Motor Coaches}, London E2 (LN)
116674	SY 9249	Duple	54884	C29F	9/49	WD Tod, Mid Calder (MN)
116678						Exported to Izmir (O-TR)
116893 *	HOD 70	Duple	54553	C29F	10/49	Western National, Exeter (DN) 591
116903	EBW 299	Strachan		C29F	11/49	EHA Oliver, Long Hanborough (OX)
116911	KFM 841	Duple	54557	C29F	11/49	Crosville MS, Chester (CH) SL41
116921	HDA 109	Duple	54899	C29F	10/49	RHJ Salisbury (Salisbury Bros) {Blackhawk Coaches}, Darlaston (ST)
116933	SRF 212	Duple	46500	C29F	9/49	WS Rowbotham, Harriseahead (ST) 3
116943 *	KAH 938	Duple	54784	B30F	10/49	Eastern Counties, Norwich (NK) B938
116947	?	Duple	52644	B30F	-/49	Kuwait Oil Co (O-KWT)
116982	CRN 712	Duple	54900	C29F	10/49	G Clayton & N Murray (Clayton & Murray) {Majestic Motors}, Preston (LA)
116992	FUN 955	Duple	43993	C29F	9/49	Mrs D Challoner, Moss (DH)
117000	HDK 60	Trans-United		C27F	11/49	AB & H Johnson, Shaw (LA)
117011	AGR 416	Pearson		C28F	-/--	Close, Wilks & Barnfather, High Pittington (DM)
117022	DPR 667	Lee		C29F	1/50	Mrs AM Macklin {Antelope Tours}, Sherborne (DT)
117032	ADJ 778	Duple	50958	C29F	10/49	T Glover, Haydock (LA)
117036	?	Mulliner		B--F	-/--	Basra Petroleum Co (O-IRQ)
117071	MUM 276	Duple	50547	C29F	-/49	Wallace Arnold Tours Ltd, Leeds (WR)
117081	DST 528	Mulliner	T495	B31F	10/49	Ardgour & Acharacle Motor Services Ltd, Fort William (IV)
117089	FUJ 131	Duple	43227	C29F	9/49	Jones Coachways Ltd, Market Drayton (SH) 33
117100	FDM 914	Mulliner	T499	B28F	10/49	W Bellis & Son, Buckley (FT)
117111 *	LMN 361	Pearson		C26F	8/49	GC Gale {Gale's Western Motors}, Peel (IM)
117121	CCF 11	Pearson		C28F	12/49	RW Richardson & HE Rawlinson {Burton Coaches}, Haverhill (SK)
117125						Exported to Rotterdam (O-NL)
117160	BKS 179	Mulliner	T500	B28F	11/49	TM Anderson {Anderson's Bus Service}, Bonchester Bridge (RH)
117170	GWN 220	Mulliner	T493	C29F	6/50	TJ Short, Morriston (GG)
117179	KFM 842	Duple	54558	C29F	11/49	Crosville MS, Chester (CH) SL42
117189	UMY 82	Mulliner	T489	B31F	-/--	Middlesex County Council (XMX)
117200	JRT 913	Mulliner	T502	B31F	9/49	RO Simonds, Botesdale (EK)
117210	LTU 670	Duple	54367	C29F	1/50	R Bullock & Co (Transport) Ltd, Cheadle (CH)
117214	?	Duple	52645	B30F	-/49	Kuwait Oil Co (O-KWT)
117245						Exported to Suva (O-FJI)
117249 *	EBW 124	Duple	46248	C29F	10/49	AR Taylor, Bicester (OX) 4
117259	SY 9265	Duple	54897	C29F	9/49	Pentland Garage Ltd, Loanhead (MN)
117267 *	NBB 828	Duple	54522	C29F	9/49	Moordale Bus Services Ltd, Newcastle (ND) 10
117278	MAF 811	Duple	49368	C27F	10/49	Mrs A Fry, Tintagel (CO)
117289 *	FFW 188	Duple	54707	C29F	5/50	Lincolnshire RCC, Bracebridge Heath (KN) 734
117299 *	FFW 189	Duple	54706	C29F	6/50	Lincolnshire RCC, Bracebridge Heath (KN) 735
117483	?	Duple	52646	B30F	-/49	Kuwait Oil Co (O-KWT)
117514	HYG 870	Duple	54922	C29F	5/49	FW Balme {Balme's Coaches}, Otley (WR)
117518 *	ONO 90	Duple	54708	C29F	5/50	Eastern National, Chelmsford (EX) 4069
117528	KFM 843	Duple	54559	C29F	11/49	Crosville MS, Chester (CH) SL43
117536	KLC 250	Duple	44251	C29F	-/49	A Jones {Popular Coaches}, London E14 (LN)
117547 *	AEC 543	Trans-United		C27F	-/51	CA Smith {Silver Badge}, Bowness-on-Windermere (WT)
117558	KJJ 739	Duple	44827	C27F	1/50	HJ Phillips & Sons Ltd, London SW11 (LN) 1003
117568						Exported to Suva (O-FJI)
117572						Exported to Alexandria (O-ET)
117607	?	?		van	-/--	Ferguson Radio Corporation, Enfield (GMX)
117617	?	?		library	-/--	Derbyshire County Council (GDE)
117625	UHX 713	Duple	46978	C29F	-/50	CW Banfield, London SE15 (LN)

C1252/150

117636	?	?		van	-/--	L Wolberg, London N1 (GLN)
117647 *	ONO 91	Duple	54709	C29F	5/50	Eastern National, Chelmsford (EX) 4070
117657	NBB 906	Duple	54873	C29F	10/49	G Galley (Galley's Motors), Newcastle (ND)
117661						Exported to Alexandria (O-ET)
117696	?	?		van	-/--	IWHT Ltd, Sowerby Bridge (GWR)
117706	?	?		van	-/--	FG Alexander, London N21 (GLN)
117714	ONO 92	Duple	54710	C29F	5/50	Eastern National, Chelmsford (EX) 4071
117725	?	?		lorry	-/--	F Handcock & Son, Allendale (?GSN?)
117736	LTT 138	Duple	46955	C29F	9/49	RC & AC Hopkins {Blue Moorland Coaches}, Dawlish (DN)
117745 *	KAH 939	Duple	54785	B30F	10/49	Eastern Counties, Norwich (NK) B939
117750	?	Duple	52648	B30F	-/--	Kuwait Oil Co (O-KWT)
117785	JRM 112	Duple	54915	C26F	10/49	E Hartness {Hartness Bus & Coach Service}, Penrith (CU)
117795	UMY 955	Duple	46856	C29F	10/49	Northern Roadways Ltd, Glasgow (LK)
117803	JNX 197	Duple	54741	C29F	10/49	CC Hill, Studley (WK)
117814	MKE 584	Duple	54443	B30F	11/49	Dartford & Stone Hospital (XKT)
117825	KYH 23	Duple	52428	C27F	3/50	George Ewer & Co Ltd {Grey Green}, London N16 (LN)
117835	HOD 71	Duple	54713	C29F	10/49	Western National, Exeter (DN) 592
117839						Exported to Antwerp (O-B)
117873	?	?		van	-/--	Fisher Filling Station, Birmingham (GWK)
117883	LTB 147	Duple	54914	C29F	10/49	T Holmes, Bamber Bridge (LA)
117891 *	unregd	Duple	55062	C29F	-/49	Vauxhall (experimental vehicle)
118082	HDK 15	Duple	50262	C29F	10/49	Yelloway Motor Services Ltd, Rochdale (LA)
118093	KUP 234	Duple	54726	C29F	10/49	M Harrison & Sons {Cream Coaches}, Wingate (DM)
118103 *	HOD 72	Duple	54712	C29F	10/49	Western National, Exeter (DN) 593
118107						Exported to Izmir (O-TR)
118143	KFM 844	Duple	54714	C29F	12/49	Crosville MS, Chester (CH) SL44
118149	HER 307	Mulliner	T507	B31F	9/49	E Towgood & Sons Ltd, Sawston (CM)
118153						Exported to Mombasa (O-EAK)
118161 *	LYB 125	Duple	54923	C29F	10/49	BJ Chinn {English Rose Coaches}, Wincanton (SO)
118173 *	MHU 416	Duple	44173	C29F	5/50	Wessex Coaches Ltd, Bristol (GL)
118183	OMX 420	LCMW		B26R	5/50	Middlesex County Council (XMX)
118193						Exported to Izmir (O-TR)
118197	HOD 73	Duple	54711	C29F	10/49	Western National, Exeter (DN) 594
118232						Exported to Mombasa (O-EAK)
118238	CCF 67	Mulliner	T503	B28F	9/49	NS Rule, Boxford (WF)
118242	FUT 362	Thurgood	608	C29F	3/50	AW & JW Farrow (AW Farrow & Son), Melton Mowbray (LE)
118250	LPO 96	Duple	55157	B31F	c1/50	West Sussex County Council (XWS)
118261	SY 9278	Duple	54920	C29F	-/49	W Hunter, Loanhead (MN)
118272	UHX 606	Thurgood	597	C29F	9/49	FE Hughes {Grosvenor Coaches}, Enfield (MX)
118282	?	Duple	52649	B30F	-/--	Kuwait Oil Co (O-KWT)
118286	LMN 546	Mulliner	T509	B31F	4/50	Isle of Man Road Services Ltd, Douglas (IM) 43
118321	JS 8710	Mulliner	T505	B31F	-/50	WD MacKenzie, Garve (RY)
118327	HWO 909	Duple	54086	C29F	10/49	Liberty Motors Ltd, Cardiff (GG) 9
118331	FCO 345	Mulliner	T506	B28F	9/49	Millbrook Steamboat & Trading Co Ltd (CO)
118339	?	?	?	?	10/49	Rapport (wholesaler), Cardiff (GGG)
118350	HOT 810	Duple	46618	C29F	3/50	Liss & District Omnibus Co Ltd, Liss (HA) 162
118362	GBE 128	Mulliner	T508	B31F	10/49	C Bannister {Isle Coaches}, Owston Ferry (LI)
118371	?	Duple	52647	B20F	-/49	Kuwait Oil Co (O-KWT)
118375 *	KUP 240	Duple	44301	C29F	-/49	H Frazer Ltd {Dale Coaches}, Swalwell (DM)
118410	PEV 307	Duple	46219	C29F	12/49	Classique Coaches Ltd, London E10 (LN) 34
118420 *	UMY 170	Duple	55525	C29F	-/--	AE Proctor Ltd, Hanworth (MX)
118428	KGU 667	Duple	49985	B27F	1/50	Metropolitan Police, London SW1 (XLN)
118439	FUJ 221	Duple	49236	C29F	10/49	Salopia Saloon Coaches Ltd, Whitchurch (SH) 74
118450	LTT 690	Duple	46945	C29F	3/50	Falkland Garages Ltd, Torquay (DN)
118460						Exported to Rotterdam (O-NL)
118464	DVL 269	Duple	54866	C29F	10/49	CF Trott, Nettleham (LI)
118499	FET 205	Duple	50630	C29F	10/49	E Brown, Wickersley (WR)
118689	EBW 130	Duple	43883	C29F	10/49	R Jarvis, Middle Barton (OX)
118697 *	JWR 415	Duple	54747	B31F	12/49	Storthes Hall Hospital, Huddesrsfield (XWR)
118699		see 118697				
118708	HWO 910	Duple	54087	C29F	10/49	Liberty Motors Ltd, Cardiff (GG) 10

C1252/151

118719	GVJ 94	Mulliner	T516	B31F	9/49	WE Morgan {Wye Valley Motors}, Hereford (HR)
118729						Exported to Antwerp (O-B)
118733 *	JTX 220	Duple	54721	C29F	4/50	DC Evans {Cyril Evans}, Senghenydd (GG)
118753	?	?	?	?	9/49	Hamlen, Midford (GSO)
118772	UHX 714	Duple	44764	C29F	-/49	J, J, J Jnr & E Clarke {Clarke's Luxury Coaches}, London E16 (LN)
118778 *	GBE 167	Duple	54925	C29F	4/50	Enterprise (Scunthorpe) Passenger Services Ltd {Enterprise} (LI) 148
118786	GDL 366	Duple	43989	C29F	6/50	Shotters Ltd, Brighstone (IW)
118797	EVD 969	Duple	54924	C29F	10/49	Daniel Henderson & Sons, Carstairs (LK)
118809	DFV 663	Duple	54926	C29F	4/50	F Standerwick, Blackpool (LA)
118818						Exported to Alexandria (O-ET)
118822	HNM 348	Duple	50319	C29F	11/49	GE Costin, Dunstable (BD)
118855	KAH 940	Duple	54786	B30F	11/49	Eastern Counties, Norwich (NK) B780
118863	LTT 913	Duple	43367	C29F	10/49	RW Cure {Sunbeam Motor Tours}, Torquay (DN)
118873	CCB 150	Trans-United		FC29F	3/50	Ribblesdale Coachways Ltd, Blackburn (LA) 33
118883	JWR 23	Duple	43954	C29F	10/49	EL Thompson {Advance}, Swinefleet (WR)
118893	FUJ 357	Duple	49237	C29F	10/49	JT, FW & GE Whittle {JT Whittle & Sons}, Highley (SH)
118904	LBP 275	Duple	54695	C29F	c10/49	EJ Carter {Reliance Coaches}, Plummers Plain (WS) 4
118911	?	Mulliner		B--F	-/50	Gibraltar Motor Hire Services (O-GBZ)
118944						Exported to Copenhagen (O-DK)
118952	KVO 494	Duple	49486	C24F	5/50	Barton Transport, Chilwell (NG) 590
118962	KFM 845	Duple	54808	C29F	12/49	Crosville MS, Chester (CH) SL45
118972	UMY 96	Duple	52044	C25F	1/50	BEA, Ruislip (MX) 11..
118982	ECT 190	Duple	54763	C27F	11/49	WH Patch (Cream Bus Service), Stamford (KN) 18
118986	DTY 419	Mulliner	T519	B31F	10/49	AA Hollings {Hollings Garage & Engineering Works}, Wallsend-on-Tyne (ND)
118993	FT 6795	Duple	54771	C29F	-/--	G Chapman {Priory Motor Coach Co}, North Shields (ND) 49
119000						Exported to Piraeus (O-GR)
119033 *	?	?		B24-	-/--	Original operator unknown (O-GR)
119041 *	KYH 22	Duple	52429	C29F	3/50	George Ewer & Co Ltd {Grey Green}, London N16 (LN)
119051	KFM 846	Duple	54809	C29F	12/49	Crosville MS, Chester (CH) SL46
119061	KFM 847	Duple	54810	C29F	12/49	Crosville MS, Chester (CH) SL47
119071	DPR 300	Duple	48258	C29F	10/49	A Pearce & Co, Cattistock (DT)
119075	JTX 177	Duple	54095	C29F	11/49	S Protheroe, Porthcawl (GG)
119082	LTU 727	Duple	55004	C29F	3/50	Watson's (Winsford) Motor Services Ltd (CH)
119089 *	60-155	?		B24-	-/--	Original operator unknown (O-GR)
119301 *	?	?		B24-	-/--	Original operator unknown (O-GR)
119310	DTY 515	Mulliner	T533	B28F	10/49	JH Batty & Sons {Wansbeck Motor Services}, Ashington (ND)
119320	PEV 990	Duple	47599	C29F	3/50	H Monk, Bishop's Stortford (HT)
119330	MHN 592	Mulliner	T522	B31F	10/49	EG James & RW Mosley {Croft Spa Motor Services}, Croft Spa (NR)
119343	SH 8692	Duple	51048	C29F	10/49	Alexander Wait & Sons, Chirnside (BW)
119350	?	?		h/box	-/--	David Brown Tractors Ltd, Huddersfield (GWR)
119353	EEA 830	Duple	47779	C29F	1/50	Hills Tours Ltd, West Bromwich (ST) 18
119358, 119391						Exported to Izmir (O-TR)
119399	?			van	-/--	Joynson, Holland & Co, High Wycombe (GBK)
119409	HBT 880	Plaxton	585	C26F	1/50	E Milburn {Leavening Motor Services}, Leavening (ER)
119419 *	NTN 841	Plaxton	569	FC30F	4/50	G Galley (Galley's Motors), Newcastle (ND)
119429	KXU 775	Duple	54724	C29F	-/50	Cliff's Saloon Coaches Ltd, London SE9 (LN)
119433	JTG 954	Mulliner	T521	B31F	10/49	Afan Transport Co Ltd, Port Talbot (GG)
119440	?	?		h/box	-/--	FL Cunnell, Didcot (GBE)
119447	?	?		?	-/--	M Alajaji & Sons (O-BRN)
119480	?	?		?	-/--	M Alajaji & Sons (O-BRN)
119488	PEV 408	Duple	46206	C29F	1/50	ER, TW & AC Lodge, High Easter (EX)
119498	MHU 603	Mulliner	T515	B31F	10/49	Winford Orthopaedic Hospital, Winford (XSO)
119507	?	?		van	-/--	Flinn & Sons Ltd (dyers), Fishergate (GWS)
119518	HOD 74	Duple	54842	C29F	10/49	Western National, Exeter (DN) 595
119522	JS 8579	Mulliner	T524	B31F	4/50	Galson-Stornoway Motor Services Ltd, Stornoway (RY)
119529	SS 7360	Duple	54987	C29F	10/49	DM Armstrong, Ormiston (EL)
119536, 119569						Exported to Budapest (O-H)
119577	HOD 75	Duple	54844	C29F	10/49	Western National, Exeter (DN) 596

C1252/152

119587	MHU 417	Duple	54911	C27F	10/49	Bristol Corporation (XGL) 860
119596	KPW 176	Duple	46348	C29F	1/50	W Rudling, Shipdham (NK)
119607	HBT 779	Mulliner	T526	?	10/49	TH Freeman & Son Ltd, Brough (ER)
119611	GFY 451	Duple	54878	C29F	10/49	Southport & Birkdale Motor Carriage Co {Gore}, Southport (LA)
119618	NPG 750	Duple	49156	C29F	12/49	Conway Hunt Ltd, Ottershaw (SR)
119625	HB-324	?		B31F	5/50	Niemisen Linjat Oy, Padasjoki (O-FIN)
119658 *	VR 8009	Ørum-Pedersen		B27F	4/50	Hjørring Turistfart, Hjørring (O-DK)
119666	GVJ 190	Duple	54483	C29F	10/49	PHE Tummey {Llangrove Coach Services}, Llangrove (HR)
119676	KUP 481	Mulliner	T543	B28F	10/49	Scurr's Motor Services Ltd, Stillington (DM)
119685	UMY 191	Mulliner	T530	B31F	10/49	Middlesex County Council (XMX)
119697	FJB 267	Duple	54859	C29F	12/49	S Townsend, Crowthorne (BE)
119700	DDO 242	Mulliner	T528	B31F	10/49	CA Sharp, Boston (LI)
119713 - 119724						Exported to Sydney (O-AUS)
119887	JDF 768	Mulliner	T527	B28F	10/49	SK & F Silvey {Silvey's Coaches}, Epney (GL)
119894 *	D-17003	Hainje		B30-	-/49	DABO, Meppel (O-NL) 14
119927						Exported to Rotterdam (O-NL)
119935	MHU 49	Duple	54772	B30F	12/49	Bristol Tramways (GL) 207
119945 *	HRK 76	Duple	54343	C29F	12/49	HV Freemantle & H Dobson {Progress Coaches}, Sanderstead (SR)
119954	LTB 804	Duple	52494	C29F	3/50	T Cunliffe, Heywood (LA)
119965	MKE 126	Mulliner	T491	?	10/49	Leybourne Grange Hospital, West Malling (XKT)
119969 *	GBE 478	Mulliner	T537	B31F	3/50	Enterprise (Scunthorpe) Passenger Services Ltd {Enterprise} (LI) 150
119976	LAL 698	Allsop		FC29F	7/50	LW Evans, East Kirkby (NG)
119983						Exported to Rotterdam (O-NL)
120006 *	?	Van Eck		B32-	-/50	ALAD, Wyken Aalburg (O-NL) 21
120015 *	?	Bochanen		B30-	-/50	Snelle Vliet, Alblasserdam (O-NL) 24
120024 *	VML 334	Duple	55051	C29F	-/49	Wright, Bicester (XOX)
120034 *	EF 9219	Plaxton	568	FC30F	1/50	Bee-Line Continental Tours Ltd, Newcastle (ND)
120044	MHU 50	Duple	54773	B30F	12/49	Bristol Tramways (GL) 208
120054	UHX 715	Duple	47971	C29F	3/50	FWB Smith {Argosy Super Coaches}, London SE15 (LN)
120058	DFV 727	Duple	55029	C29F	2/50	J Abbott & Sons (Blackpool) Ltd (LA)
120065	SRF 852	Duple	49245	C29F	2/50	GH Austin & Sons Ltd {Happy Days}, Stafford (ST) 50
120072						Exported to Rotterdam (O-NL)
120113	GYS 985	Duple	54756	C29F	10/49	SCWS Ltd, Glasgow (LK)
120123	NPG 655	Duple	44460	C26F	11/49	ER Gudge {Comfy Coaches}, Farnham (SR)
120132	?	?		van	-/--	Brittania Wire Works, Whaley Bridge (GDE)
120143	EBL 960	Duple	44450	C29F	10/49	Windsorian Motor Coach Services Ltd, Windsor (BE) 60
120147	KNE 780	Duple	49718	C29F	-/49	C Holt Ltd, Manchester (LA) 13
120154	HHO 855	Duple	47836	C29F	c9/49	Barfoot Bros {Princess Coaches}, Southampton (HA)
120161, 120193						Exported to Rotterdam (O-NL)
120202 *	HOD 76	Duple	54843	C29F	10/49	Western National, Exeter (DN) 597
120212	CGS 766	Mulliner	T523	B28F	11/49	AS & WT Whyte {Bankfoot Motor Co}, Bankfoot (PH)
120221	GEW 874	Duple	43296	C29F	11/49	SV Robinson, Kimbolton (HN)
120232	KGU 668	Duple	49986	B27F	1/50	Metropolitan Police, London SW1 (XLN)
120236	GWS 466	Duple	54734	C29F	11/49	Edinburgh Corporation (MN) X22
120243	MUM 790	Duple	50642	C29F	12/49	TS Heaps & Sons, Leeds (WR)
120250 *	60-783	Tangalakis		B24-	-/--	Original operator unknown (O-GR)
120260		see120250				
120282 *	?	Mantadakis		B24-	-/--	Original operator unknown (O-GR)
120291 *	HOD 77	Duple	54845	C29F	10/49	Western National, Exeter (DN) 598
120481	?	?		van	-/--	Yorks & Lancs Dry Cleaners Co Ltd, York (GWR)
120490	?	?		van	-/--	JW Glass, Liverpool (GLA)
120500	GED 257	?		lorry	1/50	Peter Walker & Son (Warrington & Burton) Ltd (brewers), Warrington (GCH)
120503	HGA 401	Plaxton	586	C29F	11/49	Northern Roadways Ltd, Glasgow (LK)
120510	LTB 453	Duple	55033	C29F	10/49	W Robinson & Sons, Great Harwood (LA) 53
120519 *	GZ-48317	Domburg	164	C34F	2/50	Pool, Amsterdam (O-NL) 6
120551						Exported to Helsinki (O-FIN)
120560	PEV 369	Duple	48769	C29F	2/50	Classique Coaches Ltd, London E10 (LN) 35
120570 *	UMY 560	Duple	52151	C29F	11/49	Gainsborough Coaches Ltd, Stanmore (MX)

C1252/153

120578	HFS 248	Duple	55053	C29F	12/49	St Cuthbert's Co-operative Association Ltd, Edinburgh (MN) 14
120589	DFK 443	Duple	49466	C29F	12/49	Downes (Worcester) Ltd (WO)
120600						Exported to Antwerp (O-B)
120606	FSA 232	Duple	55052	C27F	10/49	N Watt (A Watt & Sons), Tarland (AD)
120609	GBC 777	Crawford, Prince & Johnson		C27F	1/50	AE Hercock, Leicester (LE)
120641						Exported to Antwerp (O-B)
120650	DFV 802	Duple	55166	C29F	3/50	JF Elsworth, Blackpool (LA)
120660	UMY 95	Duple	52229	C29F	11/49	E Curtis & Hearn, London NW7 (LN)
120668 *	HOD 80	Duple	54848	C29F	11/49	Western National, Exeter (DN) 1401
120678	MHU 51	Duple	54774	B30F	12/49	Bristol Tramways (GL) 209
120682	JNX 589	Duple	54860	C29F	11/49	Priory Garage & Coaches Ltd, Leamington Spa (WK)
120689	?	?		van	1/50	New Day Furnishing Stores Ltd, Levenshulme (GLA)
120694	2458	G Zammit		B32F	9/50	Route Bus Service (O-M)
120697, 120730						Exported to Rotterdam (O-NL)
120739 *	JTX 358	Mulliner	T525	B31F	3/50	AE & FR Brewer {Brewer's Motor Services}, Caerau (GG)
120749						Exported to Malta
120757	?	Mulliner	T517	?	11/49	Lappet Manufacturing Co {Lapcol}, Calder Vale (XLA)
120767	DJA 480	Duple	50486	C29F	1/50	R Bullock & Co (Transport) Ltd, Cheadle (CH)
120771 *	GBE 477	Mulliner	T529	B31F	3/50	Enterprise (Scunthorpe) Passenger Services Ltd {Enterprise} (LI) 149
120778	JWR 463	Duple	50364	C29F	11/49	JJ Longstaff, Mirfield (WR)
120783	FUJ 219	Mulliner	T520	B31F	12/49	J & HG Phillips {J Phillips & Son}, Rhostyllen (DH)
120786						Exported to Rotterdam (O-NL)
120819 *	D-17006	Hainje		B29-	-/50	DABO, Meppel (O-NL) 25
120828 *	HOD 78	Duple	54846	C29F	10/49	Western National, Exeter (DN) 599
120838	JDF 737	Mulliner	T532	B31F	11/49	ACJ Perrett {Perrett's Coaches}, Shipton Oliffe (GL)
120846						Exported to Bangkok (O-T)
120856	VML 321	Duple	54870	C29F	11/49	John Laing (contractor), Borehamwood 428
120860	PHK 911	Duple	55061	C29F	3/50	Watson Luxury Coaches, London E13 (LN)
120868	CCF 462	Thurgood	607	C29F	12/49	Corona Coaches Ltd, Acton (WF) 26
120872	GCA 221	Duple	46504	C29F	12/49	JB Pye Ltd, Rhos-on-Sea (DH)
120875, 120908						Exported to Rotterdam (O-NL)
120917	?	?		l/stock	-/--	R Young, Oakham (GRD)
120927	BEE 806	Duple	54901	C29F	1/50	GA Smith, South Thoresby (LI)
120935 *	MHU 915	Mulliner	T531	B30F	4/50	Bristol Tramways (GL) 219
120945	DAG 284	Mulliner	Z38	B31F	-/50	R Taylor & Sons, Douglas (LK)
120955	GCY 363	Mulliner	T536	C29F	-/50	WG Richards, Neath (GG)
120959	FUJ 425	Duple	49244	C29F	-/49	JH Titley & GH Turner, Shrewsbury (SH)
120964	?	Hainje		B29F	-/49	LABO, Leeuwarden (O-NL) 9
121111	GX-17797	Den Oudsten	1816	B30-	3/50	De Harde, Amsterdam (O-NL) 10
121114 *	HOD 79	Duple	54847	C29F	10/49	Western National, Exeter (DN) 1400
121123	EVY 44	Duple	50476	C29F	4/50	RP & LC Gorwood, East Cottingwith (ER)
121132	GBE 509	Duple	55584	C29F	11/49	AE Brown, Caistor (LI)
121142	KAH 941	Duple	54787	B30F	12/49	Eastern Counties, Norwich (NK) B941
121146 *	DHJ 625	Duple	54827	C29F	-/49	Westcliff-on-Sea MS (EX)
121153 *	SS 7376	Duple	54209	C29F	11/49	McKinlay, Prestonpans (XEL)
121161						Exported to Helsinki (O-FIN)
121202 *	60-136	?		B24-	-/--	Original operator unknown (O-GR)
121207	FUJ 564	Duple	49238	C29F	-/49	SC & J Vagg {Vagg's Motors}, Knockin Heath (SH)
121213	DJN 548	Duple	54828	C29F	-/49	Westcliff-on-Sea MS (EX)
121221						Exported to Bangkok (O-T)
121231	FVA 61	Duple	54697	C29F	-/49	DS MacPhail, Newarthill (LK)
121237	MPP 245	Duple	46334	C29F	10/49	JW & RFP Hayfield (Hayfield Bros), Newport Pagnell (BK)
121242	JDG 4	Duple	55585	C29F	11/49	Warner's Motors Ltd, Tewkesbury (GL)
121250 *	61-117	?		B24-	-/--	Original operator unknown (O-GR)
121288	LBP 500	Duple	44873	C29F	c11/49	CF Gates {Silver Queen Coaches}, Worthing (WS)
121291	JTX 36	Duple	48081	C29F	11/49	ME Turner, Gowerton (GG)
121294	A-55140	?		B---	-/49	Original operator unknown (O-N)
121301	GVJ 197	Duple	54485	C29F	12/49	ED, GE & Mrs ME Harrison {Broadway Coaches}, Broadway (WO)

121308	KXV 524	Mulliner	?	-/--	Ministry of Works (GOV)
121316	F-17308	?	B---	12/49	Original operator unknown (O-N)
121324	KXV 518	Mulliner	?	-/--	Ministry of Works (GOV)
121330	KXV 535	Mulliner	?	3/50	Ministry of Works (GOV)
121336	KXV 512	Mulliner	B32F	2/50	Ministry of Works (GOV)
121376	KXV 521	Mulliner	?	2/50	Ministry of Works (GOV)
121380					Exported to Karachi (O-PK)
121383	HX-24154	Bochanen	B30-	-/--	MEGGA, Sliedrecht (O-NL) 20
121390	LYC 10	Mulliner	T534 B29F	12/49	Hutchings & Cornelius Services Ltd {H & C}, South Petherton (SO)
121397	JHP 895	Duple	47996 C29F	4/49	H & H Motorways Ltd {Bunty}, Coventry (WK)
121434 #P.111		RE&C	B33D	-/--	Buses Ltd, Hamilton (O-NZ)
121584					Exported to Rotterdam (O-NL)
121593	DDO 529	Duple	55170 C29F	1/50	RL Cropley {Blue Glider Bus Service}, Sutterton (LI)
121599	MKX 927	Duple	49420 C25F	11/49	Jeffways Coaches & Station Taxis Ltd, High Wycombe (BK)
121605	?	?	h/box	-/--	J & R Mansfield, Ashby-de-la-Zouch (GLE)
121645	TRE 94	Mulliner	T471 DP26F	3/50	RG & MC Bassett & Mrs HM Latham, Tittensor (ST) 4
121652 *	?	De Groot	B33-	-/50	Blanker, Middelburg (O-NL) 7
121659	BS 3405	Mulliner	Z39 B28F	1/50	MT Spence, St Margaret's Hope (OK)
121666	MHU 992	Duple	54834 C29F	3/50	Bristol Tramways (GL) 220
121674	DST 566	Duple	55169 C29F	11/49	M Grant, Fort Augustus (IV)
121682	TRE 95	Mulliner	T480 DP26F	11/49	RG & MC Bassett & Mrs HM Latham, Tittensor (ST) 5
121688					Exported to Karachi (O-PK)
121694	LTC 388	Duple	55167 C29F	11/49	Lansdowne Garage (Morecambe) Ltd (LA)
121732	NRB 891	Duple	55168 C29F	11/49	FH Doughty, Brimington (DE)
121739 *	B-24997	Hainje	B29-	-/49	LABO, Leeuwarden (O-NL) 11
121746	MHU 993	Duple	54835 C29F	3/50	Bristol Tramways (GL) 221
121753	KXV 819	Duple	52436 C29F	12/49	Fallowfield & Britten Ltd, London E8 (LN)
121761					Exported to Thessalonika (O-GR)
121769	HWO 881	Duple	54088 C29F	9/49	Liberty Motors Ltd, Cardiff (GG) 11
121775	?	?	h/box	-/--	F Carter, Wetherby (GWR)
121781 *	GHR 206	Duple	48890 C29F	11/49	L Sheppard, Broadtown (WI)
121818					Exported to Lagos (O-WAN)
121822	GDL 432	Duple	44029 C29F	11/49	Fountain Garage Ltd, Cowes (IW)
121829 *	?	?	B24-	-/--	Original operator unknown (O-GR)
121836	JDF 971	Duple	54986 C29F	12/49	EC Young {Cotswold Coaches}, Stow-on-the-Wold (GL)
121843	BNH 603	Mulliner	T544 B28F	11/49	Manfield & Son, Northampton (XNO)
121854 *	P-40910	Kusters	B30-	8/50	Bom, Venlo (O-NL) 4
121859	DDO 324	Duple	46302 C29F	11/49	JW, JT & WE Camplin {Holme Delight Bus Service}, Donington (LI)
121865	DJN 740	Duple	48354 C24F	4/50	Stanway Coaches (Southend) Ltd (EX)
121871	GVJ 264	Mulliner	T538 B31F	11/49	WE Morgan {Wye Valley Motors}, Hereford (HR)
121906	?	Duple	52624 B30F	-/--	East African Railways, Dar-es-Salaam (O-EAT)
121908	LMN 551	Duple	51119 C29F	10/49	JA Moore {Moore's Motors}, Port Erin (IM)
121919 *	?	?	B30-	-/51	Van Rossum, Montfoort (O-NL) 3
121926	LJH 643	Duple	46245 C29F	-/50	Brunt's Coaches Ltd, Bell Bar (HT)
121933	MHU 994	Duple	54836 C29F	3/50	Bristol Tramways (GL) 222
121948 *	?	Domburg	165 C29F	3/50	Pool, Amsterdam (O-NL) 7
121951	FBU 777	Duple	54368 C29F	11/49	W Brunt & J Howarth, Chadderton (LA)
121955	KAH 942	Duple	54788 B30F	12/49	Eastern Counties, Norwich (NK) B942
121961	KFJ 683	Duple	46963 C29F	5/50	Regent Coaches (Teignmouth) Ltd (DN)
121995					Exported to Lagos (O-WAN)
122181	FET 279	Duple	51036 C29F	12/49	C Riley, Rotherham (WR)
122188 *	GX-17798	Den Oudsten 1817 B30-		3/50	De Harde, Amsterdam (O-NL) 11
122195	MHU 999	Duple	54841 C27F	5/50	Bristol Tramways (GL) 227
122202	UMY 559	Duple	46857 C29F	11/49	Northern Roadways Ltd, Glasgow (LK)
122211					Exported to Rotterdam (O-NL)
122218 *	MHU 996	Duple	54838 C29F	3/50	Bristol Tramways (GL) 224
122224	MHU 995	Duple	54837 C29F	3/50	Bristol Tramways (GL) 223
122230 *	MHU 944	Duple	50309 C29F	5/50	Wessex Coaches Ltd, Bristol (GL)
122264	AGR 321	Duple	50151 C29F	11/49	Humphrey Bros {Progressive}, Brandon Colliery (DM)
122270	UMY 699	Duple	55522 C29F	-/--	Mossrose Coaches Ltd, Waltham Abbey (EX)
122277	?	Mulliner	B--F	-/50	Gibraltar Motor Hire Services (O-GBZ)

122284	UMY 63	Duple	50232	C29F	1/50	Ardley Bros Coaches Ltd, London N17 (LN)
122291	DFV 801	Duple	55524	C29F	12/49	S Swarbrick Ltd, Cleveleys (LA)
122299	K-19075	De Groot		B33-	3/50	De Harde, Amsterdam (O-NL) 64
122308	?	?		van	-/--	New Day Furnishing Stores Ltd, Levenshulme (GLA)
122313 *	E-18804	Domburg	166	DP30F	1/50	ONOG, Oldenzaal (O-NL) 18
122319	?	?		van	-/--	W Richardson, Stretford (GLA)
122359 *	FUJ 500	Duple	54487	C29F	10/49	Corvedale Motor Services Ltd, Ludlow (SH) 29
122366						Exported to Copenhagen (O-DK)
122373	?	?		van	-/--	Road Haulage Executive, London NW1 (GLN)
122380	?	?		van	-/--	W Gardner, Bristol (GGL)
122389	JTX 343	Duple	54718	C29F	12/49	HJ Uphill, Caerau (GG)
122397						Exported to Copenhagen (O-DK)
122403	?	?		van	-/--	J White (Shopfitters) Ltd, Gateshead (GDM)
122409	?	?		van	-/--	Elliot Bros (Berwick) Ltd (GND)
122448	KBJ 194	Duple	49340	C29F	12/49	F Wightman, Saxmundham (EK)
122456						Exported to Rotterdam (O-NL)
122463	KAH 943	Duple	54789	B30F	12/49	Eastern Counties, Norwich (NK) B943
122470	HOT 806	Duple	47889	C29F	3/50	Hants & Sussex Motor Services Ltd, Emsworth (HA) 163
122476						Exported to Karachi (O-PK)
122479 *	GX-17796	Den Oudsten	1815	B30-	1/50	De Harde, Amsterdam (O-NL) 9
122487	HWY 819	Duple	54749	C29F	3/50	Kildare Coaches Ltd, Adwick le Street (WR)
122493	GBE 848	Plaxton	571	FC30F	1/50	Mellers Coaches Ltd, Goxhill (LI)
122499	KPW 986	Duple	54099	C29F	7/50	MJ Eagle, Castle Acre (NK)
122501 *	KGU 563	Plaxton	?	FC30F	-/49	Charles Rickards Ltd {Gray Coaches}, London W2 (LN)
122585 - 122596						Exported to Melbourne (O-AUS)
122719	EX 6653	Plaxton	570	FC30F	1/50	WJ Haylett {Felix Coaches}, Great Yarmouth (NK) 8
122726 *	E-48066	Hainje		B30-	3/50	NWH, Zwartsluis (O-NL) 82
122733	MHU 997	Duple	54839	C27F	3/50	Bristol Tramways (GL) 225
122740	AYJ 499	Plaxton	587	C29F	11/49	R Dickson jnr, Dundee (AS) 9
122746						Exported to Karachi (O-PK)
122750 *	G-29577	Roset		-30-	-/50	Oosterom, Beverwijk (O-NL) 1
122756	KVF 261	Plaxton	572	FC30F	2/50	Culling & Son (Norwich) Ltd {Claxton & District}, Claxton (NK)
122762	MHU 998	Duple	54840	C27F	5/50	Bristol Tramways (GL) 226
122768	JWT 24	Mulliner	T548	B30F	2/50	J & R Laycock {E Laycock & Sons}, Barnoldswick (WR) 47
122808	NPJ 762	Mulliner	T541	?	12/49	Lipscombe {Dorking Coaches}, Dorking (SR)
122815 *	?	?		B30-	-/--	PJ de Visser, Dordrecht (O-NL) 3
122822	JP 8036	Duple	49529	C29F	12/49	R Gray (Gray Bros) {Streamline Coaches}, Wigan (LA)
122829	KXX 22	Duple	50001	C29F	-/50	EJ, LM & HH Clark {Eastern Belle Motor Coaches}, London E3 (LN)
122834	?	Mulliner		B--F	-/--	Original operator unknown (O-WAN)
122837						Exported to Rotterdam (O-NL)
122845	BCP 612	Duple	51189	C29F	2/50	Brearley's Tours Ltd, Halifax (WR)
122851	LDE 997	Duple	55586	C29F	11/49	DJ Jones & Son Ltd, Crymmych (PE)
122857	KUP 537	Duple	44924	C29F	11/49	G Westwell, Felling-on-Tyne (DM)
122897 *	NPJ 590	Mulliner	T540	B32F	11/49	Redhill Group Hospitals, Earlswood (XSR)
122904	P-47838	De Groot		B33-	2/50	Göbbels, Posterholt (O-NL) 7
122911 *	FUT 58	Duple	46605	C29F	3/50	L Pole & Sons Ltd, Syston (LE)
122920	EO 9151	Duple	55601	C27F	-/50	EJ Thompson {Pearl White}, Barrow-in-Furness (LA)
122924	KXU 990	Duple	55523	C29F	-/49	Fountain Group Hospital Management Committee, London SW17 (XLN)
122929						Exported to Rotterdam (O-NL)
122934	?	Mulliner		B--F	-/--	Original operator unknown (O-WAN)
122940	LTB 906	Duple	55589	C29F	1/50	T Holden, Chorley (LA)
122946	FAP 9	Duple	54271	C27F	1/50	Killick & Vincent, Dallington (ES)
122988	HOR 403	Duple	47568	C29F	c10/49	D Jones {Doug Jones Coaches}, Winchester (HA)
122993						Exported to Rotterdam (O-NL)
123000	LTA 903	Duple	54796	C29F	11/49	Southern National, Exeter (DN) 1427
123007						Exported to Rotterdam (O-NL)
123013	LTA 904	Duple	54797	C29F	11/49	Southern National, Exeter (DN) 1428
123016 *	E-48065	Hainje		B29-	3/50	NWH, Zwartsluis (O-NL) 81
123024						Exported to Rotterdam (O-NL)

123030	LUO 634	Duple	49374	C29F	1/50	JH Clark {Tally Ho! Coaches}, East Allington (DN)
123032		see 123036				
123036 *	UMY 704	Duple	44054	C29F	3/50	Essex County Coaches Ltd, London E15 (LN)
123076	HDA 788	Thurgood	618	C19F	3/50	Worthington Motor Tours Ltd, Birmingham (WK)
123083 *	H-63994	De Groot		B33-	-/48	Daniels {States Express}, Rotterdam (O-NL) 8
123090 *	?	Groenewold		B32-	-/50	BAB, Rijswijk (O-NL)
123097	DPR 606	Duple	55590	C29F	1/50	Swanage Coaches Ltd, Chickrell (DT)
123107 *	MKK 40	Duple	47951	C29F	1/50	A Saxby & Sons Ltd {Enterprise}, Margate (KT)
123112, 123114						Exported to Rotterdam (O-NL)
123126	LTA 905	Duple	54798	C29F	12/49	Southern National, Exeter (DN) 1429
123130	?	Mulliner	T546	B32-	12/49	Sir Robert McAlpine & Sons Ltd (contractor), London W1
123166 *	MHU 52	Duple	54775	B30F	4/50	Bristol Tramways (GL) 210
123173 *	?	Domburg	168	C30F	4/50	FC van der Toorren {Lido Tours}, Amsterdam (O-NL) 2
123180 *	P-16510	De Groot		B33-	2/50	Jacobs, Nuth (O-NL) 15
123187	JNX 783	Duple	46999	C29F	12/49	Gee & Harrison Ltd, Middleton (WK)
123192	JTX 266	Duple	54720	C29F	11/49	Pugh & Stanton, Ogmore Vale (GG)
123285 - 123296						Exported to Melbourne (O-AUS)
123349		see 123449				
123381 *	HX-42162	Roset		B30-	-/50	Beuk, Noordwijk (O-NL) 12
123384 *	M-1800	Roset		B33-	-/50	Sloot, Winterswijk (O-NL) 7
123389	DWH 470	Duple	55035	C29F	1/50	J Davies, Leigh (LA) 18
123395	HDA 787	Thurgood	619	C18F	4/50	Worthington Motor Tours Ltd, Birmingham (WK)
123435	?	Mulliner	T545	B32-	12/49	Sir Robert McAlpine & Sons Ltd (contractor), London W1
123442 *	?	?		B24-	-/--	Original operator unknown (O-GR)
123449 *	?	?		B24-	-/--	Original operator unknown (O-GR)
123456 *	LNK 510	Duple	46726	C29F	-/50	Brunt's Coaches Ltd, Bell Bar (HT)
123461	MAU 23	Duple	49800	C29F	4/50	A Skill {Skill's Coaches}, Nottingham (NG) 23
123470 *	?	?		B28-	-/--	Original operator unknown (O-GR)
123472 *	?	?		B24-	-/--	Original operator unknown (O-GR)
123478	NPJ 349	Duple	43477	C29F	12/49	Cooke's Coaches (Stoughton) Ltd (SR) 16
123484	LTC 110	Duple	50505	C29F	1/50	W Robinson & Sons, Great Harwood (LA) 65
123524 *	HTM 20	Duple	55646	C29F	1/50	FD Bailey, Turvey (BD)
123531 *	?	?		B24-	-/--	Original operator unknown (O-GR)
123538 *	?	?		B24-	-/--	Original operator unknown (O-GR)
123545 *	?	?		B24-	-/--	Original operator unknown (O-GR)
123553 *	53-639	?		B24-	-/--	Original operator unknown (O-GR)
123561 *	G-53909	Domburg	183	C30F	5/50	C de Jong, Hem (O-NL) 4
123567	HOT 807	Duple	46619	C29F	3/50	Hants & Sussex Motor Services Ltd, Emsworth (HA) 164
123573						Exported to Rotterdam (O-NL)
123613	KGU 669	Duple	49987	B27F	1/50	Metropolitan Police, London SW1 (XLN)
123620	DTY 730	Mulliner	T549	B28F	1/50	E Marshall & Co Ltd {Crown Coaches}, Birtley (ND)
123627	FUJ 690	Duple	49240	C29F	4/49	RW Carpenter {Valley Motor Services}, Bishop's Castle (SH)
123634	LTA 906	Duple	54800	C29F	12/49	Southern National, Exeter (DN) 1430
123645	LTA 907	Duple	54799	C29F	12/49	Southern National, Exeter (DN) 1431
123647	?	?		lorry	-/--	London Felt Co Ltd, St Mary's Cray (GKT)
123650	?	Mulliner	T547	B32-	12/49	Sir Robert McAlpine & Sons Ltd (contractor), London W1
123656 *	MLA 240	Duple	54928	C--F	-/--	British Films Ltd, London SW17 (XLN)
123662 *	SW 8039	Duple	55603	C29F	3/50	W & A Campbell, Gatehouse of Fleet (KK)
123682		see 123662				
123702 *	MHU 53	Duple	54776	B30F	4/50	Bristol Tramways (GL) 211
123709	?	Duple	52625	B30F	4/50	East African Railways, Dar-es-Salaam (O-EAT)
123715	LYC 188	Duple	55678	C29F	1/50	E Giles {Venture}, South Petherton (SO)
123722	?	?		van	-/--	Helix Spring Co, Northallerton (GNR)
123731	ACC 724	(Pearson ?)		FC29F	5/50	J Williams & Son {Red Garage}, Portmadoc (CN)
123735	KXV 320	Duple	50238	C29F	-/15	AC Coaches Ltd, London SE15 (LN)
123739 *	MHN 823	Mulliner	T535	B31F	12/49	R Handley {JC Handley & Son}, Middleham (NR)
123745	HSF 727	Duple	55606	C29F	8/50	Dunnett Bros, Edinburgh (MN)
123751	NNW 819	Duple	50635	C29F	12/49	JA Hudson Ltd, Leeds (WR)
123791	?	?		van	-/--	C Murray, Bury (GLA)

C1252/157

123798	HDA 784	Duple	55588	C29F	3/50	L Barnett {Pathfinder}, Coseley (ST)
123938 *	JXX 468	?		?	11/49	Ministry of Supply (GOV)
123973	KEL 467	Lee		C29F	5/50	G Willmott Ltd {Wells City Coaches}, Wells (SO)
123980	DAG 347	Mulliner	T514	B31F	1/50	D Liddell, Auchinleck (AR)
123988						Exported to Copenhagen (O-DK)
123999 *	?	?		van	-/--	Venture Transport (Hendon) Ltd, London NW2 (GLN)
124001	LTA 908	Duple	54801	C29F	12/49	Southern National, Exeter (DN) 1432
124004	?	?		van	-/--	Wilkie & Paul Ltd (metal box manufacturers), Edinburgh (GMN)
124008	FNV 280	Duple	46721	C29F	12/49	LJ Adams {Buckby's Coaches}, Rothwell (NO)
124048 *	?	?		B24-	-/--	Original operator unknown (O-GR)
124055	UMY 267	Duple	44397	C29F	-/--	RG Flexman {Flexman's Coaches}, Southall (MX)
124060 *	?	?		B24-	-/--	Original operator unknown (O-GR)
124066	LTA 909	Duple	54802	C29F	12/49	Southern National, Exeter (DN) 1433
124076	CCF 470	Duple	43536	C29F	1/50	WA, E & V Jolly, Norton (WF)
124083 *	KOC 923	Duple	46286	C29F	3/50	Burley's Garage Ltd, Birmingham (WK)
124090 *	?	?		B24-	-/--	Original operator unknown (O-GR)
124094	KXV 536	Mulliner		B29F	2/50	Ministry of Works (GOV)
124099	KXV 537	Mulliner		B29F	2/50	Ministry of Works (GOV)
124143						Exported to Karachi (O-PK)
124147 *	60-032	?		B24D	-/--	Original operator unknown (O-GR)
124149						Exported to Antwerp (O-B)
124152	?	Mulliner		?	-/--	Ministry of Supply (GOV)
124156	KXV 600	Mulliner		?	4/50	Ministry of Supply (GOV)
124176	?	Mulliner		?	-/--	Ministry of Supply (GOV)
124180	FO 5798	Duple	49243	C29F	12/49	Williams & Wooding, Knighton (RR)
124183 *	GX-17179	Den Oudsten	1822	B30-	4/50	De Harde, Amsterdam (O-NL) 12
124187	FVN 299	Duple	51177	C29F	1/50	Hardwick's Services Ltd, Snainton (NR)
124189						Exported to Karachi (O-PK)
124192	?	Mulliner	T550	?	5/50	Vickers Armstrong, Weybridge (XSR)
124230						Exported to Copenhagen (O-DK)
124237	NPK 447	Mulliner	T551	B30F	-/50	Roberts & Dickson {Ashford Belle}, Ashford (SR)
124242						Exported to Copenhagen (O-DK)
124248	FVA 9	Duple	55156	C29F	12/49	McAteer & Son, Broomhouse (LK)
124258	LUO 270	Duple	54506	C27F	5/50	Woolacombe & Mortehoe Motor Co Ltd, Woolacombe (DN)
124262	FUJ 463	Mulliner	Z42	B31F	12/49	JT, FW & GE Whittle {JT Whittle & Sons}, Highley (SH)
124265	F-30052	?		B---	3/50	Karl Medgård, Nesbyen (O-N)
124272	HGA 995	Duple	54757	C29F	-/50	SCWS Ltd, Glasgow (LK)
124276	HWP 520	Duple	47640	C29F	12/49	CW Shuker {Lady Edith}, Halesowen (WO)
124281						Exported to Oslo (O-N)
124322	GDL 489	Duple	48858	C29F	3/50	Moss Motor Tours (Sandown, I.W.) Ltd (IW)
124328 *	LTC 855	Duple	55628	C29F	5/50	Kia-Ora Motor Services Ltd, Morecambe (LA)
124334 *	?			B24-	-/--	Original operator unknown (O-GR)
124339	?	Mulliner		?	-/--	Original operator unknown (O-WAN)
124349	KNF 974	Duple	49751	C29F	1/50	E Shipley, Ashton-under-Lyne (LA)
124356 *	?	Avraam		B24-	-/--	Original operator unknown (O-GR)
124363	AEJ 323	Duple	55607	C29F	12/49	E & J Lloyd-Jones {Lloyd-Jones Bros}, Pontrhydygroes (CG)
124367 *	MHU 54	Duple	54777	B30F	4/50	Bristol Tramways (GL) 212
124372	LDV 483	Duple	54905	C25F	3/50	HD Gourd & Son, Bishopsteignton (DN)
124497 - 124508						Exported to Melbourne (O-AUS)
124581	LTC 681	Duple	54369	C29F	1/50	Warburton Bros (Bury) Ltd, Tottington (LA)
124588 *	EVH 283	Duple	55165	C29F	3/50	Hanson's Buses Ltd, Huddersfield (WR) 275
124592	C-16132	?		B18-	7/50	Original operator unknown (O-WAN)
124598	MHN 826	Duple	50674	C29F	12/49	Percival Bros (Coaches) Ltd, Richmond (NR)
124607	HWF 201	Duple	49816	C29F	12/49	J & J Boddy {Boddy's Motors}, Bridlington (ER)
124615	Z-5069	?		B---	-/50	Original operator unknown (O-WAN)
124622	?	Mulliner		?	-/--	Original operator unknown (O-WAN)
124626	HWP 637	Duple	47597	C29F	4/50	ED, GE & Mrs ME Harrison {Broadway Coaches}, Broadway (WO)
124631	FMO 92	Duple	54893	C29F	12/49	OR Tibble {Pioneer Motor Services}, St Mary Bourne (HA)
124672	LYB 941	Duple	55645	C29F	12/49	CT & LT Bond {Tor Coaches}, Street (SO)

124679	DTY 719	Duple	54770	C29F	3/50	Robson & Atkinson, Stocksfield-on-Tyne (ND) 4
124683						Exported to Oslo (O-N)
124689	?	Mulliner		?	-/--	Original operator unknown (O-WAN)
124699	KXV 308	Duple	50273	C29F	-/50	CW Banfield, London SE15 (LN)
124706	D-25505	BRK		B30-	2/50	Henrik Flygind, Elverum (O-N)
124713	KVO 975	Duple	49487	C24F	9/49	Barton Transport, Chilwell (NG) 592
124717	UMY 333	Duple	44009	C29F	-/50	CG Lewis {CG Lewis Safety Coaches}, London SE10 (LN)
124722	LTA 910	Duple	54803	C29F	12/49	Southern National, Exeter (DN) 1434
124763	MCV 311	Duple	54466	C29F	12/49	NA Whitfield {Whitfield's Motor Service}, Goonhavern (CO)
124770	GVJ 376	Duple	54488	C29F	12/49	Hereford Motor Co Ltd (HR) 11
124774	K-2910	Gumpen		B---	3/50	Songdalens Billag AS, Songdalen (O-N)
124780	KXW 927	Duple	44414	C29F	-/--	AJC Giles {Viola Motor Coaches}, London SE16 (LN)
124790 *	LTA 911	Duple	54804	C29F	12/49	Southern National, Exeter (DN) 1435
124797	L-22006	?		B13FV	4/50	Sigurd Østrem, location unknown (O-N)
124804 *	?	Duple	50799	C16F	-/50	Original operator unknown (O-EAK)
124808	LTA 912	Duple	54805	C29F	12/49	Southern National, Exeter (DN) 1436
124813	EBW 300	Duple	48296	C29F	1/50	OA Slatter, Long Hanborough (OX) 22
124849	?	Mulliner		?	-/--	Ministry of Supply (GOV)
124854	R-753	Rasmussen		B24C	5/50	AS Bilruta Os-Bergen, Bergen (O-N)
124861	KYH 24	Duple	52430	C27F	3/50	George Ewer & Co Ltd {Grey Green}, London N16 (LN)
124865	W-8366	?		B---	6/50	Aksel Andreassen, Andenes (O-N)
124871	NNW 871	Duple	50548	C29F	-/50	Wallace Arnold Tours Ltd, Leeds (WR)
124881	OMX 276	LCMW		B26R	11/50	Middlesex County Council (XMX)
124888	V-109	?		B25-	5/50	Sigvart Holstad, Steinkjer (O-N)
124895	KAA287	Duple	50800	C16F	4/50	OTC, Nairobi (O-EAK)
124899	?	?		van	-/--	Parker Knoll Ltd (furniture manufacturers), High Wycombe (GBK)
124904	HJW 103	Duple	48048	C24F	5/50	Worthington Motor Tours Ltd, Birmingham (WK)
124940	H-8021	?		B---	3/50	Øst-Telemarkens Auto, Saudland (O-N)
124945 *	?	?		B24-	-/--	Original operator unknown (O-GR)
124952	NNW 870	Duple	50610	C29F	-/50	Ives & Milner, Leeds (WR)
124956 *	65-350	?		B24-	-/--	Original operator unknown (O-GR)
124962	GAW 58	Plaxton	592	C29F	3/50	W, WE & JR Fisher, Bronington (FT)
124972	DAG 298	Duple	54882	C29F	-/50	JT Maguire & Sons, Dalmellington (AR)
124979 *	61-811	?		B24-	-/--	Original operator unknown (O-GR)
124986	?	?		van	-/--	JW Street, Levenshulme (GLA)
124990 *	KOH 77	Willenhall		C31F	3/50	EWF MacMullen, Birmingham (WK)
124995 *	HDA 727	Mulliner	(AL1 ?)	C28F	4/50	CR Hughes {Pebley Beach Coaches}, Wroughton (WI)
125039	KXV 561	Mulliner		?	2/50	Ministry of Works (GOV)
125043						Exported to Piraeus (O-GR)
125052	?	Mulliner		?	-/--	Ministry of Supply (GOV)
125058						Exported to Copenhagen (O-DK)
125065	KAA289	Duple	50801	C16F	4/50	OTC, Nairobi (O-EAK)
125070	KXV 562	Mulliner		B29F	-/--	Ministry of Works (GOV)
125074	?	Mulliner		?	-/--	Ministry of Supply (GOV)
125084	HJW 268	Duple	48051	C18F	5/50	Worthington Motor Tours Ltd, Birmingham (WK)
125090	HJW 269	Duple	48052	C18F	5/50	Worthington Motor Tours Ltd, Birmingham (WK)
125161 - 125172						Exported to Sydney (O-AUS)
125298	OBB 343	Pearson		FC31F	5/50	J&T Hunter (Washington) Ltd, Washington (DM)
125302						Exported to Antwerp (O-B)
125311	?	?		van	-/--	D&H Transport, London N15 (GLN)
125317						Exported to Antwerp (O-B)
125324						Exported to Bangkok (O-T)
125329 #	?	?		h/box	-/--	HR Richmond {Epsom Coaches}, Epsom (GSR)
125333	JTX 205	Duple	44341	C29F	2/50	Edwards Bros (Beddau) Ltd (GG)
125336						Exported to Antwerp (O-B)
125343	SH 8855	Duple	55675	C29F	12/49	TF Buckle & Son, Duns (BW)
125349	DTY 780	Duple	46597	C29F	5/50	GR & F Longstaff, Broomhill (ND)
125389	KAH 944	Duple	54790	B30F	1/50	Eastern Counties, Norwich (NK) B944
125393 *	?	Domburg	170	C34F	3/50	Elshout, Giessen (O-NL)
125402	?	?		lorry	-/--	A Price & Sons Ltd, Burscough Bridge (GLA)
125408						Exported to Copenhagen (O-DK)

125415					Exported to Bangkok (O-T)
125420	VME 297	Gurney Nutting		C29F	6/50 CW Banfield, London SE15 (LN)
125424	?	?		van	-/-- R Davies Haulage Ltd, London E14 (GLN)
125427					Exported to Copenhagen (O-DK)
125434	KFM 849	Duple	54812	C29F	1/50 Crosville MS, Chester (CH) SL49
125439	DFK 717	?		van	3/50 Quality Cleaners Ltd, Worcester (GWO)
125472					Exported to Mauritius
125479					Exported to Kingston (O-JA)
125486 *	GCA 388	Duple	49242	C29F	1/50 WT & E Keeler, Wrexham (DH)
125495 *	60-995	?		B24-	-/-- Original operator unknown (O-GR)
125502	KFM 848	Duple	54811	C29F	12/49 Crosville MS, Chester (CH) SL48
125509	LTB 907	Duple	55677	C29F	1/50 J Lamb, Upholland (LA)
125514	FUT 339	Duple	55162	C29F	12/49 Windridge, Sons & Riley Ltd {Victory}, Ibstock (LE) 12
125518	KOC 974	Duple	46529	C29F	12/49 L & FG Myatt {Avon Coaches}, Birmingham (WK) 17
125526 *	62-378	?		B24-	-/50 Original operator unknown (O-GR)
125530	AGR 945	Pearson		FC31F	-/-- L Rodgers {Station Taxis}, Redcar (NR)
125531		see 123531			
125563					Exported to Mauritius
125570 *	?	?		B28-	-/-- Original operator unknown (O-GR)
125577	LFM 387	Duple	54814	C29F	2/50 Crosville MS, Chester (CH) SL50
125586 *	60-776	Tournikiotis		B24-	-/-- Original operator unknown (O-GR)
125593	CCB 201	Plaxton	588	C29F	1/50 E & JC Alderson Ltd, Settle (WR)
125600	HOD 83	Duple	54852	C29F	1/50 Western National, Exeter (DN) 1404
125605	HGB 131	Duple	55030	C27F	-/50 Cotter's Motor Tours Ltd, Glasgow (LK)
125606		see 125605			
125610	LFM 388	Duple	54813	C29F	2/50 Crosville MS, Chester (CH) SL51
125617 *	68-833	?		B24-	-/-- Original operator unknown (O-GR)
125621 *	LFM 389	Duple	54815	C29F	2/50 Crosville MS, Chester (CH) SL52
125651	LFM 390	Duple	54816	C29F	2/50 Crosville MS, Chester (CH) SL53
125659 *	60-941	?		B24-	-/-- Original operator unknown (O-GR)
125670	LTD 986	Pearson		C29F	5/50 H Entwistle & Son (Price of Wales Tours), Morecambe (LA)
125676	?	?		?	-/-- Jose Hellin Abellan, Murcia (O-E)
125683	KNG 320	Duple	43375	C29F	1/50 Coach Services 1947 (Thetford) Ltd (NK)
125690	KVF 172	Duple	52418	C29F	1/50 F, PW & CE Thompson {Eniway Coaches}, Dereham (NK)
125695	KAH 945	Duple	54791	B30F	1/50 Eastern Counties, Norwich (NK) B945
125700	CCB 175	Duple	44275	C29F	3/50 Lewis Cronshaw Ltd, London NW4 (LN)
125707					Exported to Rotterdam (O-NL)
125711 *	?	De Groot		B33-	-/50 CITO Tours BV, Axel (O-NL) 15
125746	EM 4637	Duple	50968	C29F	1/50 T Lawrenson Ltd, Bootle (LA)
125752 *	H-53179	Groenewold		B34-	-/50 BAB, Rijswijk (O-NL) 2
125759					Exported to Malta
125767 *	P-43642	De Groot		B33-	-/50 Nijsten-Souren, Simpelveld (O-NL) 9
125775	FUJ 832	Duple	49246	C29F	12/49 Greatrex Motor Coaches Ltd, Stafford (ST) 59 Robin
125782 *	CCB 186	Duple	50979	C29F	3/50 Ribblesdale Coachways Ltd, Blackburn (LA)
125786 #	?	?		h/box	-/-- HR Richmond {Epsom Coaches}, Epsom (GSR)
125792 *	KUP 711	Duple	54769	C29F	12/49 T Cook, Consett (DM)
125799					Exported to Rotterdam (O-NL)
125801 - 125812					Exported to Port Elizabeth (O-ZA)
125885 - 125896					Exported to Melbourne (O-AUS)
125971	LFM 461	Plaxton	589	C29F	1/50 AE & RI Niddrie, Middlewich (CH)
126005	FNV 500	Duple	46575	C29F	12/49 York Bros (Northampton) Ltd (NO) 25
126011	K-5534	?		B---	3/50 Original operator unknown (O-DK)
126018 #	?	?		h/box	-/-- HR Richmond {Epsom Coaches}, Epsom (GSR)
126027	K-3001	?		B26-	2/50 AS Lillesand Ruta, Lillesand (O-N)
126034	LFM 391	Duple	54818	C29F	2/50 Crosville MS, Chester (CH) SL54
126041 *	KAH 946	Duple	54792	B30F	2/50 Eastern Counties, Norwich (NK) B946
126046	?	?		van	1/50 J Brand & Sons Ltd, Farnborough (GHA)
126051	U-4647	?		B--FV	3/50 Petter A Husby {Skaunruten}, Skaun (O-N)
126058	DWH 870	Duple	55034	C27F	5/50 Lomax Bros (Transport) Ltd, Bolton (LA)
126096					Exported to Malta
126102	I-2595	?		B---	4/50 L/L Setesdal Automobilrutor, Byglandsfjord (O-N)
126109	LFM 392	Duple	54820	C29F	2/50 Crosville MS, Chester (CH) SL55

C1252/159

C1252/160

126118	K-8100	OCA		B29-	3/50	Lars Skailand {Øvstefjellruta}, location unknown (O-N)
126125	LFM 393	Duple	54819	C29F	2/50	Crosville MS, Chester (CH) SL56
126132	LFM 394	Duple	54817	C29F	2/50	Crosville MS, Chester (CH) SL57
126137	FBU 829	Duple	54370	C29F	3/50	G Barlow & Sons Ltd, Oldham (LA)
126142	GCY 503	Duple	55683	C29F	1/50	R Jones, Ystradgynlais (BC)
126149	JP 8079	Duple	49531	C29F	1/50	Stringfellow Bros {Silver Queen}, Wigan (LA)
126187						Exported to Karachi (O-PK)
126200 *	MHU 55	Duple	54778	B30F	5/50	Bristol Tramways (GL) 213
126209 *	LC-16-13	ST Guarda		B28D	2/50	Sociedade de Transportes Lda, Guarda (O-P) 18
126216	LMN 771	Duple	51120	C29F	12/49	WE Kelly {Victoria}, Abbeylands (IM)
126223	?	?		lorry	-/--	J & T Peters Ltd, Glazebury (GCH)
126227 *	HOD 81	Duple	54850	C29F	11/49	Western National, Exeter (DN) 1402
126240	DHV 617	Duple	44887	C29F	2/50	JW Armstrong & C Downey {Silvertown Coaches}, London E16 (LN)
126278						Exported to Karachi (O-PK)
126284 *	LC-16-14	Martins & Caetano	DP27D		2/50	Amândio Paraiso, Fornos de Algodres (O-P) 17
126291	DFV 960	Duple	48075	C29F	12/49	S Swarbrick Ltd, Cleveleys (LA)
126300						Exported to Helsinki (O-FIN)
126475 *	HOD 82	Duple	54849	C29F	1/50	Western National, Exeter (DN) 1403
126482	KFD 347	Duple	49870	C29F	1/50	Holden's Garage Ltd, Netherton (WO)
126487	OMX 333	Duple	55629	C29F	1/50	Rayner {West London Coachways}, Ashford (MX)
126492	DFV 974	Duple	55643	C29F	2/50	Lansdowne Motors Ltd, Fleetwood (LA)
126499	MPP 627	Duple	55720	C29F	1/50	TJ Brown & JF Grout {Lee & District Motor Services}, Chesham (BK)
126537						Exported to Kingston (O-JA)
126543 *	D-6820	Medema		B29-	-/48	Harmanni, Assen (O-NL) 14
126550	HJW 104	Duple	48049	C24F	5/50	Worthington Motor Tours Ltd, Birmingham (WK)
126559 *	B-29022	Jongerius		B---	-/50	ZWH, Balk (O-NL) 22
126566	MHN 837	Mulliner	Z43	B31F	2/50	Favourite Direct Services Ltd, Bishop Auckland (DM) 16
126573	FUT 489	Duple	55710	C29F	2/50	AA Oliver {Luxicoaches}, Loughborough (LE)
126578 *	EY 9392	Duple	44257	C29F	1/50	T Jones {T Jones & Sons}, Menai Bridge (AY)
126583	?	?		van	-/--	F Chapman & Sons Ltd, London SE20 (GLN)
126590	MHN 836	Duple	50687	C29F	1/50	Favourite Direct Services Ltd, Bishop Auckland (DM) 15
126627						Exported to Rotterdam (O-NL)
126639	JTX 488	Duple	55735	C29F	1/50	J Roberts, Caerphilly (GG)
126649 *	?	De Groot		B33-	-/50	Verhoeven, Budel (O-NL) 4
126656	HWY 957	Duple	50626	C29F	11/49	JJ Longstaff, Mirfield (WR) 4
126663	KXV 317	Duple	54887	C29F	1/50	Osborne & Fairman Ltd {Morden Travel}, Morden (SR)
126668 *	KUO 926	Duple	54851	C29F	1/50	Western National, Exeter (DN) 1405
126673	OMX 356	Duple	52045	C25F	1/50	BEA, Ruislip (MX) 1121
126680	EDP 757	Duple	44507	C29F	2/50	AE Smith {Smith's Coaches}, Reading (BE)
126720						Exported to Karachi (O-PK)
126725	FUJ 915	Duple	49247	C29F	12/49	AL Jones & Co Ltd {Victoria Coaches}, Madeley (SH)
126731 *	N-45396	Domburg	171	B34-	3/50	Laarakkers, Sambeek (O-NL) 6
126742	LTA 745	Duple	54855	C29F	1/50	Western National, Exeter (DN) 1406
126746	LUO 427	Duple	42366	C29F	1/50	J, EM & AB Geddes {Burton Cars}, Brixham (DN)
126753 *	?	Domburg	189	C34F	4/51	Boers, Nieuwleusen (O-NL) 1
126761	GDL 538	Duple	43629	C29F	5/50	Seaview Services Ltd, Seaview (IW) 12
126769	KYF 616	Mulliner		?	4/50	Ministry of Works (GOV)
126777	KXV 592	Mulliner		?	-/--	Ministry of Works (GOV)
126814						Exported to Karachi (O-PK)
126816	KXV 563	Mulliner		B--F	3/50	Ministry of Works (GOV)
126822 *	H-81557	Domburg	173	C34F	5/50	Keesen en Langhout, Alphen aan de Rijn (O-NL) 4
126833	KXW 635	Mulliner		?	5/50	Ministry of Supply (GOV)
126837	?	Mulliner		?	-/--	Ministry of Supply (GOV)
126844						Exported to Rotterdam (O-NL)
126852	KXW 636	Mulliner	Z45	B23F	8/50	London County Council (XLN) 1622
126860	KXV 633	Mulliner	Z49	B23F	8/50	London County Council (XLN) 1619
126868	KXW 634	Mulliner	Z48	B23F	8/50	London County Council (XLN) 1620
126961 - 126972						Exported to Melbourne (O-AUS)
127082	KXW 635	Mulliner	Z44	B30F	8/50	London County Council (XLN) 1621
127083						Exported to Port Harcourt (O-WAN)
127089						Exported to Rotterdam (O-NL)
127100	KXW 637	Mulliner	Z46	B23F	7/50	London County Council (XLN) 1623

127104	KXW 642	Mulliner	Z51	B23F	7/50	London County Council (XLN) 1625
127113						Exported to Rotterdam (O-NL)
127117 *	KXW 646	Mulliner	Z54	B23F	8/50	London County Council (XLN) 1629
127119		see 127117				
127127	KXW 645	Mulliner	Z53	B23F	8/50	London County Council (XLN) 1628
127134	KXW 644	Mulliner	Z52	B30F	7/50	London County Council (XLN) 1627
127139		see 127134				
127178	KXW 638	Mulliner	Z47	B23F	7/50	London County Council (XLN) 1624
127184						Exported to Madrid (O-E)
127195	KXW 643	Mulliner	Z50	B23F	8/50	London County Council (XLN) 1626
127199	SB 8052	Duple	54421	C29F	4/50	Dunoon Motor Services Ltd, Dunoon (AL)
127206						Exported to Madrid (O-E)
127214	MWB 104	Duple	46767	C29F	1/50	JO Andrew Ltd, Sheffield (WR)
127222	DFV 976	Duple	55730	C29F	1/50	S Clare, Blackpool (LA)
127229 *	LAL 235	Duple	49488	C24F	5/50	Barton Transport, Chilwell (NG) 591
127264						Exported to Lagos (O-WAN)
127269 *	GHR 553	Duple	46240	C29F	1/50	J Mapson & Sons, Swindon (WI)
127275 *	LA-16-30	?		DP29D	2/50	Francisco João Cota, Porto (O-P)
127286 *	GCY 412	Duple	54089	C29F	4/50	United Welsh, Swansea (GG) 972
127290	BSN 259	Duple	54907	C29F	1/50	C McAteer, Dumbarton (DB)
127297						Exported to Helsinki (O-FIN)
127305 *	MHU 56	Duple	54779	B30F	5/50	Bristol Tramways (GL) 214
127313	UMY 447	Duple	44055	C29F	-/--	Essex County Coaches Ltd, London E15 (LN)
127320	KXY 630	Duple	44537	C29F	3/50	Fallowfield & Britten Ltd, London E8 (LN)
127355						Exported to Karachi (O-PK)
127360	KVM 500	Duple	49674	C29F	1/50	Auty's Tours Ltd, Bury (LA)
127366						Exported to Madrid (O-E)
127377	FVN 471	Duple	54340	C29F	1/50	Begg's Luxury Coaches Ltd, Thornaby-on-Tees (NR)
127381	EDY 44	Plaxton	590	C29F	2/50	H Phillips {Empress Coaches}, Hastings (ES)
127391						Exported to Madrid (O-E)
127396	MWB 122	Duple	46766	C29F	1/50	JW Fantom, Sheffield (WR)
127404	NPK 860	Duple	49504	C29F	1/50	RG Harwood, Weybridge (SR) 8
127411	JP 8295	Pearson		C29F	5/50	Pownall Bros, Golbourne (LA) 1
127446	DHV 645	Duple	44400	C29F	-/50	Grange & Sons {Broadway Coaches}, London E6 (LN)
127451	?	?		van	-/--	G Goldman & Sons Ltd, London N1 (GLN)
127457						Exported to Sevilla (O-E)
127468	MHW 937	Duple	46387	C29F	3/50	AH Fielding {Empress Coaches}, Bristol (GL)
127479						Exported to Sevilla (O-E)
127487	GVJ 490	Duple	54489	C29F	1/50	Yeomans Private Hire Ltd, Hereford (HR) 81
127495	LTA 746	Duple	54853	C29F	1/50	Western National, Exeter (DN) 1407
127670	?	?		van	-/--	WS Gill, Spennymoor (GDM)
127697						Exported to Karachi (O-PK)
127704	OMX 357	Duple	52046	C25F	1/50	BEA, Ruislip (MX) 1122
127710, 127715						Exported to Rotterdam (O-NL)
127726 *	LTA 747	Duple	54856	C29F	1/50	Western National, Exeter (DN) 1408
127731 #	?	?		h/box	-/--	HR Richmond {Epsom Coaches}, Epsom (GSR)
127737						Exported to Rotterdam (O-NL)
127745 *	LTA 748	Duple	54854	C29F	1/50	Western National, Exeter (DN) 1409
127753	LNK 144	Duple	50324	C29F	-/50	N & S Coaches Ltd, Kibworth (LE)
127760	KXV 318	Duple	50281	C29F	1/50	Osborne & Fairman Ltd {Morden Travel}, Morden (SR)
127792	?	?		van	-/--	J Grant & Co, Edinburgh (GMN)
127801 *	(D-17007 ?)	Hainje		B30-	1/50	DABO, Meppel (O-NL) 27
127807 *	?	?		h/box	4/50	Metropolitan Police, London SW1 (GLN)
127818	LTA 749	Duple	54857	C29F	6/50	Western National, Exeter (DN) 1410
127829						Exported to Rotterdam (O-NL)
127837	GSR 23	Duple	55731	C29F	2/50	Hunter & Nelson, Arbroath (AS)
127845	?	?		van	-/--	Eastmans Dyers & Cleaners Ltd, W3 (GLN)
127852	LTA 750	Duple	54858	C29F	6/50	Western National, Exeter (DN) 1411
127883	MWB 105	Duple	46309	C29F	1/50	EH Sims, Sheffield (WR)
127892						Exported to Rotterdam (O-NL)
127898						Exported to Karachi (O-PK)
127909	KCD 736	Duple	54570	C29F	1/50	T Camping, Brighton (ES)
127920						Exported to Rotterdam (O-NL)
127928 *	MHU 57	Duple	54780	B30F	5/50	Bristol Tramways (GL) 215

127936	AXG 498	Duple	55050	B31F	2/50	Middlesbrough Education Committee (XNR)
127943	KGH 587	Duple	54982	B31F	1/50	British Broadcasting Corporation {BBC}, London SW4 (XLN)
127974						Exported to Karachi (O-PK)
127983						Exported to Rotterdam (O-NL)
127989	KEL 40	Duple	44835	C29F	3/50	Shamrock & Rambler Motor Coaches Ltd, Bournemouth (HA)
127994	LFM 395	Duple	54821	C29F	2/50	Crosville MS, Chester (CH) SL58
128000	KGH 588	Duple	54983	B31F	1/50	British Broadcasting Corporation {BBC}, London SW4 (XLN) B588
128011						Exported to Rotterdam (O-NL)
128019	GAW 21	Duple	49241	C29F	1/50	A & RA Price {Excelsior}, Wrockwardine Wood (SH)
128027	HOT 808	Duple	46433	C29F	3/50	Hants & Sussex Motor Services Ltd, Emsworth (HA) 165
128034	LFM 396	Duple	54822	C29F	2/50	Crosville MS, Chester (CH) SL59
128063	EX 6700	Duple	44890	C29F	4/50	Reynolds Garage Ltd {Metropolitan Coaches}, Great Yarmouth (NK)
128071	JM 9103	Duple	55794	C29F	1/50	SF & TW Faulkner {Brown's Luxury Coaches}, Ambleside (WT)
128076						Exported to Kingston (O-JA)
128082						Exported to Karachi (O-PK)
128087	LFM 397	Duple	54823	C29F	2/50	Crosville MS, Chester (CH) SL60
128097	MWB 292	Duple	46768	C29F	1/50	Mrs G Hibberd, Sheffield (WR)
128099		see 128097				
128106	KXY 500	Pearson		FC31F	6/50	WE & SG Blunt {Mitcham Belle Motor Coaches}, Mitcham (SR)
128118	KVF 333	Duple	48152	C29F	1/50	JC Brown {Norfolk Coachways}, Attleborough (NK)
128126						Exported to Helsinki (O-FIN)
128154	DTK 503	Lee		C29F	6/50	RW Toop, WJ Ironside & PW Davis {Bere Regis & District}, Dorchester (DT)
128162	LTD 62	Duple	55721	C29F	12/49	Lansdowne Garage (Morecambe) Ltd (LA)
128167 *	E-48067	Hainje		B30-	4/51	NWH, Zwartsluis (O-NL) 30
128173						Exported to Karachi (O-PK)
128178	KVF 324	Duple	54981	C29F	2/50	J Parker & Sons, Hindolveston (NK)
128190 *	HZ-16196	Den Oudsten	1824	B30-	6/50	Eltax, Leiden (O-NL) 96
128194	HJW 105	Duple	48050	C24F	5/50	Worthington Motor Tours Ltd, Birmingham (WK)
128213 - 128224						Exported to Sydney (O-AUS)
128309 - 128320						Exported to Melbourne (O-AUS)
128409	DTK 346	Lee		C29F	4/50	RW Toop, WJ Ironside & PW Davis {Bere Regis & District}, Dorchester (DT)
128412 *	GBE 974	Duple	54829	C29F	6/50	Lincolnshire RCC, Bracebridge Heath (KN) 760
128416	LFM 398	Duple	54824	C29F	2/50	Crosville MS, Chester (CH) SL61
128421	HOT 809	Duple	55752	C29F	3/50	Hants & Sussex Motor Services Ltd, Emsworth (HA) 166
128426						Exported to Barcelona (O-E)
128437	DTK 636	Lee		C29F	6/50	RW Toop, WJ Ironside & PW Davis {Bere Regis & District}, Dorchester (DT)
128443						Exported to Barcelona (O-E)
128448	LFM 399	Duple	54825	C29F	2/50	Crosville MS, Chester (CH) SL62
128458	MKL 51	Duple	46397	C29F	2/50	White & Farmer {Swanley Coaches}, Crockenhill (KT)
128470 *	FBU 915	Duple	54371	C29F	2/50	Hilditch's Tours Ltd, Oldham (LA)
128504	KXY 989	Duple	47757	C29F	4/50	V Bingley (Bingley Bros) {Sceptre Coaches}, London W6 (LN)
128512	DTK 935	Lee		C29F	5/50	RW Toop, WJ Ironside & PW Davis {Bere Regis & District}, Dorchester (DT)
128522	HDA 999	Duple	49248	C29F	1/50	Harman's Motor Services Ltd, Wolverhampton (ST)
128527	KOE 967	Duple	55809	C29F	3/50	Smith's Imperial Coaches Ltd, Birmingham (WK)
128533						Exported to Barcelona (O-E)
128539	HSP 255	Duple	55737	C29F	2/50	R Cameron, Cowdenbeath (FE)
128547						Exported to Karachi (O-PK)
128552						Exported to Barcelona (O-E)
128561	BRC 188	Duple	44376	C29F	2/50	Moss & Smith, Macclesfield (CH)
128595	EUH 894	Duple	55811	C29F	1/50	ER Forse, Cardiff (GG)
128603	JWT 848	Duple	43952	C29F	3/50	W Simpson, Ripon (WR) 10

128608					Exported to Barcelona (O-E)
128614	DTY 955	Duple	50087	C29F	1/50 JT Beverley, Bedlington (ND)
128619	SB 8057	Duple	55753	C27F	2/50 C Fitzpatrick {Azure Blue Line}, Dunoon (AL)
128633					Exported to Barcelona (O-E)
128637 *	EFR 32	Duple	55644	C29F	2/50 Enterprise Motors (Blackpool) Ltd (LA)
128640					Exported to Karachi (O-PK)
128652	OMX 455	Duple	46858	C29F	2/50 Northern Roadways Ltd, Glasgow (LK)
128694	HWP 926	Duple	55650	B29F	2/50 Worcestershire Constabulary (XWO)
128699					Exported to Barcelona (O-E)
128705 *	VME 227	Duple	55795	C29F	-/-- Garner's Coaches Ltd, London W5 (LN)
128710 *	MHW 936	Duple	55736	C29F	5/50 Wessex Coaches Ltd, Bristol (GL)
128716					Exported to Barcelona (O-E)
128726	?	?		goods	1/50 Wright Bros, Birkenhead (GCH)
128731					Exported to Mauritius
128735 *	KFJ 695	Duple	55816	C29F	5/50 Way & Son, Crediton (DN)
128743		see 128746			
128746	CHL 679	Duple	50554	C29F	3/50 G Illingworth, Crigglestone (WR)
128785	?	?		van	-/-- Crosby Spring Interiors Ltd (furniture manufactuers), St Helens (GLA)
128790					Exported to Barcelona (O-E)
128796	HJW 106	Duple	48947	C24F	5/50 Worthington Motor Tours Ltd, Birmingham (WK)
128909	MWB 301	Duple	50297	C29F	6/50 WH & F Crossland, Sheffield (WR)
128915					Exported to Barcelona (O-E)
128924	LAL 618	Duple	55842	C29F	-/50 ES & RN Pitchford {Minster Garage}, Southwell (NG)
128934	UMY 449	Duple	43928	C29F	3/50 Valliant Direct Coaches Ltd, London W5 (LN)
128942	FSA 589	Mulliner	T484	B31F	1/50 JC Keir, Huntly (AD)
128984	DJN 991	Duple	55711	B31F	2/50 Runwell Hospital, Wickford (XEX)
128989					Exported to Rotterdam (O-NL)
128995	KRH 934	Duple	51180	C29F	5/50 Green's Auto Services (East Yorkshire) Ltd, Doncaster (WR)
129000	?	?		van	-/-- J Johnson & Son, Northwich (GCH)
129006					Exported to Rotterdam (O-NL)
129011	?	?		van	-/-- GT Culpitt (wholesale florists), London N1 (GLN)
129021					Exported to Mauritius
129025	DTY 954	Duple	50073	C29F	-/50 Bedlington & District Luxury Coaches Ltd, Ashington (ND)
129033	KYU 90	Duple	55799	B30F	-/50 University College Hospital, London NW1 (XLN)
129065	JP 8139	Duple	55826	C29F	2/50 J Lamb, Upholland (LA)
129075 *	DTY 810	Duple	44119	C29F	-/50 R Armstrong, Westerhope (ND) 76
129080 *	(D-12496 ?)	Hainje		B30-	-/-- DABO, Meppel (O-NL) 29
129086	JDG 898	?		van	2/50 RL Dance & Co Ltd (removals), Cheltenham (GGL)
129091	GCA 544	Duple	49250	C27F	2/50 A Mates, Chirk (DH)
129115	?	?		van	-/-- M Epstein, London EC2 (GLN)
129118	GAY 500	Plaxton	594	C29F	5/50 R, SL & AH Wheildon (R Wheildon & Sons), Castle Donington (LE)
129125					Exported to Rotterdam (O-NL)
129127	NPL 750	Duple	46558	C29F	4/50 GF & BS Graves {GF Graves & Son}, Redhill (SR)
129130	?	?		van	-/-- Fitt Bros, Norwich (GNK)
129163	NUA 258	Duple	50549	C29F	-/50 Wallace Arnold Tours Ltd, Leeds (WR)
129173	FF 7716	Duple	49251	C29F	3/50 WD Pugh & Sons, Towyn (ME)
129183	LAL 440	Duple	55651	C29F	3/50 W, WW & JA Gash {W Gash & Sons}, Elston (NG) B10
129193 *	DTY 811	Duple	44120	C29F	4/50 R Armstrong, Westerhope (ND) 77
129309 - 129320					Exported to Melbourne (O-AUS)
129370 *	FBU 927	Duple	54372	C29F	3/50 Joseph Dyson Ltd {Broadway Motors}, Oldham (LA)
129377	LUO 839	Duple	46408	C29F	1/50 SK Hill, Stibb Cross (DN)
129402		see 129462			
129419	LE-16-30	?		DP31D	2/50 Agostinho Sousa e Vaz, Angra do Heroísmo (O-AZ)
129422 *	AHC 222	Duple	55648	C27F	2/50 RL & PJ Jackson {Palmerston Coaches}, Eastbourne (ES) 10
129432	MWB 310	Duple	55680	C29F	2/50 EH Sims, Sheffield (WR)
129442	DVL 789	Duple	55825	C29F	5/50 Green's Auto Services (East Yorkshire) Ltd, Doncaster (WR)
129451 *	UMY 448	Duple	47759	C29F	2/50 H & C, Garston (HT)
129462 *	LE-16-31	Murteira		B29D	2/50 Agostinho Sousa e Vaz, Angra do Heroísmo (O-AZ)

129471	MKL 509	Duple	47941	C29F	3/50	RH Sims {Marion Coaches}, Margate (KT)
129473	GAW 46	Mulliner	Z55	DP28F	1/50	G Edwards, Bwlchgwyn (DH)
129522	NHN 266	Mulliner	AL02	C29F	4/50	TW Stephenson {Stephenson Bros}, High Etherley (DM)
129526	LNK 403	Duple	55857	C29F	2/50	TR Barker {Barker's Coaches/Garden City Coaches}, Hitchin (HT)
129532 *	DJR 344	Mulliner	AL03	C29F	4/50	CR Robson, Smelting Syke (ND)
129537	KVF 447	Duple	47909	C29F	4/50	NJ Peeke-Vout, Caston (NK)
129541	JTX 591	Mulliner	T542	B30F	2/50	GB Smith, Cymmer (GG)
129552						Exported to Montevideo (O-ROU)
129559	KYH 25	Duple	52431	C27F	3/50	George Ewer & Co Ltd {Grey Green}, London N16 (LN)
129562						Exported to Mauritius
129602	?	?		van	-/--	S Robbins Ltd, Rugby (GWK)
129614	LLT 332	Duple	51233	C29F	6/50	Wallis Hire Service Ltd {Dartmouth Coaches}, London SE23 (LN)
129618	OBB 327	?		library	-/50	Newcastle-upon-Tyne City Libraries (GND)
129624	LYD 410	Duple	46357	C27F	5/50	LC Munden {Airborne Coaches}, Bridgwater (SO)
129628	MMA 488	Duple	50943	C29F	5/50	AE Bowyer & Son Ltd, Northwich (CH)
129641	GHR 850	Duple	44714	C29F	3/50	E Drew, Highworth (WI)
129645						Exported to Montevideo (O-ROU)
129654						Exported to Mauritius
129693	CCF 648	Duple	55878	C29F	2/50	HS Theobald & Son, Long Melford (WF)
129704	HJW 107	Duple	48948	C24F	5/50	Worthington Motor Tours Ltd, Birmingham (WK)
129707	GWS 468	Duple	54736	C29F	2/50	Edinburgh Corporation (MN) X24
129714	GWS 467	Duple	54735	C29F	2/50	Edinburgh Corporation (MN) X23
129718						Exported to Mauritius
129732	VMV 126	Duple	48232	C29F	-/--	Pall Mall Car Hire {Pamalhire}, London SW1 (LN)
129736						Exported to Antwerp (O-B)
129745						Exported to Mauritius
129784	PPU 767	Duple	47725	C29F	1/50	L Little & ML Leader {Lansdowne Luxury Coaches}, London E11 (LN)
129796 *	JWT 703	Duple	51192	C29F	3/50	Ripponden & District Motors Ltd (WR)
129800	GVJ 596	Duple	54490	C29F	12/49	WE Morgan {Wye Valley Motors}, Hereford (HR)
129974	?	Duple	50809	C29F	-/--	Exported to unknown overseas location
129978 *	KXY 638	Duple	49023	C29F	2/50	Fallowfield & Britten Ltd, London E8 (LN)
130010 *	HOT 759	Duple	46620	C29F	3/50	Sunbeam Coaches (Loxwood) Ltd (WS) 167
130011						Exported to Antwerp (O-B)
130012						Exported to Singapore
130055	DHH 886	Mulliner	AL13	C24F	6/50	Blair & Palmer Ltd, Carlisle (CU) B42
130059	ONU 972	Duple	50533	C29F	3/50	E, E & H Webster {E Webster & Sons}, Hognaston (DE)
130065						Exported to Singapore
130070	JWT 841	Duple	55587	B31F	2/50	West Riding Constabulary (XWR)
130083	FNV 705	Duple	46567	C29F	3/50	KW Services Ltd, Daventry (NO) B8
130095						Exported to Singapore
130103	MKL 260	Duple	54402	C29F	3/50	G & GWJ Chapman {Chapman & Son}, Lenham Heath (KT)
130146	LTD 45	Duple	55822	C29F	3/50	T Towler (Lytham) Ltd (LA)
130150	FUT 784	Duple	43893	C29F	1/50	C & M Lester (Lester Bros), Long Whatton (LE)
130156						Exported to Malaya
130161	GWS 469	Duple	54737	C29F	2/50	Edinburgh Corporation (MN) X25
130175 *	FDR 244	Mulliner	Z58	B31F	3/50	Blake's Bus Services Ltd, Delabole (CO)
130180 *	?	Jonckheere	5874	C27-	1/50	Lison, Ghent (O-B)
130186						Exported to Malaya
130194 *	SS 7486	Duple	54879	C29F	2/50	JB Stark, Dunbar (EL)
130237	KYE 308	Duple	44854	C27F	2/50	HJ Phillips & Sons Ltd, London SW11 (LN) 1004
130241	HSC 317	Duple	55054	C29F	1/50	St Cuthbert's Co-operative Association Ltd, Edinburgh (MN) 15
130249	?	Mulliner		B--F	-/--	Original operator unknown (O-WAN)
130252	KEL 41	Duple	55527	C29F	3/50	Shamrock & Rambler Motor Coaches Ltd, Bournemouth (HA)
130265 *	LTD 981	Duple	55823	C29F	3/50	Farnworth's Motor Services Ltd, Blackburn (LA)
130277	?	Duple	50805	C25F	-/50	Meralli Bus Services Ltd, Nairobi (O-EAK)
130284 *	JAB 214	Pearson		C29F	5/50	Samuel Johnson (Supreme) Ltd, Stourbridge (WO)
130328	?	?		van	-/--	FG Alexander, London N21 (GLN)

C1252/165

130332	DST 800	Duple	55885	C29F	3/50	Alexander Sutherland & Sons {Skye Cars}, Broadhead, Skye (IV)
130338	?	?		van	-/--	FG Alexander, London N21 (GLN)
130343	JAX 325	Duple	43909	C29F	4/50	El Peake, Pontnewynydd (MH)
130357		see 135037				
130359	GMR 4	Duple	54106	C29F	3/50	AH Razey {Amport & District Motor Services}, Thruxton (HA)
130364						Exported to Antwerp (O-B)
130368						Exported to Mauritius
130575	KVR 320	Duple	49741	C29F	3/50	A Mayne & Son Ltd, Manchester (LA)
130579	VME 741	Duple	48147	C29F	-/50	Lacey's (East Ham) Ltd, London E6 (LN)
130585						Exported to Mauritius
130590	JTX 625	Duple	55901	C29F	3/50	Mrs SA Bebb, Llantwit Fardre (GG)
130603	JUE 383	Duple	55896	C29F	3/50	Priory Garage & Coaches Ltd, Leamington Spa (WK)
130606	KFJ 684	Duple	46964	C29F	5/50	Greenslades, Exeter (DN)
130615						Exported to Mauritius
130666 *	ACC 712	Duple	55766	C29F	6/51	OR Williams & Son {Whiteways}, Waenfawr (CN)
130670	GCY 757	Duple	48276	C29F	3/50	DW & EM Isaac (DW Isaac & Sons), Landore (GG)
130676						Exported to Mauritius
130681 *	DTY 995	Duple	51411	C29F	4/50	R Armstrong, Westerhope (ND) 80
130701	KUP 927	Duple	44328	C29F	3/50	R & J Armstrong and Mrs M Wardle {Cowling's Bus Service}, Ebchester (DM)
130705						Exported to Montevideo (O-ROU)
130745	NHN 42	Duple	50702	C29F	3/50	F Scott {Scott's Greys Coaches}, Darlington (DM) 68
130757	LMN 885	Duple	51121	C29F	1/50	T Moore {Moerzone}, Douglas (IM) 2
130761	GRY 54	Duple	47878	C29F	3/50	ET Straw, Leicester (LE)
130767						Exported to Singapore
130772	MFM 185	Plaxton	595	C29F	8/50	Needham {Davenport Motor Hire}, Stockport (CH)
130785	DTK 256	Duple	55827	C29F	3/50	CA Adams (Adams Bros) {Victory Tours}, Sixpenny Handley (DT)
130797						Exported to Suva (O-FJI)
130805 *	LYC 731	Duple	55905	C29F	3/50	OGA Lyons {Blagdon Lioness}, Blagdon (SO)
130847						Exported to Montevideo (O-ROU)
130852	MKO 138	Plaxton	573	FC30F	6/50	EG Weeks {Valedene Coaches}, Sutton Valence (KT)
130860	FTH 100	Duple	48337	C29F	3/50	HE Clarke (Clarke Bros) {Capel Evan Express}, Capel Evan (CR)
130863	GAW 236	Duple	43244	C27F	2/50	DJ Hampson {Hampson's Luxury Coaches}, Oswestry (SH) 22
130876	KCD 947	Duple	55529	C29F	-/50	RG Johnston {Unique Coaches}, Brighton (ES)
130888						Exported to Suva (O-FJI)
130896 *	CCB 298	Duple	50982	C29F	2/50	Brook Electric Motors, Huddersfield (XWR)
130938	GDL 617	Duple	49017	C29F	4/50	SH, AC, PH & AR Randall (H Randall & Sons), Bonchurch (IW)
130942	?	Mulliner		?	1/50	Anglo-Iranian Oil Co, Sunbury (XMX)
130949	?	Duple	50804	C25F	-/50	Meralli Bus Services Ltd, Nairobi (O-EAK)
130953	EF 9295	Duple	43700	C24F	3/50	Bee-Line Continental Tours Ltd, Newcastle (ND)
130966 *	EF 9296	Duple	43699	C24F	3/50	Bee-Line Continental Tours Ltd, Newcastle (ND)
130978	?	Mulliner		?	-/--	Original operator unknown (O-WAN)
130986	GDL 616	Duple	43990	C29F	6/50	Shotters Ltd, Brighstone (IW)
131031	?	Mulliner	T504	B32-	2/50	Sir Robert McAlpine & Sons Ltd (contractor), London W1
131034	HOT 339	Duple	46227	C27F	3/50	DG Grace {Graceline Coaches}, Alresford (HA)
131040	GDL 618	Duple	44100	C29F	3/50	West Wight Motor Bus Co Ltd, Totland Bay (IW)
131045 *	KBJ 721	Duple	55820	C29F	4/50	Mrs M Moyse {Nightingale Coaches}, Beccles (EK)
131052		see 131058				
131058	HEW 150	Duple	55813	C29F	4/50	SV Robinson, Kimbolton (HN)
131070						Exported to Helsinki (O-FIN)
131078						Exported to Suva (O-FJI)
131101 - 131112						Exported to Melbourne (O-AUS)
131270 *	?	NZMB		-25-	-/51	Mount Cook & Southern Lakes Tourist Co, Christchurch (O-NZ) 48
131301	NUA 533	Duple	55883	C29F	4/50	JB Midgely & Son Ltd, Leeds (WR)
131305	MKL 635	Duple	55620	C29F	3/50	White & Farmer {Swanley Coaches}, Crockenhill (KT)

131311	SB 8075	Duple	54692	C27F	3/50	Air Industrial Developments Ltd {Gold Line}, Dunoon (AL)
131316	EDP 924	Duple	43565	C29F	3/50	AE Smith {Smith's Coaches}, Reading (BE)
131329	?	?		goods	3/50	Staffordshire County Council Education (GST)
131341, 131349						Exported to Suva (O-FJI)
131392 *	ACC 629	Duple	55471	C29F	3/50	Penmaenmawr Motor Co Ltd (CN)
131396	?	?		van	-/--	G Davis Ltd, Great Yarmouth (GNK)
131402	VME 733	Duple	55977	C29F	3/50	L Manny Ltd, London SW9 (LN)
131407 *	MWB 497	Duple	50390	C29F	3/50	CG Littlewood, Sheffield (WR)
131420	GNT 517	Plaxton	597	C29F	6/50	Greatrex Motor Coaches Ltd, Stafford (ST) 66
131432	?	Jonckheere	5870	C28-	5/50	Fedesrspeil, Differdange (O-L)
131440						Exported to Suva (O-FJI)
131469 *	JAB 213	Duple	47639	C29F	3/50	Samuel Johnson (Supreme) Ltd, Stourbridge (WO)
131482	WMX 27	Mulliner	Z62	B31F	4/50	Middlesex County Council (XMX)
131486	MAU 577	Duple	47731	C29F	4/50	A Camm {Camm's Coaches}, Nottingham (NG) 12
131492						Exported to Singapore
131497	NVK 434	Duple	50105	C29F	-/50	Moordale Bus Services Ltd, Newcastle (ND) 11
131510	GAW 360	Duple	49257	C29F	5/51	AJ Boulton {Arthur Boulton's Bus Service}, Cardington (SH)
131522						Exported to Singapore
131526 *	KEL 94	Duple	55528	C29F	3/50	Shamrock & Rambler Motor Coaches Ltd, Bournemouth (HA)
131574	KYE 535	Duple	44538	C29F	3/50	Fallowfield & Britten Ltd, London E8 (LN)
131584	WMX 35	Mulliner	Z61	B31F	4/50	Middlesex County Council (XMX)
131589	VME 925	Duple	48287	C29F	-/--	W Grier & J Wilkinson {Lucky Line Coaches}, Edgware (MX)
131596						Exported to Penang (O-MAL)
131602 *	DJA 971	Duple	54373	C29F	3/50	EC Morley & W Pickford {Great Moor Coaches}, Stockport (CH)
131614	AEN 63	Duple	47784	C29F	3/50	Auty's Tours Ltd, Bury (LA)
131621						Exported to Antwerp (O-B)
131664	SB 8085	Mulliner	T553	B26F	3/50	DT & J McPhail, Kilberry (AL)
131675	LNK 693	Duple	55910	C29F	3/50	Smiths (Buntingford) Ltd (HT)
131680	JRM 651	Duple	56017	C29F	3/50	E & L Titterington, Blencow (CU)
131686	FBO 57	Duple	55899	C29F	3/50	EG Falconer & PW Watts, Llanishen (GG)
131691	GED 624	?		lorry	2/50	Peter Walker & Son (Warrington & Burton) Ltd (brewers), Warrington (GCH)
131901						Exported to Penang (O-MAL)
131905						Exported to Helsinki (O-FIN)
131956	GVJ 724	Duple	54484	C29F	2/50	Miss I Baynham, Ross-on-Wye (HR)
131960	KBJ 712	Mulliner	T552	C28F	3/50	Combs Coaches Ltd, Ixworth (EK)
131963	AYJ 666	Duple	56016	C29F	1/50	GB Fyffe, Dundee (AS)
131970	DWH 871	Duple	54374	C27F	4/50	Lomax Bros (Transport) Ltd, Bolton (LA)
131988, 131995						Exported to Suva (O-FJI)
132035						Exported to Karachi (O-PK)
132039	LTD 953	Duple	56024	C29F	3/50	Mercers (Longridge) Ltd (LA)
132048	GFU 140	Duple	43884	C29F	1/50	JE Vessey, Hibaldstow (LI)
132053	FVA 513	Duple	56029	C29F	3/50	Daniel Henderson & Sons, Carstairs (LK)
132062	GAW 464	Duple	55791	B30F	3/50	JT, FW & GE Whittle {JT Whittle & Sons}, Highley (SH)
132072	OPA 798	Duple	44461	C29F	3/50	ER Gudge {Comfy Coaches}, Farnham (SR)
132081	?	Mulliner		B--F	-/--	Anglo Iranian Oil Co, location unknown (O-IR)
132084	DWH 709	Duple	55036	C27F	3/50	JR Woodhouse & TH Barton {W & B Coaches}, Sandiacre (NG)
132120 *	JWW 933	Mulliner	AL09	C30F	5/50	JT Hey {Silver Star}, Carleton (WR)
132124	MKO 207	Duple	55840	C29F	5/50	GM Welch, Gillingham (KT)
132127		see 132124				
132130		see 132120				
132136	LAL 564	Duple	49558	C29F	4/50	FL Lees {Lees Motorways}, Worksop (NG)
132141	VME 732	Duple	46859	C29F	-/50	Northern Roadways Ltd, Glasgow (LK)
132150	VME 742	Duple	44056	C29F	3/51	Essex County Coaches Ltd, London E15 (LN)
132157						Exported to Karachi (O-PK)
132165	FT 6905	Duple	50135	C29F	-/50	G Chapman {Priory Motor Coach Co}, North Shields (ND) 59
132170	?	Mulliner		B--F	-/--	Anglo Iranian Oil Co, location unknown (O-IR)

132208	FMO 583	Duple	44160	C29F	3/50	W & G Chandler, Wantage (BE)
132215	JDG 989	Duple	47957	C29F	3/50	CAJ Scarrott {Luxury Coaches}, Stow-on-the-Wold (GL)
132224	PTW 268	Duple	55886	C29F	3/50	HL Stracy, Little Baddow (EX)
132229	VMV 691	Duple	55800	C29F	3/50	Mono Containers Ltd, London NW10 (XLN)
132238 *	MHU 58	Duple	54781	B30F	5/50	Bristol Tramways (GL) 216
132249						Exported to Mauritius
132253 *	JWU 307	Duple	55879	C29F	4/50	Clifford Lunn, Rothwell (WR)
132258						Exported to Santiago (O-RCH)
132296						Exported to Mauritius
132303 *	JUE 860	Duple	46694	C29F	3/50	RS Webb, Armscote (WK)
132312 *	MHU 59	Duple	54782	B30F	5/50	Bristol Tramways (GL) 217
132317	SS 7501	Duple	56030	C29F	3/50	W Cleghorn, Haddington (EL)
132323	JTX 193	Duple	55898	C29F	11/49	Humphreys Garages (Pontypridd) Ltd (GG)
132344						Exported to Santiago (O-RCH)
132377	?	Mulliner		B--F	-/--	Original operator unknown (O-WAN)
132379	FMO 743	Duple	55776	C29F	3/51	Berkshire Constabulary (XBE)
132384 *	GBE 975	Duple	54830	C29F	6/50	Lincolnshire RCC, Bracebridge Heath (KN) 761
132391	EFX 231	(Lee ?)		B29F	8/50	Dorset County Council Education (XDT)
132497 - 132508						Exported to Melbourne (O-AUS)
123593		see 123595				
132595	LGC 729	Duple	56034	C29F	4/50	Camden Coaches Ltd, Edgware (MX)
132597, 132612						Exported to Dar-Es-Salaam (O-EAT)
132620	LYC 782	Duple	56031	C29F	4/50	Western Engineering & Motor Services {WEMS}, Weston-super-Mare (SO) 51
132625 *	GBE 976	Duple	54831	C29F	6/50	Lincolnshire RCC, Bracebridge Heath (KN) 762
132660						Exported to Barcelona (O-E)
132663 *	GBE 977	Duple	54832	C29F	7/50	Lincolnshire RCC, Bracebridge Heath (KN) 763
132670 *	LTA 914	Duple	54806	C29F	3/50	Southern National, Exeter (DN) 1438
132680 *	GBE 978	Duple	54833	C29F	7/50	Lincolnshire RCC, Bracebridge Heath (KN) 764
132685 #	RN 494	Duple	?	B20F	-/50	Admiralty (Royal Navy) (GOV)
132692		see 132694				
132694 *	LNN 147	Duple	55738	C29F	3/50	Clark's Coaches (Epperstone) Ltd (NG)
132701 #	RN 492	Duple	?	B20F	-/50	Admiralty (Royal Navy) (GOV)
132709 *	EFR 185	Duple	55824	C29F	4/50	A Newton & Son, Blackpool (LA)
132744						Exported to Barcelona (O-E)
132751	?	?		van	-/--	JH Hunt & Co (High Wycombe) Ltd (furniture manufacturers) (GBK)
132759 *	FDR 295	Duple	49378	C29F	4/50	Embankment Motor Co (Plymouth) Ltd (DN)
132768 #	RN 493	Duple	?	B20F	-/50	Admiralty (Royal Navy) (GOV)
132773	GAW 759	Mulliner	Z56	B31F	4/50	JT, FW & GE Whittle {JT Whittle & Sons}, Highley (SH)
132785	DJR 485	Pearson		C29F	5/50	JO Merson, Morpeth (ND)
132789						Exported to Karachi (O-PK)
132797 *	MRL 70	Duple	54467	C29F	3/50	RA Richards {Truronian}, Truro (CO)
132802	D-14858	BRK		B29-	-/50	Syver C Haakerud, Austmarka (O-N)
132839						Exported to Karachi (O-PK)
132844	GCY 837	Mulliner	AL07	C29F	5/50	EJ Jenkins & Sons {Streamline Coaches}, Swansea (GG)
132848	NHN 326	Mulliner	AL10	C29F	5/50	Anderson Bros {Blue Belle}, Evenwood (DM)
132861	JUE 823	Duple	46898	C29F	3/50	De Luxe Buses Ltd, Mancetter (WK)
132870	HWF 557	Duple	54325	C29F	3/50	J Broadbent, Stamford Bridge (ER) 18
132876						Exported to Antwerp (O-B)
132882	LAH 75	Duple	55817	C29F	3/50	LL Parnell, West Rudham (NK)
132888						Exported to Penang (O-MAL)
132928 *	HJW 128	Duple	56074	C29F	5/50	RD Cox, Bilston (ST)
132936	NHN 325	Mulliner	AL11	C28F	4/50	H Atkinson, Ingleby Arncliffe (NR)
132949	CCB 349	Duple	50980	C29F	1/50	H Kirkham (F Kirkham & Son), Church (LA)
132952						Exported to Penang (O-MAL)
132958 *	LTA 913	Duple	54807	C29F	3/50	Southern National, Exeter (DN) 1437
132969						Exported to Montevideo (O-ROU)
132973	VME 109	Duple	50233	C29F	3/50	Ardley Bros Coaches Ltd, London N17 (LN)
132976	5294	Barbara		B32C	11/51	Route Bus Service (O-M)
133073 *	P.424	Auckland TB		B33F	-/52	Auckland Transport Board (O-NZ) 143
133074 *	P.607	North Shore		B33F	-/50	North Shore Transport Co Ltd, Takapuna (O-NZ) 7
133075 *	P1.179	Transport BS		B35F	12/50	Transport BS Ltd, Auckland (O-NZ) 6

133076	P.606	North Shore		B33F	-/50	North Shore Transport Co Ltd, Takapuna (O-NZ) 6
133077 *	P.357	Auckland TB		B30F	6/52	Auckland Transport Board (O-NZ) 22
133078						Exported to Wellington (O-NZ)
133079 *	P.568	Suburban		B33F	-/50	Suburban Buses Ltd, Te Papapa (O-NZ) 17
133080						Exported to Wellington (O-NZ)
133081	H7.489	?		tower	-/--	Auckland Transport Board (O-NZ) 4
133082 *	P.396	Auckland TB		B33F	4/51	Auckland Transport Board (O-NZ) 62
133083 *	P.407	Auckland TB		B33F	7/51	Auckland Transport Board (O-NZ) 122
133084 *	P.582	Suburban		B33F	12/50	Suburban Buses Ltd, Te Papapa (O-NZ) 41
133195						Exported to Malta
133203	BJV 140	Duple	44989	C29F	4/50	A & AE Blackbourn Ltd {Granville Tours}, Grimsby (LI) 161
133216	VME 87	Duple	54746	B31F	4/50	Middlesex County Council (XMX)
133219	HOT 532	Duple	43349	C29F	c2/50	GC, FW & GR Warren {Altonian Coaches}, Alton (HA)
133225	GAW 581	Duple	55792	B30F	3/50	Jones Coachways Ltd, Market Drayton (SH) 34
133232						Exported to Montevideo (O-ROU)
133238 *	MHU 60	Duple	54783	B30F	5/50	Bristol Tramways (GL) 218
133244						Exported to Lagos (O-WAN)
133284 #	RN 508	Duple	?	B30F	-/50	Admiralty (Royal Navy) (GOV)
133292	NHN 188	Duple	55858	C29F	3/50	EG James & RW Mosley {Croft Spa Motor Services}, Croft Spa (NR)
133305	LTA 915	Duple	55913	C29F	3/50	Southern National, Exeter (DN) 1439
133308 #	RN 495	Duple	?	B20F	-/50	Admiralty (Royal Navy) (GOV)
133314	VME 744	Duple	43929	C29F	3/50	Valliant Direct Coaches Ltd, London W5 (LN)
133320						Exported to Helsinki (O-FIN)
133326	FMO 627	Duple	46316	C29F	3/50	Tom Tappin Ltd {Travel Rambler}, Wallingford (BE)
133332	VME 303	Duple	55026	C29F	3/50	George Wimpey (contractor), London W6
133372 #	RN 513	Duple	?	B30F	-/50	Admiralty (Royal Navy) (GOV)
133380	LTA 916	Duple	55912	C29F	3/50	Southern National, Exeter (DN) 1440
133393	GRY 222	Duple	48003	C29F	3/50	J Peet {Tudor Coaches}, Leicester (LE)
133396	?	Duple	50806	C27F	-/50	Meralli Bus Services Ltd, Nairobi (O-EAK)
133557 - 133568						Exported to Melbourne (O-AUS)
133582	LTA 918	Duple	55914	C29F	3/50	Southern National, Exeter (DN) 1442
133592	L-22026	?		B---	-/--	Thorvald Hamre, Moi (O-N)
133594	EFX 232	(Lee ?)		B29F	8/50	Dorset County Council Education (XDT)
133600	LTA 917	Duple	55911	C29F	3/50	Southern National, Exeter (DN) 1441
133640	?	Duple	50807	C27F	-/50	Meralli Bus Services Ltd, Nairobi (O-EAK)
133648	SX 6901	Duple	54908	C29F	3/50	McMillan & Muir, Livingston Station (WL)
133661	DRS 493	Duple	54985	C29F	3/50	JW Duguid {Swallow Tours}, Aberdeen (AD)
133664	?	Duple	50803	C29F	-/--	Shell Petroleum Co, Port of Spain (O-TT)
133670	KYE 905	Duple	52432	C29F	3/50	George Ewer & Co Ltd {Grey Green}, London N16 (LN)
133676	VMV 701	Duple	55027	C29F	4/50	George Wimpey (contractor), London W6
133682	T-5802	?		B---	9/50	Original operator unknown (O-N)
133688	VME 200	Duple	44398	C29F	-/--	RG Flexman {Flexman's Coaches}, Southall (MX)
133728						Exported to Mauritius
133736	VME 745	Duple	55969	C29F	-/--	E Evans {Evan Evan Tours}, London WC1 (LN)
133749	GDL 667	Duple	48795	C29F	3/50	H Paul (H Paul & Son), Ryde (IW) 6
133752						Exported to Mauritius
133758	HTM 986	Duple	56067	C29F	4/50	OA Bartle & Co, Potton (BD) B/50/5
133764	L-14267	?		B---	9/50	Opstad Arbeidsleir, location unknown (O-N)
133770	LDV 477	Duple	56049	C29F	3/50	RL Walls & Son, Dartmouth (DN)
133776	WMC 3	LCMW		B26R	3/51	Middlesex County Council (XMX)
133811						Exported to Antwerp (O-B)
133816						Exported to Dar-Es-Salaam (O-EAT)
133824	KVR 994	Duple	49756	C29F	4/50	Sykes' Motor Tours Ltd, Sale (CH)
133837 *	VME 161	Duple	55709	C29F	-/--	Fox & Hart Ltd {Hounslow Star Coaches}, Hounslow (MX)
133840 *	LTA 922	Duple	55918	C29F	3/50	Southern National, Exeter (DN) 1446
133851						Exported to Basra (O-IRQ)
133857						Exported to Dar-Es-Salaam (O-EAT)
133863	NVK 849	Duple	50107	C29F	5/50	S Featonby {Shotton Bus Co}, Shotton Colliery (DM)
133868	TRE 753	Duple	49239	C29F	5/50	GH Austin & Sons Ltd {Happy Days}, Stafford (ST) 56
133903	VME 605	Duple	52090	C29F	-/--	Venture Transport (Hendon) Ltd, London NW2 (LN)
133911	LTE 312	Duple	56078	C25F	4/50	IJ Curwen & Sons Ltd, Lancaster (LA)

133924 *	LAD 192	Pearson		FC31F	9/51 ACJ Perrett {Perrett's Coaches}, Shipton Oliffe (GL)
133927 #	RN 509	Duple	?	B30F	-/50 Admiralty (Royal Navy) (GOV)
133932	KOH 250	Duple	44287	C29F	3/50 Dalton's Garage Ltd, Birmingham (WK)
133944 #	RN 496	Duple	?	B20F	-/50 Admiralty (Royal Navy) (GOV)
133947	I-8887	?		B---	7/50 Original operator unknown (O-N)
133951 *	LTA 919	Duple	55915	C29F	3/50 Southern National, Exeter (DN) 1443
133992 *	LTA 920	Duple	55916	C29F	3/50 Southern National, Exeter (DN) 1444
134000	JS 8852	Duple	56085	C29F	5/50 D Noble & Sons, Muir of Ord (RY)
134013 *	MMN 18	Pearson		C29F	3/50 JR Crellin {Castle Rushen Motors}, Castletown (IM)
134016 #	RN 497	Duple	?	B30F	-/50 Admiralty (Royal Navy) (GOV)
134022	HTM 721	Duple	49209	C29F	3/50 HJ Hill {Bedfordia Coaches}, Kempston (BD)
134028					Exported to Helsinki (O-FIN)
134034 #	RN 498	Duple	?	B30F	-/50 Admiralty (Royal Navy) (GOV)
134040 *	?	Mulliner	T555	?	-/50 Perkins Engines Co Ltd, Peterborough (XCM)
134080					Exported to Penang (O-MAL)
134088	LTA 923	Duple	55920	C29F	4/50 Southern National, Exeter (DN) 1447
134101	GED 492	Duple	50400	C29F	4/50 F Sykes {F Sykes & Sons}, Warrington (LA)
134104					Exported to Penang (O-MAL)
134110	MUM 455	Duple	50550	C29F	-/49 Wallace Arnold Tours Ltd, Leeds (WR)
134116	T-1061	?		B29-	-/-- O Djupvik, Gurskøy (O-N)
134122	KYE 924	Duple	55762	C29F	5/50 Fallowfield & Britten Ltd, London E8 (LN)
134128	TRF 953	Plaxton	578	C29F	7/50 Greatrex Motor Coaches Ltd, Stafford (ST) 67 Nuthatch
134162	?	Mulliner	T556	?	-/50 Perkins Engines Co Ltd, Peterborough (XCM)
134168					Exported to Karachi (O-PK)
134177	I-8879	?		B9FV	-/-- T Waaland, Nesgrenda (O-N)
134189	VMV 702	Duple	55028	C29F	4/50 George Wimpey (contractor), London W6
134192					Exported to Karachi (O-PK)
134198	ETL 221	Plaxton	579	C29F	6/50 CW Blankley {Gem Luxury Coaches}, Colsterworth (KN)
134420 #	K-8115	OCA		B25-	7/50 Torkel Bakke og Sigurd Sigbjørnsen (Bakkeruta) (O-N)
134426 *	LTA 921	Duple	55917	C29F	3/50 Southern National, Exeter (DN) 1445
134432	LTA 924	Duple	55919	C29F	4/50 Southern National, Exeter (DN) 1448
134472	KYK 110	Duple	56091	C29F	-/-- J Gaine {Wayfarer Coaches}, London SE3 (LN)
134482	OJO 895	Dutfield		C29F	5/50 PC Skinner {Percival's Coaches}, Oxford (OX) 27
134493	GVJ 832	Duple	54491	C29F	4/50 FC Cottrell {Cottrell's Coaches}, Mitcheldean (GL)
134502	LTA 925	Duple	55921	C29F	4/50 Southern National, Exeter (DN) 1449
134508	?	Duple	50808	B30F	-/50 Wilhelm Nielsen, Tórshavn (O-FR)
134514	NDH 663	Plaxton	593	C29F	6/50 Pearson's Motorways Ltd, Walsall (ST)
134521	DTK 536	Duple	46250	C29F	6/50 RW Toop, WJ Ironside & PW Davis {Bere Regis & District}, Dorchester (DT)
134559	KAD 61	Duple	56104	C29F	3/50 HJ Flint, Nettleton (WI)
134567	KYE 464	Duple	44838	C29F	4/50 Keith & Boyle (London) Ltd {Orange Luxury Coaches}, London EC2 (LN) Wasp
134580	DWH 750	Duple	51028	C29F	4/50 ET Butterworth Ltd {Pathfinder}, Blackpool (LA)
134583					Exported to Tanga (O-EAT)
134589	KAO 77	Duple	56088	C27F	5/50 W & I Moffat, Cleator Moor (CU)
134595	B-9864	?		B29-	7/50 Marie Hansen, Slangsvoll (O-N)
134601					Exported to Karachi (O-PK)
134639	GCA 747	Duple	49261	C29F	4/50 SE & R Owen {Owen Bros}, Rhostyllen (DH)
134642	CCF 649	Duple	55970	C29F	4/50 EJ Mulley {Mulley's Motorways}, Ixworth (WF) 31
134650	HVE 242	Duple	49030	C29F	4/50 Premier Travel Ltd, Cambridge (CM) 80
134661	FBK 559	Pearson		C29F	6/50 CAW Salmon {Unity Coaches}, Portsmouth (HA)
134665	DJR 264	Duple	50084	C29F	4/50 WM Appleby & JD Jordan {A & J Coaches}, Bedlington (ND)
134673	B-9846	?		B---	8/50 Helge Røstad, Våler (O-N)
134687	ORA 281	Duple	44513	C29F	4/50 ET White & Sons Ltd, Calver (DE)
134698	LPT 858	Pearson		FC31F	11/50 N Hitch {Thornley Luxury Coaches}, Thornley (DM)
134730	MPP 658	Duple	55904	C27F	12/49 JC Chastell & DG Gray {The Dean Bus Service}, Cookham Dean (BE)
134738 *	EFR 226	Duple	56105	C29F	4/50 Whiteside Ltd, Blackpool (LA)
134753	LTA 756	Duple	56057	C29F	6/50 Western National, Exeter (DN) 1417
134761					Exported to Lisbon (O-P)
134775	JP 8415	Duple	49950	C29F	6/50 W Liptrot (Coaches) Ltd, Bamfurlong (LA)
134786 *	LTA 926	Duple	55922	C29F	4/50 Southern National, Exeter (DN) 1450

135021	GAW 755	Mulliner	Z59	B31F	3/50	JT, FW & GE Whittle {JT Whittle & Sons}, Highley (SH)
135025	DE-16-73	Ogame		B29D	4/50	Comissão de Acção Social, Lisboa (O-P)
135029	DAG 578	Mulliner	Z57	B31F	5/50	R Taylor & Sons, Douglas (LK)
135037	ECT 912	Duple	43457	C29F	4/50	Sharpe's Motors (Heckington) Ltd (LI)
135045	LTA 751	Duple	56052	C29F	6/50	Western National, Exeter (DN) 1412
135055 *	61-522	?		B24-	-/--	Original operator unknown (O-GR)
135067						Exported to Karachi (O-PK)
135078	VME 226	Duple	52047	C29F	4/50	BEA, Ruislip (MX) 1123
135113 *	62-574	?		B28-	9/50	Original operator unknown (O-GR)
135118	GDM 266	Duple	43607	C29F	4/50	Rhyl United Coachways Ltd, Rhyl (FT) B8
135125	HJW 267	Duple	48949	C24F	5/50	Worthington Motor Tours Ltd, Birmingham (WK)
135133	VME 574	Duple	49443	C29F	-/50	TJ Brown & JF Grout {Lee & District Motor Services}, Chesham (BK)
135146 *	?	?		B24-	-/--	Original operator unknown (O-GR)
135155	KVU 914	Duple	54376	C29F	4/50	Sharp's Motor Services (Manchester) Ltd (LA)
135166	GAJ 2	Duple	44882	C29F	4/50	Saltburn Motor Services Ltd, Saltburn (NR) 14
135206	KYE 781	Duple	56098	C29F	4/50	Car Contracts, London SE5 (XLN)
135213	GAW 819	Duple	49256	C29F	4/50	WH & W Lowe (JE Lowe & Sons) {Tulip Coaches}, Hadley (SH)
135221 *	?	?		h/box	-/--	Taylor of Rottingdean Ltd (GES)
135229 *	70-200	?		B24-	-/--	Original operator unknown (O-GR)
135243	REV 972	Thurgood	643	C29F	6/50	WG Amos {J Amos & Son}, Belchamp St Paul (EX)
135254 *	LTA 752	Duple	56053	C29F	5/50	Western National, Exeter (DN) 1413
135289	R-1217	?		B8FV	6/50	LL Eksingedalsruta, Modalen (O-N)
135294 #	RN 512	Duple	?	B30F	-/50	Admiralty (Royal Navy) (GOV)
135300 *	NAE 71	Duple	46320	C29F	5/50	Wessex Coaches Ltd, Bristol (GL)
135309	KAD 122	Duple	55887	C29F	5/50	ATW Ayland, Westbury-on-Severn (GL)
135317						Exported to Antwerp (O-B)
135325 *	NUB 175	Duple	55880	C29F	4/50	H Austin (Coaches) Leeds Ltd (WR)
135331	GOW 541	Duple	56126	C29F	c4/50	H Whapshare {Winchester & District}, Winchester (HA)
135342	GMR 750	Mulliner	AL05	C29F	6/50	D Cornelius {Melrose Coaches}, Warminster (WI)
135377						Exported to Alexandria (O-ET)
135389	HDK 305	Duple	49496	C29F	4/50	Kershaw's Luxury Tours Ltd, Rochdale (LA)
135397 *	LTA 753	Duple	56054	C29F	4/50	Western National, Exeter (DN) 1414
135405						Exported to Alexandria (O-ET)
135413	LUR 409	Thurgood	642	C29F	6/50	CW Jones {Enterprise Bus Service}, Kimpton (HT)
135419	MKN 981	Duple	49043	C29F	-/50	Grundon's Coaches Ltd, London SE9 (LN)
135430	DJR 159	Duple	51046	C29F	5/50	WF Wilkinson {Swift Motor Service}, Ashington (ND)
135477	GDL 702	Duple	46339	C29F	5/50	Mrs V Pearce {White Heather}, Ryde (IW)
135485	?	?		van	-/--	Copplestone Unsworth Co Ltd, Liverpool (GLA)
135493						Exported to Alexandria (O-ET)
135537 - 135548						Exported to Bombay (O-IND)
135705 *	EHJ 300	Duple	48355	C29F	5/50	LA Daniel {West Leigh Motor Coaches}, Leigh-on-Sea (EX)
135711 *	LTA 754	Duple	56055	C29F	5/50	Western National, Exeter (DN) 1415
135722 *	DCK 410	Duple	56109	C29F	4/50	Farnworth's Motor Services Ltd, Blackburn (LA)
135750						Exported to Alexandria (O-ET)
135758	DJL 52	Duple	56186	C29F	5/50	JR Flatt & Sons Ltd, Long Sutton (LI)
135769	LRO 486	Duple	52232	C29F	-/50	N & S Coaches Ltd, Kibworth (LE)
135777 *	MMN 57	Duple	51125	C29F	3/50	RH Corkill, Onchan (IM)
135785						Exported to Alexandria (O-ET)
135793 #	RN 511	Duple	?	B30F	-/50	Admiralty (Royal Navy) (GOV)
135799	HOU 377	Duple	47890	C29F	5/50	Hants & Sussex Motor Services Ltd, Emsworth (HA) 181
135810	VME 296	Duple	43803	C29F	-/50	Gilbert's Luxury Coaches Ltd, London EC1 (LN)
135846	VMV 138	Duple	48233	C29F	-/--	Pall Mall Car Hire {Pamalhire}, London SW1 (LN)
135857	NHN 327	Mulliner	AL12	C29F	5/50	Anderson Bros {Blue Belle}, Evenwood (DM)
135865	GAY 237	Duple	56122	C29F	4/50	W Housden, Loughborough (LE) 6
135873						Exported to Alexandria (O-ET)
135881 *	LTF 965	Mulliner	AL15	C29F	7/50	S Morris, Kirkby Lonsdale (WT)
135888	?	Mulliner		B--F	-/--	Anglo Iranian Oil Co, location unknown (O-IR)
135898	?	?		goods	7/50	Brown, Chester (GCH)
135934	PVW 216	Duple	52176	C29F	5/50	Leighton Coach Co Ltd, Ilford (EX)
135948	DES 200	Duple	55594	C29F	5/50	D McIntosh & Sons, Errol (PH)

C1252/171

135953	VME 495	Duple	44790	C29F	-/--	EA & ER Webber (Webber Bros) {Empire's Best}, London N22 (LN) 22
135961 *	62-878	Gerakotellis		B24-	-/--	Original operator unknown (O-GR)
135967		see 135969				
135969	GCY 957	Duple	51403	C29F	4/50	R Parkhouse & Sons, Penclawdd (GG)
135975	EDB 39	Duple	50495	C29F	5/50	Stockport Coachways, Manchester (LA)
135986	LTA 755	Duple	56056	C29F	6/50	Western National, Exeter (DN) 1416
136221						Exported to Piraeus (O-GR)
136237	GFU 501	Duple	56025	C29F	5/50	M Williams {Trent Motors}, Scunthorpe (LI)
136245 *	JAB 661	Duple	49993	C29F	5/50	CCO Powell, Dunley (WO)
136253						Exported to Piraeus (O-GR)
136261	TRF 228	Duple	47711	C29F	5/50	JW Genner, Quarry Bank (ST)
136267	MKO 67	Mulliner	AL04	C29F	5/50	Omnia Transporters Ltd, Bromley (KT)
136278	BJV 292	Duple	55801	C27F	4/50	FA & WR Stark (FA Stark and Sons), Tetney (LI) 10
136311						Exported to Karachi (O-PK)
136318	GAW 870	Duple	49258	C29F	4/50	H Carter {Reliance}, Ironbridge (SH)
136325 *	GAJ 259	Duple	54745	C29F	5/50	SF Wilson, Helmsley (NR)
136333	KYE 309	Duple	49544	C27F	2/50	HJ Phillips & Sons Ltd, London SW11 (LN) 1005
136335		see 136333				
136343 *	68-624	?		B24-	-/50	Original operator unknown (O-GR)
136349	?	?		van	-/--	Taylor Bros, Pemberton (GLA)
136355	?	?		van	-/--	S Turner, Whitley Bay (GND)
136367						Exported to Antwerp (O-B)
136390 #	?	Jonckheere	5861	C27-	3/50	Bailly, Ans (O-B)
136406	EVH 664	Duple	50360	C29F	3/50	Chapman's Ivy Coaches Ltd, Milnsbridge (WR)
136413	LYD 311	Duple	56124	C29F	6/50	PJ Riggs {Vista Coaches}, Clutton (SO)
136421	LTA 757	Duple	56058	C29F	6/50	Western National, Exeter (DN) 1418
136429						Exported to Helsinki (O-FIN)
136437	GCA 848	Mulliner	T539	B31F	5/50	SE & R Owen {Owen Bros}, Rhostyllen (DH)
136443	OS 7567	Duple	56082	C29F	-/50	G McKeand, Kirkinner (WN)
136452	H-6670	Wattenberg		B---	7/50	Stavdal og Haugen {Skien-Ryggen}, Skien (O-N)
136494	GDM 369	Duple	54999	C29F	6/50	P & O Lloyd, Bagillt (FT)
136501	FTH 369	Duple	55637	C29F	5/50	JD Evans & CA Jones {Gwalia Bus Service}, Llanybyther (CR)
136509	EF 9408	Duple	55859	C29F	5/50	Richardson Bros, West Hartlepool (DM)
136517	X-767	?		B7FV	7/50	Hans W Bjørnsund, Nerala (O-N)
136525	EVH 719	Duple	50415	C29F	3/50	Hanson's Buses Ltd, Huddersfield (WR) 276
136528	TMM 829	Duple	55045	C29F	-/50	Dicks, London NW10 (LN)
136541						Exported to Helsinki (O-FIN)
136582 *	OPC 286	Duple	47997	C29F	5/50	HR Richmond {Epsom Coaches}, Epsom (SR)
136589	GMR 513	Duple	48063	C29F	5/50	TD Barnes, Aldbourne (WI)
136597	?	?		van	-/--	Crosby Spring Interiors Ltd (furniture manufactuers), St Helens (GLA)
136605						Exported to Helsinki (O-FIN)
136613	HVB 153	Duple	44526	C29F	5/50	John Bennett (Croydon) Ltd (SR) 4
136628	JWW 572	Duple	49325	C29F	5/50	JW Kitchin & Sons Ltd, Pudsey (WR)
136661 *	PVX 16	Duple	46336	C29F	5/50	CF Barnes (CF Barnes & Son) {Progress Coach Services}, Clacton-on-Sea (EX)
136670						Exported to Karachi (O-PK)
136677	NUB 395	Duple	50643	C29F	11/50	TS Heaps & Sons, Leeds (WR)
136685	KOJ 862	Duple	48950	C29F	5/50	Worthington Motor Tours Ltd, Birmingham (WK)
136693 *	63-033	Petrakis		B24-	10/50	Original operator unknown (O-GR)
136701 - 136712						Exported to Bombay (O-IND)
136869	KOJ 863	Duple	48951	C29F	5/50	Worthington Motor Tours Ltd, Birmingham (WK)
136877	OPC 809	Duple	56079	C29F	5/50	WD Hall Ltd, London SW19 (LN)
136887 *	?	?		B24-	-/--	Original operator unknown (O-GR)
136925 *	LTA 758	Duple	56059	C29F	5/50	Western National, Exeter (DN) 1419
136926		see 136925				
136933	MRL 552	Duple	44444	C29F	5/50	Blewett's Ltd {Crimson Tours}, Hayle (CO)
136941	EX 6754	Duple	47845	C29F	4/50	Yaxley & Sayers Ltd {Grangeway Coaches}, Great Yarmouth (NK)
136949						Exported to Santiago (O-RCH)
136957	?	?		van	-/--	W & M Duncan Ltd (chocolatiers), Edinburgh (GMN)

136965	GFU 700	Duple	46488	C29F	6/50	C, JE, T & T Hudson {Hudson's Bus Co}, Horncastle (LI) 29
136975						Exported to Santiago (O-RCH)
137005	LTA 759	Duple	56060	C29F	5/50	Western National, Exeter (DN) 1420
137012	?	?		van	-/--	W & M Duncan Ltd (chocolatiers), Edinburgh (GMN)
137019	HDK 337	Duple	50263	C27F	5/50	Yelloway Motor Services Ltd, Rochdale (LA)
137033	K-7168	?		B28-	8/50	De Sammenslutede Bilruter AS, Farsund (O-N)
137047	VME 277	Duple	52048	C29F	5/50	BEA, Ruislip (MX) 1124
137050	?	?		van	-/--	R Aytoun Ltd (meat purveyors), Dalkeith (GMN)
137054 *	RN 499	Duple	?	B30F	-/50	Admiralty (Royal Navy) (GOV)
137061	C-17734	?		B---	6/50	Brd. Nitteberg, Sørumsand (O-N)
137095	CCB 516	Plaxton	580	C29F	6/50	Roberts Tours (Blackburn) Ltd (LA) 36
137102 *	LRO 296	Duple	48824	C29F	5/50	Picton & Gibbs Ltd {Vanguard Coaches}, Garston (HT)
137109	JWD 261	Duple	48059	C29F	5/50	J Lloyd & Son Ltd, Nuneaton (WK) 26
137117	DTK 936	Lee		C29F	5/50	RW Toop, WJ Ironside & PW Davis {Bere Regis & District}, Dorchester (DT)
137125	H-7540	?		B---	6/50	Isnius Aspheim, Vestre Melum (O-N)
137149						Exported to Singapore
137152	LTF 346	Duple	54377	C29F	5/50	GW Haigh, Mossley (LA)
137183	FRX 533	Duple	46416	C29F	6/50	WF Carter & Sons Ltd {Alpha Coaches}, Maidenhead (BE)
137190	HGE 156	Duple	54758	C29F	3/50	SCWS Ltd, Glasgow (LK)
137198	FMO 880	Duple	55777	C29F	5/50	EJ Spratley {Blue Star}, Mortimer (BE)
137205	KAD 880	Mulliner	AL14	C29F	7/50	EC Young {Cotswold Coaches}, Stow-on-the-Wold (GL)
137213						Exported to Alexandria (O-ET)
137221	BGL 373	Duple	55821	C29F	5/50	J & G Browning, Box (WI)
137236						Exported to Alexandria (O-ET)
137274	KOJ 484	Duple	55814	C27F	5/50	Sandwell Motor Co Ltd, Birmingham (WK)
137278						Exported to Singapore
137285	LOD 529	Duple	56050	C27F	5/50	CW Good {The Doves Motor Tours}, Beer (DN)
137293 *	KEL 95	Duple	55875	C29F	3/50	Shamrock & Rambler Motor Coaches Ltd, Bournemouth (HA)
137484 *	KXV 564	?	?		3/50	Ministry of Works (GOV).
137517						Exported to Alexandria (O-ET)
137525	LNN 331	Duple	49489	C24F	6/50	Barton Transport, Chilwell (NG) 593
137540						Exported to Alexandria (O-ET)
137578 *	KEL 657	Duple	44446	C29F	8/50	Excelsior Coaches Ltd, Bournemouth (HA) 37
137585	FSA 927	Duple	56033	C29F	5/50	JD Smith, Inverurie (AD)
137594						Exported to Mombasa (O-EAK)
137598	CCB 524	Duple	50981	C29F	5/50	NW & F Barnes & J Garside (Mark Barnes & Sons), Haslingden (LA)
137601						Exported to Antwerp (O-B)
137610	LYD 825	Duple	55531	C29F	6/50	TE Herring {W Herring & Son}, Burnham-on-Sea (SO)
137617	PS 1977	Mulliner	T558	B28F	5/50	Irvine Bros, Dunrossness (SD)
137624	MKO 60	Duple	47948	C29F	6/50	PG Warren, Ticehurst (ES)
137665	GDL 754	Duple	55876	C29F	5/50	FW Read {Read's Tours}, Ryde (IW)
137672	JAB 867	Duple	49926	C29F	5/50	S Wright, Kidderminster (WO)
137682 *	CCB 528	Duple	55630	C29F	-/50	Lewis Cronshaw Ltd, London NW4 (LN)
137686						Exported to Mombasa (O-EAK)
137689						Exported to Helsinki (O-FIN)
137703	HGE 219	Duple	54759	C29F	7/50	SCWS Ltd, Glasgow (LK)
137705	GAY 692	Duple	48319	C29F	5/50	L Pole & Sons Ltd, Syston (LE)
137750	DCK 565	Duple	56157	C29F	5/50	GE Barnes {Premier Motor Tours}, Preston (LA)
137753	FNJ 136	Duple	56188	C29F	6/50	PG Warren, Ticehurst (ES)
137760	KNY 195	Duple	56063	C29F	5/50	DJ Gray {W Gray & Sons}, Tonteg (GG)
137769	KAH 947	Duple	54793	B30F	7/50	Eastern Counties, Norwich (NK) B847
137773 #	RN 501	Duple	?	B30F	-/50	Admiralty (Royal Navy) (GOV)
137776	?	Mulliner		B--F	-/--	Anglo Iranian Oil Co, location unknown (O-IR)
137785	BEP 691	Duple	49255	C29F	5/50	Mid-Wales Motorways Ltd, Newtown (MO)
137792	?	?		h/box	-/--	Hardwick Arabian Stud, Birmingham (GWK)
137799	JWW 520	Duple	56207	C29F	5/50	FW Balme {Balme's Coaches}, Otley (WR)
137826	KYK 875	Duple	44539	C29F	2/51	Fallowfield & Britten Ltd, London E8 (LN)
137833 *	HCJ 151	Duple	54492	C29F	6/50	PW Jones, Burley Gate (HR)
137840						Exported to Alexandria (O-ET)

C1252/172

137848	CCF 669	Duple	48972	C29F	6/50	HC Chambers & Son Ltd {Chambers & Sons}, Bures (WF)
137886 *	VMY 685	Spurling		shop	11/50	Navy, Army & Air Force Institutes (NAAFI) (GLN)
137893 *	KAH 948	Duple	54794	B30F	7/50	Eastern Counties, Norwich (NK) B948
137902	ONO 93	Duple	56072	C29F	6/50	Eastern National, Chelmsford (EX) 4072
137906	AGR 826	Duple	50220	C29F	5/50	Cowell Bros, Southwick (DM) 17
137909						Exported to Alexandria (O-ET)
137922 *	KXJ 287	Duple	49721	C29F	5/50	Morecambe Motors Ltd {Silver Grey} (LA)
137925	LOD 78	Duple	49339	C27F	5/50	T & W Parker {Blue Coaches}, Ilfracombe (DN)
137932	MHY 810	Duple	56161	C27F	2/50	Bristol Co-operative Society Ltd {Queen of the Road}, Bristol (GL) 37
137939		see 137932				
137974 #	?	Jennings		library	-/50	Derbyshire County Council (GDE)
137981	?	?		van	-/--	Flinn & Sons Ltd (dyers), Fishergate (GWS)
137990	LPT 392	Mulliner	T559	B30F	5/50	F Wilson, Hunwick (DM)
137994	LTE 626	Duple	56158	C29F	5/50	G Smith, Hoghton (LA)
137997	K-2951	?		B---	8/50	Original operator unknown (O-N)
138001 - 138012						Exported to Bombay (O-IND)
138160	KYK 996	Duple	50298	C29F	-/50	A Jones {Popular Coaches}, London E14 (LN)
138171	PVX 300	Duple	55975	C29F	5/50	Mossrose Coaches Ltd, Waltham Abbey (EX)
138172	FVA 713	Duple	56015	C29F	5/50	P & T Tennant, Forth (LK)
138180 *	KXV 575	?		?	4/50	Ministry of Works (GOV)
138211 *	KNY 759	Mulliner	Z60	B31F	6/50	GH Long & Sons {Glendale Garage}, Colbren (GG)
138225	GAY 526	Duple	56159	C29F	5/50	AA Oliver {Luxicoaches}, Loughborough (LE)
138228 #	RN 502	Duple	?	B30F	-/50	Admiralty (Royal Navy) (GOV)
138233	FTH 201	Duple	48334	C27F	5/50	West Wales Coach Services Ltd, Tycroes (CR) 56
138236						Exported to Accra (O-WAC)
138240	ONO 94	Duple	56073	C29F	6/50	Eastern National, Chelmsford (EX) 4073
138244	FO 6021	Duple	49260	C29F	5/50	TA Owen, Knighton (RR)
138251 *	NAE 72	Duple	46321	C29F	5/50	Wessex Coaches Ltd, Bristol (GL)
138294	PS 1991	Mulliner	T560	B28F	5/50	J Peterson, Ollaberry (SD)
138307	GNT 140	Mulliner	T557	B31F	6/50	J & HG Phillips {J Phillips & Son}, Rhostyllen (DH)
138310						Exported to Karachi (O-PK)
138314	DJN 551	Duple	56071	C29F	-/50	Westcliff-on-Sea MS (EX)
138317						Exported to Tanga (O-EAT)
138326 *	DJD 217	Mulliner	AL16	C30F	6/50	Barnardo's Homes, Woodford Bridge (XEX)
138332	?	?		van	-/--	Suters Ltd (department store), Uxbridge (GMX)
138339	LTF 359	Duple	49530	C29F	4/50	J Davies, Leigh (LA) 20
138381 *	NUG 11	Duple	50607	C29F	5/50	Tattersall's Garage Ltd, Gisburn (WR)
138389	GFU 712	Duple	56220	C29F	6/50	JA Hankins {Reliance}, Scunthorpe (LI)
138398						Exported to Mombasa (O-EAK)
138401 - 138412						Exported to Bombay (O-IND)
138450	SY 9516	Duple	56083	C29F	5/50	RD Prentice (J Thomson & Son), West Calder (MN)
138454 #	RN 503	Duple	?	B30F	-/50	Admiralty (Royal Navy) (GOV)
138463	RHK 308	Thurgood	644	C29F	6/50	E Benjamin & E Brandon {Our Bus Service}, Grays (EX) 27
138470	KYE 310	Duple	49545	C27F	5/50	HJ Phillips & Sons Ltd, London SW11 (LN) 1099
138477 *	504 HTE	Pearson		C29F	12/51	Brockhall Institution, Langho (XLA)
138518	TMM 627	Duple	46860	C29F	-/50	Northern Roadways Ltd, Glasgow (LK)
138525	GAW 85	Duple	49253	C29F	6/50	Salopia Saloon Coaches Ltd, Whitchurch (SH) 79
138534	GAY 564	Duple	55906	C29F	5/50	HR Hipwell {Prestwells}, Woodhouse Eaves (LE)
138542	HJW 647	Duple	48952	C29F	6/50	Worthington Motor Tours Ltd, Birmingham (WK)
138714	MHY 904	Duple	56162	C24F	2/50	Bristol Co-operative Society Ltd {Queen of the Road}, Bristol (GL) 38
138718	MMN 215	Duple	51123	C29F	4/50	Mrs EA Cretney (AR Cretney){Burleigh}, Douglas (IM) 3
138731	?	?		goods	4/50	SCWS (GLK)
138735	LLT 122	Duple	54378	C29F	-/--	CW Banfield, London SE15 (LN)
138772	LUR 510	Duple	46246	C29F	-/50	Brunt's Coaches Ltd, Bell Bar (HT)
138779	ACC 849	Duple	46498	C29F	6/50	FVP Pritchard {DM Coaches}, Llanrug (CN)
138788 #	RN 505	Duple	?	B30F	-/50	Admiralty (Royal Navy) (GOV)
138792	HOU 627	Duple	48134	C29F	5/50	Hants & Sussex Motor Services Ltd, Emsworth (HA) 168
138794		see 138984				
138801	?	?		library	-/--	Warwickshire County Council (GWK)

138808	NHN 576	Duple	55860	C29F	6/50	Summerson Bros {The Eden}, West Auckland (DM)
138850						Exported to Karachi (O-PK)
138857	MRL 776	Duple	54463	C29F	6/50	WH Hawkey, Newquay (CO)
138866 *	GWN 359	Mulliner	AL08	DP29F	-/50	TJ Short, Morriston (GG)
138870 *	GDL 796	Duple	56102	C29F	7/50	Southern Vectis, Newport (IW) 221
138882 *	TMM 168	Duple	56234	C29F	-/50	Garner's Coaches Ltd, London W5 (LN)
138889	SY 9523	Duple	54898	C29F	5/50	Pentland Garage Ltd, Loanhead (MN)
138896 *	MYA 234	Mulliner	T561	B31F	6/50	WH Green, Batcombe (SO)
138938						Exported to Karachi (O-PK)
138941 *	JAA 367	Vickers (Portsmouth)		C29F	8/50	R Miller jnr {Santoy Coaches}, Fair Oak (HA)
138945	FVD 39	Duple	55031	C29F	7/50	Park's Thistle Coaches, Hamilton (LK)
138954	GAY 769	Duple	46901	C29F	6/50	HJ & AJ Barkus (Barkus & Son), Woodhouse Eaves (LE)
138958	KYK 195	Duple	49546	C27F	5/50	United Service Transport Co Ltd, London SW9 (LN) 1081
138970	?	Mulliner		B31-	7/50	Middlesex County Council (XMX)
138977 *	GDL 797	Duple	56101	C29F	6/50	Southern Vectis, Newport (IW) 222
138984 *	KYF 896	Duple	44925	C29F	-/50	J Tripp {Barnsbury Coaches}, London N7 (LN)
139004	?	?		lorry	-/--	Malmesbury & Parsons Dairies Ltd, Bournemouth (GHA)
139011 *	GDL 779	Duple	56087	C29F	6/50	Southern Vectis, Newport (IW) 219
139018	EFR 388	Duple	56106	C29F	5/50	Marshall & Son (Blackpool) Ltd (LA)
139062 *	GDL 793	Duple	56100	C29F	6/50	Southern Vectis, Newport (IW) 220
139069	HGE 590	Duple	54760	C29F	5/50	SCWS Ltd, Glasgow (LK)
139078	LUR 103	Duple	48831	C29F	6/50	AE Moule {Blue Cream Coaches}, Ashwell (HT)
139082 *	PVX 607	Duple	47864	C29F	5/50	FR Harris {Harris's Coaches}, Grays (EX)
139094						Exported to Karachi (O-PK)
139173 - 139184						Exported to Bombay (O-IND)
139282 #	RN 504	Duple		B30F	-/50	Admiralty (Royal Navy) (GOV)
139289	KRT 227	Duple	47624	C29F	7/50	RO Simonds, Botesdale (EK)
139298	GNT 296	Duple	49263	C29F	5/50	AT Brown, Trench (SH)
139302	LNG 643	Mulliner	AL06	C29F	8/50	W Reynolds & Sons {Maroon Coaches}, Overstrand (NK)
139314	EHS 464	Duple	56090	C29F	6/50	Daniel Ferguson Ltd {Victor}, Renfrew (RW) 31
139321	AEJ 642	Duple	56032	C29F	7/50	J Edmunds {Gwalia Motors}, Llangeitho (CG)
139328 *	GDL 798	Duple	56103	C29F	7/50	Southern Vectis, Newport (IW) 223
139369						Exported to Antwerp (O-B)
139377	FBK 749	Duple	56160	C29F	7/50	White Heather Transport Ltd, Southsea (HA)
139386	JAB 905	Duple	49857	C29F	6/50	TB Morris & R Maggs {M & M Coaches}, Kidderminster (WO)
139390 *	FRX 313	Duple	56127	C29F	-/50	Thames Valley, Reading (BE) 604
139400	KNY 422	Duple	55902	C29F	6/50	LH Starkey, Ton Pentre (GG)
139409 #	RN 506	Duple	?	B30F	-/50	Admiralty (Royal Navy) (GOV)
139416	LFM 400	Duple	56130	C29F	6/50	Crosville MS, Chester (CH) SL63
139423	HVE 980	Duple	55877	C29F	6/50	Percival's Motors (Cambridge) Ltd (CM)
139457						Exported to Helsinki (O-FIN)
139465	FNV 999	Duple	46516	C29F	6/50	Royal Blue Coach & Transport Ltd, Pytchley (NO)
139474	DJR 564	Duple	50071	B30F	6/50	R Tait, Kirkwhelpington (ND)
139478	EFK 133	?		van	8/50	Quality Cleaners Ltd, Worcester (GWO)
139488	GMW 1	Duple	54267	C29F	6/50	CH Thomas, Calne (WI)
139497						Exported to Barbados
139504	HOU 361	Duple	44804	C29F	c5/50	Creamline Motor Services (Bordon) Ltd (HA)
139511	LFM 401	Duple	56131	C29F	6/50	Crosville MS, Chester (CH) SL64
139553	HCJ 152	Duple	54493	C29F	6/50	WE Morgan {Wye Valley Motors}, Hereford (HR)
139562	SO 9258	Mulliner	T562	B28F	7/50	AJ Hay, Elgin (MR)
139566 *	FJY 180	Mulliner	AL17	C29F	8/50	Blake's (Continental) Tours Ltd, Plymouth (DN)
139578	HDT 888	Duple	50565	C29F	6/50	R Fretwell Ltd, Bentley (WR)
139584	?	?		van	-/--	Crosby Spring Interiors Ltd (furniture manufactuers), St Helens (GLA)
139592	GAY 726	Duple	43524	C29F	6/50	R & WE Adams {Blue Bird}, Market Harborough (LE)
139600	ORB 218	Duple	47789	C29F	6/50	JB Laban, Melbourne (DE)
139714		see 139716				
139716	KYK 812	Duple	50239	C29F	6/50	AC Coaches Ltd, London SE15 (LN)
139724	JTX 572	Duple	55971	C29F	6/50	DJ Gray {W Gray & Sons}, Tonteg (GG)

139732	KYW 330	?	-28-	8/50	Home Office (GOV)
139742					Exported to Alexandria (O-ET)
139748					Exported to Barbados
139755	KYW 331	?	?	7/50	Ministry of Supply (GOV)
139763	KYW 329	?	B28F	-/--	Royal Ordnance Factory, Chorley (GOV)
139771	KYW 332	Whitson	B28F	-/--	Home Office (GOV)
139849 - 139860					Exported to Bombay (O-IND)
139972	KYW 337	?	?	7/50	Ministry of Supply (GOV)
139980	KBJ 533	Duple	55907	C29F	7/50 WW Ling {Mid-Suffolk Bus}, Brockford (EK)
139988	GDL 812	Duple	47569	C29F	6/50 Moss Motor Tours (Sandown, I.W.) Ltd (IW)
139998					Exported to Alexandria (O-ET)
140004					Exported to Barbados
140011 *	URF 662	Duple	56597	B30F	2/51 Greatrex Motor Coaches Ltd, Stafford (ST) 73 Redwing II
140019	KAO 265	Duple	56232	C29F	6/50 Lake Hotel Coaches Ltd, Keswick (CU)
140027	SL 3474	Duple	56081	C29F	7/50 W Dawson, Sauchie (CK)
140060	ERD 334	Duple	43566	C29F	6/50 AE Smith {Smith's Coaches}, Reading (BE)
140067	LUR 511	Duple	56259	C29F	-/50 Brunt's Coaches Ltd, Bell Bar (HT)
140076	VME 103	Duple	56121	C29F	6/50 H & G Beach, Staines (MX)
140086					Exported to Antwerp (O-B)
140092					Exported to Accra (O-WAC)
140099	FVA 842	Duple	56080	C29F	7/50 J Galloway, Harthill (LK)
140107	GNT 316	Mulliner	T554	B31F	8/50 Salopia Saloon Coaches Ltd, Whitchurch (SH) 81
140115	JBT 170	Duple	49827	C29F	6/50 J & J Boddy {Boddy's Motors}, Bridlington (ER)
140148	DJN 552	Duple	56142	C29F	-/50 Westcliff-on-Sea MS (EX)
140156 *	GFU 859	Duple	56147	C29F	7/50 Lincolnshire RCC, Bracebridge Heath (KN) 768
140163	LNG 324	Plaxton	598	C29F	6/50 W Carter, Marham (NK)
140174	?	Mulliner		B--F	-/-- Anglo Iranian Oil Co, location unknown (O-IR)
140180					Exported to Karachi (O-PK)
140187	LFM 402	Duple	56132	C29F	7/50 Crosville MS, Chester (CH) SL65
140195	LUR 503	Thurgood	646	C29F	7/50 W Hodge & Sons, Much Hadham (HT)
140203	REV 90	Duple	47861	C29F	6/50 Dagenham Coaching Service, Dagenham (EX)
140236					Exported to Karachi (O-PK)
140244	?	Mulliner	T518	B32-	6/50 Sir Robert McAlpine & Sons Ltd (contractor), London W1
140248	JWX 100	Duple	55881	C29F	7/50 F Oade, Heckmondwike (WR)
140252	LNN 875	Duple	44254	C29F	7/50 Mrs R Butler {Butler Bros}, Kirkby-in-Ashfield (NG)
140262					Exported to Karachi (O-PK)
140268	?	?		van	5/50 British Broadcasting Corporation {BBC}, London SW4 (GLN)
140275	GFU 856	Duple	56144	C29F	7/50 Lincolnshire RCC, Bracebridge Heath (KN) 765
140283	HJW 648	Duple	48953	C29F	7/50 Worthington Motor Tours Ltd, Birmingham (WK)
140291	HOU 863	Duple	46621	C29F	7/50 Hants & Sussex Motor Services Ltd, Emsworth (HA) 182
140337 - 140348					Exported to Bombay (O-IND)
140528					Exported to Mombasa (O-EAK)
140536	DJN 553	Duple	56143	C29F	7/50 Westcliff-on-Sea MS (EX)
140544	KUF 326	Duple	50228	C29F	-/50 RG Johnston {Unique Coaches}, Brighton (ES) 26
140554	EFX 290	Duple	46351	C29F	7/50 RW Toop, WJ Ironside & PW Davis {Bere Regis & District}, Dorchester (DT)
140560	GBU 142	Duple	54380	C29F	7/50 Hilditch's Tours Ltd, Oldham (LA)
140567	FEA 270	Duple	55815	C29F	7/50 Hills Tours Ltd, West Bromwich (ST) 22
140575	?	?		van	-/-- Ely's (Wimbledon) Ltd (department store), London SW19 (GSR)
140583	GNT 428	Duple	49264	C29F	6/50 W Smith Snr, G, FJC & W Smith Jnr {W Smith & Sons}, Donnington Wood (SH)
140615	?	Mulliner		B--F	-/-- Anglo Iranian Oil Co, location unknown (O-IR)
140618	GFU 857	Duple	56145	C29F	7/50 Lincolnshire RCC, Bracebridge Heath (KN) 766
140624					Exported to Dar-Es-Salaam (O-EAT)
140632	LPX 150	Duple	48349	C29F	c6/50 AW Buckingham {Buck's Luxury Coaches}, Worthing (WS)
140636	ETL 373	Duple	56260	C29F	8/50 Delaine Coaches Ltd, Bourne (KN) 32
140643					Exported to Dar-Es-Salaam (O-EAT)
140648	LTJ 215	Duple	56264	C29F	8/50 Middleton Tower Holiday Camp, Morecambe (XLA)

C1252/176

140655	LTF 682	Duple	56185	C27F	7/50	JH Battersby & Son Ltd {Blue Belle Coaches}, Morecambe (LA)
140663	MYA 8	Duple	56125	C29F	7/50	EA Whittle & Co, Highbridge (SO)
140671	SB 8159	Duple	56089	C29F	5/50	A Johnston Ltd, Campbeltown (AL)
140703						Exported to Alexandria (O-ET)
140712						Exported to Trinidad
140720	LFJ 18	Duple	56226	C29F	7/50	PW Steer {Bow Belle}, Bow (DN)
140724 *	GFU 858	Duple	56146	C29F	7/50	Lincolnshire RCC, Bracebridge Heath (KN) 767
140730	RHK 890	?		l/stock	8/50	Cabinet Industries Ltd, London E4 (GLN)
140737	LPT 816	Plaxton	?	FC31F	-/50	A & JR Corbett (A Corbett & Son), Bishop Auckland (DM)
140743	?	?	?		-/--	United Services (dealer), Portsmouth
140751	LNG 403	Duple	55818	C29F	7/50	W Carter, Marham (NK)
140759	EHS 350	Duple	56064	C29F	7/50	Garner's Buses (Bridge of Weir) Ltd, Bridge of Weir (RW) 10
140789						Exported to Alexandria (O-ET)
140798 #	RN 507	Duple	?	B30F	-/50	Admiralty (Royal Navy) (GOV)
140806	KYK 815	Duple	50272	C29F	-/50	R, RG & T Warner {T Warner & Sons}, Milford (SR)
140812	MRL 863	Duple	48014	C29F	7/50	Grenville Motors Ltd, Camborne (CO)
140818	MYA 524	Duple	48070	C29F	7/50	RE Wake {Wake's Services}, Sparkford (SO)
140822 *	FRX 314	Duple	56128	C29F	-/50	Thames Valley, Reading (BE) 605
140828	GNT 429	Duple	49267	C29F	7/50	SC & J Vagg {Vagg's Motors}, Knockin Heath (SH)
140836	REV 213	Duple	44712	C29F	8/50	FC Moore {Viceroy}, Saffron Walden (EX)
140844	KEL 677	Duple	56154	C24F	7/50	Hants & Dorset, Bournemouth (HA) 685
140879	KOK 625	Duple	56263	C29F	6/50	Dalton's Garage Ltd, Birmingham (WK)
140888						Exported to Alexandria (O-ET)
140896	EVH 882	Duple	50416	C29F	7/50	Hanson's Buses Ltd, Huddersfield (WR) 277
140900	MDE 666	Duple	49265	C29F	8/50	WG Richards {Richards Bros}, Moylgrove (PE)
140909	MTA 159	Duple	54507	C20F	7/50	CT Burfitt {Grey Coaches}, Ilfracombe (DN)
140913						Exported to Singapore
140919	?	?	?	van	-/--	Shrewsbury Transport Co Ltd (GSH)
140927	HJW 649	Duple	48954	C29F	6/50	Worthington Motor Tours Ltd, Birmingham (WK)
140935 *	GFU 860	Duple	56148	C29F	7/50	Lincolnshire RCC, Bracebridge Heath (KN) 769
140970						Exported to Singapore
140976	HJW 680	Duple	48955	C29F	7/50	Worthington Motor Tours Ltd, Birmingham (WK)
140985 *	LSM 335	Duple	56094	B30F	1/51	T Rae & Sons {Boreland Bus Service}, Boreland (DF)
140988	LFM 404	Duple	56134	C29F	7/50	Crosville MS, Chester (CH) SL67
140997	LFM 403	Duple	56133	C29F	7/50	Crosville MS, Chester (CH) SL66
141013 - 141024						Exported to Bombay (O-IND)
141193 - 141204						Exported to Melbourne (O-AUS)
141218	?	Mulliner		B--F	-/--	Original operator unknown (O-WAN)
141223	CCB 676	Duple	56471	C29F	8/50	J Wearden & Sons Ltd, Blackburn (LA) 10
141231 *	MMN 343	Duple	51124	C29F	5/50	JE Cowell {Kensington Motors}, Douglas (IM)
141239	CCB 654	Duple	51390	C29F	-/50	Lewis Cronshaw Ltd, London NW4 (LN)
141279	?	Mulliner		B--F	-/--	Original operator unknown (O-WAN)
141289	MFM 37	Duple	56136	C29F	7/50	Crosville MS, Chester (CH) SL69
141292	MTV 24	Duple	48079	C29F	7/50	A Skill {Skill's Coaches}, Nottingham (NG) 24
141301	LNA 367	Duple	49748	C29F	7/50	Moss & Smith, Macclesfield (CH)
141306	DJR 665	Duple	50111	C29F	-/50	EA Raisbeck & Sons, Bedlington (ND)
141311	LOD 533	Duple	49311	C29F	7/50	Coombes (Plymouth) Ltd {Princess Tours} (DN)
141319	EFX 493	Lee		C29F	8/50	CA Adams (Adams Bros) {Victory Tours}, Sixpenny Handley (DT)
141327	?	?	?	l/stock	-/--	JH Jennings & Sons Ltd, Sandbach (GCH)
141362	EHM 332	Duple	44888	C29F	11/50	JW Armstrong & C Downey {Silvertown Coaches}, London E16 (LN)
141368						Exported to Antwerp (O-B)
141377	DVG 806	Duple	48893	C29F	7/50	RG Brown {Broadland Luxury Coaches}, Norwich (NK)
141380	NAF 69	Duple	49376	C29F	7/50	Pearce's Motors Ltd, Polperro (CO)
141389	EVH 883	Duple	50417	C29F	8/50	Hanson's Buses Ltd, Huddersfield (WR) 278
141394						Exported to Karachi (O-PK)
141399	MFM 36	Duple	56135	C29F	7/50	Crosville MS, Chester (CH) SL68
141407	SO 9111	Duple	55976	C29F	7/50	D MacKay {MacKay's Tours}, Granton-on-Spey (MR)
141415	MWE 729	Duple	50384	C29F	8/50	W, E & E Warrington {Eagle Coaches}, Sheffield (WR)
141450						Exported to Mombasa (O-EAK)

C1252/177

141456 *	VMK 20	Duple	55631	C29F	7/50	H & G Beach, Staines (MX)
141465	DES 382	Duple	56096	C29F	8/50	Loch Katrine Steamboat Co Ltd, Callander (PH)
141468 *	JAA 485	Duple	55972	C29F	8/50	Sunbeam Coaches (Loxwood) Ltd (WS) 183
141477	HJW 809	Duple	56489	C29F	6/50	J Leadbetter {Pinfold De-Luxe}, Bloxwich (ST)
141482	GBU 196	Duple	54379	C29F	7/50	Shearings Tours Ltd, Oldham (LA)
141487	LNN 877	Duple	51384	C29F	-/50	Clark's Coaches (Epperstone) Ltd (NG)
141495	GUN 54	Duple	49254	C29F	8/50	T Price {T Price & Son}, Southsea (DH)
141503						Exported to Mombasa (O-EAK)
141538	LPT 651	Duple	44605	C29F	8/50	G Pennington {Cosy Coaches/Meadowfield Motor Co}, Meadowfield (DM)
141544						Exported to Mombasa (O-EAK)
141553	OPF 924	Duple	43475	C29F	8/50	Conway Hunt Ltd, Ottershaw (SR)
141556	MYA 525	Duple	56478	C27F	8/50	RE Wake {Wake's Services}, Sparkford (SO)
141565	KTG 377	Duple	56035	C29F	10/50	M David, Pontycymmer (GG)
141570	KYK 814	Duple	50274	C29F	-/50	CW Banfield, London SE15 (LN)
141575	MFM 38	Duple	56137	C29F	7/50	Crosville MS, Chester (CH) SL70
141583						Exported to Mombasa (O-EAK)
141591	FRX 700	Duple	56026	C29F	8/50	CH Stout {Valentine Coaches}, Shalbourne (WI)
141626	WMX 6	LCMW		B26R	-/51	Middlesex County Council (XMX)
141631						Exported to Karachi (O-PK)
141641	EFX 337	Duple	46932	C29F	8/50	W Otton & Son, Cranborne (DT)
141644	EUD 38	Duple	54329	C29F	8/50	AR Taylor, Bicester (OX)
141653	EFR 535	Duple	56107	C29F	8/50	Whittaker Bros (Blackpool) Ltd (LA)
141658	SY 9561	Duple	56179	C29F	8/50	Pentland Garage Ltd, Loanhead (MN)
141663	DAG 739	Duple	55908	C29F	8/50	R Taylor & Sons, Douglas (LK)
141671 *	GAJ 588	Duple	50585	C29F	8/50	JE Robinson, Carlton Husthwaite (NR)
141679	PS 1999	Mulliner	T563	B28F	7/50	J Watt, Reawick (SD)
141857 - 141868						Exported to Port Elizabeth (O-ZA)
141917						Exported to Penang (O-MAL)
141923 *	JWY 669	Duple	55909	C29F	9/50	GT Owen, Upper Boddington (NO)
141932	JAX 827	Duple	55903	C29F	8/50	C Collier {Collier's Garage}, Abertillery (MH)
141936	KAD 882	Duple	55995	C29F	8/50	WG & RA Miles {Miles Bros}, Guiting Power (GL)
141945	EVH 578	Duple	56183	C29F	8/50	Hanson's Buses Ltd, Huddersfield (WR) 279
141949	GRY 896	Duple	49200	C29F	8/50	WH Smith (Coal and Transport) Ltd, Leicester (LE)
141954	AEG 615	Duple	55889	C29F	8/50	E Shaw, Maxey (SP)
141962	NHT 84	Duple	44809	C29F	8/50	JG Vincent {Severn Valley Motors}, Bristol (GL)
141970						Exported to Penang (O-MAL)
142006 *	VMK 155	Duple	56488	C29F	-/50	Fox & Hart Ltd {Hounslow Star Coaches}, Hounslow (MX)
142021 *	FRX 315	Duple	56129	C29F	-/50	Thames Valley, Reading (BE) 606
142025	HCJ 273	Duple	54494	C29F	8/50	Miss I Baynham, Ross-on-Wye (HR)
142034	KEL 678	Duple	56155	C24F	-/50	Hants & Dorset, Bournemouth (HA) 686
142038	VMK 193	Duple	52050	C29F	10/50	BEA, Ruislip (MX) 1126
142043						Exported to Karachi (O-PK)
142051	MTB 533	Duple	49522	C29F	8/50	J Lamb, Upholland (LA)
142059	GDM 448	Duple	43608	C29F	4/50	Rhyl United Coachways Ltd, Rhyl (FT) B9
142090	?	Mulliner		B--F	-/--	Anglo Iranian Oil Co, location unknown (O-IR)
142093	VMK 9	Duple	49276	C29F	8/50	Bexleyheath Transport Co Ltd (LN)
142103	LNG 555	Duple	48153	C29F	8/50	JC Brown {Norfolk Coachways}, Attleborough (NK)
142108	EFR 517	Duple	56474	C29F	8/50	J Abbott & Sons (Blackpool) Ltd (LA)
142112	OBB 568	Duple	50078	C29F	8/50	E Marshall & Co Ltd {Crown Coaches}, Birtley (ND)
142121	KNY 672	Mulliner	T564	B31F	7/50	AE & FR Brewer {Brewer's Motor Services}, Caerau (GG)
142125	BJV 590	Duple	44991	C24F	8/50	A & AE Blackbourn Ltd {Granville Tours}, Grimsby (LI) 163
142130						Exported to Karachi (O-PK)
142138	KNX 33	Duple	56501	C29F	8/50	Johnson's (Henley) Ltd, Henley-in-Arden (WK)
142146 *	NHN 626	Duple	55861	C29F	8/50	Scurr's Motor Services Ltd, Stillington (DM)
142179 *	GFW 84	Duple	56151	C29F	8/50	Lincolnshire RCC, Bracebridge Heath (KN) 772
142182	GFW 83	Duple	56150	C29F	8/50	Lincolnshire RCC, Bracebridge Heath (KN) 771
142192 *	GFW 82	Duple	56149	C29F	8/50	Lincolnshire RCC, Bracebridge Heath (KN) 770
142197 *	GNT 806	Duple	49266	C29F	8/50	RH & SJ Foxall {Robert Foxall & Sons}, Bridgnorth (SH)
142345	KLJ 505	Duple	55530	C29F	8/50	Shamrock & Rambler Motor Coaches Ltd, Bournemouth (HA)

C1252/178

142354	SB 8280	Duple	52225	C29F	10/50	West Coast Motor Service Co, Campbeltown (AL)
142358	MFM 43	Duple	56152	C29F	8/50	Crosville MS, Chester (CH) SL75
142363	ERJ 25	Duple	54381	C29F	9/50	Sykes' Motor Tours Ltd, Sale (CH)
142371 *	RHK 843	Duple	47572	C29F	3/51	Mrs LA Bennett {Went's Coaches}, Boxted (EX)
142379	?	Mulliner		B--F	-/--	Anglo Iranian Oil Co, location unknown (O-IR)
142414						Exported to Alexandria (O-ET)
142425	LLW 32	Duple	50278	C29F	7/50	EG Hewitt {Premier Coaches}, Watford (HT)
142429 *	MTV 31	Duple	55652	C29F	c7/50	JE Sisson {Basford Transport Driving School}, Nottingham (XNG)
142433	KDD 517	Duple	55773	C29F	9/50	ACJ Perrett {Perrett's Coaches}, Shipton Oliffe (GL)
142442	GAY 951	Duple	51228	C29F	8/50	D Jacques, Coalville (LE)
142446	GWN 471	Duple	56503	C29F	9/50	G Harris {Abernant Transport}, Glyn Neath (GG)
142451	KTG 107	Duple	56266	B30F	9/50	Thomas & Evans {Corona soft drinks}, Porth (XGG)
142459	OPE 242	Duple	44894	C29F	8/50	WE & SG Blunt {Mitcham Belle Motor Coaches}, Mitcham (SR)
142467						Exported to Alexandria (O-ET)
142494	ORB 45	Duple	55653	C29F	9/50	GE Taylor {My Lady Coaches}, Crich (DE)
142499	?	?	?	?	-/--	VM Garinan, Santa Cruz (O-E)
142507	MFM 44	Duple	56153	C29F	5/51	Crosville MS, Chester (CH) SL76
142511	TMM 377	Duple	51182	C29F	-/--	T & WJ Palmer {Ferndale Coaches}, London E6 (LN)
142515	LPT 550	Duple	56475	C29F	8/50	GE Barker, Annfield Plain (DM)
142519	GRY 904	Duple	48306	C29F	-/50	J Smith, Leicester (LE)
142523	JWY 560	Duple	50617	C29F	8/50	L & G Kenworthy, Hoyland Common (WR)
142529	?	Mulliner		B--F	-/--	Anglo Iranian Oil Co, location unknown (O-IR)
142535	EX 6837	Duple	44891	C29F	8/50	Reynolds Garage Ltd {Metropolitan Coaches}, Great Yarmouth (NK)
142539	EFX 173	Duple	49201	C29F	9/50	FC Hoare {Bluebird Coaches}, Chickrell (DT)
142546	LUR 219	Duple	56267	C29F	7/50	EG Hewitt {Premier Coaches}, Watford (HT)
142551	?	Mulliner		B--F	-/--	Anglo Iranian Oil Co, location unknown (O-IR)
142579 *	EFR 561	Duple	56108	C29F	8/50	Lansdowne Motors Ltd, Fleetwood (LA)
142584						Exported to Antwerp (O-B)
142592	GJU 163	Duple	56525	C29F	9/50	G Howlett, Quorn (LE) 8
142596	?	Mulliner	T566	B32-	7/50	Sir Robert McAlpine & Sons Ltd (contractor), London W1
142601	GMW 758	Duple	48887	C29F	9/50	PJ & D Card, Devizes (WI)
142604 *	VMK 156	Duple	47668	C29F	-/50	Garner's Coaches Ltd, London W5 (LN)
142608	KOL 193	Duple	48108	C29F	6/50	Burley's Garage Ltd, Birmingham (WK)
142614	GUN 286	Duple	54158	C29F	8/50	Mrs MA Evans {MA Evans & Sons}, Wrexham (DH)
142620	TMM 191	Duple	52049	C29F	9/50	BEA, Ruislip (MX) 1125
142625	MFM 39	Duple	56138	C29F	5/51	Crosville MS, Chester (CH) SL71
142630	FEA 420	Duple	49859	C29F	8/50	Hills Tours Ltd, West Bromwich (ST) 23
142636	LNA 776	Duple	49749	C29F	9/50	Rigby's Ltd, Patricroft (LA)
142663 *	LLW 31	Duple	55532	C29F	3/51	Essex County Coaches Ltd, London E15 (LN)
142668						Exported to Antwerp (O-B)
142679	MDE 777	Duple	56486	C29F	8/50	DJ Morrison Ltd, Tenby (PE) 32
142680 *	EBA 857	Duple	54382	C29F	8/50	JW Fieldsend Ltd, Salford (LA)
142684	HSF 646	Duple	56491	C29F	2/50	Mills Bros, Edinburgh (MN)
142688	NHT 820	Duple	47769	C29F	8/50	Mrs A Ball (H Ball) {Eagle Coaches}, Bristol (GL)
142692 *	MTA 554	Duple	56048	C29F	9/50	J Potter & Sons Ltd {Tor Bus Service}, Haytor (DN)
142698	HDK 542	Duple	50264	C29F	8/50	Yelloway Motor Services Ltd, Rochdale (LA)
142833 - 142844						Exported to Copenhagen (O-DK)
142932	GNT 969	Duple	43249	C29F	9/50	T France, Llanymynech (MO)
142936 *	KEL 679	Duple	56156	C24F	9/50	Hants & Dorset, Bournemouth (HA) 687
142942	?	?		van	6/50	British Broadcasting Corporation {BBC}, London SW4 (GLN)
142947	FRX 310	Duple	55778	C29F	8/50	Tom Tappin Ltd {Travel Rambler}, Wallingford (BE)
142974	?	?	?	?	-/--	Ministry of Supply (GOV)
142980						Exported to Antwerp (O-B)
142988	?	?	?	?	-/--	Ministry of Supply (GOV)
142992	?	?	?	?	-/--	Ministry of Supply (GOV)
142996	KYW 344	Whitson		B--F	10/50	Ministry of Supply (GOV)
143000	KYW 335	Whitson		B28F	2/50	Ministry of Supply (GOV)
143017 *	LUR 490	Duple	50328	C29F	-/50	Weatherley {Ruislip Luxury Coaches}, Ruislip (MX)
143020 #	?	Jennings		library	-/50	Derbyshire County Council (GDE)

C1252/179

143023 *	NHN 733	Duple	50695	C29F	9/50	F Lockey & Son, St Helens Auckland (DM)
143025	MKP 810	Duple	54403	C29F	10/50	PWJ Jessop, Frinstead (KT)
143028	CGV 134	Duple	49125	C29F	9/50	AW Towler & Sons Ltd, Brandon (WF)
143032	AEN 342	Duple	55037	C29F	3/51	Auty's Tours Ltd, Bury (LA)
143049	MFM 40	Duple	56139	C29F	5/51	Crosville MS, Chester (CH) SL72
143059		see 143049				
143064	T-5931	?		B21FV	2/51	Surnadal Billag NS, Surnadal (O-N) 31
143072	GNT 470	Duple	54154	C29F	8/50	J & H Coppenhall Ltd, Sandbach (CH) 17
143076	URE 216	Duple	48245	C29F	10/50	Greatrex Motor Coaches Ltd, Stafford (ST) 68 Housemartin
143080	JHO 213	Duple	55973	C29F	1/51	Hants & Sussex Motor Services Ltd, Emsworth (HA) 184
143084	CHL 687	Duple	50570	C29F	8/50	CW Illingworth {Belle View Coaches}, Wakefield (WR)
143097	JBT 229	Duple	49839	C29F	12/50	H, N & A Giles, RA Falkingham and F Danby {Giles Bros}, Withernsea (ER)
143101	HCJ 345	Duple	54496	C29F	9/50	Yeomans Private Hire Ltd, Hereford (HR) 83
143105	OPJ 200	Duple	48839	C29F	10/50	Walton on Thames Motor Co Ltd (SR)
143108	JS 9020	Duple	56540	B30F	10/50	Western Lewis Coaches Ltd, Stornoway (RY)
143111	?	Mulliner	T565	B32-	7/50	Sir Robert McAlpine & Sons Ltd (contractor), London W1
143115 *	LLW 133	Duple	56485	C29F	8/50	N & S Coaches Ltd, Kibworth (LE)
143142	LPX 909	Duple	55828	C29F	9/50	HE Bleach, Lavant (WS)
143147						Exported to Lisbon (O-P)
143155	GUJ 20	Duple	54155	C29F	9/50	AL Jones & Co Ltd {Victoria Coaches}, Madeley (SH)
143159	KNY 731	Duple	56499	C29F	8/50	F Manning & Sons Ltd, Aberdare (GG)
143163	JHO 212	Duple	46622	C29F	1/51	Hants & Sussex Motor Services Ltd, Emsworth (HA) 185
143167	?	?		van	-/--	Earnshaw Bros & Booth {Nu-Lyne Furniture}, Burnley (GLA)
143171	?	?		van	-/--	A Ryan, London E7 (GLN)
143177	FJY 622	Mulliner	AL18	C29F	11/50	FG Trathen & Son, Yelverton (DN)
143183	?	?		lorry	-/--	J Rannoch Ltd, Elmswell (GSK)
143187	?	?		van	-/--	Parker Knoll Ltd (furniture manufacturers), High Wycombe (GBK)
143192	?	Mulliner	T567	B32-	7/50	Sir Robert McAlpine & Sons Ltd (contractor), London W1
143199 *	OBB 600	Plaxton	574	C30F	8/50	Bee-Line Continental Tours Ltd, Newcastle (ND)
143226 *	EX 6830	Duple	44990	C29F	9/50	Norfolk Motor Services Ltd, Great Yarmouth (NK) 162
143231	EG-16-89	Soares		DP27D	11/50	Américo António Martins Soares, Fânzeres (O-P) 13
143239	KYE 455	Duple	56479	C29F	-/50	Hutchinson {Woodside Coaches}, London SE25 (LN)
143243	GUJ 21	Duple	43822	C29F	8/50	RB & R Charles (Charles Bros) {Charles Motor Services}, Cleobury Mortimer (SH)
143247	SX 7007	Duple	56511	C29F	9/50	W McLucas jnr, South Queensferry (WL)
143251	JHO 945	Duple	46623	C29F	3/51	BS Williams, Emsworth (HA) 187
143255	MFM 42	Duple	56141	C29F	5/51	Crosville MS, Chester (CH) SL74
143261	FVD 141	Duple	56567	C29F	10/50	I Hutchison {Hutchison's Coaches}, Overtown (LK)
143267	MTC 755	Duple	56577	C29F	3/51	Lansdowne Garage (Morecambe) Ltd (LA)
143271	GUJ 218	Duple	43315	C24F	9/50	WR & T Hoggins (WR Hoggins & Sons) {Pilot}, Wrockwardine Wood (SH)
143277	KAC 251	Duple	48060	C29F	9/50	J Lloyd & Son Ltd, Nuneaton (WK) 30
143283	NHT 227	Duple	56233	B30F	9/50	Bristol Corporation (XGL) 863
143312	OBB 746	Duple	50068	C29F	9/50	W Guest {Billingham Car Co}, Billingham-on-Tees (DM)
143316						Exported to Alexandria (O-ET)
143319 *	HGG 935	Plaxton	577	C33F	7/50	Northern Roadways Ltd, Glasgow (LK)
143323	ORB 279	Duple	56529	C29F	10/50	JB Laban, Melbourne (DE)
143328	KDD 72	Duple	46418	C29F	9/50	Tetbury Passenger Transport Co Ltd {Ivory Coaches}, Tetbury (GL)
143332	LLW 837	Duple	55978	C29F	-/--	AR Holder & Son Ltd, London SE8 (LN)
143338	DJD 477	Duple	44057	C29F	3/51	Essex County Coaches Ltd, London E15 (LN)
143340	KON 536	Duple	48956	C29F	7/50	Worthington Motor Tours Ltd, Birmingham (WK)
143347						Exported to Alexandria (O-ET)
143352	MMN 467	Duple	51129	C29F	7/50	GC Gale {Gale's Western Motors}, Peel (IM)
143356	TMM 378	Duple	43930	C29F	3/51	Valliant Direct Coaches Ltd, London W5 (LN)
143362	GKW 395	Duple	56504	C29F	9/50	Highroyds Hospital, Menston (XWR)

C1252/180

143368	LUR 446	Duple	49884	C29F	9/50 TH Kirby, Bushey Heath (HT)
143396	KYW 336	Mulliner		B28F	-/50 Ministry of Supply (GOV)
143400	?	Mulliner		B--F	-/-- Anglo Iranian Oil Co, location unknown (O-IR)
143631	?	?	?		-/-- Ministry of Supply (GOV)
143640	?	?		?	-/-- Ministry of Supply (GOV)
143642	2538 RN	Mulliner		B28F	-/50 Admiralty (Royal Navy) (GOV)
143646	GJU 181	Duple	56524	C29F	9/50 AA Oliver {Luxicoaches}, Loughborough (LE)
143652	RTW 523	Duple	56506	B30F	10/50 Essex County Council (XEX)
143659	?	Mulliner		B--F	-/-- Anglo Iranian Oil Co, location unknown (O-IR)
143664	LLW 42	Duple	55533	C29F	10/50 V Bingley (Bingley Bros) {Sceptre Coaches}, London W6 (LN)
143668	SVX 838	Duple	44713	C29F	9/51 FC Moore {Viceroy}, Saffron Walden (EX)
143674	VMK 259	Duple	50234	C29F	10/50 Ardley Bros Coaches Ltd, London N17 (LN)
143680	DJR 871	Duple	56500	B30F	5/51 C Moffit, Acomb (ND) 9
143708 *	HGG 934	Plaxton	576	C33F	7/50 Northern Roadways Ltd, Glasgow (LK)
143712					Exported to Antwerp (O-B)
143715	MMN 422	Duple	51128	C29F	6/50 WC Shimmin {Silver Star}, Douglas (IM) 3
143720	NLG 134	Duple	55472	C29F	9/50 Yates Tours Ltd, Runcorn (CH)
143724	BTS 242	Duple	56510	C29F	9/50 R Dickson jnr, Dundee (AS) 10
143728	KDD 155	Duple	54495	C29F	10/50 AW Gillett {Gillett's Coaches}, Winchcombe (GL)
143735	JBY 804	Duple	54345	C29F	3/51 C Barber & Sons Ltd, Mitcham (SR) 14
143741	LPT 723	Duple	50116	C29F	9/50 GH, S & JB Atkinson (GH Atkinson & Sons) {General Omnibus Services}, Chester-le-Street (DM)
143748	KTG 317	Duple	55900	C29F	10/50 WA & R Edwards, Llantrisant (GG)
143752	JNP 258	Duple	49473	C29F	10/50 H & WB Jones {Jones Bros}, Upton-on-Severn (WO)
143758	MTA 744	Duple	48300	C29F	6/51 NH Ashton {Ashtonville Coaches}, Halwill (DN)
143764	AEN 300	Duple	47785	C29F	10/50 Auty's Tours Ltd, Bury (LA)
143792	MTD 242	Duple	56578	C29F	10/50 Lansdowne Garage (Morecambe) Ltd (LA)
143796					Exported to Antwerp (O-B)
143799	URE 680	Duple	54157	C29F	11/50 GH Austin & Sons Ltd {Happy Days}, Stafford (ST) 69
143804 *	LNG 323	Duple	48156	C29F	11/50 JC Brown {Norfolk Coachways}, Attleborough (NK)
143808	NHU 345	Duple	56235	C29F	10/50 EJ Kear {Duchess}, Bristol (GL) 2
143812	VMK 200	Duple	48850	C29F	5/51 FE Hughes {Grosvenor Coaches}, Enfield (MX)
143816	RVW 370	Duple	55632	C29F	10/50 Bridge Haulage (Coachway Luxury Travel), Thundersley (EX)
143829	URE 550	Duple	43894	C29F	8/50 CE & WH Nickolls (H Nickolls & Sons), Milford (ST)
143832	JWX 884	Duple	56505	C29F	9/50 JB Maddison {Drake's Tours}, Scholes (WR)
143836	JAA 741	Duple	46434	C29F	8/50 Hants & Sussex Motor Services Ltd, Emsworth (HA) 186
143842 *	VMK 721	Duple	49283	C29F	-/50 M Logan {Diamond Bus Service}, South Moor (DM)
143848	NBH 746	Duple	48919	C29F	10/50 EJ Sargeant {Slough Coaching Services}, Slough (BK)
143876 *	LUC 645	Duple	50279	C29F	1/51 Keith & Boyle (London) Ltd {Orange Luxury Coaches}, London EC2 (LN) Georgia
143880					Exported to Alexandria (O-ET)
143883	JM 9696	Duple	49076	C29F	9/50 RW Stainton & Sons, Kendal (WT)
143888	JWY 50	Duple	56512	C29F	9/50 FW Balme {Balme's Coaches}, Otley (WR)
143892	AHF 893	Duple	54161	C29F	1/51 CH Dorning {Wallasey Motorways}, Wallasey (CH)
143896	MFM 41	Duple	56140	C29F	5/51 Crosville MS, Chester (CH) SL73
143903	NMN 273	?		shop	5/51 Manx Co-operative Society, Douglas (GIM)
143909	LKH 429	Duple	49832	C29F	10/50 DW Burn, H Tyler & EG Russell {Grey de Luxe}, Kingston-upon-Hull (ER)
143916	LRR 814	Duple	56523	C29F	10/50 G Gittins, Mansfield Woodhouse (NG)
143920	GFW 674	Duple	55729	C27F	10/50 E & F Adams {E Adams & Son}, Saltfleet (LI)
143926 *	FDP 299	Duple	55774	C29F	6/50 AE Smith {Smith's Coaches}, Reading (BE)
143932	BBR 223	Duple	50158	C29F	10/50 J Robson, Shotton Colliery (DM)
143960	?	?		library	-/-- Warwickshire County Council (GWK)
143964					Exported to Alexandria (O-ET)
143967	SEV 777	Duple	56593	C29F	3/51 Wiffen's Coaches Ltd, Finchingfield (EX)
143972	BJV 591	Duple	46924	C24F	10/50 A & AE Blackbourn Ltd {Granville Tours}, Grimsby (LI) 164
143976	?	?		shop	-/-- Chester Co-operative Society (GCH)
143980	KDD 866	Duple	54498	C29F	1/51 FC Cottrell {Cottrell's Coaches}, Mitcheldean (GL)
143987	NUM 13	Duple	50560	C29F	10/50 Roy Neill Ltd, Leeds (WR)
143993	EPR 572	(Lee ?)		B29F	7/51 Dorset County Council Education (XDT)

144000 *	MPT 409	Duple	46907	C29F	3/51 J Iveson & Son, Esh (DM)
144011		see 140011			
144235	?	?		van	-/-- Ipswich Co-operative Society (GSK)
144238	?	?		shop	-/-- Whiston Co-operative Society (GLA)
144244	LNB 238	Duple	56518	B30F	10/50 Manchester Corporation Education Committee (XLA)
144272	JP 8530	Duple	49941	C29F	10/50 E & T Eaves {Eavesway Tours}, Ashton-in-Makerfield (LA)
144276	?	Mulliner		B--F	-/-- Anglo Iranian Oil Co, location unknown (O-IR)
144281	JYG 418	Duple	56531	C29F	10/50 Bolton-by-Bowland Motor Services Ltd (LA)
144284	OS 7715	Duple	56605	C29F	-/50 A MacLean, Port William (WN)
144288	GNT 746	Duple	43323	C29F	7/50 Corvedale Motor Services Ltd, Ludlow (SH)
144292	?	?		shop	-/-- Stalybridge Co-operative Society (GCH)
144296	FJY 469	Duple	55844	C29F	10/50 J Hoare & Sons {The Ivy}, Ivybridge (DN)
144300	MAR 776	Duple	56534	C29F	-/50 WH Harrison, Welwyn (HT)
144312	LND 185	Duple	56582	C29F	10/50 J Stubbs {Empress Coaches}, Manchester (LA)
144316	JNP 990	Duple	56513	C29F	10/50 WD Smith {Fernhill Heath Motors}, Fernhill Heath (WO)
144322	NHN 919	Duple	56494	C29F	2/51 JH Dowson {Safety Coach Service}, Frosterley (DM)
144328	KRT 578	Duple	48870	C29F	10/50 Combs Coaches Ltd, Ixworth (EK)
144354	?	Mulliner		B--F	-/-- Anglo Iranian Oil Co, location unknown (O-IR)
144356 *	MKP 557	Duple	56527	C29F	8/50 JE Mannifield {Camden Coaches}, Sevenoaks (KT)
144360	?	Mulliner		B--F	-/-- Anglo Iranian Oil Co, location unknown (O-IR)
144364	EPR 835	(Lee ?)		B29F	1/52 Dorset County Council Education (XDT)
144367					Exported to Izmir (O-TR)
144368	?	?		van	-/-- C Goodman & Sons Ltd, London SE17 (GLN)
144372	GBU 374	Duple	54931	C29F	4/51 G Barlow & Sons Ltd, Oldham (LA)
144376	EJT 792	Duple	48790	C29F	3/51 EA Seager {Enterprise Coaches}, Sherborne (DT)
144380	?	?		van	-/-- H Slade & Co, St Albans (GHT)
144384	OPH 528	Duple	56532	C29F	10/50 Finch & Lewis {Ashtead Streamline}, Ashtead (SR)
144396	URF 968	Duple	56596	C29F	1/51 St George's Mental Hospital, Stafford (XST)
144400	FTH 935	Duple	48336	C29F	10/50 JL Davies & E Jones, Glanamman (CR)
144406	?	?		?	-/-- Ministry of Supply (GOV)
144407	?	?		?	-/-- Ministry of Supply (GOV)
144440	?	?		?	-/-- Ministry of Supply (GOV)
144444	?	Mulliner		B--F	-/-- Anglo Iranian Oil Co, location unknown (O-IR)
144447	?	?		?	-/-- Ministry of Supply (GOV)
144452	?	?		?	-/-- Ministry of Supply (GOV)
144456	FT 7009	Duple	50134	C29F	-/51 G Chapman {Priory Motor Coach Co}, North Shields (ND) 60
144460 *	GUJ 289	Duple	54159	C29F	10/50 Roberts Coaches Ltd, Crewe (CH)
144464	LPW 503	Duple	56208	C29F	7/51 GV Carter {BM & KT Carter}, Litcham (NK)
144468	HEW 500	Duple	56533	C29F	4/50 H Lee {Whippet Coaches}, Hilton (HN)
144480	MAR 67	Duple	49960	C29F	10/50 WJ Carter, Royston (HT)
144484	?	?		van	-/-- Bowater Sales Co Ltd (paper manufacturer), SE1 (GLN)
144490	CCB 861	Duple	50983	C29F	1/51 Ribblesdale Coachways Ltd, Blackburn (LA)
144496	LTE 901	Duple	56560	C29F	5/51 Atkinson & Co {Dreadnought Motors}, Morecambe (LA)
144549 - 144551					Exported to Copenhagen (O-DK)
144552 *	VE 8008	Ørum-Pedersen		B25C	3/51 Albert Kristensen, Kolind (O-DK)
144553	JA 8081	?		C28C	12/50 Tejn Turistfart, Tejn (O-DK)
144554 - 144560					Exported to Copenhagen (O-DK)
144711, 144718					Exported to Izmir (O-TR)
144721	EUD 284	Duple	52145	C29F	5/51 RC Surman, Chinnor (OX)
144726	NKE 433	Duple	49270	C29F	10/50 CJ Greenough {Dartford Coaches}, Dartford (KT)
144730 *	LLX 425	Duple	56528	C29F	10/50 Car Contracts, London SE5 (XLN)
144734	SX 7039	Duple	56542	C29F	10/50 J McCabe, Winchburgh (WL)
144738	GET 7	Duple	51221	C29F	10/50 W Smart, Greasborough (WR)
144742 *	JKV 575	Duple	56517	C29F	9/50 Midland Theatre Group, Coventry (WK)
144748	GFW 963	Duple	56566	C29F	11/50 WK Harsley {Excelsior Coaches}, Scotter (LI)
144754	EFR 740	Duple	56544	C29F	1/51 S Swarbrick Ltd, Cleveleys (LA)
144758	FCX 63	Duple	50361	C29F	9/50 Central Garage Co (Marsden) Ltd, Uppermill (WR)
144764	OEH 621	Duple	54685	C29F	10/50 AJ, WH & LW Jeffreys {W Jeffreys & Sons}, Goldenhill (ST)
144770	GVN 18	Duple	55634	C29F	1/51 JB Johnson, Helmsley (NR)
144804					Exported to Izmir (O-TR)
144807	?	?		van	-/-- ICI, Grangemouth (GSN)

C1252/182

144812	LUC 642	Duple	55534	C29F	3/51	WE & SG Blunt {Mitcham Belle Motor Coaches}, Mitcham (SR)
144816	MYA 657	Duple	56236	C29F	10/50	CT & LT Bond {Tor Coaches}, Street (SO)
144820	DCS 981	Duple	56601	C29F	-/51	Arrol Motors (Maybole) Ltd (AR)
144824	KRT 853	Duple	51393	C27F	4/51	RO Simonds, Botesdale (EK)
144828	VMK 568	Duple	49441	C29F	-/--	Luton Car Deliveries, Luton (XBD)
144834	GJU 912	Duple	56572	C29F	1/51	AW & JW Farrow (AW Farrow & Son), Melton Mowbray (LE)
144840	HYS 16	Duple	56606	C29F	11/50	Lowland Motorways Ltd, Glasgow (LK) 7
144844	BEP 882	Duple	54165	B30F	3/51	Mid-Wales Motorways Ltd, Newtown (MO)
144850 *	(WMC 26 ?)	Mulliner	T568	B31F	9/50	Middlesex County Council (XMX)
144856						Exported to Izmir (O-TR)
144888	?	Mulliner		B--F	-/--	Anglo Iranian Oil Co, location unknown (O-IR)
144891	BVV 418	Duple	46517	C29F	10/50	RG & T Wesley, Stoke Goldington (BK)
144896	GUJ 291	Duple	54163	B30F	10/50	TH & T Hyde {T Hyde & Son}, Welsh Frankton (SH)
144900	GJU 462	Duple	54912	C29F	10/50	OC Bishop, Coalville (LE)
144904	JWY 927	Duple	50559	C29F	1/51	L & G Kenworthy, Hoyland Common (WR)
144908	CGV 583	Duple	43945	C29F	10/50	NS Rule, Boxford (WF)
144912	MYD 444	Duple	56580	C29F	3/51	EG Bryant, Monksilver (SO)
144918	GUN 489	Duple	54162	B30F	11/50	WJ Hanmer {WJ Hanmer & Sons}, Southsea (DH)
144924	GUJ 290	Duple	54156	C29F	10/50	DC & AN Jones (DC Jones & Sons), Ruabon (DH)
144928	MTD 399	Duple	56576	C29F	3/51	Kia-Ora Motor Services Ltd, Morecambe (LA)
144934	LPX 672	Duple	46784	C29F	c7/50	EJ Carter {Reliance Coaches}, Plummers Plain (WS)
144940	KDD 846	Duple	56238	C27F	10/50	GJ Miller {GJ Miller & Son}, Cirencester (GL)
144968	?	Mulliner		B--F	-/--	Anglo Iranian Oil Co, location unknown (O-IR)
144971 *	GBL 200	Duple	55779	C29F	11/50	WA Perdue {Chiltonian Motors}, Chilton Foliat (WI)
144976 *	GED 797	Duple	56530	C29F	10/50	J Fairhurst, Warrington (CH)
144980	JWY 831	Duple	55927	C29F	10/50	Kildare Coaches Ltd, Adwick le Street (WR)
144984	GUJ 356	Duple	49262	C29F	9/50	D & J Gittins, Crickheath (SH)
144988	HFH 538	Duple	56613	C29F	10/50	Bayliss Coaches & Transport Ltd {Rover Motor Services}, Dymock (GL)
144992	JOR 619	Duple	46624	C29F	4/51	Liss & District Omnibus Co Ltd, Liss (HA) 189
144998	JNP 872	Duple	49871	C29F	10/50	WH Hayes {Doreen Coaches}, Lye (WO)
145004	JHO 946	Duple	56568	C29F	3/51	BS Williams, Emsworth (HA) 188
145008 *	HCJ 452	Duple	54497	C29F	7/50	WE Morgan {Wye Valley Motors}, Hereford (HR)
145014	NKJ 221	Duple	48983	C29F	10/50	DJ Reeves {Reeves Taxis & Coaches}, Faversham (KT)
145048	MWJ 998	Duple	54744	C29F	11/50	Hirst & Sweeting Ltd, Sheffield (WR)
145056	T-6176	Solheimdal		B27-	5/51	Straumsnes Billag, Straumsnes (O-N)
145059	EHH 96	Duple	51158	C29F	8/50	W Colquhoun, Carlisle (CU)
145064 *	EFV 448	Duple	56627	C29F	3/51	Batty-Holt Touring Service Ltd, Blackpool (LA)
145068 *	ORB 767	Duple	44802	C29F	8/50	GW Bull, Tideswell (DE)
145072	ENL 154	Duple	50074	C29F	10/50	AA Hollings {Hollings Garage & Engineering Works}, Wallsend-on-Tyne (ND)
145076	JWY 863	Duple	50475	C29F	11/50	GE & DJ Sykes, Appleton Roebuck (WR)
145080	CGV 691	Duple	56581	C29F	10/50	BA Taylor & Sons, Bildeston (WF)
145086	LNC 324	Duple	49683	C29F	10/50	GW Cartledge {Supreme Red Coaches}, Rhyl (FT)
145092	JS 9239	Duple	56624	B30F	5/51	J Mitchell {Mitchell's Transport Parcel Service}, Stornoway (RY)
145096	JFG 233	Duple	56558	C29F	1/51	D Meldrum, Dunfermline (FE)
145197 - 145204						Exported to Melbourne (O-AUS)
145205	WJB 465	CAC	?	B35D	-/--	Jordan, location unknown, Tas (O- AUS)
145206 - 145208, 145293 - 145304						Exported to Melbourne (O-AUS)
145366	BCN 943	Duple	50094	C29F	10/50	Mayfair Luxury Coaches Ltd, Gateshead (DM) 7
145372	KTX 48	Duple	56599	C29F	3/51	C Lewis & J Jacob, Maesteg (GG)
145404	?	Mulliner		B--F	-/--	Anglo Iranian Oil Co, location unknown (O-IR)
145412	GDM 644	Duple	56062	C29F	1/51	W Cooper & Sons, Prestatyn (FT)
145416	EUD 126	Duple	48775	C29F	6/51	AE Butler, Henley-on-Thames (OX)
145418	LXL 909	Duple	56620	C29F	12/50	Russian Trade Delegation, London N6 (XLN)
145420	DJL 677	Duple	47581	C29F	10/50	R Kime & JH Jackson, Folkingham (LI)
145423	?	Mulliner		B--F	-/--	Anglo Iranian Oil Co, location unknown (O-IR)
145428	BBR 320	Duple	50152	C29F	11/50	G Bridges, Sunderland (DM)
145431	MYB 33	Duple	56553	C29F	10/50	HR, J & Miss V Gunn {Safeway Services}, South Petherton (SO)

145434	BDC 387	Duple	50676	C29F	11/50	A Ayton, South Bank (NR)
145440	GPY 554	Duple	55944	C29F	1/51	Mrs F Walker & Son, Brompton (NR)
145444	AJC 41	Duple	55491	C29F	3/51	R Hughes-Jones {Express Motors}, Rhostryfan (CN)
145450	GDM 676	Duple	54167	C29F	1/51	GW Cartledge {Supreme Red Coaches}, Rhyl (FT)
145453	LVO 146	Duple	48158	C29F	10/50	F Gilbert {Victory}, East Markham (NG)
145456	LRR 601	Duple	55654	C29F	10/50	WE, RE and RN Brumpton {WE Brumpton & Sons}, Dunham-on-Trent (NG)
145488 *	?	Van Leersum		B32-	-/--	FC van der Toorren {Lido Tours}, Amsterdam (O-NL) 5
145491 #	?	Jennings		library	-/50	Derbyshire County Council (GDE)
145500	HDK 491	Duple	51354	C29F	3/51	H Threlfall, Failsworth (LA)
145504	OPK 244	Duple	56594	C29F	10/50	WHG & RS Blackburn (Blackburn Bros), Godalming (SR)
145508	SEV 700	Duple	55869	C29F	1/51	Ashdown's Luxury Coaches Ltd, Danbury (EX) 44
145512	ECL 190	Duple	48284	C29F	3/51	RG Brown {Broadland Luxury Coaches}, Norwich (NK)
145518	KNX 718	Duple	55160	C29F	1/51	Priory Garage & Coaches Ltd, Leamington Spa (WK)
145528	FPM 124	Duple	49347	C29F	1/51	Ashline Ltd {Ashline Coaches}, Tonbridge (KT)
145534	OHN 132	Duple	50673	C29F	1/51	Crowe Bros, Osmotherley (NR)
145540	ERG 164	Duple	56575	C29F	12/50	James Paterson & Co (Motor Hirers) Ltd, Aberdeen (AD)
145569	FTH 816	Duple	56537	C29F	10/50	LT & WH Evans (E Evans & Sons), Llangennech (CR)
145572						Exported to Antwerp (O-B)
145579	OBH 100	Duple	56036	C29F	1/51	F Soul (Soul Bros), Olney (BK)
145587	GUJ 389	Duple	49361	C29F	9/50	RH & SJ Foxall {Robert Foxall & Sons}, Bridgnorth (SH)
145595						Exported to Lindi (O-EAT)
145605 *	KDD 989	Duple	56237	C29F	11/50	TAP Goulding & JA Payne {Sherstonian Coaches}, Sherston (WI)
145611 *	VMK 161	Duple	48215	C29F	-/50	JWH, EAG & WHR Hall (Hall Bros) {Ickenham Coaches}, Hillingdon (MX)
145624						Exported to Lindi (O-EAT)
145653	KOP 702	Duple	56514	C29F	9/50	A Winwood {Alwyn Coaches}, Birmingham (WK)
145656						Exported to Antwerp (O-B)
145660	HTR 144	Duple	56585	C27F	c11/50	PFV Summerbee {Sumerbee's Motor Coaches}, Southampton (HA)
145670	GWN 707	Duple	49422	C29F	11/50	Griff Fender (Swansea) Ltd (GG)
145671						Exported to Dar-Es-Salaam (O-EAT)
145675 *	?	Roset		B34-	-/--	CW van Leuven, Zwijndrecht (O-NL) 3
145684 *	CEP 4	Duple	43941	C29F	2/51	TR Morris, Llanfyllin (MO)
145687	SS 7691	Duple	44270	C29F	10/50	A Dunsmuir, Tranent (EL)
145695	HVJ 203	Duple	54500	C29F	2/51	WE Morgan {Wye Valley Motors}, Hereford (HR)
145707	MTT 44	Duple	43370	C29F	9/50	AE Townsend {Townsend's Tours}, Torquay (DN)
145708						Exported to Dar-Es-Salaam (O-EAT)
145737	LKD 246	Duple	50961	C29F	1/51	Liver Cars Ltd, Liverpool (LA)
145740	?	Mulliner		B--F	-/--	Anglo Iranian Oil Co, location unknown (O-IR)
145744	OPJ 584	Duple	46287	C29F	10/50	A Plumridge, Lowfield Heath (WS)
145752	HSG 231	Duple	55159	C29F	10/50	Halley Coaches (Bathgate) Ltd, Edinburgh (MN)
145759						Exported to Karachi (O-PK)
145771	AFL 49	Duple	47910	C29F	1/51	JW Bingham & E Easton, Newborough (SP)
145779	EDB 535	Duple	50487	C29F	1/51	R Bullock & Co (Transport) Ltd, Cheadle (CH)
145785	SJ 1340	Duple	56604	C29F	1/51	Gordon Bros {Gordon's Motors}, Lamlash (BU)
145791	MAR 190	Duple	56487	C29F	10/50	FN Darvill {Norman's Coaches}, Watford (HT)
145801 - 145812, 145849 - 145860, 145945 - 145956						Exported to Melbourne (O-AUS)
146061	MTC 756	Duple	56559	C29F	-/50	Kia-Ora Motor Services Ltd, Morecambe (LA)
146064	?	Mulliner		B--F	-/--	Anglo Iranian Oil Co, location unknown (O-IR)
146068	MTT 214	Duple	43372	C29F	12/50	Court Garages (Torquay) Ltd (DN)
146075 *	GUT 55	Duple	48210	C29F	5/51	AA Oliver {Luxicoaches}, Loughborough (LE)
146082	?	Mulliner		B--F	-/--	Anglo Iranian Oil Co, location unknown (O-IR)
146094	GUX 10	Duple	54166	B30F	1/51	Greatrex Motor Coaches Ltd, Stafford (ST) 72 Kittiwake II
146098						Exported to Karachi (O-PK)
146102 *	GKY 750	Duple	56574	B--F	1/51	Bradford Corporation Education Committee (XWR) 026
146108	NBH 941	Duple	48806	B30F	2/51	JRG Dell {Rover Bus Service}, Lye Green (BK)
146115	EUD 448	Duple	46833	C29F	11/50	Back's Coaches (Witney) Ltd (OX)
146145	OPK 510	Duple	56571	C29F	10/50	Cooke's Coaches (Stoughton) Ltd (SR) 19
146148						Exported to Alexandria (O-ET)

C1252/184

146151	LUV 870	Duple	56583	C29F	3/51	Fallowfield & Britten Ltd, London E8 (LN)
146160	RVW 100	Duple	56507	C29F	1/51	Ashdown's Luxury Coaches Ltd, Danbury (EX) 43
146163	MAR 510	Duple	54729	C29F	1/51	Brunt's Coaches Ltd, Bell Bar (HT)
146179 *	LUW 75	Duple	52424	C29F	1/51	Dryer's Coaches Ltd, London E17 (LN)
146183	FDN 777	Duple	52283	C29F	1/51	HC Fawcett, York (NR)
146193	MJH 255	Duple	56013	C29F	2/51	JR Street, Hertford (HT)
146200						Exported to Karachi (O-PK)
146227	NAF 678	Duple	56477	C29F	4/51	Harper, Son & Kellow {Reliance Bus Service}, St Agnes (CO)
146231						Exported to Alexandria (O-ET)
146233		see 146236				
146236	GUX 133	Duple	54168	C29F	2/51	AJ Evans & JE Lewis {Minsterley Motor Co}, Minsterley (SH)
146244	MYC 442	Duple	56617	C29F	2/51	JH Fursland & Co Ltd {Pride of Bridgwater}, Bridgwater (SO)
146247						Exported to Alexandria (O-ET)
146251						Exported to Penang (O-MAL)
146262	GUX 188	Duple	43245	B30F	1/51	JW, WHF & GW Lloyd, Oswestry (SH) 9
146267	NS 2401	Duple	56614	C29F	2/51	S MacGregor, Dornoch (SU)
146277 *	GBU 393	Duple	54932	C29F	c9/50	Hilditch's Tours Ltd, Oldham (LA)
146284	GBL 182	Duple	54768	C29F	1/51	L Stevens, Charney Bassett (BE)
146316						Exported to Helsinki (O-FIN)
146320	SB 8378	Duple	54693	C27F	1/51	Air Industrial Developments Ltd {Gold Line}, Dunoon (AL)
146328	MTD 289	Duple	49525	C29F	1/51	J Lamb, Upholland (LA)
146331	KRM 244	Duple	56611	C29F	-/51	Lake Hotel Coaches Ltd, Keswick (CU)
146335						Exported to Penang (O-MAL)
146347	LRR 655	Duple	49490	C24F	5/51	Barton Transport, Chilwell (NG) 594
146351	GWV 296	Duple	48264	C29F	11/50	W & G Chandler, Wantage (BE)
146361 *	MPT 410	Duple	56618	C29F	1/51	J Iveson & Son, Esh (DM)
146368	ERD 808	Duple	43567	C29F	3/51	AE Smith {Smith's Coaches}, Reading (BE)
146393, 146400						Exported to Helsinki (O-FIN)
146404	EBL 962	Duple	44451	C29F	-/50	Windsorian Motor Coach Services Ltd, Windsor (BE) 62
146412	MTE 987	Duple	56612	C29F	3/51	EM Pickwick & Sons, Radcliffe (LA)
146415	GUX 134	Duple	56621	C29F	2/51	RW Carpenter {Valley Motor Services}, Bishop's Castle (SH)
146425	EM 5107	Duple	56616	C29F	3/51	T Lawrenson Ltd, Bootle (LA)
146431						Exported to Rotterdam (O-NL)
146435	ENL 224	Duple	50081	C29F	1/51	R Weymes, Stamfordham (ND)
146445	KNX 470	Duple	48262	C29F	5/51	Wainfleet Motor Services Ltd, Nuneaton (WK)
146452	GWM 812	Duple	56640	C27F	2/51	Southport & Birkdale Motor Carriage Co {Gore}, Southport (LA)
146484	?	Mulliner		B--F	-/--	Anglo Iranian Oil Co, location unknown (O-IR)
146488	AEJ 813	Duple	46591	C29F	1/51	H Daniell & Sons, Aberystwyth (CG)
146496	PWL 559	Duple	44283	C29F	2/51	H Crapper & Son Ltd, Oxford (OX) 35
146504	GUX 186	Duple	43977	C29F	1/51	DJ Hampson {Hampson's Luxury Coaches}, Oswestry (SH) 23
146509	FTH 943	Duple	46594	C29F	4/51	TJ Jones, Newcastle Emlyn (CR)
146515	MBP 900	Duple	56573	B30F	c1/51	West Sussex County Council Education Dept (XWS)
146520						Exported to Karachi (O-PK)
146529	JDA 298	Duple	56626	C29F	2/51	Worthington Motor Tours Ltd, Birmingham (WK)
146535	EJN 22	Duple	48356	C29F	-/51	RE Cook, Westcliff-on-Sea (EX)
146561	?	Mulliner		B--F	-/--	Anglo Iranian Oil Co, location unknown (O-IR)
146568 *	?	De Groot		B33-	-/51	ALAD, Wyken Aalburg (O-NL) 22
146572	EHV 65	Duple	56061	B29F	2/51	East Ham County Borough Council (XLN)
146580	LUW 615	Duple	55763	C29F	3/51	Fallowfield & Britten Ltd, London E8 (LN)
146590	LUW 90	Duple	55535	C29F	1/51	AC Coaches Ltd, London SE15 (LN)
146593	KTG 935	Duple	56598	C29F	1/51	HJ Uphill, Caerau (GG)
146599						Exported to Karachi (O-PK)
146649 - 146654						Exported to Melbourne (O-AUS)
146655 *	P1.126	Buses		B33F	-/--	Buses Ltd, Hamilton (O-NZ)
146656 - 144660, 146745 - 146756						Exported to Melbourne (O-AUS)
146795	LSM 44	Duple	51289	C29F	1/51	M Green {Green's Motor Hirers}, Lochmaben (DF)

(74898) The Burton Cars fleet from Brixham was always well turned out, as shown by KTT254, an unusual Woodall Nicholson 29 seat bus. The company also operated a double decker and later some large capacity Bedford service buses on its network of stage services. (Alan Cross, John Shearman collection)

(76646) Not all the Bedford OBs operating in Ireland were delivered new to local operators with locally built bodies. JUR493 is a Thurgood bodied OB that was new to Hewitt's Premier Coaches fleet in Watford before travelling 'across the water' to join the fleet of Renehan's. (Omnibus Society, John Parke)

(77048) Trans-United was a coachbuilder set up by a consortium of operators in the Rochdale area. HWR584 was new to Wild of Barnoldswick, a town that has changed allegiances between Lancashire and West Yorkshire over the years. It later moved more firmly into Yorkshire to the fleet of Bronte Coaches of Howarth. (John Cockshott)

(79221) The Wounded Warriors Welfare Committee of Leeds bought this Wilks & Meade bodied Bedford OB as transport for their charges. When not in service, it was usually to be found at the Wallace & Arnold garage in Leeds, where it was based and serviced. (John Cockshott)

(80765) House's of Watlington bought a considerable number of Bedford OBs, and before that OWBs. These were used on stage services in and around the Reading area, where DBW534 with Duple Vista coachwork is seen in March 1963 with the imposing frontage of Reading (Southern) Station in the background. (Geoffrey Morant, courtesy Richard Morant)

(88128) The Lancashire based coachbuilder Santus bodied just four OBs. Three of them were forward control conversions with full fronted bodywork. JTF965 started life with Wall's Motor Tours of Wigan, where Santus were based, but later moved to Brown's of Hundred House in Radnorshire. (Omnibus Society, Roy Marshall)

(88210) Ellis & Bull of Moreton in Marsh, Gloucestershire operated a Duple bodied WTB well into the 1960s, but also ran HDG859, a Whitson bodied OB new to Perrett's Coaches of nearby Shipton Oliffe. The WTB outlasted the OB, testament to Duple's excellent build quality. (Omnibus Society, Roy Marshall, Norris-Cull collection)

(93222&93226) This pair of OBs were part of a larger fleet operated in New Zealand by the Auckland Transport Board. Both P.408 and P.403 (424 and 413) carried bodies built in the ATB's own workshops. They were originally numbered 124 and 113. (Brian Schrieb)

(93224) Another New Zealand OB, this time operated by the North Shore Transport Company, who were also responsible for its body. P.604 was numbered 4 in the NST fleet, which included other British manufacturers, when such influence was strong. (Brian Schrieb)

(unknown) Portuguese operators also purchased British chassis in considerable quantities in the decade after the war. The grandly named Viacao Mecanica de Carnaxide bought this OB with unknown, but doubtless Portuguese, coachwork. (Unknown source)

(94757) For a short period in 1948 - just four months - the Duple Mk V Service Coach was offered in response to Governmental requests for material cutbacks. With no side flare, no opening roof and generally simpler trim, the coaches had a slightly Spartan look to them. SJ1243 was new to the Isle of Arran operator, Lennox Motor Services of Whiting Bay. (Geoffrey Morant, courtesy Richard Morant)

(96735) Another Duple Mk V Service Coach is seen here in July 1963 at Cheltenham Bus Station; HDG973 being operated by one of many Cotswold operators to use the Bus Station, in this case Miles of Guiting Power. (Roy Marshall)

(97341) Not satisfied by the more Spartan looks of the Duple Mk V Service Coach, some operators modified the appearance, as can be seen here on LKK59. New to Ashline Coaches of Tonbridge, the coach had moved to the fleet of Dengate & Sons of Beckley in neighbouring Sussex. (Roy Marshall)

(101496) Not all OBs were delivered new to PSV operators. LHY371, a Mulliner bodied bus complete with wooden slatted seats, was purchased by Clifton College School in Bristol, one of a small fleet of OWBs and OBs they operated on various school duties. (Geoffrey Morant, courtesy Richard Morant)

(103971) Whilst the Allsop bodied buses of Booth & Fisher are the best known examples from that coachbuilder, they also bodied two forward control conversions of OBs for local operators. Wain of Mansfield bought KRR107 in 1949, but it later passed to Bott of Sileby, a Leicestershire operator. (Omnibus Society, Norris-Cull collection)

(117835) The Southern and Western National fleets, and their associated company, Royal Blue, operated many standard Duple Vista bodied Bedford OBs. HOD71 (592) was a very typical example in a very typical South West seaside pose – believed to be at Perranporth. You can almost feel the hot sun beating down. (Omnibus Society, JH Aston, John Clarke collection)

(118719) Another company long associated with Bedford OBs is the Wye Valley Motors fleet based in Hereford. GVJ94 was a bus bodied example, built by Mulliner, though the Company operated many other combinations of coachbuilder and seating. It is seen in Hereford's rudimentary bus station in July 1967. (Roy Marshall)

(120606) FSA232 was another OB new to a Tarland operator, but this time it was a Duple Vista bodied example and the first operator was A Watt & Sons. The photograph was taken in June 1973, by which time it was operating for Sinclair of Newtonmore. It appears that a little remedial work has been carried out on the door panelling. (Geoffrey Morant, courtesy Richard Morant)

(124147) This 1952 photograph shows 60.032, a Greek OB with bodywork by an unknown coachbuilder. It was operating for Fokida Intercity KTEL on the old local road from Lidoriki to Amfissa City, Central Greece. (Mr Konstantinos Rellos family collection, courtesy Rodolivos Publications)

(128448) Crosville was another BTC company to operate Bedford OBs with Duple Vista bodies. When these were sold off they found ready buyers, one of who was Bengry's Primrose Motor Services of Leominster, Herefordshire. Bengry's bought a Jersey registered OB in 1967, reregistering it with an 'E' suffix number. (Roy Marshall)

(unknown) The Singapore Traction Company were regular purchasers of British chassis and these two Bedford OBs (STC183 and STC157) were typical of their 1940s/1050s intake, as was the Albion Victor just visible behind the large black car. (Peter Tulloch collection)

(unknown) Meralli Ltd from Nairobi, Kenya bought quite a fleet of complete vehicles, choosing Duple as their preferred coachbuilder. However a quick look at these three vehicles on the quayside bound for Mombasa shows quite a number of detail differences from the standard body, e.g. the roof racks and the rear doors for a mail compartment. (The Omnibus Society)

(135254) A couple of Western National's OBs saw a further life as open sided seafront buses operating for Lincolnshire RCC. This view shows LTA 752 in 1971 branded, in modern parlance, for the Ingoldmells Village service. (Roy Marshall)

(H&S3024) Haines & Strange, a Cheltenham dealer, built up a Bedford OB from new parts, giving it the chassis number H&S3024, the number being their telephone number. The resultant chassis received a standard Duple Vista body and joined the fleet of Bowles of Ford in Gloucestershire as their LDF833. (Colin F Martin)

(146361) The Shetland Isles can sometimes be bathed in glorious sunshine, as this photo testifies. Eunson, Virkie operated MPT410 Bedford OB, a 1951 with Duple Vista C29F bodywork. The photograph was taken in August 1973 on the roadside at Virkie, the coach having been acquired from Heaviside of Sunderland in January 1959. (Donald Hudson)

(28606) This publication also covers other early postwar Bedford passenger vehicles. AGS676 is an SMT bodied Bedford MLZ, one of six new to the Loch Katrine Steamboat Company of Callander. Later many of these small buses were to be found on the Scottish Islands, this one passing to the Trustees of T R Manson, West Sandwick, Shetland. (Roy Marshall)

(97293) SB7744 was one of a pair of Bedford OLAZ, with a Binnie bodies. SB7744 (and its sister SB7743) started life with Air Industrial Developments Ltd {Gold Line}, Dunoon, but by the time of the photograph appears to have moved to another unidentified operator. (Unknown photographer)

(121902) MTO683 was a staff bus for Boot's (the Chemists) at their Bulwell headquarters in Nottingham. The small Bedford K bus, looking very smart with its polished radiator, carried a Spurling 11 seat body with semi-luxury seats. (John Shearman collection)

(236943) In 1951 Percival Brothers of Richmond, North Yorkshire, bought a pair of 24 seat Mulliner bodied Bedford OLAZ coaches. Although seated as coaches, they saw plenty of service on Percival's network of stage services, being ideally suited to the narrow roads in the area. (Phil Moth, John Shearman collection)

(245827) MacBrayne's major purchase in 1952 consisted of a large batch of 22 Bedford OLAZ chassis, fitted with Duple bodies derived from the prototype 'Sportsman' style. Some seated 25, such as KGB268 (157), whilst others had a mail compartment reducing their passenger carrying capacity. (Geoffrey Morant, courtesy Richard Morant)

(JCB58) John C Beadle developed a chassisless bus which was powered by various makes of engine and transmission, of which Bedford was one. HOD63 (2012) was a Bedford-Beadle delivered to Western National in July 1949. (Omnibus Society, JH Aston, John Clarke collection)

(JCB122) Only two Bedford-Beadle chassisless buses did not enter service initially with Tilling Group companies. The pair entered the fleet of SK & F Silvey of Epney, a small village near Gloucester. The first of the pair, HFH368, is seen at Gloucester Bus Station, ready to depart for Saul, on one of the routes operated by Silvey's Coaches. (John Cockshott)

146805	NAF 934	Duple	51216	C29F	3/51	CN Rickard {Penryn & Falmouth Motor Co}, Penryn (CO)
146812	LNA 310	Duple	49709	C29F	1/51	J Prophet, Heaton Chapel (CH)
146844						Exported to Helsinki (O-FIN)
146848	HCJ 861	Duple	54499	C29F	1/51	Miss I Baynham, Ross-on-Wye (HR)
146856	VMK 278	Duple	44657	C29F	-/51	T Gibson {Lily Coaches}, London N9 (LN)
146864	NLG 482	Duple	56519	C29F	3/51	Northwich Transport {Haslington Coaches}, Haslington (CH)
146869	PNU 406	Duple	49448	C29F	3/51	GW Bull, Tideswell (DE)
146875						Exported to Karachi (O-PK)
146879	EFK 224	Duple	56261	C29F	3/51	Downes (Worcester) Ltd (WO)
146889	LUP 114	Duple	56562	C29F	3/51	GH, S & JB Atkinson (GH Atkinson & Sons) {General Omnibus Services}, Chester-le-Street (DM) 3
146896	JNP 864	Duple	47712	C29F	3/51	CW Shuker {Lady Edith}, Halesowen (WO)
146928						Exported to Helsinki (O-FIN)
146932 *	LCD 236	Duple	55536	C29F	3/51	RG Johnston {Unique Coaches}, Brighton (ES) 27
146940						Exported to Lagos (O-WAN)
146948	MYB 711	Duple	56239	C29F	1/51	GT & LT Bond {Tor Coaches}, Street (SO)
146953	GJF 503	Duple	52282	C29F	1/51	AA Mason, Leicester (LE)
146959	GUX 189	Duple	56631	C29F	1/51	Jones Coachways Ltd, Market Drayton (SH) 36
146963	GWV 297	Duple	48266	C29F	11/50	C Harrison & Sons, Swindon (WI)
146973	GWV 101	Duple	44097	C29F	2/51	BC Leather, Maiden Bradley (WI)
146980	HUK 328	Duple	56608	B30F	1/51	R, H & SJ Foxall {Robert Foxall & Sons}, Bridgnorth (SH)
147006						Exported to Lagos (O-WAN)
147012, 147019						Exported to Singapore
147024	ERJ 427	Duple	54933	C29F	3/51	JW Fieldsend Ltd, Salford (LA)
147032	RVW 157	Duple	56584	B30F	1/51	Walthamstow Borough Council (XEX)
147037	JYG 538	Duple	50606	C29F	1/51	H Murgatroyd & Son, Thruscross (WR)
147043	MDV 825	Duple	56615	C29F	4/51	NC Born {Born's Tours}, Northlew (DN)
147047 *	KOV 827	Duple	43384	C29F	10/50	Burley's Garage Ltd, Birmingham (WK)
147057	DMS 234	Duple	56586	C29F	1/51	Gillespie Bros, Bonnybridge (SN)
147064	MYC 801	Duple	56622	C27F	4/51	J & W Hawkins (Hawkins Bros) {Scarlet Pimpernel Coaches}, Minehead (SO)
147090	RTW 222	Duple	43530	C27F	1/51	Moore Bros (Kelvedon) Ltd (EX)
147096						Exported to Rotterdam (O-NL)
147100 *	LVO 85	Duple	49491	C24F	5/51	Barton Transport, Chilwell (NG) 595
147137 - 147148, 147245 - 147256						Exported to Melbourne (O-AUS)
147336	JM 9852	Duple	51316	C29F	1/51	E Nelson & Son, Arnside (WT)
147344						Exported to Penang (O-MAL)
147349	LUC 646	Duple	50351	C29F	2/51	Keith & Boyle (London) Ltd {Orange Luxury Coaches}, London EC2 (LN) Zinnia
147355 *	MTA 917	Duple	56579	C29F	1/51	Heybrook Bay Motor Services Ltd, Down Thomas (DN)
147359	PPC 275	Duple	48139	C29F	1/51	H Howard, West Byfleet (SR)
147369, 147375						Exported to Mombasa (O-EAK)
147488	?	Mulliner		B--F	-/--	Anglo Iranian Oil Co, location unknown (O-IR)
148584	E-15556	?		B12FV	3/51	AL Etnedal Bilruter, Etnedal (O-N)
152382	E-15581	Fjeldhus		B29C	4/51	AL Torpa Bilruter, Torpa (O-DK)
152481 *	B-29024	Jongerius		B30-	-/51	ZWH, Balk (O-NL) 24
152593	?	Duple	50810	C29F	4/51	Weerakoon Bros Ltd, Colombo (O-CL)
153641 *	?	Verheul	6873	B33-	3/51	Citosa, Zoetermeer (O-NL) 4712
153757	?	Duple	56644	C29F	-/--	Ceylon Touring Co, Colombo (O-CL)
154037	?	Duple	56645	C29F	-/--	Ceylon Touring Co, Colombo (O-CL)
154147	?	Duple	56646	C29F	-/--	Ceylon Touring Co, Colombo (O-CL)
154236	?	Duple	56647	C29F	-/--	Ceylon Touring Co, Colombo (O-CL)
154240	?	Duple	56648	C29F	-/--	Ceylon Touring Co, Colombo (O-CL)
154310 *	B-29023	Jongerius		B30-	-/51	ZWH, Balk (O-NL) 23
154333	?	Duple	56649	C29F	-/--	Ceylon Touring Co, Colombo (O-CL)
154403 *	HX-45883	Bochanen		B30-	-/51	MEGGA, Sliedrecht (O-NL) 23
154721 *	?	Verheul	6872	B33-	3/51	Citosa, Zoetermeer (O-NL) 4711

C1252/186

Unidentified Chassis

The following vehicles will almost certainly appear in the preceding main listing, but in the absence of chassis numbers the entries cannot be matched

a. UK vehicles
The following were among those supplied to Ministry of Supply (GOV) for use by civilian Government Departments

?	KGH 871	?	?	-/--
?	KGH 885	?	?	-/--
?	KGH 955	Mulliner	B30F	c/48
?	KGT 81	Mulliner	B28F	4/49
?	KGT 82	?	B--F	-/--
?	KGT 90	?	?	-/--
?	KGT 91	?	?	-/--
?	KGT 92	?	?	-/--
?	KGT 98	?	B28F	11/49
?	KYW 333	Whitson	B28F	-/50

The following were among those supplied to Admiralty (Royal Navy)(GOV)

?	* 599 RN	?	B32F	-/45
?	* 585 RN	?	B32F	-/--

A non-PSV which cannot be traced in Bedford records - it may have been an OL
    MPK 477   ?   caravan c1/49 Sir Malcom Campbell, Reigate (VSR) Bluebird

The following are known only by their subsequent registrations; all are believed to have originally carried military registrations. Those marked ++ could in fact have been Bedford OWBs

++	?	?	?	B30F	-/-- Originally Royal Air Force (RAF) (GOV). Re-registered EET 35 1948 (C Riley, Rotherham (WR))
	?	(Mulliner ?)	B--F	-/-- Re-registered PCH 175 1958 (Ford & Weston (contractor), Derby & Cheltenham)
++	?	Mulliner	B--F	-/-- Re-registered PPA 934 1951 (Vacuum Oil Co, Ottershaw (XSR))
++	?	?	B32F	-/-- Re-registered WOJ 828 5/58 (RM Douglas Ltd (contractor), Birmingham 405)
++	?	?	B32F	-/-- Re-registered XOC 38 at an unknown date (RM Douglas Ltd (contractor), Birmingham 439)
++	?	?	B--F	-/-- Re-registered XOC 41 at an unknown date (RM Douglas Ltd (contractor), Birmingham 442 as B28F)
++	?	?	B32F	-/-- Re-registered YOF 234 at an unknown date (RM Douglas Ltd (contractor), Birmingham 454)
	?	?	?	-/-- Rebodied Belle FC30F and re-registered YBJ 871 7/58 (BR Shreeve Ltd {Belle Coaches}, Lowestoft (NK)); chassis number recorded incorrectly as 14279. Shreeve purchased several ex military OBs and this could possibly have been 12749, ex RAF.
	?	?	B--F	-/-- Re-registered YRC 419 4/62 (Ford & Weston (contractor), Derby & Cheltenham)
	?	?	B--F	-/-- Re-registered 542 GMG at unknown date (unknown operator)

The following are known only by their subsequent registrations

?	?	C--F	-/-- Exported to Gibraltar and re-registered G12141 8/59.
?	Duple	? C29F	-/-- Re-registered J 5980 3/52 (W Le Marinel {Favourite Tours}, St Helier, Jersey (CI))
?	Duple	? C29F	-/-- Re-registered J 6477 4/56 (J Jones {Maple Leaf Tours}, St Helier, Jersey (CI))
?	Duple	? C29F	-/-- Re-registered WNR 647 11/60 (Ratby Engineering, Peckleton Common (XLE)); reportedly ex Channel Islands, but not traced as such
?	(Mulliner ?)	B32F	c/48 Exported to Cyprus and re-registered TAQ 596 8/58

. Irish vehicles

FI 4022	?	B--F	-/48 M Hogan {Shamrock Bus Service}, Thurles (EI)
FI 3910	Ryan	B26F	-/48 M Hogan {Shamrock Bus Service}, Thurles (EI)
FI 4515	Shamrock	B26F	-/49 M Hogan {Shamrock Bus Service}, Thurles (EI)
FI 4991	Shamrock	B31F	-/50 M Hogan {Shamrock Bus Service}, Thurles (EI)
HI 4569	GJ Roberts	B26F	-/47 R Campion {Princess Bus Service}, Clonmel (EI)

C1252/187

?	HI 4939	GJ Roberts	B28F	-/48	R Campion {Princess Bus Service}, Clonmel (EI)
?	HI 5692	GJ Roberts	B28F	-/49	R Campion {Princess Bus Service}, Clonmel (EI)
?	* IP 5589	GJ Roberts	B20F	-/47	JJ Kavanagh & Sons {Kavanagh Bus Service}, Urlingford (EI)
?	IP 5726	GJ Roberts	B26F	-/48	T Nolan, Callan (EI)
?	IP 6517	GJ Roberts	B26F	-/50	T Nolan, Callan (EI)
?	KI 3429	Cahill	B26F	-/48	Dunmore Bus Service, Dunmore (EI)
?	NI 5254	Ryan	C29F	-/50	Scraggs, Bray (EI)
?	NI 5255	Ryan	C29F	-/50	Scraggs, Bray (EI)
?	ZB 8127	Ryan	B24F	-/48	Donogue, Castletown (EI)
?	ZJ 4945	GJ Roberts	B24F	-/49	Irish Racing Board, Dublin (XEI)

c. Overseas vehicles – where registrations are known

?	1016	Grice	B--F	-/--	Hume Street South Bus Service, Toowoomba, Qld (O-AUS)
?	3194	CAC	? FB31D	by6/49	WAGT, Perth, WA (O-AUS) 42
?	3340	CAC	? FB31D	by6/49	WAGT, Perth, WA (O-AUS) 43
?	* 3453	CAC	? FB33F	9/53	Riverton Bus Service, Riverton, WA (O-AUS) 3
?	10.14	CAC	? FB31D	by6/48	WAGT, Perth, WA (O-AUS) 33
?	21.965	CAC	? FB31D	by6/49	WAGT, Perth, WA (O-AUS) 41
?	31.729	CAC	? FB31D	by6/48	WAGT, Perth, WA (O-AUS) 31
?	31.730	CAC	? FB31D	by6/48	WAGT, Perth, WA (O-AUS) 30
?	31.732	CAC	? FB31D	by6/48	WAGT, Perth, WA (O-AUS) 32
?	31.735	CAC	? FB31D	by6/49	WAGT, Perth, WA (O-AUS) 35
?	31.738	CAC	? FB31D	by6/49	WAGT, Perth, WA (O-AUS) 38
?	31.740	CAC	? FB31D	by6/49	WAGT, Perth, WA (O-AUS) 40
?	* 31.824	CAC	? FB33F	-/49	United Buses Pty Ltd, Claremont, WA (O-AUS) 24
?	31.825	CAC	? FB31D	-/49	United Buses Pty Ltd, Claremont, WA (O-AUS) 25
?	* 45.157	CAC	? FB29F	-/51	Beam Transport Ltd, Redcliffe, WA (O-AUS) 57
?	* 45.158	CAC	? FB28F	-/51	Beam Transport Ltd, Redcliffe, WA (O-AUS) 58
?	* 45.159	CAC	? FB28F	-/50	Beam Transport Ltd, Redcliffe, WA (O-AUS) 59
?	* 45.160	CAC	? FB34F	-/50	Beam Transport Ltd, Redcliffe, WA (O-AUS) 60
?	* 45.161	CAC	? FB34F	-/51	Beam Transport Ltd, Redcliffe, WA (O-AUS) 61
?	45.315	CAC	? FC--F	-/--	Tourist Omnibus Service, location unknown, WA (O-AUS)
?	* (45.071 ?)	CAC	? ?	-/--	Pioneer Omnibus Co, Cottesloe, WA (O-AUS) 11
?	451.903	Grice	B27F	7/46	Hume Street South Bus Service, Toowoomba, Qld (O-AUS)
?	(614850 ?)	?	C---	-/--	Anna Cars, unknown location (O-B)
?	* 729144	Van Hool	? C36F	-/50	Original operator unknown (O-B)
?	A 28.384	Sorø	B27F	/47	Østbanen, Hårlev (O-DK)
?	A 4382	Sorø	B27F	-/48	Østbanen, Hårlev (O-DK)
?	* A 7193	Duple	? C26F	c-/49	OTC, Nairobi (O-EAK)
?	B-9854	Fjeldhus	C---	-/50	Marie Hansen, Slangsvoll (O-N)
?	C 3114	?	B26	2/50	Danish State Railways, Copenhagen (O-DK) 274
?	CF-10-70	?	B---	-/--	Viacao Mecanica de Carnaxide Lda, Carnaxide (O-P)
?	* D 1512	?	B---	-/51	ONDA, Montevideo (O-ROU) 102
?	* DR1214	CAC	? FB33F	7/50	Kalamunda Bus Service, Kalamunda, WA (O-AUS) 14
?	* DR1240	CAC	? FB33F	3/51	Kalamunda Bus Service, Kalamunda, WA (O-AUS) 15
?	DS6	CAC	? ?	-/--	Churches of Christ Native Mission, Norseman, WA (O-AUS)
?	DS 9738	?	?	-/--	OTC, Dar-Es-Salaam (O-EAT)
?	E 9370	Sorø	B25C	-/48	Johs. Eskesen, Stenlille (O-DK)
?	GN1225	CAC	? ?	-/--	MacRobertson Millar Airlines, Perth, WA (O-AUS)
?	* GZ-60874	Met	B29-	-/46	TESO, Den Burg (O-NL) 6
?	H 17.002	?	B27C	4/47	Danish State Railways, Copenhagen (O-DK) 73
?	H 19.304	Ørum-Pedersen	B27C	-/47	Møns Omnibusser, Mon (O-DK) 04
?	H 19.305	Sorø	B27C	-/47	Møns Omnibusser, Mon (O-DK) 05
?	H 19.306	Sorø	B27C	-/47	Møns Omnibusser, Mon (O-DK) 06
?	H 7015	Duple	? C10F	-/47	OTC, Nairobi (O-EAK)
?	* H 8156	Duple	? ?	-/47	Original operator unknown
?	* H 9926	Duple	? C--F	-/48	OTC, Nairobi (O-EAK) 20
?	H-3051	Wattenberg	B25	-/50	Karl Bunkholt, Gjerpen (O-N)
?	HB 31.516	Ørum-Pedersen	B--C	by-/51	"Gamle Olfert", København (O-DK)

C1252/188

?	* HZ-85662	Jongman	B29	-/50	NAL, Ter Aar (O-NL) 13
?	* J 1727	Ørum-Pedersen	B29C	-/49	DBJ (Bornholm Railways), Rønne (O-DK) 01
?	J6498	?	B--F	c1947	South Johore Omnibus Co., Johor Bahru (O-MAL)
?	J9649	?	B--F	c1950	Alec Bus Co, Johore Baharu (O-MAL)
?	K-9000	?	B---	by-/50	Olav G Osen {Osenruta}, Sira (O-N)
?	K.9891	Duple	? B—D	-/--	Uganda Transport Co Ltd, Kampala (O-EAU)
?	* KA 2102	?	?	-/--	OTC, Kampala (O-EAU)
?	* KA 6953	Duple	? C--F	-/50	OTC, Nairobi (O-EAK) 8
?	* KBB 665	?	B---	-/49	Green Line Ltd, unknown location (O-EAK)
?	* KBC 426	?	B---	-/49	Green Line Ltd, unknown location (O-EAK)
?	* KBD 299	Duple	? B32-	-/50	Meralli Bus Services Ltd, Nairobi (O-EAK)
?	* KBD 356	Duple	? B32-	-/50	Meralli Bus Services Ltd, Nairobi (O-EAK)
?	* KBD 357	Duple	? B32-	-/50	Meralli Bus Services Ltd, Nairobi (O-EAK)
?	KW.15	CAC	? FB--D	-/--	MacRobertson Millar Airlines, Perth, WA (O-AUS)
?	* L 297	?	B---	-/46	ONDA, Montevideo (O-ROU) 28
?	LFW244	CAC	? FB--F	-/--	Original operator unknown (O-AUS)
?	* M-85614	?	?	9/50	Original operator not known (O-E)
?	* M-79787	?	?	-/48	Salustino Gomez, Madrid (O-E)
?	* M-79788	?	?	-/48	Salustino Gomez, Madrid (O-E)
?	* M-80877	?	?	-/49	Club Atletico de Madrid (O-E)
?	* M-80896	?	?	-/49	Joaquin Cobo, Madrid (O-E)
?	mo4266	(Syd Wood ?)	B--F	-/--	original operator unknown, NSW (O-AUS)
?	N-25216	De Groot	B31	-/48	Clarys (De Postduif), Ossendrecht (O-NL) 3
?	* N-80613	Van Eck	B33-	-/52	ALAD, Wyken Aalburg (O-NL) 25
?	O 74	Elite	T31	by-/50	Elite Bus Co, Hothersal Turning (O-BDS)
?	OD.111	CAC	? FB—F	-/--	Warrnambool Bus Lines, Warrnambool, Vic (O-AUS) 32
?	Ø 7715	?	B29-	11/48	Danish State Railways, Copenhagen (O-DK) 171
?	Ø 7873	?	B27-	5/47	Danish State Railways, Copenhagen (O-DK) 74
?	Ø 7979	?	B27-	5/47	Danish State Railways, Copenhagen (O-DK) 75
?	Ø 8673	?	B27	2/50	Danish State Railways, Copenhagen (O-DK) 295
?	Ø 8675	?	B29-	12/48	Danish State Railways, Copenhagen (O-DK) 172
?	* P.605	North Shore	B33F	-/50	North Shore Transport Co Ltd, Takapuna (O-NZ) 5
?	* P.624	North Shore	B33F	-/54	North Shore Transport Co Ltd, Takapuna (O-NZ) 25
?	P-42007	?	B25-	-/46	Ghielen, Helden-Beringe (O-NL) 7
?	P4421	?	B---	c-/49	Penang Yellow Bus Co, Penang (O-MAL)
?	P4775	?	B26-	c1950	Hin Co, Georgetown (O-MAL)
?	* s.794	Modern	?	-/--	Mount Cook & Southern Lakes Tourist Co, Christchurch (O-NZ) F36
?	S3012	?	B--C	c-/45	Keppel Co (O-SGP)
?	SC3223	?	B---	c-/48	Keppel Co (O-SGP)
?	STC157	?	B---	-/--	Singapore Traction Co (O-SGP)
?	STC183	?	B---	-/--	Singapore Traction Co (O-SGP)
?	STC217	?	B---	by-/51	Singapore Traction Co (O-SGP)
?	T-1104	Ødegård	B26C	-/49	Indreviks Rutebiler (O-N)
?	TF-6692	San Andres	B--D	c/48	Transportes de San Andres, San Andres (O-E)
?	TF-6953	San Andres	B--D	-/50	Transportes de San Andres, San Andres (O-E)
?	TN-707	?	B---	-/--	Turun Euroliikenne Oy, Turku (O-FIN)
?	U 14.580	?	B29-	11/48	Danish State Railways, Copenhagen (O-DK) 180
?	UAN550	CAC	? FB27F	-/--	Original operator unknown (O-AUS)
?	* v1.933	?	B33F	-/--	North Shore Transport Co Ltd, Takapuna (O-NZ)
?	* v3.718	?	?	-/46	Marlborough Scenic Tours, Picton (O-NZ)
?	V-21752	Ayats	241 B28-	-/49	Santiago, Barcelona (O-E)
?	W2491	?	-30-	-/49	Johan Carlsen, Seterstøa st. (O-N)
?	* W 2491	Duple	? C--F	-/47	Kenya Bus Services (Mombasa) Ltd (O-EAK)
?	W 4458	Duple	? C--F	-/47	OTC, Nairobi (O-EAK) 15
?	W 4459	Duple	? C--F	-/47	OTC, Nairobi (O-EAK) 16
?	W 4640	Duple	? B30-	-/49	Meralli Bus Services Lrd, Nairobi (O-EAK)
?	W 5070	?	B---	-/49	Green Line Ltd, unknown location (O-EAK)
?	* W 5073	Duple	? C--F	-/47	OTC, Nairobi (O-EAK) 17
?	WB.616	?	B--F	-/--	Unknown operator, Wongan Hills (O-AUS) Miss Wongan
?	X22.271	Aarhus	B??-	9/48	AHTJ, Aarhus (O-DK)
?	Y 9596	?	B28-	10/48	Danish State Railways, Copenhagen (O-DK) 170
?	Y 9649	?	B27	3/50	Danish State Railways, Copenhagen (O-DK) 294

? Y.340 CAC ? FB27F -/-- Unknown operator, York (O-AUS)

d. Overseas Vehicles – where neither chassis number nor original registration are known
(Vehicles are listed in approximate alphabetical order of country)

Five CAC FB31D bodied vehicles delivered by 6/48 to WAGT, Perth, WA (O-AUS), four of which carried fleet numbers 34, 36, 37 and 39

Two CAC FB31FR bodied vehicles delivered to Hendersons Bus Service, Bunbury, WA (O-AUS). These both passed to Coopers Bus Service, Benger, WA (O-AUS), where one was rebuilt as FB32F and registered H548, and the other was converted to FB35F and re-registered H1309.

An unidentified B—F body was carried by an OB supplied new as Carilla Bus Service, Carilla, WA (O-AUS) 4

CAC body M231 was carried by an OB at one time with an unknown operator in Port Hedland, WA (O-AUS)

Of two other CAC-bodied OBs, one was built as FB27F for an unknown Australian operator and the other with unknown seating for Hancock & Wright, Wittenoom, WA (O-AUS)

Although the chassis cannot be confirmed as OB, the following Bedfords were delivered as shown:
Jonckheere 5542 C27- 3/48 Pullman Cars, Liège (O-B)
Jonckheere 5603 C27- 7/48 Touring Cars, Leuven (O-B)
Jonckheere 5881 C27- 2/50 Vanden Eynde, Brussels (O-B)
Jonckheere 5963 C27- 6/50 De Schedevallei SPRL, Eine (O-B)
Jonckheere 5984 C24- 6/50 SA Voyages Henri Fontaine, Brussels (O-B)

A Van Hool C—D body was fitted to a 1951 OB for Pam Vermeulen {Pam Cars}, Antwerp (O-B) 6

A Louis Maes C26- body was carried by an OB for Pullman Cars, (Hasselt ?) (O-B) and exhibited at a Belgian motor show when new

Liberty Motor Transport, from an unknown location in Barbados, was operating an OB by 1950

Two vehicles delivered to Escuelas Pias, Barcelona (O-E) in 1950 with Ayats C--- bodies 294, 295

A vehicle delivered to Ricardo Martin, Barcelona (O-E) in 1950 with Ayats C--- body 298

Duple C—F body 50802 was supplied to OTC, Nairobi (O-EAK)

A locally built B--- body was supplied on a 1949 OB chassis as OTC, Nairobi (O-EAK) 18

Of two further Duple C—F bodies supplied to that same operator, one carried fleet number 3 when placed in service in 1948; it later received a Chevrolet oil engine and was re-registered KBB 178 by 3/51. The other was numbered 19 and was re-registered KBE 799 by 1952.

Three Churchill C30F bodied OBs delivered to BOAC in 1947 for use in Alexandria (O-ET), Jerusalem (O-IL) and Tripoli (O-LAR)

Heino Toivo, from an unknown location in Finland, ran a B18F vehicle, new in 1952

Duple bodies 50767 and 52634 were fitted to unknown chassis for export to Iraq and the Near East respectively.

A Repstad body was carried by a 1950 OB with Syver C Haakerud, Austmarke (O-N)

A Verheul B29- body was carried by a 1947 OB with PG Ganzewinkel, Maarheeze (O-NL). It was re-registered NB-62-92 at an unknown date. Its chassis number is recorded as 5A128936A, which may indicate some rebuilding.

An Eaddy & Taylor B—F bodied OB served at some time with Webbs Motors Ltd, Whangarei (O-NZ) 4; it was re-registered DZ.5985 in 1965.

Emslie & Flockton bodied a 1948 OB which at some time operated with Glenorchy Motors, Glenorchy (O-NZ)

A Johnson & Smith C20F bodied OB was supplied to Alexandra Motors, Alexandra (O-NZ)

A Magee C—F bodied OB served at some time as Edwards Motors, Auckland (O-NZ) 20

A Modern C20- bodied OB built in 1949 served at some time as Turnbulls Coaches Ltd, Dunedin (O-NZ) 3

Another Modern-bodied vehicle served at some time as Aorangi Motors, Pleasant Point (O-NZ) 4 and was re-registered AH.6363 in 1965.

Original owners are not known for four NZMB C—F bodied OBs which served at some time as nos 31 – 34 in the fleet of Edwards Motors, Auckland (O-NZ)

An NZMB B—F body was fitted to an OB at some time operating as Tui Motors Ltd, Te Puke (O-NZ) 24

A further NZMB body was carried by an OB at some time with Gibson's Motors, New Plymouth (O-NZ)

A Stratford B24F body was carried by a 1949 OB at some time with George Duke Co Ltd, location unknown (O-NZ); it was re-registered EP.2425 in 1965.

Another Stratford body was carried by an OB at some time with JC Hills, Hawera (O-NZ)

Although not confirmed as the first owner, Transport BS Ltd, Auckland (O-NZ) fitted their own bodies to two OBs in their fleet: no 7 (of 1949) and no 5 (1950)

A Wilton body was carried by an OB at some time with Rogers, Ongaonga (O-NZ)

Other known OBs about which information is particularly incomplete are the following:
    Bentley's Motors, Waihaha (O-NZ) at some time ran a 1947 B20F-bodied OB
    Blains, Ashburton (O-NZ) at some time operated a 1948 OB
    Burling's Bus Service, Waihaha (O-NZ) at some time operated a 1950 OB
    Eastern Buses Ltd, Bucklands Beach (O-NZ) ran OBs numbered 2 and 4
    Johnston's Blue Motors, Auckland (O-NZ) was running a C25F-bodied OB by1955, with fleet no 6
    L Osborne, Taumarunui (O-NZ) operated a 1947 OB
    Madge Motors Ltd, Palmerston North (O-NZ) operated an OB with fleet number 15
    Midland, Christchurch (O-NZ) ran an OB with fleet number 71
    Northern Motor Bus Co, Whangarei (O-NZ) 11 was a 25-seat OB
    The Passenger Transport Co Ltd, Otahuhu (O-NZ) at some time ran an OB with fleet number 35
    CP Ritchie, Waihi (O-NZ) is known to have operated an OB
    Suburban Bus Lines, Westport (O-NZ) at some time ran an OB as its fleet number 3
    Teddy's Motors, Waerenga (O-NZ) at some time operated an OB
    Thorn's Passenger Service, Mercer (O-NZ) at some time ran an OB
    Transport BS Ltd, Auckland (O-NZ): another unidentified OB operated as fleet number 15
    Tui Motors Ltd, Te Puke (O-NZ) ran an OB with fleet number 9
    Unknown owners in New Zealand operated OBs known only as follows:
        a. Re-registered CZ.5980 in 1965; it was at some time a Non-PSV
        b. Re-registered DT.1315 in 1965; it was at some time a Non-PSV
        c. Re-registered EH.2884 in 1965
        d. Re-registered EJ.1721 in 1965
        e. Re-registered MT.5293 in 1965; became a Non-PSV by 1989
        f. Re-registered NJ.105 in 1965; latterly a Non-PSV

Karachi Road Transport Corporation (O-PK) was operating an open-top double-deck OB by 1950

Duple B—F bodies 52582/3/4 were fitted to unknown chassis for export to Trinidad.

C1252/191

NOTES

General Notes

Contemporary Press reports noted 20 vehicles with Mulliner utility-style bodies arriving at Beira in June 1947. It is assumed that these were the vehicles with chassis numbered between 41190 and 49126 delivered to Nyasaland Transport Co Ltd, Blantyre (O-EAN) at that time; the company's records indicate that 12 more Mulliner-bodied 32-seaters arrived in 1947; of this further batch only two have been specifically identified. Thirty further OBs were bodied as 32-seaters by Fath & Co, Bulawayo for the same operator in 1948 and a further 15 were being similarly bodied later in the same year; the records indicate that the company was considering diverting some or all of these Fath-bodied vehicles to other customers as the state of the roads in Nyasaland was proving too harsh for the OBs. None of these vehicles can be directly traced in Bedford records, but it is likely that there were regular diversions of chassis between customers or even countries in East Africa.

In February 1946 Uganda Transport Co Ltd announced that they were expecting 30 Bedford OBs with Duple Almet B28D bodies. It is thought that the order materialised as 26 chassis (numbered between 15065 and 45691) with Duple bodies 41839 - 41864. Most have previously been recorded as B8D, the remainder as B32F (which is how an extract from Duple records show the whole batch). Contemporary press photographs show that B28D is correct. The bodies comprised two passenger compartments, hence the dual doors. The forward compartment was fitted with 8 upholstered seats, while the main compartment had slatted wooden seats for a further 20.

Bedford records have 26 OB chassis, numbered between 25677 and 59475, as exported to Hong Kong, some to Hong Kong & Shanghai Hotels, which is believed to have acted as a dealer; it is likely that all these vehicles were supplied to Kowloon Motor Bus Co, but in the absence of confirmation, the chassis are noted only as Exported to Hong Kong.

Mulliner bodies 41779 - 41819 carried by the 1946 batch of OB chassis (17249 being numerically the first) for Anglo-Iranian Oil Co, Abadan (O-IR) were sub-contracted by Duple, and carried Duple numbers

15066/7/70: Bedford records indicate intended for Uganda Transport Co, Kampala (O-EAU). The order of the registration and fleet numbers require confirmation

17214, 28304, 30294, 34826, 61189, 66607, 66821, 68897, 69377, 70306, 71593, 73144, 74021, 75035, 75647, 86714, 87605, 88631, 99145 103240, 106420, 113861, 117000, 121434, 134420, 136390: These chassis, along with others more specifically noted, have not been traced in Bedford records

17297, 18729, 18737: one of these 1946 OBs for Gibraltar was registered G4746

19824, 22997, 23085, 23245, 23333, 23421, 23464, 23673, 23731, 23761, 23772, 23819, 23848, 24455, 24485, 24497 for Anglo-Iranian Oil Co, Abadan (O-IR): All given as Duple but assumed to be the batch sub-contracted to Mulliner, with Duple order numbers in the range 41820 - 41835

21325 – 21336 are specifically noted as having been supplied in ckd form; there are likely to have been many others exported in this form.

29011, 29424, 29478, 29525, 29641: Not traced beyond Mulliner; they may have received goods bodywork, or been exported

32823, 32874, 62378, 64348: Duple records have as intended for Alton Bros (Trimdon) Ltd (DM)

33441, 33795, 33884, 70382: Bedford records have as intended for Wallace Arnold Tours Ltd, Leeds (WR) who acquired Barker; Duple has Barker

34828, 36102, 36280, 57822, 60060, 65698, 72999: Bedford records have as intended for Shearings Tours Ltd, Oldham (LA)

41872, 43955, 45851, 49495, 59423, 62029, 62762, 66088, 66711: Bedford records have as intended for Eclipse Transport, Manchester - status unknown, but linked with most Junction bodies

43121, 43199, 43447, 60741, 66968: These BEA coaches had extra large rear luggage compartments, hence the lower seating capacity

43301, 47112, 62778, 92387, 114801: Bedford and Duple records have as intended for J & C Williams (J Williams & Son), Wrockwardine Wood (SH) - maybe in error

45465, 125329, 125786, 126018, 127731: HR Richmond was also a PSV operator

53554, 56760, 59866, 65866, 68601, 103280, 103357: Bedford records have as intended for Enterprise & Silver Dawn, Scunthorpe (LI)

58801, 63622, 76613, 92701: Bedford and Duple records have as intended for Greenslades, Exeter (DN) - parent company of both Belcher and Regent

85701, 86995, 88281: These Ministry of Supply vehicles were noted as based in Liverpool

105959, 105968, 106899, 107741, 107783, 115348, 118173: Ordered by Morning Star Motor Services Ltd, Bristol (GL) before Wessex was formed

132685, 132701, 132768, 133284, 133308, 133372, 133927, 133944, 134016, 134034, 135294, 135793, 137054, 137773, 138228, 138454, 138788, 139282, 139409, 140798: The Duple bodies were almost certainly numbered 52585/6, 52626 - 29, 52675 - 88 in unknown order

137974, 143020, 145491: Two of these Derbyshire County Council libraries were registered ONU 97 and 98

Duple records show body numbers 46164 - 46188 allocated to OBs for Pamalhire operations in East Africa, but there are no traces of any chassis being supplied. The order is assumed to have been cancelled.

The Duple-bodied 14-seat touring coaches supplied to Overseas Touring Co Ltd for use in East Africa were noted as having "tropical refinements", with a double-framed aluminium body structure, with insulation between the framing and with teak timber.

Individual Notes

11008	(P.351) Re-registered V2.546 at an unknown date; re-registered EH.2881 1965
11009	(2900) Chassis number also recorded as 13015 - now known to be the engine number
11015	(P.962) Re-registered P1.533 at an unknown date
11016	(P1.133) Also recorded as new to Suburban Buses Ltd, Te Papapa (O-NZ) 38 with Suburban B33F body. Re-registered EH.3023 1965
11021	(FTG 400) Complete vehicle had been delivered 11/45, but the vehicle was not registered until 1946
11027	(EBM 615) Originally an experimental chassis, bodied c1946 for use as a Vauxhall staff bus with Duple body 41990 from chassis 37204. Registered EBM 615, but probably used on only on Trade Plates. Re-registered LMN 147 (Hamill's Garage Ltd, Douglas) 1949. (Registration EBM 615 then transferred to chassis 26003)
11037	(V1.632) Howie not confirmed as original operator
11045	(RAF 208529) Re-registered 00 AC 02 1/50
11046	(RAF 119773) Re-registered 01 AC 87 1/50
11047	(RAF 119779) Re-registered 00 AC 04 1/50
11048	(RAF 119780) Re-registered 00 AC 05 1/50
11049	(RAF 120733) Re-registered 00 AC 06 1/50
11054	(P.350) Re-registered EY.9857 1965
11058	(?) Re-registered 1071.IC at an unknown date, and re-registered KO.2760 1965
11067	(?) Re-registered PB-58-95 with BPM, Rotterdam (O-NL) 2 at an unknown date
11068	(?) Re-registered JLR 468 2/48 (unknown operator)
11069	(?) Re-registered J 8232 by 8/47 (Jersey Motor Transport (CI) 18)
11070	(RAF 208539) Re-registered 00 AC 07 1/50. Sold in Cyprus and re-registered TAS 621 2/59
11071	(RAF 208536) Re-registered 00 AC 08 1/50
11072	(RAF 208543) Re-registered 00 AC 09 1/50
11073	(RAF 119776) Re-registered 00 AC 10 1/50
11074	(RAF 208541) Re-registered 00 AC 11 1/50
11075	(RAF 208544) Re-registered 00 AC 12 1/50
11091	(634) Rebuilt to forward control 2/57
11093	(?) Originally used as an "experimental" vehicle by Duple
11096	(CNV 668) Bedford and Duple records have as intended for RLH & A Seamarks (Seamarks Bros), Rushden (NO)
11103	(P.352) Re-registered P2.484 and V2.412 at unknown dates; re-registered EY.840 or EY.841 1965
11109	(RAF 208545) Re-registered 00 AC 13 1/50
11110	(RAF 208542) Re-registered 00 AC 14 1/50
11111	(S.306) Re-registered S.493 at an unknown date

11724	(?) Re-registered EN.3002 1965
11725	(P.339) Re-registered EH.2882 1965
11727	(RAF 209744) Re-registered 00 AC 15 1/50
11728	(RAF 209732) Re-registered 00 AC 16 1/50
11729	(RAF 209733) Re-registered 00 AC 17 1/50
11730	(RAF 209731) Re-registered 00 AC 18 1/50
12009	(RAF 209734) Re-registered 00 AC 19 1/50
12017	(CE 7021) Re-registered IC 474 2/49
12028	(?) Re-registered DZ.5058 1965
12035	(?) Re-registered v2.420 at an unknown date; re-registered EW.1838 1965
12038	(S.307) Re-registered CT.9786 1965
12047	(RAF 209737) Re-registered 00 AC 20 1/50
12049	(RAF 208548 ?) RAF records show same registration for chassis 12049 and 12742. Re-registered 00 AC 21 1/50
12052	(RAF 209741) Re-registered 00 AC 22 1/50
12059	(1292) The original body was a rebuild from that previously carried by a Packard; rebodied Mallett B32F 8/53
12076	(P.576) Re-registered v1.830 and v3.348 at unknown dates; re-registered EH.9840 or EH.9850 1965
12081	(P.575) Re-registered P2.425 at an unknown date
12092	(P.126) Re-registered EW.5975 1965
12702	(?) Chassis number recorded as 12072; Bedford records have 12702
12709	(v1.828) Chassis number recorded as 12079; Bedford records have 12709. Re-registered v3.347 at an unknown date. Fleet number also recorded as 38
12714	(FT 5651) Carried the prototype post-war Duple Vista body
12722	(CE 5575) Re-registered IC 588 1950
12740	(RAF 208547) Re-registered 00 AC 23 1/50
12742	(RAF 208548 ?) RAF records show same registration for chassis 12049 and 12742. Re-registered 00 AC 24 1/50
12743	(RAF 209739) Re-registered 00 AC 25 1/50. Re-registered STG 227 1955 (J Hemmings, Llanharan (GG) as B28F)
12744	(RAF 208549) Re-registered 00 AC 26 1/50
12745	(RAF 208552) Re-registered 00 AC 27 1/50
12748	(RAF 208551) Re-registered 00 AC 28 1/50. Re-registered WOJ 826 5/58 (RM Douglas Ltd (contractor), Birmingham)
12749	(RAF 208550) Re-registered 00 AC 29 1/50. Just possibly re-registered YBJ 871 - see page 186
12753	(CE 7292) Re-registered IC 678 2/51
12766	(?) Chassis number recorded as 12765; Bedford records have 12766
12784	(DCA 574) Originally allocated registration CUX 663, but seemingly not operated as such
13406	(RAF 208553) Re-registered 00 AC 30 1/50. Re-registered WOJ 830 6/58 (RM Douglas Ltd (contractor), Birmingham 407)
13407	(RAF 208554) Re-registered 00 AC 31 1/50
13448	(RAF 208559) Re-registered 00 AC 32 1/50
13452	(RAF 208556) Re-registered 00 AC 33 1/50
13459	(RAF 208564) Re-registered 00 AC 34 1/50
13463	(RAF 208557) Re-registered 00 AC 35 1/50
13464	(RAF 208555) Re-registered 00 AC 36 1/50
13471	(RAF 208566) Re-registered 00 AC 37 1/50
13472	(RAF 208558) Re-registered 00 AC 38 1/50
13475	(RAF 208565 ?) Registration needs confirmation; re-registered RUJ 205 9/58 (G Scoltock {Premier Coaches}, Much Wenlock (SH))
13480	(LMY 893) Re-registered J 5721 5/51 (F Hopkins {Favourite Tours}, St Helier, Jersey (CI))
13481	(HLX 833) Exported to Cyprus and re-registered TAB 498 11/56
13490	(DDL 928) Exported to Cyprus and re-registered TAK 38 10/57
13498	(CE 7885) Re-registered IC 2581 8/53
13500	(RAF 95848) Re-registered 00 AC 39 1/50
13715	(?) Chassis number not traced in Bedford records but taken from Motor Taxation records – possible error for 18715? Re-registered NGY 421 11/54 (unknown operator)
14121	(?) Chassis number not traced in Bedford records but taken from Motor Taxation records. Re-registered LRC 423 1/58 (Ford & Weston (contractor), Derby & Cheltenham)
14204	(RAF 95849) Re-registered 00 AC 40 1/50
14208	(RAF 95850) Re-registered 00 AC 41 1/50
14210	(RAF 208561) Re-registered 00 AC 42 1/50
14216	(RAF 208560) Re-registered 00 AC 43 1/50
14217	(RAF 208563) Re-registered 02 AC 02 1/50. Re-registered UOU 302 12/58 (unknown operator)

14219	(RAF 95851) Re-registered 00 AC 44 1/50
14220	(RAF 208562) Re-registered 00 AC 45 1/50
14286	(?) Re-registered CV 4186 3/54
15054	(CRX 857) Motor Taxation records have chassis number as 15074 (believed to be CRX 858); Bedford records have 15054
15057	(J 11593) Re-registered GJF 396 9/50 (WH Millward & WH Starmer {Barwell Coaches}, Leicester (LE))
15058	(FT 5681) Exported to Ceylon 8/53 and re-registered CV 3486 11/53
15061	(FT 5666) Exported to Cyprus and re-registered TM 389 3/55
15070	(A 4828) Perkins oil engine fitted and renumbered 15 by 11/51
15074	(CRX 858) Motor Taxation records have 15074 as CRX 857 (see 15054)
15075	(CSA 234) Exported to Cyprus and re-registered TAC 319 12/56
15085	(GEL 502) Originally allocated registration HLY 560, but seemingly not operated as such
15087	(GEL 500) Originally allocated registration HLY 558, but seemingly not operated as such
15430	(P.766) Not traced in Bedford records. Re-registered P1.654 at an unknown date
15917	(CUJ 38) Exported to Cyprus and re-registered L 183 11/54
15959	(KPD 956) Exported to Cyprus and re-registered TX 844 6/56
15963	(RAF 208642) Re-registered 00 AC 46 1/50
15966	(RAF 209765) Re-registered 00 AC 47 1/50
15968	(RAF 209766) Re-registered 00 AC 48 1/50
15970	(RAF 209779) Re-registered 00 AC 49 1/50
15972	(RAF 208595) Re-registered 00 AC 50 1/50
15973	(RAF 209768) Re-registered 00 AC 51 1/50
15974	(RAF 208567) Re-registered 00 AC 52 1/50
15976	(RAF 209776) Re-registered 00 AC 53 1/50
15977	(RAF 208634) Re-registered 00 AC 54 1/50. Re-registered XDE 864 4/58 (WG Richards (Richards Bros), Moylgrove (PE) as B28F)
15979	(RAF 209770) Re-registered 00 AC 55 1/50
15982	(RAF 208568) Re-registered 00 AC 56 1/50
15983	(RAF 208578) Re-registered 00 AC 57 1/50
15984	(RAF 209767) Re-registered 00 AC 58 1/50
15985	(RAF 209773) Re-registered 00 AC 59 1/50
15986	(RAF 208569) Re-registered 00 AC 60 1/50
15988	(RAF 209772) Re-registered 00 AC 61 1/50. Sold in Cyprus and re-registered TW 39 2/56
15990	(RAF 209777) Re-registered 00 AC 62 1/50
15991	(RAF 209763) Re-registered 00 AC 63 1/50. Sold in Cyprus and re-registered TAJ 352 9/57
15992	(RAF 208629) Re-registered 00 AC 64 1/50
15994	(RAF 209769) Re-registered 00 AC 66 1/50
15995	(RAF 208575) Re-registered 00 AC 65 1/50
15997	(RAF 208570) Re-registered 00 AC 67 1/50
15999	(RAF 208571) Re-registered 00 AC 68 1/50
16601	(RAF 208572) Re-registered 00 AC 69 1/50. Sold in Cyprus and re-registered TAG 445 7/57
16603	(RAF 209761) Re-registered 00 AC 70 1/50. Rebuilt to forward control, rebodied Belle FC30F and re-registered URT 287 for BR Shreeve Ltd {Belle Coaches}, Lowestoft (SK) 7/56
16604	(RAF 208581) Re-registered 00 AC 71 1/50
16605	(RAF 209778) Re-registered 00 AC 72 1/50
16607	(RAF 209775) Re-registered 00 AC 73 1/50. Re-registered 691 CRA 10/56 (Booth & Fisher Ltd, Halfway (DE) as B30F)
16608	(RAF 209790) Re-registered 00 AC 74 1/50. Re-registered KJA 800 10/56 (mobile shop)
16610	(RAF 208579) Re-registered 00 AC 75 1/50
16612	(RAF 208621) Re-registered 00 AC 76 1/50
16614	(RAF 208596) Re-registered 00 AC 77 1/50
16616	(RAF 209795) Re-registered 00 AC 78 1/50
16617	(RAF 209782) Re-registered 00 AC 79 1/50
16618	(RAF 208597) Re-registered 00 AC 80 1/50
16620	(RAF 208639) Re-registered 00 AC 81 1/50.
16621	(RAF 209784) Re-registered 00 AC 82 1/50
16623	(RAF 208618) Re-registered 00 AC 83 1/50. Re-registered XOP 722 2/59 (RM Douglas Ltd (contractor), Birmingham 451)
16625	(RAF 208643) Re-registered 00 AC 84 1/50. Re-registered 3293 BT 9/60 (CHC Phillips, Shiptonthorpe (ER))
16627	(RAF 208580) Re-registered 00 AC 85 1/50
16629	(RAF 208635) Re-registered 00 AC 86 1/50
16630	(RAF 208622) Re-registered 00 AC 87 1/50

16631	(?) Believed to have been re-registered JGF 836 1946 (AERE, Harwell (GOV)) (chassis no quoted as 16031)
16633	(RAF 208608) Re-registered 00 AC 88 1/50
16634	(RAF 208607) Re-registered 00 AC 89 1/50
16636	(RAF 208612) Re-registered 00 AC 90 1/50
16638	(RAF 208632) Re-registered 00 AC 91 1/50
16639	(RAF 208592) Re-registered 00 AC 92 1/50. Sold in Cyprus and re-registered TAG 317 7/57
16641	(RAF 208900) Re-registered 00 AC 93 1/50
16642	(RAF 209792) Re-registered 00 AC 94 1/50
16643	(RAF 208609) Re-registered 00 AC 95 1/50
16644	(RAF 208633) Re-registered 00 AC 96 1/50
16645	(RAF 208604) Re-registered 00 AC 97 1/50
16647	(RAF 208577) Re-registered 00 AC 98 1/50
16648	(RAF 208605) Re-registered 00 AC 99 1/50
16649	(RAF 208576) Re-registered 01 AC 00 1/50
16650	(RAF 208574) Re-registered 01 AC 01 1/50
16651	(RAF 208610) Re-registered 01 AC 02 1/50
16652	(RAF 208602) Re-registered 01 AC 03 1/50
16655	(RAF 208582 ?) Registration needs confirmation
16656	(RAF 208603) Re-registered 01 AC 04 1/50
16657	(RAF 208583) Re-registered 01 AC 05 1/50. Re-registered PNY 259 9/54 (H Thomas, Pontardawe (GG))
16658	(RAF 208584) Re-registered 01 AC 06 1/50
16659	(RAF 208606) Re-registered 01 AC 07 1/50
16660	(RAF 208591) Re-registered 01 AC 08 1/50
16661	(RAF 208611) Re-registered 01 AC 09 1/50
16663	(RAF 208640) Re-registered 01 AC 10 1/50
16664	(RAF 208636) Re-registered 01 AC 11 1/50
16665	(RAF 208599) Re-registered 01 AC 12 1/50
16666	(RAF 208638) Re-registered 01 AC 13 1/50
16667	(RAF 208585) Re-registered 01 AC 14 1/50. Re-registered WOJ 829 6/58 (RM Douglas Ltd (contractor), Birmingham 406)
16668	(RAF 209771) Re-registered 01 AC 15 1/50
16669	(RAF 209774) Re-registered 01 AC 16 1/50
16671	(RAF 208600) Re-registered 01 AC 17 1/50
16672	(RAF 208587) Re-registered 01 AC 18 1/50
16673	(RAF 208586) Re-registered 01 AC 19 1/50
16674	(RAF 208588) Re-registered 01 AC 20 1/50
16675	(RAF 208613) Re-registered 01 AC 21 1/50
16676	(RAF 209780) Re-registered 01 AC 22 1/50
16677	(RAF 208589) Re-registered 01 AC 23 1/50
16679	(RAF 208590) Re-registered 01 AC 24 1/50
16680	(RAF 208593) Re-registered 01 AC 25 1/50
16681	(RAF 209781) Re-registered 01 AC 26 1/50
16682	(RAF 208594) Re-registered 01 AC 27 1/50
16683	(RAF 209785) Re-registered 01 AC 28 1/50
16684	(RAF 208601 ?) Registration needs confirmation
16685	(RAF 209783) Re-registered 01 AC 29 1/50
16689	(5190800) The original registration had an unknown prefix letter. Re-registered 50 YP 85 1949
17206	(CJY 538) Exported to Ceylon and re-registered CV 3570 11/53
17219	(GEL 503) Originally allocated registration HLY 561, but seemingly not operated as such
17223	(GEL 509) Originally allocated registration HLY 568, but seemingly not operated as such
17247	(GYC 892) Exported to Cyprus and re-registered TW 411 3/56
17259	(GEL 507) Originally allocated registration HLY 566, but seemingly not operated as such
17263	(CJY 535) Exported to Ceylon and re-registered CV 3327 9/53
17264	(GEL 510) Originally allocated registration HLY 569, but seemingly not operated as such
17272	(GEL 504) Originally allocated registration HLY 562, but seemingly not operated as such. Exported to Cyprus and re-registered TAA 750 9/56
17275	(GEL 508) Originally allocated registration HLY 567, but seemingly not operated as such. Exported to Cyprus and re-registered TX 433 5/56
17276	(FUP 669) Exported to Cyprus and re-registered TAG 897 7/57
17278	(GEL 501) Originally allocated registration HLY 559, but seemingly not operated as such
17280	(JTT 719) Exported to Cyprus and re-registered TW 412 5/56
17284	(FUP 723) Exported to Cyprus and re-registered TR 988 10/55

17288	(GEL 505) Originally allocated registration HLY 563, but seemingly not operated as such.
17295	(GEL 506) Originally allocated registration HLY 565, but seemingly not operated as such
18701	(RAF 209793) Re-registered 01 AC 33 1/50
18702	(RAF 208616) Re-registered 01 AC 34 1/50
18703	(RAF 209786) Re-registered 01 AC 35 1/50
18704	(RAF 208617) Re-registered 01 AC 36 1/50
18706	(RAF 209794) Re-registered 01 AC 37 1/50
18711	(JRA 737) Exported to Cyprus by 10/59
18712	(DVJ 22) Rebuilt to forward control as FDP30F between 1955 and 1957 (Corvedale Motor Co, Ludlow (SH) 5)
18714	(?) Rebodied Duple C29F (127/8) and re-registered ASY 804 1952 (W Hunter, Loanhead (MN))
18715	(RAF 208631) Re-registered 01 AC 38 1/50. See also 13715
18716	(RAF 208624) Re-registered 01 AC 39 1/50. Re-registered 349 ETD 3/58 as a mobile shop (Woosey, Lowton (XLA))
18717	(RAF 209797) Re-registered 01 AC 40 1/50. Re-registered UVP 595 5/57 (unknown operator)
18718	(RAF 209787) Re-registered 01 AC 41 1/50
18719	(RAF 209788) Re-registered 01 AC 42 1/50
18720	(RAF 209789) Re-registered 01 AC 43 1/50. Sold in Cyprus and re-registered TAT 469 4/59
18722	(RAF 209791) Re-registered 01 AC 44 1/50
18723	(?) Re-registered YOF 235 5/59 (RM Douglas Ltd (contractor), Birmingham 455)
18724	(RAF 208625) Re-registered 01 AC 45 1/50
18725	(?) Re-registered 01 AC 46 1/50
18726	(RAF 208619) Re-registered 01 AC 47 1/50
18727	(RAF 209798) Re-registered 01 AC 48 1/50
18728	(RAF 208620) Re-registered 01 AC 49 1/50
18730	(RAF 208623) Re-registered 01 AC 50 1/50. Re-registered 245 BOB 3/60 (unknown operator)
18731	(RAF 208626) Re-registered 01 AC 51 1/50
18733	(RAF 209799) Re-registered 01 AC 52 1/50. Re-registered FES 129 6/53, body rebuilt by McLennan as B30F (A & C McLennan, Spittalfied (PH) 68)
18734	(RAF 209804) Re-registered 01 AC 53 1/50
18735	(RAF 208641) Re-registered 01 AC 54 1/50
18736	(RAF 209796) Re-registered 01 AC 55 1/50
18738	(RAF 208628) Re-registered 01 AC 56 1/50
18762	(RAF 208637) Re-registered 01 AC 57 1/50
18786	(5190808) The original registration had an unknown prefix letter. Re-registered 50 YP 84 1949
18791	(6062632) The original registration had an unknown prefix letter. Re-registered 50 YP 33 1949
19809	(CUJ 30) Duple records show seating as C29F; confirmation that this carried a bus body is required
19825	(812 RN) Re-registered 14 BT 47 at an unknown date
19826	(RAF 209802) Bedford records have as intended for Admiralty (Royal Navy) (GOV). Re-registered 01 AC 58 1/50
19827	(?) Rebuilt to forward control, rebodied Shreeve FC30F and re-registered 341 JRT for BR Shreeve Ltd {Belle Coaches}, Lowestoft (SK) 7/61
19832	(698 RN) Re-registered 248 FDE c9/59 (OJ Edwards (OJ Edwards & Sons), Maenclochog (PE))
19844	(RAF 209803) Re-registered 01 AC 59 1/50
19847	(?) Re-registered HOR 608 1950 (Air Service Training Corps, Hampshire (XHA))
20801	(718 RN) Sold in Cyprus and re-registered AP 219 4/58
20802	(DC-11-81) Rebodied Feirense DP27D 1/60
20803	(RAF 209801) Bedford records have as intended for Admiralty (Royal Navy) (GOV). Re-registered 01 AC 60 1/50
20807	(744 RN) Re-registered XOC 39 10/58 (RM Douglas Ltd (contractor), Birmingham 440)
20811	(?) Probably re-registered XOC 36 9/58 (RM Douglas Ltd (contractor), Birmingham 437) (Motor Taxation records give chassis number 20611 - assumed to be this vehicle)
20814	(?) Re-registered MDG 750 7/53 (DJ & LW Edwards {WT Edwards & Sons}, Joy's Green (GL) as B28F)
20821	(CUJ 29) Duple records show seating as C29F; confirmation that this carried a bus body is required. Exported to Cyprus and re-registered TX 621 5/56
21305	(HHA 434) Exported to Cyprus and re-registered TAA 749 9/56
21468	(GMN 699) Re-registered SUX 980 5/59 (RCW Smith, Shrewsbury (SH))
21505	(GYD 80) Exported to Cyprus and re-registered TX 943 6/56
21539	(JRA 710) Exported to Cyprus and re-registered TAE 590 5/57
21567	(GTC 651) Exported to Cyprus and re-registered TAC 343 12/56
21588	(JDH 858) Re-registered J 14198 4/53 (WL Jones {Len's Tours}, St Helier, Jersey (CI))
22049	(?) Re-registered VMB 321 7/55 (Mulcaster (Contractor), Haslington)
22334	(EOU 856) Bedford records have as intended for AE Butler {Cove Saloon Coaches & Cars}, Farnborough (HA); Duple has AE Butler, Bagshot (SR). Probably the same person?

C1252/197

22407	(FUO 534) Duple records have as intended for SF Carter, North Petherton (SO)
22804	(HWJ 180) Carried a pre-war body, probably from Bedford WTB DWB 192
22892	(EU 8097) Bedford and Duple records have as intended for Ford & Reames, Brynmawr (BC). Exported to Cyprus and re-registered TG 790 11/53; re-registered TCP 187 5/65
23046	(HUU 430) Exported to Cyprus and re-registered TAG 238 7/57
23206	(KFC 820) Bedford records have as Duple, but not traced in Duple records
23228	(DDT 244) Exported to Cyprus and re-registered TAR 26 9/58
23316	(KBB 766) Body number needs confirmation
23382	(1560) Re-registered AY 59 10/58 (WP Simon, Alderney (CI))
23489	(CVH 239) Not traced in Bedford records; Duple records confirm OB 23489 which is a good chronological fit
23684	(BTY 380) Probably FC30F ?
23888	(?) Re-registered 37 JBB at an unknown date (unknown operator)
23937	(II-12-01) Rebodied Alfredo Caetano C30F and renumbered 12 2/63
24161	(EYG 100) Exported to Cyprus and re-registered TBE 44 7/60
24422	(JS 7166) Body believed built by operator using SMT spares - confirmation required
24428	(JS 7297) Body believed built by operator using SMT spares - confirmation required
24436	(?) Sold in Ceylon and re-registered CV 5271 6/55
25155	(?) Sold in Ceylon and re-registered CV 4910 11/54
25185	(818 RN) Re-registered 14 BT 49 at an unknown date
25196	(813 RN) Re-registered 14 BT 48 at an unknown date
25303	(CUJ 656) Exported to Cyprus and re-registered TAE 401 4/57
25333	(FAB 202) Re-registered J 6579 5/50 (LA Jones {Jersey Tours}, St Helier, Jersey (CI))
25367	(?) Sold in Ceylon and re-registered CV 6218 3/56
25373	(751 RN) Re-registered 14 BT 50 at an unknown date. Chassis not traced in Bedford records - probably the vehicle listed as 25378.
25378	(?) Possibly the vehicle listed as 25373
25510	(LWL 252) Carried a pre-war body, origin unknown; rebodied Duple C29F (49379) 2/51. Exported to Cyprus and re-registered TDL 904 11/67
25592	(EDL 283) Exported to Cyprus and re-registered TAY 624 11/59
25599	(GUO 114) Carried a pre-war body, origin unknown
25799	(EBM 606) Bedford records have as Duple, but not traced in Duple records; a candidate for body 41900
26003	(EBM 615) Chassis believed to have been used initially by Vauxhall Motors. Registration transferred from chassis 11027 when the unidentified Duple body was fitted. This is a candidate for body 41900.
26245	(855 RN) Re-registered XOC 37 9/58 (RM Douglas Ltd (contractor), Birmingham 438)
26304	(CUJ 657) Exported to Cyprus and re-registered TAD 854 3/57
26388	(GUR 985) Bedford records have as intended for A Livermore, Barley (HT) before that business was acquired by Richmond
26436	(?) Re-registered KAW 346 (Corvedale Motor Co, Ludlow (SH) 10) as B30F; this was given in C1251 as OWB 26436, but OB 26436 now appears to be a more likely candidate
26484	(CUJ 658) Exported to Cyprus and re-registered TAE 782 5/57
26532	(808 RN) Re-registered 14 BT 46 at an unknown date
26570	(?) Sold in Ceylon and re-registered CV 5222 2/55
26641	(E-45613) Re-registered NB-50-19 at an unknown date
26654	(JVT 965) Tatton reported body built "in Luton"
26690	(E-45614) Re-registered NB-50-20 at an unknown date
26820	(CVH 317) Carried the pre-war body from former Huddersfield Leyland Cub VH 7891
26856	(HD-12-07) Rebodied UTIC (Lisboa) 1296 DP30D 2/64
26869	(796 RN) Re-registered WOJ 831 6/58 (RM Douglas Ltd (contractor), Birmingham 408)
27096	(?) To NSB Vestfoldrutene, Vestfold (O-N) registered Z-8056 11/52
28038	(FAA 987) Exported to Cyprus and re-registered TAB 580 11/56
28461	(KNW 455) Re-registered J 1355 4/55 (LA Chapman {Jersey Tours}, St Helier, Jersey (CI))
28507	(FAA 244) Exported to Cyprus and re-registered TAB 222 10/56
28512	(FOY 321) Exported to Cyprus and re-registered TBE 770 8/60
28545	(EBM 616) Later with OM & PL Hooks, PO Francis & PM Dugmore, Great Oakley (EX)
28607	(DJB 279) Duple records have chassis number as 28697; Bedford records have 28607
28640	(HXB 719) Exported to Cyprus and re-registered TV 965 2/56
28657	(HXB 724) Exported to Cyprus and re-registered TAR 23 9/58
28689	(KPH 478) Exported to Cyprus and re-registered TW 144 2/56
28701	(GUR 664) Bedford records have as intended for CW Sworder {Walkern Garage}, Walkern (HT). Exported to Cyprus and re-registered TW 531 3/56
28890	(HXB 718) Exported to Cyprus and re-registered TAA 332 8/56
29436	(K-17856) Re-registered NB-26-00 at an unknown date
29490	(K-17857) Re-registered NB-26-01 at an unknown date

29496	(K-17858) Re-registered (NB-26-02 ?) at an unknown date, but this registration also claimed by 29573
29513	(DBU 341) Exported to Cyprus and re-registered TAK 377 11/57
29573	(K-17859) Re-registered (NB-26-02 ?) at an unknown date, but this registration also claimed by 29496
29629	(FHP 782) Later had Ford front panel and GMC engine
29653	(HTB 728) Carried a pre-war body from an unidentified Opel Blitz in Mayers' fleet
29806	(BCB 785) As this 1946 chassis carried a 1948 body and registration, it has been queried as a re-body; this seems not to have been the case.
29948	(HLB 149) Body given as Cancelled in Duple record!
30073	(KNW 639) Exported to Cyprus and re-registered TAD 660 3/57
30079	(EBT 240) Recorded as Roe, but seems unlikely
30085	(HUW 164) Carried a pre-war Duple body, probably from Ansell's Opel EXO 524
30307	(DBU 386) Bedford records have as intended for Gregory & Richards, Oldham (LA), subsequently controlled by Renton
30340	(GMN 798) Re-registered 9734 E 4/59 (H Bown, Birmingham (WK))
30373	(KPJ 389) Exported to Cyprus and re-registered TAN 307 3/58
30382	(KTW 244) Exported to Cyprus and re-registered TAP 400 5/58
30664	(EGD 448) Passed to Lochs Motor Transport Ltd, Stornoway (RY), probably from one of its constituent operators in 5/47. Motor Taxation records show chassis number as 30644; Bedford records have 30664.
31103	(KTW 243) Exported to Cyprus and re-registered TAP 399 5/58
31121	(KNW 902) Diverted new from Enterprise & Silver Dawn, Scunthorpe (LI)
31145	(DAW 473) Exported to Cyprus and re-registered TAD 858 3/57
31160	(JUO 874) Bedford records have as intended for T & W Parker, Ilfracombe (DN)
31679	(DCO 558) Exported to Cyprus and re-registered TAC 847 2/57
32150	(EGD 150) Body has been claimed as Waveney (could only be so if second hand); probably a similarly styled Mulliner body
32185	(FDV 210) Duple records have as intended for Moor & Son, South Molton (DN); this was a dealer
32323	(Q.489.923) O'Brien not confirmed as original operator
32329	(WVF.767) Re-registered VA.7778 at an unknown date
32359	(KTW 242) Exported to Cyprus and re-registered TY 238 6/56
32368	(GZ-60875) Not traced in Bedford records. Re-registered NJ-48-58 at an unknown date.
32426	(J 6986) Chassis delivered to Safety Coach Service (1940) Ltd, St Helier, Jersey (CI) 9/46 but not bodied until sold to JMT 1947. Re-registered LTR 336R by 1982; re-registered LSU 857 1988
32433	(DBD 151) Exported to Cyprus and re-registered TAF 398 6/57
32764	(GPT 492) Exported to Cyprus and re-registered TAC 342 12/56
32809	(DBU 688) Duple records have as intended for Shearing Tours Ltd, Oldham (LA). The body has been recorded erroneously as Duple
33016	(GUO 398) Exported to Cyprus c1960
33030	(JKX 555) Later DP29F (bus seats)
33038	(?) Not traced with Eastern National. Just possibly used by Beadle in constructing Beadle-Bedford prototype LNO 150 ?
33185	(CTH 636) Exported to Ceylon and re-registered CV 3488 11/53
33264	(CVH 241) Exported to Ceylon and re-registered CV 3904 2/54
33337	(BTY 656) Exported to Cyprus and re-registered TM 519 3/55
33485	(HFM 28) Exported to Ceylon 8/54 and re-registered CV 4921 1/55
33634	(EMJ 62) Has also been recorded as EMJ 82 in error. Exported to Cyprus and re-registered TAW 887 8/59
33706	(BTY 631) Exported to Ceylon and re-registered CV 3926 1/54
33737	(GBJ 375) Carried 1929 body of unknown make from Graham Dodge VE 1075
33915	(BTY 629) Exported to Ceylon and re-registered CV 3487 11/53
33990	(KUA 182) Exported to Cyprus and re-registered TU 223 11/55
34017	(MML 496) Exported to Cyprus and re-registered TBA 175 1/60
34106	(DTP 308) Body has also been claimed as Lee
34549	(FO 4711) Body destroyed in accident; rebodied Duple C29F (54481) 11/49 for FOJ & RJ Bevan (Bevan Bros) {Soudley Valley Coaches}, Soudley (GL)
34828	(DBU 689) Re-registered FBU 171 6/49 (reason unknown)
34870	(BHV 793) Bedford and Duple records have as intended for CJ Worsley {Brownie Saloon Coaches}, London E18 (LN)
34884	(CFR 878) Rebodied Thurgood C27F (706) for O Porter, Dummer (KT) 1/52
34904	(FFS 855) Body built by Duple but sent to SMT for jig purposes; originally intended for SMT (MN) where it would have been C156
35042	(DBK 944) Body built by operator using the body frame from either a Leyland Cub or a Harrington body from a former Southdown TSM

C1252/199

35233	(BHV 792) Bedford and Duple records have as intended for CJ Worsley {Brownie Saloon Coaches}, London E18 (LN)
35291	(FT 5884) Chassis was depatched 10/46; date to service not known
35399	(JKE 386) Recorded as ordered by Carey Bros, New Romney (KT)
35427	(MMT 864) Re-registered J 6595 7/52 (H Swanson {Redline Tours}, St Helier, Jersey (CI) 14)
35683	(?) Re-registered PP-294 at an unknown date
35757	(D 171) Chassis number recorded as 35737: Bedford records have 35757
35802	(EJW 258) Chassis number also recorded (PD16) as 35823. Bedford records show 35802
35911	(FFY 628) Bedford records have as intended for Blundell Coaches (Southport) Ltd (LA). Has been recorded with a KB body, but these were not built until later in the 1950s
36005	(DNT 569) Probably FC30F ?
36215	(HFJ 149) Re-registered UMN 137 10/55 (E Miller, Port St Mary (IM))
36335	(?) Not traced in Bedford records. Exported to Cyprus and re-registered TAK 842 11/57
36471	(HMN 347) Bedford records have as intended for "Ford/Holdsworth", Stockport - probably a dealer
36893	(GTJ 947) Diverted new from Enterprise & Silver Dawn, Scunthorpe (LI)
37049	(HCD 465) Bedford and Duple records have as intended for HK Hart {Alpha Coaches}, Brighton (ES)
37150	(KUB 745) Diverted new from Enterprise & Silver Dawn, Scunthorpe (LI)
37204	(DNT 731) Initially with Mulliner (unregistered) for jig purposes with Duple body 41990; then rebodied Mulliner SP80 B32F for Commercial Motor Show, and registered DNT 731 for Whittle. The Duple body was the transferred to chassis 11027.
37290	(MMP 815) Exported to Cyprus and re-registered TBB 23 2/60
37298	(RRF 799) Chassis had been delivered 10/46, but the vehicle was not registered until 1949
38386	(HFJ 150) Duple records have as intended for Greenslades, Exeter (DN), Regent's parent company
38554	(FWW 742) Exported to Ceylon 12/51 and re-registered CV 822 3/52
38584	(LHK 325) Bedford records have as intended for J Root, Ongar, Essex status unknown; Duple has Ongar Motors.
38752	(HYB 284) Exported to Cyprus and re-registered TW 632 3/56
39240	(FWY 494) Bedford and Duple records have as intended for TAV Scadding {White Lion Motorways}, Wotton-under-Edge (GL), with booked registration GAD 966
39260	(FWY 495) Bedford and Duple records have as intended for TAV Scadding {White Lion Motorways}, Wotton-under-Edge (GL), with booked registration GAD 967
39269	(HYC 60) Carried a pre-war Duple Hendonian body, origin unknown, rebuilt (by Longwell Green?)
39349	(BES 700) Body described as "by SMT for Duple"
39438	(DAW 552) Chassis number also recorded as 39428. Bedford records have 39438 as the Vagg vehicle with 39428 as shown above
39467	(HUU 722) Exported to Cyprus and re-registered TAB 40 10/56
39497	(GTJ 245) Exported to Cyprus and re-registered TAF 401 6/57
39538	(FHO 456) Exported to Ceylon and re-registered CV 45 8/51
39708	(MMP 584) Bedford records have as intended for Church, London E10, status unknown; Duple has Unique.
39766	(JKJ 971) Suggested as Duple, but not traced in Duple records. Possibly a locally-built body to Duple design
39850	(FOR 732) Bedford records have as intended for AE Butler, Bagshot (SR)
40202	(CVH 986) Exported to Ceylon and re-registered CV1051 3/52
40263	(EMJ 334) Exported to Cyprus and re-registered TAY 553 11/59
40297	(HUU 723) Exported to Cyprus and re-registered TAB 77 10/56
40451	(JAU 10) Exported to Cyprus and re-registered TY 219 6/56
40481	(KVK 89) Bedford and Duple records have as intended for Bedlington & District Luxury Coaches Ltd, Ashington (ND)
40491	(HYE 553) Exported to Cyprus and re-registered TL 628 1/55
40500	(DFW 90) Exported to Cyprus and re-registered TV 105 12/55
40541	(BCK 189) Re-registered HMN 711 7/47 (TH Kneen, Douglas); re-registered LMN 972 2/50 (JA & LQ Kneen {A & L Kneen}, Douglas (IM))
40601	(KVK 51) Bedford and Duple records have as intended for Bedlington & District Luxury Coaches Ltd, Ashington (ND)
40631	(MMY 847) Re-registered J 6160 5/50 (UV Noel {Waverley Tours}, St Martin, Jersey (CI))
40770	(HUU 724) Exported to Cyprus and re-registered TAF 936 6/57
40781	(GTJ 247) Bedford records have as intended for Hanson's Buses Ltd, Huddersfield (WR). Exported to Cyprus and re-registered TAJ 12 9/57
40811	(JKK 322) Possibly carried a pre-war body
40830	(3088) Re-registered AY 59 12/55 (WP Simon, Alderney (CI))
40851	(3087) Re-registered AY 59 2/55 (WP Simon, Alderney (CI))
40941	(DNT 523) Bedford records have as intended for Jones Coachways Ltd, Market Drayton (SH)
40991	(EJW 915) Bedford records have as intended for Worthington Motor Tours Ltd, Wolverhampton (ST)

C1252/200

41031	(KMA 468) Bedford records have as intended for Murphy (dealer), Leicester
41077	(DBK 461) Exported to Cyprus and re-registered TBB 21 2/60
41111	(FWW 745) Exported to Cyprus and re-registered TAQ 594 8/58
41121	(FWW 744) Exported to Ceylon and re-registered CV 821 3/52
41512	(YJ 9093) Bedford and Duple records have as intended for Stuart Bros {J Lawson}, Methven (FE)
41562	(FHO 790) Exported to Cyprus and re-registered TU 222 11/55
41641	(DUJ 185) Bedford records have as intended for AE Parker, Clun (SH)
41652	(GDD 415) Exported to Cyprus and re-registered TX 423 5/56
41692	(K-19341) Re-registered NB-50-35 at an unknown date. Chassis number recorded as 41693; Bedford records have 41692
41760	(K-19343) Re-registered NB-31-19 at an unknown date
41811	(JKM 536) Rebodied Duple C29F (51900) 1949
41850	(K-19342) Re-registered NB-12-22 at an unknown date
42008	(FWY 311) It had been suggested that the vehicle originally carried a body which was transferred to Bedford WTL DWT 250 in 3/51, when this Plaxton body was fitted. It now seems this Plaxton body was fitted from new.
42077	(DAP 807) Re-registered J 13802 4/50 (Seymour Services Ltd {Mascot Motors}, St Helier, Jersey (CI))
42236	(SB 6907) Exported to Ceylon and re-registered CV 1675 9/52
42269	(JX 9549) Exported to Ceylon and re-registered CV 5272 5/55
42281	(HUU 726) Exported to Cyprus and re-registered TAB 130 10/56
42370	(?) Not traced in Bedford records. Motor Taxation records give chassis 57/42370 when re-registered 423 DTB 7/58 (Evangel Express, Radcliffe (XLA))
42427	(GMA 904) GMA 904 is recorded as an OB with Altrincham; as Bedford records have chassis 42427 delivered to that operator, the linkage is assumed
42461	(BCK 329) Exported to Ceylon and re-registered CV 3950 1/54
42490	(HND 739) Body given as Cancelled in Duple record!
42839	(FDV 383) Carried a pre-war body, origin unknown
42917	(FHO 864) Exported to Cyprus c1960
42987	(HYY 900) Suggested as Duple, but not traced in Duple records
43007	(MRF 632) Has been recorded (3PD1) as 43077, as given by Duple; Bedford records have 43007. Exported to Cyprus and re-registered TW 81 2/56
43018	(JWB 892) Exported to Cyprus and re-registered TBC 495 4/60
43060	(DBD 907) Exported to Cyprus and re-registered TAP 502 5/58
43072	(OML 813) Exported to Cyprus and re-registered TAR 22 9/58
43187	(HTB 80) Exported to Cyprus and re-registered TAG 209 7/57
43277	(HUO 688) Exported to Cyprus and re-registered TW 577 3/56
43312	(P-39749) Re-registered NB-58-06 at an unknown date
43469	(HDE 542) Exported to Cyprus and re-registered TX 885 6/56
43494	(DMO 248) Motor Taxation records have chassis as 43194. Bedford records have 43494
43527	(DMO 349) Bedford and Duple records have as intended for Tenaplas, Pangbourne (XBE)
43590	(OML 915) Re-registered J 1761 5/58 (J Jones {Maple Leaf Tours}, St Helier, Jersey (CI))
44096	(HUO 689) Exported to Cyprus and re-registered TW 540 3/56
44107	(GTJ 613) Bedford records have as intended for Holdsworth & Hanson (Leeds) Ltd (WR); Duple has Broughton & Walker
44129	(EBD 856) Bedford records have as intended for Jones & Allen, Corby (NO)
44181	(EBX 77) Bedford records have as intended for Gravell (Dealer), Kidwelly 1/47 for bodying as a cattle truck. It is possible that Gravell built the coach body, or arranged for it to be built locally
44309	(OML 742) Bedford and Duple records have as intended for H & G Beach Ltd, Staines (MX)
44347	(EBE 307) Possibly delivered to Johnson as a cattle truck and rebodied as shown in 1951; it may however have been bodied as a coach from new
44395	(HUO 690) Exported to Cyprus and re-registered TW 495 3/56
44421	(HYF 378) Exported to Cyprus and re-registered TBA 626 1/60
44438	(OML 743) Exported to Cyprus and re-registered TV 262 1/56
44444	(OML 543) There are two bodies numbered 46605 in Duple records! - see also FUT 58
44540	(HYE 927) Exported to Cyprus and re-registered TBD 896 7/60
44551	(HUO 691) Exported to Cyprus and re-registered TBA 28 1/60
44645	(EJ 8108) Re-registered VMN 809 3/57 (EC Hamill, Onchan (IM))
44699	(HXW 496) Bedford and Duple records have as intended for Luxitours (Blackpool) Ltd (LA). Exported to Cyprus and re-registered TAA 881 10/56
44710	(PRF 167) Bedford records have as intended for NC Kendrick, Dudley (WO)
44739	(HUO 683) Exported to Cyprus and re-registered TW 698 3/56
44749	(DBE 812) Exported to Cyprus and re-registered TAF 466 6/57
44761	(HUO 693) Exported to Cyprus and re-registered TAV 845 7/59
44767	(P-36194) Re-registered NB-91-99 at an unknown date

C1252/201

44775	(HUO 692) Rebuilt as open-sided (nearside only) sea-front runabout by Lincolnshire RCC, Bracebridge Heath (KN) 1959
44784	(HNE 512) Suggested as Duple, but not traced in Duple records
44845	(BBV 351) Bedford records have as intended for Leaver, Blackburn, Lancashire, status unknown
44857	(HUO 684) Exported to Cyprus and re-registered TW 684 3/56
44863	(FWX 696) Probably carried a second-hand body, maybe Duple
45093	(v1.805) Re-registered EH.9858 1965. Original registration also quoted as v1.855
45095	(P1.398) Re-registered P1.134 at an unknown date
45098	(P.619) Re-registered EY.3887 1965
45104	(v1.835) Re-registered v4.904 at an unknown date; re-registered EH.9856 1965. Also given as BP.6890 at an unknown date
45210	(H-413) To Ødegaardens Bilruter AS, Ødegaardens Verk (O-N), registered H-4509 -/59
45239	(DBE 808) Exported to Cyprus and re-registered TAB 666 11/56
45325	(DBE 809) Exported to Cyprus and re-registered TAF 529 6/57
45456	(JX 9674) Exported to Ceylon and re-registered CV 6386 5/56
45480	(DBE 810) Exported to Cyprus and re-registered TAH 816 9/57
45490	(KRB 65) Exported to Ceylon and re-registered CV 2936 5/53
45541	(OML 603) Re-registered J 1445 5/58 (J Jones {Maple Leaf Tours}, St Helier, Jersey (CI))
45610	(H 7442) Chevrolet oil engine fitted by 12/52
45598	(DNT 763) Carried the pre-war body from Opel JRF 285
45729	(GUP 979 ?) Motor Taxation records have chassis number 50557 for GUP 979; Bedford records have no such OB - but they do have OB 45729 as intended for the Constabulary (see also 43487, GUP 978). Maybe a horsebox?
45746	(BCK 647) Exported to Ceylon and re-registered CV 1474 4/52
45768	(FOR 633) Exported to Cyprus and re-registered TAK 972 12/57
45778	(FOR 634) Exported to Cyprus and re-registered TAK 971 12/57; rebuilt as forward control with new locally built FB--F body
45826	(CBW 722) Bedford and Duple records have as intended for RC Surman, Chinnor (OX)
45920	(HUO 685) Exported to Cyprus and re-registered TW 685 3/56
45968	(DCX 301) Exported to Ceylon and re-registered CV 1292 4/52
46069	(GMJ 499) Bedford records have as intended for Palmer, Luton, believed to have been the owner of N&S. Chassis had been delivered 5/47, but the vehicle did not enter service until 1949
46111	(EDL 840) Body reportedly transferred from a Lancia, possibly by Margham or Heaver
46124	(FBC 933) Bedford records have as intended to be a van for Davis Haulage, London E14 (GLN)
46146	(ERY 721) Carried the pre-war body from Opel CRY 436
46181	(FBC 931) Bedford records have as intended to be a van for Davis Haulage, London E14 (GLN). Motor Tax gives chassis 51143 (probably engine no). Seemingly rebuilt to forward control, rebodied Belle FC30F 5/59 and re-registered 495 ART for B R Shreeve {Belle Coaches}, Lowestoft (SK), using the 51143 chassis no.
46336	(BCK 982) Exported to Cyprus and re-registered TU 221 11/55
46363	(DBU 936) Bedford records have as intended for Platt, Manchester (GLA) as a furniture van
46369	(HRT 298) Rebodied Belle FC30F 1955. It has been suggested that the original body may have been by Churchill.
46375	(158) Possibly initially registered 2590 (until 12/47). The body may have been by Mulliner, sub-contracted from Duple.
46709	(DBU 870) Bedford records have as intended for Platt, Manchester (GLA) as a furniture van
46713	(GRU 110) Bedford records have as intended for "Excelsior, Lymington"; Duple has Excelsior Coaches Ltd, Bournemouth (HA). Excelsior is assumed to have been involved in its dealing capacity
46779	(AHL 970) Exported to Ceylon and re-registered CV 4672 10/54
46889	(HMN 439) Duple records have as intended for EA Winwood, London E10 (LN), with booked registration OML 604; Bedford records have Kneen.
46966	(KRB 66) Chassis number aslo claimed as 45966. Bedford and Duple records both have 46966
47042	(HFD 609) Bedford records have as intended for AT Hardwick {Glider Coaches}, Bilston (ST)
47099	(JP 6376) Bedford records have as intended for Grimshaw & Culsham, Wigan (GLA) as a lorry
47172	(JTB 207) Re-registered LMN 958 2/58 (EC Hamill, Onchan (IM))
47176	(NRF 268) Bedford records have as intended for Blackheath & District Motor Services Ltd (WO). Carried pre-war body from Bedford WTB CAC 632.
47200	(ECA 166) Exported to Cyprus and re-registered TBN 574 10/61
47252	(PRE 759) Probably carried a secondhand body
47265	(FBM 339) Bedford and Duple records have as intended for GE Costin, Dunbstable (BD). Chassis number shown incorrectly in Motor Taxation records as 47765
47295	(DBE 815) Exported to Cyprus and re-registered TAF 530 6/57
47300	(FA 8543) Exported to Cyprus and re-registered TAQ 908 9/58

47362	(?) Smith was a PSV operator, but the chassis is not recorded in that fleet; it may have been diverted for use as a goods vehicle
47418	(SME 8) Bedford records have as intended for Wright Bros (London) Ltd, London W7. Re-registered OMN 304 5/52 (JR Crellin {Castle Rushen Motors}, Castletown (IM))
47484	(HNE 960) Bedford records have as intended to be a furniture van with Sharp
47494	(DCX 627) Exported to Cyprus and re-registered TAG 960 8/57
47814	(HYP 722) Carries plates LTA 755 for display purposes in preservation
47864	(DBE 817) Exported to Cyprus and re-registered TAB 472 10/56
47874	(HFM 30) Exported to Ceylon 8/54 and re-registered CV 4756 11/54
48005	(FDV 548) Duple order number reportedly allocated for SMT built body
48035	(HTD 492) Probably FC30F. Bedford records have as intended for Fleet Motors, St Annes, Lancashire, possibly a dealer
48140	(?) Although Britten was a PSV operator, this was probably a goods vehicle
48159	(DPY 708) Exported to Cyprus and re-registered TBF 36 9/60
48331	(ACP 562) Bedford records have as intended for Broughton & Walker Ltd, Great Harwood (LA)
48392	(HTC 600) Seemingly diverted new from Y Helliwell & Sons Ltd, Nelson (LA)
48423	(EDL 638) Gardner 4LK oil engine fitted at unknown date (requiring an extended bonnet), followed by Perkins P6 oil engine. Exported to Cyprus 7/63
48483	(?) Although City Coach Co was a PSV operator, this was probably a goods vehicle
48501	(EFU 375) Chassis number also recorded as 48507. Bedford records have 48501
48673	(v1.840) Re-registered v4.602 at an unknown date; re-registered EH.9856 1965
48675	(s.805) Re-registered s.20 at an unknown date
48678	(GVT 19358) Re-registered DU.7333 1965
48679	(GVT 18306) Re-registered EH.2888 1965
48684	(s.322) Re-registered s.404 at an unknown date
48948	(HUO 694) Exported to Cyprus and re-registered TAY 35 10/59
48973	(?) The operator has also been given as Cattle, Manchester (GLA)
48992	(NRF 301) Carried the pre-war body from Bedford WTB BBU 62
49001	(JWJ 16) Exported to Cyprus and re-registered TAK 57 10/57
49048	(OMT 968) Re-registered J 9477 4/55 (R Cotrel {Gorey Coaches}, St Martin, Jersey (CI))
49057	(LVW 650) Exported to Cyprus and re-registered TAB 497 11/56
49325	(NRE 614) Re-registered J 12204 4/56 (LA Chapman {Jersey Tours}, St Helier, Jersey (CI))
49368	(HFM 31) Exported to Ceylon 8/54
49376	(HUO 668) Exported to Cyprus and re-registered TAF 467 6/57
49530	(LBB 165) Bedford records have as intended for E Marshall & Co Ltd, Newcastle-on-Tyne (ND)
49536	(DBE 813) Exported to Cyprus and re-registered TAB 492 10/56
49570	(EMW 145) The Lee body possibly used some components from a utility body
49610	(MRA 315) Exported to Cyprus and re-registered TW 631 3/56
49618	(FE-13-33) Later rebodied (details unknown) and renumbered 5 at an unknown date
49653	(KUM 173) Exported to Cyprus and re-registered TU 667 11/55
49713	(AL-13-34) Rebodied UTIC (Porto) DP27D (no 783/1) and renumbered 28 5/69
49738	(HVU 674 ?) HVU 674 is recorded as C26F OB with Altrincham; as Bedford records have chassis 49738 delivered to that operator, the linkage is assumed
49748	(JTC 395) Final operator was Burnacre Weaving Co, Garstang (GLA) 1/58; it MAY have carried a bus body at one time?
49772	(JCV 612) Bedford and Duple records have as intended for JH Dingle, West Looe (CO) before that business was acquired by Pearce
49791	(JP 6243) Exported to Cyprus and re-registered TU 220 11/55
49817	(DUJ 253) Exported to Cyprus and re-registered TAA 748 9/56
49925	(OMT 537) Exported to Cyprus and re-registered TBA 695 1/60
49967	(FOT 352) Exported to Cyprus and re-registered TX 391 5/56
49995	(LPU 624) Exported to Cyprus and re-registered TAP 395 5/58
50020	(JWJ 399) Exported to Cyprus and re-registered TBE 791 8/60
50043	(LPU 623) Exported to Cyprus and re-registered TAP 397 5/58
50099	(HMN 835) Bedford records have as intended for Clague, Douglas (IM) - which Clague is not specified
50261	(GAO 465) Exported to Cyprus c1954
50280	(SMT 100) Bedford records have as intended for Willesden Borough Council (XLN)
50299	(BCK 895) Bedford and Duple records have as intended for Ireland & Sons Ltd {Red Rose Garages}, Lancaster (LA)
50493	(P.626) Re-registered v2.281 at an unknown date, and EW.4656 1965
50495	(P.577) Re-registered P2.424 at an unknown date
50497	(?) Re-registered EK.6490 1965. With JL Richardson, Greerton (O-NZ) by 1965
50499	(P.181) Chassis number recorded as 50490: assumed to be that given in Bedford records as 50499. Re-registered EW.9527 1965

50500	(P.373) Re-registered P2.527 at an unknown date
50502	(P.366) Re-registered P2.455 at an unknown date
50504	(?) Smith not confirmed as original operator
50619	(P-36198) Re-registered NB-50-95 at an unknown date
50713	(P-39843) Re-registered NB-01-35 at an unknown date
50750	(AFB 266) Bedford records have as intended for Peradin's Bonded Rubber, Freshford (XSO)
50760	(HYP 723) Exported to Cyprus and re-registered TCD 604 9/63
50817	(JWJ 531) Exported to Ceylon and re-registered CV 1390 3/52
50950	(OMT 552) Exported to Cyprus and re-registered TAY 675 11/59
50957	(HFM 33) Exported to Ceylon 8/54
51001	(HMN 511) Bedford and Duple records have as intended for Cowell, Peel (IM) - which Cowell is not specified
51196	(P-36202) Re-registered NB-30-09 at an unknown date. Chassis number recorded as 51198; Bedford records have 51196
51231	(DBE 816) Exported to Cyprus and re-registered TAF 468 6/57
51305	(BDO 338) Exported to Cyprus and re-registered TAE 987 5/57
51331	(KUM 172) Bedford and Duple records have as intended for Enterprise & Silver Dawn, Scunthorpe (LI)
51359	(HYK 236) Exported to Cyprus and re-registered TAX 227 9/59
51424	(DRX 296) Exported to Cyprus and re-registered TAA 754 9/56
51479	(EX 5760) Bedford records have as intended for FA Sayer {Grangeway Coaches}, Caister (NK) which merged with the Yaxley business in 1948; Duple records have "Grangeway". Exported to Cyprus and re-registered TAK 37 10/57
51628	(CDB 896) Exported to Cyprus and re-registered TAY 979 11/59
51923	(FBC 930) Bedford records have as intended for J Bradshaw & Sons Ltd, Sturton-by-Stow (GLI), probably for use as a goods vehicle
51952	(EDL 850) Exported to Cyprus and re-registered TAA 751 9/56
51972	(HRT 299) Rebodied Belle FC30F 1957
51986	(BBV 483) Bedford records have as intended for J Wearden & Sons Ltd, Blackburn (LA); Duple records have Whitehurst
52049	(FCY 390) Chassis had been delivered 5/47, but the vehicle was not registered until 1948
52426	(JAH 171) Longford is most unlikely body given geographical location; no other OB/Longfords are known
52539	(JTB 771) Bedford records have as intended for Mills & Seddon Ltd, Farnworth (LA)
52549	(OMT 553) Exported to Cyprus and re-registered TBD 230 6/60
52616	(GAO 466) Exported to Cyprus and re-registered TAP 536 5/58
52720	(GTX 3) Thomas is not the BET company of the same name
52767	(CFV 847) Bedford records have as intended for Mills & Seddon Ltd, Farnworth (LA), with a Trans-United body. NMU bodywork has also been suggested.
52834	(HUO 698) Exported to Cyprus and re-registered TAW 596 8/59
52846	(JKO 674) Bedford records have as intended for G Taylor, Strood (KT); Duple has Medway Belle
53419	(HDV 754) Recorded as carrying a pre-war Duple body, ex Western National Leyland Cub and later rebodied Tiverton C26F. Now believed to have carried a Tiverton rebuild body from new, source unknown
53428	(KRB 67) Exported to Ceylon and re-registered CV 2930 5/53
53454	(HYN 420) Re-registered J 14234 5/53 (F Hopkins {Favourite Tours}, St Helier, Jersey (CI))
53534	(CFV 846) Bedford records have as intended for Mills & Seddon Ltd, Farnworth (LA)
53544	(JYA 8) Exported to Ceylon 2/56 and re-registered CV 6417 5/56
54457	(LDH 45) Exported to Cyprus and re-registered TY 291 6/56; rebodied locally as FB--F
54534	(HTD 190) Re-registered J 15538 4/54 (J Jones {Maple Leaf Tours}, St Helier, Jersey (CI))
54649	(P-35308) Re-registered NB-57-89 at an unknown date
54661	(LJO 756) Exported to Cyprus and re-registered TAD 821 3/57
54727	(GWR 46) Exported to Cyprus and re-registered TV 817 2/56
54744	(P-36203) Re-registered NB-19-31 at an unknown date
54822	(KRB 68) Exported to Ceylon and re-registered CV 2611 3/53
54851	(P-39844) Chassis number recorded as 54581; Bedford records have 54851
54934	(D-16286) Re-registered NB-27-16 at an unknown date
54956	(HMN 600) Re-registered GNM 976 10/48 (AS Stockman {Icknield Coaches}, Tring (HT))
54965	(KKX 99) Bedford records have Arnold as first operator, but also on record as new to Pilot Coaches (High Wycombe) Ltd (BK)
54978	(?) Perkins P6 oil engine fitted and re-registered KBJ 180 1/51 (Kenya Bus Services (Mombasa) Ltd 43)
55241	(E-37754) Re-registered NB-37-33 at an unknown date
55306	(GHP 581) Exported to Cyprus and re-registered TAJ 262 9/57
55324	(E-37756) Re-registered NB-37-34 at an unknown date
55357	(?) Re-registered NB-27-15 at an unknown date

55365	(LPG 191) Rebodied Gurney Nutting C29F 9/52 following accident damage
55373	(EX 5818) Exported to Cyprus and re-registered TAM 743 2/58
55381	(JWJ 532) Exported to Ceylon and re-registered CV 982 3/52
55421	(FWM 33) Bedford records have as intended for F Standerwick {Crown Motors}, Southport (LA)
55443	(?) Re-registered NB-27-17 at an unknown date
55451	(KUM 998) Probably FC30F ?
55467	(HVO 691) Ordered by Mrs ER Thacker, Mansfield Woodhouse (NG) before business taken over by Gittins
55531	(SME 617) Exported to Cyprus and re-registered TBG 707 12/60
55546	(HYO 706) Re-registered J 11079 5/52 (H Swanson {Redline Tours}, St Helier, Jersey (CI) 12)
55604	(HNY 566) Bedford records have as intended for Thomas Bros, Port Talbot (GG); actually licensed to their Afan Transport subsidiary.
55618	(DUX 74) Exported to Cyprus and re-registered TBC 501 4/60
55631	(GDG 467) Bedford records have as intended for Miss I Baynham, Ross-on-Wye (HR); Duple has Bayliss. Exported to Cyprus and re-registered TAH 814 8/57
55651	(BBV 809) Body has also been claimed as Pearson C26F, seemingly in error
55665	(HTE 624) Bedford records have as intended for JN Davies & Co, Skerton (LA). Exported to Cyprus and re-registered TY 255 6/56
55723	(EMW 788) The Lee body possibly used some components from a utility body
55739	(MHK 525) Mulliner records have chassis number as 55737; Bedford records have 55739
55865	(HVU 243) Exported to Cyprus and re-registered TAD 511 3/57
55894	(FFS 856) Rebuilt to forward control and rebodied Burlingham FC24F (5500) 1953
55995	(LPG 109) Exported to Cyprus and re-registered TBA 534 1/60
56154	(FOU 936) Exported to Cyprus and re-registered TCG 848 c1964; rebodied locally as FB33-
56173	(GOV 580) Exported to Cyprus and re-registered TV 572 1/56
56177	(GZ-25926) Re-registered NB-55-03 at an unknown date
56183	(FWO 614) Exported to Cyprus and re-registered TR 327 8/55
56529	(HYP 209) Exported to Cyprus and re-registered TAX 226 9/59
56538	(K-19052) Re-registered NB-28-39 at an unknown date
56597	(?) Re-registered NB-72-21 at an unknown date
56605	(JWJ 533) Exported to Ceylon and re-registered CV 1183 6/52
56619	(CFV 415) Bedford records have as intended for F Standerwick, Blackpool (LA)
56678	(GDG 700) Bedford and Duple records have as intended for CAJ Scarrott {Luxury Coaches}, Stow-on-the-Wold (GL)
56685	(HMN 601) Exported to Cyprus and re-registered TBJ 586 3/61
56709	(L-34219) Re-registered NB-55-70 at an unknown date
56802	(D-16933) Re-registered NB-27-19 at an unknown date
56826	(BRN 190) Re-registered JMN 773 6/48 (TH Kneen, Douglas (IM)); re-registered 281 HWR 1964 (mobile shop, Swansea (GGG))
56860	(DTP 948) Exported to Cyprus and re-registered TL 919 2/55
56881	(SMF 632) Exported to Cyprus and re-registered TBB 19 2/60
57004	(E-37757) Re-registered NB-37-35 at an unknown date
57031	(JTU 888) Re-registered KMN 854 4/49 (HB Clague, Douglas (IM))
57100	(?) Re-registered NB-27-18 at an unknown date
57117	(SMF 410) Seating also quoted as FC26F
57131	(P-41539) Re-registered NB-19-13 at an unknown date
57252	(K-20257) Re-registered NB-28-06 at an unknown date
57321	(KRB 69) Exported to Ceylon and re-registered CV 2340 1/53
57329	(HZ-43871) Re-registered PB-13-86 at an unknown date
57356	(HYR 257) Exported to Cyprus and re-registered TV 607 1/56
57384	(K-20256) Re-registered NB-46-91 at an unknown date
57430	(JAL 30) Chevrolet oil engine fitted 1951
57476	(E-27960) Re-registered NB-37-36 at an unknown date
57485	(HYP 211) Exported to Cyprus and re-registered TAY 168 10/59
57511	(GWT 716) Perkins oil engine fitted an unknown date
57536	(LPU 628) Exported to Cyprus and re-registered TAP 396 5/58
57557	(A-35170) Re-registered NB-80-21 at an unknown date
57673	(FFS 863) Rebuilt to forward control and rebodied Burlingham FC24F (5507) 1953
57684	(HPT 917) Mulliner records have chassis number as 57694; Bedford records have 57684
57691	(FFS 864) Rebuilt to forward control and rebodied Burlingham FC24F (5510) 1953
57777	(KWB 5) Full front to be confirmed
57797	(KWB 6) Full front to be confirmed
57801	(FFS 865) Rebuilt to forward control and rebodied Burlingham FC24F (5508) 1953
57808	(FFS 858) Rebuilt to forward control and rebodied Burlingham FC24F (5502) 1953

C1252/205

57816	(FFS 857) Rebuilt to forward control and rebodied Burlingham FC24F (5501) 1953
57858	(EFU 575) Probably FC30F ?
57878	(FFS 862) Rebuilt to forward control and rebodied Burlingham FC24F (5506) 1953
57882	(FFS 861) Rebuilt to forward control and rebodied Burlingham FC24F (5505) 1953
57897	(FFS 860) Rebuilt to forward control and rebodied Burlingham FC24F (5504) 1953
57918	(FFS 859) Rebuilt to forward control and rebodied Burlingham FC24F (5503) 1953
57959	(GWT 403) Exported to Ceylon and re-registered CV 1052 3/52
57970	(HYR 297) Re-registered J 12213 4/56 (LA Chapman {Jersey Tours}, St Helier, Jersey (CI))
57991	(EU 8714) Exported to Ceylon and re-registered CV 4665 11/54
58139	(HUO 686) Exported to Cyprus and re-registered TW 494 3/56
58228	(HYR 298) Exported to Cyprus and re-registered TAC 709 1/57
58247	(N-20761) Re-registered NB-51-86 at an unknown date
58259	(HEL 412) Bedford records have as intended for AP Downs, Worcester Park (SR). Originally allocated registration HYR 2, but seemingly not operated as such
58317	(?) Re-registered NB-27-22 at an unknown date
58366	(?) Re-registered NB-95-62 at an unknown date
58381	(?) Although Venture was a PSV operator, this was probably a goods vehicle
58425	(E-34070) Re-registered NB-37-38 at an unknown date
58463	(M-29849) Re-registered NB-80-58 at an unknown date
58618	(E-48219) Re-registered NB-30-66 at an unknown date
58685	(?) Re-registered NB-91-27 at an unknown date
58704	(KRB 70) Exported to Ceylon and re-registered CV 2949 5/53
58715	(E-33637) Re-registered NB-37-37 at an unknown date
58720	(FFS 868) Rebuilt to forward control and rebodied Burlingham FC24F (5512) 1953
58753	(K-19049) Re-registered NB-28-36 at an unknown date
58777	(JNB 53) Bedford records have as intended for Macclesfield Coachways (CH), an operator associated with Altrincham Coachways
58812	(K-20258) Re-registered NB-31-20 at an unknown date
58817	(SB 7161) Bedford records have as intended for C Fitzpatrick {Azure Blue Line}, Dunoon (AL), with whom Hartley was associated
58826	(JP 6591) Re-registered KMN 661 2/49 (EC Hamill, Onchan (IM))
58850	(A 32264) Re-registered NB-80-20 at an unknown date
58889	(HXJ 496) Bedford records have as intended for Timperley Coach (Subsidiaries) Ltd, Wilmslow (CH)
58909	(P-34004) Re-registered NB-16-11 at an unknown date
58923	(KLG 391) Re-registered KMN 744 3/49 (A & R Caine Ltd, Laxey (IM))
58937	(CWH 525) Body could be Booth as operator received two others from that builder; it could however have carried the pre-war Shearing body from Bedford WTB CDK 996
58947	(?) Re-registered NB-27-74 at an unknown date
58985	(EMO 6) Bedford records have as intended to be a horsebox with Moore
59087	(?) Re-registered EP.28 1965. Jamieson is not confirmed as original operator
59088	(?) Madge is not confirmed as original operator
59089	(?) Re-registered ER.9694 1965
59090	(P.680) Re-registered EH.3017 1965
59091	(P.915) Re-registered v2.099 at an unknown date
59093	(?) Re-registered v2.417 at an unknown date; re-registered DY.8303 1965
59096	(P.358) Re-registered EW.9225 1965
59120	(D-16997) Re-registered NB-27-34 at an unknown date
59151	(?) Re-registered NB-52-85 at an unknown date
59164	(JMN 138) Exported to Cyprus and re-registered TBN 336 9/61
59197	(CHH 508) Bedford records have as intended for E Hartness {Hartness Bus & Coach Service}, Penrith (CU)
59207	(?) Re-registered NB-26-95 at an unknown date
59246	(K-4314) Re-registered NB-26-99 at an unknown date
59281	(FFS 866) Rebuilt to forward control and rebodied Burlingham FC24F (5509) 1953
59305	(D-16995) Re-registered NB-27-27 at an unknown date
59326	(FFS 867) Rebuilt to forward control and rebodied Burlingham FC24F (5511) 1953
59647	(KHW 987) Exported to Cyprus and re-registered TBA 147 1/60
59696	(JNB 146) Bedford records have as intended for Macclesfield Coachways (CH), an operator associated with Altrincham Coachways
59722	(KA 4910) Perkins P6 oil engine fitted and re-registered KBL 502 4/52
59737	(EBL 647) Carried a pre-war body, origin unknown
59759	(?) Noakes was a PSV operator. May have been diverted elsewhere, probably with a goods body
59793	(DVH 133) Carried the 1938 Duple body from the operator's Dodge SBF BVH 187
59818	(?) Re-registered KBB 429 1/50

59841	(GAO 467) Perkins P6 oil engine fitted 1949. Exported to Cyprus and re-registered TAP 398 5/58	
59866	(KUM 999) Re-registered LMN 971 2/50 (E Bradshaw & Son Ltd {West End Garage}, Ramsey (IM))	
59890	(CRD 979) Body transferred to OB FUJ 500 with RB Talbott {Barry's Coaches}, Moreton-in-Marsh (GL) c1963	
59924	(AEE 764) Exported to Cyprus and re-registered TBH 559 1/61	
59931	(FBT 900) Exported to Cyprus and re-registered TBB 257 2/60	
59983	(KA 4909) Perkins P6 oil engine fitted and re-registered KBK 694 2/52	
60011	(W 125) Chevrolet oil engine fitted by 12/52	
60020	(CWH 640) Bedford records have as intended for W Knowles & Sons, Bolton (LA)	
60034	(EFU 361) Exported to Cyprus and re-registered TAD 789 1/58	
60093	(SMF 530) Bedford and Duple records have as intended for Venture Transport (Hendon) Ltd, London NW2 (LN). Re-registered MMN 177 4/50 (Corkhill's Garage Ltd, Onchan (IM))	
60125	(FWX 547) Exported to Cyprus and re-registered TAC 120 12/56	
60337	(HFM 35) Exported to Ceylon and re-registered CV 4794 12/54	
60347	(E-48059) Re-registered NB-37-40 at an unknown date	
60371	(DHS 192) Exported to Cyprus and re-registered TM 119 2/55	
60395	(DTP 878) Re-registered J 8404 3/60 (W Turner {Premier Tours, St Helier, Jersey (CI))	
60406	(M-29850) Re-registered NB-80-59 at an unknown date	
60495	(JWJ 538) Exported to Ceylon and re-registered CV 1176 6/52	
60528	(E-48218) Re-registered NB-30-65 at an unknown date	
60560	(HYR 587) Exported to Cyprus and re-registered TAY 167 10/59	
60600	(D-16996) Re-registered NB-27-31 at an unknown date	
60749	(TMG 94) Bedford records have as intended for Venture Transport (Hendon) Ltd, London NW2 (LN). Exported to Cyprus and re-registered TBH 121 12/60	
60773	(E-48058) Re-registered NB-37-39 at an unknown date	
60805	(E-18800) Re-registered NB-55-17 at an unknown date	
60821	(L-34220) Re-registered PB-35-95 at an unknown date	
60885	(CFV 970) Bedford records have as intended for C Booth (Builders) Ltd, Bolton (LA)	
60894	(FBC 932) Bedford records have as intended for CH Butter, Childs Ercall (SH)	
60902	(A-39774) Re-registered NB-80-12 at an unknown date	
60935	(HYR 776) Re-registered J 5625 3/52 (UV Noel {Waverley Tours}, St Martin, Jersey (CI))	
60943	(FWM 197) Possibly not used by Howard and diverted new to Blundells Coaches (Southport) Ltd (LA). Body also given as K.W. Bedford records have as intended for F Standerwick {Crown Motors}, Southport (LA)	
60975	(EAW 112) Carried the pre-war body from Bedford WTB UJ 8725	
60991	(LTN 376) Bedford records have as intended for Marshall & Co Ltd, Newcastle-upon-Tyne (ND)	
61064	(LTN 680) Body has also been claimed as ACB	
61101	Re-registered DY.9725 1965; with Leabourn Passenger Service, Kaiwaka (O-NZ) by 12/70	
61107	(P.367) Re-registered P1.652 at an unknown date; re-registered EW.4284 1965	
61111	(V2.071) Re-registered V4.474 at an unknown date	
61236	(K-20244) Re-registered NB-27-00 at an unknown date	
61265	(CFV 678) Bedford records have as intended for F Standerwick, Blackpool (LA)	
61289	(PRF 84) Bedford records have as intended for A Janes {Bert Janes}, Stourbridge (WO)	
61338	(LJO 757) Registration later transferred to OB GBL 200	
61354	(EWN 19) Exported to Cyprus and re-registered TW 471 3/56	
61401	(HUO 687) Exported to Cyprus and re-registered TV 329 1/56	
61425	(A-39244) Re-registered NB-80-13 at an unknown date	
61450	(?) Noakes was a PSV operator. May have been diverted elsewhere, probably with a goods body	
61466	(A-39689) Re-registered NB-80-11 at an unknown date. Chassis number recorded as 61446; Bedford records have 61466	
61474	(E-48060) Re-registered NB-37-41 at an unknown date	
61661	(D-16998) Re-registered NB-27-47 at an unknown date	
61769	(E-48061) Re-registered NB-37-42 at an unknown date	
61779	(OMY 384) Bedford and Duple records have as intended for AC Susans {Fountain Luxury Coaches}, Twickenham (MX). Re-registered UMN 670 3/56 (E Bradshaw & Son Ltd {West End Garage}, Ramsey (IM))	
61795	(CL 9649) Re-registered CV 1205 5/52	
61957	(KAF 110) Exported to Cyprus and re-registered TW 579 3/56	
62013	(LVT 317) Bedford records have as intended for H Nickolls, Milford (ST)	
62055	(JAR 976) Exported to Cyprus and re-registered TAE 448 4/57	
62087	(FWW 598) Exported to Cyprus and re-registered TAD 121 2/57	
62144	(ACP 730) Bedford records have as intended for Denroy Coaches Ltd, Hebden Bridge (WR). Body recorded as SMT when vehicle was in EMTA. Exported to Ceylon and re-registered CV 3432 10/53	

C1252/207

62184	(ORE 944) Bedford records have as intended for AJ, WH & LW Jeffreys {W Jeffreys & Sons}, Goldenhill (ST)
62249	(GAB 754) Exported to Cyprus and re-registered TR 987 10/55
62314	(MTW 263) Re-registered J 14396 5/53 (WL Jones {Len's Tours}, St Helier, Jersey (CI))
62330	(CNL 262) Carried the pre-war body from Leyland Cub FPT 182 (originally registered FM 7001)
62427	(HTJ 913) New to Ribchester as a box van; rebodied Plaxton FC30F (564) 3/49
62802	(JWJ 540) Exported to Ceylon and re-registered CV 1784 9/52
62850	(GAO 468) Exported to Cyprus c1954
62875	(CJA 520) Bedford records have as intended for Ford, Reddish, status unknown
62907	(CJA 521) Bedford records have as intended for Ford, Reddish, status unknown
62930	(?) Chassis number recorded as 82930, assumed to be that given in Bedford records as 62930
62988	(EJU 397) Mulliner records have as intended for Windridge, Sons & Riley {Victory}, Ibstock (LE); Bedfords records have Smeeton
63020	(LAE 275) Carried the pre-war body from Opel EHY 444
63085	(TMG 169) Exported to Ceylon and re-registered CV 4097 3/54
63101	(FGD 818 ?) Registration variously quoted as FGD 818 or FGE 460
63141	(?) Mulliner records have as intended for HR Cropley {Safety Coaches}, Fosdyke (LI). Bedford records have RL Cropley {Blue Glider}, Sutterton (LI). No record with either operator.
63155	(HFJ 836) Exported to Cyprus and re-registered TAP 139 4/58. Rebodied Trimbakiri FB35F 11/68
63376	(EFU 362) Exported to Cyprus and re-registered TAG 183 6/57
63463	(P1.221) Re-registered EL.9172 1965
63464	(P1.223) Re-registered EW.8672 1965
63466	(P1.891) Re-registered DX.2962 1965
63469	(P.375) Re-registered EH.9854 1965
63710	(JXA 925) Exported to Cyprus and re-registered TU 719 11/55
63732	(DUH 110) Rebodied Duple C29F (55674) 1950 (following accident). Exported to Cyprus and re-registered TAX 251 9/59
63792	(SML 958) Bedford and Duple records have as intended for A Livermore, Barley (HT) before that business was acquired by Richmond
63823	(FWW 599) Exported to Cyprus and re-registered TAD 122 2/57
63840	(LPU 615) Exported to Cyprus and re-registered TAC 795 1/57
63880	(HNY 868) Carried a Jeffreys "Van-cum-Bus" body
64097	(G60xx) Registration from G6052 - 6054 batch
64168	(G60xx) Registration from G6052 - 6054 batch
64265	(HB-938) Later with Kolmilinjat Oy, Punkalaidun (O-FIN)
64307	(JAH 888) Body has also been claimed as both Belle and Churchill ! Photographic evidence casts doubt on both of these
64332	(LVK 381) Re-registered NTN 195 10/49 after accident rebuild by Modern Coachcraft. Exported to Cyprus 11/60
64421	(G60xx) Registration from G6052 - 6055 batch. Either 64421 or 64533 was G 6055
64533	(G60xx) Registration from G6052 - 6055 batch. Either 64421 or 64533 was G 6055
64721	(EWN 863) Exported to Cyprus and re-registered TV 263 1/56
64743	(DVN 799) Re-registered JMN 453 2/48 (EC Hamill, Onchan (IM))
64759	(GAO 469) Exported to Cyprus c1954
64823	(HTJ 347) Exported to Cyprus and re-registered TAQ 907 9/58
64929	(MVW 68) There are two bodies numbered 440 in Thurgood records! - see also MVW 556
64937	(CTL 275) Exported to Cyprus and re-registered TAG 55 6/57
65017	(JNA 611) Davies has not been identified as a PSV operator, and is therefore assumed to have been a non-PSV operator
65091	(RA-152) Later with Kossilan Liikenne, location unknown (O-FIN)
65201	(P.374) Re-registered v1.836 and v4.372 at unknown dates; re-registered EH.9855 1965
65202	(P.628) Re-registered v2.266 at an unknown date; re-registered EW.4657 1965
65206	(P1.191) Re-registered P1.104 at an unknown date
65208	(P.371) Re-registered P2.457 at an unknown date
65209	(?) Registration has been claimed as P.767, but this appears to have been 65210
65210	(P.767) Registration P.767 also claimed by 65209. Re-registered EW.9200 1965
65211	(S1.047) Re-registered V.398 and V1.219 at unknown dates. Johnstons not confirmed as original operator
65392	(TL-802) Later with Alinen Aarne, location unknown (O-FIN)
65400	(JP 6692) Bedford records have as intended for Grocott, Upholland, Lancashire), status unknown
65515	(HUP 737) Exported to Cyprus and re-registered TBM 431 7/61
65641	(EAW 275) Re-registered J 3074 3/56 (JO Manning {JBS}, St Helier, Jersey (CI))
65923	(EEA 500) Exported to Ceylon and re-registered CV 831 3/52
65988	(FJW 110) Exported to Cyprus and re-registered TY 220 6/56

66004	(HFD 945)	Bedfords records have as intended for Mrs FG Mason, Darlaston (ST)
66020	(JFJ 14)	Exported to Cyprus and re-registered TAM 159 1/58
66028	(DUH 627)	Body has also been claimed as Pearson. Bedfords records have as intended for Cheam Hire, Cheam, Surrey, status unknown
66153	(JAF 837)	Exported to Cyprus and re-registered TBH 171 1/61
66187	(SX 6218)	Re-registered J 702 7/53 (H Swanson {Redline Coaches}, St Helier, Jersey (CI) 15)
66207	(GRM 910)	Exported to Cyprus 1/64
66219	(DTP 929)	Exported to Cyprus and re-registered TBA 468 1/60
66230	(FWM 196)	Possibly not used by Howard and diverted new to Blundells Coaches (Southport) Ltd (LA)
66294	(MVW 556)	There are two bodies numbered 440 in Thurgood records! - see also MVW 68
66305	(BCB 263)	Bedford records have as intended for J Wearden & Sons Ltd, Blackburn (LA)
66438	(MBB 262)	Exported to Cyprus and re-registered TX 888 6/56
66630	(JAH 570)	Body has been mistakenly claimed as Plaxton
66654	(KDE 525)	Has been recorded incorrectly as Duple. Exported to Cyprus and re-registered TX 899 6/56
66784	(GNP 278)	Exported to Cyprus and re-registered TAH 976 9/57
67119	(FFS 869)	Rebuilt to forward control and rebodied Burlingham FC24F (5513) 1953
67124	(BGS 595)	Exported to Cyprus and re-registered TAD 512 3/57
67141	(JDV 561)	Exported to Cyprus and re-registered TAC 708 1/57
67161	(JNA 920)	Exported to Cyprus and re-registered TAN 129 3/58
67190	(JMN 201)	Re-registered LMB 240 6/49 (Watson's (Winsford) Motor Services Ltd (CH))
67238	(JP 7040)	Seating also quoted as C26F, more usual for a Pearson body
67336	(TM-355)	Chassis number recorded as 67330; Bedford records have 67336
67388	(CWH 370)	Exported to Ceylon and re-registered CV 4083 3/54
67396	(JFJ 198)	Bedford records have as intended for Beal, Exeter, a dealer and owner of Central Garage
67446	(FFS 874)	Rebuilt to forward control and rebodied Burlingham FC24F (5518) 1953
67451	(FFS 870)	Rebuilt to forward control and rebodied Burlingham FC24F (5514) 1953
67468	(FFS 871)	Rebuilt to forward control and rebodied Burlingham FC24F (5515) 1953
67729	(LPU 617)	Exported to Cyprus and re-registered TAC 794 1/57
67761	(FDL 535)	Carried the pre-war body from Morris Viceroy DL 7967, but converted to C26F
67773	(CTL 460)	Exported to Cyprus and re-registered TAD 855 3/57
67776	(FFS 873)	Rebuilt to forward control and rebodied Burlingham FC24F (5517) 1953
67780	(FFS 872)	Rebuilt to forward control and rebodied Burlingham FC24F (5516) 1953
67982	(HDD 119)	Bedford records have as intended for Park Coachways (West Vale) Ltd (WR); Duple records have Fluck
68011	(KGH 389)	Motor Taxation records have chassis number as 68071; Bedford records have 68011
68256	(GX-3488)	Re-registered NB-48-52 at an unknown date
68303	(KHY 917)	Ordered by CW Jordan {Maple Leaf}, Bristol (GL) before Wessex was formed
68325	(EJU 936)	Recorded as Duple with two operators, but not traced in Duple records
68342	(HG-822)	Later with Valkeakosken Liikenne Oy, Valkeakoski (O-FIN)
68371	(JOD 354)	Bedford records have as intended for Beal, Exeter, a dealer and also owner of Teign Cars
68435	(DRV 140)	Exported to Cyprus and re-registered TBA 811 2/60
68492	(DPN 936)	Body has also been claimed as Wadham, but photographic evidence confirms Kenex
68592	(GWU 856)	Exported to Cyprus and re-registered TV 467 1/56
68663	(GWW 407)	Exported to Cyprus and re-registered TX 975 6/56
68683	(DBD 938)	Exported to Ceylon and re-registered CV 4704 10/54
68726	(P.338)	Re-registered EH.2885 1965
68728	(?)	Re-registered EK.8280 1965
68729	(P2.499)	Re-registered CW.572 1965
68730	(P.629)	Re-registered V2.280 at an unknown date; re-registered EW.4661 1965
68732	(?)	Later with W & H Motors, location unknown (O-NZ)
68735	(P2.100)	Re-registered DX.8007 or DX.3007 1965.
68736	(P3.208)	Re-registered EH.9983 1965
68887	(EFW 92)	Exported to Cyprus and re-registered TAH 826 9/57
68901	(NEV 190)	Motor Taxation records have chassis number as 68910; Bedford records have 68901
68979	(GAO 470)	Exported to Cyprus and re-registered TM 479 3/55
69127	(ECO 974)	Rebodied Duple C29F (127/4) 12/53
69142	(EWN 967)	Exported to Cyprus and re-registered TV 81 12/55
69158	(HZ-55742)	Re-registered NB-38-15 at an unknown date
69266	(EBD 300)	Duple records have chassis number as 69299; Bedford records have 69266
69483	(JXF 327)	Exported to Cyprus and re-registered TAG 434 7/57
69504	(?)	Re-registered NB-73-29 at an unknown date
69509	(P.630)	Not traced in Bedford records. Re-registered EY.3886 1965
69537	(JNB 701)	Bedford records have as intended for Hirst Tours Ltd, Longton (ST)

C1252/209

69719	(FDL 278) Re-registered J 9586 6/53 (J Jones {Maple Leaf Tours}, St Helier, Jersey (CI))
69736	(LPU 619) Exported to Cyprus and re-registered TAD 345 3/57
69885	(FMJ 544) Duple records have as intended for R Franklin {Century Bus}, Carlton (BD)
70107	(JFJ 346) Bedford records have as intended for Beal, Exeter, a dealer and also owner of Central Garage
70218	(EAJ 645) Exported to Cyprus and re-registered TAJ 13 9/57
70619	(?) Not traced in Bedford records - not confirmed as OB.
71329	(FWX 548) Exported to Cyprus and re-registered TAB 904 11/56
71406	(?) Not traced in Bedford records. Re-registered ET.176 1965. Blue Bus not confirmed as original operator
71454	(JUO 605) Exported to Cyprus and re-registered TAV 704 7/59
71950	(FBE 131) Exported to Cyprus and re-registered TAH 817 9/57
72389	(KWJ 773) Full front to be confirmed
72504	(MVW 286) Exported to Cyprus and re-registered TU 224 2/58; re-registered TAP 537 5/58
72585	(5183) Re-registered AY 59 3/62 (WP Simon, Alderney (CI))
72843	(JND 999) Bedford records have as intended for Holt, Manchester (LA) - which Holt is unspecified, although the Manchester registration supports this.
72885	(DBA 348) Body has also been claimed as Rushworth
72892	(CJA 716) Bedford records have as intended for Goddard & Buckingham Ltd, Marple (CH); Duple has Melba
73023	(5188) Re-registered AY 59 3/62 (WP Simon, Alderney (CI))
73042	(CTL 625) Exported to Cyprus 2/58
73118	(JUO 606) Exported to Cyprus and re-registered TAY 31 9/59
73174	(5190) Re-registered AY 59 2/60 (WP Simon, Alderney (CI))
73881	(FWX 550) Exported to Cyprus and re-registered TAH 820 9/57
73895	(DBD 939) Exported to Ceylon and re-registered CV 4793 12/54
74050	(EFW 501) Exported to Cyprus and re-registered TAC 476 1/57
74342	(?) Probably the vehicle supplied with a Tiverton horse/livestock carrier body to WA Ellis of Broadclyst - Flew may have been a dealer
74445	(MPB 333) Exported to Cyprus and re-registered TBA 140 1/60
74619	(JTD 999) Re-registered UMN 634 3/56 (GW Wharton {Highlander}, Douglas (IM))
74838	(FP 4771) Exported to Cyprus and re-registered TBH 259 1/61
75256	(FFS 886) Chassis number also recorded as 75286. Bedford records show 75256
75430	(FWO 620) Exported to Cyprus and re-registered TAK 417 11/57
75697	(DBD 941) Exported to Ceylon and re-registered CV 4716 10/54
75855	(GHO 942) Exported to Cyprus and re-registered TU 219 11/55
76101	(HNY 941) Bedford and Duple records have as intended for Davies Bros, Port Talbot (GG); actually licensed to their Thomas & James subsidiary. Exported to Cyprus and re-registered TL 629 1/55
76145	(5189) Re-registered AY 101 2/60 (WP Simon, Alderney (CI))
76170	(P-30078) Re-registered NB-58-14 at an unknown date
76180	(MPB 833) Exported to Cyprus and re-registered TAM 460 2/58
76363	(EA-216) Not traced in Bedford records. Linja not confirmed as original operator
76402	(45409) Rebuilt as FB33F and converted to Perkins oil engine, both on unknown dates
76562	(SO 9300) Chassis had been delivered in 1948, but vehicle not registered until 1950. If the body was indeed by SMT, this too would have been built in 1948
76591	(HOD 108) Exported to Cyprus and re-registered TV 332 1/56
77072	(HWT 629) The operator also allegedly operated identical HWT 628, but no record can be found
77090	(ECO 698) Exported to Cyprus and re-registered TX 260 4/56
77273	(?) Re-registered DS.640 1965
77278	(s.424) Re-registered EP.2551 1965. Gibson not confirmed as original operator
77279	(P3.588) Re-registered DR.6828 1965
77280	(P2.416) Re-registered DX.3014 1965
77281	(P2.413) Re-registered P3.212 at an unknown date
77612	(HOD 109) Exported to Cyprus and re-registered TW 718 3/56
77710	(KKO 745) Exported to Cyprus and re-registered TAM 836 2/58
77727	(HOD 110) Exported to Cyprus and re-registered TV 818 2/56
77794	(FHR 502) Ordered by L Alexander {Queen of the Road}, Devizes (WI), who sold out to Card
77858	(FJW 917) Mulliner records have chassis number as 74858; Bedford has 77858. Exported to Cyprus and re-registered TBQ 128 12/61
77871	(EBU 674) Bedford records have as intended for Ralph Renton Ltd, Hollinwood (LA), but seemingly operated by associate Dyson. Re-registered LMN 979 2/50 (P D Craine, Douglas (IM))
78162	(?) Re-registered NB-29-40 at an unknown date
78437	(?) Re-registered EQ.4895 1965. Martin & Vernon not confirmed as original operator
78441	(?) Re-registered CW.2211 1965. Later with OL Jenkins, unknown overseas location

78442	(P2.480) Re-registered AA.7381 1965
78446	(P.359) Re-registered V2.363 at an unknown date; re-registered BA.4004 1965
78638	(JPT 541) Exported to Cyprus and re-registered TBD 895 7/60
78729	(FCJ 915) Bedford records have as intended for AW Tipping {Victory}, Lower Wyche (WO); confirmed by Motor Taxation records, with booked registration GWP 546
78961	(FUS 606) Fitted with removable seats to allow wheelchairs to be carried
79221	(MNW 300) Later (at least) fitted with bus seats ie DP..F
79244	(CTL 967) Exported to Cyprus and re-registered TAD 859 3/57
79527	(HDF 343) Exported to Cyprus and re-registered TAZ 772 12/59
79834	(HOD 111) Exported to Cyprus and re-registered TBA 23 1/60
79928	(H-30829) Re-registered NB-56-92 at an unknown date
79937	(JYD 619) Exported to Cyprus and re-registered TAK 841 11/57
80416	(GRK 316) Exported to Cyprus and re-registered TV 338 1/56
80441	(MNU 939) Duple records have as intended for "Davenport, Hulland Ward"; this is not a known operator in the Derbyshire village of that name.
80498	(HOD 112) Exported to Cyprus and re-registered TAV 571 6/59
80598	(JBJ 791) Bedford records have as intended for G Reynolds, London N16 (GLN) as a van. Body number needs confirmation
80641	(V.459) Re-registered V2.418 at an unknown date; re-registered EY.1110 1965
80642	(H2.404) Re-registered EY.693 1965
80645	(P.601) Re-registered V1.593 and V4.799 at unknown dates; re-registered EH.2886 1965 and GJ.470 at an unknown date
80646	(?) Re-registered EH.2887 1965
80647	(P.602) Re-registered EY.8123 1965
81226	(E-18799) Re-registered NB-57-21 at an unknown date
81239	(JTC 648) Exported to Cyprus and re-registered TU 650 11/55
81251	(FWO 622) Exported to Cyprus and re-registered TQ 093 6/55
81411	(FDL 537) Exported to Cyprus (1957 ?)
81589	(HOD 37) Exported to Cyprus and re-registered TAV 974 7/59
81674	(P.632) Re-registered EY.8122 1965
81675	(V2.415) With Matakawau Motors, Waiuku (O-NZ) by 5/64
81678	(?) Re-registered EZ.2224 1965. Acquired by DG Wright, Wellsford (O-NZ) 1/99
81681	(?) Re-registered EP.2425 1965. Later with Haydon Priest, Oakura (O-NZ)
81683	(?) Re-registered EQ.4894 1965. Martin & Vernon not confirmed as original operator
81924	(HOD 39) Exported to Cyprus and re-registered TAW 498 8/59
81957	(JUR 879) Re-registered J 8520 2/50 (CB Griss {Scarlet Pimpernel Coaches}, St Helier, Jersey (CI))
82114	(JTE 484) Bedford records have as intended for WL Ibbotson, Morecambe (LA); Duple records have as intended for JN Davies & Co, Skerton (LA)
82134	(KYA 64) Exported to Cyprus and re-registered TBE 281 7/60
82181	(KTV 396) Bedford and Duple records have as intended for Talbot, Nottingham and Bateman, Nottingham respectively; the status of neither is known
82285	(JXL 560) Exported to Cyprus and re-registered TBH 184 1/61
82619	(DFR 404) Re-registered TMN 613 5/55 (F Gash {Empress}, Douglas (IM))
82743	(MPF 643) Exported to Cyprus and re-registered TAD 115 2/57
82798	(JXP 557) Exported to Cyprus and re-registered TBH 172 1/61
83100	(KYA 142) Bedford records have as intended for Binding & Payne Ltd {Dorothy's Coaches}, Clevedon (SO), absorbed into WEMS; Duple has WEMS
83244	(LKX 291) Exported to Cyprus and re-registered TBB 20 2/60
83262	(HTG 986) Thomas is not the BET company of the same name
83456	(D-8981) Re-registered NB-25-39 at an unknown date
83474	(E-48221) Re-registered NB-30-63 at an unknown date
83647	(D335) Chassis number recorded as 83947; Bedford records have 83647
83719	(EUT 619) Ran on plates EUT 169 for some time in error
83754	(EUJ 502) Exported to Cyprus and re-registered TV 399 1/56
83817	(FJF 833) Quinn is the earliest recorded operator, but the vehicle was not recorded there until 12/52. Bedford records have as intended for AGH Jordan {Jordan's Motor Services}, Blaenavon (MH)
83881	(?) Mendip Queen was also a PSV operator
84417	(J 4442) Re-registered HWO 915 c10/49 (G Williams, Blaina (MH))
84508	(?) Re-registered NB-78-84 at an unknown date
84603	(P.125) Re-registered EW.5974 1965
84606	(P.631) Re-registered V1.593 and V4.798 at unknown dates; re-registered EH.2887 1965
84607	(?) Re-registered DU.4794 1965
84612	(?) Chassis number recorded as 84812: assumed to be that given in Bedford records as 84612. Madge not confirmed as original operator

C1252/211

84790	(JKD 930) Exported to Cyprus and re-registered TBE 401 7/60
84911	(TMV 948) Bedford and Duple records have as intended for A Livermore, Barley (HT) before that business was acquired by Richmond
85057	(?) Re-registered 78891 in 1956. Later with KTEL Chania (O-GR)
85067	(HOD 42) Exported to Cyprus and re-registered TAW 499 8/59
85076	(?) Re-registered 78892 in 1956. Later with KTEL Chania (O-GR)
85096	(50-855) Re-registered 70292 in 1956. Later with KTEL Patras City (O-GR)
85143	(54-537) Re-registered Kp-776 1953 and 80153 in 1956. Later with Spyridakis (KTEL Herakleoin) (O-GR) 49
85154	(?) Re-registered 79236 in 1956. Later with KTEL Rethymnon (O-GR)
85226	(D-6194) Re-registered PB-07-87 at an unknown date
85610	(HTX 594) Carried a Jeffreys "Van-cum-Bus" body
85756	(?) Re-registered 67271 in 1956. Later with KTEL Kavala (O-GR)
85767	(?) Re-registered 67241 in 1956. Later with KTEL Kavala City (O-GR)
85788	(HHP 178) Bedford and Duple records have as intended for Ferguson tractors, Coventry whose products Standard built under licence
85922	(CCK 530) Re-registered WMN 59 5/57 (GW Wharton {Highlander}, Douglas (IM))
86302	(DHJ 22) Exported to Cyprus and re-registered TAP 394 5/58
86480	(KGP 290) Exported to Cyprus c1962
86749	(LHN 146) Exported to Cyprus and re-registered TAP 506 5/58
86843	(EVN 100) Bedford records have as intended for C Bentley, Amotherby (WR); Duple has Armstrong
87309	(GOT 513) Exported to Cyprus and re-registered TAL 91 12/57
87406	(FDT 718) Exported to Cyprus and re-registered TU 649 11/55
87438	(MPF 109) Exported to Cyprus and re-registered TAZ 783 12/59
87544	(CCK 567) Exported to Cyprus and re-registered TAN 95 3/58
87618	(LMN 1) Originally allocated registration JMN 901, but seemingly not operated as such
87633	(BCB 857) Owned by Brockholes Motor Co, Huddersfield (XWR), but operated by Brook
88128	(JTF 965) Bedford records have as intended for Entwistle, Wigan (GLA)` for bodying as a furniture van
88210	(HDG 859) Body number also recorded as 6034. Bedford records have as intended for AJF Stevens, London NW1 (GLN) for bodying as a furniture van.
88626	(KGH 913) Registration also recorded as KGH 918
88698	(BCB 872) Exported to Belgium at an unknown date
88907	(LBH 720) Has been recorded as new to Finefield Garage Ltd, Slough, possibly the supplying dealer. Bedford and Duple records both have as intended for the Sanatorium
89111	(?) Not traced in Bedford records - not confirmed as OB.
89320	(JMN 902) Re-registered 278 ABE 6/62 (Newton {Reliance}, Scunthorpe (LI))
89357	(TMK 28) Exported to Cyprus and re-registered TBE 69 7/60
89502	(HOD 46) Exported to Cyprus and re-registered TAU 967 6/59
90079	(KYB 376) Bedford records have as intended for Binding & Payne Ltd {Dorothy's Coaches}, Clevedon (SO), absorbed into WEMS; Duple has WEMS
90468	(EUT 917) Exported to Cyprus and re-registered TBM 432 7/61
90488	(LHN 211) Exported to Cyprus and re-registered TAA 328 8/56
90495	(DFR 686) Motor Taxation records have chassis number as 50123; Bedford records have 90495
90650	(NVW 220) Bedford and Duple records have as intended for Wiffen's Coaches Ltd, Finchingfield (EX)
90670	(JXT 482) Re-registered Q986 OCR 1/92; re-registered ESL 175 11/99 (with travellers)
90684	(KTU 724) Exported to Ceylon 8/53 and re-registered CV 3511 11/53
90832	(GVE 502) Bedford records have as intended for Bennett, St Neots, status unknown
90839	(KYB 378) Bedford records have as intended for Binding & Payne Ltd {Dorothy's Coaches}, Clevedon (SO), absorbed into WEMS
91162	(GEW 58) Bedford records have as intended for E Towgood & Sons Ltd, Sawston (CM)
91216	(FWO 625) Exported to Cyprus and re-registered TR 349 9/55
92189	(LPP 53) Exported to Cyprus and re-registered TBZ 463 4/63
91401	(?) Re-registered EP.2552 1965. Gibson not confirmed as original operator
91404	(?) Re-registered FE.1974 1965. Also TL.7157 at later unknown date. Edwards not confirmed as original operator
91408	(?) Re-registered FE.5761 1965
91676	(HWT 531) Exported to Cyprus and re-registered TBM 433 7/61
91854	(TMY 485) Exported to Cyprus and re-registered L 882 1/55
92133	(J 12613) Re-registered KCJ 135E 7/67 (GD Bengry {Primrose Motors}, Leominster (HR))
92195	(KGH 695) Bedford records have as intended for W Hodge & Sons, Much Hadham (HT); Duple has Wallis
92227	(FFU 104) Exported to Cyprus and re-registered TAH 818 9/57
92244	(HOD 113) Exported to Cyprus and re-registered TAU 985 6/59
92383	(?) Re-registered 76985 in 1956. Later with KTEL Messinia (O-GR) 6

92439	(?) Re-registered 20974 in 1956. Later with KTEL Attica (O-GR) 24
92482	(54-886) Re-registered A-4918 1953 and 30102 in 1956. Later with KTEL Korinthia (O-GR) 102
92493	(KTB 127) Ordered by Lancashire Electricity & Power (XLA) before formation of NWEB. Duple records give chassis number as 92494; Bedford records have 92493
92577	(?) Re-registered BM.8720 1965
92749	(?) Re-registered 46017 in 1962. Later with KTEL Fokida (O-GR)
92760	(KJH 91) Duple records have as intended for St James School, London NW9 (XLN). Re-registered MAS 427 10/02. Exported to Holland and re-registered BE 50 08 at unknown date
92875	(HOD 114) Exported to Cyprus and re-registered TBA 24 1/60
92934	(KGH 482) Ford oil engine fitted by 1966
92942	(DRJ 334) Bedford records have as intended for JR Entwistle, Wigan (GLA) as a furniture van. In fact delivered with a coach body to J W Fieldsend Ltd, Salford (LA), but not used.
93093	(NVW 835) Bedford and Duple records have as intended for Wiffen's Coaches Ltd, Finchingfield (EX)
93099	(?) Re-registered 20533 in 1956
93224	(P.604) Re-registered EY.3888 1965
93227	(P.124) Re-registered EW.5973 1965
93228	(P1.161) Also recorded with registration V1.161
93229	(P1.105) Re-registered P.1362 at an unknown date
93231	(P.809) Re-registered P1.761 at an unknown date; re-registered EX.7360 1965
93232	(P1.078) Re-registered P1.328 at an unknown date; re-registered EH.9841 1965
93291	(LUM 509) Exported to Ceylon and re-registered CV 1079 5/52
93352	(?) Re-registered 21026 in 1956. Later with KTEL Attica (O-GR) 78
93363	(FJU 191) Bedford records have as intended for F Presswick, Witham (GEX) as a furniture van.
93439	(?) Re-registered 20182 in 1956
93483	(?) Mendip Queen was also a PSV operator
93526	(?) Re-registered 62493 in 1956
93974	(FBU 7) Re-registered RMN 425 5/54 (Mrs EA Cretney (R Cretney) {Burleigh}, Douglas (IM) 2)
94225	(HOD 115) Exported to Cyprus and re-registered TAU 914 6/59
94273	(J 12830) Re-registered KCJ 398E 9/67 (CT Sargeant, Kington (HR))
94321	(?) Re-registered 20238 in 1956
94683	(GC-15-91) Rebuilt 5/67 - no details known
94733	(HOD 116) Exported to Cyprus and re-registered TAY 32 10/59
94761	(JOH 262) Exported to Ireland and re-registered IY 1947 3/77 (Crosson, Dundalk (EI))
94892	(EDR 793) Exported to Netherlands and re-registered BE-52-07 2003
94999	(DFR 699) Re-registered J 2562 3/56 (JP Birbeck {Blue Eagle Tours}, St Helier (CI) 1); exported to Cyprus 1964
95073	(KTB 521) Owned by Martin's Coaches Ltd, Salford (LA), but operated by Leigh Manufacturing
95391	(HOD 117) Exported to Cyprus and re-registered TAU 913 6/59
95396	(?) Re-registered 20136 in 1956
95893	(DRD 382) Exported to Cyprus and re-registered TBK 735 5/61
95937	(DFR 700) Re-registered J 2566 3/56 (JP Birbeck {Blue Eagle Tours}, St Helier (CI) 2); reverted to DFR 700 6/64 (Showerings Ltd, Shepton Mallett (XSO))
95977	(JP 7335) Re-registered NSV 583 by 11/84 (in preservation)
96544	(HOD 118) Exported to Cyprus and re-registered TAV 2 6/59
96712	(HAX 657) Exported to Cyprus and re-registered TAK 418 11/57
96726	(KMN 324) Exported to Cyprus and re-registered TBJ 347 3/61
96827	(DFR 701) Re-registered J 2641 3/56 (JP Birbeck {Blue Eagle Tours}, St Helier (CI) 3)
96952	(HOD 119) Exported to Cyprus and re-registered TAU 933 6/59; re-registered TBJ 620 by 10/72
97420	(DFR 706) Re-registered J 2865 3/56 (JP Birbeck {Blue Eagle Tours}, St Helier (CI) 8); reverted to DFR 706 7/64 (Ward Bros (Lepton) Ltd (WR))
97436	(LTF 845) Body has been claimed as King & Lancaster, but no such builder has been traced. An Ireland body is a possibility
97955	(KGW 126) Bedford records have as intended for W Hodge & Sons, Much Hadham (HT); Duple has Wallis
98065	(HOD 48) Exported to Cyprus and re-registered TAX 410 9/57
98461	(?) Venture Transport was also a PSV operator
98468	(HCG 244) Warren was also a PSV operator, trading as Altonian Coaches
98544	(DFR 702) Re-registered J 2609 3/56 (JP Birbeck {Blue Eagle Tours}, St Helier (CI) 4)
98547	(?) Of the four OBs delivered to Wright, one was ACM 990 with Spurling pantechnicon body
98563	(FKW 571) Fitted with bench seats
98569	(DFR 703) Re-registered J 2813 3/56 (JP Birbeck {Blue Eagle Tours}, St Helier (CI) 5); exported to Cyprus c1964
98712	(FKW 572) Fitted with bench seats
98763	(DFR 704) Re-registered J 2742 3/56 (JP Birbeck {Blue Eagle Tours}, St Helier (CI) 6)

C1252/213

98779	(JOK 557) Exported to Cyprus and re-registered TAJ 29 9/57
98950	(AEP 849) Re-registered 159 GMO 3/83; re-registered AEP 849 12/89 (in preservation)
99297	(KGT 75) Exported to Cyprus and re-registered TX 649 5/56
99380	(HFM 44) Exported to Ceylon 8/54 and re-registered CV 4703 10/54
99472	(HOD 49) Exported to Cyprus and re-registered TAU 934 6/59
99570	(?) Re-registered B-394 1952; re-registered 48366 in 1956. Later with KTEL Larissa City (O-GR) 9
100005	(DFR 705) Re-registered J 2833 3/56 (JP Birbeck {Blue Eagle Tours}, St Helier (CI) 7); reverted to DFR 705 6/64 (Showerings Ltd, Shepton Mallett (XSO))
100169	(EY 9025) Re-registered WFF 583 11/95; exported to Belgium and re-registered BCK 893 by 8/96. Chassis recorded as 111338 in Duple records, but Bedford records have 100169.
100257	(ATS 689) Re-registered 184 XUF 9/07 (in preservation); exported to Ireland and re-registered ZV 50203 2/08
100273	(FFU 594) Exported to Cyprus and re-registered TAK 306 11/57
100278	(?) Re-registered 67243 in 1956. Later with KTEL Kavala City (O-GR) 7
100347	(DFR 707) Re-registered J 2874 3/56 (JP Birbeck {Blue Eagle Tours}, St Helier (CI) 9); exported to Cyprus 1964
100360	(46-199) Re-registered 53218 in 1956
100429	(KGT 397) Bedford records have as intended for Royal Arsenal Co-operative Society, London SE18 (LN); Duple has Duval. Exported to Cyprus and re-registered TBX 935 2/63
100497	(TMY 940) Exported to Cyprus and re-registered TBD 848 7/60
100630	(A917) Chassis number also recorded as 112033, the latter not traced in Bedford records.
100887	(KGT 398) Bedford records have as intended for Royal Arsenal Co-operative Society, London SE18 (LN); Duple has Duval.
100937	(TMY 716) Duple records have as intended for W King & Sons Ltd {Emerald Coaches}, London N1 (LN). Bedford records have Dartmouth
100969	(DFR 708) Re-registered J 2773 3/56 (JP Birbeck {Blue Eagle Tours}, St Helier (CI) 10); exported to Cyprus 1964
101170	(HI-744) Not traced in Bedford records. Linjat not confirmed as original operator
101241	(ERX 534) Exported to Ceylon and re-registered CV 4671 10/54
101361	(LPU 621) Exported to Cyprus and re-registered TAD 344 3/57
101414	(CMS 47) Chassis also recorded as 101314; Bedford records have 101414
101421	(DRG 411) Chassis also recorded as 101321; Bedford records have 101421
101953	(LPU 622) Exported to Cyprus and re-registered TAD 346 3/57
101966	(JEL 276) Perkins P6 oil engine fitted 11/52; reverted to Bedford petrol engine 1957/58
102058	(EL-15-32) Rebodied Martins & Caetano B27D and renumbered 35 1/65
102204	(LKM 55) Exported to Cyprus and re-registered TAM 912 3/58
102520	(JNY 200) Bedford records have as intended for Thomas Bros, Port Talbot (GG); actually licensed to their Afan Transport subsidiary.
102572	(ETH 888) Originally allocated registration DBX 936, but seemingly not operated as such
102596	(CRN 91) Has also been recorded as CRN 96 in error. To Cyprus and re-registered TY 419 6/56
102736	(ABR 587) Exported to Cyprus and re-registered TAH 824 9/57
102775	(PV 9316) A publicity photograph shows this vehicle carrying registration PV 9136, believed to be incorrect.
103247	(SJ 1263) Body has been claimed both as SMT (too late) & Duple (not traced in records) !
103351	(CN 811) Re-registered CV 1106 1/52
103370	(UMP 95) Bedford records have as intended for Barber {Rose}, London N7 (LN), an operator within the same Group as Garner.
103401	(HBY 163) Exported to Cyprus and re-registered TV 210 12/55
103755	(KGT 77) Not traced in Bedford records; Motor Taxation records have as OB 103755
103848	(EJB 234) Exported to Cyprus and re-registered TAH 666 8/57. Motor Taxation records have 103848 as EJB 232; the version shown here is from Bedford records
103971	(KRR 107) Not traced in Bedford records; photograph confirms as OB and chassis number is a good chronological fit
103976	(DHS 939) Exported to Cyprus and re-registered TAN 691 4/58
104011	(HAA 874) Exported to Belgium after 1996 (for preservation)
104109	(JEL 578) Perkins P6 oil engine fitted 7/52; reverted to Bedford petrol engine 1957/58
104191	(JEL 277) Perkins P6 oil engine fitted 11/52; reverted to Bedford petrol engine 1957/58
104453	(VML 937) Exported to Cyprus and re-registered TBA 143 1/60
104494	(JBJ 868) Bedford records have as intended for BR Shreeve Ltd {Belle Coaches}, Lowestoft (EK); Duple has Moyse
104501	(JEL 278) Perkins P6 oil engine fitted 11/52
104543	(NJO 669) Bedford and Duple records have as intended for Wright, Bicester - probably a non-PSV operator -see also chassis 120024
104555	(FED 767) Re-registered PMN 150 2/53 (JN Clague {Broadway Coaches}, Douglas (IM));

C1252/214

	reverted to FED 767 1963 (JB Tatlock & Son Ltd, Manchester(LA))
105075	(FFU 961) Exported to Cyprus and re-registered TAM 643 2/58
105087	(CBV 353) Bedford and Duple records have as intended for J Wearden & Sons Ltd, Blackburn (LA)
105722	(JEL 579) Perkins P6 oil engine fitted 6/52; reverted to Bedford petrol engine 1957/58
105880	(?) Not traced in Bedford records; possibly an error - also recorded as KLB 104 (which is 98650)
105905	(JEL 580) Perkins P6 oil engine fitted 3/52; reverted to Bedford petrol engine 1957/58
105959	(LHY 919) Exported to Cyprus and re-registered TAV 694 7/59
105979	(JEL 581) Perkins P6 oil engine fitted 3/52; reverted to Bedford petrol engine 1957/58
106266	(EJB 232) Exported to Cyprus and re-registered TAH 911 9/57
106343	(EJB 233) Exported to Cyprus and re-registered TAH 310 8/57
106507	(HOD 120) Exported to Cyprus and re-registered TBM 948 8/61
106512	(DDB 891) Chassis number also recorded as 106518 and 106587.
	Bedford and Duple records have 106512
106519	(KDV 675) Bedford records have as intended for Wallace Arnold Tours Ltd, Leeds (WR), Ruby's parent company; Duple has Ruby
106883	(FDM 569) Chassis also recorded as 106882; Bedford records have 106883
106965	(DFV 52) Bedford and Duple records have as intended for JR Freeman {B & B Luxury Coaches}, Bispham (LA)
107047	(HOD 121) Exported to Cyprus and re-registered TBJ 624 3/61
107056	(NPC 430) Exported to Cyprus and re-registered TAZ 827 12/59
107075	(HOD 122) Exported to Cyprus and re-registered TBJ 625 3/61
107692	(FWV 427) Ordered by L Alexander {Queen of the Road}, Devizes (WI), who sold out to Card
107705	(HOD 128) Exported to Cyprus and re-registered TBQ 163 12/61
107741	(LHY 923) Exported to Cyprus and re-registered TBB 596 3/60
107783	(LHY 922) Exported to Cyprus and re-registered TAV 348 7/59
108009	(MBH 88) Although the body cannot be traced in Duple records, Bedford and photographic records clearly confirm that it carried a Duple Vista body.
108018	(LKO 209) Exported to Cyprus and re-registered TBA 628 1/60
108095	(CRN 417) Chassis number also recorded as 108096. Bedford records have 108095
108209	(FAJ 872) Exported to Cyprus 1958
108388	(DTL 965) Bedford records have as intended for RH Barney & AA Allo {Pioneer Coaches}, St Helier, Jersey (CI)
108594	(4426) Re-registered AY 59 2/64 (WP Simon, Alderney (CI))
108787	(FFW 397) Bedford records have as intended for Lincolnshire RCC, Bracebridge Heath (KN)
108830	(HOD 53) Exported to Cyprus and re-registered TAV 154 6/59
108848	(KGY 200) Exported to Cyprus and re-registered TAM 430 2/58
108872	(HOD 54) Exported to Cyprus and re-registered TAV 155 6/59
108900	(KPT 472) Duple records have as intended for JS Mowbray {Diamond Bus Service}, South Moor (DM)
109133	(FFW 182) Exported to Cyprus and re-registered TAM 429 2/58
109216	(FAJ 874) Bedford and Duple records have as intended for RB Allenby {Allenby's Coaches}, Great Ayton (NR)
109262	(FFW 398) Bedford records have as intended for Lincolnshire RCC, Bracebridge Heath (KN). Exported to Cyprus and re-registered TAM 428 2/58
109362	(FFW 183) Exported to Cyprus and re-registered TAF 853 6/57
109708	(KTE 951) Re-registered MMN 166 4/50 (JT Tasker {Waverley Coaches}, Douglas (IM))
109726	(KAH 949) Re-registered J 469 6/57 (WL Jones {Len's Tours}, St Helier, Jersey (CI))
109758	(NBB 171) Chassis number also recorded as 109748. Bedford and Duple records have 109758
110238	(FFW 309) Exported to Cyprus and re-registered TAH 821 9/57
110936	(KNC 297) Exported to Cyprus and re-registered TY 249 6/56
110940	(FBL 677) Bedford records have as intended for Jones, Binfield, Berkshire, status unknown
110947	(BGV 782) Exported to Cyprus and re-registered TBF 2 9/60
110972	(GDL 153) Exported to Cyprus and re-registered TCE 134 10/63
111060	(GUS 494) Also reported as operating with SCWS Ltd {The Skye Transport Co} from Portree (IV)
111388	(SS 7245) Bedford records have as intended for J Davidson, Auchencairn (KK).
	Rebodied Duple C29F (127/9) 1954. Original body transferred to OWB KRF 115 1954
111666	(v1.599) Also recorded as chassis 11160; neither traced in Bedford records. Re-registered v4.901 at an unknown date, and EW.4659 1965. Martello not confirmed as original operator
111804	(LYA 231) Bedford records have as intended for Binding & Payne Ltd {Dorothy's Coaches}, Clevedon (SO), absorbed into WEMS; Duple has WEMS. Exported to Cyprus and re-registered TBZ 537 4/63
111950	(ONO 89) Rebuilt as open-sided (both sides) sea-front run-about by Lincolnshire RCC, Bracebridge Heath (KN) 1959
112032	(ONO 88) Rebuilt as open-sided (both sides) sea-front run-about by Lincolnshire RCC, Bracebridge Heath (KN) 1959
112387	(HUY 97) Exported to Cyprus and re-registered TAH 973 9/57

C1252/215

112436	(KNC 385) Exported to Cyprus and re-registered TAH 825 9/57
112480	(FFW 184) Exported to Cyprus and re-registered TAM 501 2/58
112609	(KTJ 201) Exported to Cyprus and re-registered TAW 345 8/59
112640	(JXW 858) Not traced in Bedford records. Photographs show this to have had a Duple Almet body, almost certainly from the 526xx batch
112920	(HOD 130) Exported to Cyprus c12/60
112978	(HOD 131) Exported to Cyprus and re-registered TBJ 622 3/61
113025	(KJJ 516) Exported to Cyprus and re-registered TAM 391 1/58
113060	(KUR 510) Re-registered J 6013 2/52 (AA Allo {Pioneer Coaches, St Helier, Jersey (CI))
113098	(UMP 699) Bedford and Duple records have as intended for Evan Evans, London WC1 (LN)
113382	(HOD 129) Exported to Cyprus and re-registered TBJ 621 3/61
114186	(HOD 132) Exported to Cyprus and re-registered TBN 296 9/61
114210	(GDL 226) Exported to Cyprus and re-registered TCE 135 10/63
114283	(FNR 237) Exported to Cyprus and re-registered TBN 55 8/61
114304	(DTY 19) Bedford records have as intended for JM Smith, Amble(ND)
114365	(HOD 133) Exported to Cyprus and re-registered TBJ 489 3/61
114787	(HOD 134) Exported to Cyprus and re-registered TBP 892 10/61
115348	(MHT 672) ** Exported to Cyprus and re-registered TBJ 623 3/61
115748	(OPA 112) Bedford records have as intended for Oliver Taylor (Coaches) Ltd, Caterham (SR)
115829	(FFW 186) Exported to Cyprus and re-registered TAP 505 5/58
115837	(KND 569) Bedford records have as intended for Melba Motors Ltd, Reddish (CH)
115848	(FFW 187) Exported to Cyprus and re-registered TAP 507 5/58
115854	(JOP 626) Exported to Cyprus and re-registered TBM 434 7/61
116301	(HUY 655) Re-registered ASV 541 5/84; re-registered HUY 655 9/91 (in preservation)
116311	(LWJ 679) Re-registered J 766 5/56 (WL Jones {Len's Tours}, St Helier, Jersey (CI))
116464	(AGR 174) Exported to Cyprus and re-registered TU 664 11/55
116486	(HUY 856) Exported to Cyprus and re-registered TAH 972 9/57
116893	(HOD 70) Exported to Cyprus and re-registered TBJ 546 3/61
116943	(KAH 938) Exported to Cyprus and re-registered TY 946 7/56
117111	(LMN 361) Exported to Cyprus and re-registered TBN 86 8/61
117249	(EBW 124) Exported to Cyprus and re-registered TBZ 227 4/63
117267	(NBB 828) Exported to Cyprus and re-registered TBM 428 7/61
117289	(FFW 188) Exported to Cyprus and re-registered TAH 823 9/57
117299	(FFW 189) Exported to Cyprus and re-registered TAH 822 9/57
117518	(ONO 90) Exported to Cyprus and re-registered TBC 895 5/60
117547	(AEC 543) Originally allocated registration JM 9101, but seemingly not operated as such
117647	(ONO 91) Exported to Cyprus and re-registered TBC 896 5/60
117745	(KAH 939) Exported to Cyprus and re-registered TAA 524 9/56
117891	(unregd) Experimental vehicle - probably never registered. Given revised chassis no 49/4
118103	(HOD 72) Exported to Cyprus and re-registered TBB 749 3/60
118161	(LYB 125) Re-registered LWT 825 6/52 (A Hymas, Burton Leonard (WR))
118173	(MHU 416) Exported to Cyprus and re-registered TBH 204 1/61
118375	(KUP 240) Exported to Cyprus and re-registered TAW 471 8/59
118420	(UMY 170) Bedford records have as intended for AC Susans {Fountain Luxury Coaches}, Twickenham (MX); Duple has Proctor
118697	(JWR 415) Chassis number also recorded as 118699. Bedford and Duple records have 118697. Exported to Cyprus and re-registered TAB 66 10/56
118733	(JTX 220) Complete vehicle had been delivered 11/49, but the vehicle was not registered until 1950
118778	(GBE 167) Exported to Cyprus and re-registered TBA 146 1/60
119033	(?) Re-registered 76289 in 1956. Later with KTEL Lakonia (O-GR)
119041	(KYH 22) Exported to Cyprus and re-registered TAM 390 2/58
119089	(60-155) Re-registered 51122 in 1956. Later with Grillias (KTEL Arta) (O-GR)
119301	(?) Re-registered 76320 in 1956. Later with KTEL Lakonia (O-GR)
119419	(NTN 841) Exported to Cyprus and re-registered TBK 184 4/61
119658	(VR 8009) Re-registered AN 98434 4/71.
119894	(D-17003) Re-registered NB-27-26 at an unknown date
119945	(HRK 76) Exported to Cyprus and re-registered TBB 52 2/60
119969	(GBE 478) Exported to Gold Coast 11/57
120006	(?) Re-registered NB-57-60 at an unknown date. Not traced in Bedford records
120015	(?) Re-registered NB-38-44 at an unknown date
120024	(VML 334) Bedford records have as intended for A Hudson Ltd, Bicester (OX), but there is no record of the vehicle running with Hudson; Duple has Wright - not an identified PSV operator, and therefore assumed to be a non-PSV operator

120034	(EF 9219) Bedford records have as intended for C McCune {McCune's Luxury Coaches}, Stockton-on-Tees (NR)
120202	(HOD 76) Re-registered MSJ 606 5/98 (in preservation); exported to Ireland and re-registered ZV 3839 5/98 ; re-registered MSJ 606 by 5/03
120250	(60-783) Re-registered 45868 in 1956. Later with KTEL Evrytania (O-GR) 17. Chassis number recorded as 120260; Bedford records have 120250
120282	(?) Re-registered 20966 in 1956. Later with KTEL Attica (O-GR) 16
120291	(HOD 77) Exported to Cyprus and re-registered TBC 542 5/60
120519	(GZ-48317) Also recorded as NB-08-69 with Hoogeveen C34F body, unknown operator
120570	(UMY 560) Bedford records have as intended for Berney & Anthony, Edgware (MX); Duple has Gainsborough. Exported to Cyprus and re-registered TAL 138 12/57
120668	(HOD 80) Exported to Cyprus 9/62
120739	(JTX 358) Complete vehicle had been delivered 12/49, but the vehicle was not registered until 1950
120771	(GBE 477) Exported to Cyprus and re-registered TAM 499 2/58
120819	(D-17006) Re-registered NB-98-21 at an unknown date
120828	(HOD 78) Exported to Cyprus 1962
120935	(MHU 915) Ordered by SA & WF Ball {Dundry Pioneer}, Dundry (SO) before Bristol Tramways purchased that operation
121114	(HOD 79) Exported to Cyprus 9/62
121146	(DHJ 625) Exported to Cyprus and re-registered TBC 472 4/60
121153	(SS 7376) Re-registered 1949 MN 6/86 (Tours (Isle of Man) Ltd, Douglas (IM)); re-registered KSU 381 6/88; re-registered SS 7376 11/05 (in preservation)
121202	(60-136) Re-registered 45689 in 1956, Later with Prentzas (KTEL Fthiotida) (O-GR) 47. Bedford records show this chassis destined for Helsinki (O-DK)
121250	(61-117) Re-registered T-995 1952 and 75960 in 1956. Later with KTEL Argolida (O-GR) 57
121652	(?) Re-registered NB-37-85 at an unknown date
121739	(B-24997) Re-registered NB-31-95 at an unknown date
121781	(GHR 206) Exported to Cyprus and re-registered TBB 16 2/60
121829	(?) Re-registered 56063 in 1956. Later with KTEL Thessaloniki (O-GR)
121854	(P-40910) Re-registered NB-26-96 at an unknown date
121919	(?) Re-registered NB-98-74 at an unknown date
121948	(?) Re-registered NB-63-31 at an unknown date
122188	(GX-17798) Re-registered NB-58-77 at an unknown date
122218	(MHU 996) Exported to Cyprus and re-registered TBY 51 2/63
122230	(MHU 944) Exported to Cyprus and re-registered TBH 276 1/61
122313	(E-18804) Re-registered NB-57-22 at an unknown date
122359	(FUJ 500) Rebodied Duple C29F (44496) ex OB CRD 979 with RB Talbott {Barry's Coaches}, Moreton-in-Marsh (GL) c1963
122479	(GX-17796) Re-registered NB-59-33 at an unknown date
122501	(KGU 563) Not traced in Bedford records. Full front requires confirmation
122726	(E-48066) Re-registered NB-37-46 at an unknown date
122750	(G-29577) Re-registered NB-69-89 at an unknown date
122815	(?) Re-registered NB-51-37 at an unknown date
122897	(NPJ 590) Exported to Cyprus and re-registered TAB 49 10/56
122904	(P-47838) Re-registered NB-69-28 at an unknown date
122911	(FUT 58) There are two bodies numbered 46605 in Duple records! - see also OML 543
123016	(E-48065) Re-registered NB-37-45 at an unknown date
123036	(UMY 704) Chassis number also recorded as 123032. Bedford and Duple records have 123036
123083	(H-63994) Re-registered NB-30-37 at an unknown date
123090	(?) Re-registered NB-38-18 at an unknown date
123107	(MKK 40) Exported to Cyprus and re-registered TAM 870 3/58
123166	(MHU 52) Perkins P6 oil engine fitted 12/57
123173	(?) Re-registered NB-63-69 at an unknown date
123180	(P-16510) Re-registered NB-92-00 at an unknown date
123381	(HX-42162) Re-registered NB-51-68 at an unknown date
123384	(M-1800) Re-registered NB-29-21 at an unknown date
123442	(?) Re-registered 67395 in 1956. Later with KTEL Kavala (O-GR)
123449	(?) Re-registered 56063 in 1956. Later with KTEL Thessaloniki (O-GR). Chassis number recorded as 123349; Bedford records have 123449
123456	(LNK 510) Exported to Cyprus and re-registered TBB 15 2/60
123470	(?) Re-registered 67238 in 1956. Later with KTEL Kavala City (O-GR) 5
123472	(?) Re-registered 55954 in 1956, Later with KTEL Kilkis (O-GR) 54
123524	(HTM 20) Re-registered BVH 319A 7/82; re-registered 1949 MN 7/87 (Tours (Isle of Man) Ltd, Douglas (IM))

C1252/217

123531	(?) Re-registered 67700 in 1956. Later with KTEL Kavala (O-GR). Chassis number recorded as 125531; Bedford records have 123531
123538	(?) Re-registered 55612 in 1956. Later with KTEL Pella (O-GR) 12
123545	(?) Re-registered 53766 in 1956. Later with KTEL Kastoria (O-GR) 66
123553	(53-639) Re-registered 67511 in 1956. Later with KTEL Kavala (O-GR)
123561	(G-53909) Re-registered NB-59-65 at an unknown date
123656	(MLA 240) Fitted out as a mobile cinema
123662	(SW 8039) Chassis also recorded as 123682; Bedford records have 123662
123702	(MHU 53) Exported to Cyprus and re-registered TAB 489 10/56
123938	(JXX 468) Not traced in Bedford records; chassis number from Motor Taxation records
123999	(?) Venture Transport was also a PSV operator
124048	(?) Re-registered 67325 in 1956. Later with KTEL Kavala (O-GR)
124060	(?) Re-registered 53272 in 1956, Later with KTEL Kozani (O-GR) 72
124083	(KOC 923) Bedford records have as intended for JH & IV McLaughlin {Stockland Garage}, Birmingham (WK), Burley's parent company; Duple has Burley
124090	(?) Re-registered 32992 in 1956. Later with Paraschos (KTEL Lesvos) (O-GR)
124147	(60-032) Re-registered V-611 1952 and 46016 in 1956. Later with Rellos-Boviatsis (KTEL Fokida) (O-GR) 6
124183	(GX-17799) Re-registered NB-59-44 at an unknown date
124328	(LTC 855) Exported to Cyprus and re-registered TAN 690 4/58
124334	(?) Re-registered 51566 in 1956.Later with KTEL Thesprotia (O-GR)
124356	(?) Re-registered 31417 in 1956. Later with KTEL Theba (O-GR) 17
124367	(MHU 54) Perkins P6 oil engine fitted 4/58
124588	(EVH 283) Re-registered VMN 844 3/57 (R & JD Scott {R Scott & Son}, Douglas (IM))
124790	(LTA 911) Exported to Cyprus 1962
124804	(?) Probably the OB registered KAA 201 with OTC, Nairobi (O-EAK)
124945	(?) Re-registered 47786 in 1956. Later with KTEL Trikala (O-GR)
124956	(65-350) Re-registered Kp-765 1952 and 80136 in 1956. Later with KTEL Herakleion (O-GR) 35
124979	(61-811) Re-registered Kp-842 1952 and 80179 in 1956. Later with KTEL Herakleion (O-GR) 74
124990	(KOH 77) Bedford records have as intended for Supreme, Coleshill, Warwickshire, status unknown. Forward control conversion, but with half cab body
124995	(HDA 727) The body is not definitively confirmed as AL1. Initially used by Mulliner for publicity purposes as C20F; then delivered to Worthington Motor Tours Ltd, Birmingham (WK) but not used.
125393	(?) Re-registered NB-51-55 at an unknown date
125486	(GCA 388) Exported to Cyprus and re-registered TBN 825 10/61
125495	(60-995) Re-registered 70381 in 1956. Later with KTEL Achaia (O-GR) 88
125526	(62-378) Re-registered Kp-782 1952 and 80144 in 1956. Later with KTEL Herakleion (O-GR) 40
125570	(?) Re-registered 80231 in 1956. Later with KTEL Herakleion City (O-GR)
125586	(60-776) Re-registered A-5775 1952 and 30069 in 1956. Later with KTEL Korinthia (O-GR) 69
125617	(68-833) Re-registered A-4749 1952 and 30094 in 1956. Later with KTEL Korinthia (O-GR) 94
125621	(LFM 389) Exported to Cyprus and re-registered TAK 305 11/57
125659	(60-941) Re-registered 48386 in 1956. Later with KTEL Larissa (O-GR)
125711	(?) Re-registered NB-29-36 at an unknown date
125752	(H-53179) Re-registered NB-38-17 at an unknown date
125767	(P-43642) Re-registered NB-58-44 at an unknown date
125782	(CCB 186) Bedford and Duple records have as intended for Ribblesdale; has also been recorded as new to E & JC Alderson, Settle (WR)
125792	(KUP 711) Rebuilt with Ford ET style bonnet at an unknown date
126041	(KAH 946) Re-registered GCV 623 7/56 (WH Hawkey, Newquay (CO))
126200	(MHU 55) Perkins P6 oil engine fitted 3/58
126209	(LC-16-13) Rebodied UTIC (Porto) DP27D (800/1) and renumbered 23 7/69
126227	(HOD 81) Exported to Cyprus 9/62
126284	(LC-16-14) Rebodied Martins & Caetano DP27D (again) 4/62
126475	(HOD 82) Exported to Cyprus and re-registered TAR 2xx 9/58
126543	(D-6820) Re-registered NB-25-42 at an unknown date
126559	(B-29022) Re-registered NB-37-08 at an unknown date
126578	(EY 9392) Re-registered WFF 582 11/95; exported to Belgium and re-registered 5695 P by 8/98
126649	(?) Re-registered NB-52-88 at an unknown date
126668	(KUO 926) Exported to Cyprus 9/62
126731	(N-45396) Re-registered NB-48-47 at an unknown date
126753	(?) Re-registered NB-47-91 at an unknown date
126822	(H-81557) Re-registered BN-46-84 at an unknown date
127117	(KXW 646) Mulliner records have chassis number as 127119; Bedford has 127117
127229	(LAL 235) Exported to Cyprus 1963

127269	(GHR 553) Exported to Cyprus and re-registered TBB 18 2/60
127275	(LA-16-30) Rebuilt DP28D with Soares Oliveira, Baião (O-P) 16 8/54 and rebodied Martins & Caetano DP28D and renumbered 30 4/63
127286	(GCY 412) Exported to Cyprus and re-registered TV 261 1/56
127305	(MHU 56) Exported to Cyprus and re-registered TAB 493 10/56
127726	(LTA 747) Exported to Cyprus 1962
127745	(LTA 748) Exported to Cyprus 1962
127801	(D-17007 ?) Re-registered NB-27-32 at an unknown date
127807	(?) This was probably KYF 696 with Vincent body
127928	(MHU 57) Perkins P6 oil engine fitted 3/58
128167	(E-48067) Re-registered NB-37-47 at an unknown date
128190	(HZ-16296) Re-registered NB-94-86 at an unknown date
128412	(GBE 974) Exported to Cyprus and re-registered TAM 542 2/58
128470	(FBU 915) Bedford records have as intended for Shearing's Tours Ltd, Oldham (LA): Duple has Hilditch
128637	(EFR 32) Bedford and Duple records have as intended for JR Freeman {B & B Luxury Coaches}, Bispham (LA)
128705	(VME 227) Bedford records have as intended for Fox & Hart Ltd {Hounslow Star Coaches}, Hounslow (MX); Duple has Garner
128710	(MHW 936) Exported to Cyprus and re-registered TBJ 620 3/61
128735	(KFJ 695) Duple records have as intended for Warne (dealer), Exeter; Bedford records have Way
129075	(DTY 810) Exported to Cyprus and re-registered TP 774 5/55
129080	(D-12496 ?) Re-registered NB-27-33 at an unknown date
129193	(DTY 811) Exported to Cyprus and re-registered TBJ 548 3/61
129370	(FBU 927) Bedford records have as intended for Ralph Renton Ltd, Hollinwood (LA), but seemingly operated by associate Dyson; Duple has Dyson
129422	(AHC 222) Exported to Cyprus and re-registered TCD 682 9/63
129451	(UMY 448) Bedford records have as intended for Houchin, London WC2, status unknown; Duple has Charing Cross Motors, London WC1 I(LN). Exported to Cyprus and re-registered TBA 142 1/60
129462	(LE-16-31) Chassis number also recorded as 129402; Bedford records have 129462
129532	(DJR 344) Mulliner records have as intended for "Brewer" - no details known; Bedford records have Robson
129796	(JWT 703) Re-registered PMN 379 5/53 (E Bradshaw & Son Ltd {West End Garage}, Ramsey (IM))
129978	(KXY 638) Bedford and Duple records have as intended for Empress Motors Ltd, London E2 (LN)
130010	(HOT 759) Re-registered TMN 586 5/55 (JN Clague {Broadway Coaches}, Douglas (IM)); re-registered UDO 927 7/62 (D & AAP Elsey, Gosberton (LI))
130175	(FDR 244) Exported to Cyprus c1955
130180	(?) Chassis number recorded as 1310180; assumed to be 130180 which Bedfords records confirm went to Belgium
130194	(SS 7486) Ford 4-cylinder oil engine fitted in 1952
130265	(LTD 981) Duple records have as intended for JF Waterhouse, Hutton (LA). Bedford records have D Walley, Feniscowles (LA)
130284	(JAB 214) Exported to Cyprus and re-registered TAH 974 9/57
130666	(ACC 712) Exported to Ireland and re-registered 419 JZD 1978 (Lavery, Dublin (EI))
130681	(DTY 995) Exported to Cyprus and re-registered TP 992 6/55
130805	(LYC 731) Exported to Ireland and re-registered ZV 1460 3/95 (Ryan, Maycullan); returned to UK and re-registered LYC 731 1/04
130896	(CCB 298) Owned by Brockholes Motor Co, Huddersfield (XWY), but operated by Brook
130966	(EF 9296) Exported to Cyprus c1958
131045	(KBJ 721) Bedford records have as intended for BR Shreeve Ltd {Belle Coaches}, Lowestoft (EK); Duple has Moyse
131270	(?) Not traced in Bedford records. Re-registered DS.5335 1965. Mount Cook not confirmed as original operator
131392	(ACC 629) Re-registered J 3617 5/55 (UV Noel {Waverley Tours}, St Martin, Jersey (CI)); reverted to ACC 629 5/75 (J & JM Turnbull {Blue Band Motors}, Lockerbie (DF)); re-registered TRN 618A 2/86 (P & M Bibby & M Stephenson, Ingleton (NR)); re-registered ACC 629 (same operator) 7/89
131407	(MWB 497) Exported to Cyprus and re-registered TBA 145 1/60
131469	(JAB 213) Exported to Cyprus and re-registered TAH 975 9/57
131526	(KEL 94) Registration taken by KEL 95 in preservation
131602	(DJA 971) Bedford records have as intended for Green, Hazel Grove, Cheshire, status unknown; Duple has Great Moor
132120	(JWW 933) Mulliner records have chassis number as 132130; Bedford and Motor Taxation records have 132120
132238	(MHU 58) Exported to Cyprus and re-registered TAB 470 10/56

C1252/219

132253	(JWU 307) Re-registered FSV 424 by 6/90 (in preservation) and re-registered J 9151 12/94 (Classic Coach Co Ltd, St Saviour, Jersey (CI)); re-registered JWU 307 at unknown date (in preservation)
132303	(JUE 860) Re-registered 72103 9/12 in Guernsey
132312	(MHU 59) Perkins P6 oil engine fitted 12/57
132384	(GBE 975) Exported to Cyprus and re-registered TAM 392 2/58
132625	(GBE 976) Exported to Cyprus and re-registered TBB 829 2/60
132663	(GBE 977) Exported to Cyprus and re-registered TAH 819 9/57
132670	(LTA 914) Exported to Cyprus and re-registered TBB 829 3/60
132680	(GBE 978) Exported to Cyprus and re-registered TAK 303 11/57
132694	(LNN 147) Chassis number also recorded as 132692. Bedford and Duple records have 132694
132709	(EFR 185) Bedford and Duple records have as intended for JR Freeman {B & B Luxury Coaches}, Bispham (LA)
132759	(FDR 295) Exported to Cyprus and re-registered TBB 17 2/60
132797	(MRL 70) Re-registered J 18515 8/56 (H Swanson {Redline Tours}, St Helier, Jersey (CI) 17)
132928	(HJW 128) Actually owned by Price, Bilston (ST) but operated by Cox
132958	(LTA 913) Exported to Cyprus 1962
133073	(P.424) Re-registered EJ.1424 1965
133074	(P.607) Re-registered V2.264 at an unknown date; re-registered EW.4658 1965
133075	(P1.179) Re-registered EW.9199 1965
133077	(P.357) Re-registered EK.6793 1965
133079	(P.568) Re-registered V1.841 at an unknown date; re-registered EH.9857 1965
133082	(P.396) Re-registered P1.674 at an unknown date; re-registered EW.9226 1965
133083	(P.407) Re-registered P1.673 at an unknown date
133084	(P.582) Re-registered V2.381 at an unknown date
133238	(MHU 60) Exported to Cyprus and re-registered TAB 455 10/56
133837	(VME 161) Bedford records have as intended for Garner's Coaches Ltd, London W5 (LN): Duple has Fox & Hart
133840	(LTA 922) Exported to Cyprus 1962
133924	(LAD 192) Chassis had been delivered 1950; stored unbodied by operator until 1951
133951	(LTA 919) Exported to Cyprus and re-registered TBB 830 3/60
133992	(LTA 920) Exported to Cyprus and re-registered TBC 543 5/60
134013	(MMN 18) Re-registered DNP 212B 1964 (Foxall (Dealer), Stourbridge)
134040	(?) Possibly registered AFL (204 or 302 or 304 ?)
134426	(LTA 921) Exported to Cyprus 1962
134738	(EFR 226) Bedford records have as intended for F Standerwick, Blackpool (LA); Duple has Whiteside
134786	(LTA 926) Exported to Cyprus 1962
135055	(61-522) Re-registered 71241 in 1956. Later with KTEL Heleia (O-GR)
135113	(62-574) Re-registered A-7450 1952 and 33060 in 1956. Later with Kostopoulos (KTEL Mytilene City) (O-GR)
135146	(?) Re-registered 57735 in 1956. Later with KTEL Thessaloniki (O-GR)
135221	(?) Taylor was also a PSV operator
135229	(70-200) Re-registered A-5810 1952 and 30121 in 1956. Later with KTEL Korinthia (O-GR) 121
135254	(LTA 752) Rebuilt as open-sided sea-front runabout by Lincolnshire RCC, Bracebridge Heath (KN) 1960
135300	(NAE 71) Exported to Cyprus and re-registered TBH 205 1/61
135325	(NUB 175) Bedford records have as intended for James A Hudson Ltd, Leeds (WR); Duple has Austin
135397	(LTA 753) Exported to Cyprus 1962
135705	(EHJ 300) Exported to Cyprus and re-registered TBX 478 1/63
135711	(LTA 754) Exported to Cyprus 1962
135722	(DCK 410) Bedford records have as intended for D Whalley, Feniscowles (LA); Duple has Farnworth
135777	(MMN 57) Re-registered YTF 162J 1/73 (Walton-le-Dale Boys' Brigade (XLA)); exported to Netherlands re-registered BE-02-31 at unknown date
135881	(LTF 965) Mulliner records have as intended for "Woodcock" (= Woodcock's British Tours Ltd, Heskin (LA) ? - no record of the vehicle there); Bedford records have Morris
135961	(62-878) Re-registered A-7407 1952 and 32799 in 1956. Later with Velonidis (KTEL Lesvos) (O-GR) 16
136245	(JAB 661) Re-registered J 7247 5/97 (Tantivy Blue Coach Tours Ltd, St Helier, Jersey (CI))
136325	(GAJ 259) Bedford records have as intended for Hutchinson, Helmsley, North Riding, status unknown; Duple has Wilson
136343	(68-624) Re-registered O-2222 1952 and 56211 in 1956. Later with KTEL Serres (O-GR) 93
136582	(OPC 286) Re-registered J 17661 11/55 (J Jones {Maple Leaf Tours}, St Helier, Jersey (CI))
136661	(PVX 16) Exported to Cyprus by 3/69
136693	(63-033) Re-registered A-7712 1952 and 32331 in 1956. Later with Athanassiou (KTEL Samos) (O-GR)
136887	(?) Re-registered 76519 in 1956. Later with KTEL Lakonia (O-GR)
136925	(LTA 758) Duple records have chassis number as 136926; Bedford records have 136925
137054	(RN 499) Duple body almost certainly one of 52585/6, 52626 - 29, 52675 - 88

137102	(LRO 296) Perkins P6 oil engine fitted at unknown date. Exported to Japan 1990
137293	(KEL 95) Re-registered WSL 115 1/01 (in preservation); re-registered KEL 94 5/07; exported to Ireland and re-registered ZV 9400 by 6/10
137484	(KXV 564) Not traced in Bedford records; Motor Taxation records have as OB 137484
137578	(KEL 657) Exported to Cyprus and re-registered TBD 935 7/60
137682	(CCB 528) Exported to Cyprus and re-registered TBB 14 2/60
137833	(HCJ 151) Bedford and Duple records have as intended for CT Sargeant, Kington (HR)
137886	(VMY 685) Baico chassis extension
137893	(KAH 948) Re-registered GCV 213 7/56 (WH Hawkey, Newquay (CO))
137922	(KXJ 287) Bedford records have as intended for Lancashire Motor Traders (Dealer), Manchester; Duple has Morecambe Motors
138180	(KXV 575) Not traced in Bedford records; Motor Taxation records have as OB 138180
138211	(KNY 759) Mulliner records have as intended for "Thomas Bros" - no details known. Bedford records have Long
138251	(NAE 72) Exported to Cyprus and re-registered TBH 277 1/61
138326	(DJD 217) Exported to Netherlands and re-registered BE-67-57 at unknown date (in preservation)
138381	(NUG 11) Bedford and Duple records have as intended for WA Tasker & Sons Ltd, Leeds (WR)
138477	(504 HTE) Seemingly operated unregistered until 2/59 when prepared for sale
138866	(GWN 359) Mulliner records have as intended for Morgan & Evans, Cwmllynfell (GG); Bedford records have Short
138870	(GDL 796) Exported to Cyprus and re-registered TCE 132 10/63
138882	(TMM 168) Bedford records have as intended for Barber {Rose}, London N7 (LN), an operator within the same Group as Garner; Duple has Garner.
138896	(MYA 234) Ordered by FS Boyce, Batcombe (SO) before selling out to Green
138941	(JAA 367) Body has also been claimed as Withnell, although this would seem unlikely. Chassis number is also given as 158941 - too high for an OB. Motor Taxtion records suggest 138941, a good fit with DFR, but vehicle not traced in Bedford records
138977	(GDL 797) Exported to Cyprus and re-registered TCE 133 10/63
138984	(KYF 896) Chassis number also recorded as 138794. Bedford and Duple records have 138984
139011	(GDL 779) Exported to Cyprus and re-registered TCE 580 10/63
139062	(GDL 793) Exported to Cyprus 7/63
139082	(PVX 607) Exported to Cyprus and re-registered TBY 164 2/63
139328	(GDL 798) Exported to Cyprus 7/63
139390	(FRX 313) Exported to Cyprus and re-registered TAE 49 4/57
139566	(FJY 180) Exported to Cyprus and re-registered TY 469 7/56
140011	(URF 662) Duple records have chassis number as 144011; Bedford records have 140011
140156	(GFU 859) Exported to Cyprus and re-registered TAP 503 5/58
140724	(GFU 858) Exported to Cyprus and re-registered TAM 503 2/58
140822	(FRX 314) Exported to Cyprus and re-registered TAH 815 9/57
140935	(GFU 860) Exported to Cyprus and re-registered TAP 504 5/58
140985	(LSM 335) Duple records have as intended J McGregor Ltd {Brown's Motors & Coaches}, Ambleside (WT); Bedford records have Rae. Understood to have been cancelled by Brown
141231	(MMN 343) Delivered as MMN 305, but seemingly not operated as such. Exported to Ireland re-registered EZE 692 10/69 (Lavery, Dublin (EI))
141456	(VMK 20) Duple records have as intended for Rayner's Coachways Ltd, Ashford (MX); Bedford has Beach
141468	(JAA 485) Re-registered UMN 794 4/56 (Ranson's Happyways Tours Ltd, Douglas (IM))
141671	(GAJ 588) Exported to Cyprus and re-registered TBH 275 1/61
141923	(JWY 669) Bedford and Duple records have as intended for Berkeley, Lanark - status unknown
142006	(VMK 155) Bedford records have as intended for Barber {Rose}, London N7 (LN), an operator within the same Group as Fox & Hart; Duple has Fox & Hart
142021	(FRX 315) Exported to Cyprus and re-registered TAH 813 9/57
142146	(NHN 626) Exported to Cyprus and re-registered TBM 436 7/61
142179	(GFW 84) Exported to Cyprus and re-registered TAP 509 5/58
142192	(GFW 82) Exported to Cyprus and re-registered TAM 502 2/58
142197	(GNT 806) Exported to Cyprus and re-registered TBM 435 7/61
142371	(RHK 843) Re-registered 1950 MN 1987 (Tours (Isle of Man) Ltd, Douglas (IM))
142429	(MTV 31) Duple records have as intended for A Skill {Skill's Coaches}, Nottingham (NG); Bedford has Basford Transport
142579	(EFR 561) Bedford records have as intended for WB Brunskill, Accrington (LA); Duple has Lansdowne
142604	(VMK 156) Bedford records have as intended for Barber {Rose}, London N7 (LN), an operator within the same Group as Garner; Duple has Garner
142663	(LLW 31) Duple records have as intended for Carshalton & Wallington Coaches Ltd, Wallington (SR); Bedford has Essex County

C1252/221

142680	(EBA 857) Exported to Cyprus and re-registered TAM 922 3/58
142692	(MTA 554) Exported to Cyprus and re-registered TBW 428 10/61
142936	(KEL 679) Re-registered J 5149 2/96 (Classic Coach Co Ltd, St Saviour, Jersey (CI)); reverted to KEL 679 by5/02 (in preservation)
143017	(LUR 490) Exported to Cyprus and re-registered TBN 270 9/61
143023	(NHN 733) Exported to Cyprus 11/63
143115	(LLW 133) Allegedly intended for Cosy Coaches Ltd, Staines (MX) but both Bedford and Duple records have N & S as the customer
143199	(OBB 600) Probably FC30F?
143226	(EX 6830) Bedford records have as intended for A & AE Blackbourn {Grimsby Tours}, Grimsby (LI); Duple has Norfolk Motor Services
143319	(HGG 935) Baico chassis extension
143708	(HGG 934) Baico chassis extension
143804	(LNG 323) Bedford and Duple records have as intended for Pye's Garage (Blakeney) Ltd (NK)
143842	(VMK 721) Bedford records have as intended for Clayton, London N9, status unknown; Duple has Logan
143876	(LUC 645) Bedford records have as intended for Brighton Motors, Brighton, status unknown; Duple has Orange
143926	(FDP 299) Ordered by Donovan & Crane Ltd {D & C}, Yattendon (BE) and delivered as FRX 510; re-registered before entering service with Smith
144000	(MPT 409) Bedford records have as intended for JH Fursland & Co Ltd {Pride of Bridgwater}, Bridgwater (SO); Duple has Osmond's Tours & Engineering Ltd, Curry Rivel (SO)
144356	(MKP 557) Bedford records have as intended for Boakes, Sevenoaks, status unknown; Duple has Camden
144460	(GUJ 289) Bedford records have as intended for Jones Coachways Ltd, Market Drayton (SH); Duple has Roberts
144552	(VE 8008) Re-registered LX 88.075 -/71, re-registered PZ 93325 6/99
144730	(LLX 425) Exported to Cyprus 1964
144742	(JKV 575) Bedford records have as intended for Arts Council, London SW1 (XLA); Duple has Midland Theatre Group, probably sponsored by the Arts Council
144850	(WMC 26 ?) Registration also recorded as WMC 76
144971	(GBL 200) Re-registered LJO 757 11/83 (in preservation)
144976	(GED 797) Bedford and Duple records have as intended for JP & M Bell, Warrington (CH); in fact it passed to Bell in 1951
145008	(HCJ 452) Delivered in 1950 but not used until 5/51
145064	(EFV 448) Bedford and Duple records have as intended for RT & B Bolton {Ribblesdale Coachways} Blackburn (LA)
145068	(ORB 767) Original operator might have been F Pyle (Pyle Bros), Buxton (DE) as shown in Bedford records, although Duple has Bull. The vehicle is known to have been with Pyle at some stage.
145488	(?) Re-registered NB-63-71 at an unknown date
145605	(KDD 989) Duple records have as intended for Mrs K Riddiford,Thornbury (GL)
145611	(VMK 161) Exported to Cyprus and re-registered TBF 86 9/60
145675	(?) Re-registered NB-40-13 at an unknown date
145684	(CEP 4) Duple records have as intended for M Peters, Llanarmon yn al (DH)
146075	(GUT 55) Publicised by Duple as the final Vista body to be built (- not in fact true!)
146102	(GKY 750) Fitted with bench seats
146179	(LUW 75) Re-registered J 3572 3/58 (W Le Marinel (Favourite Tours}, St Helier, Jersey (CI)); To Ireland and re-registered 6651 IR at an unknown date (Irish River Hotels)(registration needs confirmation)
146277	(GBU 393) Re-registered PRA 622 3/51 (R Warhurst, Chapel-en-le-Frith (DE))
146361	(MPT 410) Duple records have as intended for JH Fursland & Co Ltd {Pride of Bridgwater}, Bridgwater (SO)
146568	(?) Re-registered NB-01-39 at an unknown date
146655	(?1.126) Bedford records have as exported to Melbourne (O-AUS)
146932	(LCD 236) Re-registered J 8338 5/59 (W Lock {St Quen's Coaches}, St Quen, Jersey (CI))
147047	(KOV 827) Bedford records have as intended for JH & IV McLaughlin {Stockland Garage}, Birmingham (WK), Burley's parent company; Duple has Burley
147100	(LVO 85) Exported to Cyprus and re-registered TBA 144 1/60
147355	(MTA 917) Exported to Cyprus and re-registered TAZ 365 12/59
152481	(B-29024) Re-registered NB-37-10 at an unknown date
153641	(?) Re-registered NB-71-67 at an unknown date.
154310	(B-29023) Re-registered NB-37-09 at an unknown date
154403	(HX-45883) Re-registered PB-00-97 at an unknown date
154721	(?) Re-registered NB-71-66 at an unknown date

- ? (599 RN) Sold in Cyprus and re-registered TAJ 91 9/57
- ? (585 RN) Sold in Malta 8/54
- ? (IP 5589) Also recorded with Ryan B25F body
- ? (3453) Perkins P6 oil engine fitted at unknown date
- ? (31.824) Perkins P6 oil engine fitted at unknown date, possibly rear-engined!
- ? (45.157) Perkins P6 oil engine fitted at unknown date
- ? (45.158) Perkins P6 oil engine fitted at unknown date
- ? (45.159) Perkins P6 oil engine fitted at unknown date
- ? (45.160) Perkins P6 oil engine fitted at unknown date
- ? (45.161) Perkins P6 oil engine fitted at unknown date
- ? (45.071 ?) Re-registered 45735 with Metro Buses Pty Ltd, Perth, WA (O-AUS) by 1954
- ? (729144) Exhibited at 1the 950 Brussels show
- ? (A 7193) To Kenya Bus Services (Mombasa) Ltd (O-EAK) 44 with Perkins P6 oil engine 1/52
- ? (D 1512) Not confirmed as OB
- ? (DR1214) Re-registered DR2214 at an unknown date and UAN223 12/58
- ? (DR1240) Re-registered DR2215 at an unknown date and UAN222 12/58
- ? (GZ-60874) Re-registered NJ-41-61 at an unknown date
- ? (H 8156) With Kenya Bus Services (Mombasa) Ltd (O-EAK) 51 by 1/51
- ? (H 9926) Chevrolet oil engine fitted by 1952
- ? (HZ-85662) Re-registered PB-07-92 at an unknown date
- ? (J 1727) Also recorded with registration Z 61
- ? (KA 2102) Overseas Touring Company records note this as a "prototype"
- ? (KA 6953) Perkins P6 oil engine fitted and re-registered KBL 146 1952
- ? (KBB 665) Neither the registration nor the operator are confirmed as the original
- ? (KBC 426) Neither the registration nor the operator are confirmed as the original
- ? (KBD 299) Also given as Duple Vista
- ? (KBD 356) Also given as Duple Vista. Chevrolet oil engine fitted by 1952
- ? (KBD 357) Also given as Duple Vista. Perkins P6 oil engine fitted 1952
- ? (L 297) Not confirmed as OB
- ? (M-85614) Later with F Canals, Fornells de la Selva (O-E)
- ? (M-79787) Not confirmed as OB
- ? (M-79788) Not confirmed as OB
- ? (M-80877) Not confirmed as OB
- ? (M-80896) Not confirmed as OB
- ? (N-80613) Re-registered NB-67-66 at an unknown date
- ? (P.605) Chassis number recorded as NST10064, possibly a rebuild. Re-registered EI.2815 1965
- ? (P.624) Chassis number recorded as NST10065 (or NST/C10065), possibly a rebuild
- ? (S.794) Mount Cook not confirmed as original operator
- ? (V1.933) North Shore not confirmed as original operator
- ? (V3.718) Re-registered DY.1334 1965. Marlborough not confirmed as original operator
- ? (W 2491) Perkins P6 oil engine fitted by 1952
- ? (W 5073) May have been new to associated operator Green Line Ltd, unknown location (O-EAK)

C1252/223

SELF-BUILD BEDFORD OB

These were new vehicles constructed by operators or dealers to OB specification using primarily new Bedford components. It is just possible that several of the vehicles listed as rebuilds in C1251, on the assumption that they used wartime chassis, may also in fact have been new builds. Conversely it is just possible that a refurbished chassis might inadvertently be included in this list.

GH1	* FEA 50 Duple	55676	C29F	4/50	Hill's Tours Ltd, West Bromwich (ST)
10004	* JDD 37 Lee		C29F	4/49	WG & RA Miles {Miles Bros}, Guiting Power (GL)
SG1/48	* JOK 365 Mulliner	T343	DP27F	3/49	JH & IV McLaughlin {Stockland Garage}, Birmingham (WK)
SG2/50	* LOC 286 Plaxton	599	C29F	3/51	JH & IV McLaughlin {Stockland Garage}, Birmingham (WK)
H&S3024	* LDF 833 Duple	127/1	C29F	7/52	TEA Bowles {Bowles Coaches}, Ford (GL)
NC7128500	* LAH 555 Duple	56182	C29F	8/50	JC Brown {Norfolk Coachways}, Attleborough (NK)

Notes:
GH1   (FEA 50) Built by Hill; GH = George Hill
10004   (JDD 37) Built by Miles; chassis number allocated by Lee Motors in their rebuild series
SG1/48   (JOK 365) Built by Stockland; SG = Stockland Garage
SG2/50   (LOC 286) Built by Stockland; SG = Stockland Garage
H&S3024   (LDF 833) Built by Haines & Strange (Dealer), Cheltenham; 3024 was H&S telephone number
NC7128500 (LAH 555) Built by Brown; NC = Norfolk Coachways

C1252/224

BEDFORD OL

The K/M/O range had been launched in 1939 and, after suspension of production during the war years, reappeared late in 1945. OL models were of 4x2 configuration, with a wheelbase of 157ins. Production continued until 1953.

The chassis number series, engine and general mechanical specification were common to all models in the K/M/O range, including OBs. Chassis designations for post-war OLs included a third letter to indicate the load carrying capacity: A for 4 ton and B for 5 ton. The fourth character of the model designation referred to the ex-works body styling, C indicating that the vehicle left the factory as a chassis/cab, D that a drop-side body of Bedford's own manufacture was fitted and Z that no body was fitted (ie a chassis/scuttle).

(It should be noted that the pre-war OL models had only 3-letter designations, omitting the A or B weight designations; for those vehicles the 5-tonners were differentiated by a suffix of 40 eg OLC/40)

BEDFORD OLAC

40844	T 4980	?	B30D	4/47	HadjiPolykroniou, Lapithos (O-CY)
40992	TN 4983	?	B27D	4/47	HadjiYianni, Akaki (O-CY)
41023	T 4949	?	B30D	4/47	Zihni, Platanisso (O-CY)
41054	T 4977	?	B30D	4/47	Pieris, Kondemenos (O-CY)
41112	T 4936	?	B30D	3/47	Georgakis, Ayios Elias (O-CY)
41145	TN 5028	?	B30D	4/47	Ellinas, Nicosia (O-CY)
41535	T 5040	?	B28D	5/47	Kallis, Karavas (O-CY)
41564	T 4985	?	B30D	5/47	Vasiliades, Zoopiyi (O-CY)
41625	T 4912	?	B23D	3/47	Houssein, Malia (O-CY)
43910	T 5049	?	B27D	5/47	Pilavakis, Pedhoulas (O-CY)
43936	T 4994	?	B25D	4/47	Volos, Vouni (O-CY)
43965	T 5119	?	B28D	5/47	Hakki, Paphos (O-CY)
44009	TN 5373	?	B30D	6/47	Kouloundis, Limassol (O-CY)
44057	* T 4998	?	lorry	4/47	Original operator unknown (O-CY)
54301	TN 5955	?	B28D	9/47	Markides, Kato Lakatamia (O-CY)
56794	* T 6250	?	lorry	11/47	Original operator unknown (O-CY)
57883	T 6307	?	B28D	11/47	Taliotis, Tsadha (O-CY)
59414	T 6415	?	B30D	12/47	Moisi, Pretori (O-CY)
59438	T 6655	?	B28D	1/48	Kiazim, Mandria (O-CY)
59631	T 6351	?	B30D	11/47	Savvides, Pano Kividhes (O-CY)
59655	T 6736	?	B28D	1/48	Xenophontos, Skarinou (O-CY)
59728	TN 6478	?	B30D	12/47	Constandinou, Paleometokho (O-CY)
62045	T 6786	?	B30D	1/48	Hadjoullas, Milia (O-CY)
62121	* TN 6713	?	lorry	1/48	Original operator unknown (O-CY)
62142	T 6719	?	B28D	1/48	HadjiArgyrou, Dhrousha (O-CY)
62234	T 6757	?	B27D	1/48	Violaris, Asha (O-CY)
64575	* T 6937	?	lorry	3/48	Original operator unknown (O-CY)
83159	T 7926	?	B29D	10/48	E.Kyriakou, Kalavasos (O-CY)
83248	T 8065	?	B30D	11/48	Savva & Portokallides, Meniko (O-CY)
83494	T 8010	?	B27D	11/48	Kyriakou, Patriki (O-CY)
84166	* T 7896	?	lorry	10/48	Original operator unknown (O-CY)
83159	T 7926	?	B29D	10/48	E.Kyriakou, Kalavasos (O-CY)
83248	T 8065	?	B30D	11/48	Savva & Portokallides, Meniko (O-CY)
83494	T 8010	?	B27D	11/48	Kyriakou, Patriki (O-CY)
84166	* T 7896	?	lorry	10/48	Original operator unknown (O-CY)
97046	TN 9246	?	B30D	10/49	Kriftis, Peristerona (O-CY)
97055	T 9166	?	B28D	9/49	Elia, Ora (O-CY)
97337	TN 8855	?	B30D	6/49	Constandinou, Paleometokho (O-CY)
97423	T 8736	?	B30D	5/49	Ppalis, Kato Zodhia (O-CY)
97429	T 8732	?	B30D	5/49	Megalmos, Kokkinotrimithia (O-CY)
94034	T 8524	?	B29D	3/49	Georghiou, Nata (O-CY)
118859	* ?	?	B24-	-/--	Original owner unknown (O-GR)
121287	* 65-374	?	B24-	-/50	Original owner unknown (O-GR)
125753	TN 9632	?	B29D	2/50	Georghiou, Sha (O-CY)
129076	T-1068	Vatne	B5FV	-/51	A/S Søre Sunnmøre Billag, Volda (O-N)
133819	* T 9997	?	lorry	5/50	Original operator unknown (O-CY)
133904	* TN 9960	?	lorry	5/50	Original operator unknown (O-CY)
210973	* TB 429	?	lorry	6/51	Original operator unknown (O-CY)

C1252/225

245193 *	TD 370	?	lorry	8/52	Original operator unknown (O-CY)
260039 *	TF 178	?	B31D	5/53	Nea EM Lapithou, Lapithos (O-CY)
260460 *	TE 786	?	tipper	3/53	Original operator unknown (O-CY)
260461 *	TF 35	?	B30D	4/53	Fella, Sotira (O-CY)
262884 *	TF 364	?	B30D	6/53	Massou, Kalokhorio (O-CY)
?	* K-3000	?	B6FV	-/49	AS Lillesand Ruta, Lillesand (O-N)
?	* KBE 230	(locally-built)	B30-	-/51	Meralli Bus Services Ltd, Nairobi (O-EAK)
?	* KBF 554	(locally-built)	B30-	-/51	Meralli Bus Services Ltd, Nairobi (O-EAK)
?	* KBJ 266	(locally-built)	B30-	12/51	Meralli Bus Services Ltd, Nairobi (O-EAK)
?	* KBJ 961	(locally-built)	?	12/51	Meralli Bus Services Ltd, Nairobi (O-EAK)
?	* KBL 86	(locally-built)	B32-	-/51	Meralli Bus Services Ltd, Nairobi (O-EAK)

BEDFORD OLAZ

35883 *	BCW 814	?	lorry	-/46	Original operator unknown (GB)
88069	SB 7743	Binnie	C18F	1/50	Air Industrial Developments Ltd {Gold Line}, Dunoon (AL)
97293	SB 7744	Binnie	C18F	2/50	Air Industrial Developments Ltd {Gold Line}, Dunoon (AL)
98386	DST 158	?	C25F	3/49	D Noble & Sons, Muir of Ord (RY)
121379 *	ACC 883	Duple	? C--F	6/50	OR Williams & Son {Whiteways}, Waenfawr (CN)
129546	KXU 333	Allweather G4355	B24F	10/50	British Railways (XLN) S238W
130324	KXU 332	Allweather G4454	B24F	7/50	British Railways (XLN) S237W
133902	TA 366	?	B30D	9/50	Skarparis, Kokkinotrimithia (O-CY)
135474	TA 054	?	B28D	6/50	Kyriacou & Neofytou, Orounda (O-CY)
135753	TA 241	?	B28D	7/50	Kallis, Karavas (O-CY)
140613 *	TA 397	?	lorry	9/50	Original operator unknown (O-CY)
141363	TA 603	?	B31D	11/50	Christofi, Charalambous & Agathangelou, Morphou (O-CY)
147770	?	Duple 1029/3	C20F	-/51	Brook Electric Motors, Huddersfield (XWR)
149725	TA 819	?	B30D	12/50	Elia, Katokopia (O-CY)
154281	TA 959	?	B30D	2/51	Hassan, Epikho (O-CY)
154374	TA 943	?	B30D	2/51	Constandinou, Paleometokho (O-CY)
201078	TB 084	?	B30D	3/51	E Kyriakou, Limassol (O-CY)
201190	TB 235	?	B30D	4/51	SP Platanistasa, Platanistasa (O-CY)
205467	TB 337	?	B29D	5/51	Kallis, Karavas (O-CY)
205477	TB 237	?	B30D	4/51	HadjiYianni, Pano Dhikomo (O-CY)
208161	TB 581	?	B29D	7/51	Charalambous, Alona (O-CY)
208171	TB 598	?	B30D	7/51	Constandinou, Paleometokho (O-CY)
213599	TB 827	?	B28D	9/51	Mavrou, Kissonerga (O-CY)
213649	TB 892	?	B30D	9/51	Elia, Kedhares (O-CY)
214796	CV 354	?	-27-	12/51	Original operator unknown (O-CL)
214804	CV 566	?	-26-	1/52	Original operator unknown (O-CL)
219267	TC 122	?	B29D	11/51	HadjiGeorghiou, Avgorou (O-CY)
219656	TC 123	?	B29D	11/51	Agros Co-operative, Agros (O-CY)
220256	CV 581	?	-27-	1/52	Original operator unknown (O-CL)
221339	OHW 292	Mulliner	? B24F	1/52	Bristol Corporation (XGL) 861
222838	TC 215	?	B30D	12/51	Pyrou, Leonarisso (O-CY)
223636	TC 279	?	B30D	12/51	Kouloundis, Limassol (O-CY)
223654	TC 182	?	B30D	12/51	Prokopi, Ayios Epiktitos (O-CY)
224958	CV 1025	?	-37-	4/52	Chandra Tours Ltd, Kandy (O-CL)
225180	TC 371	?	B29D	1/52	Costa, Pano Dhikomo (O-CY)
225259	TC 358	?	B30D	1/52	Constandinou, Paleometokho (O-CY)
227067	CV 1349	?	-27-	7/52	SCBC, location unknown (O-CL)
229456	CV 1549	?	-29-	7/52	Kalyani, location unknown (O-CL)
231085	TC 688	?	B29D	4/52	Ellinas, Nicosia (O-CY)
231814	TC 644	?	B29D	3/52	Lymbouris, Kato Dhikomo (O-CY)
233071	CV 1350	?	-27-	7/52	SCBC, location unknown (O-CL)
233715	TD 159	?	B30D	6/52	Mavrommatis, Nicosia (O-CY)
233727	CV 1348	?	-27-	7/52	SCBC, location unknown (O-CL)
233901	TC 801	?	B30D	5/52	Petrides, Politiko (O-CY)
233965	TD 093	?	B29D	6/52	Kallis, Karavas (O-CY)
234416	CV 1559	?	-29-	7/52	KMDK Bus Co Ltd, Kurunegala (O-CL)
234492	WMX 161	Mulliner	? B30F	7/52	Middlesex County Council (XMX)

235707	CV 3053	?		-29-	7/53	Maturata, unknown location (O-CL)
236291	TD 328	?		B29D	7/52	Avraamides, Pakhna (O-CY)
236369	TD 146	?		B31D	6/52	E Kyriakou, Limassol (O-CY)
236645	TD 055	?		B30D	5/52	Panayi, Angastina (O-CY)
236797	CV 1829	?		-27-	10/52	WK, location unknown (O-CL)
236865	TD 092	?		B30D	6/52	Kitsis, Angastina (O-CY)
236943	RHN 107	Mulliner	?	C24F	-/51	Percival Bros (Coaches) Ltd, Richmond (NR)
237387	RHN 108	Mulliner	?	C24F	-/51	Percival Bros (Coaches) Ltd, Richmond (NR)
237540	TD 129	?		B30D	6/52	Constandinou, Yerakies (O-CY)
239302	TD 247	?		B30D	7/52	PapaNicolaou, Stroumbi (O-CY)
239938	TD 337	?		B29D	7/52	Stavrides, Koma tou Yialou (O-CY)
240499 *	MXV 578	Duple	1023/1	C25F	-/52	Lewis (Greenwich) Ltd, London SE18 (LN)
240729	CV 2138	?		-29-	12/52	Kalyani, location unknown (O-CL)
241185	HKY 892	Roe	GO3539	B--F	1/53	Bradford Corporation Social Services (XWR) 027
241847	TD 793	?		B30D	10/52	Karayiannis, Xylophagou (O-CY)
241892	TD 516	?		B30D	8/52	Houssein, Kridhia (O-CY)
243917	TD 914	?		B30D	11/52	Houssein, Epikho (O-CY)
243936	TD 674	?		B30D	9/52	Spyrou, Kyra (O-CY)
245059	KGB 261	Duple	1026/1	C25F	9/52	David MacBrayne Ltd, Glasgow (LK) 150
245063	KGB 262	Duple	1026/2	C25F	9/52	David MacBrayne Ltd, Glasgow (LK) 151
245073	KGB 263	Duple	1026/3	C25F	9/52	David MacBrayne Ltd, Glasgow (LK) 152
245139	KGB 264	Duple	1026/4	C25F	9/52	David MacBrayne Ltd, Glasgow (LK) 153
245143	KGB 265	Duple	1026/5	C25F	9/52	David MacBrayne Ltd, Glasgow (LK) 154
245153	KGB 266	Duple	1026/6	C25F	9/52	David MacBrayne Ltd, Glasgow (LK) 155
245219	KGB 269	Duple	1026/9	C25F	9/52	David MacBrayne Ltd, Glasgow (LK) 158
245223	KGB 267	Duple	1026/7	C25F	9/52	David MacBrayne Ltd, Glasgow (LK) 156
245650	TD 624	?		B30D	9/52	Thoma, Akaki (O-CY)
245664	TD 564	?		B30D	9/52	Diogenous, Kato Pyrgos (O-CY)
245753	KGD 901	Duple	1027/1	C20FM	-/52	David MacBrayne Ltd, Glasgow (LK) 160
245827	KGB 268	Duple	1026/8	C25F	9/52	David MacBrayne Ltd, Glasgow (LK) 157
246113	KGD 902	Duple	1027/2	C20FM	9/52	David MacBrayne Ltd, Glasgow (LK) 161
246143	KGB 270	Duple	1026/10	C25F	9/52	David MacBrayne Ltd, Glasgow (LK) 159
246187	KGD 907	Duple	1027/7	C20FM	10/52	David MacBrayne Ltd, Glasgow (LK) 166
246291	KGD 903	Duple	1027/3	C20FM	10/52	David MacBrayne Ltd, Glasgow (LK) 162
246335	KGD 906	Duple	1027/6	C20FM	-/52	David MacBrayne Ltd, Glasgow (LK) 165
246361	KGD 908	Duple	1027/8	C20FM	10/52	David MacBrayne Ltd, Glasgow (LK) 167
246581	KGD 909	Duple	1027/9	C20FM	10/52	David MacBrayne Ltd, Glasgow (LK) 168
246607	KGD 910	Duple	1028/3	C14FM	10/52	David MacBrayne Ltd, Glasgow (LK) 169
246647	KGE 243	Duple	1028/2	C14FM	10/52	David MacBrayne Ltd, Glasgow (LK) 171
246673	KGD 905	Duple	1027/5	C20FM	9/52	David MacBrayne Ltd, Glasgow (LK) 164
246714	KGE 242	Duple	1028/1	C14FM	10/52	David MacBrayne Ltd, Glasgow (LK) 170
246739	KGD 904	Duple	1027/4	C20FM	10/52	David MacBrayne Ltd, Glasgow (LK) 163
247236	TD 760	?		B30D		Christoforou, Ayios Ioannis Maloundas (O-CY)
247302	TE 77	?		B30D	12/52	Theochari, Milia (O-CY)
247933	TE 172	?		B31D	12/52	Strovolos Bus Co., Strovolos (O-CY)
248000	TE 116	?		B30D	12/52	SP Pelendriou, Pelendria (O-CY)
249492	TD 843	?		B30D	10/52	Costa, Philia (O-CY)
250469	TE 319	?		B30D	1/53	Solomou, Avlona (O-CY)
250539	TE 155	?		B30D	12/52	Kyriakou, Patriki (O-CY)
250580	TE 637	?		B29D	2/53	Kallis, Karavas (O-CY)
250609	TD 931	?		B30D	11/52	Hasikos, Kato Dhikomo (O-CY)
250650	TE 34	?		B30D	11/52	Georghiou, Palekythro (O-CY)
250679	TE 283	?		B30D	1/53	Channides, Kondea (O-CY)
253801	TE 328	?		B30D	1/53	HadjiKyriakou, Kythrea (O-CY)
253869	TE 585	?		B30D	2/53	Constandinou, Paleometokho (O-CY)
253937	TE 221	?		B30D	12/52	Aristidi, Kilani (O-CY)
254209	TE 624	?		B28D	2/53	Avraam, Pakhna (O-CY)
254345	TE 666	?		B30D	3/53	Ioannou, Phasoula (O-CY)
254481	TE 349	?		B30D	1/53	Eliades, Bellapais (O-CY)
254765	TE 267	?		B29D	1/53	Nea EM Lapithou, Lapithos (O-CY)
254833	TE 634	?		B30D	2/53	Kourkoutas, Rizokarpaso (O-CY)
254901	TE 278	?		B30D	1/53	Theocharides, Kaminaria (O-CY)
254969	TE 732	?		B30D	3/53	Varnava, Perakhorio (O-CY)
255273	TE 762	?		B29D	3/53	Kalavazides, Ayios Dhimitrios (O-CY)

C1252/227

256763	TE 828	?		B30D	3/53	Pitsillos, Mia Milia (O-CY)
257515	* TE 832	?		lorry	3/53	Original operator unknown (O-CY)
?	NPO 290	Reading		C--F	c2/52	Plant Protection Ltd, Fernhurst (XWS)
?	* WMC 27	Mulliner	?	B30F	-/51	Middlesex County Council (XMX)
?	* WMX 184	Mulliner	?	B30F	3/53	Middlesex County Council (XMX)
?	* CV 1402	?		-30-	7/52	PTCK, location unknown (O-CL)

BEDFORD OLBC

18668	* P.105	Eaddy & Taylor		B33F	2/47	W Lowett Ltd, location unknown (O-NZ)
31564	* P1.911	Steel Bros		B33F	-/47	Coburn's De Luxe Motors, Greymouth (O-NZ) 3
80224	* ?	Stevens & Sons		B33F	-/49	Midland, Christchurch (O-NZ) 71
96714	B-79584	Ayats	238	C22-	-/48	Miguel Marti, Sabadell (O-E)
99200	* ?	Midland		B32F	12/49	Midland, Christchurch (O-NZ) 75
106331	* ?	?		B24-	-/--	Original owner unknown (O-GR)
114303	* 57-058	Zacharpoulos		B28-	-/--	Original owner unknown (O-GR)
115258	* ?	?		B24-	-/--	Original owner unknown (O-GR)
130245	* 62-230	?		B24-	-/--	Original owner unknown (O-GR)
132054	* ?	?		B13-	-/50	Original owner unknown (O-GR)
132582	* ?	?		B--F	-/50	Kaikohe Bus Co, Kaikohe (O-NZ)
146685	* P1.391	Buses		B33F	-/50	Buses Ltd, Hamilton (O-NZ) 37
210793	* ?	?		B35F	-/52	New Zealand Air Force (O-NZ)
?	* ?	Stevens & Sons		B33F	-/53	McGlashan Motors, Greymouth (O-NZ) 2
?	P1.915	Ben Riseley		B33F	-/47	McGlashan Motors, Greymouth (O-NZ)
?	?	Ørum-Ped	1959	B---	9/52	Ruteautomobil, Haderslev (O-DK)
?	?	Ørum-Ped	1960	B---	9/52	Ruteautomobil, Haderslev (O-DK)

BEDFORD OLBD

11119	L-34218	Hoogeveen		B31-	12/46	GVU, Utrecht (O-NL) 1
11123	K-18222	Verheul	2405	B29-	10/46	SBM, Aardenburg (O-NL) 12
11143	* B-18293	Medema		B30-	-/47	Van der Bosch, location unknown (O-NL) 2
11158	* N-67226	Allan		B31-	8/46	BBA, Breda (O-NL) 172
11160	* A-36125	Hoogeveen		B30-	-/46	Marnedie NS, Zoutkamp (O-NL) 38
11169	L-49072	De Schelde	?	B30-	10/46	NS (Nederlandse Spoorwegen), Utrecht (O-NL) 912
11175	* E-28125	ECF	076	B29-	-/48	VERA, Deventer (O-NL) 8
11208	L-49073	De Schelde	?	B30-	-/46	NS (Nederlandse Spoorwegen), Utrecht (O-NL) 913
11209	L-5014	DO&D		B30-	7/46	GVU, Utrecht (O-NL) 6
11214	L-12588	DO&D		B30-	8/46	GVU, Utrecht (O-NL) 7
11219	* HZ-85665	Den Oudsten	1600	B29-	11/46	NAL, Ter Aar (O-NL) 17
11223	* ?	?		B30-	-/46	Van Koningsbruggen, Den Helder (O-NL)
11225	GZ-22948	Verheul	5112	B32-	4/46	Maarse & Kroon, Aalsmeer (O-NL) 69
11228	GZ-22952	Verheul	5114	B32-	4/46	Maarse & Kroon, Aalsmeer (O-NL) 70
11234	L-34223	DO&D		B30-	8/46	GVU, Utrecht (O-NL) 8
11239	L-34224	DO&D		B30-	9/46	GVU, Utrecht (O-NL) 9
11242	L-49071	De Schelde	?	B30-	-/46	NS (Nederlandse Spoorwegen), Utrecht (O-NL) 911
11249	L-34222	DO&D		B30-	6/46	GVU, Utrecht (O-NL) 5
11253	* ?	Hoogeveen		B31-	-/46	Willems-Kroese, Hattem (O-NL) 1
11286	* P-19291	De Groot		B30-	-/46	Kupers, Weert (O-NL) 3
11292	* ?	?		B30-	-/46	Bruil, Gebr., Ede (O-NL) 6
11309	L-34225	DO&D		B30-	9/46	GVU, Utrecht (O-NL) 10
11337	* ?	?		B29-	-/46	Lippinkhof en Boerrigter, Losser (O-NL)
11347	L-34229	Hoogeveen		B31-	12/46	GVU, Utrecht (O-NL) 14
11372	* N-67227	Allan		B31-	1946	BBA, Breda (O-NL) 173
11377	* ?	(De Groot ?)		B31-	-/46	De Rijk, St. Willebrord (O-NL)
11413	K-18067	Ver-Av	5091	B26-	5/46	SBM, Aardenburg (O-NL) 8
11423	* K-17456	Verheul	5127	B32-	-/46	ZVTM, Terneuzen (O-NL) 226
11435	* P-31549	Allan		B31-	-/46	Mevis, Nuth (O-NL) 8
11443	* L-34227	Hoogeveen		B31-	11/46	GVU, Utrecht (O-NL) 12
11444	L-10285	Hoogeveen		B31-	1/47	GVU, Utrecht (O-NL) 15
11448	* L-34221	DO&D		B30-	5/46	GVU, Utrecht (O-NL) 4
11512	* P-14322	Hoogeveen		B30-	7/47	IAO-Römke NS, Eygelhoven (O-NL) 2
11518	* P-11412	Allan		B---	-/46	Veders & Cramers, Grevenbicht (O-NL) 17
11548	* L-34226	DO&D		B30-	10/46	GVU, Utrecht (O-NL) 11

11591	* L-34228	Hoogeveen		B31-	11/46	GVU, Utrecht (O-NL) 13
11594	* ?	?		B30-	-/46	Bruil, Gebr., Ede (O-NL)
11605	* N-67190	Allan		B31-	12/46	BBA, Breda (O-NL) 158
11789	E-26877	(Huif ?)		B---	-/--	Schutte, Zwolle (O-NL) 5
12376	* H-37323	De Schelde	?	B30-	-/46	TP-RAGOM, Ridderkerk (O-NL) 178
12459	M-71027	Verheul	5163	B25-	-/46	GVA, Arnhem (O-NL) 28
13002	* ?	?		lorry	-/46	Original operator unknown (G??)
13019	* HZ-95872	De Schelde	?	B30-	-/47	TP-ESOO, Sliedrecht (O-NL) 119
13021	* D-14625	Hainje		B---	-/46	DABO, Meppel (O-NL) 13
13025	* (N-34047 ?)	?		B31-	-/46	Verhoeven, Budel (O-NL) 2?
13291	M-71032	Verheul	5168	B25-	-/46	GVA, Arnhem (O-NL) 33
13313	* HZ-89475	Bochanen		B30-	-/46	MEGGA, Sliedrecht (O-NL) 6
(13549?)	*L-19818	Hoogeveen		B31-	-/46	Dijkhuizen, Spakenburg (O-NL) 1
13563	* N-67220	Allan		B31-	8/46	BBA, Breda (O-NL) 165
13616	* N-67221	Allan		B31-	9/46	BBA, Breda (O-NL) 166
13660	L-9155	Van Rooijen	?	B30-	-/46	Leguit, Soesterberg (O-NL) 1
13661	* N-67215	Allan		B31-	-/46	BBA, Breda (O-NL) 160
13662	B-19039	?		B26-	-/46	NTM, Heerenveen (O-NL) 503
13667	* N-67216	Allan		B31-	8/46	BBA, Breda (O-NL) 161
13673	* N-67218	Allan		B31-	9/46	BBA, Breda (O-NL) 163
13725	* HZ-95873	De Schelde	?	B30-	-/47	TP-ESOO, Sliedrecht (O-NL) 120
13740	* N-67222	Allan		B31-	-/46	BBA, Breda (O-NL) 167
13745	* L-8913	Van Rooijen N	64	B28-	8/46	TP-AV, Jutphaas (O-NL) 67
13750	* N-67217	Allan		B31-	8/46	BBA, Breda (O-NL) 162
13885	* L-32409	Van Rooijen	264	B28-	11/46	TP-AV, Jutphaas (O-NL) 68
13886	* E-45541	?		B29-	-/--	Winkel, Vriezenveen (O-NL) 4
13937	* N-67219	Allan		B31-	8/46	BBA, Breda (O-NL) 164
13958	* A-36552	Hoogeveen		B30F	-/47	ESA, Marum (O-NL) 39
13984	* ?	De Groot		B31-	-/46	Marijnissen, St Willebrord (O-NL) 3
14027	H-42474	Van Rooijen	271	B30-	-/46	Blom & Zanen {VALK}, Schoonhoven (O-NL) 6
14028	* K-3847	?		B31-	-/46	Krijger, Goes (O-NL)
14844	* ?	?		lorry	-/46	Original operator unknown (G??)
15567	* ?	?		B---	c-/46	Original operator unknown (O-NL)
15568	* K-10735	Verheul	2420	B29-	1/47	SBM, Aardenburg (O-NL) 16
15867	* ?	?		B32-	c-/46	LAD, Lobith (O-NL) 10
16049	* A-35168	Hoogeveen		B30-	-/46	ESA, Marum (O-NL) 29
16061	* ?	?		B27-	-/46	Schorfhaar, Losser (O-NL) 5
16070	* M-52119	Roset		B31F	-/46	ETAO, Tiel (O-NL) 5
16071	* E-42976	Den Oudsten	1593	B29-	11/46	TAD, Enschede (O-NL) 13
16120	* K-3346	De Groot		B29-	-/46	Picavet, Nieuw Namen (O-NL) 3
16136	* E-30678	?		B---	-/46	NWH, Zwartsluis (O-NL) 2
16141	* D-15896	Den Oudsten	1622	B23-	2/47	EDS, Enschede (O-NL) 27
16241	* K-13037*	Roset		B30-	-/46	Van der Klundert, Oud Vossemeer (O-NL) 3
16252	* E-28608	?		B---	-/46	NWH, Zwartsluis (O-NL) 3
16379	* L-49075	De Schelde	?	B30-	10/46	NS (Nederlandse Spoorwegen), Utrecht (O-NL) 915
16435	* M-20528	Den Oudsten	1608	B30-	2/47	Onze Tram, Rossum (O-NL) 2
16440	* G-32947	?		B32-	-/46	Roodt, Haarlem (O-NL) 9
16443	* GZ-1404	Verheul	2403	B29-	1/47	Maarse & Kroon, Aalsmeer (O-NL) 74
16444	* ?	Bochanen		B31-	-/47	Jans, Groot Ammers (O-NL) 5
16454	* M-53175	Den Oudsten	1609	B30-	5/47	Onze Tram, Rossum (O-NL) 3
16462	* A-35171	Hoogeveen		B30F	1946	ESA, Marum (O-NL) 30
16465	* L-33407	Den Oudsten	1588	B28-	11/46	De Haas, Veenendaal (O-NL) 9
16467	* HZ-37986	?		B---	-/46	EGAO, Hardinxveld-Giessendam (O-NL) 10
16528	* ?	Cucarwa		B30-	-/47	Streef, Culemborg (O-NL) 3
16543	GZ-1401	Verheul	5129	B32-	7/46	Maarse & Kroon, Aalsmeer (O-NL) 71
16561	* N-18828	Roset		B25-	-/46	Bolders, Ossendrecht (O-NL) 2
16563	* N-34356	Lemmens		B30-	-/46	EMA, Valkenswaard (O-NL) 44
16573	* N-34358	Lemmens		B30-	-/46	EMA, Valkenswaard (O-NL) 45
16582	* P-33085	Pennock		B26-	-/46	NAO, Roermond (O-NL) 23
16756	* E-41981	?		B---	-/46	Zinger, Enschede (O-NL) 4
16763	* ?	?		B31-	-/46	Snoeyink, Denekamp (O-NL)
16764	* N-67191	Allan		B31-	12/46	BBA, Breda (O-NL) 159
16770	* K-10734	Verheul	2408	B29-	12/46	SBM, Aardenburg (O-NL) 15
16838	* B-10793	Hainje		B30-	-/46	NOF, Dokkum (O-NL) 604

16854	* N-67129	Allan		B31-	9/46	BBA, Breda (O-NL) 169
16856	* H-14954	Den Oudsten	1589	B29-	8/46	Verhoef, Driebruggen (O-NL) 2
16896	* HZ-91335	Den Oudsten	1607	B29-	11/46	TP-De IJssel, Krimpen aan de Ijssel (O-NL) 205
16977	* P-7885	Hoogeveen		B26-	10/46	IAO-Van Kan, Nieuwenhagen (O-NL) 1
17325	* E-42977	Den Oudsten	1598	B29-	11/46	TAD, Enschede (O-NL) 14
17347	* K-17457	Verheul	5176	B32-	-/46	ZVTM, Terneuzen (O-NL) 227
17596	* B-30007	Hainje		B30-	-/46	LABO, Leeuwarden (O-NL) 18
17752	* N-67122	Allan		B31-	9/46	BBA, Breda (O-NL) 170
18039	* ?	?		B32-	-/46	Sprengers, Heeze (O-NL) 4
18100	* M-30606	Den Oudsten	1596	B29-	9/46	Veldhuis, Aalten (O-NL) 7
18102	* D-14623	Hainje		B---	-/46	DABO, Meppel (O-NL) 11
18456	M-71018	Ver-Av	5102	B25-	5/46	GVA, Arnhem (O-NL) 19
18460	* M-12475	De Schelde	?	B30-	-/47	Ballegooijen, Van (O-NL) 8
18464	M-71031	Verheul	5167	B25-	-/46	GVA, Arnhem (O-NL) 32
18512	* P-30083	Pennock		B26-	-/46	NAO, Roermond (O-NL) 22
18521	* B-12624	Hulshoff		B34-	-/46	NOF, Dokkum (O-NL) 600
18534	* K-18069	Verheul	2397	B29-	8/46	SBM, Aardenburg (O-NL) 10
18549	* ?	?		B30-	c-/46	Snoeyink, Denekamp (O-NL)
18556	* EP 9031	?		lorry	-/46	Original operator unknown (G??)
18610	M-71029	Verheul	5165	B25-	-/46	GVA, Arnhem (O-NL) 30
18614	* L-19423	Hoogeveen		B31-	-/46	WABO, Wijk bij Duurstede (O-NL) 1
18617	* M-20308	?		B26	-/46	Hendriks, Zevenaar (O-NL) 6
18776	M-71019	Ver-Av	5103	B25-	5/46	GVA, Arnhem (O-NL) 20
18813	* K-1663	Van Oers	12	B31F	7/47	Krijger, Goes (O-NL) 8
18828	* N-67144	Allan		B31-	9/46	BBA, Breda (O-NL) 168
18846	* P-36370	Verheul	5173	B31-	5/46	MBS, Gennep (O-NL) 113
18847	* A-20638	?		B---	-/--	Marnedienst, Zoutkamp (O-NL) 37
18853	* ?	?		B31-	c-/46	Meinderink, Beerzerveld (O-NL) 4
18900	* ?	?		B30-	-/47	WG de Jong, St. Annaparochie (O-NL) 10
18903	* D-14622	Hainje		B---	-/46	DABO, Meppel (O-NL) 10
18913	* L-54895	Hoogeveen		B30-	-/46	Dijkhuizen, Spakenburg (O-NL) 2
18916	P-36372	Verheul	5175	B31-	5/46	MBS (Maasbuurtspoor), Gennep (O-NL) 115
18919	* ?	?		B30-	-/46	Bruil, Gebr., Ede (O-NL) 1
18923	* ?	Krijgsheld		B29-	-/46	Boer, Westerbork (O-NL)
18926	M-71017	Ver-Av	5101	B25-	5/46	GVA, Arnhem (O-NL) 18
18928	* HZ-9854	Den Oudsten	1691	B31-	1/48	Van Eldik, Gouda (O-NL) 4
19018	* A-34558	Smit Appingedam		B33F	-/46	DAM, Appingedam (O-NL) 86
19021	* G-36142	Van Wessem		B30-	-/46	MEA, Koog aan de Zaan (O-NL) 4
19027	* N-67121	Allan		B31-	8/46	BBA, Breda (O-NL) 171
19038	P-36371	Verheul	5174	B31-	5/46	MBS (Maasbuurtspoor), Gennep (O-NL) 114
19046	M-71033	Verheul	5169	B25-	-/46	GVA, Arnhem (O-NL) 34
19053	* ?	Hainje		B31-	-/47	DABO, Meppel (O-NL) 8
19120	* ?	?		B32-	-/46	Snoeyink, Denekamp (O-NL)
19128	* D-14624	Hainje		B---	-/46	DABO, Meppel (O-NL) 12
19136	* K-12218	Verheul	2398	B29-	-/46	ZVTM, Terneuzen (O-NL) 11
19339	* A-36551	Hoogeveen		B30F	-/47	ESA, Marum (O-NL) 38
19347	* HZ-88668	?		B---	c-/46	Snelle Vliet, Alblasserdam (O-NL) 20
19351	* GZ-39393	Smit Joure		B26-	-/--	van der Wijst, Den Helder (O-NL) 2
19354	* ?	Lemmens		B30-	-/46	Koning, Veendam (O-NL) 1
19357	* HZ-10293	Verheul	6286	B30-	-/48	MEGGA, Sliedrecht (O-NL) 17
19372	* G-58158	Den Oudsten	1599	B29-	10/46	ENHABO, Zaandam (O-NL) 19
19613	* D-2244	?		B---	-/46	Pieper, Nieuw Schoonebeek (O-NL) 1
19620	* N-15872	Domburg	143	DP28F	5/46	Hoefnagels, Roosendaal (O-NL) 14
19629	* K-8797	Plaum		B28-	-/46	Van Oeveren, Zierikzee (O-NL) 4
19632	* ?	?		B31-	-/46	Bleijering, Wijk en Aalburg (O-NL) 8
19701	* M-16484	?		B25-	-/46	Ballegooijen, Van (O-NL) 3
19706	* P-3537	Jongerius		B30-	-/46	Van der Biesen, Kerkrade (O-NL) 5
19710	* N-71216	De Groot		B31-	-/46	ALAD, Wyken Aalburg (O-NL) 10
19787	* ?	?		B31-	-/46	HJ Heijligers, Afferden (O-NL)
19794	GZ-1402	Verheul	5128	B32-	6/46	Maarse & Kroon, Aalsmeer (O-NL) 72
19856	* ?	?		B30-	-/46	Bruil, Gebr., Ede (O-NL)
19861	* ?	?		B30-	-/46	Bruil, Gebr., Ede (O-NL)
19886	* K-9763	Verheul	2402	B28-	-/46	Van Oeveren, Zierikzee (O-NL) 5
20110	* ?	Hoogeveen		B31-	-/46	R Dijkstra, Epe (O-NL) 21

20193	* E-18246	?		B30-	-/--	WATO, Nijverdal (O-NL) 1
20204	M-71030	Verheul	5166	B25-	-/46	GVA, Arnhem (O-NL) 31
20211	* K-18926	Allan		B31-	12/46	AMZ-De Baar & Leendertse, Wemeldinge (O-NL) 47
20273	* B-19038	?		B26-	-/46	NTM, Heerenveen (O-NL) 506
20285	* B-8151	?		B31-	-/46	Jager's Touringcarbedrijf, Heerenveen (O-NL) 3
20354	* L-49074	De Schelde	?	B30-	-/46	NS (Nederlandse Spoorwegen), Utrecht (O-NL) 914
20361	* K-17458	Verheul	5177	B32-	-/46	ZVTM, Terneuzen (O-NL) 228
20370	* B-29027	Jongerius		B30F	-/46	ZWH, Balk (O-NL) 27
20373	P-36368	Verheul	5171	B31-	5/46	MBS (Maasbuurtspoor), Gennep (O-NL) 111
20406	P-3134	Den Oudsten	1597	B30-	11/46	Derksen, Venray (O-NL) 1
20438	* N-19645	?		B29-	-/46	EMA, Valkenswaard (O-NL) 47
20443	* B-29923	Jongerius		B30F	-/46	LAB, Leeuwarden (O-NL) 15
20448	* H-97930	Den Oudsten	1620	B30-	1/47	Blom & Zanen, Oudewater (O-NL) 24
20455	* P-30082	Ver-Av	5092	B26-	-/46	NAO, Roermond (O-NL) 20
20524	* A-29858	?		B---	-/--	Marnedienst, Zoutkamp (O-NL) 36
20533	* N-34241	?		B31-	-/46	Van Asten, Budel (O-NL) 8
20536	* E-41604	Den Oudsten	1595	B29-	9/46	Arke & Ten Barge, Enshede (O-NL) 17
20605	* ?	?		B30-	-/46	Bruil, Gebr., Ede (O-NL) 2
20616	* ?	?		B31-	-/46	Han van Gelder (contractor), Hattem (O-NL)
20638	N-75025	De Schelde	?	B30-	-/46	Vitesse, 's Hertogenbosch (O-NL) 360
20642	HZ-92674	ZABO	171	B28-	10/46	TP-Ropdel, Kinderdijk (O-NL) 8
20707	* N-67189	Allan		B31-	12/46	BBA, Breda (O-NL) 157
20713	* HZ-46038	ZABO	160	B26-	7/46	TP-RAGOM, Ridderkerk (O-NL) 177
20729	M-71034	Verheul	5170	B25-	6/46	GVA, Arnhem (O-NL) 35
20850	* ?	Hoogeveen		B31-	-/46	OAD, Holten (O-NL) 4
20936	* P-17886	Hoogeveen		B29-	-/46	IAO-Van Kan, Niuwenhagen (O-NL) 5
20945	* ?	?		B31-	-/46	AL Fassbender, Eerde (O-NL) 14?
21381	* A-35169	Hoogeveen		B30F	-/47	ESA, Marum (O-NL) 31
21960	* P-30635	De Groot		B30-	-/46	Kupers, Weert (O-NL) 4
21975	* HZ-91333	Smit Appingedam		B27-	-/49	Snelle Vliet, Alblasserdam (O-NL) 21
22047	* ?	De Groot		B31-	-/46	Auto Omnibusdienst, Utrecht (O-NL)
22052	* K-18221	Verheul	2399	B26-	9/46	SBM, Aardenburg (O-NL) 11
22185	* L-29905	Hoogeveen		B29-	-/46	De Haas, Veenendaal (O-NL) 10
22195	*	Verheul	?	B29-	-/46?	Kleuterhuis/Kabouterhuis?, Amsterdam (school) (O-NL)
22281	* P-20320	Verheul	2414	B28-	-/47	GABM, Maastricht (O-NL) 23
22297	* GZ-81202	De Schelde	?	B30-	6/47	Maarse & Kroon, Aalsmeer (O-NL) 47
22578	* GZ-81201	De Schelde	?	B30-	5/47	Maarse & Kroon, Aalsmeer (O-NL) 46
22740	* N-71215	De Groot		B31-	-/46	ALAD, Wyken Aalburg (O-NL) 12
22929	N-67156	Allan		B31-	9/46	BBA, Breda (O-NL) 179
23017	* N-71219	De Groot		B31-	-/46	ALAD, Wyken Aalburg (O-NL) 11
23098	* L-16667	Van Rooijen	126	B30-	12/46	TP-AV, Jutphaas (O-NL) 69
23105	* HZ-84378	ZABO	159	B26-	7/46	TP-RAGOM, Ridderkerk (O-NL) 175
23252	* A-36519	Hoogeveen		B30-	-/47	ESA, Marum (O-NL) 37
23258	* ?	Cucarwa		B26F	-/46	ETAO, Tiel (O-NL)
23275	* ?	?		B31-	c-/46	Snoeyink, Denekamp (O-NL)
23340	K-18068	Ver-Av	5093	B26-	5/46	SBM, Aardenburg (O-NL) 9
23346	* HZ-95871	Hoogeveen		B31-	-/47	TP-ESOO, Sliedrecht (O-NL) 121
23353	* H-42052	Met		B30-	-/46	Pasteur, Den Haag (O-NL) 6
23358	* E-25017	ECF	062	B30-	11/46	Kolkman, Deventer (O-NL) 6
23368	P-36369	Verheul	5172	B31-	5/46	MBS (Maasbuurtspoor), Gennep (O-NL) 112
23428	* ?	Lemmens		B30-	-/46	VADAH, Echt (O-NL) 22
23438	* B-29924	Jongerius		B30F	-/46	LAB, Leeuwarden (O-NL) 16
23443	D-8981	Harmanni		B---	-/46	Harmanni, Assen (O-NL) 1
23636	* GZ-1403	Verheul	2400	B29-	9/46	Maarse & Kroon, Aalsmeer (O-NL) 73
23641	* HZ-86192	ZABO	170	B28-	9/46	TP-RopdeL, Kinderdijk (O-NL) 7
23651	* ?	?		B30-	c-/46	T Kool, Leerdam (O-NL)
23729	* ?	?		B31-	c-/46	Original operator unknown (O-NL)
23812	* A-36126	Hoogeveen		B30-	-/46	Marnedienst, Zoutkamp (O-NL) 39
23817	* ?	Allan		B31-	c-/46	Krijger, Goes (O-NL) 11
23822	* P-20675	Van Oers	8	B31F	5/47	Schurgers, Maastricht (O-NL) 8
23827	* ?	Den Oudsten	1594	B29-	9/46	Arke & Ten Barge, Enschede (O-NL) 18
24103	* ?	Hainje		B30-	-/46	LABO, Leeuwarden (O-NL) 17
24282	* H-35171	De Schelde	?	B30-	-/47	TP-RAGOM, Ridderkerk (O-NL) 179
25168	* N-75027	De Schelde	?	B30-	-/46	Vitesse, 's Hertogenbosch (O-NL) 362

25183	* HZ-96415	De Schelde	? B30-	3/47	RTM, Zierikzee (O-NL) 5
25272	* HZ-96416	De Schelde	? B30-	4/47	RTM, Zierikzee (O-NL) 6
25287	* M-17514	De Schelde	? B30-	-/47	Ballegooijen, Van (O-NL) 9
25292	* N-75029	De Schelde	? B30-	-/46	Vitesse, 's Hertogenbosch (O-NL) 364
25307	HZ-92675	ZABO	177 B30-	1/47	TP-RopdeL, Kinderdijk (O-NL) 9
25463	* N-75030	De Schelde	? B30-	-/46	Vitesse, 's Hertogenbosch (O-NL) 365
25542	* N-75026	De Schelde	? B30-	-/46	Vitesse, 's Hertogenbosch (O-NL) 361
25567	* L-54229	De Schelde	? B30-	-/47	TP-AV, Jutphaas (O-NL) 73
25573	* G-79511	De Schelde	BF2-3 B30-	2/47	NHADO, Bergen Binnen (O-NL) 7
25685	* ?	?	B31-	c-/46	Pulleman, Oude Tonge (O-NL)
25802	* ?	?	B30-	c-/46	TESO, Den Burg (O-NL) 7
25898	N-75028	De Schelde	? B30-	-/46	Vitesse, 's Hertogenbosch (O-NL) 363
25906	* P-38386	Allan	B31-	-/46	GABM, Maastricht (O-NL) 14
26006	* ?	Allan	B30-	-/45	De Vos Tours (Van Oosterom), Oss (O-NL) 3
26037	* HZ-96417	De Schelde	? B30-	4/47	RTM, Zierikzee (O-NL) 7
26045	* M-75026	De Schelde	? B30-	-/46	ETAO, Tiel (O-NL) 7
26159	* M-18698	De Schelde	? B30-	-/47	Ballegooijen, Van (O-NL) 7
26166	* M-12478	De Schelde	? B30-	-/47	Ballegooijen, Van (O-NL) 6
26287	* K-17855	Verheul	2401 B29-	-/46	ZVTM, Terneuzen (O-NL) 12
27956	* GAO 3	Duple	5438/2 B24F	10/46	E Hartness {Hartness Bus & Coach Service}, Penrith (CU)
29009	* ?	Allan	B30-	-/46	Staatsmijnen, Limburg (O-NL) 18
32374	* ?	Jongerius	B31-	c-/46	Fikse, Oostendorp/Doorpijk (O-NL)
54091	* ?	?	lorry	-/47	Original operator unknown (G??)
?	A-36549	?	B26-	-/47	ESA, Marum (O-NL)
?	B-30008	Hainje	B29-	-/46	LABO, Leeuwarden (O-NL) 19
?	D-14498	Hoogeveen	B31-	-/46	EDS, Hoogeven (O-NL) 17
?	D-14499	Hoogeveen	B31-	-/46	EDS, Hoogeven (O-NL) 18
?	D-14500	Hoogeveen	B31-	-/46	EDS, Hoogeven (O-NL) 19
?	D-14502	Hoogeveen	B31-	-/46	EDS, Hoogeven (O-NL) 20
?	D-15890	Hoogeveen	B31-	-/46	EDS, Hoogeven (O-NL) 21
?	D-15891	Hoogeveen	B31-	-/46	EDS, Hoogeven (O-NL) 22
?	D-15892	Den Oudsten	1611 B23-	12/46	EDS, Hoogeven (O-NL) 23
?	D-15893	Den Oudsten	1612 B23-	12/46	EDS, Hoogeven (O-NL) 24
?	D-15894	Den Oudsten	1613 B23-	12/46	EDS, Hoogeven (O-NL) 25
?	D-15895	Den Oudsten	1614 B23-	1/47	EDS, Hoogeven (O-NL) 26
?	D-15897	Den Oudsten	1623 B23-	2/47	EDS, Hoogeven (O-NL) 28
?	D-15898	?	B23-	-/47	EDS, Hoogeven (O-NL) 29
?	GZ-33316	Verheul	2419 B29-	-/46	Spijkers, Amsterdam (O-NL) 3
?	HX-3277	Bakker, Montfoort	B30-	-/46	Beuk, Noordwijk (O-NL) 7
?	HZ-89476	?	B30-	-/46	MEGGA, Sliedrecht (O-NL)
?	M-37282	Verheul	2404 B29-	-/46	GTW, Doetinchem (O-NL) 20
?	M-37472	Verheul	2407 B29-	-/46	GTW, Doetinchem (O-NL) 21
?	M-37537	Verheul	2410 B29-	-/46	GTW, Doetinchem (O-NL) 22
?	M-37751	Verheul	2413 B29-	-/46	GTW, Doetinchem (O-NL) 23
?	M-38354	Verheul	2417 B29-	-/46	GTW, Doetinchem (O-NL) 24
?	M-71015	Ver-Av	5099 B25-	4/46	GVA, Arnhem (O-NL) 16
?	M-71016	Ver-Av	5100 B25-	5/46	GVA, Arnhem (O-NL) 17
?	M-71020	Verheul	5156 B25-	5/46	GVA, Arnhem (O-NL) 21
?	M-71021	Verheul	5157 B25-	-/46	GVA, Arnhem (O-NL) 22
?	M-71022	Verheul	5158 B25-	-/46	GVA, Arnhem (O-NL) 23
?	M-71023	Verheul	5159 B25-	-/46	GVA, Arnhem (O-NL) 24
?	M-71024	Verheul	5160 B25-	-/46	GVA, Arnhem (O-NL) 25
?	M-71025	Verheul	5161 B25-	-/46	GVA, Arnhem (O-NL) 26
?	M-71026	Verheul	5162 B25-	-/46	GVA, Arnhem (O-NL) 27
?	M-71028	Verheul	5164 B25-	-/46	GVA, Arnhem (O-NL) 29
?	* ?	Allan	B30-	-/46	JH Geelen Vaals (O-NL) 46
?	?	Verheul	2411 B---	-/46	AKU-ENKA, Ede (O-NL)
?	?	Verheul	2415 B---	-/46	AKU-ENKA, Ede (O-NL)
?	?	Verheul	2416 B---	-/46	AKU-ENKA, Ede (O-NL)
?	?	?	B---	-/46	ETAO, Tiel (O-NL) 4

Note: It is curious that the many vehicles for operators in the Netherlands listed above are recorded as OLBD; as may be deduced from the introductory remarks to these OL lists, OLBDs were equipped with drop-side bodies of

C1252/232

Bedford's own manufacture. It would actually have been more logical for them to have been unbodied OLBZ models. An error in the records cannot be ruled out.

BEDFORD OLBZ

150125	T-1087	?	B7CV	3/51	AS Eidsdal Rutebillag, Eidsal (O-N)
204618	E-6389	PSK	B--CV	-/51	Lesja Ysteris Bilruter (O-N)
233229	CV 1801	?	-27-	9/52	Jaffna, location unknown (O-CL)
261112	?	Ørum-Ped 2028	B---	-/53	Bernh. Pedersen, Stubbekøbing (O-DK)

MISCELLANEOUS BEDFORD OLs, where full chassis designations are unknown

a. OLA chassis

20865	TN 4055	?	B30D	7/46	PapaCharalambous, Skylloura (O-CY)
21016	TN 4044	?	B27D	7/46	Yiangou, Kalopanayiotis (O-CY)
21058	* TN 4042	?	lorry	6/46	Original operator unknown (O-CY)
21943	T 4219	?	B30D	8/46	Stylianou, Letimbou (O-CY)
22026	* T 4045	?	lorry	7/46	Original operator unknown (O-CY)
22169	* T 4051	?	lorry	7/46	Original operator unknown (O-CY)
22253	* T 4043	?	lorry	7/46	Original operator unknown (O-CY)
22590	T 4132	?	B30D	7/46	Stylianou, Arakapas (O-CY)
30663	B-2732	?	B28-	12/47	Gunnar Riseberg, location unknown (O-N)
?	TN 4044	?	B27D	7/46	Yiangou, Kalopanayiotis (O-CY)

b. OLB chassis

37684	* ?	?	?	-/46	Original operator unknown (O-NZ)
53124	J 1732	Rønne	C29C	6/48	DBJ (Bornholm Railways), Rønne (O-DK) 13
63413	* P1.002	Midland	B33F	-/--	Midland, Christchurch (O-NZ) 66
85484	* P1.003	Midland	B33F	-/49	Midland, Christchurch (O-NZ) 72
90323	* ?	Midland	B33F	-/49	Midland, Christchurch (O-NZ) 68
119658	P 10.287	Ørum-Pedersen	B27F	4/50	Hjørring Privatbaner, Hjørring (O-DK) 23
121434	* P1.111	RE&C	B33D	-/51	Buses Ltd, Hamilton (O-NZ) 14
136825	* ?	?	?	-/50	Original operator unknown (O-NZ)
146688	V.886	?	B31F	-/51	JS Norquay, Rangiriri (O-NZ)
148582	A 17.530	Sorø	B--F	12/50	Herlev Ruterne AS, Herlev (O-DK) 7
151510	A 17.538	Sorø	B--F	6/51	Herlev Ruterne AS, Herlev (O-DK)
187749	* ?	RE&C	B30F	-/--	WJ Wheeler & Sons Ltd, Penrose (O-NZ) 12
213392	H-15715	Wattenberg	B21C	11/51	Olav Merkebekk, Drangedal (O-N)
219114	S-2326	?	B5FV	-/51	Kjøs Auto, Hornindal (O-N)
233234	CV 2427	?	-27-	2/53	Gunasekara, Horana (O-CL)
233244	CV 2153	?	-29-	11/52	Anandu Tours Ltd, Kandy (O-CL)
251951	?	?	?	-/--	Waikato Services Ltd, Port Waiakato (O-NZ)
259522	K 30.065	Ørum-Ped 2027	C25C	4/54	Lars Iversen, Rødovre (O-DK)
?	C 3367	?	B25-	9/47	Danish State Railways, Copenhagen (O-DK) 100
?	* JA 8029	Ørum-Ped 1928	C25C	4/52	Tejn Turistfart, Tejn (O-DK) 64
?	MC 90.083	Rønne	C25C	by/51	Evald Kruse, Nakskov (O-DK)
?	MK 94.276	Rønne	C25C	-/52	Henning Svendsen, Aakirkeby (O-DK)
?	* P1.113	?	?	-/--	Waugh, Gisborne (O-NZ)
?	* R-1224	Auto 1923	B--C	-/53	LL Eksingedalsruta, Modalen (O-N)
?	U 14.517	?	B25-	10/48	Danish State Railways, Copenhagen (O-DK) 152
?	X 22.523	?	B25-	7/48	Danish State Railways, Copenhagen (O-DK) 151
?	?	Crawley Ridley	B28F	-/50	Weld Motors Ltd, Palmerston North (O-NZ) 8
?	?	Crawley Ridley	B28F	-/50	Weld Motors Ltd, Palmerston North (O-NZ) 1
?	* ?	McWhinnie	B30F	-/--	Ecroyd's Garage & Transport, Hawarden (O-NZ)
?	?	Pomeroy	B33F	-/--	Findlay Motors, Taupo (O-NZ) 1
?	?	Ørum-Ped 1917	B---	-/52	De Graa Busser, Rønde (O-DK)
?	?	Ørum-Ped 1928	B---	-/52	PC Poulsen, Thisted (O-DK)

c. OLA or OLB chassis

15365	* ?	RE&C	B31F	-/46	WJ Wheeler & Sons Ltd, Penrose (O-NZ) 13
16800	* ?	Cheetham & Borwick	B--F	-/--	Original operator unknown (O-AUS)
23305	* TW 807	?	lorry	-/46	Original operator unknown (O-CY)
23325	* ?	?	lorry	-/--	War Department (GOV)

C1252/233

32368	* GZ-60875	Met		B29-	-/46	TESO, Den Burg (O-NL) 3
40374	* ?	?		B29-	-/--	Lambers, Ommen (O-NL)
79661	* TN 7831	?		lorry	9/48	Original operator unknown (O-CY)
80559	* ?	?		lorry	-/48	Original operator unknown (G??)
115269	* ?	?		B28-	-/--	Original owner unknown (O-GR)
115277	* ?	Smytliadis		B28-	-/--	Original owner unknown (O-GR)
125531	* ?	?		B24-	-/--	Original owner unknown (O-GR)
130247	* 61-929	?		B24-	-/--	Original owner unknown (O-GR)
131124	* 63-507	?		B24-	-/--	Original owner unknown (O-GR)
132051	* 62-292	?		B24-	-/--	Original owner unknown (O-GR)
144516	* ?	?		B24-	-/--	Original operator unknown (O-GR)
147604	* ?	?		B24-	-/--	Original owner unknown (O-GR)
168604	* ?	Verheul	6874	B29-	3/51	NHADO, Bergen Binnen (O-NL)
?	* A-8463	?		?	-/49	Original operator unknown (O-E)
?	B-78928	Ayats	388	C20-	-/52	Molist, Barcelona (O-E)
?	HMJ 971	?		B24-	7/49	Original operator unknown
?	NHU 254	?		C--F	12/50	Bristol Corporation (XGL)
?	* P2.776	?		B--F	-/50	D Salt, Birkenhead (O-NZ)
?	PM-7566	Ayats	243	B33-	-/49	Villafranca & Cardona, Mahon (O-E)
?	* TL 745	?		lorry	c-/50	Original operator unknown
?	V-21284	Ayats	368	C33D	-/52	Motor Union, Palma (O-E)
?	V-21727	Ayats	336	C33-	-/51	Empresa Clar, Palma (O-E)
?	V-21779	Ayats	319	C33-	-/51	Jaime Sestre, Palma (O-E)
?	V-22166	Ayats	367	C33D	-/52	Motor Union, Palma (O-E)
?	?	Ayats	209	C38-	-/48	Transportes Santa Maria, Suria (O-E)
?	?	Ayats	334	C---	-/51	Andalucia Express, La Linea (O-E)
?	?	Ayats	335	C30-	-/51	Villafranca & Cardona, Mahon (O-E)
?	?	Jonckheere	5606	C23	7/48	FD D'Hondt, Hoboken (O-B)

NOTES

Bedford OLACs
44057	(T 4998) New as a lorry. To Gavriel, Yeroskipou (O-CY) as B27D 1/48
56794	(T6250) New as a lorry. To Omer, Paphos (O-CY) as B27D 12/48
62121	(TN 6713) New as a lorry. To Thrasyvoulou, Morphou (O-CY) as B28D 10/51
64575	(T 6937) New as a lorry. To Tsangaris, Paralimni (O-CY) as B28D 9/49
84166	(T 7896) New as a lorry. To Georghiou, Vatili (O-CY) as B30D 1/54
84166	(T 7896) New as a lorry. To Georghiou, Vatili (O-CY) as B30D 1/54
118859	(?) Re-registered 33001 in 1956. Later with KTEL Limnos (O-GR) 6
121287	(65-374) Re-registered KP-785 in 1952 and 80123 in 1956. Later with KTEL Herakleion (O-GR) 22
133819	(T 9997) New as a lorry. To Nicolettis, Lysi (O-CY) as B30D 3/60
133904	(TN 9960) New as a lorry. To Christoforou, Lythrodhonda (O-CY) as B29D 3/52
210973	(TB 429) New as a lorry. To Savvides, Larnaca (O-CY) as B30D 6/58
245193	(TD 370) New as a lorry. To Anastasi, Lythrodhonda (O-CY) as B29D 10/55
260460	(TE 786) (OLAC) New as a tipper. To Nicolaou, Kapedhes (O-CY) as B30D 10/53

Bedford OLAZs
35883	(BCW 814) New as a lorry in UK. To Liveras, Argates (O-CY) 12/57, re-registered TAL 118 and bodied locally as B30F
121379	(ACC 883) Carried a pre-war Duple body, modified to resemble a post-war Vista
140613	(TA 397) New as a lorry. To Foris, Palekhori (O-CY) as B30D 5/55
240499	(MXV 578) Believed to have been used initially as a Bedford demonstrator
257515	(TE 832) New as a lorry. To Demosthenous, Ephtagonia (O-CY) as B29D 3/54
?	(CV 1402) Chassis number recorded as 23301, missing a digit
?	(HMJ 971) Presumed to have been an OL. Motor Taxation records have chassis number 109932; this clashes with an export OB chassis.
?	(WMC 27) Chassis number partially recorded as "2344"
?	(WMX 184) One of the Middlesex County Council vehicles is believed to have had Mulliner body Z97

Bedford OLBCs
18668	(P.105) Believed new as lorry. Re-registered P1.565 at an unknown date; re-registered EW.2087 1965
31564	(P1.911) Re-registered P3.010 at an unknown date; re-registered DH.882 at an unknown date after 1965
80224	(?) Re-registered DT.6198 1965
99200	(?) Re-registered DU.7332 1965

106331   (?) Re-registered 67364 in 1956. Later with KTEL Kavala (O-GR)
114303   (57-058) Re-registered 70340 in 1956. Later with KTEL Patris City (O-GR)
115258   (?) Re-registered 45725 in 1956. Later with KTEL Fthiotida (O-GR)
130245   (62-230) Re-registered 70410 in 1956. Later with KTEL Achaia (O-GR) 89
132054   (?) Re-registered 80129 in 1956. Later with KTEL Herakleion (O-GR) 28
132582   (?) Re-registered P2.776 and V2.348 at unknown dates
146685   (P1.391) Re-registered EW.9541 1965. Chassis also recorded as 146655
210793   (?) Re-registered EJ.2270 at an unknown date after 1965
?   (?) (The Stevens & Sons-bodied vehicle was re-registered DX.536 1965

Bedford OLBDs
11143   (B-18293) Re-registered NB-32-09 at unknown date
11158   (N-67226) Re-registered NB-33-31 at unknown date
11160   (A-36125) Re-registered NB-73-78 at unknown date
11175   (E-28125) Re-registered NB-41-51 at unknown date
11219   (HZ-85665) Re-registered PB-07-95 at unknown date
11223   (?) Re-registered NB-54-85 at unknown date
11253   (?) Re-registered PB-16-46 at unknown date
11286   (P-19291) Re-registered NB-37-50 at unknown date
11292   (?) Re-registered NB-24-68 at unknown date
11337   (?) Re-registered NB-53-90 at unknown date
11372   (N-67227) Re-registered NB-33-32 at unknown date
11377   (?) Re-registered NB-57-37 at unknown date
11423   (K-17456) Re-registered NB-25-98 at unknown date
11435   (P-31549) Re-registered NB-19-30 at unknown date
11443   (L-34227) Re-registered NB-58-75 at unknown date
11448   (L-34221) Re-registered NB-53-57 at unknown date
11512   (P-14322) Re-registered NB-51-87 at unknown date
11518   (P-11412) Re-registered NB-08-89 at unknown date
11548   (L-34226) Re-registered NB-04-51 at unknown date
11591   (L-34228) Re-registered NB-28-28 at unknown date
11594   (?) Re-registered NB-24-72 at unknown date
11605   (N-67190) Re-registered NB-33-17 at unknown date
12376   (H-37323) Re-registered NB-78-22 at unknown date
13002   (?) Rebodied Thurgood 516 C29F and re-registered GVE 586 11/48 (BC Kenzie, Shepreth (CM))
13019   (HZ-95872) Re-registered NB-78-23 at unknown date
13021   (D-14625) Re-registered NB-15-73 at unknown date
13025   ((N-34047 ?)) Re-registered NB-49-84 at unknown date
13313   (HZ-89475) Re-registered NB-98-18 at unknown date
(13549 ?)   (L-19818) Re-registered NB-30-38 at unknown date
13563   (N-67220) Re-registered NB-33-24 at unknown date
13616   (N-67221) Re-registered NB-33-25 at unknown date
13661   (N-67215) Re-registered NB-33-19 at unknown date
13667   (N-67216) Re-registered NB-33-20 at unknown date
13673   (N-67218) Re-registered NB-33-22 at unknown date
13725   (HZ-95873) Re-registered NB-78-20 at unknown date
13740   (N-67222) Re-registered NB-33-26 at unknown date
13745   (L-8913) Re-registered NB-78-14 at unknown date
13750   (N-67217) Re-registered NB-33-21 at unknown date
13885   (L-32409) Re-registered NJ-84-72 at unknown date
13886   (E-45541) Re-registered NB-48-71 at unknown date
13937   (N-67219) Re-registered NB-33-23 at unknown date
13958   (A-36552) Re-registered NB-72-85 at unknown date
13984   (?) Re-registered NB-57-47 at unknown date
14028   (K-3847) Re-registered NB-29-69 at unknown date
14844   (?) Rebodied Beccols C29F and re-registered GVJ 86 c9/49 (L Sheppard, Broadtown (WI))
15567   (?) Re-registered NB-78-19 at unknown date; later with TP-AV, Jutphaas (O-NL) 73
15568   (K-10735) Re-registered NF-28-54 at unknown date
15867   (?) Re-registered NB-97-07 at unknown date
16049   (A-35168) Re-registered NB-72-76 at unknown date
16061   (?) Re-registered NB-51-45 at unknown date
16070   (M-52119) Re-registered NB-54-93 at unknown date
16071   (E-42976) Re-registered NB-31-02 at unknown date
16120   (K-3346) Re-registered NB-29-79 at unknown date

16136	(E-30678) Re-registered NB-37-44 at unknown date
16141	(D-15896) Re-registered NB-38-38 at unknown date
16241	(K-13037*) Re-registered NB-26-97 at unknown date
16252	(E-28608) Re-registered NB-37-43 at unknown date
16379	(L-49075) Re-registered M-70135, later PB-55-75, both at unknown dates
16435	(M-20528) Re-registered NB-70-58 at unknown date
16440	(G-32947) Re-registered NB-72-00 at unknown date
16443	(GZ-1404) Re-registered NB-90-43 at unknown date
16444	(?) Re-registered NB-93-36 at unknown date
16454	(M-53175) Re-registered NB-70-59 at unknown date
16462	(A-35171) Re-registered NB-72-77 at unknown date
16465	(L-33407) Re-registered NB-42-45 at unknown date
16467	(HZ-37986) Re-registered NB-38-46 at unknown date
16528	(?) Re-registered NB-57-13 at unknown date
16561	(N-18828) Re-registered NB-54-42 at unknown date
16563	(N-34356) Re-registered NB-69-79 at unknown date
16573	(N-34358) Re-registered NB-69-78 at unknown date
16582	(P-33085) Re-registered NB-24-96 at unknown date
16756	(E-41981) Re-registered NB-48-38 at unknown date
16763	(?) Re-registered NB-30-87 at unknown date
16764	(N-67191) Re-registered NB-33-18 at unknown date
16770	(K-10734) Re-registered NB-71-80 at unknown date
16838	(B-10793) Re-registered NB-53-62 at unknown date
16854	(N-67129) Re-registered NB-33-28 at unknown date
16856	(H-14954) Re-registered NB-11-78 at unknown date
16896	(HZ-91335) Re-registered NB-00-98 at unknown date. Chassis number also given as 16996
16977	(P-7885) Re-registered NB-53-59 at unknown date
17325	(E-42977) Re-registered NB-31-03 at unknown date
17347	(K-17457) Re-registered NB-25-99 at unknown date
17596	(B-30007) Re-registered NB-31-99 at unknown date
17752	(N-67122) Re-registered NB-33-29 at unknown date
18039	(?) Re-registered NB-51-90 at unknown date
18100	(M-30606) Re-registered NB-97-53 at unknown date
18102	(D-14623) Re-registered NB-27-34 at unknown date
18460	(M-12475) Re-registered NB-54-05 at unknown date
18512	(P-30083) Re-registered NB-38-79 at unknown date
18521	(B-12624) Re-registered NB-63-08 at unknown date
18534	(K-18069) Re-registered NB-15-42 at unknown date
18549	(?) Re-registered NB-30-91 at unknown date
18556	(EP 9031) Rebodied Mulliner T337 C29F in 1949 to order of WH Hailstone, Church Stoke (MO) but diverted to J Williamson {The Green Bus Service}, Shrewsbury (SH)
18614	(L-19423) Re-registered NB-57-91 at unknown date
18617	(M-20308) Re-registered NB-52-64 at unknown date
18813	(K-1663) Re-registered NB-29-66 at unknown date
18828	(N-67144) Re-registered NB-33-27 at unknown date
18846	(P-36370) Re-registered NB-15-42 at unknown date
18847	(A-20638) Re-registered NJ-67-49 at unknown date
18853	(?) Re-registered PB-11-27 at unknown date
18900	(?) Re-registered NB-37-71 at unknown date
18903	(D-14622) Re-registered NB-27-23 at unknown date
18913	(L-54895) Re-registered NB-30-39 at unknown date
18919	(?) Re-registered NB-24-69 at unknown date
18923	(?) Re-registered NB-51-51 at unknown date
18928	(HZ-9854) Re-registered RB-07-58 at unknown date
19018	(A-34558) Re-registered NB-72-96 at unknown date
19021	(G-36142) Re-registered NB-64-88 at unknown date
19027	(N-67121) Re-registered NB-33-30 at unknown date
19053	(?) Re-registered NB-37-32 at unknown date
19120	(?) Re-registered NB-17-50 at unknown date
19128	(D-14624) Re-registered NB-27-25 at unknown date
19136	(K-12218) Re-registered NB-25-96 at unknown date
19339	(A-36551) Re-registered NB-72-84 at unknown date
19347	(HZ-88668) Re-registered NB-38-40 at unknown date
19351	(GZ-39393) Re-registered NB-64-26 at unknown date

19354	(?) Re-registered NB-16-69 at unknown date
19357	(HZ-10293) Re-registered PB-00-94 at unknown date
19372	(G-58158) Re-registered NB-48-64 at unknown date
19613	(D-2244) Re-registered NB-27-03 at unknown date
19620	(N-15872) Re-registered NB-54-81 at unknown date. Possibly a lorry with unknown owner until 1949
19629	(K-8797) Re-registered NB-26-30 at unknown date
19632	(?) Re-registered PB-18-44 at unknown date
19701	(M-16484) Re-registered NB-54-02 at unknown date
19706	(P-3537) Re-registered NB-16-98 at unknown date
19710	(N-71216) Re-registered NB-52-52 at unknown date
19787	(?) Re-registered NB-52-30 at unknown date
19856	(?) Re-registered NB-24-71 at unknown date
19861	(?) Re-registered NB-24-73 at unknown date
19886	(K-9763) Re-registered NB-26-31 at unknown date
20110	(?) Re-registered NB-53-51 at unknown date
20193	(E-18246) Re-registered NB-30-59 at unknown date
20211	(K-18926) Re-registered NB-28-43 at unknown date
20273	(B-19038) Re-registered NB-93-13 at unknown date
20285	(B-8151) Re-registered NB-13-79 at unknown date
20354	(L-49074) Re-registered NB-50-99 at unknown date
20361	(K-17458) Re-registered NF-71-15 at unknown date
20370	(B-29027) Re-registered NJ-02-48 at unknown date
20438	(N-19645) Re-registered NB-01-93 at unknown date
20443	(B-29923) Re-registered NB-35-31 at unknown date
20448	(H-97930) Re-registered NB-70-52 at unknown date
20455	(P-30082) Re-registered NB-38-78 at unknown date
20524	(A-29858) Re-registered NB-73-77 at unknown date
20533	(N-34241) Re-registered NB-49-88 at unknown date
20536	(E-41604) Re-registered NB-32-99 at unknown date
20605	(?) Re-registered NB-24-70 at unknown date
20616	(?) Re-registered NB-55-63 at unknown date
20707	(N-67189) Re-registered NB-33-16 at unknown date
20713	(HZ-46038) Re-registered NB-90-32 at unknown date
20850	(?) Re-registered NB-46-48 at unknown date
20936	(P-17886) Re-registered NB-10-70 at unknown date
20945	(?) Re-registered NB-72-16 at unknown date
21381	(A-35169) Re-registered NB-72-78 at unknown date
21960	(P-30635) Re-registered NB-37-51 at unknown date
21975	(HZ-91333) Re-registered NB-38-41 at unknown date
22047	(?) Re-registered NB-28-51 at unknown date
22052	(K-18221) Re-registered NB-15-72 at unknown date
22185	(L-29905) Re-registered NB-42-46 at unknown date
22195	( ) Re-registered NB-38-64 at unknown date
22281	(P-20320) Re-registered NB-53-86 at unknown date
22297	(GZ-81202) Re-registered NJ-41-63 at unknown date
22578	(GZ-81201) Re-registered NJ-41-62 at unknown date
22740	(N-71215) Re-registered NB-52-53 at unknown date
23017	(N-71219) Re-registered NB-52-73 at unknown date
23098	(L-16667) Re-registered NB-78-15 at unknown date
23105	(HZ-84378) Re-registered NB-90-31 at unknown date
23252	(A-36519) Re-registered NB-72-83 at unknown date
23258	(?) Re-registered NB-56-44 at unknown date
23275	(?) Re-registered NB-30-86 at unknown date
23346	(HZ-95871) Re-registered NB-76-94 at unknown date
23353	(H-42052) Re-registered NB-38-14 at unknown date
23358	(E-25017) Re-registered NB-41-46 at unknown date
23428	(?) Re-registered NB-24-92 at unknown date
23438	(B-29924) Re-registered NB-35-32 at unknown date
23636	(GZ-1403) Re-registered NB-90-44 at unknown date
23641	(HZ-86092) Re-registered NB-28-61 at unknown date
23651	(?) Re-registered PB-44-05 at unknown date
23729	(?) Re-registered NB-25-46 at unknown date. Later with Harmanni, Assen (O-NL) 21
23812	(A-36126) Re-registered NB-73-79 at unknown date
23817	(?) Re-registered NB-29-68 at unknown date

C1252/237

23822	(P-20675) Re-registered NB-22-80 at unknown date
23827	(?) Re-registered NB-31-39 at unknown date
24103	(?) Re-registered NF-99-53 at unknown date
24282	(H-35131) Re-registered NB-78-21 at unknown date
25168	(N-75027) Re-registered NB-51-76 at unknown date
25183	(HZ-96415) Re-registered NB-63-79 at unknown date
25272	(HZ-96416) Re-registered NB-17-00 at unknown date
25287	(M-17514) Re-registered NB-57-27 at unknown date
25292	(N-75029) Re-registered NB-09-61 at unknown date
25463	(N-75030) Re-registered NJ-02-83 at unknown date
25542	(N-75026) Re-registered NB-25-55 at unknown date
25567	(L-54229) Re-registered NB-78-19 at unknown date
25573	(G-79511) Re-registered NJ-41-35 at unknown date
25685	(?) Re-registered NB-82-96 at unknown date
25802	(?) Re-registered NB-68-03 at unknown date
25906	(P-38386) Re-registered NB-53-85 at unknown date
26006	(?) Re-registered NB-37-78 at unknown date
26037	(HZ-96417) Re-registered NB-82-38 at unknown date
26045	(M-75026) Re-registered NJ-23-48 at unknown date
26159	(M-18698) Re-registered NB-57-26 at unknown date
26166	(M-12478) Re-registered NB-57-25 at unknown date
26287	(K-17855) Re-registered NB-25-97 at unknown date
27956	(GAO 3) Carried the pre-war body from Bedford WTL VN 7462
29009	(?) Re-registered NB-96-01 at unknown date
32374	(?) Re-registered NB-80-53 at unknown date
54091	(?) Rebodied C25F (unknown builder) and re-registered ERX 734 3/49 (W&G Chandler, Wantage (BE))
?	(?) Re-registered PB-02-01 at an unknown date
21058	(TN 4042) New as a lorry. To Orphanou, Ayia Marina (O-CY) as B29D 3/49
22026	(T 4045) New as a lorry. To Pastellis, Mandria (O-CY) as B25D 5/48
22169	(T 4051) New as a lorry. To Sevastides, Mandria (O-CY) as B27D 4/47
22253	(T 4043) New as a lorry. To Souleyman, Kyrenia (O-CY) as B30D 3/51
37684	(?) Re-registered GZ.3356 at unknown date after 1966. Later with RW Green, Whenuapai, Auckland (O-NZ)
63413	(P1.002) Date new given as 1954; maybe the date of conversion from a goods vehicle? Re-registered P1.203 at an unknown date. Re-registered EH.3279 at an unknown date after 1965
85484	(P1.003) Re-registered P1.602 at an unknown date
90323	(?) Re-registered EH.2892
121434	(P1.111) Re-registered P1.370 at an unknown date
136825	(?) Re-registered HU.2404 1965
187749	(?) Date new recorded as 1944 - cannot be correct.
?	(JA 8029) Chassis number recorded as 26744; probably 26744x, rather than a rebuild of a 1946 chassis
?	(P1.113) Re-registered EM.494 1965
?	(R-1224) Chassis number recorded as 24930L, presumably in error
?	The McWhinnie-bodied vehicle was re-registered DT.6195 1965

Bedford OLs (exact models unknown)
15365	(?) (OL-Z) Re-registered EY.3882 1965
16800	(?) Later in Tempe Museum (O-AUS)
23305	(TW 807) New as a lorry. To Paphitis, Mandres (O-CY) as B30D 4/56
23325	(?) (OL-C). New as a War Department (GOV) lorry. To Lefkaritis, Larnaca (O-CY) as B29D and re-registered T 7237 5/52
32368	(GZ-60875) (Assumed OL--). Re-registered NJ-48-58 at unknown date
40374	(?) (Assumed OL--). Re-registered NB-41-27 at unknown date
79661	(TN 7831) (OLAC ?) New as a lorry. To Angeli, Mitsero (O-CY) as B28D (6/60?)
80559	(?) Rebodied Armoury and re-registered KMN 938 4/49 (J Broadbent {Safeway}, Ramsey (IOM))
115269	(?) (Assumed OL--). Re-registered 32701 in 1956. Later with KTEL Chios City (O-GR) 5
115277	(?) (Assumed OL--). Re-registered 32702 in 1956. Later with KTEL Chios City (O-GR) 19
125531	(?) (Assumed OL--). Re-registered 67700 in 1956. Later with KTEL Kavala (O-GR)
130247	(61-929) (Assumed OL--). Re-registered 70372 in 1956. Later with KTEL Achaia (O-GR) 77
131124	(63-507) (Assumed OL--). Re-registered 70472 in 1956. Later with KTEL Achaia (O-GR) 93
132051	(62-292) (Assumed OL--). Re-registered 70404 in 1956. Later with KTEL Achaia (O-GR) 79
144516	(?) (Assumed OL--). Re-registered 55320 in 1956. Later with KTEL Imathia (O-GR)
147604	(?) (Assumed OL--). Re-registered 67908 in 1956. Later with KTEL Drama (O-GR)

168604 (?) Chassis number also recorded as 169604. Recorded as an OB but the chassis number indicates an OL. Re-registered NB-63-62 at an unknown date.
? (A-8463) Rebodied Ayats 632 C28- (Motor Union, Palma (O-E)) -/58
? (P2.776) Chassis number recorded in error as C13258
? (TL 745) (OLAD ?). New as a lorry. To Hassan, Vatili (O-CY) as B30D 8/60

C1252/239

BEDFORD ML

The K/M/O range had been launched in 1939 and after suspension of production during the war years reappeared late in 1945. ML models were of 4x2 configuration, with a wheelbase of 143 ins, designed for operation as 2 or 3-tonners. Production continued until 1953.

The chassis number series, engine and general mechanical specification were common to all models in the K/M/O range, including OBs.

The third character of the model designation referred to the ex-works body styling, C indicating that the vehicle left the factory as a chassis/cab, D that a drop-side body of Bedford's own manufacture was fitted and Z that no body was fitted (ie a chassis/scuttle). It is probable that many other MLs served as non-PSV passenger-carriers, although details have not been located.

BEDFORD MLC

32425	* T 4732	?		B25D	2/47	Agros Motor Co, Agros (O-CY)
32425	* T 4806	?		B25D	2/47	Nicolaou, Yialousa (O-CY)
33095	T 4862	?		B24D	3/47	Arsiotis, Yialousa (O-CY)
36652	* TN 4562	?		lorry	1/47	Original owner unknown (O-CY)
37166	TN 5313	?		B27D	6/47	Stephanides, Strovolos (O-CY)
53788	T 5849	?		B25D	8/47	Karacostas, Bellapais (O-CY)
53832	TN 5983	?		B26D	9/47	Therapontas, Kythrea (O-CY)
53867	T 5840	?		B25D	8/47	Mouharrem, Yeroskipou (O-CY)
53911	TN 5832	?		B27D	8/47	Zacharia, Kythrea (O-CY)
59409	T 6694	?		B26D	1/48	Vasiliades, Asgata (O-CY)
62331	T 6992	?		B21D	3/48	Thoma, Sanidha (O-CY)
63313	* T 6817	?		tipper	2/48	Original owner unknown (O-CY)
63614	* T 6999	?		lorry	3/48	Original owner unknown
66185	TN 6531	?		B25D	12/47	Zekki, Peristerona (O-CY)
66324	T 6970	?		B22D	3/48	Georghiou, Anoyira (O-CY)
83409	* T 8045	?		lorry	11/48	Original owner unknown (O-CY)
90187	B-79346	Ayats	237	C18-	-/48	Miguel Marti, Sabadell (O-E)
93398	T 8494	?		B25D	3/49	Aristides, Kilani (O-CY)
93409	TN 9057	?		B28D	8/49	EL Aglandjias, Aglandjia (O-CY)
93428	TN 8500	?		B28D	3/49	Petrou, Aphania (O-CY)
113684	* ?	Touw		B21-	-/49	Gebr. Hurks {De Peilkaan}, Breda (O-NL) 12
148855	* K-12532	Domburg	192	C22F	3/51	Tissing, 's-Gravenpolder (O-NL) 1
202409	?	Jonckheere	6094	C18F	3/51	Pauly et Graven {SADAR}, La Calamine (O-B)
209326	* TB 415	?		lorry	6/51	Original owner unknown (O-CY)
211559	* N-79178	Van Oers	56	C21F	8/51	Hurks {De Peilkaan}, Breda (O-NL) 16
220852	FFX 458	Lee		B20F	4/52	Dorset County Council (XDT)
225593	* N-13161	Jongerius		B21	3/52	Van Morkhoven, Tilburg (O-NL) 8
225739	FJT 86	Lee		B20F	7/52	Dorset County Council (XDT)
239950	TD 419	?		B25D	8/52	Arsos Co-operative, Arsos (O-CY)
255795	* N-38119	Van Oers	64	C21F	5/53	Balemans, Breda (O-NL) 19
259974	TF 446	?		B23D	6/53	Savva, Kyrenia (O-CY)
260006	TF 626	?		B25D	7/53	Fagoundri, Rizokarpaso (O-CY)
262584	TF 216	?		B25D	5/53	Matteou, Rizokarpaso (O-CY)

BEDFORD MLD

15853	* DBT 959	Rounding		B16F	-/46	W Norris, Driffield (ER)
17800	* HKM 175	?		-14-	2/46	LP Brenchley, Laddingford (KT)
21642	* HKM 914	?		-14-	6/46	WG Norris, Wouldham (KT)
116013	* LKP 961	?		LB14-	9/49	J Diprose {Belmont Coaches}, Goudhurst (KT)
121283	EG 9990	?		-12-	-/50	W Prior, Sutton (CM)

BEDFORD MLZ

25141	AGS 672	SMT	B19F	6/47	Loch Katrine Steamboat Co Ltd, Callander (PH)
25462	AGS 673	SMT	B19F	5/47	Loch Katrine Steamboat Co Ltd, Callander (PH)
26670	SB 6697	SMT	B19F	6/46	R & A Cowe, Tobermory, Mull (AL)
27414	FFS 854	SMT	B18-	2/47	M MacLennan, Govig, Harris (IV)

C1252/240

27472	SB 6920	(SMT ?)	B14F	-/47	J & H Caskie, Bowmore, Islay (AL)
27596	EGG 760	SMT	B14F	1/47	SCWS Ltd {The Skye Transport Co}, Portree (IV)
27698	AGS 674	SMT	B19F	7/47	Loch Katrine Steamboat Co Ltd, Callander (PH)
28378	BST 700	SMT	B19F	2/47	A Sutherland {Skye Cars}, Broadford (IV)
28484	AGS 675	SMT	B19F	4/47	Loch Katrine Steamboat Co Ltd, Callander (PH)
28511	AGS 677	SMT	B19F	4/47	Loch Katrine Steamboat Co Ltd, Callander (PH)
28579	SB 6937	(SMT ?)	B14F	4/47	Air Industrial Developments Ltd {Gold Line}, Dunoon (AL)
28606	AGS 676	SMT	B19F	-/47	Loch Katrine Steamboat Co Ltd, Callander (PH)
30152	SB 6919	SMT	B14F	6/47	R & A Cowe, Tobermory, Mull (AL)
31667	EYS 629	SMT	B19F	5/47	SCWS Ltd {The Skye Transport Co}, Portree (IV)
36284	EYS 630	SMT	B14F	5/47	SCWS Ltd {The Skye Transport Co}, Portree (IV)
36373	FGA 463	SMT	B19F	6/47	SCWS Ltd {The Skye Transport Co}, Portree (IV)
93413	T 8640	?	B23D	4/49	Theocharides, Kaminaria (O-CY)
93995 *	JUP 809	Burlingham	C14F	3/49	R & J Armstrong and Mrs M Wardle {Cowling's Bus Service}, Ebchester (DM)
124319	T 9526	?	B25D	1/50	Ahmet, Larnaca (O-CY)
124738	TN 9583	?	B25D	2/50	Giorgi, Asha (O-CY)
130013	LYH 616	Reall	B22F	-/51	London County Council (XLN) 1631
130195	LYH 617	Reall	B22F	-/51	London County Council (XLN) 1632
130285 *	LYH 618	Reall	B22F	-/51	London County Council (XLN) 1633
130914	T 9956	?	B25D	5/50	Kitsis, Angastina (O-CY)
130922	T 9865	?	B25D	5/50	Mehmet, Geunyeli (O-CY)
132636	LYH 619	Reall	B22F	-/51	London County Council (XLN) 1634
132734	LYH 620	Reall	B22F	-/51	London County Council (XLN) 1635
135007	LYH 621	Reall	B22F	-/51	London County Council (XLN) 1636
135359	LYH 622	Reall	B22F	-/51	London County Council (XLN) 1637
137648	LYH 623	Reall	B22F	-/51	London County Council (XLN) 1638
139056	LYH 624	Reall	B22F	-/51	London County Council (XLN) 1639
140956	LYH 625	Reall	B22F	-/51	London County Council (XLN) 1640
140968	TA 351	?	B25D	8/50	Piperides, Galata (O-CY)
152417	TA 973	?	B25D	2/51	Isaia, Loutros (O-CY)
152623	TA 972	?	B27D	2/51	PapaMichael, Psevdhas (O-CY)
153987	TB 026	?	B25D	2/51	Kleanthous, Kambia (O-CY)
154001	TB 012	?	B25D	2/51	Phani, Koutsovendis (O-CY)
204742	TB 189	?	B27D	3/51	PapaVarnava, Palekythro (O-CY)
204747	TB 159	?	B27D	3/51	Christodoulou, Trakhoni (O-CY)
211026	TB 467	?	B25D	6/51	Pieri, Kondemenos (O-CY)
211050	TB 606	?	B25D	7/51	Kallis, Karavas (O-CY)
213189	TB 860	?	B25D	9/51	Neophytou, Constandinou & Matsouka, Paleomylos (O-CY)
213517	TB 832	?	B25D	9/51	Christodoulou, Lyso (O-CY)
220146	TC 155	?	B25D	12/51	SP Tris Elion, Tris Elies (O-CY)
220269	TC 080	?	B25D	11/51	Makariou, Letimbou (O-CY)
222841	CV 862	?	-25-	3/52	Mawatagame Tours Ltd, location unknown (O-CL)
224270	TC 204	?	B28D	12/51	Panayi, Leonarisso (O-CY)
224326	TC 124	?	B25D	11/51	Theocharides, Kaminaria (O-CY)
226180	CV 1306	?	-22-	6/52	IMBC, location unknown (O-CL)
229846	CV 1328	?	-23-	6/52	IMBC, location unknown (O-CL)
234298	TC 753	?	B26D	4/52	Kitsis, Angastina (O-CY)
238695	TD 157	?	B24D	6/52	Kouspos, Pakhna (O-CY)
239035	TD 376	?	B26D	8/52	Strovolos Bus Co, Strovolos (O-CY)
240276	TD 484	?	B25D	8/52	Kleanthous & Himonas, Vasa Kilaniou (O-CY)
240348	TD 508	?	B25D	8/52	Louca, Khoulou (O-CY)
241861	TD 330	?	B25D	7/52	Nea EM Lapithou, Lapithos (O-CY)
242424	TD 494	?	B25D	8/52	Tsentas, Karavas (O-CY)
245374	TD 552	?	B27D	9/52	Hadji Mehmet, Tziaos (O-CY)
245430 *	TD 492	?	lorry	8/52	Original owner unknown (O-CY)
245449	TD 497	?	B27D	8/52	Ahmed, Larnaca (O-CY)
245454	TD 872	?	B25D	10/52	Liassi, Ayios Epiktitos (O-CY)
246122	TD 626	?	B25D	9/52	Ioannides, Kyperounda (O-CY)
246133	TD 514	?	B25D	8/52	Skarparis, Kokkinotrimithia (O-CY)
247897	TD 681	?	B25D	9/52	Christodoulou, Salamiou (O-CY)
247936	TD 775	?	B25D	10/52	Nicolaou, Yialousa (O-CY)

C1252/241

249201	TD 981	?	B25D	11/52	Kalli, Liopetri (O-CY)
249215	TE 24	?	B24D	11/52	Malakounides, Yialousa (O-CY)
251227	TE 258	?	B24D	1/53	Perivolia Co-op Farming Society, Perivolia (O-CY)
251248	TE 201	?	B25D	12/52	Kapera, Xerovounos (O-CY)
262527	TF 186	?	B26D	5/53	Kyriacou, Kythrea (O-CY)
?	JS 7324	SMT	B19F	6/47	Original owner unknown
?	JS 7325	SMT	B19F	6/47	Original owner unknown
?	JS 7326	SMT	B19F	6/47	P MacRitchie, Uig (RY)
?	JS 7327	SMT	B19F	6/47	J MacMillan, Lemreway (RY)

MISCELLANEOUS BEDFORD MLs, where full chassis designations are unknown

22819	KNO 773	?	20/goods	4/46	RG Knight, Harold Wood (EX)
24617	SJ 1072	?	B20F	7/46	R & A Cowe, Tobermory, Mull (AL)
62660	T 6850	?	B25D	2/48	Pieri, Kondemenos (O-CY)
62758	T 6846	?	B24D	2/48	E Kyriakou, Kalavasos (O-CY)
63247	TN 6904	?	B28D	3/48	Georghiou, Aglandjia (O-CY)
63518	* T 6860	?	lorry	2/48	Original owner unknown (O-CY)
88849	BG-15-26	?	DP20F	10/48	Escola de Regentes Agrícolas de Santarém (O-P)
117233	KXW 648	Reall	B22F	-/50	London County Council (XLN)
119003	HOR 704	Vickers (Portsmouth)	C16F	2/50	Glider & Blue Motor Services Ltd, Bishop's Waltham (HA) 20
144269	?	Jonckheere 6004	B18-	8/50	L Denis {Malmedy Cars}, Malmedy (O-B)
156368	* ?	?	lorry	-/51	War Department (GOV)
?	* GAO 81	Willowbrook 2383	B20F	11/46	E Hartness {Hartness Bus & Coach Service}, Penrith (CU)
?	* ?	?	C--F	-/--	Mostyn & Kenilworth Hotels, Eastbourne (XES)

NOTES

Bedford MLC
32425 (T 4732) Same chassis number also claimed by T 4806
32425 (T 4806) Same chassis number also claimed by T 4732
36652 (TN 4562) New as a lorry. To Panteli, Aradhippou (O-CY) as B23D 2/58
63313 (T 6817) New as a tipper. To Antoniou, Pyrgos (O-CY) as B23D 7/48
63614 (T 6999) New as a lorry. To Evangelou, Xylophagou (O-CY) 1/53
83409 (T 8045) New as a lorry. To Vasilidaes, Zoopiyi (O-CY) as B25D 7/49
113684 (?) Re-registered NB-75-33 at unknown date
148855 (K-12532) Re-registered NB-00-66 at unknown date
209326 (TB 415) Unknown owner (O-CY) as B25D 4/53
211559 (N-79178) Re-registered NB-58-67 at unknown date
225593 (N-13161) Re-registered NB-39-21 at unknown date
255795 (N-38119) Re-registered NB-77-11 at unknown date

Bedford MLD
15853 (DBT 959) Probably originally carried goods bodwork. Bus body by 1949
17800 (HKM 175) Originally carried goods bodywork; probably latterley a lorry/bus
21642 (HKM 914) Originally carried goods bodywork; probably latterley a lorry/bus
116013 (LKP 961) First registered as Goods/Hackney

Bedford MLZ
93995 (JUP 809) Carried the pre-war body from Northern General Commer Centaur CN 6107
130285 (LYH 618) Became a PSV with Mrs EA Potten, Whitstable (KT) as B14F 8/61
245430 (TD 492) New as a lorry. To Michael, Avgorou (O-CY) as B25D 12/53

Bedford MLs (exact models unknown)
63518 (T 6860) New as a lorry. To Charalambous, Xylophagou (O-CY) as B25D 12/50
156368 (?) New as a lorry. To Georghiou, Limnatis (O-CY) as B13D, re-registered TAF 554 6/57
? (GAO 81) Carried pre-war body from Commer WE 9079
? The vehicle for Mostyn & Kenilworth Hotels: Bedford publicity records this as a 143ins wheelbase chassis (=ML), but a photograph suggests it was more probably a KZ

C1252/242

BEDFORD K

The K/M/O range had been launched in 1939 and after suspension of production during the war years reappeared late in 1945. K models were of 4x2 configuration, with a wheelbase of 120 ins, and designed for loads of up to 30cwt. Production continued until 1953.

The chassis number series, engine and general mechanical specification were common to all models in the K/M/O range, including OBs.

The second character of the model designation referred to the ex-works body styling, C indicating that Bedford produced the vehicle as a chassis/cab, D that a drop-side body of Bedford's own manufacture was fitted, and Z indicating that neither cab nor body was fitted (ie supplied as a chassis/scuttle).

Many other Ks operated for a wide variety of passenger-carrying non-PSV uses, including estate buses, hotel buses, and with utility, local authority and ambulance services; details of individual vehicles have however not been located, apart from the representative selection shown below. It is probable that all of those were KZs with the possible exception of 143420, believed to have been a KC.

48389	* SB 7979	?	B7-	2/50	Original operator unknown
48926	KHU 739	?	B12-	4/49	Bristol Corporation (XGL)
51199	5519CB5	Spurling	B11DR	by7/47	BOAC, Marseilles (O-F)
54952	A-15682	Spurling	B11DR	9/47	BEA, Oslo (O-N)
82692	* GNM 261	?	van	-/--	Original operator unknown
85986	* TMV 320	SMT	C11F	10/48	BEA, Ruislip (MX) 2053
90794	TMK 571	Spurling	B7D	-/49	Valliant Direct Coaches Ltd, London W5 (LN)
96499	TMY 248	Spurling	B11D	3/49	BEA, Ruislip (LN) 2020
100993	SB 7719	(Munro ?)	B7F	5/49	M Munro, Lochbuie, Mull (AL)
116028	* JXX 327	?	B7F	c/50	? (GOV)
121902	MTO 683	Spurling	DP11D	c/50	Boots Drug Co, Nottingham (XNG)
140038	A 730	?	B13-	12/50	Cyprus Police, Nicosia (O-CY)
140212	A 816	?	B13-	12/50	Cyprus Police, Nicosia (O-CY)
141508	A 729	?	B13-	12/50	Cyprus Police, Nicosia (O-CY)
145565	KYW 727	Spurling	B11D/R	9/47	BEA, Oslo (O-N)
147628	KYW 740	Spurling	B6-	3/51	AWRE, Aldermaston (GOV)
149657	* ?	(Spurling ?)	B13-	-/50	War Department (GOV)
153420	* ?	?	?	-/51	Unknown operator (O-NZ)
208607	?	?	B--C	5/51	Unknown operator (O-N)
232395	* JFH 760	Spurling	B9F	2/52	Rotol Airscrews Ltd, Gloucester (XGL)
244053	NGK 245	Spurling	C7FM	9/52	Ministry of Supply (GOV)
248440	NGK 246	Spurling	B12-	9/52	Ministry of Supply (GOV)
248920	E 294	Spurling	B11D	1/53	British Middle East Office, Nicosia (O-CY)
249660	E 293	Spurling	B11D	1/53	British Middle East Office, Nicosia (O-CY)
?	DS 8041	?	?	-/48	OTC, Dar-Es-Salaam (O-EAT) 13
?	DSA 599	?	?	-/49	OTC, Dar-Es-Salaam (O-EAT) 20
?	DSA 789	?	?	-/49	OTC, Dar-Es-Salaam (O-EAT)
?	H 9041	?	?	-/--	OTC, Dar-Es-Salaam (O-EAT)
?	H 9537	?	?	-/--	OTC, Mombasa (O-EAK)
?	KAA 901	?	?	-/51	OTC, Mombasa (O-EAK)
?	KAA 902	?	?	-/51	OTC, Mombasa (O-EAK)
?	KAA 903	?	C7-	1/51	OTC, Mombasa (O-EAK)
?	KAA 904	?	C7-	1/51	OTC, Mombasa (O-EAK)
?	KBE 856	?	?	by3/51	OTC, Nairobi (O-EAK)
?	NGK 863	Spurling	?	-/52	Ministry of Supply (GOV)
?	W 3233	?	?	-/49	Gibbs Auto Tours (1947) Ltd, Nairobi (O-EAK) 42
?	W 3234	?	?	-/49	Gibbs Auto Tours (1947) Ltd, Nairobi (O-EAK) 41
?	W 3235	?	?	-/49	Gibbs Auto Tours (1947) Ltd, Nairobi (O-EAK) 40
?	W 3236	?	?	-/49	Gibbs Auto Tours (1947) Ltd, Nairobi (O-EAK) 43
?	W 3358	?	?	-/49	Gibbs Auto Tours (1947) Ltd, Nairobi (O-EAK) 44
?	W 3359	?	?	-/49	Gibbs Auto Tours (1947) Ltd, Nairobi (O-EAK) 45
?	W 3360	?	?	-/49	Gibbs Auto Tours (1947) Ltd, Nairobi (O-EAK) 32
?	?	Allweather	C11-	by3/47	Nyasaland Transport Co., Blantyre (O-EAN)
?	?	Fath	B---	by3/47	Nyasaland Transport Co., Blantyre (O-EAN)
?	* ?	NZMB	B13F	-/52	New Zealand Air Force (O-NZ)

C1252/243

NOTES
48389 (SB 7979) The final owner was JDS Cursitor, Colonsay (AL)
82692 (GNM 261) Converted to 7-seat PSV at unknown date and operated by Manson, West Sandwick (SD)
85986 (TMV 320) BEA operated this as a non-PSV crew-bus in Orkney
116028 (JXX 327) Later with Pentland Hotel, Thurso (CS)
149657 (?) Not confirmed as a K type. To British Middle East Office, Nicosia (O-CY)
153420 (?) Re-registered HR.5346 1965
232395 (JFH 760) Re-registered PFF 777 (in preservation) 7/94
? The NZMB-bodied vehicle for the New Zealand Air Force was re-registered OC 1562 and DPT 632 with Wanganui Heritage Coachlines (O-NZ) by 10/12

Duple bodies 53470 to 53646 were fitted to an export order of Bedford KZ chassis. The majority have been described as "pick-ups"; while it could be assumed that these were purely for goods use, such needs would normally be met by standard Bedford products. The fact that Duple was involved suggests these were rather more sophisticated, quite possibly with a passenger compartment. All were supplied to the Anglo-Iranian Oil Co for use in Iraq. For the record, the Duple bodies (and KZ chassis numbers) were as follows:

Ch No	Du B No	Ch No	Du B No	Ch No	Du B No	Ch No	Du B No
84934	53495	100821	53522	109148	53562	114163	53606
85629	53504	101318	53524	109738	53560	114179	53607
85636	53492	101377	53526	109747	53568	114245	53608
85739	53496	101541	53517	109829	53563	115218	53610
85982	53497	101639	53523	109896	53566	115307	53609
87770	53471	101937	53525	109902	53564	115718	53611
88263	53470	102019	53521	109911	53565	116097	53612
96578	53483	102551	53520	109978	53567	116257	53617
96605	53477	102633	53518	110521	53569	116336	53613
96664	53488	102715	53519	110527	53570	116419	53614
96750	53473	102797	53515	110534	53571	116425	53615
96777	53476	103095	53516	110985	53573	116441	53616
96836	53475	103131	53534	110991	53574	116530	53618
96863	53472	103587	53527	110999	53572	116611	53623
96922	53474	103885	53535	111327	53576	116619	53622
96949	53484	104517	53528	111330	53575	116691	53619
97008	53486	104599	53530	111395	53579	116882	53621
97035	53479	104681	53529	111653	53578	116953	53624
97094	53485	104763	53536	111661	53577	116969	53620
97300	53478	105049	53531	111729	53580	117058	53625
97387	53489	105213	53533	111735	53581	117131	53628
97473	53505	105295	53532	111743	53584	117147	53627
97669	53481	105377	53537	111811	53582	117220	53626
97749	53482	105675	535xx	111817	53583	117489	53632
97913	53480	105757	53546	112412	53585	117508	53631
97999	53490	105839	535xx	112428	53586	117589	53630
98085	53487	105921	53543	112494	53590	117597	53629
98434	53494	106207	53542	112510	53587	117678	53637
98521	53491	106371	535xx	112576	53589	117691	53636
98607	53493	106927	535xx	112592	53588	117767	53635
98697	53498	106931	53540	112660	53592	117779	53638
98736	53499	106936	53538	112678	53591	118227	53642
98822	53500	107009	53545	113361	53601	118300	53634
98903	53501	107018	535xx	113377	53598	118316	53633
98910	53502	107080	53544	113443	53599	118389	53641
98920	53503	107158	53539	113538	53594	118405	53640
98989	53507	107476	53541	113540	53602	118478	53639
99961	53506	108058	535xx	113542	53604	118494	53643
100043	53509	108262	535xx	113607	53596	118740	53644
100125	53508	108271	535xx	113622	53597	129511	53645
100207	53510	108330	535xx	113689	53593	129578	53646
100289	53511	108340	535xx	113999	53595	132009	53647
100371	53513	108644	535xx	114003	53600		
100453	53514	108655	53561	114081	53603		
100739	53512	108715	535xx	114097	53605		

C1252/244

(Note: Body numbers shown 535xx were in the range 53547 to 53559, but one chassis number for that block is unknown)

Further known similar vehicles are as follows:

77657	Duple 50767	The protype vehicle for the Anglo-Iranian Oil Co contract
85113	Duple 50740	Ango Iranian Oil Co, Iraq
99352	Duple 53654	United Africa Co, East Africa - probably in Kenya
99430	Duple 53655	United Africa Co, East Africa - probably in Kenya

The records of Nyasaland Transport Co Ltd, Blantyre (O-EAN) indicate that 22 Bedford KZ with Allweather 11 seat bodies were placed in service in 1947

BEDFORD JCV

Unlike the other models covered in this publication, the JCV was not part of the K/M/O range, although it too had first appeared in 1939, with production resuming in 1945.

The JCV was intended for use as a 10/12cwt van, and the chassis had a wheelbase of 105 ins. It was fitted with a Bedford 1442cc petrol engine, rated at 12hp. A variant offered by Bedford was for the van body to be converted by Martin Walter to provide 6 passenger seats; this conversion was known as the Utilecon.

8235	HTD 72	Martin Walter	B6-	5/47	W Robinson & Son, Great Harwood (LA)
13177	JTF 262	Martin Walter	B6-	8/48	W Robinson & Son, Great Harwood (LA)

C1252/245

BEADLE CHASSISLESS VEHICLES INCORPORATING BEDFORD RUNNING UNITS

John C Beadle of Dartford, Kent, produced four prototype fully-fronted light-alloy chassis-less vehicles in 1946, each using running units from a different manufacturer. These were a Bedford (LNO 150), a Commer (HKK 26), a Dennis Ace (FNG 818) and a Leyland Cub (FUO 481).

Production commenced in 1948. Listed below are those vehicles constructed using Bedford running units, including the standard 3519cc 28hp petrol engine; apart from the final three, all went to Tilling Group companies.

All of the Beadle chassis-less vehicles shared a common numbering scheme, vehicles using running units of other manufacture accounting for gaps in the following list.

Beadle also produced 75 bodies (numbers C104 to C178) on standard OB chassis; all went to Tilling companies and are detailed in the main OB listing.

JCB3	* LNO 150	B33R	11/46	Eastern National, Chelmsford (EX) 3924
JCB31	HOD 123	B35R	-/48	Southern National, Exeter (DN) 2001
JCB32	JFM 990	B35R	-/48	Crosville MS, Chester (CH) SC18
JCB33	JFM 991	B35R	-/48	Crosville MS, Chester (CH) SC19
JCB34	HOD 124	B35R	1/49	Southern National, Exeter (DN) 2002
JCB35	HOD 125	B35R	2/49	Southern National, Exeter (DN) 2003
JCB36	HOD 126	B35R	2/49	Southern National, Exeter (DN) 2004
JCB37	HOD 127	B35R	2/49	Southern National, Exeter (DN) 2005
JCB38	HOD 58	B35R	2/49	Southern National, Exeter (DN) 2007
JCB39	HOD 59	B35R	2/49	Southern National, Exeter (DN) 2008
JCB40	HOD 60	B35R	2/49	Southern National, Exeter (DN) 2009
JCB41	* HPW 801	B35R	3/49	Eastern Counties, Norwich (NK) CB816
JCB42	* HPW 802	B35R	3/49	Eastern Counties, Norwich (NK) CB817
JCB43	* HPW 803	B35R	3/49	Eastern Counties, Norwich (NK) CB818
JCB44	NVX 525	B33R	3/49	Eastern National, Chelmsford (EX) 4011
JCB45	NVX 526	B33R	6/49	Eastern National, Chelmsford (EX) 4012
JCB46	NVX 527	B33R	7/49	Eastern National, Chelmsford (EX) 4013
JCB47	FFU 157	B35R	3/49	Lincolnshire RCC, Bracebridge Heath (KN) 722
JCB48	FFU 158	B35R	3/49	Lincolnshire RCC, Bracebridge Heath (KN) 723
JCB49	FFU 159	B35R	4/49	Lincolnshire RCC, Bracebridge Heath (KN) 724
JCB50	* HPW 804	B35R	5/49	Eastern Counties, Norwich (NK) CB819
JCB51	* HPW 805	B35R	7/49	Eastern Counties, Norwich (NK) CB820
JCB52	* HPW 806	B35R	7/49	Eastern Counties, Norwich (NK) CB821
JCB53	NVX 528	B33R	3/49	Eastern National, Chelmsford (EX) 4014
JCB54	NVX 529	B33R	6/49	Eastern National, Chelmsford (EX) 4015
JCB55	NVX 530	B33R	7/49	Eastern National, Chelmsford (EX) 4016
JCB56	HOD 61	B35R	7/49	Western National, Exeter (DN) 2010
JCB57	HOD 62	B35R	7/49	Western National, Exeter (DN) 2011
JCB58	HOD 63	B35R	7/49	Western National, Exeter (DN) 2012
JCB59	FFU 160	B35R	7/49	Lincolnshire RCC, Bracebridge Heath (KN) 725
JCB60	FFU 161	B35R	7/49	Lincolnshire RCC, Bracebridge Heath (KN) 726
JCB61	FFU 162	B35R	7/49	Lincolnshire RCC, Bracebridge Heath (KN) 727
JCB62	* HPW 807	B35R	8/49	Eastern Counties, Norwich (NK) CB822
JCB63	* HPW 808	B35R	8/49	Eastern Counties, Norwich (NK) CB823
JCB64	* HPW 809	B35R	8/49	Eastern Counties, Norwich (NK) CB824
JCB65	HOD 64	B35R	-/49	Western National, Exeter (DN) 2013
JCB66	HOD 65	B35R	-/49	Western National, Exeter (DN) 2014
JCB67	HOD 66	B35R	-/49	Western National, Exeter (DN) 2015
JCB68	* HPW 810	B35R	9/49	Eastern Counties, Norwich (NK) CB825
JCB69	* HPW 811	B35R	9/49	Eastern Counties, Norwich (NK) CB826
JCB70	* HPW 812	B35R	9/49	Eastern Counties, Norwich (NK) CB827
JCB71	HOD 67	B35R	8/49	Western National, Exeter (DN) 2016
JCB72	HOD 68	B35R	8/49	Western National, Exeter (DN) 2017
JCB73	HOD 69	B35R	-/49	Western National, Exeter (DN) 2018
JCB74	NVX 531	B33R	9/49	Eastern National, Chelmsford (EX) 4017
JCB75	NVX 532	B33R	9/49	Eastern National, Chelmsford (EX) 4018
JCB76	NVX 533	B33R	10/49	Eastern National, Chelmsford (EX) 4019
JCB77	* HPW 813	B35R	10/49	Eastern Counties, Norwich (NK) CB828
JCB78	* HPW 814	B35R	10/49	Eastern Counties, Norwich (NK) CB829

JCB79 *	HPW 815	B35R	10/49	Eastern Counties, Norwich (NK) CB830
JCB80 *	HPW 816	B35R	10/49	Eastern Counties, Norwich (NK) CB831
JCB116	KYH 957	van	-/50	Danish Bacon Co, London (GLN)
JCB122	HFH 368	B35R	6/50	SK & F Silvey {Silvey's Coaches}, Epney (GL)
JCB156	HFH 702	B35R	11/50	SK & F Silvey {Silvey's Coaches}, Epney (GL)

Notes:
JCB3   (LNO 150) Prototype. Just possibly used Bedford OB chassis 33038 as a source of componentry.
JCB41   (HPW 801) Received Gardner 4LK engine in 1952
JCB42   (HPW 802) Received Gardner 4LK engine in 1952
JCB43   (HPW 803) Received Gardner 4LK engine in 1952
JCB50   (HPW 804) Received Gardner 4LK engine in 1952
JCB51   (HPW 805) Received Gardner 4LK engine in 1952
JCB52   (HPW 806) Received Gardner 4LK engine in 1952
JCB62   (HPW 807) Received Gardner 4LK engine in 1952
JCB63   (HPW 808) Received Gardner 4LK engine in 1952
JCB64   (HPW 809) Received Gardner 4LK engine in 1950
JCB68   (HPW 810) Received Gardner 4LK engine in 1952
JCB69   (HPW 811) Received Gardner 4LK engine in 1952
JCB70   (HPW 812) Received Gardner 4LK engine in 1952
JCB77   (HPW 813) Received Gardner 4LK engine in 1950
JCB78   (HPW 814) Received Gardner 4LK engine in 1950
JCB79   (HPW 815) Received Gardner 4LK engine in 1950
JCB80   (HPW 816) Received Gardner 4LK engine in 1950

REGISTRATION TO CHASSIS NUMBER CROSS REFERENCE
(UK & Irish Civilian Registrations Only)

An * denotes a re-registered vehicle

Reg	Chassis	Reg	Chassis	Reg	Chassis	Reg	Chassis
AS 1930	105014	EU 8714	57991	FT 5651	12714	HG 9240	52463
DJ 9464	20831	EU 8758	59875	FT 5666	15061	HG 9241	66622
DJ 9730	41971	EU 8793	64105	FT 5679	17287	HI 4180	?
DS 2275	5826	EU 9170	81420	FT 5680	17294	HI 4569	?
EF 7577	17270	EU 9533	98634	FT 5681	15058	HI 4939	?
EF 7578	15081	EU 9833	111015	FT 5784	24245	HI 5692	?
EF 7579	17296	EU 9895	115437	FT 5785	24699	HI 5828	105693
EF 7580	17282	EX 5500	34602	FT 5794	22287	ID 3507	15035
EF 7663	25966	EX 5501	34630	FT 5795	23055	IH 5806	16695
EF 7664	25121	EX 5508	29466	FT 5820	34004	IH 5807	16698
EF 7665	25166	EX 5566	29165	FT 5828	33400	IH 5808	16699
EF 7666	25048	EX 5621	40361	FT 5829	33646	IL 4579	105342
EF 7778	32823	EX 5626	40641	FT 5884	35291	IN 6485	103269
EF 7779	32874	EX 5627	41502	FT 5885	35281	IP 4862	18763
EF 7955	36039	EX 5760	51479	FT 5892	34997	IP 5113	30583
EF 7992	48517	EX 5777	50138	FT 5893	36257	IP 5589	?
EF 8093	55201	EX 5818	55373	FT 5894	35488	IP 5726	?
EF 8132	62378	EX 5870	56916	FT 5895	36155	IP 6517	?
EF 8165	58695	EX 5874	58639	FT 5896	36089	IY 1947 *	94761
EF 8223	58468	EX 5900	59479	FT 5974	45815	JC 7729	17291
EF 8254	64348	EX 6000	65179	FT 6102	55732	JC 7732	17202
EF 8336	69590	EX 6031	61932	FT 6281	66848	JC 7734	17248
EF 8616	92847	EX 6148	65511	FT 6282	69840	JC 8317	41862
EF 8891	109281	EX 6324	97427	FT 6358	77544	JC 8451	50655
EF 8983	112937	EX 6526	114198	FT 6526	92433	JC 8464	48343
EF 9219	120034	EX 6653	122719	FT 6642	105811	JC 8509	57410
EF 9295	130953	EX 6700	128063	FT 6795	118993	JC 8725	58217
EF 9296	130966	EX 6754	136941	FT 6905	132165	JC 8745	57349
EF 9408	136509	EX 6830	143226	FT 7009	144456	JC 8845	58405
EG 7358	42032	EX 6837	142535	GL 8583	15014	JC 8887	64243
EG 9990	121283	EY 8600	72997	GL 9200	24872	JC 8898	59357
EJ 7671	15089	EY 9025	100169	GR 9196	49665	JC 8924	67724
EJ 8108	44645	EY 9392	126578	GR 9615	64597	JC 9621	92404
EJ 8620	61434	FA 8543	47300	GR 9616	58898	JC 9712	96481
EJ 9403	87485	FF 6711	79450	GR 9682	67847	JC 9825	99373
EJ 9693	100265	FF 6737	56672	GR 9748	63872	JE 7906	13425
EM 4077	50741	FF 7716	129173	GR 9805	74131	JE 7925	18707
EM 4227	58598	FI 3910	?	GR 9967	66664	JE 7984	17292
EM 4507	102152	FI 4022	?	GV 9759	15911	JE 8578	32206
EM 4637	125746	FI 4070	79563	GV 9861	18710	JE 8712	30716
EM 5107	146425	FI 4515	?	GV 9865	12720	JK 9188	26964
EN 8923	45353	FI 4991	?	GV 9866	20830	JK 9589	48124
EN 8955	49073	FO 4654	21836	GV 9928	21484	JM 5699	11028
EN 8956	51398	FO 4711	34549	GV 9970	18760	JM 6497	44062
EN 9871	116564	FO 4712	36447	HB 6144	18746	JM 6548	35245
EO 8906	99692	FO 4777	39180	HB 6145	18748	JM 6677	49247
EO 9151	122920	FO 4785	39408	HB 6146	18750	JM 6731	43536
EP 8950	15914	FO 4842	40951	HB 6147	18772	JM 7090	60519
EP 9031	18556	FO 5069	59319	HB 6361	38673	JM 7327	75270
EP 9387	38782	FO 5127	64870	HB 6362	38613	JM 8031	97056
EP 9388	39230	FO 5416	89438	HB 6536	72407	JM 8477	109720
EP 9548	46764	FO 5506	97070	HB 6538	44072	JM 9103	128071
EP 9588	49301	FO 5513	95949	HB 6539	41712	JM 9696	143883
EP 9982	63236	FO 5731	111110	HB 6629	66236	JM 9852	147336
EU 7942	11083	FO 5798	124180	HB 6648	85315	JP 5946	38742
EU 7948	12712	FO 6021	138244	HC 8218	72518	JP 5950	42257
EU 8097	22892	FP 4207	17220	HC 9178	101327	JP 6242	47187
EU 8535	51555	FP 4771	74838	HC 9888	114135	JP 6243	49791
EU 8541	53597	FP 4997	102514	HG 8641	29942	JP 6376	47099

JP 6500	56983	PS 1977	137617	SB 8280	142354	SX 6518	98375
JP 6522	26724	PS 1991	138294	SB 8378	146320	SX 6525	99557
JP 6523	53491	PS 1999	141679	SE 6725	86414	SX 6901	133648
JP 6591	58826	PV 8172	57790	SH 8394	88102	SX 7007	143247
JP 6692	65400	PV 8242	60503	SH 8570	105239	SX 7039	144734
JP 6750	66776	PV 8261	57594	SH 8692	119343	SY 8104	42371
JP 6751	64124	PV 8831	85173	SH 8855	125343	SY 8172	42851
JP 6752	67284	PV 9136 see PV 9316		SJ 1042	18708	SY 8240	36924
JP 6876	72832	PV 9316	102775	SJ 1072	24617	SY 8483	65098
JP 6878	30523	PV 9371	109693	SJ 1081	40212	SY 8499	65585
JP 6921	65523	PV 9636	115464	SJ 1082	110308	SY 8812	85584
JP 7017	80703	RC 9963	50646	SJ 1113	44880	SY 8878	88725
JP 7018	76660	RN 492	132701	SJ 1119	49670	SY 8975	96645
JP 7040	67238	RN 493	132768	SJ 1120	37138	SY 9044	101249
JP 7299	92776	RN 494	132685	SJ 1125	43244	SY 9207	114058
JP 7335	95977	RN 495	133308	SJ 1168	65050	SY 9249	116674
JP 7509	101324	RN 496	133944	SJ 1243	94757	SY 9265	117259
JP 7562	106273	RN 497	134016	SJ 1263	103247	SY 9278	118261
JP 7941	110352	RN 498	134034	SJ 1288	111345	SY 9516	138450
JP 8036	122822	RN 499	137054	SJ 1340	145785	SY 9523	138889
JP 8079	126149	RN 501	137773	SK 3033	38564	SY 9561	141658
JP 8139	129065	RN 502	138228	SK 3073	51470	VV 9042	12020
JP 8295	127411	RN 503	138454	SK 3384	92212	WI 2117	16696
JP 8415	134775	RN 504	139282	SL 2970	32563	WI 2317	52824
JP 8530	144272	RN 505	138788	SL 3073	54811	XG 8276	13493
JS 6924	12025	RN 506	139409	SL 3305	104172	XG 9631	62891
JS 6963	17204	RN 507	140798	SL 3474	140027	XS 5822	25613
JS 7166	24422	RN 508	133284	SO 6882	5899	XS 6185	57667
JS 7297	24428	RN 509	133927	SO 8176	62664	XS 6564	94127
JS 7326	?	RN 511	135793	SO 8770	107200	YJ 8332	22870
JS 7327	?	RN 512	135294	SO 9111	141407	YJ 8446	22311
JS 7693	65009	RN 513	133372	SO 9258	139562	YJ 8447	22418
JS 7766	69954	SB 6697	26670	SO 9300	76562	YJ 8524	22584
JS 7796	72209	SB 6704	18759	SS 5568	6047	YJ 8939	33499
JS 7799	70550	SB 6705	19801	SS 5610	5543	YJ 9064	43970
JS 7853	76009	SB 6785	32836	SS 6192	13427	YJ 9093	41512
JS 7899	78239	SB 6825	38406	SS 6556	54632	YJ 9190	45372
JS 8089	89529	SB 6826	38287	SS 6690	64815	YJ 9291	43211
JS 8159	91300	SB 6827	38475	SS 6785	69146	ZB 8127	?
JS 8208	102281	SB 6828	38346	SS 6786	70399	ZH 7684	73447
JS 8232	99565	SB 6907	42236	SS 6817	73682	ZH 9892	58962
JS 8579	119522	SB 6919	30152	SS 7023	66711	ZH 9893	68288
JS 8710	118321	SB 6920	27472	SS 7041	91841	ZH 9894	68363
JS 8852	134000	SB 6937	28579	SS 7237	109966	ZH 9895	71063
JS 9020	143108	SB 7161	58817	SS 7245	111388	ZH 9896	71121
JS 9239	145092	SB 7180	65114	SS 7360	119529	ZH 9897	71974
JV 9032	12769	SB 7183	64807	SS 7376	121153	ZJ 4945	?
JV 9375	18743	SB 7264	78322	SS 7486	130194	ABR 6	83731
JX 9549	42269	SB 7470	87745	SS 7501	132317	ABR 143	75935
JX 9550	42202	SB 7611	97849	SS 7691	145687	ABR 226	89697
JX 9673	44656	SB 7709	108757	SU 4894	60362	ABR 587	102736
JX 9674	45456	SB 7719	100993	SU 5267	93030	ABR 752	107153
JX 9967	51885	SB 7743	88069	SW 7172	47107	ACC 88	108625
KI 3429	?	SB 7744	97293	SW 7187	44834	ACC 238	115197
NI 5254	?	SB 7765	106348	SW 7449	73999	ACC 629	131392
NI 5255	?	SB 7779	108282	SW 7747	106328	ACC 712	130666
NS 1953	12771	SB 7799	112905	SW 7944	116367	ACC 724	123731
NS 1984	25245	SB 7809	114028	SW 8039	123662	ACC 849	138779
NS 2050	43558	SB 8023	111306	SX 5901	44141	ACC 883	121379
NS 2283	110978	SB 8052	127199	SX 5925	43109	ACF 54	15901
NS 2401	146267	SB 8057	128619	SX 6103	59127	ACF 72	45704
OS 7567	136443	SB 8075	131311	SX 6151	60157	ACF 181	25340
OS 7715	144284	SB 8085	131664	SX 6203	65074	ACF 272	38228
PS 1407	15088	SB 8159	140671	SX 6218	66187	ACF 669	40650

C1252/249

ACF 672	39583	AJV 454	80759	BCF 411	75390	BHV 741	35357
ACF 680	33098	AJV 656	85239	BCF 573	80005	BHV 792	35233
ACH 850	68050	AKS 314	65963	BCH 280	111130	BHV 793	34870
ACM 990	(98547 ?)	AMS 944	25040	BCK 189	40541	BJD 4	30385
ACN 288	50025	ANH 252	51135	BCK 190	40380	BJD 5	28060
ACP 509	59382	ANH 698	60583	BCK 328	41532	BJD 6	30689
ACP 562	48331	ANH 831	66905	BCK 329	42461	BJD 7	30671
ACP 729	57462	ASD 961	12710	BCK 330	43502	BJD 815	51064
ACP 730	62144	ASN 465	66313	BCK 331	44026	BJL 341	63617
ACP 760	73865	ASN 502	66753	BCK 535	45571	BJL 342	63718
ADJ 57	68245	ASV 541 *	116301	BCK 551	44415	BJL 705	71793
ADJ 778	117032	ASY 804 *	18714	BCK 552	47950	BJN 475	24604
ADO 270	17213	ATL 885	11098	BCK 647	45746	BJR 268	34079
AEB 49	57939	ATS 186	65850	BCK 799	50931	BJR 450	44262
AEB 204	62474	ATS 294	81855	BCK 800	50903	BJR 643	51222
AEC 543	117547	ATS 408	86011	BCK 894	50912	BJR 679	44678
AEE 158	45442	ATS 689	100257	BCK 895	50299	BJR 802	34636
AEE 578	56099	AVV 654	96805	BCK 982	46336	BJR 803	36083
AEE 760	57286	AVV 669	92428	BCN 170	97403	BJR 825	48218
AEE 764	59924	AVV 814	98032	BCN 192	99458	BJR 946	52981
AEE 966	66281	AVV 882	103222	BCN 943	145366	BJR 947	52662
AEG 615	141954	AVV 941	96232	BCP 368	115655	BJR 956	50704
AEJ 145	110580	AWG 989	39668	BCP 612	122845	BJT 168	11035
AEJ 323	124363	AWG 990	39681	BCS 981	52040	BJT 169	11041
AEJ 642	139321	AWG 991	39623	BCT 54	17218	BJT 170	11023
AEJ 813	146488	AWG 992	45266	BCT 55	17222	BJT 171	11019
AEN 63	131614	AWG 993	52976	BCT 188	21516	BJT 217	11660
AEN 300	143764	AWG 994	52994	BCW 814	35883	BJT 470	15096
AEN 342	143032	AWG 995	53322	BDC 387	145434	BJT 471	15001
AEP 76	69878	AWG 996	52987	BDO 89	48904	BJT 472	15083
AEP 551	83176	AWG 997	42804	BDO 338	51305	BJT 889	15918
AEP 849	98950	AWG 998	54925	BDO 539	54602	BJT 890	15078
AFB 266	50750	AWG 999	42437	BDO 540	54524	BJT 891	15098
AFB 455	63178	AXG 498	127936	BDO 574	54571	BJT 892	15047
AFB 730	73528	AYJ 499	122740	BDO 644	56612	BJT 893	15909
AFB 939	78400	AYJ 666	131963	BDT 659	5530	BJT 894	15039
AFL 49	145771	BAG 574	24864	BEB 121	108560	BJT 901	20835
AGL 449	89515	BBR 223	143932	BEE 100	103556	BJT 902	20837
AGR 174	116464	BBR 320	145428	BEE 551	116642	BJT 943	21716
AGR 321	122264	BBV 84	30274	BEE 806	120927	BJV 140	133203
AGR 416	117011	BBV 148	42179	BEP 157	110318	BJV 292	136278
AGR 826	137906	BBV 351	44845	BEP 691	137785	BJV 590	142125
AGR 945	125530	BBV 483	51986	BEP 882	144844	BJV 591	143972
AGS 215	12022	BBV 514	51963	BES 700	39349	BKS 97	113569
AGS 672	25141	BBV 520	52806	BES 789	51727	BKS 179	117160
AGS 673	25462	BBV 809	55651	BES 790	42359	BMS 93	54917
AGS 674	27698	BBV 896	56849	BES 876	36936	BMS 94	54946
AGS 675	28484	BCB 7	61231	BES 973	45742	BMS 95	55315
AGS 676	28606	BCB 50	64496	BFK 574	47231	BMS 96	55251
AGS 677	28511	BCB 84	62826	BFK 857	47064	BMS 97	70545
AGV 194	48203	BCB 96	58000	BGL 373	137221	BMS 98	70538
AGV 653	57784	BCB 97	58304	BGS 69	54515	BMS 99	70603
AGV 957	64146	BCB 169	68987	BGS 433	65425	BMS 293	59115
AGV 967	64372	BCB 263	66305	BGS 480	66193	BMS 931	70312
AHC 222	129422	BCB 286	70791	BGS 536	41040	BMS 932	70558
AHE 957	50289	BCB 476	75297	BGS 537	64235	BNH 603	121843
AHF 81	50053	BCB 542	77461	BGS 538	58874	BNL 642	12718
AHF 82	56200	BCB 684	83195	BGS 595	67124	BNL 673	12061
AHF 893	143892	BCB 785	29806	BGS 721	74845	BNL 674	20822
AHL 970	46779	BCB 857	87633	BGV 155	90958	BNL 675	20833
AJC 41	145444	BCB 858	89090	BGV 261	95880	BNL 676	21634
AJL 289	33073	BCB 872	88698	BGV 719	108247	BNL 894	18754
AJV 91	68006	BCB 965	91238	BGV 782	110947	BNL 929	15076
AJV 190	71777	BCF 339	70305	BGV 845	112837	BNL 930	15092

BPR 398	23792	BWG 39	73977	CCS 511	90241	CFX 728	54735
BPR 399	23873	BWG 40	73969	CCS 857	100333	CFX 977	57240
BPR 400	23697	BWG 41	75317	CCT 596	55287	CGS 45	103854
BPR 401	23704	BWG 42	75084	CCT 954	58840	CGS 134	68815
BPR 402	23496	BWG 43	75320	CDB 322	34662	CGS 285	112633
BPR 403	23658	BWG 244	75999	CDB 323	35937	CGS 339	109268
BPR 500	26279	BWG 245	76441	CDB 680	50732	CGS 423	114626
BPR 501	27852	BWG 246	76466	CDB 717	48301	CGS 566	115418
BRC 188	128561	BWG 247	75945	CDB 799	51253	CGS 572	116278
BRN 61	54552	BWG 248	76285	CDB 896	51628	CGS 766	120212
BRN 62	49886	BWG 540	103439	CDO 851	91763	CGV 134	143028
BRN 190	56826	BWG 983	99928	CDO 921	92792	CGV 583	144908
BRN 361	56636	CAG 37	65162	CDP 231	17285	CGV 691	145080
BRN 362	57952	CAG 89	65195	CDP 232	17210	CHH 508	59197
BRN 494	58691	CAN 155	57599	CDP 233	18744	CHJ 76	42416
BRN 495	60069	CAN 260	60132	CDP 234	19802	CHJ 415	49930
BRN 497	64783	CBL 502	5490	CDP 235	19808	CHL 679	128746
BRN 498	67437	CBN 748	51934	CDP 236	17207	CHL 687	143084
BRN 499	67370	CBU 418	6430	CDP 768	34726	CHS 895	41558
BRN 500	68264	CBV 67	95385	CDP 769	36144	CHS 896	36812
BRN 565	67365	CBV 274	101278	CDT 759	12006	CJA 440	64953
BRN 654	67375	CBV 353	105087	CDT 772	13416	CJA 520	62875
BRN 710	68311	CBV 509	106561	CDY 294	18787	CJA 521	62907
BRN 791	69804	CBV 618	109798	CDY 737	52454	CJA 707	73552
BRN 837	73200	CBV 857	116065	CDY 946	63229	CJA 716	72892
BRN 958	76226	CBW 522	40680	CEP 4	145684	CJD 40	77187
BRN 962	77123	CBW 722	45826	CES 163	60330	CJL 35	96270
BRN 963	75531	CBX 810	11092	CES 447	67488	CJL 130	99311
BRS 603	22167	CCB 150	118873	CES 473	88983	CJL 647	110270
BRS 638	24517	CCB 175	125700	CES 721	67482	CJN 299	83357
BRS 718	28435	CCB 186	125782	CES 926	103064	CJN 361	73098
BRS 719	28157	CCB 201	125593	CFE 957	54496	CJR 255	82122
BRS 856	28413	CCB 298	130896	CFK 274	57522	CJR 449	85061
BSD 139	54410	CCB 349	132949	CFK 363	74359	CJR 455	87547
BSN 259	127290	CCB 516	137095	CFK 448	79043	CJR 530	88711
BST 173	15907	CCB 524	137598	CFK 872	90963	CJR 696	92962
BST 700	28378	CCB 528	137682	CFN 623	37080	CJR 832	94744
BST 854	46988	CCB 654	141239	CFN 624	37091	CJT 185	58446
BTK 624	44045	CCB 676	141223	CFR 735	33140	CJT 596	64081
BTK 866	44687	CCB 861	144490	CFR 878	34884	CJT 864	68449
BTS 242	143724	CCF 11	117121	CFR 879	36458	CJY 317	12021
BTY 63	24333	CCF 67	118238	CFR 977	52672	CJY 531	17246
BTY 64	25128	CCF 462	120868	CFV 66	45537	CJY 532	17224
BTY 187	17205	CCF 470	124076	CFV 128	51017	CJY 533	15960
BTY 202	18781	CCF 648	129693	CFV 167	52852	CJY 534	17211
BTY 203	18792	CCF 649	134642	CFV 194	52869	CJY 535	17263
BTY 348	23359	CCF 669	137848	CFV 208	49867	CJY 536	17268
BTY 380	23684	CCK 30	77170	CFV 237	49895	CJY 537	17277
BTY 533	25787	CCK 31	79407	CFV 415	56619	CJY 538	17206
BTY 626	32932	CCK 32	81994	CFV 617	59294	CMS 47	101414
BTY 627	32960	CCK 486	49427	CFV 677	60951	CMS 103	105005
BTY 628	33617	CCK 487	50799	CFV 678	61265	CMS 316	110304
BTY 629	33915	CCK 528	84898	CFV 827	67432	CNL 151	50827
BTY 630	33826	CCK 529	82897	CFV 839	69813	CNL 252	53313
BTY 631	33706	CCK 530	85922	CFV 840	67815	CNL 262	62330
BTY 656	33337	CCK 567	87544	CFV 846	53534	CNL 263	80793
BTY 823	32190	CCK 572	86459	CFV 847	52767	CNL 312	54697
BUD 279	11024	CCK 589	86023	CFV 851	68894	CNL 417	56844
BUD 522	20829	CCK 590	88789	CFV 893	69754	CNL 566	57624
BVG 190	6112	CCK 591	93043	CFV 970	60885	CNL 832	61008
BVG 722	17245	CCK 927	96984	CFV 994	74689	CNL 947	66458
BVL 338	11081	CCL 687	43477	CFV 995	52878	CNL 973	63808
BVV 239	112558	CCL 888	49263	CFW 829	11105	CNV 668	11096
BVV 418	144891	CCS 330	87374	CFW 833	12004	CPM 450	11082

CPM 895	22396	CTL 490	69911	CWH 640	60020	DBK 944	35042
CPM 963	21309	CTL 625	73042	CWH 694	68655	DBM 59	39/OB/1
CPN 183	17271	CTL 941	77625	CWH 817	61499	DBN 51	66047
CPR 425	76452	CTL 967	79244	CWH 821	77547	DBN 157	90475
CPR 693	75034	CTY 7	66842	CWH 923	73049	DBN 252	92688
CPR 923	80863	CTY 146	57199	DAG 284	120945	DBN 627	102117
CPY 821	11657	CTY 168	68225	DAG 298	124972	DBN 677	103228
CPY 822	11658	CTY 265	69759	DAG 347	123980	DBT 959	15853
CRD 36	40421	CTY 303	69994	DAG 578	135029	DBU 78	25518
CRD 37	40761	CTY 535	76520	DAG 739	141663	DBU 79	25606
CRD 591	50034	CTY 580	71757	DAJ 178	29188	DBU 341	29513
CRD 592	51818	CTY 605	49557	DAJ 216	28468	DBU 386	30307
CRD 593	55229	CTY 753	66614	DAJ 590	38633	DBU 530	40470
CRD 594	56022	CTY 754	59416	DAJ 738	33723	DBU 536	41632
CRD 595	58414	CTY 811	74930	DAJ 846	33111	DBU 594	25549
CRD 596	61684	CUD 365	56818	DAP 807	42077	DBU 688	32809
CRD 649	49483	CUD 568	57388	DAV 614	42314	DBU 689	34828
CRD 678	51174	CUD 647	61522	DAW 41	26413	DBU 788	36280
CRD 842	56570	CUD 724	57631	DAW 346	28482	DBU 836	36102
CRD 978	58631	CUD 825	69151	DAW 349	34815	DBU 870	46709
CRD 979	59890	CUD 900	64437	DAW 469	35835	DBU 887	45861
CRG 517	33659	CUJ 29	20821	DAW 470	35861	DBU 888	51269
CRG 682	43267	CUJ 30	19809	DAW 471	34062	DBU 889	51611
CRG 736	43154	CUJ 38	15917	DAW 472	34740	DBU 890	52887
CRG 991	58670	CUJ 46	21306	DAW 473	31145	DBU 902	51583
CRN 90	93545	CUJ 619	23404	DAW 474	33365	DBU 936	46363
CRN 91	102596	CUJ 652	26291	DAW 475	30313	DBW 67	88030
CRN 136	103275	CUJ 654	25580	DAW 550	35203	DBW 372	77530
CRN 158	101599	CUJ 655	25290	DAW 552	39438	DBW 534	80765
CRN 159	102079	CUJ 656	25303	DAW 589	35143	DBW 576	80924
CRN 417	108095	CUJ 657	26304	DAW 746	37816	DBW 612	81945
CRN 438	114555	CUJ 658	26484	DAW 766	36320	DBW 613	82194
CRN 440	109184	CUX 527	11029	DAW 922	39527	DBW 854	85251
CRN 501	112527	CUX 528	11031	DAW 938	40931	DBX 152	44017
CRN 502	112535	CUX 589	12001	DAY 499	11099	DBX 579	51592
CRN 503	112929	CUX 591	11039	DAY 752	12780	DBX 677	44534
CRN 504	112866	CUX 592	12024	DBA 348	72885	DBX 850	55950
CRN 505	113637	CUX 614	12717	DBD 150	30698	DBX 862	54608
CRN 506	113955	CUX 760	13413	DBD 151	32433	DCA 574	12784
CRN 712	116982	CUX 804	18755	DBD 500	36345	DCA 643	17216
CRS 44	61516	CUX 995	18740	DBD 907	43060	DCA 644	17266
CRS 808	79901	CVA 242	17255	DBD 933	41952	DCJ 474	11033
CRV 436	20828	CVD 148	38544	DBD 936	68033	DCJ 776	17242
CRV 983	33001	CVD 695	38267	DBD 937	68669	DCJ 777	17243
CRX 546	11097	CVG 219	56783	DBD 938	68683	DCK 410	135722
CRX 547	12005	CVH 239	23489	DBD 939	73895	DCK 565	137750
CRX 857	15054	CVH 240	23504	DBD 940	73858	DCL 151	85854
CRX 858	15074	CVH 241	33264	DBD 941	75697	DCL 804	111704
CSA 234	15075	CVH 317	26820	DBE 95	18742	DCO 99	19816
CSA 472	15905	CVH 986	40202	DBE 346	13428	DCO 553	32083
CST 42	55699	CVH 987	40236	DBE 653	18795	DCO 554	30960
CST 343	65842	CVH 988	39838	DBE 773	21304	DCO 555	32078
CST 511	66103	CVH 989	42134	DBE 808	45239	DCO 556	31261
CTH 200	18780	CVL 789	74076	DBE 809	45325	DCO 557	30356
CTH 201	20838	CVN 71	17208	DBE 810	45480	DCO 558	31679
CTH 636	33185	CVN 153	17214	DBE 811	45504	DCS 981	144820
CTK 178	80017	CVN 208	15902	DBE 812	44749	DCT 303	83440
CTK 210	83280	CVN 564	18709	DBE 813	49536	DCT 994	95459
CTK 524	83998	CWH 266	62956	DBE 814	47350	DCX 256	44276
CTK 548	88387	CWH 267	60190	DBE 815	47295	DCX 257	45335
CTL 67	62859	CWH 340	66498	DBE 816	51231	DCX 301	45968
CTL 166	63296	CWH 370	67388	DBE 817	47864	DCX 424	51867
CTL 275	64937	CWH 525	58937	DBK 461	41077	DCX 626	47977
CTL 460	67773	CWH 558	76434	DBK 623	36333	DCX 627	47494

C1252/252

DCX 628	47317	DFU 400	29605	DJN 740	121865	DNT 735	45296
DCX 738	58768	DFU 435	31000	DJN 991	128984	DNT 763	45598
DCX 884	68499	DFV 47	105026	DJR 159	135430	DNT 879	47112
DCX 964	65433	DFV 52	106965	DJR 264	134665	DNT 880	47147
DDB 394	88026	DFV 175	108131	DJR 344	129532	DNV 810	54467
DDB 501	90073	DFV 242	109960	DJR 485	132785	DNV 983	56624
DDB 801	103362	DFV 456	113001	DJR 564	139474	DOD 530	6998
DDB 847	105361	DFV 663	118809	DJR 665	141306	DOD 531	7224
DDB 891	106512	DFV 727	120058	DJR 871	143680	DOD 532	7100
DDB 959	108033	DFV 801	122291	DJT 241	108161	DOD 533	6059
DDL 874	11106	DFV 802	120650	DJT 376	111797	DOD 534	8951
DDL 924	13488	DFV 960	126291	DJT 995	114299	DOD 535	9074
DDL 928	13490	DFV 974	126492	DJU 210	17203	DOD 536	9083
DDL 929	15072	DFV 976	127222	DJU 532	21611	DOD 537	9056
DDM 262	18741	DFW 90	40500	DJU 831	24612	DOD 543	6402
DDM 783	42449	DFW 131	40755	DJY 6	54716	DOD 544	6595
DDM 981	48302	DFW 182	41602	DJY 810	60352	DOD 545	6189
DDN 450	75061	DFW 207	42247	DKG 12	46838	DOD 546	6220
DDN 777	69787	DFW 765	46977	DMO 246	26178	DOD 547	6083
DDO 242	119700	DFW 993	49800	DMO 247	31390	DOD 548	7122
DDO 324	121859	DFX 57	93652	DMO 248	43494	DOD 549	6708
DDO 529	121593	DFX 144	94144	DMO 249	47206	DOD 550	5422
DDP 117	62094	DFX 458	96866	DMO 250	62370	DOD 551	9011
DDP 295	65328	DFX 932	105190	DMO 251	63599	DOD 552	8918
DDP 561	59445	DHH 886	130055	DMO 349	43527	DOD 553	9022
DDP 632	75850	DHJ 22	86302	DMO 351	44586	DPM 267	59963
DDP 912	82840	DHJ 23	90066	DMO 422	45420	DPM 371	56741
DDR 744	47088	DHJ 24	94371	DMR 835	11713	DPM 945	63334
DDT 244	23228	DHJ 229	91397	DMS 234	147057	DPM 946	63897
DDY 383	90768	DHJ 464	99401	DNL 272	102649	DPN 936	68492
DEA 230	55536	DHJ 623	103900	DNL 351	104665	DPR 300	119071
DEA 410	60757	DHJ 624	104564	DNL 580	108360	DPR 477	115248
DEA 940	81323	DHJ 625	121146	DNL 601	107529	DPR 606	123097
DEA 996	87451	DHM 69	86396	DNL 676	111918	DPR 667	117022
DES 200	135948	DHM 352	95521	DNL 690	108819	DPY 113	42981
DES 382	141465	DHM 402	96062	DNR 53	30658	DPY 708	48159
DET 51	22360	DHM 657	98055	DNT 26	39477	DRD 74	86038
DET 94	26509	DHM 769	106829	DNT 27	39657	DRD 382	95893
DET 779	56909	DHS 86	47137	DNT 28	40571	DRD 426	97781
DET 961	67861	DHS 192	60371	DNT 49	39507	DRD 605	104026
DFE 392	91326	DHS 537	76988	DNT 59	36482	DRD 820	107763
DFE 708	102070	DHS 629	84867	DNT 90	39378	DRG 411	101421
DFE 750	105230	DHS 933	99549	DNT 146	40979	DRG 529	105865
DFK 248	113674	DHS 939	103976	DNT 147	40661	DRJ 92	49403
DFK 443	120589	DHV 216	115973	DNT 241	39649	DRJ 334	92942
DFK 717	125439	DHV 617	126240	DNT 417	42971	DRP 100	55937
DFR 95	78873	DHV 645	127446	DNT 418	45361	DRP 101	56830
DFR 242	82033	DJA 480	120767	DNT 419	43301	DRP 289	56931
DFR 404	82619	DJA 971	131602	DNT 420	44117	DRP 722	61409
DFR 655	93570	DJB 117	28258	DNT 421	44650	DRP 900	63608
DFR 686	90495	DJB 279	28607	DNT 422	44387	DRS 493	133661
DFR 699	94999	DJB 379	31007	DNT 523	40941	DRV 27	66861
DFR 700	95937	DJB 406	30332	DNT 533	41742	DRV 140	68435
DFR 701	96827	DJB 410	30974	DNT 556	40901	DRV 685	75993
DFR 702	98544	DJB 786	41070	DNT 569	36005	DRV 931	64138
DFR 703	98569	DJD 217	138326	DNT 570	35433	DRX 296	51424
DFR 704	98763	DJD 477	143338	DNT 571	36013	DRX 723	54798
DFR 705	100005	DJF 671	13415	DNT 606	41022	DSA 896	64888
DFR 706	97420	DJL 52	135758	DNT 662	40860	DSR 391	26990
DFR 707	100347	DJL 677	145420	DNT 672	42337	DSR 500	24596
DFR 708	100969	DJN 548	121213	DNT 673	42816	DST 158	98386
DFR 827	100191	DJN 551	138314	DNT 674	42292	DST 478	114678
DFR 987	102130	DJN 552	140148	DNT 675	42012	DST 528	117081
DFU 224	29519	DJN 553	140536	DNT 731	37204	DST 566	121674

Code	Number	Code	Number	Code	Number	Code	Number
DST 800	130332	DUT 149	45396	EAW 275	65641	EBW 49	114391
DTH 435	65311	DUT 345	39564	EAW 280	63044	EBW 124	117249
DTH 903	71397	DUT 448	39827	EAW 281	64985	EBW 130	118689
DTH 960	58293	DUT 630	45873	EAW 283	66262	EBW 299	116903
DTH 999	73901	DUX 74	55618	EAW 285	67810	EBW 300	124813
DTK 256	130785	DUX 160	57257	EAW 394	69352	EBX 77	44181
DTK 346	128409	DUX 337	54893	EAW 511	70189	EBX 511	80322
DTK 503	128154	DUX 355	56955	EAW 637	71439	EBX 666	61072
DTK 536	134521	DUX 356	57293	EAW 653	71303	EBX 831	86754
DTK 636	128437	DUX 357	57680	EAW 857	71651	ECA 166	47200
DTK 935	128512	DUX 473	57543	EAW 858	72649	ECA 231	49765
DTK 936	137117	DUX 584	58224	EAW 859	72974	ECA 621	55845
DTL 224	102035	DUX 585	61249	EAY 50	49843	ECA 907	60415
DTL 264	100953	DUX 586	60927	EAY 605	51241	ECA 963	62241
DTL 772	111886	DUX 587	61693	EAY 848	41881	ECJ 65	39358
DTL 965	108388	DUX 601	59972	EAY 881	57086	ECJ 116	39398
DTP 149	34753	DUX 786	62696	EAY 882	57279	ECJ 144	40671
DTP 212	54802	DUX 945	62778	EBA 857	142680	ECJ 151	41551
DTP 218	55220	DVA 987	64445	EBC 221	20832	ECJ 282	43457
DTP 308	34106	DVD 166	70388	EBC 883	39171	ECJ 389	44663
DTP 413	57336	DVD 401	83969	EBC 909	39487	ECJ 777	51147
DTP 416	55976	DVD 536	73476	EBC 980	40740	ECJ 845	49783
DTP 417	55982	DVG 806	141377	EBD 300	69266	ECJ 897	51379
DTP 877	64856	DVH 81	62753	EBD 567	72824	ECL 190	145512
DTP 878	60395	DVH 133	59793	EBD 856	44129	ECO 384	73128
DTP 929	66219	DVH 169	66214	EBD 900	74909	ECO 456	72645
DTP 948	56860	DVH 183	66727	EBE 307	44347	ECO 698	77090
DTY 19	114304	DVH 210	68387	EBE 435	51054	ECO 746	57011
DTY 225	114914	DVH 217	68919	EBE 788	56145	ECO 801	77559
DTY 419	118986	DVH 434	74943	EBK 257	89313	ECO 974	69127
DTY 515	119310	DVH 531	76861	EBL 42	64113	ECO 997	66809
DTY 719	124679	DVH 837	83793	EBL 349	60439	ECR 57	29748
DTY 730	123620	DVH 916	90137	EBL 430	60536	ECT 190	118982
DTY 780	125349	DVJ 22	18712	EBL 647	59737	ECT 912	135037
DTY 810	129075	DVJ 759	35370	EBL 952	66720	ECX 79	93450
DTY 811	129193	DVJ 760	35257	EBL 954	89774	ECX 80	93602
DTY 954	129025	DVJ 767	35459	EBL 960	120143	ECX 81	93963
DTY 955	128614	DVJ 859	36913	EBL 962	146404	ECX 82	95476
DTY 995	130681	DVL 269	118464	EBL 967	67260	ECX 83	96812
DUD 127	93970	DVL 789	129442	EBM 606	25799	ECX 412	103155
DUD 385	101570	DVN 24	53445	EBM 615	11027	ECX 413	104100
DUD 522	104625	DVN 37	52405	EBM 615	26003	ECX 430	104735
DUD 755	111263	DVN 715	51709	EBM 616	28545	ECX 484	105877
DUD 762	110662	DVN 754	59938	EBM 760	21919	ECX 566	108291
DUD 810	111258	DVN 799	64743	EBO 431	90164	ECX 599	108834
DUH 110	63732	DVY 948	102228	EBT 172	28867	ECX 983	116386
DUH 627	66028	DWH 470	123389	EBT 240	30079	ECY 458	40391
DUJ 97	49958	DWH 709	132084	EBU 13	34093	ECY 702	45879
DUJ 185	41641	DWH 750	134580	EBU 24	54830	ECY 803	47224
DUJ 197	48165	DWH 870	126058	EBU 106	55883	EDA 691	32633
DUJ 216	49143	DWH 871	131970	EBU 157	57822	EDA 693	31157
DUJ 251	48940	DWV 82	17293	EBU 223	65698	EDA 694	32976
DUJ 252	49107	DWV 260	24154	EBU 294	66929	EDA 695	34182
DUJ 253	49817	DWV 776	26233	EBU 296	64832	EDA 696	33928
DUJ 254	49878	DYS 933	12002	EBU 301	69529	EDB 39	135975
DUJ 296	50629	EAJ 14	63344	EBU 449	67225	EDB 535	145779
DUJ 436	50836	EAJ 645	70218	EBU 503	60060	EDK 965	12071
DUJ 483	51280	EAJ 679	68823	EBU 578	77025	EDL 140	23112
DUJ 684	54477	EAJ 680	71056	EBU 595	77488	EDL 141	23196
DUJ 931	55658	EAO 177	5560	EBU 674	77871	EDL 256	23785
DUJ 933	54707	EAP 447	79483	EBU 709	67210	EDL 257	23880
DUJ 934	55579	EAW 112	60975	EBU 771	72999	EDL 283	25592
DUJ 935	56590	EAW 131	65553	EBU 865	87529	EDL 284	26522
DUN 903	41828	EAW 225	63678	EBU 984	89081	EDL 285	28500

C1252/254

EDL 375	30093	EFU 247	61996	EJW 257	35822	EPY 860	81484
EDL 376	30117	EFU 361	60034	EJW 258	35802	ERD 334	140060
EDL 445	36069	EFU 362	63376	EJW 259	36500	ERD 808	146368
EDL 446	35446	EFU 375	48501	EJW 260	36836	ERG 164	145540
EDL 447	35891	EFU 571	57113	EJW 713	41922	ERJ 25	142363
EDL 448	35338	EFU 575	57858	EJW 714	39299	ERJ 427	147024
EDL 475	40371	EFU 655	64791	EJW 715	39319	ERP 45	68575
EDL 618	43579	EFU 656	67274	EJW 804	43289	ERP 922	107458
EDL 637	49489	EFU 662	64299	EJW 915	40991	ERX 7	89711
EDL 638	48423	EFU 772	62281	EJY 146	100437	ERX 284	93371
EDL 639	49521	EFU 858	70332	EJY 250	103444	ERX 534	101241
EDL 640	51544	EFV 448	145064	EJY 737	106594	ERX 734 *	54091
EDL 641	57018	EFW 91	71980	EKG 501	106316	ERX 848	100490
EDL 642	57159	EFW 92	68887	EKG 702	110598	ERY 576	46766
EDL 708	44714	EFW 119	70697	EKU 726	38277	ERY 636	47849
EDL 761	46941	EFW 414	73027	EKW 874	55461	ERY 721	46146
EDL 808	50192	EFW 501	74050	EKY 703	58284	ERY 722	49358
EDL 809	50845	EFX 173	142539	EMJ 62	33634	ERY 861	50157
EDL 840	46111	EFX 231	132391	EMJ 334	40263	ESA 920	97798
EDL 850	51952	EFX 232	133594	EMJ 999	43391	ESL 175 *	90670
EDL 918	55349	EFX 290	140554	EMO 5	75410	ETH 180	94396
EDL 942	55799	EFX 337	141641	EMO 6	58985	ETH 545	101982
EDL 956	55389	EFX 493	141319	EMO 524	84871	ETH 888	102572
EDL 973	57024	EGD 150	32150	EMO 735	90249	ETH 984	105804
EDM 203	60463	EGD 448	30664	EMR 107	46948	◄ETL 221	134198 ►
EDM 327	49195	EGG 760	27596	EMR 335	51638	ETL 373	140636
EDM 783	76847	EGG 789	40731	EMR 601	50109	ETP 806	114230
EDM 935	76230	EGG 790	40581	EMR 870	54391	EUD 38	141644
EDP 95	115670	EGG 791	37193	EMW 59	51876	EUD 126	145416
EDP 757	126680	EGG 792	37168	EMW 96	54576	EUD 284	144721
EDP 924	131316	EHH 96	145059	EMW 141	56054	EUD 448	146115
EDR 345	87039	EHJ 300	135705	EMW 145	49570	EUE 421	11731
EDR 561	90559	EHM 332	141362	EMW 165	57402	EUE 798	17244
EDR 792	95062	EHR 74	42191	EMW 490	57212	EUH 894	128595
◄EDR 793	94892 ►	EHR 801	44170	EMW 788	55723	EUJ 118	70225
EDT 208	52567	EHS 350	140759	EMW 939	60982	EUJ 279	82084
EDT 409	56041	EHS 464	139314	ENL 154	145072	EUJ 441	82208
EDT 666	60830	EHV 65	146572	ENL 224	146435	EUJ 502	83754
EDW 541	66375	EJB 167	71598	ENR 176	69545	EUJ 593	85051
EDW 691	76087	EJB 232	106266	ENR 262	70733	EUJ 691	86056
EDY 44	127381	EJB 233	106343	ENR 294	72926	EUJ 832	88782
EEA 160	92743	EJB 234	103848	ENR 428	73920	EUJ 855	86828
EEA 400	63368	EJB 242	104017	ENR 429	73988	EUK 533	48315
EEA 480	107118	EJB 271	73613	ENR 840	75940	EUK 534	51075
EEA 500	65923	EJB 369	72272	ENR 935	76999	EUK 535	51185
EEA 830	119353	EJB 460	67839	ENT 102	73662	EUK 540	55597
EED 618	52031	EJB 503	73579	ENT 283	76023	EUK 892	56078
EET 35 *	?	EJB 628	74847	ENT 284	76257	EUK 893	56577
EET 261	80846	EJF 39	52906	ENT 731	76166	EUN 51	61669
EET 572	95084	EJF 778	63246	ENT 808	72915	EUN 87	63214
EET 951	109677	EJF 919	58439	ENT 866	77127	EUN 88	64566
EEW 974	55638	EJN 22	146535	ENT 876	77567	EUN 176	62338
EFK 133	139478	EJT 792	144376	ENT 963	77654	EUN 318	67938
EFK 224	146879	EJU 136	58125	ENT 964	78868	EUN 612	65569
EFR 32	128637	EJU 164	60455	ENV 250	79423	EUN 626	72553
EFR 185	132709	EJU 319	62022	ENV 309	85041	EUT 65	77475
EFR 226	134738	EJU 397	62988	ENX 893	12003	EUT 145	78817
EFR 388	139018	EJU 691	61418	EOT 404	11063	EUT 160	82025
EFR 517	142108	EJU 694	61613	EOT 784	15913	EUT 169 see EUT 619	
EFR 535	141653	EJU 699	64749	EOU 856	22334	EUT 284	79347
EFR 561	142579	EJU 786	64283	EOW 870	63278	EUT 619	83719
EFR 740	144754	EJU 822	67167	EPR 572	143993	EUT 851	89347
EFU 70	44194	EJU 936	68325	EPR 835	144364	EUT 880	87397
EFU 82	58328	EJW 75	34795	EPY 809	77721	EUT 917	90468

C1252/255

EUT 923	88395	FAA 241	28269	FBL 677	110940	FDL 240	67910
EUX 7	89613	FAA 242	28288	FBL 756	111761	FDL 278	69719
EUX 8	89768	FAA 243	28349	FBL 779	113661	FDL 318	71259
EUX 26	76915	FAA 244	28507	FBM 339	47265	FDL 354	72487
EUX 149	91603	FAA 863	29700	FBO 57	131686	FDL 432	75501
EUX 203	92387	FAA 921	26219	FBT 200	49202	FDL 455	77463
EUX 320	92862	FAA 987	28038	FBT 402	52472	FDL 535	67761
EUX 369	94020	FAB 202	25333	FBT 900	59931	FDL 537	81411
EUX 474	94722	FAB 463	28975	FBT 967	67328	FDL 577	83182
EUX 557	95858	FAB 498	30055	FBU 7	93974	FDL 581	83340
EUX 618	96147	FAB 930	36178	FBU 27	94977	FDL 627	85158
EUX 758	97962	FAC 527	33206	FBU 117	99451	FDL 640	75013
EUX 922	99631	FAC 726	34733	FBU 171 *	34828	FDL 655	83091
EUY 356	11661	FAC 892	36128	FBU 376	109764	FDL 656	85342
EUY 592	12767	FAJ 749	105354	FBU 493	114825	FDL 676	87567
EUY 855	38396	FAJ 851	107614	FBU 777	121951	FDL 713	89333
EUY 994	17267	FAJ 872	108209	FBU 829	126137	FDL 773	92298
EVA 540	92879	FAJ 874	109216	FBU 915	128470	FDL 802	91827
EVA 974	102212	FAM 210	72320	FBU 927	129370	FDL 842	96558
EVD 51	100947	FAM 250	73666	FBX 54	110252	FDL 869	97714
EVD 683	115245	FAM 313	72685	FBX 240	112623	FDL 905	99618
EVD 969	118797	FAP 9	122946	FBX 535	116295	FDL 969	102693
EVH 283	124588	FAW 40	101997	FCA 139	68613	FDM 554	105251
EVH 578	141945	FAW 46	101591	FCA 383	80946	FDM 569	106883
EVH 664	136406	FAW 277	102760	FCA 498	87022	FDM 695	108040
EVH 719	136525	FAW 375	101332	FCA 506	85148	FDM 914	117100
EVH 882	140896	FAW 498	104473	FCA 555	87007	FDN 777	146183
EVH 883	141389	FAW 523	101699	FCJ 14	65633	FDP 299	143926
EVJ 74	54420	FAW 531	108369	FCJ 353	72510	FDR 244	130175
EVJ 439	56990	FAW 532	107661	FCJ 354	73394	FDR 295	132759
EVJ 441	57106	FAW 620	103033	FCJ 752	74835	FDT 102	73518
EVJ 572	58833	FAW 762	106911	FCJ 780	71898	FDT 718	87406
EVJ 923	64089	FAW 994	108618	FCJ 781	77199	FDT 788	66824
EVN 100	86843	FAX 324	41738	FCJ 915	78729	FDV 8	47141
EVN 485	91223	FAX 325	41542	FCO 111	114217	FDV 210	32185
EVY 44	121123	FAY 102	92411	FCO 345	118331	FDV 233	46821
EWD 229	22783	FAY 549	95437	FCR 985	46172	FDV 383	42839
EWF 402	44252	FAY 599	98391	FCX 63	144758	FDV 548	48005
EWF 631	50610	FAY 675	97869	FCY 152	72548	FDV 591	46955
EWF 644	52019	FAY 691	74994	FCY 390	52049	FDV 628	48401
EWN 5	49677	FAY 797	98849	FCY 435	80501	FEA 50	GH1
EWN 18	56777	FAY 954	102294	FCY 949	92396	FEA 270	140567
EWN 19	61354	FAY 980	100183	FDA 122	55623	FEA 420	142630
EWN 368	56511	FBC 465	72561	FDA 256	55713	FED 175	76601
EWN 863	64721	FBC 597	76513	FDA 258	55758	FED 399	86861
EWN 917	67204	FBC 904	76874	FDA 461	60838	FED 422	93396
EWN 967	69142	FBC 905	77640	FDA 536	60084	FED 767	104555
EWV 155	62491	FBC 930	51923	FDD 832	13423	FER 241	43426
EWV 378	63816	FBC 931	46181	FDD 863	12019	FER 841	45448
EWV 389	66156	FBC 932	60894	FDG 107	20840	FES 129 *	18733
EWV 655	68329	FBC 933	46124	FDG 108	21301	FET 205	118499
EWV 967	69405	FBD 200	111119	FDG 128	23373	FET 279	122181
EWX 273	11043	FBD 311	113069	FDG 343	21551	FEW 55	57050
EWX 274	11034	FBD 788	116291	FDK 570	40551	FEW 800	81233
EWX 943	11080	FBE 131	71950	FDK 571	42089	FFD 480	12026
EWY 35	12715	FBE 215	81343	FDK 572	48551	FFG 741	48083
EWY 61	12723	FBE 853	89431	FDK 573	55480	FFH 8	51026
EYG 100	24161	FBE 924	90566	FDK 682	52653	FFH 293	57564
EYS 629	31667	FBE 981	91790	FDL 23	57946	FFH 399	64396
EYS 630	36284	FBJ 870	17260	FDL 43	59235	FFH 551	71036
EZE 692 *	141231	FBK 559	134661	FDL 68	58401	FFH 781	79672
FAA 238	28204	FBK 749	139377	FDL 69	55591	FFS 247	33417
FAA 239	28226	FBL 401	108784	FDL 154	63352	FFS 548	41648
FAA 240	28250	FBL 515	109170	FDL 239	67289	FFS 589	41611

FFS 854	27414	FFW 437	109368	FKW 571	98563	FPW 92	17221
FFS 855	34904	FFX 458	220852	FKW 572	98712	FPY 228	111111
FFS 856	55894	FFY 628	35911	FMJ 544	69885	FPY 296	111925
FFS 857	57816	FFY 776	57762	FMJ 694	72024	FPY 559	115184
FFS 858	57808	FFY 949	65674	FMJ 933	73038	FRK 443	41061
FFS 859	57918	FFY 950	65690	FMO 92	124631	FRM 88	11659
FFS 860	57897	FGA 463	36373	FMO 583	132208	FRW 67	29442
FFS 861	57882	FGA 566	45251	FMO 627	133326	FRX 310	142947
FFS 862	57878	FGD 203	57741	FMO 743	132379	FRX 313	139390
FFS 863	57673	FGD 815	63101	FMO 880	137198	FRX 314	140822
FFS 864	57691	FGD 888	66958	FMR 140	86927	FRX 315	142021
FFS 865	57801	FGE 343	65950	FMR 168	86470	FRX 533	137183
FFS 866	59281	FGE 384	64509	FMR 236	89411	FRX 700	141591
FFS 867	59326	FGE 460	63101	FMR 791	92949	FRY 12	66012
FFS 868	58720	FGE 835	65408	FMW 40	96649	FRY 295	86951
FFS 869	67119	FGE 836	64907	FMW 144	100154	FRY 481	92240
FFS 870	67451	FGE 837	66398	FMW 503	99944	FRY 684	93565
FFS 871	67468	FHO 456	39538	FMW 730	102567	FRY 932	100482
FFS 872	67780	FHO 494	35413	FNG 931	13440	FSA 232	120606
FFS 873	67776	FHO 595	41781	FNJ 136	137753	FSA 589	128942
FFS 874	67446	FHO 790	41562	FNP 336	39141	FSA 927	137585
FFS 875	68626	FHO 864	42917	FNP 411	42056	FSC 186	35192
FFS 876	73450	FHP 782	29629	FNP 909	42122	FSC 723	43379
FFS 877	73378	FHR 25	75245	FNR 237	114283	FSF 507	43550
FFS 878	73412	FHR 502	77794	FNT 88	109119	FSG 280	57268
FFS 879	73561	FHR 839	82626	FNT 89	111843	FSG 815	59430
FFS 880	73652	FHR 876	68293	FNT 449	112398	FSP 181	54543
FFS 881	75481	FJB 364	112392	FNT 593	113093	FSP 300	43322
FFS 882	75603	FJB 267	119697	FNT 851	114381	FSP 327	58133
FFS 883	75610	FJF 663	109928	FNT 861	114801	FSP 898	66937
FFS 884	75620	FJF 833	83817	FNV 280	124008	FSR 333	108312
FFS 885	76555	FJT 86	225739	FNV 500	126005	FSV 424 *	132253
FFS 886	75256	FJU 191	93363	FNV 705	130083	FTG 99	11036
FFS 887	76531	FJU 810	110392	FNV 999	139465	FTG 353	11104
FFS 901	51497	FJU 817	111779	FOD 25	68238	FTG 392	11020
FFS 902	52510	FJU 950	112006	FOD 697	72546	FTG 393	11062
FFS 903	52577	FJW 100	67834	FOD 945	72313	FTG 400	11021
FFS 904	52586	FJW 101	58269	FOR 567	45229	FTG 446	12068
FFU 104	92227	FJW 102	58623	FOR 633	45768	FTG 536	15915
FFU 121	92855	FJW 103	63628	FOR 634	45778	FTG 628	18757
FFU 157	JCB47	FJW 104	58430	FOR 732	39850	FTG 629	18766
FFU 158	JCB48	FJW 105	62459	FOR 741	47884	FTG 630	18767
FFU 159	JCB49	FJW 106	61764	FOR 817	47116	FTH 100	130860
FFU 160	JCB59	FJW 107	66368	FOR 907	48578	FTH 201	138233
FFU 161	JCB60	FJW 108	62233	FOT 19	49186	FTH 369	136501
FFU 162	JCB61	FJW 109	63320	FOT 20	49436	FTH 816	145569
FFU 347	97063	FJW 110	65988	FOT 214	47014	FTH 935	144400
FFU 352	96875	FJW 111	68019	FOT 215	55792	FTH 943	146509
FFU 594	100273	FJW 112	70128	FOT 237	48116	FTM 367	58660
FFU 852	102529	FJW 113	67523	FOT 256	47998	FTM 994	63750
FFU 874	102662	FJW 114	66125	FOT 285	48169	FTX 237	20827
FFU 961	105075	FJW 115	69743	FOT 352	49967	FTX 453	23712
FFW 182	109133	FJW 196	70204	FOT 432	36166	FTX 773	32195
FFW 183	109362	FJW 198	72481	FOU 375	56160	FUE 992	49688
FFW 184	112480	FJW 199	71918	FOU 483	56692	FUJ 131	117089
FFW 185	112445	FJW 915	74528	FOU 728	41911	FUJ 219	120783
FFW 186	115829	FJW 916	74522	FOU 936	56154	FUJ 221	118439
FFW 187	115848	FJW 917	77858	FOW 692	105115	FUJ 357	118893
FFW 188	117289	FJW 918	74918	FOY 321	28512	FUJ 425	120959
FFW 199	117299	FJW 939	76066	FOY 322	28577	FUJ 463	124262
FFW 224	109180	FJY 180	139566	FOY 323	28556	FUJ 500	122359
FFW 309	110238	FJY 469	144296	FPM 124	145528	FUJ 564	121207
FFW 397	108787	FJY 622	143177	FPW 26	15094	FUJ 690	123627
FFW 398	109262	FKV 475	48246	FPW 27	17262	FUJ 832	125775

FUJ 915	126725	FWO 486	41622	GAB 2	57078	GBJ 375	33737
FUN 309	101478	FWO 611	42952	GAB 167	57194	GBL 182	146284
FUN 310	102744	FWO 612	43028	GAB 168	57167	GBL 200	144971
FUN 394	103930	FWO 613	54861	GAB 497	58607	GBM 302	76926
FUN 415	105272	FWO 614	56183	GAB 728	59254	GBP 628	12054
FUN 562	109347	FWO 615	58157	GAB 754	62249	GBT 103	64362
FUN 570	107451	FWO 616	63133	GAC 767	58177	GBT 110	61087
FUN 661	111716	FWO 617	63654	GAD 141	30130	GBU 142	140560
FUN 939	114890	FWO 618	70889	GAD 559	38495	GBU 196	141482
FUN 955	116992	FWO 619	73193	GAD 560	38702	GBU 374	144372
FUO 92	21599	FWO 620	75430	GAD 781	38307	GBU 393	146277
FUO 264	22204	FWO 621	77648	GAJ 2	135166	GBY 85	55858
FUO 534	22407	FWO 622	81251	GAJ 259	136325	GBY 567	57469
FUP 499	13439	FWO 623	83157	GAJ 588	141671	GBY 800	63646
FUP 521	12007	FWO 624	85949	GAM 338	116446	GCA 221	120872
FUP 522	12797	FWO 625	91216	GAM 477	115962	GCA 388	125486
FUP 567	12057	FWP 656	54486	GAO 3	27956	GCA 544	129091
FUP 615	15041	FWP 769	54766	GAO 81	?	GCA 747	134639
FUP 669	17276	FWP 847	55717	GAO 465	50261	GCA 848	136437
FUP 723	17284	FWR 199	22024	GAO 466	52616	GCE 69	56854
FUP 794	20825	FWR 300	22061	GAO 467	59841	GCE 413	60118
FUP 795	21311	FWS 629	71966	GAO 468	62850	GCE 422	63173
FUP 817	17279	FWT 646	31037	GAO 469	64759	GCE 842	66667
FUP 954	15079	FWU 231	31896	GAO 470	68979	GCG 284	63557
FUP 993	12793	FWU 584	34692	GAO 522	41592	GCG 334	51083
FUS 606	78961	FWV 424	107770	GAO 595	42827	GCG 512	68414
FUT 58	122911	FWV 427	107692	GAO 861	42929	GCG 618	61507
FUT 339	125514	FWV 429	109682	GAW 21	128019	GCG 735	71672
FUT 362	118242	FWW 596	52924	GAW 46	129473	GCG 749	69577
FUT 489	126573	FWW 597	57275	GAW 58	124962	GCG 823	60797
FUT 784	130150	FWW 598	62087	GAW 85	138525	GCG 873	69961
FUY 579	33125	FWW 599	63823	GAW 236	130863	GCG 874	70377
FUY 580	29472	FWW 742	38554	GAW 360	131510	GCG 886	65546
FUY 707	49601	FWW 743	39289	GAW 464	132062	GCG 981	71262
FUY 950	49099	FWW 744	41121	GAW 581	133225	GCJ 251	105157
FVA 9	124248	FWW 745	41111	GAW 755	135021	GCJ 297	106336
FVA 61	121231	FWW 902	42941	GAW 759	132773	GCJ 298	105729
FVA 513	132053	FWX 161	43993	GAW 819	135213	GCJ 969	115958
FVA 713	138172	FWX 547	60125	GAW 870	136318	GCV 213 *	137893
FVA 842	140099	FWX 548	71329	GAX 9	45909	GCV 623 *	126041
FVB 383	47271	FWX 549	71318	GAX 189	53401	GCY 153	116634
FVC 651	41142	FWX 550	73881	GAX 531	54625	GCY 363	120955
FVD 39	138945	FWX 696	44863	GAX 587	55944	GCY 412	127286
FVD 141	143261	FWX 723	44006	GAY 237	135865	GCY 503	126142
FVF 4	17290	FWX 846	44212	GAY 500	129118	GCY 757	130670
FVF 160	21693	FWY 311	42008	GAY 526	138225	GCY 837	132844
FVJ 274	82825	FWY 494	39240	GAY 564	138534	GCY 957	135969
FVJ 548	90502	FWY 495	39260	GAY 692	137705	GDA 498	84958
FVJ 664	91593	FYF 798	6727	GAY 726	139592	GDA 700	84527
FVJ 704	94648	FYG 4	50081	GAY 769	138954	GDA 720	82725
FVN 299	124187	FYG 74	50683	GAY 951	142442	GDA 721	74992
FVN 471	127377	FYG 148	51668	GBC 777	120609	GDA 722	85572
FWF 489	70283	FYG 809	52795	GBE 128	118362	GDA 779	86292
FWF 646	71868	FYY 830	5844	GBE 167	118778	GDA 780	87722
FWM 33	55421	FYY 831	9077	GBE 477	120771	GDA 781	88038
FWM 151	64380	FYY 832	6607	GBE 478	119969	GDA 892	88142
FWM 196	66230	FYY 833	9038	GBE 509	121132	GDA 893	88607
FWM 197	60943	GAA 210	57343	GBE 848	122493	GDA 967	87636
FWM 332	80316	GAA 232	58236	GBE 974	128412	GDA 981	85782
FWM 917	96626	GAA 548	60512	GBE 975	132384	GDA 982	98957
FWN 91	96240	GAA 549	61989	GBE 976	132625	GDA 983	100251
FWN 280	101660	GAA 762	63117	GBE 977	132663	GDA 984	102161
FWN 561	106500	GAA 872	52500	GBE 978	132680	GDA 985	102049
FWN 795	110427	GAA 940	42112	GBJ 205	39572	GDA 986	102122

C1252/258

GDD 200	38168	GEL 503	17219	GJU 462	144900	GOP 992	42067
GDD 415	41652	GEL 504	17272	GJU 912	144834	GOR 120	80952
GDD 479	42101	GEL 505	17288	GJW 563	99936	GOR 136	69380
GDD 670	41701	GEL 506	17295	GJW 882	103139	GOR 376	77456
GDE 687	18758	GEL 507	17259	GJW 883	102064	GOR 653	83436
GDF 4	44514	GEL 508	17275	GJW 884	102199	GOR 824	68058
GDF 73	47278	GEL 509	17223	GKF 464	39131	GOR 880	81847
GDF 222	47340	GEL 510	17264	GKF 465	39220	GOT 286	84814
GDF 748	47988	GEL 714	26112	GKV 784	78830	GOT 513	87309
GDF 789	52068	GEL 792	28134	GKW 395	143362	GOT 514	86325
GDG 58	53589	GER 72	73336	GKY 750	146102	GOT 784	91310
GDG 368	44561	GER 422	77691	GMA 904	42427	GOU 361	95372
GDG 392	56001	GET 7	144738	GMJ 267	102580	GOU 721	94672
GDG 467	55631	GEW 1	86727	GMJ 335	104462	GOU 791	99639
GDG 700	56678	GEW 58	91162	GMJ 389	105713	GOU 887	100071
GDG 717	57441	GEW 300	100940	GMJ 499	46069	GOU 888	99543
GDG 877	57124	GEW 874	120221	GMJ 559	105021	GOV 398	44286
GDK 39	59347	GFD 322	29200	GMJ 667	109190	GOV 399	44456
GDK 288	65883	GFD 323	29780	GMN 699	21468	GOV 580	56173
GDK 317	80933	GFD 442	35924	GMN 798	30340	GOV 959	46004
GDK 564	94818	GFD 859	47031	GMN 799	30262	GOW 541	135331
GDK 810	109253	GFH 176	92140	GMR 4	130359	GOW 871	89795
GDK 852	111124	GFJ 632	29712	GMR 513	136589	GOY 234	68569
GDL 14	104571	GFJ 867	34543	GMR 750	135342	GOY 503	71613
GDL 75	107035	GFJ 953	41152	GMW 1	139488	GPT 17	15056
GDL 102	108384	GFU 140	132048	GMW 758	142601	GPT 99	18747
GDL 137	110422	GFU 501	136237	GNG 61	38257	GPT 154	22371
GDL 153	110972	GFU 700	136965	GNK 274	22879	GPT 206	25179
GDL 193	112847	GFU 712	138389	GNK 593	21528	GPT 207	25252
GDL 226	114210	GFU 856	140275	GNM 976 *	54956	GPT 208	23391
GDL 366	118786	GFU 857	140618	GNP 76	61637	GPT 390	29543
GDL 432	121822	GFU 858	140724	GNP 278	66784	GPT 488	31396
GDL 489	124322	GFU 859	140156	GNP 702	68274	GPT 489	32884
GDL 538	126761	GFU 860	140935	GNP 703	68336	GPT 490	31655
GDL 616	130986	GFW 82	142192	GNP 704	68087	GPT 491	32207
GDL 617	130938	GFW 83	142182	GNP 813	69764	GPT 492	32764
GDL 618	131040	GFW 84	142179	GNP 860	71168	GPT 718	32583
GDL 667	133749	GFW 674	143920	GNP 871	72495	GPT 775	31297
GDL 702	135477	GFW 963	144748	GNP 996	73471	GPT 883	34972
GDL 754	137665	GFY 451	119611	GNT 140	138307	GPW 48	42001
GDL 779	139011	GGE 530	100244	GNT 296	139298	GPW 559	45258
GDL 793	139062	GGG 143	104646	GNT 316	140107	GPW 568	47022
GDL 796	138870	GGG 269	101485	GNT 428	140583	GPW 774	45668
GDL 797	138977	GHN 938	15924	GNT 429	140828	GPY 554	145440
GDL 798	139328	GHN 942	15904	GNT 470	143072	GRK 316	80416
GDL 812	139988	GHO 53	72183	GNT 517	131420	GRM 378	57367
GDM 266	135118	GHO 54	72334	GNT 746	144288	GRM 491	60382
GDM 369	136494	GHO 170	62680	GNT 806	142197	GRM 604	61305
GDM 448	142059	GHO 321	74065	GNT 969	142932	GRM 910	66207
GDM 644	145412	GHO 322	73983	GNX 530	63829	GRM 914	65131
GDM 676	145450	GHO 786	67896	GNY 338	40920	GRO 205	11714
GDT 255	109289	GHO 941	75948	GNY 509	40511	GRO 206	11723
GDV 133	51649	GHO 942	75855	GNY 718	43346	GRR 19	12759
GDV 584	54439	GHP 581	55306	GNY 856	45204	GRR 436	13435
GDV 923	55752	GHP 937	56769	GOE 257	21941	GRT 221	52644
GDV 940	55728	GHR 206	121781	GOE 258	22251	GRT 434	55473
GED 256	110258	GHR 553	127269	GOE 259	22001	GRT 457	55541
GED 257	120500	GHR 850	129641	GOG 877	26426	GRT 516	56029
GED 492	134101	GJF 396 *	15057	GOG 878	26628	GRU 63	41982
GED 624	131691	GJF 503	146953	GOH 80	21896	GRU 100	45896
GED 797	144976	GJH 2	13437	GOM 82	33970	GRU 101	47236
GEL 500	15087	GJH 766	12798	GOM 412	24945	GRU 102	47449
GEL 501	17278	GJU 163	142592	GON 500	39121	GRU 103	52897
GEL 502	15085	GJU 181	143646	GON 800	40321	GRU 104	54839

GRU 110	46713	GUN 286	142614	GWN 707	145670	GYS 985	120113
GRU 158	39309	GUN 489	144918	GWO 53	64501	HAA 557	92768
GRU 159	39329	GUO 82	29176	GWO 876	94846	HAA 558	93639
GRY 54	130761	GUO 83	29261	GWP 39	78978	HAA 559	88802
GRY 222	133393	GUO 84	29285	GWP 101	68382	HAA 560	90157
GRY 896	141949	GUO 114	25599	GWP 421	82174	HAA 561	91388
GRY 904	142519	GUO 398	33016	GWP 577	86739	HAA 562	90657
GSC 988	94593	GUO 778	36245	GWP 842	89677	HAA 563	100776
GSF 384	97325	GUP 30	39418	GWR 28	54567	HAA 564	100707
GSG 410	107068	GUP 195	40966	GWR 46	54727	HAA 596	104659
GSM 722	41832	GUP 364	36358	GWR 365	56659	HAA 597	104489
GSP 249	95556	GUP 365	36400	GWS 139	111861	HAA 631	105169
GSR 23	127837	GUP 942	44720	GWS 463	114275	HAA 874	104011
GTB 539	12756	GUP 978	43487	GWS 464	114965	HAB 891	98941
GTB 564	17212	GUR 622	28108	GWS 465	116045	HAB 919	96015
GTC 651	21567	GUR 623	25893	GWS 466	120236	HAC 980	88900
GTE 289	30124	GUR 664	28701	GWS 467	129714	HAD 151	57660
GTE 551	32772	GUR 941	28012	GWS 468	129707	HAD 216	61540
GTE 552	33750	GUR 985	26388	GWS 469	130161	HAD 267	62103
GTF 644	37180	GUS 247	112371	GWT 206	57314	HAD 270	62047
GTG 74	47322	GUS 494	111060	GWT 340	57572	HAD 314	48271
GTG 155	48098	GUS 949	115286	GWT 403	57959	HAD 380	62273
GTG 322	46241	GUT 55	146075	GWT 509	57437	HAD 866	67302
GTG 438	48045	GUX 10	146094	GWT 533	46206	HAD 953	67537
GTJ 245	39497	GUX 133	146236	GWT 716	57511	HAF 797	15922
GTJ 246	39596	GUX 134	146415	GWU 633	67346	HAF 798	15100
GTJ 247	40781	GUX 186	146504	GWU 653	58390	HAH 171	55924
GTJ 612	43945	GUX 188	146262	GWU 855	66243	HAH 338	56722
GTJ 613	44107	GUX 189	146959	GWU 856	68592	HAH 825	58274
GTJ 947	36893	GUY 122	64967	GWU 857	69894	HAL 511	28356
GTM 128	92830	GUY 393	68583	GWU 913	66036	HAO 389	74137
GTM 272	92705	GUY 602	61079	GWV 101	146973	HAO 487	77405
GTM 358	94931	GVB 190	91878	GWV 296	146351	HAR 556	36203
GTX 3	52720	GVE 502	90832	GWV 297	146963	HAR 557	36187
GTX 69	55341	GVE 574	94317	GWW 100	66921	HAR 648	26496
GTX 154	55397	GVE 586 *	13002	GWW 292	67518	HAX 452	92125
GTX 194	55917	GVF 421	52435	GWW 407	68663	HAX 657	96712
GTX 208	62346	GVF 534	48450	GWW 532	67461	HAX 824	102234
GTX 263	54671	GVF 900	53580	GWW 612	69949	HAX 828	100318
GTX 274	57093	GVJ 41	116357	GWW 928	68606	HBJ 10	60765
GTX 439	62305	GVJ 86 *	14844	GWW 929	68441	HBJ 750	72295
GTX 551	57064	GVJ 94	118719	GWW 930	68618	HBP 852	35848
GTX 584	58333	GVJ 190	119666	GWX 66	75865	HBP 872	36424
GTX 774	62885	GVJ 197	121301	GWX 74	82045	HBP 873	37038
GTX 778	62152	GVJ 264	121871	GWX 79	77184	HBP 999	37026
GTX 911	60544	GVJ 376	124770	GWX 156	67934	HBT 584	116653
GUE 207	67132	GVJ 490	127487	GWX 192	74422	HBT 779	119607
GUE 353	71244	GVJ 596	129800	GWX 796	65384	HBT 880	119409
GUE 785	76141	GVJ 724	131956	GWX 927	71663	HBY 163	103401
GUJ 20	143155	GVJ 832	134493	GWX 968	68230	HCD 465	37049
GUJ 21	143243	GVN 18	144770	GWY 207	76469	HCD 607	39388
GUJ 218	143271	GVO 765	28234	GWY 654	59827	HCE 426	104094
GUJ 289	144460	GVP 875	51388	GYB 640	11032	HCG 20	105096
GUJ 290	144924	GWF 250	95869	GYB 993	11030	HCG 244	98468
GUJ 291	144896	GWF 290	88970	GYC 330	17283	HCG 298	102725
GUJ 356	144984	GWF 358	99479	GYC 892	17247	HCG 372	82299
GUJ 389	145587	GWF 687	102243	GYD 39	18751	HCG 581	106993
GUK 8	106953	GWF 741	103945	GYD 80	21505	HCG 601	106355
GUK 135	113861	GWK 76	62208	GYD 353	20834	HCG 946	111937
GUK 315	102611	GWK 493	64210	GYD 354	21576	HCG 947	112363
GUK 316	105658	GWM 812	146452	GYD 502	21978	HCJ 151	137833
GUK 317	106397	GWN 220	117170	GYG 134	74947	HCJ 152	139553
GUK 657	110346	GWN 359	138866	GYG 936	84548	HCJ 273	142025
GUN 54	141495	GWN 471	142446	GYS 708	115833	HCJ 345	143101

HCJ 452	145008	HFJ 150	38386	HJW 648	140283	HNG 99	57395
HCJ 861	146848	HFJ 151	38485	HJW 649	140927	HNG 407	62168
HCV 312	18752	HFJ 152	35324	HJW 680	140976	HNG 625	57748
HDA 109	116921	HFJ 153	34991	HJW 809	141477	HNG 626	57963
HDA 727	124995	HFJ 507	55565	HKA 648	32353	HNG 953	62842
HDA 784	123798	HFJ 575	55900	HKD 875	34781	HNK 47	44894
HDA 787	123395	HFJ 834	58801	HKF 93	49950	HNK 95	44683
HDA 788	123076	HFJ 835	63622	HKF 544	53517	HNM 348	118822
HDA 999	128522	HFJ 836	63155	HKK 593	11061	HNN 810	43402
HDD 119	67982	HFM 28	33485	HKK 709	12754	HNP 27	100715
HDD 182	70294	HFM 29	47468	HKL 61	15060	HNP 114	103824
HDD 187	68931	HFM 30	47874	HKM 15	15048	HNP 301	103565
HDD 230	69496	HFM 31	49368	HKM 175	17800	HNP 592	105197
HDD 251	69552	HFM 32	49503	HKM 914	21642	HNP 736	108779
HDD 691	72970	HFM 33	50957	HKN 750	17269	HNX 687	94659
HDE 542	43469	HFM 34	51895	HKX 377	11025	HNY 167	64773
HDE 657	43436	HFM 35	60337	HKX 651	12064	HNY 168	65064
HDE 733	30731	HFM 36	60386	HKX 654	13492	HNY 221	65463
HDF 192	77607	HFM 37	63694	HKY 892	241185	HNY 328	68463
HDF 343	79527	HFM 38	63742	HLB 149	29948	HNY 337	68299
HDF 413	59423	HFM 39	76155	HLJ 171	67182	HNY 432	64880
HDG 302	82575	HFM 40	76176	HLJ 273	70075	HNY 566	55604
HDG 325	88120	HFM 41	75544	HLJ 600	59705	HNY 746	71209
HDG 574	90593	HFM 42	75347	HLJ 800	63109	HNY 763	61040
HDG 734	92424	HFM 43	75440	HLX 831	12772	HNY 768	73071
HDG 798	91202	HFM 44	99380	HLX 832	12758	HNY 868	63880
HDG 816	92332	HFM 45	99536	HLX 833	13481	HNY 941	76101
HDG 859	88210	HFS 248	120578	HLX 834	14297	HOB 251	47008
HDG 973	96735	HGA 401	120503	HLX 835	14300	HOB 941	50243
HDG 988	94677	HGA 995	124272	HLX 836	14296	HOD 37	81589
HDK 15	118082	HGB 131	125605	HLX 837	15050	HOD 38	81598
HDK 60	117000	HGE 156	137190	HLX 838	15003	HOD 39	81924
HDK 60	117000	HGE 219	137703	HLX 839	13476	HOD 40	82007
HDK 305	135389	HGE 590	139069	HLX 840	14298	HOD 41	82706
HDK 337	137019	HGG 934	143708	HLY 556	15052	HOD 42	85067
HDK 491	145500	HGG 935	143319	HLY 557	15005	HOD 43	85230
HDK 542	142698	HGK 446	52941	HLY 564	17256	HOD 44	87707
HDT 888	139578	HGK 447	56194	HMN 152	42146	HOD 45	88595
HDV 75	57043	HGP 514	15044	HMN 153	45430	HOD 46	89502
HDV 320	56749	HHA 431	20839	HMN 217	54612	HOD 47	97318
HDV 415	55413	HHA 432	21650	HMN 253	45792	HOD 48	98065
HDV 416	56996	HHA 433	19815	HMN 277	46348	HOD 49	99472
HDV 496	56895	HHA 434	21305	HMN 347	36471	HOD 50	100087
HDV 751	60788	HHA 435	21307	HMN 426	51775	HOD 51	101345
HDV 754	53419	HHA 436	21670	HMN 439	46889	HOD 52	101509
HEL 160	56563	HHN 10	15045	HMN 468	50233	HOD 53	108830
HEL 161	61701	HHN 751	32298	HMN 511	51001	HOD 54	108872
HEL 162	64976	HHN 980	39876	HMN 569	44152	HOD 55	116496
HEL 412	58259	HHO 164	112295	HMN 600	54956	HOD 56	116545
HEL 775	70319	HHO 324	115354	HMN 601	56685	HOD 58	JCB38
HEL 776	76674	HHO 346	113011	HMN 634	46077	HOD 59	JCB39
HER 307	118149	HHO 698	116032	HMN 658	48560	HOD 60	JCB40
HEW 150	131058	HHO 855	120154	HMN 711 *	40541	HOD 61	JCB56
HEW 500	144468	HHP 178	85788	HMN 774	57978	HOD 62	JCB57
HFD 541	62729	HJW 103	124904	HMN 835	50099	HOD 63	JCB58
HFD 609	47042	HJW 104	126550	HMN 994	54992	HOD 64	JCB65
HFD 643	63539	HJW 105	128194	HNC 867	40871	HOD 65	JCB66
HFD 945	66004	HJW 106	128796	HND 739	42490	HOD 66	JCB67
HFH 368	JCB122	HJW 107	129704	HNE 512	44784	HOD 67	JCB71
HFH 538	144988	HJW 128	132928	HNE 960	47484	HOD 68	JCB72
HFH 702	JCB156	HJW 267	135125	HNF 68	52087	HOD 69	JCB73
HFJ 147	44583	HJW 268	125084	HNF 802	41872	HOD 70	116893
HFJ 148	36003	HJW 269	125090	HNF 805	43955	HOD 71	117835
HFJ 149	36215	HJW 647	138542	HNF 810	45851	HOD 72	118103

C1252/261

HOD 73	118197	HOU 863	140291	HSF 646	142684	HUF 454	55703
HOD 74	119518	HOY 263	114289	HSF 727	123745	HUF 635	46301
HOD 75	119577	HPO 431	40410	HSG 231	145752	HUF 892	65026
HOD 76	120202	HPO 501	39753	HSM 501	64429	HUK 328	146980
HOD 77	120291	HPP 773	23285	HSM 535	65147	HUO 108	38376
HOD 78	120828	HPP 774	23068	HSM 543	66946	HUO 221	38465
HOD 79	121114	HPT 47	49118	HSP 255	128539	HUO 222	38643
HOD 80	120668	HPT 74	54505	HTB 80	43187	HUO 376	40289
HOD 81	126227	HPT 190	50775	HTB 193	45391	HUO 668	49376
HOD 82	126475	HPT 191	51564	HTB 247	46158	HUO 669	49419
HOD 83	125600	HPT 356	52482	HTB 248	46164	HUO 670	59834
HOD 108	76591	HPT 381	52625	HTB 410	50894	HUO 671	60181
HOD 109	77612	HPT 504	57865	HTB 411	51442	HUO 672	65171
HOD 110	77727	HPT 505	65352	HTB 728	29653	HUO 673	65473
HOD 111	79834	HPT 642	57360	HTB 739	46727	HUO 674	65481
HOD 112	80498	HPT 917	57684	HTC 577	51163	HUO 675	67753
HOD 113	92244	HPW 180	68800	HTC 578	51461	HUO 676	67952
HOD 114	92875	HPW 555	69323	HTC 600	48392	HUO 677	67996
HOD 115	94225	HPW 801	JCB41	HTC 661	52711	HUO 678	70143
HOD 116	94733	HPW 802	JCB42	HTC 690	53500	HUO 679	70148
HOD 117	95391	HPW 803	JCB43	HTC 863	50637	HUO 680	71836
HOD 118	96544	HPW 804	JCB50	HTD 72	8235	HUO 681	101958
HOD 119	96952	HPW 805	JCB51	HTD 190	54534	HUO 682	101988
HOD 120	106507	HPW 806	JCB52	HTD 200	55877	HUO 683	44739
HOD 121	107047	HPW 807	JCB62	HTD 492	48035	HUO 684	44857
HOD 122	107075	HPW 808	JCB63	HTD 658	52748	HUO 685	45920
HOD 123	JCB31	HPW 809	JCB64	HTE 528	57145	HUO 686	58139
HOD 124	JCB34	HPW 810	JCB68	HTE 624	55665	HUO 687	61401
HOD 125	JCB35	HPW 811	JCB69	HTE 958	57617	HUO 688	43277
HOD 126	JCB36	HPW 812	JCB70	HTF 74	56649	HUO 689	44096
HOD 127	JCB37	HPW 813	JCB77	HTF 255	58788	HUO 690	44395
HOD 128	107705	HPW 814	JCB78	HTF 878	60781	HUO 691	44551
HOD 129	113382	HPW 815	JCB79	HTG 116	71497	HUO 692	44775
HOD 130	112920	HPW 816	JCB80	HTG 171	75071	HUO 693	44761
HOD 131	112978	HPW 901	68457	HTG 528	79253	HUO 694	48948
HOD 132	114186	HPW 985	71713	HTG 613	83790	HUO 695	49476
HOD 133	114365	HRH 50	42167	HTG 679	62762	HUO 696	49513
HOD 134	114787	HRH 834	48923	HTG 986	83262	HUO 697	51045
HOD 135	116575	HRK 76	119945	HTJ 278	66249	HUO 698	52834
HOD 441	65001	HRL 25	21493	HTJ 279	66703	HUO 699	61572
HOD 930	78226	HRL 75	21752	HTJ 280	69523	HUO 700	63549
HOF 757	54988	HRL 178	22083	HTJ 316	67279	HUP 245	48186
HOH 920	57498	HRM 48	86917	HTJ 317	67351	HUP 283	60431
HOH 922	56969	HRM 411	94055	HTJ 325	68807	HUP 376	61925
HOJ 662	58498	HRO 1	47048	HTJ 347	64823	HUP 417	60724
HOM 78	65376	HRO 150	48295	HTJ 748	60717	HUP 574	65530
HOM 886	71692	HRO 260	49696	HTJ 841	66268	HUP 697	65560
HON 255	72060	HRO 281	47045	HTJ 913	62427	HUP 737	65515
HON 861	74482	HRO 679	50004	HTJ 957	66898	HUP 796	69303
HOP 554	76840	HRO 821	51790	HTJ 979	59464	HUP 842	49213
HOR 403	122988	HRO 998	53483	HTM 20	123524	HUP 859	66474
HOR 608 *	19847	HRR 192	36026	HTM 368	115361	HUP 891	65449
HOR 704	119003	HRR 421	45699	HTM 721	134022	HUP 982	71130
HOT 339	131034	HRR 422	44805	HTM 986	133758	HUR 106	49281
HOT 532	133219	HRR 553	49021	HTR 144	145660	HUR 664	57187
HOT 759	130010	HRR 973	51516	HTX 594	85610	HUR 755	55786
HOT 806	122470	HRR 995	51534	HTX 659	94012	HUU 426	24510
HOT 807	123567	HRT 298	46369	HTX 753	95543	HUU 427	23215
HOT 808	128027	HRT 299	51972	HTX 890	96977	HUU 428	24959
HOT 809	128421	HRU 62	84786	HUC 194	15091	HUU 429	25078
HOT 810	118350	HRU 190	87466	HUE 163	78143	HUU 430	23046
HOU 361	139504	HRU 269	89704	HUE 382	98864	HUU 431	23294
HOU 377	135799	HRW 186	90221	HUE 400	99464	HUU 432	24252
HOU 627	138792	HSC 317	130241	HUE 911	113546	HUU 433	25621

HUU 721	39447	HWU 623	101503	HYE 555	53375	HYP 209	56529
HUU 722	39467	HWU 800	102684	HYE 762	66106	HYP 210	56703
HUU 723	40297	HWU 965	103861	HYE 927	44540	HYP 211	57485
HUU 724	40770	HWU 996	113391	HYF 378	44421	HYP 559	56546
HUU 725	41168	HWW 322	103058	HYF 530	44357	HYP 560	56533
HUU 726	42281	HWW 412	100850	HYF 531	44202	HYP 681	57205
HUW 164	30085	HWW 580	107133	HYF 532	47335	HYP 686	58758
HUY 97	112387	HWW 642	103073	HYF 906	42326	HYP 687	58792
HUY 655	116301	HWW 650	103237	HYF 971	47067	HYP 688	58743
HUY 856	116486	HWW 703	104581	HYG 23	111275	HYP 689	58971
HVB 153	136613	HWX 212	115651	HYG 870	117514	HYP 690	58952
HVC 288	103206	HWX 243	105816	HYG 911	116407	HYP 720	55805
HVE 242	134650	HWY 637	112518	HYH 556	45755	HYP 721	61710
HVE 980	139423	HWY 682	113666	HYH 557	46015	HYP 722	47814
HVF 160	57871	HWY 819	122487	HYH 563	45996	HYP 723	50760
HVF 544	73113	HWY 957	126656	HYH 570	48416	HYP 724	71412
HVF 750	76120	HXB 711	28602	HYH 912	51407	HYP 725	81218
HVF 926	76199	HXB 712	28713	HYH 919	55293	HYP 775	55552
HVJ 203	145695	HXB 713	28797	HYK 192	45714	HYP 847	57529
HVM 97	51828	HXB 714	28563	HYK 235	48912	HYP 891	56149
HVM 98	52757	HXB 715	28879	HYK 236	51359	HYP 901	57448
HVM 99	52815	HXB 716	28406	HYK 237	54906	HYR 1	58172
HVM 103	51573	HXB 717	28650	HYK 836	47290	HYR 7	61490
HVM 393	48467	HXB 718	28890	HYK 910	47212	HYR 257	57356
HVO 387	53365	HXB 719	28640	HYK 991	36824	HYR 297	57970
HVO 594	54640	HXB 720	28451	HYK 992	38188	HYR 298	58228
HVO 596	54585	HXB 721	29297	HYK 993	38178	HYR 330	52491
HVO 691	55467	HXB 722	29273	HYL 143	46849	HYR 522	62402
HVR 631	57610	HXB 723	28987	HYL 144	47904	HYR 523	62939
HVU 243	55865	HXB 724	28657	HYL 787	48089	HYR 524	63012
HVU 879	63053	HXB 725	28672	HYL 788	49705	HYR 525	62980
HWD 978	112024	HXB 726	28921	HYL 789	49643	HYR 526	63262
HWE 475	12782	HXB 727	30802	HYL 797	50204	HYR 527	64057
HWE 562	18788	HXB 728	31097	HYL 798	51213	HYR 528	65826
HWF 201	124607	HXJ 103	55871	HYL 799	50922	HYR 529	65940
HWF 557	132870	HXJ 496	58889	HYL 800	51093	HYR 587	60560
HWJ 180	22804	HXW 113	40401	HYM 648	55283	HYR 774	60911
HWJ 484	29665	HXW 496	44699	HYM 685	51452	HYR 776	60935
HWJ 621	26400	HXX 631	36055	HYN 420	53454	HYR 782	63595
HWJ 622	26124	HXX 632	35966	HYN 461	55501	HYR 783	63517
HWJ 649	28595	HXX 633	35816	HYN 467	61645	HYS 16	144840
HWJ 650	28625	HXX 828	41962	HYN 468	62972	HYU 786	61750
HWO 881	121769	HXX 972	38317	HYN 469	60576	HYY 900	42987
HWO 909	118327	HXY 214	38722	HYN 470	65601	JAA 367	138941
HWO 910	118708	HXY 215	38732	HYN 479	53464	JAA 485	141468
HWO 915 *	84417	HYB 40	38445	HYN 480	53385	JAA 741	143836
HWP 520	124276	HYB 284	38752	HYN 688	55491	JAB 213	131469
HWP 637	124626	HYB 285	38764	HYN 699	56976	JAB 214	130284
HWP 926	128694	HYB 288	38524	HYN 700	56938	JAB 661	136245
HWR 130	97730	HYB 646	41821	HYO 97	54401	JAB 867	137672
HWR 181	85083	HYB 894	40971	HYO 197	54429	JAB 905	139386
HWR 225	91784	HYB 984	42347	HYO 263	55212	JAD 198	95897
HWR 259	94276	HYC 60	39269	HYO 264	55428	JAD 770	103304
HWR 584	77048	HYC 769	46801	HYO 265	55486	JAD 798	103392
HWR 616	62745	HYC 840	48324	HYO 271	56120	JAD 832	110638
HWT 93	89495	HYC 918	40691	HYO 272	56542	JAF 235	38663
HWT 531	91676	HYD 134	50940	HYO 495	55277	JAF 236	38693
HWT 629	77072	HYD 848	54703	HYO 496	55260	JAF 415	38653
HWT 736	95472	HYD 963	55611	HYO 690	54785	JAF 830	26317
HWT 738	97935	HYE 297	46878	HYO 706	55546	JAF 831	30136
HWU 170	94807	HYE 300	48441	HYO 981	54887	JAF 832	32996
HWU 479	98706	HYE 552	39819	HYO 985	55832	JAF 833	45822
HWU 480	98871	HYE 553	40491	HYO 988	56814	JAF 834	46998
HWU 593	96473	HYE 554	50855	HYO 990	57455	JAF 835	45887

C1252/263

JAF 836	51768	JDH 518	15063	JKE 386	35399	JNB 701	69537
JAF 837	66153	JDH 813	23347	JKE 392	37002	JNB 858	71699
JAH 171	52426	JDH 858	21588	JKF 340	90748	JNB 888	69400
JAH 463	80523	JDH 917	23272	JKH 531	69727	JNC 388	72372
JAH 570	66630	JDV 317	62394	JKJ 555	39210	JNC 398	65141
JAH 888	64307	JDV 561	67141	JKJ 957	35472	JNC 626	74410
JAH 899	78310	JDV 562	68401	JKJ 971	39766	JND 404	78906
JAL 30	57430	JDV 754	65366	JKK 322	40811	JND 999	72843
JAL 123	57036	JDV 789	67110	JKK 426	41801	JNE 247	67359
JAL 592	61548	JDV 912	67743	JKK 668	44036	JNE 607	82654
JAL 708	61257	JEL 32	69237	JKK 952	36382	JNE 878	77697
JAO 144	105267	JEL 107	101555	JKM 55	41902	JNF 767	86033
JAO 380	112377	JEL 276	101966	JKM 83	39734	JNG 108	82097
JAR 111	56944	JEL 277	104191	JKM 270	44798	JNG 276	86381
JAR 426	60050	JEL 278	104501	JKM 282	47054	JNG 551	88691
JAR 559	59856	JEL 437	105033	JKM 536	41811	JNK 143	64218
JAR 905	61800	JEL 483	104747	JKO 590	54382	JNK 356	64538
JAR 954	59996	JEL 578	104109	JKO 674	52846	JNK 487	69294
JAR 976	62055	JEL 579	105722	JKO 754	54775	JNK 713	67568
JAT 11	50883	JEL 580	105905	JKO 758	55688	JNN 174	66764
JAT 12	51784	JEL 581	105979	JKO 789	55964	JNN 253	64477
JAU 10	40451	JEL 718	106589	JKR 36	56141	JNN 573	69845
JAU 804	62688	JFD 460	100421	JKR 163	56072	JNN 656	61048
JAU 808	61717	JFD 673	105974	JKR 510	57417	JNN 712	67218
JAX 325	130343	JFG 233	145096	JKR 636	56729	JNN 960	71074
JAX 827	141932	JFH 760	232395	JKR 970	61475	JNP 258	143752
JBH 400	29794	JFJ 14	66020	JKT 210	54756	JNP 864	146896
JBJ 728	105279	JFJ 15	73541	JKV 575	144742	JNP 872	144998
JBJ 791	80598	JFJ 178	67196	JKX 555	33030	JNP 990	144316
JBJ 868	104494	JFJ 179	55508	JLG 991	32564	JNX 197	117803
JBP 856	62362	JFJ 180	69970	JLJ 127	109248	JNX 589	120682
JBT 170	140115	JFJ 181	63312	JLJ 128	109335	JNX 783	123187
JBT 229	143097	JFJ 198	67396	JLR 468 *	11068	JNY 83	100175
JBY 804	143735	JFJ 259	76613	JMA 17	31013	JNY 200	102520
JCD 176	69711	JFJ 260	60870	JMA 201	45313	JNY 273	103521
JCD 370	73170	JFJ 261	68687	JMB 461	50120	JNY 332	103042
JCD 371	73538	JFJ 346	70107	JMB 717	49238	JNY 521	104150
JCD 424	74830	JFJ 386	81905	JMN 106	68842	JNY 634	104637
JCD 900	85850	JFJ 867	92701	JMN 113	57226	JNY 766	107733
JCV 30	42907	JFJ 939	105898	JMN 122	59488	JNY 771	108746
JCV 525	46867	JFM 990	JCB32	JMN 126	66873	JNY 918	107536
JCV 606	49385	JFM 991	JCB33	JMN 127	66913	JOC 550	81816
JCV 612	49772	JGF 836 *	(16631 ?)	JMN 128	69217	JOD 87	69561
JCV 629	46731	JHA 136	29507	JMN 129	58342	JOD 354	68371
JCV 645	35950	JHA 264	22792	JMN 130	58855	JOD 479	76883
JCV 917	51154	JHN 116	43357	JMN 132	64275	JOD 640	80407
JDA 298	146529	JHN 250	45784	JMN 133	74034	JOD 810	81334
JDD 37	10004	JHN 624	51839	JMN 138	59164	JOE 668	86100
JDD 612	108862	JHN 625	52690	JMN 201	67190	JOF 332	88990
JDD 680	111679	JHN 626	52595	JMN 399	66679	JOF 693	92108
JDD 920	114148	JHN 744	55779	JMN 438	74936	JOH 262	94761
JDE 6	56866	JHN 902	55838	JMN 446	81472	JOK 11	97410
JDE 226	62111	JHO 212	143163	JMN 453 *	64743	JOK 365	SG1/48
JDE 479	64186	JHO 213	143080	JMN 773 *	56826	JOK 557	98779
JDE 487	67738	JHO 945	143251	JMN 902	89320	JOK 660	98579
JDE 889	75450	JHO 946	145004	JMN 936	83896	JOL 298	103469
JDF 306	112562	JHP 193	116000	JNA 4	56629	JOL 998	103526
JDF 398	105108	JHP 895	121397	JNA 611	65017	JOP 626	115854
JDF 737	120838	JHU 830	21303	JNA 920	67161	JOP 710	111868
JDF 768	119887	JHY 308	34706	JNA 932	67414	JOR 619	144992
JDF 971	121836	JJO 656	11094	JNB 53	58777	JPO 200	64258
JDG 4	121242	JKB 944	66402	JNB 146	59696	JPP 455	44297
JDG 898	129086	JKD 930	84790	JNB 234	68858	JPP 513	45620
JDG 989	132215	JKE 165	37104	JNB 600	59987	JPT 4	66364

C1252/264

JPT 101	72558	JTF 262	13177	JUR 830	82659	JXC 935	85604
JPT 490	77882	JTF 414	85776	JUR 879	81957	JXC 981	63864
JPT 529	56035	JTF 605	91704	JUV 297	61365	JXC 985	63670
JPT 541	78638	JTF 965	88128	JVF 528	102766	JXC 989	66299
JPT 677	88050	JTG 129	112600	JVF 843	106233	JXC 990	66325
JPT 725	80964	JTG 280	112617	JVM 873	90150	JXD 221	65106
JPT 957	87725	JTG 622	116375	JVO 148	82217	JXD 486	68850
JPW 519	95448	JTG 933	115240	JVO 329	82714	JXD 528	72877
JPW 964	99625	JTG 954	119433	JVO 390	74972	JXD 635	67532
JPX 15	59802	JTJ 903	92476	JVO 749	86932	JXD 637	67547
JPX 500	77733	JTT 719	17280	JVR 497	92326	JXD 650	66224
JPX 523	79852	JTT 964	25033	JVT 330	12023	JXD 750	69366
JPX 867	85181	JTT 965	24952	JVT 965	26654	JXE 60	69272
JRA 476	15920	JTU 13	55819	JVU 269	65666	JXE 459	70211
JRA 580	13411	JTU 42	56716	JVU 774	97853	JXE 462	70102
JRA 710	21539	JTU 170	57645	JWA 348	31645	JXE 463	70231
JRA 737	18711	JTU 381	58865	JWA 809	35029	JXE 464	70238
JRB 953	23037	JTU 457	52739	JWB 274	41521	JXE 570	73097
JRH 268	80589	JTU 888	57031	JWB 892	43018	JXE 571	61032
JRL 265	53356	JTV 774	58930	JWD 261	137109	JXE 572	60027
JRL 513	56135	JTX 36	121291	JWE 41	42896	JXE 573	63766
JRL 635	57138	JTX 177	119075	JWE 211	44369	JXE 574	69869
JRM 112	117785	JTX 193	132323	JWE 876	51800	JXE 575	71353
JRM 651	131680	JTX 220	118733	JWJ 16	49001	JXE 590	71165
JRO 101	69310	JTX 266	123192	JWJ 399	50020	JXE 641	68349
JRO 375	69214	JTX 305	125333	JWJ 531	50817	JXE 649	71172
JRO 511	73610	JTX 343	122389	JWJ 532	55381	JXE 879	70194
JRO 591	69409	JTX 358	120739	JWJ 533	56605	JXE 956	62435
JRR 114	74151	JTX 488	126639	JWJ 534	56837	JXF 327	69483
JRR 830	78665	JTX 572	139724	JWJ 535	57699	JXH 163	71417
JRT 41	108174	JTX 591	129541	JWJ 536	58162	JXH 361	72278
JRT 913	117200	JTX 625	130590	JWJ 537	60447	JXH 363	73594
JSM 267	89620	JUE 383	130603	JWJ 538	60495	JXH 366	74900
JSM 272	88809	JUE 823	132861	JWJ 539	60854	JXH 400	72700
JTB 139	65834	JUE 860	132303	JWJ 540	62802	JXH 545	73620
JTB 140	67920	JUF 74	90251	JWR 23	118883	JXH 555	76149
JTB 207	47172	JUF 637	105734	JWR 415	118697	JXH 623	75928
JTB 210	67925	JUF 808	109808	JWR 463	120778	JXH 630	82552
JTB 262	57889	JUM 543	24691	JWR 899	74354	JXH 634	85934
JTB 286	68467	JUM 717	23303	JWT 24	122768	JXH 635	85944
JTB 292	67824	JUO 324	43981	JWT 703	129796	JXH 637	88306
JTB 639	68092	JUO 600	63393	JWT 841	130070	JXH 649	74327
JTB 770	53340	JUO 601	65082	JWT 848	128603	JXH 650	74146
JTB 771	52539	JUO 602	69859	JWU 307	132253	JXH 662	66168
JTC 12	51126	JUO 603	71117	JWW 520	137799	JXH 663	61377
JTC 248	66379	JUO 604	71224	JWW 572	136628	JXH 664	60471
JTC 267	71884	JUO 605	71454	JWW 933	132120	JXH 666	71071
JTC 293	71807	JUO 606	73118	JWX 100	140248	JXH 718	74363
JTC 451	73132	JUO 607	75437	JWX 884	143832	JXH 719	74425
JTC 487	73389	JUO 608	76097	JWY 50	143888	JXH 720	57262
JTC 525	71345	JUO 609	76253	JWY 560	142523	JXJ 299	100415
JTC 526	70325	JUO 691	41731	JWY 669	141923	JXL 47	73685
JTC 648	81239	JUO 874	31160	JWY 831	144980	JXL 166	75845
JTC 920	74348	JUP 104	84804	JWY 863	145076	JXL 376	74597
JTD 714	81257	JUP 326	88192	JWY 927	144904	JXL 478	74581
JTD 726	77109	JUP 327	88893	JXA 701	62217	JXL 547	76854
JTD 840	79055	JUP 432	89982	JXA 925	63710	JXL 558	83704
JTD 999	74619	JUP 566	61653	JXB 321	63725	JXL 560	82285
JTE 35	70119	JUP 600	95532	JXB 322	64160	JXM 468	77043
JTE 36	70746	JUP 609	95350	JXC 640	63274	JXN 558	76959
JTE 323	49495	JUP 809	93995	JXC 931	66138	JXN 559	77094
JTE 353	81568	JUR 181	77539	JXC 932	67312	JXN 560	80074
JTE 396	82813	JUR 493	76646	JXC 933	72624	JXN 840	77483
JTE 484	82114	JUR 824	81384	JXC 934	75955	JXN 936	80955

C1252/265

JXN 937	81302	JYB 190	60147	KAW 346 *	26436	KFM 439	100109
JXN 938	86841	JYB 258	62443	KBB 766	23316	KFM 838	115683
JXN 939	87733	JYB 351	63004	KBB 767	23259	KFM 839	105333
JXN 940	88371	JYB 856	64404	KBH 47	47940	KFM 840	115676
JXP 54	83367	JYB 925	49221	KBH 173	49565	KFM 841	116911
JXP 58	83257	JYB 950	67574	KBH 384	48907	KFM 842	117179
JXP 453	80275	JYC 339	71078	KBJ 194	122448	KFM 843	117528
JXP 525	87017	JYC 439	71150	KBJ 533	139980	KFM 844	118143
JXP 557	82798	JYC 612	72951	KBJ 712	131960	KFM 845	118962
JXR 795	88317	JYC 990	73397	KBJ 721	131045	KFM 846	119051
JXT 381	87364	JYD 201	77400	KBP 749	94351	KFM 847	119061
JXT 390	86307	JYD 426	74667	KBP 800	94297	KFM 848	125502
JXT 481	89586	JYD 619	79937	KBP 993	96798	KFM 849	125434
JXT 482	90670	JYG 418	144281	KCD 736	127909	KGB 261	245059
JXT 483	91338	JYG 538	147037	KCD 947	130876	KGB 262	245063
JXT 529	94105	JYP 490	82265	KCV 244	71447	KGB 263	245073
JXT 614	75615	KAC 251	143277	KCV 355	70639	KGB 264	245139
JXT 615	75020	KAD 61	134559	KCV 569	74157	KGB 265	245143
JXT 886	90859	KAD 122	135309	KCV 688	74912	KGB 266	245153
JXT 896	90762	KAD 880	137205	KDD 72	143328	KGB 267	245223
JXT 898	85883	KAD 882	141936	KDD 155	143728	KGB 268	245827
JXT 901	85843	KAF 110	61957	KDD 517	142433	KGB 269	245219
JXT 902	87796	KAF 221	61596	KDD 846	144940	KGB 270	246143
JXT 903	83422	KAF 451	62499	KDD 866	143980	KGD 901	245753
JXT 904	93284	KAF 484	57829	KDD 989	145605	KGD 902	246113
JXT 905	93309	KAF 559	64920	KDE 525	66654	KGD 903	246291
JXT 960	75625	KAF 882	66289	KDE 875	96789	KGD 904	246739
JXU 473	91376	KAF 883	62176	KDH 801	48337	KGD 905	246673
JXU 488	95963	KAF 912	66484	KDH 802	48510	KGD 906	246335
JXU 548	91861	KAF 986	69316	KDH 803	50176	KGD 907	246187
JXU 550	75630	KAF 992	52558	KDH 804	57518	KGD 908	246361
JXU 561	82535	KAH 535	108638	KDH 805	57843	KGD 909	246581
JXU 562	82543	KAH 555	66075	KDH 806	64574	KGD 910	246607
JXU 584	85750	KAH 938	116943	KDV 440	59778	KGE 242	246714
JXU 592	90039	KAH 939	117745	KDV 477	89593	KGE 243	246647
JXU 600	90046	KAH 940	118855	KDV 649	103995	KGH 310	91767
JXU 601	90059	KAH 941	121142	KDV 675	106519	KGH 321	91129
JXU 602	89054	KAH 942	121955	KDV 991	105651	KGH 330	92306
JXU 606	85661	KAH 943	122463	KEL 40	127989	KGH 389	68011
JXW 858	112640	KAH 944	125389	KEL 41	130252	KGH 481	92153
JXW 862	109846	KAH 945	125695	KEL 94	131526	KGH 482	92934
JXW 863	109857	KAH 946	126041	KEL 94 *	137293	KGH 483	92281
JXW 865	109884	KAH 947	137769	KEL 95	137293	KGH 484	94842
JXW 870	109872	KAH 948	137893	KEL 467	123973	KGH 485	95097
JXW 872	109878	KAH 949	109726	KEL 657	137578	KGH 486	96703
JXX 327	116028	KAH 950	109802	KEL 677	140844	KGH 487	96898
JXX 460	111218	KAH 951	110434	KEL 678	142034	KGH 587	127943
JXX 461	111187	KAH 952	110960	KEL 679	142936	KGH 588	128000
JXX 464	111176	KAH 953	111054	KEV 836	11064	KGH 638	62029
JXX 466	111142	KAH 954	111691	KFC 820	23206	KGH 695	92195
JXX 468	123938	KAH 955	113496	KFD 347	126482	KGH 720	96155
JXX 470	112305	KAH 956	113405	KFJ 683	121961	KGH 893	81550
JXX 473	114632	KAH 957	114066	KFJ 684	130606	KGH 906	85762
JXX 474	114664	KAH 958	114880	KFJ 695	128735	KGH 910	94190
JXX 475	114636	KAL 255	90741	KFM 429	105795	KGH 911	93001
JXX 487	114640	KAL 412	92917	KFM 430	106582	KGH 913	88626
JYA 8	53544	KAL 652	94637	KFM 431	106892	KGH 918 see KGH 913	
JYA 109	56008	KAL 683	96050	KFM 432	110649	KGH 922	86816
JYA 268	57307	KAO 77	134589	KFM 433	110680	KGK 419	97788
JYA 387	57550	KAO 265	140019	KFM 434	111382	KGK 425	88873
JYA 630	57071	KAR 67	82272	KFM 435	111786	KGK 457	97496
JYA 839	60592	KAR 224	85967	KFM 436	111855	KGK 458	95560
JYA 880	60323	KAR 510	83746	KFM 437	99647	KGK 459	96133
JYB 136	61949	KAR 550	89522	KFM 438	100093	KGK 466	97988

C1252/266

KGN 204	96780	KGY 264	112453	KKM 733	74613	KNY 195	137760
KGN 207	99610	KGY 265	112474	KKN 414	69902	KNY 422	139400
KGN 431	97886	KGY 266	111968	KKN 752	76964	KNY 672	142121
KGN 432	97972	KGY 267	112691	KKO 193	74538	KNY 731	143159
KGN 433	101690	KGY 268	112638	KKO 745	77710	KNY 759	138211
KGN 434	104653	KGY 269	113016	KKR 221	80837	KOC 923	124083
KGN 435	108603	KGY 270	112995	KKR 815	87561	KOC 974	125518
KGN 436	111224	KHK 178	13478	KKT 590	87379	KOD 965	114111
KGN 596	98785	KHN 79	58729	KKX 28	50788	KOE 967	128527
KGN 597	100326	KHN 335	70847	KKX 40	51991	KOH 77	124990
KGN 598	101406	KHT 345	43513	KKX 99	54965	KOH 250	133932
KGN 773	100236	KHT 346	46832	KKX 812	62915	KOJ 484	137274
KGN 971	98795	KHT 566	39793	KKX 866	61015	KOJ 862	136685
KGP 290	86480	KHT 717	47311	KLB 103	101668	KOJ 863	136869
KGT 62	96289	KHU 28	49630	KLB 104	98650	KOK 625	140879
KGT 68	85701	KHU 129	50693	KLB 491	115765	KOL 193	142608
KGT 69	84021	KHU 176	29484	KLC 250	117536	KON 536	143340
KGT 70	96459	KHU 470	51687	KLG 48	64556	KOP 702	145653
KGT 74	91655	KHU 739	48926	KLG 49	67866	KOV 827	147047
KGT 75	99297	KHU 996	33224	KLG 70	57603	KPC 658	17261
KGT 76	97765	KHW 121	55524	KLG 391	58923	KPD 329	12795
KGT 77	103755	KHW 501	56902	KLG 529	57912	KPD 956	15959
KGT 78	100865	KHW 578	64315	KLJ 505	142345	KPE 455	18773
KGT 79	86772	KHW 869	58356	KLK 495	95985	KPE 959	18756
KGT 86	99290	KHW 987	59647	KMA 93	63774	KPH 478	28689
KGT 93	97761	KHY 318	62081	KMA 98	71930	KPJ 389	30373
KGT 96	97772	KHY 917	68303	KMA 371	72239	KPJ 390	32004
KGT 97	96568	KJA 800 *	16608	KMA 378	74070	KPK 549	37015
KGT 99	89061	KJH 91	92760	KMA 468	41031	KPK 951	35131
KGT 138	99282	KJH 492	97489	KMB 246	65891	KPO 714	103819
KGT 139	100858	KJH 731	98856	KMB 956	73697	KPP 190	62200
KGT 155	100882	KJJ 188	96218	KMN 324	96726	KPP 251	65034
KGT 397	100429	KJJ 314	113415	KMN 530	100408	KPP 253	65609
KGT 398	100887	KJJ 315	113472	KMN 531	103982	KPP 706	69705
KGT 406	103902	KJJ 316	113486	KMN 532	107139	KPP 918	67267
KGT 426	99998	KJJ 317	113420	KMN 533	111773	KPT 96	105701
KGT 610	109275	KJJ 318	113467	KMN 661 *	58826	KPT 194	104482
KGT 611	109374	KJJ 319	113593	KMN 744 *	58923	KPT 197	105639
KGT 612	109380	KJJ 516	113025	KMN 854 *	57031	KPT 307	105741
KGT 888	103310	KJJ 518	114928	KMN 938 *	80559	KPT 472	108900
KGT 889	104078	KJJ 738	114539	KNA 208	104789	KPT 646	110674
KGT 895	108226	KJJ 739	117558	KNC 297	110936	KPT 903	114903
KGT 898	107627	KKC 10	110966	KNC 385	112436	KPU 730	25560
KGU 563	122501	KKE 173	61442	KND 388	66088	KPU 859	25587
KGU 584	103124	KKE 282	61392	KND 445	115443	KPU 871	26846
KGU 600	105321	KKE 472	61556	KND 569	115837	KPW 176	119596
KGU 652	103319	KKE 478	63525	KNE 780	120147	KPW 986	122499
KGU 658	104066	KKE 704	63532	KNF 974	124349	KPX 600	113555
KGU 659	104719	KKE 802	65577	KNG 83	112541	KRA 504	40223
KGU 666	116053	KKE 944	62947	KNG 320	125683	KRB 65	45490
KGU 667	118428	KKE 986	64459	KNG 492	115337	KRB 66	46966
KGU 668	120232	KKH 127	105886	KNK 57	99528	KRB 67	53428
KGU 669	123613	KKH 293	109939	KNK 870	106254	KRB 68	54822
KGU 670	94913	KKJ 933	64518	KNN 314	100400	KRB 69	57321
KGW 126	97955	KKK 342	68973	KNN 377	103116	KRB 70	58704
KGW 419	105947	KKK 373	58453	KNO 723	22819	KRH 934	128955
KGY 53	112011	KKL 691	72196	KNU 581	31248	KRL 294	80580
KGY 57	112896	KKM 90	72479	KNU 857	33901	KRL 771	84504
KGY 199	109972	KKM 131	72614	KNW 455	28461	KRL 984	81829
KGY 200	108848	KKM 178	71584	KNW 639	30073	KRM 244	146331
KGY 251	110560	KKM 222	71766	KNW 902	31121	KRO 511	107592
KGY 252	110503	KKM 358	60552	KNX 33	142138	KRO 517	110264
KGY 253	110668	KKM 471	74441	KNX 470	146445	KRO 689	111943
KGY 255	111042	KKM 472	77006	KNX 718	145518	KRR 107	103971

KRR 297	110416	KUB 745	37150	KWB 826	69774	KYD 815	109295
KRR 631	112699	KUF 326	140544	KWB 936	70719	KYE 308	130237
KRT 227	139289	KUG 666	49860	KWE 293	71619	KYE 309	136333
KRT 578	144328	KUG 757	45626	KWE 337	72225	KYE 310	138470
KRT 853	144824	KUM 82	52785	KWJ 634	83908	KYE 455	143239
KSM 142	113584	KUM 83	53508	KWJ 773	72389	KYE 464	134567
KSU 381 *	121153	KUM 172	51331	KXJ 287	137922	KYE 535	131574
KTA 17	83467	KUM 173	49653	KXU 332	130324	KYE 781	135206
KTA 435	84971	KUM 797	96993	KXU 333	129546	KYE 905	133670
KTA 713	86391	KUM 998	55451	KXU 775	119429	KYE 924	134122
KTB 121	94229	KUM 999	59866	KXU 990	122924	KYF 616	126769
KTB 127	92493	KUO 160	98760	KXV 308	124699	KYF 696	(127807 ?)
KTB 521	95073	KUO 260	96970	KXV 317	126663	KYF 896	138984
KTB 649	96511	KUO 674	100968	KXV 318	127760	KYH 22	119041
KTC 535	100162	KUO 888	101262	KXV 320	123735	KYH 23	117825
KTC 627	106981	KUO 926	126668	KXV 512	121336	KYH 24	124861
KTC 642	101435	KUP 10	113347	KXV 518	121324	KYH 25	129559
KTC 987	103193	KUP 107	115375	KXV 521	121376	KYH 957	JCB116
KTD 179	100101	KUP 153	115329	KXV 524	121308	KYK 110	134472
KTD 462	104740	KUP 234	118093	KXV 535	121330	KYK 195	138958
KTE 951	109708	KUP 240	118375	KXV 536	124094	KYK 812	139716
KTF 235	108841	KUP 481	119676	KXV 537	124099	KYK 814	141570
KTG 107	142451	KUP 537	122857	KXV 561	125039	KYK 815	140806
KTG 317	143748	KUP 711	125792	KXV 562	125070	KYK 875	137826
KTG 377	141565	KUP 927	130701	KXV 563	126816	KYK 996	138160
KTG 935	146593	KUR 123	113077	KXV 564	137484	KYU 90	129033
KTJ 201	112609	KUR 238	115697	KXV 575	138180	KYW 329	139763
KTJ 236	111136	KUR 510	113060	KXV 592	126777	KYW 330	139732
KTJ 720	116590	KUR 857	115425	KXV 600	124156	KYW 331	139755
KTO 459	76696	KVF 172	125690	KXV 635	126833	KYW 332	139771
KTT 254	74898	KVF 261	122756	KXV 819	121753	KYW 335	143000
KTT 492	90930	KVF 324	128178	KXW 633	126860	KYW 336	143396
KTT 882	95305	KVF 333	128118	KXW 634	126868	KYW 337	139972
KTU 724	90684	KVF 447	129537	KXW 635	127082	KYW 344	142996
KTU 882	88229	KVK 51	40601	KXW 636	126852	KYW 740	147628
KTV 17	78715	KVK 89	40481	KXW 637	127100	LAD 192	133924
KTV 396	82181	KVK 678	42044	KXW 638	127178	LAE 223	69467
KTW 91	17286	KVM 500	43334	KXW 642	127104	LAE 275	63020
KTW 212	21302	KVO 148	127360	KXW 643	127195	LAE 622	73180
KTW 236	27969	KVO 494	114876	KXW 644	127139	LAE 845	74631
KTW 237	28376	KVO 975	118952	KXW 645	127127	LAF 186	86369
KTW 238	29460	KVR 320	124713	KXW 646	127117	LAF 407	89404
KTW 239	32155	KVR 994	130575	KXW 648	117233	LAF 978	94140
KTW 240	31650	KVT 63	133824	KXW 927	124780	LAH 75	132882
KTW 241	31636	KVT 119	39151	KXW 964	114125	LAH 555	NC7128500
KTW 242	32359	KVT 120	38791	KXX 2	122829	LAL 235	127229
KTW 243	31103	KVT 121	39111	KXY 500	128106	LAL 440	129183
KTW 244	30382	KVT 385	39200	KXY 630	127320	LAL 564	132136
KTW 846	21859	KVT 540	43087	KXY 638	129978	LAL 618	128924
KTW 855	26748	KVT 628	43256	KXY 989	128504	LAL 698	119976
KTX 48	145372	KVU 914	46931	KYA 64	82134	LAU 18	86485
KUA 181	33795	KVW 60	135155	KYA 142	83100	LBB 165	49530
KUA 182	33990	KVW 948	25878	KYA 528	81918	LBB 234	44476
KUA 183	34151	KVW 949	33170	KYB 8	87493	LBB 235	45275
KUA 184	34529	KVW 950	33589	KYB 46	87644	LBB 236	47930
KUA 185	32213	KVW 951	33812	KYB 376	90079	LBB 237	49833
KUA 186	34469	KVW 952	33839	KYB 378	90839	LBH 57	73468
KUA 187	33884	KVW 953	34455	KYB 568	90775	LBH 107	75361
KUA 188	34616	KVX 739	34479	KYB 836	94286	LBH 720	88907
KUA 189	34562	KWA 729	30104	KYB 989	95016	LBH 757	74516
KUA 190	34649	KWB 5	57984	KYC 193	97860	LBP 275	118904
KUA 510	33441	KWB 6	57777	KYC 386	98720	LBP 500	121288
KUB 11	40461	KWB 334	57797	KYC 926	101607	LCD 236	146932
KUB 477	92788		65649	KYD 575	105178	LCV 404	99318

C1252/268

LCV 810	103028	LKM 55	102204	LNK 510	123456	LPU 629	58679
LDE 400	105987	LKM 379	102678	LNK 693	131675	LPW 503	144464
LDE 997	122851	LKM 743	102654	LNN 147	132694	LPX 150	140632
LDF 833	H&S3024	LKN 257	106245	LNN 331	137525	LPX 672	144934
LDH 45	54457	LKN 546	105630	LNN 875	140252	LPX 909	143142
LDV 477	133770	LKN 550	106863	LNN 877	141487	LRA 310	58487
LDV 483	124372	LKN 941	108086	LNO 150	JCB3	LRA 443	60479
LEH 132	50873	LKN 948	106437	LNO 177	41790	LRB 158	63206
LEH 339	66414	LKO 209	108018	LNW 31	53554	LRB 191	64469
LFJ 18	140720	LKO 239	108239	LNW 623	57924	LRB 222	66161
LFM 387	125577	LKO 520	110592	LNW 825	50978	LRB 284	59899
LFM 388	125610	LKP 835	114793	LNW 827	56760	LRB 749	66082
LFM 389	125621	LKP 961	116013	LNW 829	65866	LRB 750	64154
LFM 390	125651	LKR 32	112354	LNW 830	68601	LRB 751	64178
LFM 391	126034	LKT 824	116553	LOC 286	SG2/50	LRB 790	71485
LFM 392	126109	LKX 40	81244	LOD 78	137925	LRC 423 *	14121
LFM 393	126125	LKX 291	83244	LOD 529	137285	LRE 640	11712
LFM 394	126132	LLG 806	97350	LOD 533	141311	LRE 641	11107
LFM 395	127994	LLT 122	138735	LPB 4	43177	LRE 642	11095
LFM 396	128034	LLT 332	129614	LPB 250	44519	LRE 794	12066
LFM 397	128087	LLW 31	142663	LPB 722	36995	LRF 654	28529
LFM 398	128416	LLW 32	142425	LPB 723	36847	LRF 714	21622
LFM 399	128448	LLW 42	143664	LPB 748	44871	LRL 660	110509
LFM 400	139416	LLW 133	143115	LPC 62	40308	LRL 941	111048
LFM 401	139511	LLW 837	143332	LPC 851	34917	LRO 296	137102
LFM 402	140187	LLX 425	144730	LPC 938	47163	LRO 486	135769
LFM 403	140997	LMA 174	102602	LPC 939	47092	LRR 601	145456
LFM 404	140988	LMB 240 *	67190	LPD 847	49912	LRR 655	146347
LFM 461	125971	LMG 988	12785	LPD 906	44242	LRR 814	143916
LGC 729	132595	LMN 1	87618	LPE 123	50014	LSM 44	146795
LHK 325	38584	LMN 147 *	11027	LPE 442	49593	LSM 335	140985
LHN 146	86749	LMN 261	115181	LPF 249	47475	LSU 857 *	32426
LHN 211	90488	LMN 361	117111	LPG 109	55995	LTA 86	112459
LHN 475	97705	LMN 546	118286	LPG 154	55814	LTA 169	112943
LHN 640	101256	LMN 551	121908	LPG 191	55365	LTA 697	114222
LHN 756	104071	LMN 771	126216	LPH 403	56789	LTA 745	126742
LHN 965	107471	LMN 885	130757	LPH 482	58252	LTA 746	127495
LHN 966	107187	LMN 958 *	47172	LPK 54	61973	LTA 747	127726
LHN 967	107109	LMN 971 *	59866	LPL 780	66174	LTA 748	127745
LHT 285	76922	LMN 972 *	40541	LPO 96	118250	LTA 749	127818
LHT 543	61604	LMN 979 *	77871	LPP 53	91289	LTA 750	127852
LHT 721	80534	LMY 254	21409	LPP 549	98881	LTA 751	135045
LHU 605	84953	LMY 449	23966	LPP 683	102040	LTA 752	135254
LHU 948	89606	LMY 450	24857	LPP 943	103146	LTA 753	135397
LHW 139	88963	LMY 462	25574	LPT 392	137990	LTA 754	135711
LHY 64	64542	LMY 681	20824	LPT 550	142515	LTA 755	135986
LHY 350	101487	LMY 682	21310	LPT 651	141538	LTA 756	134753
LHY 371	101496	LMY 725	21308	LPT 723	143741	LTA 757	136421
LHY 918	105618	LMY 760	18749	LPT 816	140737	LTA 758	136925
LHY 919	105959	LMY 770	18774	LPT 858	134698	LTA 759	137005
LHY 920	105968	LMY 893	13480	LPU 615	63840	LTA 903	123000
LHY 921	106899	LNA 310	146812	LPU 616	67555	LTA 904	123013
LHY 922	107783	LNA 367	141301	LPU 617	67729	LTA 905	123126
LHY 923	107741	LNA 776	142636	LPU 618	68699	LTA 906	123634
LJH 643	121926	LNB 238	144244	LPU 619	69736	LTA 907	123645
LJO 756	54661	LNC 324	145086	LPU 620	69986	LTA 908	124001
LJO 757	61338	LND 185	144312	LPU 621	101361	LTA 909	124066
LJO 757 *	144971	LNG 323	143804	LPU 622	101953	LTA 910	124722
LKD 246	145737	LNG 324	140163	LPU 623	50043	LTA 911	124790
LKH 429	143909	LNG 403	140751	LPU 624	49995	LTA 912	124808
LKJ 966	99394	LNG 555	142103	LPU 625	51257	LTA 913	132958
LKK 35	101339	LNG 643	139302	LPU 626	52933	LTA 914	132670
LKK 42	94988	LNK 144	127753	LPU 627	51757	LTA 915	133305
LKK 59	97341	LNK 403	129526	LPU 628	57536	LTA 916	133380

LTA 917	133600	LUG 14	79823	MAF 811	117278	MHU 992	121666
LTA 918	133582	LUM 509	93291	MAR 67	144480	MHU 993	121746
LTA 919	133951	LUM 520	97079	MAR 190	145791	MHU 994	121933
LTA 920	133992	LUM 613	90130	MAR 510	146163	MHU 995	122224
LTA 921	134426	LUM 614	88820	MAR 776	144300	MHU 996	122218
LTA 922	133840	LUO 270	124258	MAS 427 *	92760	MHU 997	122733
LTA 923	134088	LUO 427	126746	MAU 23	123461	MHU 998	122762
LTA 924	134432	LUO 634	123030	MAU 577	131486	MHU 999	122195
LTA 925	134502	LUO 839	129377	MBB 262	66438	MHW 936	128710
LTA 926	134786	LUP 114	146889	MBB 263	65931	MHW 937	127468
LTB 147	117883	LUR 103	139078	MBH 88	108009	MHX 450	20836
LTB 453	120510	LUR 219	142546	MBP 900	146515	MHY 810	137932
LTB 804	119954	LUR 409	135413	MCV 311	124763	MHY 904	138714
LTB 906	122940	LUR 446	143368	MDE 666	140900	MJH 255	146193
LTB 907	125509	LUR 490	143017	MDE 777	142679	MJO 283	64251
LTC 110	123484	LUR 503	140195	MDG 750 *	20814	MJO 923	72012
LTC 388	121694	LUR 510	138772	MDH 681	105185	MKE 126	119965
LTC 681	124581	LUR 511	140067	MDV 825	147043	MKE 584	117814
LTC 855	124328	LUV 870	146151	MEV 321	41130	MKK 40	123107
LTD 45	130146	LUW 75	146179	MEV 352	51857	MKL 51	128458
LTD 62	128162	LUW 90	146590	MEV 408	54448	MKL 260	130103
LTD 953	132039	LUW 615	146580	MFC 340	53411	MKL 509	129471
LTD 981	130265	LVK 181	63036	MFC 951	55765	MKL 635	131305
LTD 986	125670	LVK 381	64332	MFM 36	141399	MKN 981	135419
LTE 312	133911	LVK 593	73456	MFM 37	141289	MKO 60	137624
LTE 626	137994	LVO 85	147100	MFM 38	141575	MKO 67	136267
LTE 901	144496	LVO 146	145453	•MFM 39	142625 •	MKO 138	130852
LTF 346	137152	LVT 317	62013	MFM 40	143049	MKO 207	132124
LTF 359	138339	LVT 485	68944	MFM 41	143896	MKP 557	144356
LTF 682	140655	LVW 59	45289	MFM 42	143255	MKP 810	143025
LTF 845	97436	LVW 152	47377	MFM 43	142358	MKX 322	115979
LTF 965	135881	LVW 258	46910	MFM 44	142507	MKX 427	114565
LTJ 215	140648	LVW 490	49057	MFM 185	130772	MKX 927	121599
LTN 376	60991	LVW 952	51321	MHK 525	55739	MLA 240	123656
LTN 582	63188	LVW 953	51734	MHN 81	109258	MMA 488	129628
LTN 680	61064	LWA 121	87317	MHN 192	111342	MME 174	21420
LTN 942	64412	LWB 647	100355	MHN 255	109175	MME 738	18739
LTO 19	98770	LWJ 679	116311	MHN 442	115875	MME 742	23475
LTO 246	104707	LWL 252	25510	MHN 509	116475	MME 743	24684
LTO 715	108111	LWT 825 *	118161	MHN 592	119330	MME 744	25091
LTT 44	115870	LXL 909	145418	MHN 823	123739	MME 745	25136
LTT 138	117736	LYA 166	110566	MHN 826	124598	MMH 618	34809
LTT 690	118450	LYA 231	111804	MHN 836	126590	MMH 619	34930
LTT 913	118863	LYB 121	115740	MHN 837	126566	MML 496	34017
LTU 670	117210	LYB 125	118161	MHT 597	112567	MMN 18	134013
LTU 727	119082	LYB 941	124672	MHT 672	115348	MMN 57	135777
LTV 21	112551	LYC 10	121390	MHU 49	119935	MMN 166 *	109708
LTV 522	115422	LYC 188	123715	MHU 50	120044	MMN 177 *	60093
LTW 251	44669	LYC 731	130805	MHU 51	120678	MMN 215	138718
LTW 461	47133	LYC 782	132620	MHU 52	123166	MMN 343	141231
LTW 552	47153	LYD 311	136413	MHU 53	123702	MMN 422	143715
LUA 467	59229	LYD 410	129624	MHU 54	124367	MMN 467	143352
LUA 541	68097	LYD 825	137610	MHU 55	126200	MMP 169	36269
LUA 591	69944	LYH 616	130013	MHU 56	127305	MMP 170	36232
LUB 12	67475	LYH 617	130195	MHU 57	127928	MMP 578	38356
LUB 251	70382	LYH 618	130285	MHU 58	132238	MMP 579	38366
LUB 359	78098	LYH 619	132636	MHU 59	132312	MMP 584	39708
LUB 360	83446	LYH 620	132734	MHU 60	133238	MMP 585	38604
LUB 500	67972	LYH 621	135007	MHU 193	116397	MMP 808	37245
LUB 550	75516	LYH 622	135359	MHU 416	118173	MMP 809	37276
LUB 564	59391	LYH 623	137648	MHU 417	119587	MMP 811	35383
LUC 642	144812	LYH 624	139056	MHU 603	119498	MMP 812	34958
LUC 645	143876	LYH 625	140956	MHU 915	120935	MMP 813	36435
LUC 646	147349	MAF 446	116456	MHU 944	122230	MMP 814	36901

C1252/270

MMP 815	37290	MPU 394	61677	MWB 104	127214	NNU 461	105349
MMT 506	38218	MPU 504	61346	MWB 105	127883	NNW 819	123751
MMT 507	38198	MRA 311	49610	MWB 122	127396	NNW 870	124952
MMT 508	38208	MRA 599	68845	MWB 292	128097	NNW 871	124871
MMT 524	39742	MRA 602	88117	MWB 301	128909	NPA 73	103483
MMT 525	40560	MRA 610	83295	MWB 310	129432	NPA 308	103111
MMT 861	35161	MRB 354	91691	MWB 497	131407	NPC 214	108322
MMT 862	35223	MRB 765	95361	MWE 729	141415	NPC 416	106948
MMT 863	35310	MRB 934	97876	MWJ 998	145048	NPC 430	107056
MMT 864	35427	MRF 301	40721	MXV 578	240499	NPD 239	112001
MMT 865	34843	MRF 632	43007	MYA 8	140663	NPD 271	111722
MMT 866	35179	MRL 70	132797	MYA 234	138896	NPE 376	110556
MMT 875	38435	MRL 552	136933	MYA 524	140818	NPE 380	110401
MMT 876	38520	MRL 776	138857	MYA 525	141556	NPF 479	103936
MMT 877	38574	MRL 863	140812	MYA 657	144816	NPG 655	120123
MMT 878	38297	MSJ 606 *	120202	MYB 33	145431	NPG 750	119618
MMT 879	37115	MTA 159	140909	MYB 711	146948	NPG 948	116075
MMT 880	37258	MTA 554	142692	MYC 442	146244	♦NPJ 349	123478 ♦
MMY 668	41101	MTA 744	143758	MYC 801	147064	NPJ 590	122897
MMY 680	42472	MTA 917	147355	MYD 444	144912	NPJ 762	122808
MMY 696	42157	MTB 533	142051	NAE 71	135300	NPK 447	124237
MMY 847	40631	MTC 755	143267	NAE 72	138251	NPK 860	127404
MNO 290	56796	MTC 756	146061	NAF 69	141380	NPL 750	129127
MNO 901	57579	MTD 242	143792	NAF 678	146227	NPO 290	?
MNU 79	65978	MTD 289	146328	NAF 934	146805	NPU 424	81402
MNU 80	66060	MTD 399	144928	NBB 171	109758	NPU 437	59132
MNU 81	66113	MTE 987	146412	NBB 828	117267	NRB 122	114870
MNU 82	68069	MTN 233	92681	NBB 906	117657	NRB 262	116271
MNU 83	68486	MTO 683	121902	NBH 746	143848	NRB 891	121732
MNU 84	69186	MTT 44	145707	NBH 941	146108	NRE 74	47283
MNU 336	74103	MTT 214	146068	NDH 663	134514	NRE 234	46771
MNU 512	72074	MTV 24	141292	NEV 190	68901	NRE 614	49325
MNU 686	68764	MTV 31	142429	NEV 248	72896	NRF 175	54982
MNU 687	68927	MTW 263	62314	NEV 387	73489	NRF 268	47176
MNU 688	69374	MTW 498	63282	NEV 861	76269	NRF 301	48992
MNU 689	69358	MTW 819	67886	NFC 850	82886	NRF 409	54680
MNU 690	68838	MTW 868	66689	NGK 245	244053	NRF 410	56642
MNU 929	43918	MTW 879	66816	NGK 246	248440	NRF 552	56091
MNU 931	51913	MUA 346	99386	NGY 421 *	(13715 ?)	NSV 583 *	95977
MNU 939	80441	MUA 596	101270	NHK 286	70152	NTN 195 *	64332
MNW 300	79221	MUA 633	106871	NHN 42	130745	NTN 841	119419
MPA 796	69488	MUG 344	110586	NHN 188	133292	NTW 330	86683
MPB 333	74445	MUG 868	114582	NHN 266	129522	NTW 368	85220
MPB 550	71849	MUG 869	114979	NHN 325	132936	NTW 706	89535
MPB 666	73185	MUG 873	103280	NHN 326	132848	NTW 911	45547
MPB 833	76180	MUG 874	103357	NHN 327	135857	NUA 258	129163
MPE 59	76941	MUM 276	117071	NHN 576	138808	NUA 533	131301
MPF 109	87438	MUM 455	134110	NHN 626	142146	NUB 175	135325
MPF 368	81393	MUM 790	120243	NHN 733	143023	NUB 395	136677
MPF 643	82743	MVK 148	101443	NHN 919	144322	NUG 11	138381
MPG 750	85353	MVK 501	104728	NHT 641	141962	NUM 13	143987
MPG 970	89424	MVW 62	44175	NHT 227	143283	NVK 434	131497
MPH 621	76865	MVW 68	64929	NHT 820	142688	NVK 849	133863
MPK 477	?	MVW 155	67946	NHU 254	?	NVW 220	90650
MPK 639	98484	MVW 285	66331	NHU 345	143808	NVW 835	93093
MPL 640	102286	MVW 286	72504	NJO 669	104543	NVX 129	94116
MPP 245	121237	MVW 287	90872	NKE 433	144726	NVX 525	JCB44
MPP 627	126499	MVW 387	66800	NKJ 221	145014	NVX 526	JCB45
MPP 658	134730	MVW 515	55709	NLG 134	143720	NVX 527	JCB46
MPT 409	144000	MVW 556	66294	NLG 482	146864	NVX 528	JCB53
MPT 410	146361	MVX 376	70820	NMN 273	143903	NVX 529	JCB54
MPU 61	62411	MVX 508	71745	NNO 186	78156	NVX 530	JCB55
MPU 62	62923	MVX 596	72612	NNO 222	78595	NVX 531	JCB74
MPU 348	61458	MVX 923	71863	NNO 229	74895	NVX 532	JCB75

C1252/271

NVX 533	JCB76	OMY 385	61296	PPC 275	147359	SMF 605	58187
NVX 677	94042	OMY 386	61322	PPU 767	129784	SMF 632	56881
NVX 782	96119	OMY 410	62297	PRA 622 *	146277	SMF 654	58371
NVX 822	96027	OMY 520	63848	PRE 128	74490	SMF 655	58308
NWL 804	91874	OMY 556	62005	PRE 333	74540	SMF 954	57374
OBB 327	129618	OMY 617	63287	PRE 498	78375	SMF 957	56060
OBB 343	125298	OMY 740	62721	PRE 569	76070	SMF 960	48368
OBB 568	142112	OMY 837	58349	PRE 587	75337	SMF 961	56110
OBB 600	143199	OMY 838	58646	PRE 759	47252	SMK 294	114812
OBB 746	143312	ONO 84	108118	PRF 48	81297	SML 144	66340
OBH 100	145579	ONO 85	108741	PRF 84	61289	SML 276	64912
OEH 621	144764	ONO 86	108764	PRF 167	44710	SML 400	69796
OEV 889	100338	ONO 87	112050	PRF 559	59681	SML 467	68394
OHK 668	100723	ONO 88	112032	PRF 560	62467	SML 468	68936
OHK 973	103199	ONO 89	111950	PRF 561	65915	SML 469	64049
OHK 976	103987	ONO 90	117518	PRF 655	85832	SML 622	69471
OHN 132	145534	ONO 91	117647	PTW 268	132224	SML 623	69444
OHW 292	221339	ONO 92	117714	PVW 216	135934	SML 696	64726
OJO 895	134482	ONO 93	137902	PVX 16	136661	SML 699	69229
OML 125	40590	ONO 94	138240	PVX 300	138171	SML 700	66343
OML 126	41172	ONO 177	102146	PVX 607	139082	SML 958	63792
OML 127	35267	ONO 711	106430	PWL 559	146496	SMT 100	50280
OML 198	40841	ONO 975	104583	REV 90	140203	SMY 140	66968
OML 312	44703	ONU 97	?	REV 213	140836	SMY 152	73590
OML 543	44444	ONU 98	?	REV 972	135243	SMY 239	74450
OML 603	45541	ONU 972	130059	RHK 308	138463	SMY 256	58240
OML 665	44526	OPA 112	115748	RHK 843	142371	SMY 257	59672
OML 742	44309	OPA 113	115759	RHK 890	140730	SMY 262	74506
OML 743	44438	OPA 798	132072	RHN 107	236943	SMY 294	76476
OML 813	43072	OPC 286	136582	RHN 108	237387	SMY 547	78337
OML 825	43568	OPC 809	136877	RMN 425 *	93974	SMY 559	75524
OML 912	43906	OPE 242	142459	RRE 325	93658	SMY 560	76019
OML 915	43590	OPF 924	141553	RRE 506	94310	SMY 583	73942
OMN 304 *	47418	OPH 528	144384	RRF 729	103550	SMY 586	76548
OMP 141	46029	OPJ 200	143105	RRF 799	37298	SMY 587	79545
OMP 142	46063	OPJ 584	145744	RTW 222	147090	SMY 590	78823
OMP 143	44466	OPK 244	145504	RTW 523	143652	SMY 602	88880
OMP 248	45638	OPK 510	146145	RUJ 205 *	13475	SMY 864	72177
OMP 249	45946	OPU 853	109100	RVW 100	146160	SMY 911	72422
OMP 250	46854	ORA 281	134687	RVW 157	147032	SMY 916	74056
OMT 31	47259	ORB 45	142494	RVW 370	143816	SMY 919	72569
OMT 149	50215	ORB 218	139600	SEV 700	145508	SMY 920	69573
OMT 150	57174	ORB 279	143323	SEV 777	143967	SRE 12	106573
OMT 462	52950	ORB 767	145068	SME 8	47418	SRF 212	116933
OMT 463	54870	ORE 359	61587	SME 9	47182	SRF 234	115954
OMT 537	49925	ORE 944	62184	SME 96	43121	SRF 852	120065
OMT 544	50090	ORF 90	65617	SME 97	43199	STG 227 *	12743
OMT 551	51370	ORF 497	66422	SME 271	43447	SUX 980 *	21468
OMT 552	50950	ORF 564	71266	SME 280	55559	SVX 838	143668
OMT 553	52549	ORF 833	66119	SME 553	60741	TMG 94	60749
OMT 602	67560	ORF 840	72630	SME 617	55531	TMG 119	79374
OMT 820	48106	PCH 175 *	?	SME 624	56559	TMG 167	72366
OMT 834	51349	PEV 307	118410	SME 652	54897	TMG 168	68355
OMT 961	47894	PEV 369	120560	SMF 8	56962	TMG 169	63085
OMT 968	49048	PEV 408	119488	SMF 380	57906	TMG 197	73086
OMT 969	49547	PEV 885	115786	SMF 407	56046	TMG 244	75541
OMX 276	124881	PEV 990	119320	SMF 410	57117	TMG 497	91251
OMX 333	126487	PFF 777 *	232395	SMF 413	65336	TMG 725	76687
OMX 356	126673	PHK 911	120860	SMF 527	61281	TMG 732	82488
OMX 357	127704	PMN 150 *	104555	SMF 530	60093	TMG 998	80855
OMX 420	118183	PMN 379 *	129796	SMF 585	59188	TMK 28	89357
OMX 455	128652	PNU 406	146869	SMF 596	57233	TMK 31	89684
OMY 378	62120	PNY 259 *	16657	SMF 597	59139	TMK 112	93695
OMY 384	61779	PPA 934 *	?	SMF 604	49851	TMK 238	94908

C1252/272

TMK 272	97038	TRF 953	134128	UVP 595 *	18717	VML 988	109209
TMK 282	98041	UDO 927 *	130010	VMB 321 *	22049	VML 989	111029
TMK 318	97946	UHX 102	112852	VME 87	133216	VMN 809 *	44645
TMK 430	96961	UHX 131	111288	VME 103	140076	VMN 844 *	124588
TMK 571	90704	UHX 191	113940	VME 109	132973	VMV 126	129732
TMK 635	97452	UHX 269	115986	VME 161	133837	VMV 138	135846
TMK 638	94829	UHX 285	99922	VME 200	133688	VMV 691	132229
TMK 639	96719	UHX 286	112469	VME 226	135078	VMV 701	133676
TMK 640	99699	UHX 306	116541	VME 227	128705	VMV 702	134189
TMK 731	95012	UHX 429	115259	VME 277	137047	VMY 685	137886
TMM 168	138882	UHX 430	113976	VME 296	135810	WFF 582 *	126578
TMM 191	142620	UHX 606	118272	VME 297	125420	WFF 583 *	100169
TMM 377	142511	UHX 712	116664	VME 303	133332	WMC 3	133776
TMM 378	143356	UHX 713	117625	VME 495	135953	WMC 26	144850
TMM 627	138518	UHX 714	118772	VME 574	135133	WMC 27	?
TMM 829	136528	UHX 715	120054	VME 605	133903	WMC 76	144850
TMN 586 *	130010	UHX 833	113961	VME 732	132141	WMN 59 *	85922
TMN 613 *	8261	UMN 137 *	36215	VME 733	131402	WMX 6	141626
TMV 8	83931	UMN 634 *	74619	VME 741	130579	WMX 27	131482
TMV 35	85347	UMN 670 *	61779	VME 742	132150	WMX 35	131584
TMV 182	84983	UMN 794 *	141468	VME 744	133314	WMX 161	234492
TMV 320	85986	UMP 78	106425	VME 745	133736	WMX 184	?
TMV 502	91680	UMP 79	106491	VME 925	131589	WOJ 528 *	?
TMV 503	92313	UMP 80	108053	VMK 9	142093	WOJ 826 *	12748
TMV 505	93378	UMP 81	108306	VMK 20	141456	WOJ 828 *	?
TMV 597	90228	UMP 82	107549	VMK 155	142006	WOJ 829 *	16667
TMV 726	89340	UMP 95	103370	VMK 156	142604	WOJ 830 *	13406
TMV 728	88997	UMP 96	107655	VMK 161	145611	WOJ 831 *	26869
TMV 729	87291	UMP 416	113429	VMK 193	142038	WNR 647	?
TMV 941	85246	UMP 520	108753	VMK 200	143812	WSL 115 *	137293
TMV 948	84911	UMP 522	110334	VMK 259	143674	XDE 864 *	15977
TMV 950	83334	UMP 531	109714	VMK 278	146856	XOC 36 *	20811
TMV 989	85327	UMP 532	113501	VMK 568	144828	XOC 37 *	26245
TMV 990	81867	UMP 695	106986	VMK 721	143842	XOC 38 *	?
TMV 999	87656	UMP 697	110483	VML 2	70161	XOC 39 *	20807
TMY 26	96891	UMP 698	114371	VML 100	91617	XOC 41 *	?
TMY 55	98967	UMP 699	113098	VML 101	90677	XOP 722 *	16623
TMY 81	98935	UMP 831	105893	VML 102	93624	YBJ 871 *	(12749 ?)
TMY 107	100080	UMP 832	107670	VML 103	97698	YOF 234 *	?
TMY 173	96518	UMY 63	122284	VML 221	100783	YOF 235 *	18723
TMY 218	94030	UMY 82	117189	VML 232	104184	YRC 419 *	?
TMY 248	96499	UMY 95	120660	VML 290	113651	9734 E *	30340
TMY 277	96530	UMY 96	118972	VML 301	107748	3293 BT *	16625
TMY 359	104179	UMY 170	118420	VML 302	111879	1949 MN *	121153
TMY 485	91854	UMY 191	119685	VML 321	120856	1949 MN *	123524
TMY 493	103288	UMY 193	116630	VML 334	120024	1950 MN *	142371
TMY 494	104163	UMY 267	124055	VML 401	113509	278 ABE *	89320
TMY 495	107027	UMY 333	124717	VML 574	72053	495 ART *	46181
TMY 699	105823	UMY 447	127313	VML 575	72693	245 BOB *	18730
TMY 700	103474	UMY 448	129451	VML 576	76678	691 CRA *	16607
TMY 716	100937	UMY 449	128934	VML 592	80432	423 DTB *	42370
TMY 717	105103	UMY 559	122202	VML 643	83382	349 ETD *	18716
TMY 718	106553	UMY 560	120570	VML 663	87461	248 FDE *	19832
TMY 719	108189	UMY 699	122270	VML 664	89074	542 GMG *	?
TMY 720	109102	UMY 704	123036	VML 786	92157	159 GMO *	98950
TMY 806	101584	UMY 853	115772	VML 797	94382	504 HTE	138477
TMY 938	98631	UMY 955	117795	VML 804	97334	281 HWR *	56826
TMY 939	98846	UOU 302 *	14217	VML 936	104143	37 JBB *	23888
TMY 940	100497	URE 216	143076	VML 937	104453	341 JRT *	19827
TMY 941	98382	URE 550	143829	VML 938	104059	419 JZD *	10566
TRE 94	121645	URE 680	143799	VML 948	106479	184 XUF *	100257
TRE 95	121682	URF 662	140011	VML 949	108003	BVH 319A *	123524
TRE 753	133868	URF 968	144396	VML 976	108165	TRN 618A *	131392
TRF 228	136261	URT 287 *	16603	VML 977	108196	DNP 212B *	134013

C1252/273

TRN 618A *	131392	3087	40851	J 1761 *	43590	J 8404 *	60395
KCJ 135E *	92133	3088	40830	J 1879	79440	J 8520 *	81957
KCJ 398E *	94273	3089	41161	J 2562 *	94999	J 9151 *	132253
YTF 162J *	135777	3090	40821	J 2566 *	95937	J 9477 *	49048
LTR 336R *	32426	3117	30226	J 2609 *	98544	J 9586 *	69719
Q986 OCR *	90670	3118	31908	J 2641 *	96827	J 10278	71707
		3458	33376	J 2742 *	98763	J 10584	72977
Alderney		3460	31380	J 2773 *	100969	J 10585	73190
AY 59 *	23382	4101	30485	J 2813 *	98569	J 11079 *	55546
AY 59 *	40830	4414	105646	J 2833 *	100005	J 11590	15043
AY 59 *	40851	4426	108594	J 2865 *	97420	J 11592	17215
AY 59 *	72585	5181	70827	J 2874 *	100347	J 11593	15057
AY 59 *	73023	5182	72578	J 3074 *	65641	J 11594	72633
AY 59 *	73174	5183	72585	J 3572 *	146179	J 11595	72620
AY 59 *	108594	5184	76076	J 3590	80006	J 11888	79364
		5185	75989	J 3617 *	131392	J 11982	84149
Guernsey		5186	77409	J 4442	84417	J 12204 *	49325
261	35168	5187	70813	J 5149 *	142936	J 12213 *	57970
1292	12059	5188	73023	J 5296	80784	J 12613	92133
1557	24340	5189	76145	J 5625 *	60935	J 12614	92220
1558	23960	5190	73174	J 5721 *	13480	J 12829	94360
1560	23382	5191	84059	J 5980 *	?	J 12830	94273
1833	17258	5192	79382	J 6013 *	113060	J 13802 *	42077
1864	22228	72103 *	132303	J 6160 *	40631	J 14198 *	21588
1951	29502			J 6477 *	?	J 14396 *	62314
2411	35115	Jersey		J 6579 *	25333	J 14234 *	53454
2441	34898	J 469 *	109726	J 6595 *	35427	J 15538 *	54534
2818	43166	J 702 *	66187	J 6986	32426	J 17661 *	136582
2819	43097	J 766 *	116311	J 7247 *	136245	J 18515 *	132797
2851	43367	J 1355 *	28461	J 8232 *	11069		
2877	43412	J 1445 *	45541	J 8338 *	146932		

C1252/274

HISTORICAL COUNTY CODES

GOV Government Department

AD	Aberdeenshire	KK	Kirkcudbrightshire
AH	Armagh	KN	Kesteven division of Lincolnshire
AL	Argyllshire	KS	Kinross-shire
AM	Antrim	KT	Kent
AR	Ayrshire	LA	Lancashire
AS	Angus	LC	Lincoln (City)
AY	Isle of Anglesey	LE	Leicestershire
BC	Brecknockshire	LI	Lindsey division of Lincolnshire
BD	Bedfordshire	LK	Lanarkshire
BE	Berkshire	LN	London Postal area
BF	Banffshire	LY	Londonderry
BK	Buckinghamshire	ME	Merionethshire
BU	Buteshire	MH	Monmouthshire
BW	Berwickshire	MN	Midlothian
CG	Cardiganshire	MO	Montgomeryshire
CH	Cheshire	MR	Morayshire
CI	Channel Islands	MX	Middlesex
CK	Clackmannanshire	ND	Northumberland
CM	Cambridgeshire	NG	Nottinghamshire
CN	Caernarvonshire	NK	Norfolk
CO	Cornwall	NN	Nairnshire
CR	Carmarthenshire	NO	Northamptonshire
CS	Caithness	NR	North Riding of Yorkshire
CU	Cumberland	OK	Orkney Islands
DB	Dunbartonshire	OX	Oxfordshire
DE	Derbyshire	PB	Peebles-shire
DF	Dumfries-shire	PE	Pembrokeshire
DH	Denbighshire	PH	Perthshire
DM	County Durham	RD	Rutland
DN	Devon	RH	Roxburghshire
DO	Down	RR	Radnorshire
DT	Dorset	RW	Renfrewshire
EI	Eire	RY	Ross-shire & Cromarty
EK	East Suffolk	SD	Shetland Islands
EL	East Lothian	SH	Shropshire
ER	East Riding of Yorkshire	SI	Selkirkshire
ES	East Sussex	SN	Stirlingshire
EX	Essex	SO	Somerset
EY	Isle of Ely	SP	Soke of Peterborough
FE	Fife	SR	Surrey
FH	Fermanagh	ST	Staffordshire
FT	Flintshire	SU	Sutherland
GG	Glamorgan	TY	Tyrone
GL	Gloucestershire	WF	West Suffolk
HA	Hampshire	WI	Wiltshire
HD	Holland division of Lincolnshire	WK	Warwickshire
HN	Huntingdonshire	WL	West Lothian
HR	Herefordshire	WN	Wigtownshire
HT	Hertfordshire	WO	Worcestershire
IM	Isle of Man	WR	West Riding of Yorkshire
IV	Inverness	WS	West Sussex
IW	Isle of Wight	WT	Westmorland
KE	Kincardineshire	YK	York (City)

Note: A 'G' prefix (eg GAD) indicates the operator was a Goods operator (in this case in Aberdeenshire).

C1252/275

INTERNATIONAL CODES USED IN THIS PUBLICATION

Code	Country	Code	Country	Code	Country
O-AUS	Australia	O-FR	Faeroe Islands	O-PE	Peru
O-B	Belgium	O-GBZ	Gibraltar	O-PK	Pakistan
O-BDS	Barbados	O-GR	Greece	O-PY	Paraguay
O-BRG	British Guiana	O-H	Hungary	O-RA	Argentina
O-BRN	Bahrain	O-HK	Hong Kong	O-RCH	Chile
O-BS	Bahamas	O-IC	Canary Islands	O-RI	Indonesia
O-BUR	Burma	O-IL	Palestine	O-ROU	Uruguay
O-CL	Ceylon	O-IND	India	O-S	Sweden
O-CO	Columbia	O-IR	Iran	O-SGP	Singapore
O-CY	Cyprus	O-IRQ	Iraq	O-SUD	Sudan
O-DK	Denmark	O-JA	Jamaica	O-T	Thailand
O-E	Spain	O-KWT	Kuwait	O-TR	Turkey
O-EAK	Kenya	O-LAR	Libya	O-TT	Trinidad
O-EAN	Nyasaland	O-M	Malta	O-WAC	Gold Coast
O-EAT	Tanganyika	O-MA	Morocco	O-WAL	Sierre Leone
O-EAU	Uganda	O-MAL	Malaya	O-WAN	Nigeria
O-ET	Egypt	O-N	Norway	O-YV	Venezuela
O-F	France	O-NL	Netherlands	O-ZA	South Africa
O-FIN	Finland	O-NZ	New Zealand		
O-FJI	Fiji	O-P	Portugal		

ABBREVIATED OPERATORS NAMES

Abbreviated Name	Full name
AHTJ, Aarhus (O-DK)	AHTJ (Aarhus-Hammel-Thorsø Jernbane), Aarhus (O-DK)
AICASA, Las Palmas (O-IC)	AICASA (Autobuses Interurbanos Canarios SA), Las Palmas (O-IC)
ALAD, Wyken Aalburg (O-NL)	ALAD (Altena's Locale Autodienst), Wyken Aalburg (O-NL)
AMZ	AMZ (BV Auto-Maatschappij Zeeland)
BBA, Breda (O-NL)	BBA (Brabantsche Buurtspoorwegen en Autodiensten), Breda (O-NL)
Christofi, Charalambous et al, Morphou (O-CY)	Christofi, Charalambous & Agathangelou, Morphou (O-CY)
DABO, Meppel (O-NL)	DABO (NV Drentsche Auto-Bus Onderneming), Meppel (O-NL)
DAM, Appingedam (O-NL)	DAM (Damster Auto Maatschappij), Appingedam (O-NL)
EDS, Hoogeveen (O-NL)	EDS (Eerste Drentsche Stoomtramweg-Maatschappij), Hoogeveen (O-NL)
EGAO, Hardinxveld-Giessendam (O-NL)	EGAO (Eerste Giessendamsche Autobus Onderneming, Firma WA van den Heuvel), Hardinxveld-Giessendam (O-NL)
EMA, Valkenswaard (O-NL)	EMA (Eerste Meierijsche Autobedrijf NV), Valkenswaard (O-NL)
ENHABO, Zaandam (O-NL)	ENHABO (Eerste Noord-Hollandse Autobus Onderneming), Zaandam (O-NL)
ESA, Marum (O-NL)	ESA (Elema-Stollenga's Autodiensten), Marum (O-NL)
ETAO, Tiel (O-NL)	ETAO (Eerste Tielse Autobus Onderneming), Tiel (O-NL)
GABM, Maastricht (O-NL)	GABM (Gemeentelijk Autobussenbedrijf Maastricht), Maastricht (O-NL)
GTW, Doetinchem (O-NL)	GTW (Geldersche Tramwegen), Doetinchem (O-NL)
GVA, Arnhem (O-NL)	GVA (Gemeente Vervoerbedrijf Arnhem), Arnhem (O-NL)
GVU, Utrecht (O-NL)	GVU (Gemeentelijk Vervoerbedrijf Utrecht), Utrecht (O-NL)
IAO (O-NL)	IAO (NV Internationale Autobusonderneming)
LAB, Leeuwarden (O-NL)	LAB (Leeuwarder Auto Bedrijf), Leeuwarden (O-NL)
LABO, Leeuwarden (O-NL)	LABO (Leeuwarder Autobus Onderneming), Leeuwarden (O-NL)
LAD, Lobith (O-NL)	LAD (Lobitsche Auto-Dienst), Lobith (O-NL)
Maarse & Kroon, Aalsmeer (O-NL)	NV Autobusonderneming Maarse & Kroon, Aalsmeer (O-NL)
MEA, Koog aan de Zaan (O-NL)	MEA (NV Maatschappij tot Exploitatie van Autobussen en Autobusondernemingen), Koog aan de Zaan (O-NL)
MEGGA, Sliedrecht (O-NL)	MEGGA (NV Maatschappij tot Exploitatie van Goede en Goedkope Autobusdiensten), Sliedrecht (O-NL)
Midland, Christchurch (O-NZ)	Midland Motorways Services Ltd, Christchurch (O-NZ)
NAL, Ter Aar (O-NL)	NAL (Nieuwkoop-Alphen-Leiden), Ter Aar (O-NL)
NAO, Roermond (O-NL)	NAO (Nedam's Autobus Onderneming NV), Roermond (O-NL)

NHADO, Bergen (O-NL) — NHADO (Noord-Hollandse Auto-Dienst Onderneming Bergen-Binnen), Bergen (O-NL)
NOF, Dokkum (O-NL) — NOF (Noord-Oost-Freische Autobusonderneming), Dokkum (O-NL)
NTM, Heerenveen (O-NL) — NTM (Nederlandsche Tramweg Maatschappij), Heerenveen (O-NL)
NWH, Zwartsluis (O-NL) — NWH (NV Vervoermaatschappij De Noord West Hoek), Zwartsluis (O-NL)
OAD, Holten (O-NL) — OAD (OVeijsselsche Autobus Diensten BV), Holten (O-NL)
OMT [various East Africa locations] — Overseas Motor Transport Ltd
ONDA, Montevideo (O-ROU) — ONDA (Organisation Nacional Des Autobuses), Montevideo (O-ROU)
OTC [various East Africa locations] — Overseas Touring Company (East Africa) Ltd
Øst-Telemarkens Auto, Saudland (O-N) — AS Øst-Telemarkens Automobilselskab, Saudland (O-N)
Pauly et Graven {SADAR}, La Calamine (O-B) — SA des Autobus Regionaux Pauly et Graven (SADAR), La Calamine (O-B)
RTM, Zierikzee (O-NL) — RTM (NV Rotterdamse Tramweg Maatschappij), Zierikzee (O-NL)
SBM, Aardenburg (O-NL) — SBM (Stoomtram-Maatschappij Breskens-Maldeghem NV), Aardenburg (O-NL)
SCWS Ltd — Scottish Co-operative Wholesale Society Ltd
SPAP Railways (O-GR) — Piraeus, Athens & Peloponnese Railways, Athens (O-GR)
TAD, Enschede (O-NL) — Firma JW Bos & Zn "Twentsche Autobusdienst (TAD)", Enschede (O-NL)
TESO, Den Burg (O-NL) — TESO (NV Texel's Eigen Stoomboot Onderneming), Den Burg (O-NL)
TP-AV, Jutphaas (O-NL) — TP-AV (Twee Provincien Autobusdiensten "Vereeniging"), Jutphaas (O-NL)
TP-De IJssel, Krimpen aan de Ijssel (O-NL) — TP-De Ijssel (Twee Provincien De Ijssel), Krimpen aan de Ijssel (O-NL)
TP-ESOO, Sliedrecht (O-NL) — TP-ESOO (Twee Provincien Eerste Sliedrechtse Omnibus Onderneming), Sliedrecht (O-NL)
TP-RAGOM, Ridderkerk (O-NL) — TP-RAGOM (Twee Provincien Ridderkerksche Autogarage en Omnibusmaatschappij), Ridderkerk (O-NL)
TP-RopdeL, Kinderdijk (O-NL) — TP-RopdeL (Twee Provincien Reederij op de Lek), Kinderdijk (O-NL)
VADAH, Echt (O-NL) — VADAH (Vaassen's Auto Diensten en Auto Handel), Echt (O-NL)
VALK, Schoonhoven (O-NL) — Stichting Vereenigd Autovervoer in Lopiker- en Krimpenerwaard (VALK), Schoonhoven (O-NL)
VERA, Deventer (O-NL) — Fa Verenigde Autobusbedrijven (Ver A), Deventer (O-NL)
WABO, Wijk bij Duurstede (O-NL) — WABO (Werkhovense Autobus Onderneming), Wijk bij Duurstede (O-NL)
WATO, Nijverdal (O-NL) — WATO (Wierdensche Algemeene Transport Onderneming), Nijverdal (O-NL)
Willems-Kroese, Hattem (O-NL) — Willems-Kroese, v/h H van Gelder, Hattem (contractor) (O-NL)
ZVTM, Terneuzen (O-NL) — ZVTM (Zeenwsch -Vlaamasche Tramweg-Maatschappij NV), Terneuzen (O-NL)
ZWH, Balk (O-NL) — ZWH (Autobedrijf "De Zuidwesthoek"), Balk (O-NL)

ABBREVIATED COACH BUILDERS NAMES

Auckland TB	Auckland Transport Board
ACB	Associated Coachbuilders
CAC	Commonwealth Aircraft Corporation
DOD	Den Oudsten & Domburg
ECF	Van Ereton
NMU	Northern Motor Utilities
Ørum-Ped	Ørum-Pedersen
RE&C	Reevely, Ellis & Collingwood
Transport BS	Transport Bus Services
Ver-Av	Verheul-Aviolanda

ABBREVIATED BODY STYLES

h/box	horse-box
l/stock	livestock carrier, generally cattle wagon
tower	tower wagon
prison	prison van